Canadian
Families Today

Third Edition

Canadian
Families Today
New Perspectives

EDITED BY
David Cheal
Patrizia Albanese

OXFORD
UNIVERSITY PRESS

Oxford University Press is a department of the University of Oxford.
It furthers the University's objective of excellence in research, scholarship,
and education by publishing worldwide. Oxford is a registered trade mark of
Oxford University Press in the UK and in certain other countries.

Published in Canada by
Oxford University Press
8 Sampson Mews, Suite 204,
Don Mills, Ontario M3C 0H5 Canada
www.oupcanada.com

First Edition published in 2007
Second Edition published in 2010

Library and Archives Canada Cataloguing in Publication

Canadian families today : new perspectives / edited by David
Cheal and Patrizia Albanese. — 3rd ed.

Includes bibliographical references and index.
ISBN 978-0-19-544936-5

1. Families—Canada — Textbooks. 2. Family policy—Canada—
Textbooks. 3. Families—Economic aspects—Canada—Textbooks.
I. Cheal, David J. II. Albanese, Patrizia

Cover image: Cultura/Moof/Stock Image/Getty Images

Printed and bound in Canada
5 6 — 17 16

CONTENTS

CONTRIBUTORS

Patrizia Albanese is a Professor of Sociology, Interim Director of the PhD in Policy Studies at Ryerson University, in Toronto, and President-elect of the Canadian Sociological Association. She is a book series co-editor with Lorne Tepperman (Oxford University Press), co-editor of Sociology: A Canadian Perspective (Oxford, 2012), and co-author of Making Sense: A Student's Guide to Research and Writing – Social Sciences (Oxford, 2012), Youth & Society (Oxford, 2011) and More Than It Seems: Household Work and Lifelong Learning (Women's Press, 2010). She is the author of Child Poverty in Canada (Oxford, 2010), Children in Canada Today (Oxford, 2009), and Mothers of the Nation (U of T Press, 2006). She has been working on a number of research projects which share a focus on understanding family policies in Canada and families under stress.

Neena L. Chappell, PhD, FRSC, tier 1 Canada Research Chair in Social Gerontology, is a professor of sociology at the University of Victoria, BC. She established the research Centres on Aging at the University of Manitoba and the University of Victoria, both still world-class centres today. Her recent awards include the Betty Havens award for knowledge translation from the Canadian Institutes of Health Research and the Queen Elizabeth Diamond Jubilee Medal for contributions to gerontology. Her 9th authored book will be released in August 2013 by Oxford University Press; *Aging in Canada* focuses on meeting the needs of older adults in an aging society, appropriately and cost-effectively; it is co-authored by Marcus Hollander.

David Cheal is Professor Emeritus, University of Winnipeg. He is the author of *Families in Today's World: A Comparative Approach* (Routledge, 2008), *Sociology of Family Life* (Palgrave, 2002, and in Japanese translation by Minerva Shobo Co. Ltd., 2006), and *Family and the State of Theory* (University of Toronto Press and Harvester-Wheatsheaf Press, 1991), plus other books, book chapters, and journal articles. In addition to editing the first two editions of *Canadian Families Today*, he has edited the four volume set, *Family: Critical Concepts* (Routledge, 2003), as well as a book on aging in Canada.

Cynthia Comacchio, Professor, Department of History, Wilfrid Laurier University, has a PhD in Canadian history from the University of Guelph. Her research focuses on Canadian social and cultural history, especially the history of childhood, youth, and family. She has published three books on those subjects, most recently *The Dominion of Youth: Adolescence and the Making of Modern Canada, 1920–1950* (Wilfrid Laurier University Press, 2006), which received the Canadian History of Education Association's Founders Award for best

English-language monograph. She is currently collaborating, with Neil Sutherland, on *Ring Around the Maple: A Sociocultural History of Children and Childhood in Canada, 19th and 20th Centuries*, for WLU Press.

Andrea Doucet is the Canada Research Chair in Gender, Work, and Care and Professor of Sociology and Women's & Gender Studies at Brock University. She has published widely on themes of gender and care work, fatherhood, masculinities, parental leave policies, embodiment, reflexivity, and feminist approaches to methodologies and epistemologies. Her book *Do Men Mother?* (University of Toronto Press, 2006) was awarded the John Porter Tradition of Excellence Book Award from the Canadian Sociology Association. She is also co-author of *Gender Relations: Intersectionality and Beyond* (with Janet Siltanen, Oxford, 2008). She is currently completing two long-standing book projects—one on breadwinning mothers and caregiving fathers and a second book on reflexive and relational knowing (with Natasha Mauthner).

Margrit Eichler is Professor Emerita of the University of Toronto/Ontario Institute for Studies in Education. She has published widely in the areas of family policy, biases in research that derive from social hierarchies (e.g. sexism, racism, ableism), women's studies, and sustainability and social justice. She is a member of the Royal Society of Canada and the European Academy of Sciences.

James S. Frideres is a Professor Emeritus at the University of Calgary. He was the director of the International Indigenous Studies program and held the Chair of Ethnic Studies. His recent publications include *International Perspectives: Integration and Inclusion* with J. Biles (McGill Queens) (which is on the *Hill Times* List of top 100 books for 2012) and the 9th edition of *Aboriginal People in Canada* with R. Gadacz (Pearson, 2012).

Doreen Fumia is an Associate Professor of Sociology at Ryerson University. Her work examines lesbians and aging, identities, anti-poverty activism, and neighbourhood belonging in Toronto. She has published in the areas of lesbian motherhood, non-traditional families, informal learning, and same-sex marriage debates.

Amber Gazso is an Associate Professor of Sociology at York University. She completed her PhD in Sociology at the University of Alberta in 2006. Her current research interests include citizenship, family and gender relations, poverty, research methods, and social policy and the welfare state. Her recent journal publications focus on low-income mothers on social assistance. She is currently working on two major research projects funded by SSHRC. In one project she is exploring how diverse families make ends meet by piecing together networks of social support that include both government programs (e.g., social assistance) and community supports, and informal relations within families and with friends and neighbours. Another comparative project explores the relationship between health and income inequality among Canadians and Americans in mid-life.

Melanie Heath is Assistant Professor of Sociology at McMaster University. She is the author of *One Marriage Under God: The Campaign to Promote Marriage in America* (New York University Press, 2012). She has published articles in *Gender & Society* and *Qualitative Sociology*. Her current project on "Harm or Right? Polygamy's Contested Terrain Within and Across Borders" is funded by a five-year SSHRC Insight Grant.

Don Kerr is a Professor of Sociology at King's University College at Western University. His areas of interest are population studies and Canadian demography. His research has focused on social demography, population estimates and projections, environmental demography, the Aboriginal population, and family demography.

Karen M. Kobayashi is an Associate Professor in the Department of Sociology and the Centre on Aging at the University of Victoria. Her research interests include the economic and health dimensions of ethnic inequality in Canada, intergenerational relationships and social support in mid-to-later life families, and the socio-cultural dimensions of dementia and personhood. Her current research programs focus on the relationship between social isolation and health care utilization among older adults, access to health and social care among older visible minority immigrants, living-apart-together (LAT) relationships in adulthood, and an evaluation of *quality of care* in residential long-term care facilities. Recent work has been published in the *Journal of Aging Studies, Ethnicity and Health, Canadian Review of Sociology*, and the *Journal of Aging and Health*.

Catherine Krull is Associate Dean of the Faculty of Arts and Science and Professor of Sociology and Cultural Studies at Queen's University. She is past editor of *Cuban Studies* and current editor-in-chief of the *Canadian Journal of Latin American and Caribbean Studies*. Recent publications include *A Life in Balance? Reopening the Family-Work Debate* (with Sempruch, 2011); *Rereading Women and the Cuban Revolution*, (with Jean Stubbs, 2011); *A Measure of a Revolution: Cuba, 1959–2009* (with Soraya Castro, 2010) and *New World Coming: The 1960s and the Shaping of Global Consciousness* (with Dubinsky et al., 2009). Currently, she is working on a monograph entitled *Generations, Memory and Political Consciousness: Women's Daily Life in Cuba* and has two ongoing international SSHRC funded research projects: (1) the Cuban Diaspora in Canada and Europe, and (2) Entangled US/Cuban Terrains, 1933–1965: Memories from inside Guantanamo.

Craig McKie is a retired Professor of Sociology. He taught at the University of Western Ontario for several years, spent more than a decade working for Statistics Canada in Ottawa, latterly as Editor-in-Chief of *Canadian Social Trends*, and most recently, from 1990 until retirement, he taught in the Department of Sociology at Carleton University.

Amal Madibbo is an Assistant Professor of Sociology at the University of Calgary. Her research focuses on race and antiracism, Black Francophone immigration to Canada, and race and ethnicity in sub-Saharan Africa.

Joseph H. Michalski is an Associate Professor and Chair of the Department of Sociology, King's University College at Western. His current theoretical work and research focus on the geometry of social space in relation to behaviours as diverse as intimate partner violence, welfare, and knowledge production.

Michelle Owen, PhD, is acting coordinator of the Disability Studies Program, Associate Professor in the Department of Sociology, and director of the Global College Institute for Health and Human Potential at the University of Winnipeg. In 2011 she was given the Marsha Hanen Award for Excellence in Creating Community Awareness. She is currently working on two disability-related research projects: an investigation into how Canadian academics with multiple sclerosis negotiate the workplace, and the experience of intimate partner violence in the lives of women with disabilities. In 2008 she co-edited *Dissonant Disabilities: Women with Chronic Illnesses Explore Their Lives* (CSPI/Women's Press). She has two chapters forthcoming about violence in the lives of girls and young women with disabilities in *Gender and Beyond: An Intersectional Analysis of Violence in the Lives of Girls* (London: Althouse Press).

Aysan Sev'er is Professor Emeritus of Sociology at the University of Toronto Scarborough. Her current research focuses on extreme forms of violence against women in India and in south eastern Turkey. She is the founding editor of the *Women's Health & Urban Life Journal* and the recipient of the Canadian Person's Day Award (1998) and the Canadian Women's Studies Book Award (2004) for *Fleeing the House of Horrors* (UTP, 2002). Her most recent books are *Skeletons in Family Closets* (WLU Press, 2010, with Jan Trost from University of Upsala), *Memories that Reside in Poems* (UTSC Publishing, 2012), *Mothers, Daughters & Untamed Dragons* (Demeter Press, 2012) and *Patriarchal Murders of Women* (Mellen, upcoming).

Deborah K. van den Hoonaard is Professor of Gerontology and Canada Research Chair in Qualitative Research and Analysis at St Thomas University in Fredericton, New Brunswick. She is the author of *Qualitative Research in Action: A Canadian Primer* (OUP, 2012), *By Himself: The Older Man's Experience of Widowhood* (UTP, 2010), *The Widowed Self: The Older Woman's Journey Through Widowhood* (WLU Press, 2001), and co-author (with Will C. van den Hoonaard) of *Essentials of Thinking Ethically in Qualitative Research* (Left Coast Press, 2013) and *The Equality of Women and Men: The Experience of the Bahá'í Community of Canada* (Art Bookbindery, 2006). She is currently working on a new study of older women's experiences of widowhood.

PREFACE

The third edition of *Canadian Families Today* is an introduction to the sociology of family life that draws on a wide range of materials. In 16 chapters, 18 experts in the field cover a wide range of topics that introduce you to families in a Canadian context.

The book is organized into four parts, reflecting its main themes. Part 1 contains the introductory chapter by Patrizia Albanese, which discusses the diversity of family forms existing in Canada today, reviews different definitions of the family, and considers how the changing definition of this concept has had policy implications for access to programs and privileges or status within society. In Chapter 2, Cynthia Comacchio reviews the major changes and continuities in the history of Canadian families over the past two centuries.

Part 2 provides information about various stages and events in the life course. In Chapter 3, Melanie Heath focuses on how people form relationships. Heath discusses technological innovations that have been affecting dating and sexual relationships in recent years. Amber Gazso, in Chapter 4, focuses on becoming and being a parent of young children. She outlines some of the activities of parenting, with emphasis on how everyday practices of parenting are textured by ideological discourses in our society.

In Chapter 5, Craig McKie focuses on how families fragment through separation or divorce, but often reformulate within the context of a new union. McKie discusses post-separation hardships, but also concludes that these must be weighed against the real risks of physical and emotional trauma in relationships that are full of conflict and which are greatly diminished by separation.

Middle age and "old age," two other stages of the life course, are considered in Chapters 6 and 7. Karen Kobayashi, in Chapter 6, focuses on the transitions that mark middle age (e.g., the "empty nest," caregiving) and are triggered by the occurrence of life events in families (e.g., adult children leaving home, care for aging parents). Despite similarities, the chapter also examines some of the diversity of mid-life families. In Chapter 7, Neena Chappell highlights the central role that families play in the lives of older adults. Chappell suggests that we look to diverse countries around the world from which Canada can learn.

Part 3 of *Canadian Families Today* focuses on some of the many challenges, decisions, and strategies that families face in light of the shifting social, economic, and political contexts. In Chapter 8 Deborah K. van den Hoonaard focuses special attention on the rituals associated with marriage and death. She considers how rituals have evolved over time, and notes that individuals now exercise greater individuality in their choices about how to conduct rituals. In Chapter 9, Andrea Doucet describes patterns of paid and unpaid work in families by looking at the relationship between gender and paid work. Doucet, among other things, examines the relationship between paid and unpaid work and state policies.

Don Kerr and Joseph H. Michalski, in Chapter 10, focus on recent poverty trends affecting families today, while also considering some of the broader structural shifts in the Canadian economy and in government policies. They examine the high rates of poverty among female-headed lone-parent families and recent immigrants, and discuss the coping strategies that these families use to survive. In Chapter 11, Doreen M. Fumia discusses same-sex marriage in Canada and changes in marriage law in Canada in the form of Bill C-38—the Civil Marriages Act. She explores how concepts of "normal" and "abnormal" sexuality continue to demarcate relationships and thus still leave many Canadians as "others."

James S. Frideres and Amal Madibbo, in Chapter 12, discuss family patterns among diverse groups, including Aboriginal peoples, immigrants, and visible minorities. They explore socio-economic factors, including labour force participation and unemployment, as they affect family structure and family experiences. In Chapter 13, Michelle Owen writes about the impact that disability has on families. She begins by discussing the problem of defining disability, and then aims to show that disabled Canadians and their families, like racialized families discussed in Chapter 12, continue to be marginalized in our society.

Finally, Part 4 of the book looks at issues that, if not unique to families, are endemic to the contemporary family: violence, shifts in public policy, and questions regarding the future. Chapter 14, by Aysan Sev'er, analyzes how power differences in the family can lead to mental, physical, or sexual abuse. At the same time, she argues that the powerlessness and dependency cycles in families that make children, women, and aged persons vulnerable can be broken. Catherine Krull, in Chapter 15, discusses government policies affecting families in Canada, which she believes have a great impact on family life. She points out that Canada lacks a comprehensive national family policy, unlike some other countries around the world. In the concluding chapter, Margrit Eichler discusses what predictions of the future of the family have been like in the past, pointing out that there have been a number of spectacular misprognoses about the future of families. She concludes with predictions of her own.

Acknowledgments

Statistics Canada information is used with the permission of Statistics Canada. Users are forbidden to copy the data and redisseminate them, in an original or modified form, for commercial purposes, without permission from Statistics Canada. Information on the availability of the wide range of data from Statistics Canada can be obtained from its World Wide Web site at www.statcan.gc.ca.

David Cheal & Patrizia Albanese
February, 2013

CONCEPTUALIZING FAMILIES, PAST AND PRESENT

The first two chapters of this book provide an introduction to the study of family life in Canada. They present some the changes in the study of families, with a special focus on Canada, while presenting an overview of historical diversity in family life. Multiple perspectives on understanding families are presented, and the complexity of family life is stressed.

In Chapter 1, Patrizia Albanese discusses the diversity of family forms existing in Canada today, reviews different definitions of the family, and considers how the changing definition of this concept has had policy implications for access to programs and privileges or status within society. Albanese also introduces some of the different theories of family life and discusses the influence that theoretical assumptions have on ways of seeing the world. She examines recent changes in family life in Canada and concludes the chapter by noting that today, as in the past, Canadian families take on a number of diverse forms. The changing definition of family simply reflects a reality that change has been, and continues to be, a normal part of family life.

In Chapter 2, Cynthia Comacchio reviews the major changes and continuities in the history of Canadian families over the past two centuries. She discusses how in the past, as is the case today, "the family" as a social construct is an idealization that reinforces hierarchies of class, race, gender, and age. Throughout the chapter, she underscores the fact that, despite prevailing ideas about what properly constitutes "the family" at various points in time, Canadian families are and have been in constant flux. Comacchio makes it abundantly clear that the importance of families to both individuals and to society is a constant, both in ideal and in practice; at the same time, the form and experience of actual families have always been diverse.

Introduction to Diversity in Canada's Families: Variations in Forms, Definitions, and Theories

PATRIZIA ALBANESE

LEARNING OBJECTIVES

- To gain an overview of some changing Canadian demographic trends
- To discover that Canadian families have taken, and continue to take, diverse forms
- To see that definitions of "family" have changed over time, and are continuing to change
- To recognize the implications for defining family in certain ways—restricting who has access to programs, policies, and privileges and who does not
- To learn about some of the theories which guide our understanding of families
- To understand that theoretical orientations guide what we study and how we study it

Introduction

I am a widow and childless—well, sort of childless. I was wife number four to my late husband, 22 years my senior; and step mother to his two now-adult children from two of his previous relationships. I recently ended a relationship with a divorced man who had custody of three children and four cats. At the moment, I find myself single—but not for long, I expect. You see, I love family and family life, in all its shapes, sizes, and manifestations. I am most content living in a family. And while I have not had children of my own, helping to care for the children of others suits me just fine. So what does that make me? Pretty "normal" I think.

While the term "normal" doesn't seem appropriate in my case, neither does the word "typical," when it comes to describing anything to do with family life. What exactly does the "typical Canadian family" look like? We begin this chapter with an overview of some recent shifts and trends in family life as they are captured by broad-sweeping, national statistics. We will see that Statistics Canada data captures a considerable amount of change and diversity in family forms, but even then, we must keep in mind that it actually masks so much of the variations, fluctuations, and "oddities" that make up everyday life for millions of Canadians today.

Following a review of recent trends in family forms, we assess various definitions of family, to determine which ones, if any, actually reflect the diversity that we see and experience around us. Following that, we review theories used to help us understand and explain what is happening to, with, and in family life. We see, through the trends, definitions, and theories covered in this chapter, that change and diversity is the norm when it comes to understanding families. We will—throughout this chapter and the rest of the book—see that Statistics Canada data, while it does not paint a static picture of family structures over time, provides a tidier picture than what actually makes up the lived experiences of Canadians.

Changing Trends in the Diversity of Family Forms

In 2011 there were 9,389,700 families in Canada, up from 8,896,800 only five years before (Statistics Canada, 2012a; Milan, Vézina, and Wells, 2007). According to Canadian Census data, the number of married-couple families has risen close to 20 per cent since 1981, while the number of common-law unions has more than quadrupled since they began being counted in 1981 (Statistics Canada, 2012b). The 2011 Census revealed that married couples remained the dominant family form, making up two-thirds of all families, but as in past Census years, this number is declining with time in relation to other family forms. For example, since the 2006 Census, the number of common-law couples rose 13.9 per cent and lone-parent families increased 8.0 per cent (Statistics Canada, 2012a). The growth in the number of male lone-parent families, up 16.2 per cent since 2006, was especially striking (Statistics Canada, 2012a). But even with this increase, the number of common-law couples outnumbered lone-parent families for the first time since they began being counted in 1981.

In 2011, there were 64,575 same-sex couple families (21,015 were same-sex married couples and 43,560 were same-sex common-law couples), up 42.4 per cent since same-sex married couples started being counted in 2006 (Statistics Canada, 2012). So, after decades of political mobilizing and many legal battles, same-sex families in Canada have gone from being illegal, to being invisible, to being recognized and counted as marriages and families for the first time in the 2006 Canadian census (see Chapter 11).[1] Clearly, as a result of social change, including changes in the way we define and count families, Canadian families today come in a plurality of forms, with no one family portrait capturing this diversity.

Blended families are increasingly common, and only recently, new to the 2011 Census, being officially counted. But even before official counting, we have known that following divorces and other break-ups, we are seeing many second and subsequent unions in the form of remarriages and common-law unions. This has amounted to an increase in the number of stepfamilies in Canada today. Not surprising then, to capture changing reality, for the first time ever, the 2011 Census counted stepfamilies. It found that of the 3,684,675 couples with children, 87.4 per cent were families that included two parents and their biological or adopted children; the remaining 12.6 per cent were stepfamilies (by 2011, there were 464,335 stepfamilies; Statistics Canada, 2012a). This is up from the some 5.3 per cent of all families in Canada that were stepfamilies in 2006 (Statistics Canada, 2008a). Of the

For more on legal changes to same-sex marriage in Canada, see "Chain of Events in Canada: Bill C-38 Confronts Heteronationalism" in Chapter 11, p. 214.

Table 1.1 **Distribution (Number and Percentage) and Percentage Change of Census Families by Family Structure, Canada, 2001–2011**

Census family	2001	2006	2011	Percentage change
Total census families	8,371,020	8,896,840	9,389,700	5.5
Couple families	7,059,830	7,482,775	7,861,860	5.1
	(84.3%)	(84.1%)	(83.7%)	
Married	5,901,420	6,105,910	6,293,950	3.1
	(70.5%)	(68.6%)	(67.0%)	
Common-law	1,158,410	1,376,865	1,567,910	13.9
	(13.8%)	(15.5%)	(16.7%)	
Lone-parent families	1,311,190	1,414,060	1,527,840	8.0
	(15.7%)	(15.9%)	(16.3%)	
Female parents	1,065,360	1,132,290	1,200,295	6.0
	(12.7%)	(12.7%)	(12.8%)	
Male parents	245,825	281,775	327,545	16.2
	(2.9%)	(3.2%)	(3.5%)	

SOURCE: Statistics Canada, 2012a, p. 5 (Table 1), available at http://www12.statcan.gc.ca/census-recensement/2011/as-sa/98-312-x/98-312-x2011001-eng.pdf.

12.6 per cent of all families with children that were stepfamilies in 2011, 7.4 per cent were *simple stepfamilies*, in which all children were the biological or adopted children of only one married spouse or common-law partner; the remaining 5.2 per cent were *complex stepfamilies*, which were comprised of at least one child of both parents as well as at least one child of one parent only (Statistics Canada, 2012a). Many step-parents face a number of unique challenges and experiences. At the same time, they have much in common with other families today.

"Other" families today include transnational families—which have been around a long time, to be sure, but simply have been invisible to most. Recent years have seen an increase in interest, research, and information on **transnational, multi-local families** (Bernhard et al., 2006; Burholt, 2004; Waters, 2001). Interest in transnational families has been sparked by the growing awareness of some of the challenges faced by immigrant families, refugee claimants, foreign domestic workers from the Caribbean and Philippines, migrant workers, visa students, and individuals and families with "less-than-full" legal status (for more on immigrant families, see Chapter 12). Thousands of people living in Canada currently find themselves temporarily separated from their children and spouses as part of a strategy to secure a better economic future and opportunities for their family. Some have been called **"satellite" families** or satellite children, a term first used in the 1980s to describe Chinese children whose parents were immigrants to North America, usually from Hong Kong or Taiwan, but who have returned to their country of origin after immigration, and left children, and sometimes spouses, in Canada (Tsang et al., 2003). Researchers studying transnational families have been documenting the changes and challenges that arise from parent–child separations (for more on parenting, see Chapter 4), long-distance relationships, extended family networks providing child care, and the often emotionally charged reunifications that follow the multi-local family arrangements (Bernhard et al., 2006; Burholt, 2004; Tsang et al., 2003; Waters, 2001).

While some families find themselves living between and across households and borders, or are multi-local, others—particularly younger Canadians—find themselves increasingly unable to leave their parental homes and establish independent households.

In 1981, about 28 per cent of Canadians between the ages of 20 to 29 lived with their parents. By 2001, this increased to 41 per cent (Beaujot, 2004). In 2006, 43.5 per cent of the four million Canadians in this age range remained in or returned to live in their parental home (Milan et al., 2008). Because of changing economic circumstances and difficulty finding stable, long-term, decent-paying work (see Chapter 9 on work and families, and Chapter 10 on poverty), coupled with an increasing demand for post-secondary education and large debt loads, researchers have seen the postponement of home-leaving or a delayed **child launch** (see Chapter 6). Linked with this trend is an increase in the number of "boomerang children" or "velcro kids" (Beaupré, Turcotte, and Milan, 2006; Tyyskä, 2001; Mitchell, 1998)—young adults who leave their parental homes for work or school, only to return due to large debt loads, shifting employment prospects, or changing marital status (unions and breakups, see Chapter 5).

Table 1.2 **Counting Census Families**

Census year	Family type, number, and/or percent	Historical context; changes in census enumeration
1921	1.8 million census families	First World War; large number of war widows; first time census distinguishes between households and families
1931	86.4% married; 13.6% lone parent	Great Depression; marriage and fertility rates decline; reference to food, shared tables, and housekeeping are dropped from census; eradicating hints of women's domestic labour (Bradbury, 2000a); single-parent heads of households counted for the first time
1941	87.8% married; 12.2% lone parent	Second World War; women at work in factories; 1942 Dominion-Provincial Wartime Day Nurseries Agreement, funding daycare services in Ontario, Quebec, and Alberta
1951	90.1% married; 9.9% lone parent	Baby boom (1946–65); fertility rates increase; first time the census clearly makes it possible for single parents with children living with other families to be separately counted
1956	91.4% married; 8.6% lone parent	High marriage rates; high fertility rates, low death rates: rates of single parenthood were at their lowest
1961	91.6% married; 8.4% lone parent	High marriage rates; high fertility rates; low death rates: rates of single parenthood were at their lowest
1966	91.8% married; 8.2% lone parent	Mass marketing of birth control pill; contraception is legalized in 1969; changes in Divorce Act, 1968
1971	90.6% married; 9.4% lone parent	Was the last census year that fertility was at "replacement level" of 2:1; lone parents due to divorce now outnumber those due to widowhood
1976	90.2% married; 9.8% lone parent	Women's en mass (re)entry into labour force

(*Continued*)

Table 1.2 **Counting Census Families (Continued)**

Census year	Family type, number, and/or percent	Historical context; changes in census enumeration
1981	83.1% married; 5.6% common-law; 11.3% lone parent	First time common-law unions are enumerated
1986	80.2% married; 7.2% common-law; 12.7% lone parent	Changes in Divorce Act; in 1987, divorce rates peak
1991	77.3% married; 9.8% common-law; 13% lone parent	The number of married-couple families continues to make up a smaller proportion of all families in Canada
1996	73.7% married; 11.7% common-law; 14.5% lone parent	Number of stepfamilies sharply on the rise; number of hours spent doing unpaid housework is asked for the first time in this census
2001	70.5% married; 13.8% common-law; 15.7% lone parent	First time same-sex common-law unions are enumerated; parental leave extended
2006	68.6% married; 15.5% common-law; 15.9% lone parent	First time same-sex marriages are enumerated
2011	67.0% married; 16.7% common-law; 16.3% lone parent	First time stepfamilies and foster children are enumerated

Outlining the recent historical evolution of the Canadian Census family (which masks more than it reveals) shows that what we know actually better reflects how, what, and when we counted, and not necessarily who and what was there.

SOURCE: Bradbury 2000a, 2011; Statistics Canada, 2012b.

While many young people today may never have expected to live with their parents or in-laws into their 30s and 40s, for many new immigrants to Canada, older Canadians (see Chapter 7), or Canadians with disabilities (see Chapter 13), the extended family model and the pooling of family resources in multi-generational households is nothing new, unexpected, or alarming (Sun, 2008; Che-Alford and Hamm, 1999). A considerable amount of pooling of resources and care also happens across generations and households, especially by women, in a complex web of exchanges and support (Connidis and Kemp, 2008; Eichler and Albanese, 2007). And while *how* some of this carework happens (for example, over the Internet) may be different, *what* is done, *by whom*, and *for whom*, may not actually be new. In fact, many of Canada's "new" family forms have always existed but some have done so in the margins, in the shadows, or during specific historical and economic contexts. For example, lone-parent families and stepfamilies/remarriages are not new on the Canadian landscape (see Figure 1.1). Nor are same-sex families or transnational families, for that matter. Many of these family forms were simply not previously counted (Bradbury, 2000a, see Table 1.2). While diversity seems to best characterize Canadian families today, diversity, adaptability, conflict, and change have always—past and present—been a fact of life for Canadian families.

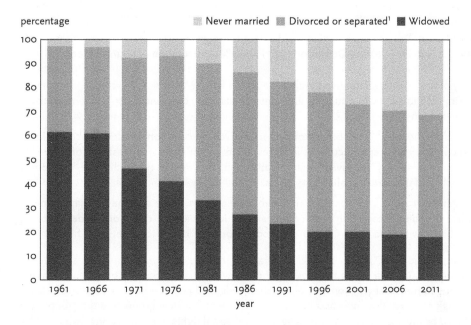

Figure 1.1 Distribution (in Percentage) of the Legal Marital Status of Lone Parents, Canada, 1961 to 2011

NOTE: 1. Divorced or separated category includes "married, spouse absent."

SOURCE: Statistics Canada, 2012b, p. 3.

Contemporary Canadian Family Studies

Studying Canadian families requires students and researchers to stay on top of legal, political, social, and economic changes at the community, sub-national/provincial, national, and international levels. As you will see throughout this book, studying Canadian families often includes understanding and studying aspects of the Canadian economy, policy shifts, changes to health care and longevity, the Internet, poverty, immigration, environmental issues, globalization, war/genocide/ethnic conflict, violence, taxation, legal changes, and human rights issues. And much of this has been sparked by what some have called the "big bang" (Cheal, 1991) in family theorizing. Before exploring the "big bang" let us first turn to what we mean by "family" and how the changing definition of this concept has had profound implications on access to programs, policies, and privilege in this country.

Changing Definitions of Family

The definition of "family" is in a constant state of flux (Holtzman, 2011) (see Box 1.1) and even judicial uses of family definitions—which one would assume to be the most comprehensive—tend to "be inconsistent, unpredictable . . ." and not always "effective"

Box 1.1

What is a Family? Evolving Definitions of "Family"—Is Everyone Accounted For?

Do any of the following definitions exclude your own family? Who else is excluded from the following definitions? Can you spot any other similarities, differences, or problems with these definitions?

Murdock (1949): . . . a social group characterized by common residence, economic co-operation and reproduction. It includes adults of both sexes, at least two of whom maintain a socially approved sexual relationship, and one or more children, own or adopted, of the sexually cohabiting adults.

Stephens (1963): . . . a social arrangement based on marriage and the marriage contract, including recognition of the rights and duties of parents, common residence for husband, wife, and children and reciprocal economic obligations between husband and wife.

Coser (1974): . . . a group manifesting the following organizational attributes: it finds its origin in marriage; it consists of husband, wife, and children born in their wedlock, though other relatives may find their place close to this nuclear group, and the group is united by moral, legal, economic, religious, and social rights and obligations.

Eichler (1983): A family is a social group which may or may not include adults of both sexes (e.g., lone-parent families), may or may not include one or more children (e.g., childless couples), who may or may not have been born in their wedlock (e.g., adopted children, or children by one adult partner of a previous union). The relationship of the adults may or may not have its origin in marriage (e.g., common-law couples), they may or may not share a common residence (e.g., commuting couples). The adults may or may not cohabit sexually, and the relationship may or may not involve such socially patterned feelings as love, attraction, and awe.

Goode (1995): Doubtless the following list is not comprehensive, but it [family] includes most of those relationships: (1) At least two adult persons of opposite sex reside together. (2) They engage in some kind of division of labor; that is, they do not both perform exactly the same tasks. (3) They engage in many types of economic and social exchanges; that is, they do things for one another. (4) They share many things in common, such as food, sex, residence, and both goods and social activities. (5) The adults have parental relations with their children, as their children have filial relations with them; the parents have some authority over children, and share with one another, while also assuming some obligations for protection, co-operation, and nurturance. (6) There are sibling relations among the children themselves, with, once more, a range of obligations to share, protect, and help one another.

Census Family (1996): Refers to a now-married couple (with or without never-married sons and/or daughters of either or both spouses), a couple living common-law (with or without never-married sons and/or daughters of either or both partners), or a lone parent of any marital status, with at least one never-married son or daughter living in the same dwelling.

Mandell and Duffy (2000): . . . a social ideal, generally referring to a unit of economic co-operation, typically thought to include only those related by blood, but revised by feminists to include those forming an economically co-operative, residential unit bound by feelings of common ties and strong emotions.

Census Family (2001): Refers to a married couple (with or without children of either or both spouses), a couple living common-law (with or without children of either or both partners), or a lone parent of any marital status with at least one child living in the same dwelling. A couple living common-law may be of opposite or same sex. "Children" in a census family include grandchildren living with their grandparent(s) but with no parents present.

Census Family (2006): Refers to a married couple (with or without children of either or both spouses), a couple living common-law (with or without children of either or both partners) or a lone parent of any marital status, with at least one child living in the same dwelling. A couple may be of opposite or same sex. "Children" in a census family include grandchildren living with their grandparent(s) but with no parents present.

Census Family (2011): . . . is composed of a married or common-law couple, with or without children, or of a lone parent living with at least one child in the same dwelling.

Vanier Institute of the Family (2012): . . . any combination of two or more persons who are bound together over time by ties of mutual consent, birth and/or adoption or place-ment and who, together, assume responsibilities for variant combinations of some of the following:

- Physical maintenance and care of group members;
- Addition of new members through procreation or adoption;
- Socialization of children;
- Social control of members;
- Production, consumption, distribution of goods and services; and
- Affective nurturance—love.

Census Family Sources: Statistics Canada, at www.statcan.ca, *Census Dictionary 1996*, *Census Dictionary 2001*, *Census Dictionary 2006*, and Statistics Canada (2012c).

(Holtzman, 2011: 620). Today one will have a difficult time identifying a conventional defi-nition of family accepted within and across academic research and disciplines, and formal or informal organizations. In fact, the adjectives used with the term "family" find more consensus on their definitions than the term has ever had. For example, most agree on the definition of a **nuclear family**, which typically includes a couple and their children, sharing the same household, but may also define one parent and his/her child(ren) (Ambert, 2006). Today, with divorce and remarriages, we are also seeing an increase in the number of **bi-nuclear families**—where children of divorced parents move and live across households. For children, the family they "belong to" or originate in is called their "family of origin" or "orientation" (Ambert, 2006). There is also the **extended family**, mentioned briefly above, in which several generations or sets of kin—grandparents, aunts, uncles, cousins—share a household. This has also come to be called a "multi-generational household." Similarly, terms like **household**, a set of related and unrelated individuals who share a dwelling, are also relatively easily defined.

At the individual level, there are likely as many definitions of "family" as there are families in this country, because the lived reality of "the family" is quite different from the reality privileged through Canadian law and social policy. At the same time, individual level explanations, like some more formal definitions, like the ones in Box 1.1 above, tend to stress the *structural* or *compositional definition* of the family (Gazso, 2009b; Eichler, 1983). These definitions do little more than answer the question: "who makes up a/the/your family"? Family researchers, beginning with key feminists like Margrit Eichler (1983), have long stressed the importance of rethinking our definitions of "the family," to instead focus on questions like "what *makes* a family?" And the Vanier Institute of the Family definition, above, tries to do some of this.

Gazso (2009b: 157), like Eichler, has highlighted the importance of including "process-based approaches" to doing family (much like West and Zimmerman's "doing gender," which assumes gender is "performative") that stress the relations, processes, and activities that individuals share and *do* together—the totality of sets of fluid practices—that make them a family (also see McDaniel and Tepperman, 2007; Morgan, 1996). This can and likely often includes parenting, intimacy, sharing resources, dividing household work and care work, making important decisions, etc. Similarly, Widmer (2010) treats families as dynamic systems of interdependencies that exist in shifting relational contexts. This allows for the analysis of ever-present tensions and conflicts, and recognizes the fluxes and flows in who is seen to make up a family at any given time.

Gazso (2009b) explains that these process-based approaches to defining and understanding families ("doing family") offer the potential to transcend heternormative, patriarchal, and Eurocentric assumptions about family life, and help capture the diversity and structural constraints embedded in cultural expectations. That said, she recognizes some of the shortcomings of this approach, noting that this approach runs "the risk of embracing individualism and agency to the point of neglecting to consider how agentic choices are shaped by social structure" (Gazso, 2009b: 158). She also reminds us that the structural/compositional definitions of the family, for better and worse, continue to inform eligibility and administration of social policies and programs, and service delivery (Gazso, 2009b: 158).

Eichler (2005: 53), writing on the definition of family, noted that "who is included in the definition of family is an issue of great importance as well as great consequence," because who we include in our definition will determine who is eligible to claim tax benefits, sponsor family members in immigration, claim insurance benefits, claim Indian status, etc.

Eichler challenges us to move beyond "who" definitions of family, which focus on group membership and family structure (a mom and a dad and their children, for example), towards a "what" definition of family, which focuses on the services and supports provided by various members. In accepting a "what" definition of family, we would then recognize, reward, and legitimize families for what they do together and for each other, rather than recognize and privilege only those who take the "proper" form, regardless of what happens behind closed doors.

All this said, there remains a disconnect between how individuals themselves, family sociologists, and social policies and policy makers define "family." It also reminds us that *legal/formal definitions*, like the census family, *social definitions* found within different organizations and social groups, and *personal definitions* of families have been created for different purposes and in different contexts, and so typically remain far apart and distinct.

How we define family has profound implications for who is actually counted as a family. Census data, for example, reflect and are constrained by which families are measured and how. As a result, we only know about the types of families we have legally accepted, defined, asked about, and counted. Quantitative studies typically mask the actual existence of all other family forms that inevitably exist (see "Case in Point" box).

In sum, when we try to define family, what is clear and constant is the variability of definitions. This tells us that "family" is a changing social construct that reflects variations in how states, institutions, and individuals understand, experience, and interact within it. Cheal (2008: 14) noted that family is "a term whose relevance is defined in social interaction and its referents vary according to the nature of that interaction." Social scientific definitions of family change about as rapidly as other definitions, and often reflect both formal and informal or subjective uses of the term (see Cheal, 2008). As you will see, each of the social scientific and theoretical approaches that follow adopts a somewhat different definition and set of assumptions about families, which in turn shape our understanding of it.

Theoretical and Methodological Approaches to Studying Families

Theories are not fixed, complete, or "once and for all" explanations of how things work or are expected to work. They neither emerge as "complete theories," nor remain the same because theory and research are intertwined (Ingoldsby et al., 2004: 2). As our understanding or theory changes, so do our research questions. Likewise, as we do research and come up with new observations that run counter to existing theories, our theories change. Even the seemingly unchanging or indisputable theories in the natural sciences are constructed in cultural contexts and so are influenced by social change. For example, there was Galileo's challenge to the widely accepted idea that the earth was flat, and the Catholic Church's profound disapproval of his work, resulting in his arrest. This shows us that at times, we accept things to be theoretically sound or "true" for a time, despite evidence to the contrary, even in the natural or "objective" sciences, because of the social climate in which we live.

CASE IN POINT
Accepting New (Old) Family Forms

"In February 2006, the documentary film *March of the Penguins* won an Academy Award as the best documentary film of 2005 . . . At the same time that the film was popular across North America, two legal debates were also capturing the attention of the Canadian public. The first was the legalization by statute of same-sex marriage in Canada in July 2005, after several successful constitutional challenges across the country to the common law definition of marriage. The second was revived attention, in light of particular community practices, to the criminalization of polygamy in Canada and, in particular, whether Criminal Code sanctions are the best way to address the troubling aspects of polygamous or plural unions. Both of these debates meant that Canadians were engaging with the legal definition of family in a more public way than had been seen in recent memory" (Calder, 2009: 56–7). Calder (2009: 57), using a framework drawn from the literature of law and film, shows that ". . .the popularity of this film is a backlash reaction to current challenges to the traditional notion of family in Canada and, in particular, to concerns that marriage, as a sexually monogamous institution, is under siege."

Polygamy—the marriage or marriage-like union of more than two partners at the same time—has existed in Canada and around the world for as long as family itself has existed. Still an illegal and clandestine family form (Section 293 of the Criminal Code renders being in a conjugal union with more than one person at the same time a crime), polygamy has recently received media attention, in part because of "the proliferation of so-called 'slippery slope' arguments in the conversations taking place about same-sex marriage" (Calder, 2009: 78). Calder (2009) notes that a second reason for renewed attention to polygamy in 2005 was the media attention to community practices in Bountiful, British Columbia, where some Mormon (Church of Jesus Christ of Latter Day Saints) residents of Bountiful, following the teachings of Joseph Smith, were practicing polygyny (a single man marrying multiple wives).

Polygamy, despite there being very few prosecutions throughout history, has been illegal in Canada since it was written into the Criminal Code in 1892. But the question remains, should loving and living in a marriage or marriage-like union with more than one person at the same time be illegal in Canada today?

Paradigm shifts, or radical shifts in scientific views, occur after *significant* data have been collected that do not fit the existing theory to the extent that a new theory is needed to fit the data. This is clearly the case in theorizing on/about families, as family theories have undergone a number of significant shifts and modifications, resulting from challenges and social change.

Theories provide us with a lens through which we look at the social world. With a shift in theory, we take on a different lens through which we try to understand the social world in general and families in particular. Theories then suggest *what* we look at and *how*, because each theory contains underlying assumptions about how the social world works—which in turn guide our research questions and methods. For example, some assume human behaviour is biologically based, and so things like the gender division of labour are not only justified and necessary, but natural, inevitable, and unchanging or unalterable. Others assume our behaviour is learned and so can be unlearned, relearned, or learned differently as products of the culture in which we live; and therefore patterns of behaviour can be constructed to support specific groups and interests, at the expense of others. For the first group of theorists, certain kinds of social change are viewed as problematic or dysfunctional, and so they seek to preserve particular existing structures and relations. Others, like those in the second group, recognize power struggles and inequities in existing structures and relations, and so seek change.

Although some approaches seemingly lend themselves to certain methods, as we will see below, it is important to note that sociologists and other family researchers *within* each theoretical tradition can and do use multiple types of methods—both qualitative and quantitative—at times, such that theories and methods do not always "line up" exactly.

Researchers may use seemingly similar methods but with different theoretical approaches, and so come to very different results. For example, anthropologists have been studying families in cross-cultural contexts, and comparative **case studies**, for a relatively long time. Within the discipline there has also been considerable variation in theorizing. For example, George Murdock (1949), who surveyed 250 human societies, concluded that the nuclear family was universal and served four basic social functions: sexual, economic, reproductive, and educational. According to Murdock, a man and woman constitute an efficient co-operating unit, whereby a man's "superior physical strength" and ability to "range further afield" to hunt and trade, complements a woman's "lighter tasks" performed in or near the home. He noted that all known societies work this way because of innate and inevitable biological facts and differences (Murdock, 1949: 7).

In contrast, Margaret Mead's comparative ethnographic research done in the South Pacific at approximately the same time is **qualitative** and descriptive in nature. Mead identified considerable variation across cultures and stressed that the division of labour in every known society rests firmly on learned behaviour and not simply on biological differences. For example, she noted that if and when men went away to work in large cities, women were left behind to do the farm labour, which, by Murdock's biological explanation, would be considered heavy male labour requiring "superior male strength." She did not dismiss or even minimize biology, but instead argued that "human beings have learned, laboriously, to be human" (Mead, 1949: 198).

Clearly, two seemingly similar cross-cultural studies of societies from around the world have come to different conclusions about family life because of differing theoretical orientations. Let us explore some of these theoretical differences.

Functionalism

In general, structural functionalist theories are based on the idea of organic ontology, which assumes that society is like a living organism or body, made up of a series of interrelated parts working together for the good of the whole. Each social institution or subsystem, like parts of the organism/body, serves specific functions, keeping society in a state of equilibrium. Individuals within the institutions, like cells in a body, fill specific and pre-scribed roles, again, for the proper functioning of the institution and society. From a func-tionalist point of view, families are institutions that serve specific functions in society, and family members are expected to fill prescribed roles within the institution for the good of society as a whole. Social change, or a challenge to the existing order, is then undesirable, at best.

Murdock's work exemplifies this approach. He believed we can best understand "the family" by examining what it does and how it functions for and within society. Talcott Parsons (1955) also studied the functions of family by looking at the roles men and women fill within them. According to Parsons, men were biologically better suited to fulfill *instru-mental functions*, that is, tasks that needed to be performed to ensure a family's physical survival, including providing for the material needs of the family by earning an income (Parsons and Bales, 1955). Women were believed to be better suited to performing *expressive functions*—the tasks involved in building emotionally supportive relationships among fam-ily members—that are needed for their psychological well-being. In other words, women were expected to fill the nurturing role.

Researchers who begin with a functionalist theoretical orientation are likely to look for cultural universals and aspects of dominant family forms and ask "What purpose do they serve?" They are also likely to look negatively upon rapid social change that could challenge or disrupt the existing social order. Much of this has been criticized, as you will see in the following discussion. More recent neo-functionalist approaches have also tried to address some of the critiques (see Swenson, 2008; White and Klein, 2008).

Marxism

The functionalist approach to the study of families was particularly popular in North America throughout the 1940s and 1950s. However, competing views also existed and some researchers studying families turned to the work of Friedrich Engels, who provided a very different explanation and approach to the study of families in *Origin of the Family, Private Property and the State* (1972 [1884]). Engels, like Marx, argued that a number of dis-tinct phases in human history shape, alter, and constrain human relations. He explained that the mode of production, or the way we organize economic life—whether the hunt-ing and gathering (foraging) in primitive communism, land-based (agrarian) feudalism, or modern industry and profit-driven capitalism—affects the way we organize social life and experience family relations. He noted in the shift away from primitive communism, characterized by a foraging/nomadic existence, that there was the absence of the notion of private ownership and relative equality between the sexes. Then, with land-based feudal-ism came a reorganization and privatization of family life and a change in power relations between the sexes. With the advent of the notion of private ownership and male control of land and other property, women lost power and control both within and outside of families. Ideally, for Marxists, the social goal is to abolish private property, re-establish communism, and return to more equitable relations between the sexes. Thus, unlike functionalists, for Marxists, gender differences in power and status, and the domination of men over women, within and outside families, is neither natural nor inevitable but rather is a product of the (re)organization of economic life. This approach, again unlike functionalism, implies that social change is a normal, and at times desirable, part of social life. For family researchers who embrace a Marxist approach, a likely goal would be to identify power relations within the home and connect them to inequities in economic relations outside it.

Symbolic Interactionism

While Marxists looked outside of families to economic forms and relations to understand what was happening within them, others have looked instead within families at social relations and interactions. That is, while Marxists saw economic forces acting on individuals and families, others, like George Herbert Mead, assumed that individuals were active agents or "doers" of social life. In other words, if you want to understand social life in general and family life in particular, you should examine how individuals construct meaning through their daily interactions with others. For example, according to Mead, understanding family involves understanding parent–child relations and "the relationship between the sexes" (Mead, 1967 [1934]: 238). Exchanges or interactions between them lead to the organization of the family and society. That is, he explained that "all such larger units or forms of human social organization as the clan or the state are ultimately based upon, and whether directly or indirectly are developments from or extensions of, the family" (ibid., 229). Therefore, in contrast to Marxism, this approach implies that the individuals and interactions within families shape the organization of family life, which in turn helps shape larger organizations like the state. Thus, if one were to do research using this theoretical approach, it is very likely that one would conduct in-depth, qualitative interviews with family members and/or observe individuals and interactions within families as they happen. At the same time, a researcher would seek to uncover the rich and complex underlying meanings of interactions and relations, often from the point of view of the individuals involved in the exchanges.

Exchange Theory

Social exchange theory is a broad theoretical framework used to examine relational processes within families. It borrows from psychology, sociology, and economics, as it seeks to explain the development, maintenance (including power), and decay of "exchange relationships" (Nakonezny and Denton, 2008). It focuses on understanding the balance between the costs and rewards that marital partners obtain when choosing to be and remain within a conjugal relationship. In this approach, marital exchange relationships are conceptualized as transactions between partners, (and the costs and rewards associated with those transactions), of valued resources—including love and affection—which culminate in individual or family-level profit or losses. The theory maintains that partners seek positive outcomes based on rewards and costs, but each partner must value the other's activities for relational solidarity to be sustained. It purports that couples who receive favourable reward/cost outcomes from each other—the distribution of rewards and costs is perceived to be fair (enough)—are more likely to develop solidarity and be more satisfied with their marriage (Homans, 1974). These are then the families that are most likely to remain together. Each partner's satisfaction with the relationship is assumed to vary directly with the perceived rewards of the marital relationship and inversely with the perceived costs (Nakonezny and Denton, 2008).

A major risk factor for a relationship's stability is at least one partner's low level of satisfaction with the distribution of costs and benefits. But satisfaction alone is not enough. The theory goes on to explain that the rewards and punishments that individual actors "administer" to each other is a key source of marital power (Nakonezny and Denton, 2008). The balance of power generally belongs to that partner who contributes the greater resources to the marriage. Inevitably then "resource differentials" produce "relationship asymmetry," which can then result in exploitation in the marital relationship (Blau, 1964). While interesting and seemingly logical, because of its emphasis on micro-level exchanges and their outcomes, this theoretical approach tends to overlook the broader social and cultural contexts that shape, constrain, and alter family life.

Family Systems Theory

Influenced by symbolic interactionism, family systems theory assumes that a family is a relatively closed system of social interactions, or a site of interacting personalities. According to this theory, which happens to be especially popular among family therapists and social workers, an individual's problems and behaviour are best understood in the context of families because it is believed that the locus of pathology is not within the person but in a system dysfunction. In other words, the family is more than a collection of individuals or interactions, it is a natural social system, "with its own rules, roles, communication patterns, and power structure" (Ingoldsby et al., 2004: 168).

Urie Bronfenbrenner's ecological theory of human development uses a systems approach to understanding family life by looking at how the home environment, or microsystem, affects child development. Bronfenbrenner's ecological model, however, explains child development as a multi-level interactive process, requiring multi-level analysis of a number of interconnected systems. His bioecological paradigm stresses the importance of reciprocal interactions between individuals and their micro- (family environment), meso- (e.g., school), exo- (institutions beyond a child's immediate environment, like a parent's workplace), and macro systems (customs, values, and laws of the culture in which we live) on developmental and socio-emotional outcomes (Bronfenbrenner, 1977). Bronfenbrenner argued that a child's immediate family environment, larger social environment, other systems, and institutions shape development. All of these interacting systems, taken together, provided an understanding of child development.

Doing research from this theoretical perspective would require the researcher to study interactions at multiple levels, modelled like a series of circles, one inside the other. One may first study a child's interactions within the home, the first and smallest circle; then the child's interactions at school, the next and slightly larger circle; then the child's neighbourhood, the next and larger circle, etc. One would try to understand how the child is affected by and affects relations within each environment or circle.

Developmental Theories

In the 1940s, some family researchers noted that, like individuals, families were influenced by developmental processes, or experienced life cycles, with clearly delineated stages (Ingoldsby et al., 2004). In a report created for the "First National Conference on the Family" called together by US President Truman, Duvall and Hill (1948) outlined a relatively new and interdisciplinary approach to the study of families. Evelyn Millis Duvall, a specialist in human development, teamed up with Reuben Hill, a family sociologist, to create the family development theory. Using Freud's work on psychosexual development, Erikson's research on psychosocial development, Piaget's theories on cognitive development, and Kohlberg's ideas on moral development, along with demographic and **longitudinal** research on families, Duvall and Hill argued that families go through a series of eight sequential or developmental stages in the family life cycle (Duvall, 1988). At each life stage—marriage, child-bearing, preschool, school, teen, launching centre, middle-aged, and aging—family members, depending on their physical maturation, are challenged by different developmental tasks and normative events, which can, at times, result in stress, crises, and critical transitions.

Duvall noted that "although the timing and duration of family life cycle stages vary widely, families everywhere try to conform to norms present in all societies in what is expected at each life cycle's stage" (ibid., 130). She explained that the family development theory was unique among theoretical frameworks because:

(a) its family life cycle dimension provides the basis for study of families over time;
(b) its emphasis on the developmental tasks of individual family members and of families at every stage of their development;
(c) its built-in recognition of family stress at critical periods in development; and
(d) its recognition ever since 1947 of the need for services, supports, and programs for families throughout their life cycles. (ibid., 133)

More recent research (Cooke and Gazso, 2009) using a life-course approach has attempted to capture life-course complexity and gender-specific experiences and trajectories, which were somewhat lacking in the original approach (see Krüger and Levy, 2001).

Biases in Traditional Approaches/Theorizing

Within many of the family theories popular throughout the first half of the twentieth century, the family was conceptualized as an important but relatively isolated unit "whose internal structures resulted mainly from negotiated action of adult members" (Krüger and Levy, 2001: 149). Most of these theories tended to treat all or most families as homogeneous, and questions about gender differences affecting experiences within families, and inequality, generally remained unasked and unanswered. Writing about this, Eichler (1997) noted that, in fact, a great deal of theorizing about families in the past contained a number of hidden assumptions and biases. She identified seven biases in past family literature and theorizing: monolithic, conservative, sexist, ageist, micro-structural, racist, and heterosexist. She noted that a number of theories tended to treat family as a monolithic structure by emphasizing uniformity of experience and universality of functions—*monolithic bias*. In other words, theories tended to under-represent the diversity of family forms that actually existed in any given society. She identified a *conservative bias*, where theorists tended to provide only a romanticized view of the nuclear family and regarded recent changes as ephemeral. A *sexist bias* was manifested in a number of ways, including the assumption that there is a "natural" division of functions between the sexes. Theorists also almost exclusively talked about families as involving exchanges between two middle-aged adults, largely excluding children and the elderly in their analysis, producing an *ageist bias*. She identified a *microstructural bias*, a tendency to treat families as encapsulated units, typically ignoring extraneous/ external factors. Theories also often devalued or outright ignored families of culturally or ethnically non-dominant groups—*racist bias*—and treated the heterosexual family as "natural," denying family status to lesbian and gay families—*heterosexist bias*. A large number of these biases have since been addressed by feminist theorizing on families.

The "Big Bang"—Feminist Theories

Feminism is not a new paradigm, and in fact has existed for as long as, if not longer than, sociology itself (for example, see Mary Wollstonecraft, 1759–97). But what is new is the force with which feminism was able to challenge existing family theories in the period following the 1960s—a period that David Cheal (1991) called "the big bang." Since then, feminist scholarship and feminist questions have charted a different course for theorizing families. Feminism "is not only an academic school of thought, it is also a broad movement for change" (Cheal, 1991: 9). Feminism took what, for a long time, have been considered intimate or "private" matters: sexuality, violence, child-rearing and care, domestic division of labour, etc., and made them public, social, and political issues—not only worthy of study, but in need of change.

For more on feminist theories, see "Feminist Explanations of Violence" in Chapter 14, p. 279.

Feminist theorizing on families generally challenges the apparently gender-neutral assumptions about family life and roles—often found in other family theories—that mask or ignore inequalities and result in negative outcomes for women. Feminists typically seek to determine who does what, for whom, and with what consequences, often assessing the differential distribution of activities, resources, and power (see Saul, 2003). Second, feminists believe that gender relations in the home and in other institutions are neither natural nor immutable, but rather historical and socio-cultural products, subject to reconstruction (Elliot and Mandel, 1998). Typically, feminists subject marriage and family to a series of profound and critical questions, challenge myths about women's roles and abilities, and advocate for change.

Having said this, there is considerable variation within feminism, as feminists themselves depart from or have developed in response to different intellectual traditions, for example, Marxism, symbolic interactionism, phenomenology, and psychoanalysis. These traditional approaches were "sooner or later all reflected in feminist analysis of family life, and they were in turn transformed by it" (Cheal, 1991: 2). As a result, within feminism there are liberal feminists, Marxist feminists, radical feminists, socialist feminists, psycho-analytic feminists, post-structural feminists, post-colonial feminists, anti-racist feminists, etc. Each focuses on a somewhat different aspect of inequality, often identifying a different source of the problem or problems, and therefore proposing different solutions. The authors of the chapters that follow reflect some of this diversity. One prominent Canadian example of feminist theorizing on families, found in this book, focuses on the notion of social reproduction. This approach draws on Marxist and socialist feminism to shed light on power and household relations in capitalist economies like ours.

Gazso (2009b) points out that for many feminist scholars the theoretical framework of social reproduction offers a sharp focus on both micro-level relations and activities that make up families, and the broader social processes that constrain them. This theoretical approach begins by pointing out that while men's paid work in the public sphere has been historically viewed as productive and socially valuable, the unpaid work so often carried out by women, which meets the care and economic needs to maintain life on a daily basis and contributes to the reproduction of labour in capitalist societies, has for the most part been undervalued and ignored (Gazso, 2009b; Bezanson and Luxton, 2006; Bezanson, 2006b; Fox and Luxton, 2001; Luxton 2001).

Researchers embracing this theoretical approach focus their attention on women's care behaviours and relations and work to highlight how women socially reproduce daily life for family members, making it possible to, among other things, allow men to engage in paid work (Fox and Luxton 2001). Gazso (2009b) notes that social reproduction includes various kinds of work—mental, manual, and emotional—aimed at providing the socially variable care necessary to maintain life and to reproduce the next generation. This theoretical approach, while keenly in tune with the resistance and agency of women from various racialized groups and class backgrounds, has been critiqued for not having done enough to analyze and recognize the experiences of those growing up in gay and lesbian families.

Queer theory has provided some additional stimulus in rethinking family theories, because most, as noted above, feminist approaches have been criticized for failing to provide an adequate analysis of lesbian and gay family experiences. For example, while feminists have done important work on family violence and on the subordination of women of different races, classes, and of other diverse backgrounds, most have failed to note that for lesbian families, "it is not their powerlessness *within* the family that marks their subordination, but rather their *denial of access to* a legitimate and socially instituted sphere of family, marriage, and parenting" (Calhoun, 2000: 139). This more critical theorizing and activism has resulted in legal and attitudinal changes; on the other hand, much remains to be done.

Conclusion

Today, as in the past, Canadian families exist in a number of very diverse forms, which, in relation to other social institutions, both aid and constrain individual family members. That is, while a variety of family forms have existed in the past, our changing definitions of family are now making it possible for us to identify, count, and validate a variety of diverse forms. At the same time, our current definitions, theories, and measurement tools are likely to miss or mask a number of family forms that actually exist but remain unrecognized and uncounted, and these family forms may become part of future definitions of family.

Our current and shifting definitions reflect changing social attitudes, economic trends, laws, and policies. At the same time, changing economic trends and social attitudes have changed the age of first marriage; the duration of a marriage; whether marriage occurs at all; family size; the sequence and spacing of life-cycle events; where families live, whether they live together or apart, or across households and/or borders; and how they live.

With changing definitions and trends there have been shifts in how family theorists and researchers study and try to understand family life. Some are critical of change, while others actively seek it. Some look within families to understand them, some look outside them, and still others look at a combination or variety of contexts. Some take a qualitative and descriptive approach, some a quantitative one, and others use both. The chapters that follow will reflect some of this diversity in approaches, as they map out and critically assess some of the trends and changes that, for better or worse, are part of the complex collage that makes up Canadian family life.

STUDY QUESTIONS

1. Find one of your family photos that best captures or characterizes what you would consider your family. What is it about that particular photo that makes it the best? Does it capture who and what makes up your family today? Five years ago? Ten years ago? Who or what is still excluded?
2. If you were forced to come up with a description of the typical Canadian family today what would it look like? Who would you include? Exclude? What are the biggest barriers to you coming up with this description?
3. What would you consider the "best" definition of family? Why?
4. Select any two theories. How do you think they would compare in their approach to and study of non-parental child care (early childhood education and care)?
5. Why do you think Canadians are postponing marriage and childbirth? What do you think is an ideal age (if any) to marry? To have children? Why?
6. If you wanted to study the domestic division of labour within families, how would you study it? Which theoretical orientation would best suit/guide your approach?

Further Readings

Carter, Sarah. 2008. *The Importance of Being Monogamous: Marriage and Nation Building in Western Canada to 1915*. Edmonton: Alberta University Press. Carter shows that as part of Canada's nation-building efforts, the monogamous ideal was imposed on a growing and varied population of dwellers. She concludes that the consequences for women that arose from the imposition of monogamy were devastating.

Eichler, Margrit. 1997. *Family Shifts: Families, Policies, and Gender Equality*. Toronto: Oxford University Press. This classic text has proven to be a major contribution to the study of Canadian families because it both traces shifts in Canadian family composition and gender roles, and identifies important theoretical and policy implications.

Ingoldsby, Bron, Suzanne Smith, and J. Elizabeth Miller. 2004. *Exploring Family Theories*. Los Angeles: Roxbury. This book provides a detailed introduction and overview of family theory and research. Following each chapter the book includes a "sample reading" or application of the theoretical approach.

McQuillan, Kevin, and Zenaida Ravanera, eds. 2006. *Canada's Changing Families*. Toronto: University of Toronto Press. This collection of studies looks at the changing composition and role of Canadian families in a broader economic context and in light of social changes.

Trovato, Frank. 2012. *Population and Society: Essential Readings.* Toronto: Oxford University Press. This text examines, among other things, the relationship between individual action and demographic phenomena including family processes like fertility, marriage, and migration.

Widmer, Eric. 2010. *Family Configurations: A Structural Approach to Family Diversity.* Burlington, VT: Ashgate. This book takes a "configurational approach" to understanding families, which focuses on the complexities and richness of familial relationships and interdependencies within families.

Websites

www.equal-marriage.ca
Canadians for Equal Marriage pursues a nationwide, bilingual campaign for rights for same-sex families. It works at the grassroots level, in the media, and in Parliament, with the goal of persuading MPs to oppose any measures to take away equal marriage.

http://dsp-psd.pwgsc.gc.ca/Collection-R/Statcan/11-008-XIE/11-008-XIE.html
Canadian Social Trends discusses the social, economic, and demographic changes affecting the lives of Canadians. It contains the latest figures for major social indicators and articles written by Statistics Canada researchers on social situations in Canada.

http://ceris.metropolis.net/frameset_e.html
It is one of five such research centres across Canada. Its goals include promoting research on the integration of immigrants into Canadian society; providing training opportunities; disseminating policy- and program-relevant research information.

www.un.org/esa/socdev/family
This United Nations Program on the Family site contains an overview of major trends affecting families worldwide, including changing family structure, aging families, and the rise of migration. It also includes access to reports and to "Family Matters," a bimonthly circular letter with information about activities related to the family from around the globe.

www.vanierinstitute.ca
The aim of the Vanier Institute of the Family is to create awareness of the importance and strengths of Canadian families and the changes and challenges they face in their structural, demographic, economic, cultural, and social diversity.

Notes

1. The Civil Marriage Act (Bill C-38), adopted on 20 July 2005, made Canada the third country in the world after Netherlands (2000) and Belgium (2003) to legalize same-sex marriages.
2. Same-sex married couples were not enumerated in 2001.

Canada's Families: Historical and Contemporary Variations

CYNTHIA COMACCHIO

LEARNING OBJECTIVES

- To review the major changes and continuities in the history of Canadian families over the past two centuries
- To discuss how "the family" is an idealization that reinforces hierarchies of class, race, gender, and age
- To reflect on "the family" as a social construction deriving from the dominant social group's anxieties and objectives at particular historical moments
- To understand that families have always varied in form and composition, despite the force of prevailing ideas about what properly constitutes "the family"

Introduction

Most people throughout history have spent at least some part of their lives in a family or a family setting. Despite common reference to "the family" as though one model and experience are universally relevant across time and place, Canadian families have always been diverse in form and composition. Other chapters detail how twenty-first century families represent such recent trends as later first marriages and childbearing; lone-parenting and childlessness by choice; common-law, same-sex, and mixed unions; multiple divorces, remarriages, and family reconstitutions. But some of the characteristics that we associate with contemporary families, such as lone-parent, joint-custody, blended or multigenerational households, international adoptions—even families with wage-earning mothers— have existed since the nation's sixteenth-century origins in New France.

The history of the family was one of the earliest offshoots of the "new social history" that emerged in universities during the turbulent 1960s. Their shared purpose was to explore the lives of ordinary people—the majority in any time and place—and to bring to light the experiences of social groups identified, and frequently marginalized, by race, gender, class, culture, and age. These lived experiences had long been ignored by traditional analyses that focused on the tiny percentile of those—largely men—who hold political and economic power. Even in histories about monarchs and prime ministers and church leaders, family backgrounds and family networks figured strongly, because families, historically, have operated as central units of society, the economy, culture, and politics. Family, in short, was an "absent presence" in earlier historical studies that family historians, frequently borrowing conceptually and methodologically from social scientists, have attempted to recover. In doing so, they inevitably touch upon the differences that have always existed, and that remain, between what family means and what family is (Comacchio, 2000: 177–8).

In keeping with the focus of this collection on Canadian families in their pluralistic contemporary forms, this chapter emphasizes the simple fact that there are many forms and meanings of family in any historical moment. The constant is that, whatever we take to be "family," it was, and remains, important to our individual, social, and national identities. Even as they change over time, as the historical and sociological literature indicates, families persist. They are elemental to self-formation as well as to social formation. And just as they underpin identity and status, class, gender, region, race, ethnicity, religion, and age are fundamental to experiences of family, past and present.

Families as Historical Actors

Even within the broad range of family experiences that has been documented for the past several centuries of Canadian history, further variations have always been found in communities distinguished by "race" and culture: Aboriginal families, Inuit families in the North, francophone Catholic families in Quebec, and immigrant families arriving from all parts of the globe. Families adapt to, and also initiate, larger demographic, economic, cultural, and political trends. They are, in short, historical actors and not merely passive recipients of changing ideas and practices. Moreover, the emotional elements of family are

---

Box 2.1
Family Sociology in Canada

The Canadian Conference on the Family, convened by Governor General Georges Vanier in 1964, led to the founding of The Vanier Institute of the Family, which continues to be an important agency for family research and policy. University of Montreal sociologist Frederick Elkin (1918–2011) was charged with preparing the nation's first "state of the art" family survey, published as *The Family in Canada: An Account of Present Knowledge and Gaps in Knowledge about Canadian Families* (1964). Elkin observed that the nation's distinctive geography and history, and its diverse class, religious, ethnic, occupational, "and other groupings," made it "much too heterogeneous" to have "one or ten or twenty distinctive family types" (Elkin, 1964: 31–2).

> Change is a key concept for any family analyst. The family, with its crucial functions, does not expire, it changes. In varying ways, it adapts and bends and of course, in turn, it influences. (Elkin, 1964: 8)

as important to self and society as are the socio-economic and cultural functions. Families are, and have ever been, at once supportive and restrictive, nurturing and oppressive, protective and abusive, innovative and conservative, liberating and entrapping. Finally, it is important to note that while the form and function of real historical families are adaptive, the symbolic power ascribed to "the family"—a power embedded in culture and memory— has remarkable endurance. The family of ideal is socially constructed and reconstructed to meet the larger needs and objectives of any given historical moment, at least as these are defined by the dominant class. Until recently, the ideal was the patriarchal, heterosexual male-breadwinner family of white Euro-Canadian middle-class custom. This particular social construction of family retains adherents even while most Canadians today do not live in families resembling the model. Notwithstanding the public force of the ideal, and that of nostalgia, many Canadians never have.

The historic centrality of families derives from their vital functions: reproduction, production, socialization, maintenance, and regulation. Aboriginal families in pre-contact times were the basis of all economic, political, and spiritual organization, in varying ways for different clans and regions, but always functioning collectively to sustain their members and the larger community. The Europeans who arrived in the sixteenth century shared this understanding of family function. The North American colonies were focused on trade with the mother countries of France and Great Britain. This economic purpose, as well as the colonists' own need to sustain themselves through agriculture and trade, necessitated that the family duties of production, as well as reproduction, also be transplanted. Yet the very process of colonization necessitated certain adaptations to "New World" conditions. Early family theorists contended that the **stem family**, or **extended family**, characterizing traditional agrarian communities was imported intact to the New World. The abundance of cheap land in North America, however, meant that the **nuclear family**, rather than being the outcome of industrialization as theorized, actually predominated. In these sparsely settled and isolated communities, the absence of any effective regulatory or policing agency made the family's role in that respect—alongside, if always subordinate to, the Church and the courts—even more important than in Europe (Dechêne, 1992: 238–9).

At the same time, the vital economic role of families as units of production, the importance of land ownership to family fortunes, and the necessary mutual reliance of family members across generations, characterized colonial family life as much as that of the mother countries. All family members were expected to work in some capacity, performing labour according to age and gender, from childhood until they "came into their own." Adulthood was signified by early marriage and family formation, usually in separate households, although often on land allotted to sons who had worked for their families without wages since childhood. In this setting, the best outcome required that each family member sacrifice self-interest for the good of the family as a whole. These were the expectations embedded in the meanings of family, reinforced by Church and law. Marriage was both a civic responsibility and an economic necessity. Women were expected to get pregnant shortly after marrying, and could look forward to new babies at regular two- or three-year intervals until at least their mid-forties. Families with as many as a dozen children, ranging in age from infancy to young adulthood, were not the average experience but were certainly not unusual (Errington, 1995: 25–6). Childlessness was considered both a tragedy and an economic hardship. Adoption, often within family and kin circles, and often without the death of both parents, was commonplace (Strong-Boag, 2006; 2011). Put simply, survival depended on family.

By mid-nineteenth century, the British North American colonies were undergoing a profound structural transformation that would greatly affect their resident families. Alongside these fundamental economic and demographic changes were political concerns that led to the Confederation, in 1867, of the Dominion of Canada. Production gradually moved out of the home and the artisanal workshop to ever-larger "manufactories." Work and domestic life were increasingly separated, at least for the more affluent. In the urban middle class, anglophone and francophone, Protestant and Catholic, family life became less concerned with economic subsistence, and more with maintaining certain living standards in the interests of "respectability," a vital middle-class objective. This model of family life was further encouraged by a "cult of domesticity," inspired by Queen Victoria and her growing family, that emphasized **separate spheres** for men and women. While retaining their traditional patriarchal authority, men belonged to the public sphere of wage labour, business, and politics. Women, newly glorified in their traditional domestic roles, were expected to use their "innate" care-giving skills to make home and family a "haven in a heartless world." More than ever before, mothers were uniquely responsible for children's upbringing in this sheltered home (Errington, 1995: 53).

Because the processes are so entwined, there is no simple way to chart the relationship of structural and familial change through time. What we can identify is the transformative impact of the **modernization** process. Modernization was augmented and accelerated by such transportation and communication advances as canals, railways, and telegraph lines, all of which facilitated the political vision of a nation "from sea unto sea" that was realized by the first decade of the twentieth century. The industrialization and urbanization at its core were further intensified by out-migration from rural areas in central Canada, where inexpensive farm land was increasingly scarce by the last quarter of the nineteenth century, making it difficult to sustain the familial custom of outfitting adult sons with land to settle their own families.

Unprecedented waves of immigration from Europe also spurred the process. Frequently utilizing the familial practice of **chain migration**, some three million newcomers arrived in Canada between 1896 and 1914. In the decade between the Dominion census of 1901 and that of 1911, the population grew by 43 per cent, the "foreign-born" accounting for 22 per cent of all Canadians. Many newcomers were intent on resettling families and kin and even entire villages, complete with their social institutions, on the prairies. Enticed by the promise of free land, opportunity, and religious tolerance, these families were critical to the vision of a prosperous modern Canada. Others, especially male migrant workers eager to make money to enrich their families overseas or perhaps to bring them to Canada after establishing themselves, joined the expanding urban proletariat (Knowles, 1997: 123–4).

Modernization also saw the traditional family functions of educating children and caring for the sick and the elderly gradually transferred out of the household to public institutions, whether funded by charity, or, eventually, by the state. The first transfer of functions to the state was schooling. Pre-industrial families were responsible for children's education, in its widest sense, through the generational transmission of both life and work skills, as well as a rudimentary literacy and numeracy. Beginning with Ontario in 1871, most provinces enacted compulsory schooling legislation that specified the ages during which children were expected to attend publicly funded schools, as well as the number of years. Because needy families could not aspire to such a protected childhood for their own, many children continued to work. The common experience in this transitional stage, despite the laws, was an erratic school attendance with "time out" to earn wages, help at home, or work on family farms (Sutherland, 2000:159–60).

There is much historical evidence to indicate that working-class families were bearing the brunt of exploitation and deprivation in the midst of the rapid socio-economic changes at the turn of the twentieth century. In 1900, infant, child, and maternal mortality, orphanhood, and early widowhood disrupted between 35 and 40 per cent of all Canadian families (Copp, 1974; Piva, 1976). Rough estimates suggest that as many as 1 in 5 babies lost their lives before their first birthdays, the majority in the first year of life. This was very much a class mortality. The children of the poor were particularly vulnerable to impure water and milk, the contagion fostered by crowded living conditions, and the expense of medical care. For women of childbearing age, maternal mortality was the second-ranked threat to life (Comacchio, 1993).

An organized response to the dislocations brought about by modernizing forces took shape in the form of an urban-based Protestant middle-class reform movement. The **Social Gospel** was inspired by the traditional Christian commitment to alleviating the suffering

For more on the notion of the male breadwinner and the "male model of employment", see "Paid Work" in Chapter 9, p. 167.

of the needy, but also by mounting middle-class anxieties about the urban slums, disease, alcoholism, infant mortality, prostitution, "racial degeneration" and other horrors, real and imagined, seen to have been unleashed (Allen, 1971; Valverde, 1991). Among the movement's members was a growing contingent of women, many of whom contended that their "innate" maternal capacity qualified them for the necessary "clean up," both material and moral, that the situation demanded. They used these **maternal feminist** arguments to pressure municipal and provincial governments to address the problems of poor families, especially those threatening children. By the 1890s, in most provinces, new laws aimed to remove boys under the age of 12 and girls under the age of 14 from paid employment and to define suitable working conditions for those of employable age but not yet adults. Because of their perceived "delicacy," and their understood maternal "vocation," women were included in this protective legislation. The "factory laws" reinforced the middle-class male breadwinner family ideal. However well-intentioned, their effect was to take away jobs from women and children for whom personal and family need meant that they had no choice but to earn wages. In the absence of social support networks, the family's material condition, not legislation, determined who would work (Ursel, 1992: 97–9; Sutherland, 2000: 24–5).

Structural changes, legislation, and new ideas about "the family" effectively redefined women and children as non-working dependants of male breadwinners. Much work, both productive and reproductive, remained in the home. Through the course of the twentieth century, however, work and family became increasingly disassociated in the public imagination and in state policy. Work was redefined as the wage labour of men functioning as primary breadwinners. Yet many women and children continued to "earn their keep" and help to sustain their families, although often in ways that were neither paid nor enumerated. On farms, women and children worked many hours in such unwaged activities as egg and dairy production; in vegetable, fruit, and small animal cultivation for domestic use and market sale; and as essential seasonal labour for sowing and harvesting. In urban working-class homes, children were kept out of school to earn or to mind younger siblings so that mothers could take paid employment. Women took in boarders or laundry or "piece work," usually sewing, often helped by their children and by the elderly family members for whom the dreaded workhouse was the only public welfare provision (Bradbury, 1993; Montigny, 1993). Because male employment continued to be seasonal and subject to regular recessionary contractions, and public welfare was scarce and inadequate, few working-class families could survive on the wages of a sole breadwinner. Moreover, the value of the daily domestic labour traditionally performed by women in caring for children, husbands, and dependent family members was undermined by the association of work with wages earned outside the home, and consequently with male labour. The result was an under-valuation of female labour both inside the home and in the marketplace, in the understanding that women's unpaid work in the home was not as important to family subsistence as that of men in the workplace. This assessment also applied to women's paid work, deemed unskilled and "menial" by virtue of being feminine.

Box 2.2
Domestic Labour and Social Reproduction

By the 1980s, Canadian feminist sociologists were actively involved in the "domestic labour debates," using historical analysis to emphasize that women's unpaid labour in the home was both productive and reproductive, and that the vital work of social reproduction did, in fact, have substantial economic value in the past as in the present. Meg Luxton's seminal work, *More Than a Labour of Love: Three Generations of Women's Work in the Home* (1980), contended that, in working-class homes, women's unpaid work often made the difference between destitution and family survival. In the present, domestic labour is still mostly "women's work" and still under-valued.

> . . . what women (and men) do, looking after their homes and the people they live with, is work that contributes, not just to the survival of their own households, but to the daily and generational maintenance of the population that sustains the formal economy. Traditionally, the unpaid work women do in their homes, looking after their families, has not been recognized as work, nor valued for its contribution to the economy, and therefore, was not taken into consideration in policy priorities. . . . recent evidence suggests that unpaid domestic labour in Canada continues to be a significant part of the economy, that women do most of it and that without the care work of families, Canadian society would not function. (Luxton, 1980: 14)

Despite the evident gap between "the family" of ideal and many real Canadian families, the male breadwinner family model represented the key to social stability and national welfare in times of socio-economic upheaval and public anxiety. This construction of "the family" clearly reflected the Euro-Canadian, middle-class, urban family experiences and ideals of the times. But it held enough aspirational appeal to less affluent Canadians that it dominated both public discourses and public policy regarding families for the better part of the twentieth century.

To understand the centrality of family on the homesteading frontier in early twentieth century Canada, we need only recall the famous words of Laurier's Minister of the Interior, **Clifford Sifton**, invoking the arrival of the "stalwart peasant in a sheepskin coat." The less-cited remainder of this familiar quote refers to the "good quality," in the day's racist terms, represented by the ideal immigrant and his "stout wife and half a dozen children." Immigration was the first priority of the Laurier years (1896–1911), but the "open door" policy encouraging immigrants of all origins is also more mythic than historic. Canadian immigration policy was racially exclusive as well as economically selective. For those deemed "undesirable" and "unassimilable"—virtually all prospective immigrants outside of Great Britain, the United States, and western Europe—official policy deliberately thwarted the establishment of certain new families, or the resettlement of existing ones. Increasingly restrictive racist regulations achieved their purpose by blocking the reproduction of Asian and South Asian families. The 1911 census showed that these immigrant communities were almost exclusively male. In 1923, the **Chinese Immigration Act** closed the doors to Chinese immigrants, including wives and children of those already in Canada, until after the Second World War (Stanley, 2011: 43–4, 136).

For more on immigration policies in Canada, see "Immigrants" in Chapter 12, pp. 229–31.

Aboriginal families inarguably suffered the most dramatic effects of all in the midst of this societal transformation and the determined political focus on "nation-building." Intent on aggressive western "settlement," the federal government ignored the fact that "the Territories" had been settled for centuries by diverse clans of Indigenous peoples. The influx of white settlers threatened their traditional family economies based on hunting, trapping, and fishing. Their social and political customs, based in extensive networks of family and kin relations, were subjected to the interference of white missionaries, traders, government agents, and settlers alike. The **scientific racism** that fuelled Victorian imperialism ensured few challenges to the notion of Aboriginal racial inferiority. The newcomers were critical of the "mixed" families of white traders and Aboriginal and Métis women that had long sustained the now-expired fur trade. These families, known as "half-breeds" or Métis according to their British or French-Canadian paternity, constituted a new society that was not recognized by successive governments as either Canadian or, after the passage of the **Indian Act** (1876), as **Status Indian**.

In striving to replicate "the family" of white middle-class ideal, the Indian Act legislated women's subordination by insisting on **patrilineage**, the primacy of reproduction, and their exclusive identification according to the "Indian" status of their husbands. Aboriginal men who married white women conferred their status on wives and children. Aboriginal women who married white men lost all privileges associated with Indian status, and their children were likewise considered "non-status" (Carter, 1999; Dickason, 2010). After the land treaties of the 1870s, the reserve system and the required transition to a farming lifestyle, without the promised training and provision, left many families in abject poverty, facing the threat of deliberate deculturation by means of imposed educational, economic, and domestic institutions, most notably the compulsory **residential schools**. Run by missionaries of both Catholic and Protestant background, their purpose was to remove children from their families and communities in order to break the cultural transmission of their languages and customs. In short, the schools forcibly distanced children from their own families in every sense. The neglect and abuse that many children suffered far from home led even

> **CASE IN POINT**
> **Indigenous Families, Past and Present**
>
> A member of the Mohawk Nation and Professor emerita of Native Studies at Trent University, Marlene Brant Castellano brings Indigenous understandings of family and history to her assessment of contemporary Aboriginal family trends:
>
> > Aboriginal families are nested in communities and nations which have seen their lands alienated, their laws dismissed as "customs" and their beliefs ridiculed. Families have been at the centre of a struggle between colonial governments bent on absorbing "Indians" into Euro-Canadian society and parents, Elders and leaders, who have been equally determined to maintain their identities as peoples with unique and continuing responsibilities in the world. The current challenges that Aboriginal families face are rooted in that history of struggle. The future trajectory of Aboriginal family life will be determined in large part by the success of Aboriginal collectives in establishing their place as peoples and nations within Canada. (Castellano, 2002: 15)

some government officials charged with the assimilation project to estimate that as many as 50 per cent did not survive to leave at the age of 14 (Miller, 1996). The tragic individual, familial, and cultural impact of the residential schools has manifested generationally into the twenty-first century.

The Shape(s) of Modern Families

Inextricably bound with modernizing processes, demographic changes have fundamentally affected the size, as well as the life course, of Canadian families over this entire period. Another "family myth" challenged by the historical evidence is that late marriage and family limitation are relatively recent developments occasioned by industrialization and urbanization, and in particular, by increasing opportunities for women in the new milieu. In pre-industrial Canada, large families were economically beneficial because all hands were needed to survive and prosper. As good land became more expensive, however, marriages were delayed so that prospective male breadwinners could earn wages "hiring out" as agricultural labourers, or working in resource industries, urban factories, or on the canals and railways. By 1900, the average age at marriage for men was 28 years, and for women, 25 years. Later ages at marriage also meant fewer children, evidenced in the corresponding reduction in family size. These demographic trends were not directly caused by the transition to industrial capitalism, for all its impact, but would soon be intensified by it (Sutherland, 2000: 14).

Also important to the decline in family size were new ideas about the nature of children and the ideal childhood. Proclaimed at once to be **"Canada's Century"** and, internationally, **"The Century of the Child,"** the new century saw the widespread circulation of middle-class ideas about childhood as a special, vulnerable, and dependent life-stage associated with play, schooling, and "character formation." The new childhood demanded more attention to individual children and consequently smaller families (Sutherland, 2000: 20–2). Although this special childhood belonged to those born into affluent families, urban living, child labour laws, and compulsory schooling made smaller families even more economically advantageous for the less fortunate. In 1901, women gave birth to an average of 4.6 children; by 1921, this had fallen to 3.5 (Wargon, 1997: 1) With the notable exception of the early post–Second World War years, the trend toward later marriage and smaller families has continued unabated to the present.

In times when marital dissolution faced tremendous religious disapproval as well as legal obstacles, it is not surprising that the social stigma against divorce was intense. The law was very restrictive: divorce was only granted with proof of adultery and then by an Act of Parliament. While no church sanctioned divorce, the Roman Catholic Church, dominant in Quebec, forbade it except by means of its own very rare annulment process. There were only 11 divorces in all Canada in 1900 (Snell, 1991: 9). This is not to say that couples did not separate, re-partner, blend families, or add to them in new relationships. Desertion was known as "the poor man's divorce." Because women's limited opportunities meant that many were truly only "a man away from poverty," common-law second marriages were probably far more numerous than statistics reveal. Many Canadians spent at least some portion of their childhood in single-parent or blended family households, consequently, although both single parenthood and remarriage were more commonly the result of the death of a spouse rather than divorce until the laws were eased in 1969 (Milan, 2000: 3).

Also noteworthy in the history of families is the expanding role of women during the past century. Ironically, just as separate spheres ideology was glorifying domesticity, new opportunities were opening up to women—at least the young and unmarried—for paid employment, higher education, and participation in the organizations that dominated public activity at the turn of the century. The roles and rights of respectable women—the "woman question"—quickly came to be equated with crisis in the family, women's "proper sphere." Women both married and unmarried joined groups such as the **Women's Christian Temperance Union** (1874), the **National Council of Women of Canada** (1893), and the rural **Women's Institutes** (1897). Employing conservative **maternal feminist** arguments to defend their "unfeminine" public involvement, and to argue for the political rights they needed to effect the reforms they wanted, these women worked toward an unprecedented female autonomy. The Great War accelerated both women's public involvement and their entry into paid labour, finally delivering the right to vote in 1918, albeit to recognize their womanly "sacrifice" for the cause rather than gender equality (Sangster, 2001: 201–3).

For anxious observers, such advances for women implied a "new day" that held dangers for "the family" by drawing them into pursuits other than marriage and motherhood. Although such prospects remained unrealized for most women, Canadians were frightened enough by the prospects alone. The Great War had cost the under-populated young nation some 66,000 men, young fathers, and would-be fathers. Added to this was the toll taken by the Spanish influenza epidemic in 1919, which hit hardest in the 20–40-year-old cohort of parents and would-be parents. Not surprisingly, the 1920s occasioned a renewed public attention to marriage and family formation, and especially to "the crisis in the family," in the interests of a much-desired return to "normalcy." Governments that had expanded their role to conduct the war continued on their own modernizing path toward the interventionist state, if slowly and reluctantly. Among their postwar priorities was safeguarding "the family." In 1920, the federal government established the Canadian Council on Child and Family Welfare (later the National Welfare Council), the largest social welfare tribunal in the land, to direct research on families and related policy initiatives. New state agencies and programs called on the rising class of "family experts," drawn from medicine, psychology, sociology, social work, and education, to formulate modern programs and policies. These were largely instructional, centred on parent, especially maternal, education. Education was considered the most effective, and least interventionist, means of promoting healthier, happier families for a productive, "efficient" modern Canada (Comacchio, 1993: 22–7). In this manner, a new relationship was forged between the state and "experts" that shaped their modern roles in, and relations with, families.

During the interwar years, some of the new "family experts" espoused **eugenics**, a pseudo-science inspired by Darwinism and premised on the notion of "selective breeding." Eugenicists strove to restrict the immigration that many felt was leading to "racial degeneration." Especially among the newly influential medical profession, many supported anti-contraception campaigns, since "race suicide," as they viewed family limitation, appeared to be largely a practice of educated middle-class "better stock" couples (McLaren, 1990: 13–17). **Pronatalism** offered the solution to the perceived crisis in the family, by definition a crisis in society. The "better stock" would be encouraged by family experts, governments, voluntary agencies, and the popular media, to marry, have children, and submit to parent education to produce model future citizens. Modern science would replace custom and "superstition," and modern experts, backed by the state, would replace the now outmoded traditional sources of childrearing wisdom found in family and community (Comacchio, 1993: 92–3).

If concerns about the "crisis in the family" were intensifying, marriage and family formation remained the choice of most Canadians, although certain "modern" trends were becoming apparent. The 1921 Census revealed a proportionately greater number of married Canadians than at any previous time on record. The 14 per cent decline in the birth rate between 1921 and 1931, however, testified to the continuous spread of birth control despite its illegality. But it also testified to the impact of urban life and the rising costs of living, as well as to the spread of new ideas about childhood, and the growing correlation of small families with better quality of life. While infant and child mortality remained high, some improvement was being effected through education and improved public health and sanitation measures, especially immunization, milk inspection, and free well-baby clinics. Longer life expectancy also increased the average length of marriages. Combined with smaller family size, this development changed the family life course, extending the time between children leaving home and the death of husband or wife. Couples who married in 1920, therefore, could expect this post-parental stage to be almost seven years longer than it was for those who married in 1900, a demographic fact with important implications for the marital relationship and old age. In fact, the plight of the elderly drew considerable public attention during the interwar years, as more Canadians lived longer, and as more families were increasingly strained to provide for their dependent elderly, especially during the Great Depression (Snell, 1996; Davies, 2003: 145).

Many of the ambitious plans calling on state expansion for family welfare purposes were seriously curtailed with the start of the Great Depression in October 1929.

A decade of unrelenting, widespread economic hardship, the Depression was effectively a gender crisis, more particularly a crisis of male unemployment, and consequently of the male-breadwinner family ideal. Estimated crudely at between 30 and 50 per cent of the male labour force (ages 14 and older) the pervasive joblessness meant that many couples could not take on the financial burdens of marriage and family. Rates of marriage fell notably during the "Dirty Thirties," from 7.5 marriages per 1,000 of the population in 1928 to 5.9 in 1932. By 1937, the birth rate had fallen to an average of 2.6 children per family, an historic low. The decline is partly explained by delayed marriages, but it was also due to deliberate family limitation by couples who simply could not feed any more children and could not envision better times (McLaren and McLaren, 1986: 65; Comacchio, 1993: 158–9).

The gap between ideal and reality became painfully evident for more Canadians than ever before when the Depression undermined the material security and quality of life of families usually unaffected by periodic economic contractions. For many, the Depression necessitated a return to an older family model, that of the interdependent family economy, that middle-class and more prosperous working-class families had been discarding. Anything that any family member could contribute by way of wages took on new importance. While this usually entailed additional employment for women, paid much less than men and consequently hired instead, it did not strike at the heart of feminine identity in the way that the loss of breadwinner status affected men (Baillargeon, 1999; Campbell, 2009). In this atmosphere of social collapse, all government policy focused on assisting men and "righting" the social order by providing jobs and "relief" for male breadwinners (Struthers, 1983).

Despite the rhetoric of state intervention, of a "**New Deal**" for the common good, the welfare measures of the Depression years were minimal. In September 1939, another national emergency presented itself. As Canadians entered into a second world war, little more than a generation after the first, the reluctant Liberal government led by William Lyon Mackenzie King recognized that its citizens, especially the young men demanded for armed service, could not be asked to fight without assurance of their families' welfare, both "for the duration" and also at war's end (Marshall, 2006: 73–4). Facing the need to support the war effort and also to address public fears about a possible postwar return to depression, the government was at last prepared to consider a national social security program. Measures to support the besieged male breadwinner family were its basis. Unemployment insurance became a reality in 1941, but it left most working women out of its provisions. In 1943, McGill University social scientist Leonard Marsh presented his seminal *Report on Social Security for Canada* to the House of Commons Committee on Reconstruction and Rehabilitation. Its entire purpose was to establish a "**social minimum**" for all Canadians as a right of citizenship and not on the basis of demonstrated need, as had historically been the case. The Marsh report emphasized that families must have an unequivocal place at the heart of all post-war welfare policy. After much controversy and public debate, the **Family Allowances Act**, the nation's first universal welfare measure, was passed in 1944. The federal government gave mothers five to eight dollars per month for each child 16 years and younger. (Marshall, 2006: 25–7). Popular support for the "baby bonus" was instrumental in assuring another Liberal electoral victory in 1945.

Unemployment insurance and family allowances marked the definitive entry by the expanding state into the traditionally sacrosanct sphere of the patriarchal family. However modern and progressive their depiction, they upheld the traditional family and the traditional conceptualization of male and female roles in the home and the labour force. The federal government would assist families by protecting male breadwinners and assuring women's role in "home-making," producing children, and nurturing them. Mothers, in effect, were on the public payroll for their work of social reproduction. Once Canadians resettled themselves after the second global conflict in less than a half-century, many would go home to a family that looked much like the family of middle-class ideal in process since the middle of the previous century.

Families at Mid-century

The 20 years following the Second World War constitute another transformative period in the history of Canadian families. The world-historic events that included the Nazi defeat in May 1945, the dropping of two atomic bombs over Japan in August that heralded the Atomic Age, the beginnings of the Cold War that pitted the "Free World" of the Western capitalist democracies against the communist tyranny of the Soviet Union's Eastern sphere, would imprint Canadian society for generations to come. When the war ended, however, most Canadians appeared only too eager to be done with crisis and settled into a nostalgic version of a kind of domesticity that few had known for some time, if ever at all. The so-called **Reconstruction** interlude saw the return of veterans to civilian life, and, just as had happened after the Great War, a renewed public emphasis on "the family" (Golz, 1993: 9–10).

Married women who had served the war effort by taking paid employment, often replacing men in skilled or otherwise heavy industrial jobs, now faced public pressure to return to the home. Wartime anxieties about juvenile delinquency due to absent fathers and working mothers also underlay public obsession with stabilizing "the family." Family reunion was undoubtedly complicated for both returned soldiers and the wives and children who had become accustomed to life without father. The divorce rate briefly rose to worrying new heights, as some proved unable to resume "normal" family life, perhaps after hasty marriages, infidelity, or simply having "grown apart" (Farhni, 2005: 189). Yet, as the **Baby Boom** that commenced in 1946 testifies, after decades of contraction in marriage and fertility rates, the public desire for a return to "normalcy" was real, and its effects were profound and long-lasting.

The 1950s mark the "golden age" of the so-called "normal" family in Canadian history, as always more normative than "normal" despite the abundant discourses about it. The "normal" grouping of husband/breadwinner, mother/homemaker and three or four healthy, well-behaved, intelligent, closely spaced children, became the icon of the day. Much of the "golden" aura of the times has to do with its relatively widespread prosperity. Years of unrealized consumer demand unleashed an economic boom. Production increased and wages rose, doubling for male factory workers between 1945 and 1955. Between 1951 and 1960, inflation and unemployment were low and personal disposable income increased by 35 per cent in current dollars. This does not mean that all participated equally in the "good times." Families headed by unskilled, non-unionized workers, women, and recently arrived immigrants, Aboriginal families, African-Canadian families, the families of unilingual francophones in Quebec, and those in disadvantaged provinces such as Newfoundland, did not share in the bounty. Postwar psychology emphasized heterosexuality and continued to label homosexuality, still illegal, as deviance (Adams, 1997: 38). But roughly a century after the original "cult of domesticity," more Canadians than in any earlier time were finally able to approximate the Victorian ideal of the male breadwinner family.

At the urging of the newly formed United Nations, the Liberal government revised the Immigration Act in 1951, allowing for a second wave of immigrants, still mostly European, to enter a nation that very much needed skills, labour, and population. Their overall youthfulness guaranteed the increase in population necessary to uphold economic prosperity and quell concerns about the crisis in the family. The postwar immigration was characterized by family sponsorship: among Italians, one of the largest groups arriving, some 90 per cent were sponsored by relatives (Iacovetta, 1993: 481; Iacovetta, 2006). With close to one million newcomers entering Canada by the mid-1950s, social agencies and government policies made concerted efforts to impress upon them the appropriate standards of "Canadian" family life, in keeping with the male breadwinner ideal (Gleason, 1999: 88).

More than any other historic development of the time, demographic trends reassured family-watchers about individual and national commitment to marriage and family formation. Between the late 1940s and the early 1960s, the years of the so-called Baby Boom, the proportion of children to the rest of the population reached its highest point in the twentieth century (Vanier, 2004: 3). By 1947, young adults were marrying earlier than they had since the late nineteenth century, at an average age of 22 years for women and 24 years for men. In that year, the starting point of the Baby Boom, the birth rate increased to 29 per 1,000 of the population (approximately 350,000 babies), higher than since before the Great Depression. It remained between 27 and 28.5 per 1,000 until 1959 (500,000 babies), after which it gradually declined. Over a period of 25 years, the Baby Boom produced about 1.5 million more births than would otherwise have occurred (about 8.6 million), an increase

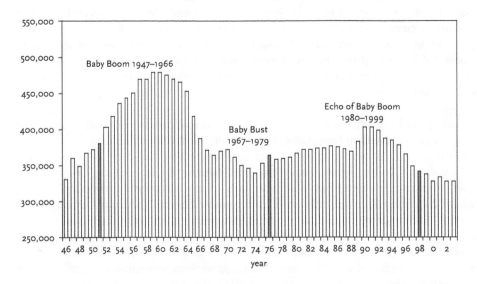

Figure 2.1 **Total Canadian Births, Baby Boom to 2003**

SOURCE: The Vanier Institute of the Family, 2004, p. 4.

of more than 18 per cent (Vanier, 2004: 3–4). During this period, a higher number of children than ever before, or since, grew up in the care of both their birth parents. The proportion of lone-parent families declined from about 14 per cent in 1931 to about 10 per cent in 1951, and then to a new low of 8.2 per cent in 1966 (Statistics Canada, 1984: Table 1).

The majority of mothers worked exclusively as full-time homemakers during the 1950s. Despite the popular attachment to this "norm" that proscribed work outside the home for women with children, this was an historic departure. As we have seen, many rural and working-class mothers had always worked, from home or outside the home, or had otherwise supplemented family income, in addition to, and frequently at the same time as, attending to the needs of husbands, the work of housekeeping, and the nurturing of dependent children. Although some women were not lured back to the kitchen by postwar government propaganda, and their numbers in the workforce continued to grow slowly during the 1950s, the participation of married women with children remained low. At its peak in 1944, the female labour force participation rate was 27 per cent, a number not reached again for nearly 20 years (Sangster, 1995: 222).

Also contributing to this family-centric social environment was intensified suburbanization. Home ownership has historically been a vital part of family formation for many Canadians, and economic prosperity was making it an increasingly accessible goal. Due to the depleted stock of housing because of the virtual absence of new construction during the Depression and the war, the time was right for low-density, inexpensive single-family housing to be built on the cheap land encircling urban centres. The federal government's commitment to supporting the postwar economy led to the establishment of the Central Mortgage and Housing Corporation to oversee and insure inexpensive mortgages. The direct outcome was the construction of one million new homes between 1945 and 1960, more than two-thirds of which were the single detached houses at the basis of the postwar family-oriented suburban communities (Harris, 2004). Suburbia became the site of a modern family life still defined by the traditional hierarchies of gender and age. Many male

---

Box 2.3
Suburban Family Life and "Home-Making" in the 1950s

Canadian family sociologists John R. Seeley, R. Alexander Sim, and Elizabeth W. Loosely published their case study of a middle-class Toronto suburb, identified as Crestwood Heights (a fictitious name), in 1956. Although they did not emphasize it, they did uncover discontent about the nature and conditions of their "full-time homemaker" status from some of the educated women they interviewed:

> Upon marriage, the woman takes charge of the home. When children come, they are her main responsibility. It was exceedingly difficult to find women in Crestwood Heights who had continued their vocations past motherhood. After marriage, the claims of the husband and, late, of the children on the woman's time and energy are so dominant that she must abandon her aspirations towards a career. . . . She was unlikely to think of motherhood itself as a career, even though she felt that she was doing a good job as wife and mother. (Seeley et al., 1956: 139–40)

breadwinners commuted a fair distance from their neighbourhoods to labour at reasonably well-paying jobs in stores, offices, sawmills, mines, and factories. During regular daytime working hours, the new, often identical, ranch bungalows and freshly paved streets of suburban enclaves were populated almost exclusively by women and children (Strong-Boag, 1991; Korinek, 2000).

In the evening, much familial interaction revolved around the new television set. By 1950, there were some 13,600 televisions in Canadian homes; 82.5 per cent of households owned a TV in 1961. The social impact of mass media, first registered in the immediate post–First World War years as film and radio became the hallmarks of modern popular culture, now made itself undeniably felt. Television signified a new epoch as much as did the atomic bomb and the Cold War. With TVs in many Canadian homes, "normalizing" ideas about home and family could be circulated readily, as television watching itself became a family activity. The CBC and Radio-Canada in Quebec specialized in such family programming as the antics of the puppet *Uncle Chichimus*, and, in French, the tragicomic saga of *La famille Plouffe*. Even with limited reception and a very restricted channel selection, many Canadians could, and did, watch such American serials as *Leave it to Beaver* and *Father Knows Best*, shows that depicted families at their glowing suburban nuclear male-breadwinner best (Sutherland, 1997).

Looking backwards, it is clear that the quick reversal in such long-term trends as higher age at marriage and smaller families was an historic aberration that would be readjusted by the late 1960s. The uniqueness of this moment within the larger context helps to explain why collective memory recalls the 1950s in such a nostalgic haze, a brief glorious moment when "family values" permeated society, and family relations were healthy and wholesome. Historians have pointed out the dark side of this "happy days" scenario. Many men had only distant relationships with their young children, as long commutes, long workdays, and the emphasis on the mother-centred home kept them away for most of the children's waking hours and vaguely sidelined in the self-enclosed nuclear family circle. Women with few personal outlets and little personal time thanks to the unrelenting pressures of modern homemaking might well find themselves suffering from what American feminist Betty Friedan, drawing upon her own experiences as a 1950s housewife, famously classified "the problem without a name" (Friedan, 1963; Strong-Boag, 1991: 504).

The children at the centre of the family universe were themselves increasingly subjected to "modern" and "scientific" personality and aptitude measures, in school, at the doctor's office, and even in the family circle, as experts widened the scope of their interventions into the nation's homes. As threats to child health declined, thanks to such wartime medical advances as antibiotics and sulfa drugs, to affordable private medical insurance and state hospital insurance, and, in large part, to prosperity, the focus on the child's healthy emotional development, and the mother's role in ensuring it, became ever stronger. Intensifying the interwar trend, child psychologists made new inroads into the schools and welfare agencies, and consequently into family life. All told, "the normal child" was stringently defined, which meant that the normal mother, in charge of the child's development, had to make herself aware of, and diligent in applying, current childrearing theories (Gleason, 1999: 84–5; Sutherland, 1997). Such mass-produced paperback manuals as that of the American paediatrician **Dr. Benjamin Spock** were ubiquitous in middle-class suburban homes across North America. Despite Dr. Spock's reassuring tones, most childrearing experts of the day blamed mothers for all the physical, emotional, and developmental "problems" that their children might face. These mixed messages about maternal influence and family life once again reflect undercurrents of a larger anxiety about shifting gender roles, age relations, and the relations of family, state and society (Adams, 1997: 18–20; Gleason, 1999: 89–90).

When the first wave of Boomers, born in 1947, entered adolescence in the 1960s, the "youth problem" that had been worrying Canadians since at least the 1920s turned into a "youthquake." High schools and post-secondary institutions expanded rapidly to accommodate the largest ever influx of young Canadians across class, racial, regional, and gender boundaries (Owram, 1996:159). This historic conjuncture of one age group sharing a cohort experience, at a time of vast social, cultural, and political turbulence across the Western world, gave new definition to age and generational relations in terms of cultural conflict. The young seemed intent on rejecting the values of their parents and elders, especially regarding sex and marriage. The political conservatism and social conformity of the 1950s gave way to a resurgence of radicalism in the New Left, in post-colonial liberation movements, in the politicization of groups historically marginalized by class, race, gender, and sexual orientation, in student protest movements, in Quebec's **Quiet Revolution** and in Aboriginal organizations (Palmer, 2008: 204–5). Although its depth was much exaggerated, the "**generation gap**" separating youth and their elders was embodied in the "hippie ethic" of the times that challenged sexual taboos and embraced "open marriage" and communal living. Needless to say, this was interpreted as a generational rejection of all that "the family" represented.

Like youth itself, however, the radical 1960s experiment was transient. Much of it was supported by the prosperity that permitted many young Canadians to finish high school, pursue further education, and find well-paying work. But the economy showed serious signs of flagging by the late 1960s, and a number of international economic shocks gave rise to the low growth, unemployment, and high inflation, characterized as "stagflation," of the 1970s. The early 1980s witnessed the worst recession since the Great Depression. Fewer young people could "come into their own" without considerable parental support and a longer stay in the parental home, the latter a modern trend already identified by the 1920s. These developments dampened youth rebellion and risk-taking, for all that the decade's "sexual revolution" would have lasting effects for individuals—especially women—and for families (Williams, 2000: 7–8).

The single most important influence on families during the 1960s and 1970s represents the outcome of an earlier trend as well: advances in the status of women. An effective female contraceptive, popularly known as The Pill, became available in Canada by 1966, finally allowing women control over their fertility and consequently their sexuality. The famous Criminal Code revisions of 1969 decriminalized contraception and consensual adult sexual relations, including homosexual relations, and also opened the way to legal abortion. Long-needed changes to divorce legislation made "no fault," uncontested divorce the new basis of marriage dissolution. The **second-wave feminism**, or "Women's Liberation" movement, of the 1970s saw the instigation of such important political pressure groups as the Committee for the Equality of Women in Canada (1966), and the National Action Committee on the Status of Women (1972). These feminist activists were instrumental in challenging gender inequality in its myriad social, economic, and political forms (Sangster, 2001: 210).

Although lone-parent families headed by women remained, as they have historically been, the largest proportion of poor families, higher-paid work opportunities for women, longer lives, and changes to the Divorce Act (1968), now made divorce a viable option for unhappy couples. In 1969, 14 per cent of all marriages ended in divorce; by 1975, the rate had doubled, reaching a peak (to date) of 36.2 per cent in 1986. More children than ever would experience at least some part of "growing up" in a lone-parent household, in shared or joint custody arrangements, and in blended families (Beaupré, Dryburgh, and Wendt, 2010). By the 1970s, as well, transnational adoptions, especially from Vietnam, China, Korea, and Guatemala, undermined historic racist legal and social barriers against "mixed" families (Strong-Boag, 2006; Dubinsky, 2010).

Most important, in its impact on both women's social position and on the families that have historically been their "vocation," was the influx of married women and mothers into the labour force. Only 1 married woman in 5 worked for wages in 1961; a decade later, the proportion was 1 in 3; by 1981, 1 of every 2 Canadian women was employed outside the home. By the early 1970s, a contracting economy highlighted by the decline of manufacturing where "men's work" was traditionally concentrated, the rising cost of living, and the historically high educational attainments of women, allowed more and better opportunities for women's employment. At the same time, the steadily rising consumerism that also characterized postwar society was demanding two incomes to maintain the standard of living that many Canadian families felt to be their due. For the less affluent and otherwise marginalized, two incomes were, as always, a matter of family need, not personal choice (Williams, 2000: 8–9).

Box 2.4
Women's Paid Labour and Contemporary Family Forms

Sociologist John F. Conway considers the development of the dual-earner family both a major contributing factor and a positive outcome of the demise of "the family" in the late twentieth century:

> The dual-earner family signals the most important social structural change since it reflects the increasing economic independence of women. The old patriarchal, traditional nuclear family was premised on the economic dependence of women—that nexus of control over women has been largely shattered . . . as women have struggled to close the gender pay gap, they have begun to gain a certain rough equality in the economic partnership with their husbands. The contribution of women's earnings to family income has increased dramatically . . . and a new growing husband/wife family has emerged—in an estimated five per cent of such families the woman is the sole earner. . . . The traditional male-headed, patriarchal single-earner husband/wife family has declined sharply to 18 per cent of husband/wife families in 2001 (comprising only 16 per cent of all families). The fall has been precipitous. This family form is obviously the one the "death of the family" theorists were talking about. (Conway, 2003: 261)

Families Approach the Millennium

As the twenty-first century dawned, the average number of children per family declined again, to 1.7, while a new demographic phenomenon, the "childless by choice" union, was making significant headway. Along with the steady increase in life expectancy, this meant that a smaller portion of the family life-course, and that of women specifically, had to be devoted exclusively to the care of infants and preschool children. While the 58.3 per cent of married mothers who worked for wages in 1980 represented an historic peak to that point, by 2000, the proportion was 80 per cent. More than two-thirds of working mothers were in the age range of 30–39 years, not coincidentally, the average age range of first marriages and first births. Most women returned to work by the end of the child's first year (Kremarek, 2000: 165). The introduction of state-supported maternity and parental leave legislation in the 1990s was vital to this "new" configuration of families. Couples not infrequently took sequential leave, permitting one parent to be the primary caregiver for the child's first year. Also "new" in historical terms was the growing, though still small, proportion of fathers who interrupted their careers to care for their children while mothers worked as sole breadwinners (Beaupré, Dryburgh, and Wendt, 2010: 32). Finally, what is probably the single most controversial of all social and legislative changes affecting families in the entire period under discussion came about with the legal recognition of same-sex marriage in the Civil Marriage Act (2005). Canada became one of only three nations worldwide to legalize same-sex unions (Luxton, 2011: 7). Perhaps most important among the demographic, socio-economic, and cultural changes that are late-century markers in the history of Canadian families are the changing ideas and corresponding practices that underlie contemporary understandings of shared parenting, involved fathering, unmarried motherhood and fatherhood, and same-sex parenting as personal choices.

The most recent demographic data confirm the historic relationship of families and societies, and cultural and structural change. The 2006 census found that some 85 per cent, accounting for nearly 27 million people, are members of "**census families**." For the first time since the Dominion Census was inaugurated in 1871, however, there were more unmarried Canadians in the "15 years and over" category than there were legally married couples, and more childless couples (43 per cent) than those with one or more children (41 per cent). Although most children resided with married parents (66 per cent), 18 per cent lived with a lone parent and 15 per cent with common-law parents. Of those 14 years and under, First Nations children were more likely to live with a lone parent, grandparent, or other relative (Statistics Canada, 2009: 53). The largest proportion of common-law families was found in Quebec, where more than one-third of different-sex unions are common-law. This is especially striking given the historical focus on marriage and family upheld by the Catholic Church and successive provincial governments (Dagenais, 2008; Vanier Institute, 2010).

Notwithstanding the endurance of families, the sociocultural developments affecting them, especially those of the past 25 years, have effectively undermined the tenacious social construction of "the family" in its idealized white middle-class form. This, too, is an historic first. Never as prevalent as it was represented to be, the male breadwinner family is now unequivocally the minority experience among Canadians of all classes, cultural backgrounds, and regions.

Conclusion

This brief overview of the history of Canadian families over the past 200 years was intended, above all, to demonstrate one key point: the importance of families to individuals and to society is a constant, both in ideal and in practice, but the form and experience of actual families have always been diverse. Families are eminently mutable. Among the major historical influences contributing to changing family forms during these two centuries are

- structural changes, particularly the late-nineteenth century shift from domestic to factory production, and, during the past 40 years, the decline of industry and the rise of digital technology;
- demographic changes sparked by later marriages, the decrease in family size, the improvements in infant mortality rates, prolonged adolescence and increasing life expectancy, single parenthood, and childless-by-choice unions;
- changes in the status of women, especially regarding higher education, professional training, wage-earning opportunities, and the gradual public acceptance of the employed wife/mother and the dual-earner family;
- the changing relations between the "private sphere" of families and the public interest increasingly represented by "experts" and the state, especially by means of family policies that have, until recently, privileged the male-breadwinner family model; and
- the contemporary societal and legal recognition of the rightful family status of so-called "non-traditional" family groups, including lone-parent, common-law, same-sex, and mixed union families.

The history of Canadian families consists of the varied stories of varying families, functioning in many different ways toward a particular objective: to be families in their own way. And some form of family experience has always been, and continues to be, the core of most of our lives. Families survive because they are individually and collectively meaningful, and infinitely adaptive to historical circumstances. Despite the multiple, ongoing changes and challenges of the past two centuries, usually interpreted in the dark language of danger and crisis, the majority of Canadians have always lived, for however much or little of their lives, in families or family settings. And this holds true for most Canadians in our own times.

STUDY QUESTIONS

1. What changes and continuities in ideals about families, and their actual forms and functions, can we trace over the roughly two centuries discussed? How do we explain the public obsession with "the family" of ideal in view of the gap between this ideal and the realities of many Canadian families?
2. How do we understand the persistence of public concern about "the family in crisis" throughout this period—and into the present—despite, as statistics reveal, the ongoing commitment to family formation by "ordinary" Canadians?

3. How has the relationship between the family and the state changed over this time? Are there continuities in that evolving relationship?

4. Women's history is not the same as the history of families, but they are clearly very closely entwined. Discuss, with consideration to contemporary as well as historical developments.

Further Readings

Baillargeon, Denyse. 1999. *Making Do: Family and Home in Montreal during the Great Depression*. Translated by Yvonne Klein. Waterloo: Wilfrid Laurier University Press. One of the earliest family histories to make use of oral testimony, this focused "case study" uncovers working-class family strategies in difficult times, highlighting the vital role of women.

Comacchio, Cynthia. 1999. *The Infinite Bonds of Family: Domesticity in Canada, 1850 to 1940*. Toronto: University of Toronto Press. Although this book follows family history only to the beginning of the Second World War, it is a comprehensive overview that fills in much of what this chapter sketches.

Comacchio, Cynthia. 2000. "'The History of Us:' Social Science, History, and the Relations of Family in Canada." *Labour/Le Travail*. Special Millennium issue. 46: 167–220. This is a literature survey tracing the evolution of sociological and historical approaches to families in Canada.

Dagenais, Daniel. 2008. *The (Un)Making of the Modern Family*. Translated by Jane Brierley. Vancouver: University of British Columbia Press. Sociologist Dagenais explores the "deconstruction" of "the family" in the past half-century and why this has incited social panic; it is especially valuable in its discussion of francophone Quebec families.

Miller, James R. 1996. *Shingwauk's Vision: A History of Native Residential Schools*. Toronto: University of Toronto Press. This is a thorough and thoughtful treatment of a tragic history that centres the recollections of the affected children and their families.

Strong-Boag, Veronica. 2011. *Fostering Nation? Canada Confronts its History of Childhood Disadvantage*. Waterloo: Wilfrid Laurier University Press. An inaugural historical study of fostering, this book shines much light on social constructions of family and how state and society support them for reasons not necessarily beneficial to children and their families.

Sutherland, Neil. 2000. *Children in English-Canadian Society: Framing the Twentieth Century Consensus*, 2nd ed. Waterloo: Wilfrid Laurier University Press. Originally published in 1976, this seminal study remains critical to understanding how and why childhood was "redefined" by the 1920s, and how class, gender and race were significant forces in framing modern childhood.

Ursel, Jane. 1992. *Private Lives, Public Policy: 100 Years of State Intervention in the Family*. Toronto: Women's Press. Sociologist Ursel situates her historical analysis of family welfare policies firmly within a gendered social reproduction framework.

Websites

www.hcyg.ca/
The History of Children and Youth Group, organized in 2004, is an affiliated committee of the Canadian Historical Association, and their website is useful for bibliographic information.

www5.statcan.gc.ca/bsolc/olc-cel/

The Statistics Canada *Canadian Social Trends* publications are quarterly reports that began publication in 1980, offering semi-annual overviews of important socio-economic and demographic trends, with much information about families; there is a helpful index of articles, and digitized copies beginning in 1998 are available. The Winter 2012 issue is the last available before its discontinuation.

www5.statcan.gc.ca/bsolc/olc-cel/

The Statistics Canada *Historical Statistics of Canada* publication is an invaluable series for historians of Canadian families, with much relevant information derived from the long-form census undertaken by the federal government every ten years until its discontinuation with the 2011 census.

www.vanierinstitute.ca/

The official website of the Vanier Institute, the foremost research institute on Canadian families, established in 1965, provides a wealth of historical and contemporary information compiled by scholars and professionals. Especially valuable are the regular publications *Profiling Canada's Families.*

THE LIFE COURSE

Family life changes over time as people have new experiences, such as the birth of a child, and as they undergo the changes associated with aging. Of course, not everyone experiences the same changes. Some people have children whereas others do not; some people get married and then later divorced, whereas other married couples remain together; and some people live long into old age while others die young. The chapters in Part II, therefore, do not pretend that everyone follows a predictable life cycle. Rather, the contributors set out some of the common changes that occur in family life and some of the stages of the life course, in order to provide a sense of how family experiences may differ at different times of life.

In Chapter 3, Melanie Heath focuses on how people form relationships, some of which result in marriage. This chapter discusses theories and ideologies of intimacy. It also shows how the legal structure of marriage has historically excluded and marginalized some Canadians based on gender, race and ethnicity, immigration status, and sexual orientation. Heath discusses technological innovations that have been affecting dating and sexual relationships among young adults. She considers why people choose to be single and the role of friendship for those who live alone, and for those in "families of choice."

Amber Gazso focuses on becoming and being a parent of young children in Canada today in Chapter 4. The chapter outlines some of the everyday activities of parenting, but at the same time shows that the everyday practices or events of parenting are intimately connected to and textured by ideological discourses, culture, individuals' participation in other social spheres (e.g., the labour market), relationships with others and social policy (e.g., child care). She highlights how differences in family structure and the sexuality of parents inform the *performance* of parenting.

In Chapter 5, Craig McKie focuses on how families fragment through separation or divorce, but often reformulate within the context of a new union. The chapter begins by reviewing the legal context for divorce and presents statistics on divorce. However, McKie notes that these statistics can be misleading because many cohabiting relationships end without legal or statistical consequences. That said, the economic and social effects of separation and divorce are almost always present and are the subject of great interest, and so they are also discussed here. McKie concludes that accounts of post-separation hardships must be weighed against the real risks of physical and emotional trauma in relationships that are full of conflict and which are greatly diminished by separation. The chapter considers how separation and divorce are often followed by the formation of new families, either lone-parent families or families that are reconstituted through new relationships.

Two stages of the life course—middle age and "old age"—are considered in Chapters 6 and 7. Karen Kobayashi, in Chapter 6, focuses on the transitions that mark middle age (e.g., the "empty nest," caregiving) and are triggered by the occurrence of life events in families (e.g., adult children leaving home, care for aging parents). Home-leaving by adult children, Kobayashi notes, has been taking longer in recent years, and in many instances adult children return to their natal home after having left. Support for aging parents is becoming a significant issue in Canada as a result of population aging. Of course, the experience of such life events as taking care of aging parents varies according to individuals' situations, and these can be quite various. The chapter therefore examines some of the diversity of mid-life families by describing the patterns of separation and divorce, remarriage, same-sex relationships, and childlessness. The chapter includes a discussion of the relationship between mid-life families and social policy.

Finally, in Chapter 7, Neena Chappell considers family life as Canadians age. Chappell highlights the central role that families play in the lives of older adults, and the role that older adults continue to play in the lives of their families. She discusses how facets of our health change as we age, in turn affecting the changing nature of family caregiving. She presents how aging families and the health care system interface, but also how they do so differently. Chappell concludes the chapter by noting that Canada should provide more and better support to family caregivers so they can continue to provide the care that they increasingly and willingly do, and suggests that we look to diverse countries around the world from which Canada can learn.

3

Intimacy, Commitment, and Family Formation

MELANIE HEATH

LEARNING OBJECTIVES

- To gain an overview of the ways that family demographics have changed in Canada

- To understand why the number of people who cohabit is increasing, why this family form is becoming more socially acceptable, and why some people choose to "live apart together"

- To learn how sociologists theorize the transformation of intimacy and the scholarly debates on the degree of change that has occurred

- To recognize how the legal structure of marriage has historically excluded and marginalized some Canadians based on gender, race and ethnicity, immigration status, and sexual orientation

- To discover the definitions of and technological innovations for dating, and the new forms of sexual relationships among adolescents and young adults

- To consider why people choose to be single, and the role of friendship for those who live alone and for those in "families of choice"

Introduction

The institutions of family and marriage have experienced both continuity and change in the past century. Family has remained a central social institution to organize individual life trajectories. Yet, the dominant patterns of family life can no longer be characterized by a routine from marriage, childbearing, and childrearing to the eventual death of a spouse. Today there is much greater diversity and transition in living arrangements and family forms involving those who cohabit, marry, separate, divorce, parent on their own, or do a combination of these. Family networks now often include parents, step-parents, same-sex partners, children conceived biologically or by artificial insemination, close friends, ex-partners, and ex-sons- and daughters-in-law.

To explain recent trends in family formation, sociologists have emphasized the increasing importance of intimacy and romantic love (Cheal, 1987; Giddens, 1992; Swidler, 2001). In "Western" societies, the historic norms for marrying have transformed from a union based on the interests of parents, kin, or community to being rooted more in emotional bonds. Historian Stephanie Coontz (2005) traces this transformation back to the Enlightenment when the rise of the "love match" revolutionized the institution of marriage. Today, marriage holds a more diminished role than it once did in society and in people's lives.

What do sociologists mean when they use the term "intimacy"? In common parlance, it is often used to mean strong emotional bonds such as love. Increasingly, sociological under-standings define it more precisely as denoting "closeness" and a state of being "special" to another person that involves self-disclosure (Jamieson, 2007). Intimacy thus represents a privileged knowledge of inner selves. Scholars in the field of social psychology study per-sonal relationships to uncover the importance of self-disclosure, partner disclosure, and partner responsiveness to what constitutes a "good" couple. Studies of "self-disclosing inti-macy" point to the benefits of mutual self-revelation for quality relationships (Jamieson, 2007). Sexual intimacy can be an important component (although not a necessary condi-tion), and scholars point to the ways that sexuality has evolved to become an expression of the self. Thus, it is central to the transformations that are taking place in intimate relation-ships (Giddens, 1992).

Expressions of love and commitment are multifaceted. For example, passionate love tends to be unsteady and can end abruptly. In contrast, commitment to someone involves a very different dimension of positive feelings for a partner and to a relationship over time. Scholars who study the meanings of love and commitment have found that relationship satisfaction is higher for companionate love than for passionate love (Hanson Frieze, 2007).

Family scholars disagree on the social consequences of transformations in intimate rela-tionships. Some argue that that the increasing importance of private intimacy is dislodg-ing civic and community engagement, whereas others view these transformations to offer heightened equality and democracy in personal life that might spread to other domains. Some view both of these to occur simultaneously. This chapter will consider how intimacy and family life has changed, looking at the debates over the causes and consequences of these transformations to North American societies.

Family Formation, Social Structures, and Change

During the past century the family system in North America has experienced vast changes in marriage and divorce rates, cohabitation, sexual behaviour, childbearing, and women's work outside the home. **Family demography** involves the study of changes in family structure—married-couple families (with or without) children, cohabiting-couple families (with or without children), single-parent families, stepfamilies, and so forth—to understand both individual and societal behaviour. Family demographers seek to answer why individuals behave as they do toward each other, and how societies compare in their family configurations and in their political, economic, and cultural institutions (Goldscheider, 1995).

How are families configured in Canada today? Based on the most recent Census estimates for 2011, the majority of all families (83.7 per cent) live as married or common-law couples in either heterosexual and same-sex relationships (Statistics Canada, 2011a). While most Canadians choose to live as a couple, we also know that the ways in which families are forming has changed dramatically. Similar to the United States and Europe, Canada has experienced substantial increases in rates of divorce, remarriage, and single parenthood, and today there is more societal acceptance of non-marital unions.

One way in which family life has changed substantially in Canada is a decrease in marriage rates. In 1961, married couples accounted for 91.6 per cent of Canadian census families. By 2011, this number had dropped to 67 per cent (Statistics Canada, 2011a). This decrease was mostly a result of the growth of common-law couples (see Figure 3.1).

Families comprised of common-law couples grew the most between 2006 and 2011, increasing 13.9 per cent compared to 3.1 per cent for married couples and 8.0 per cent for lone-parent families (Statistics Canada, 2011a). Fewer Canadian children today live with their married biological parents than in the past. Just two decades ago, 81 per cent of children aged 14 years and younger lived with their married biological parents, whereas the 2011 Census estimates that this figure has dropped to roughly 63.6 per cent (Statistics Canada, 2011a). When Canadians do marry for the first time, the average age is substantially higher than three decades ago. In 2004, the average age was 30.5 years for men and 28.5 years for women, an increase of over five years from 1970 (Vanier Institute, 2010).

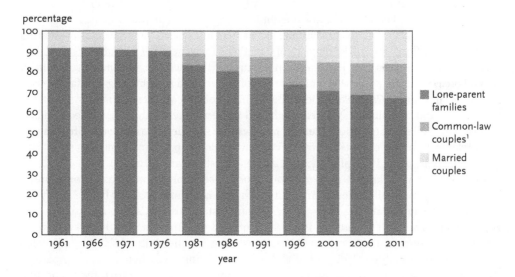

Figure 3.1 **Distribution (in percentage) of Census Families by Family Structure, Canada, 1961–2011**

source: Statistics Canada (2012). "Fifty years of families in Canada: 1961 to 2011," *Families, households and marital status, 2011 Census of Population*. Catalogue no. 98-312-X2011003; available at http://www12.statcan.gc.ca/census-recensement/ 2011/as-sa/98-312-x/98-312-x2011003_1-eng.pdf.

While there is an overall decrease in marriage, the legalization of same-sex marriage in 2005 offered the possibility for lesbians and gay men to enter the institution. There has been substantial growth in the numbers of same-sex couples reported by the Census.

For more on changing divorce law in Canada, see "The Legal Environment for Divorce in Canada" in Chapter 5, pp. 88–9.

Between 2001 and 2006, the number grew by one-third, from 34,200 to 45,345 (Milan, Vézina, and Wells, 2007). By 2011, this figure had reached 64,575 (Statistics Canada, 2011a). The Census of 2011 marked the first five-year period for which same-sex marriage has been legal across the country, and the number of same-sex married couples nearly tripled between 2006 and 2011.

Divorce increased substantially in Canada after the passage of the Divorce Act in 1968. This act expanded the grounds for divorce and made it available across the nation. From 1968 to 1995, there was a five-fold increase (Ambert, 2009). Since 1997, the divorce rate has decreased substantially and remained at a lower level with only minor yearly variations. The latest figure from Statistics Canada (2008o) estimates the risk of divorce for recently married Canadian couples at 38 per cent. There are currently no rates of divorce available for same-sex couples. Since marriage was so recently legalized for lesbians and gay men, many of these marriages may involve couples who have been in long-term relationships. Thus, the divorce rate may be initially lower for this population than for heterosexual married couples (Ambert, 2009).

Another substantial change is an increase in unmarried Canadians. For the first time in 2006, the number of unmarried individuals aged 15 and over surpassed those legally married with just over half unmarried—never legally married, divorced, widowed, or separated (Milan, Vézina, and Wells, 2007). Lone-parent homes have also increased for the last four decades. In 2011, lone-parent families represented 16.3 per cent of families, a figure that has almost doubled since 1961. Females head about eight in ten of these (Statistics Canada, 2011b).

The increase in marital breakup has meant a parallel increase in the probability of entering into a second or third union. The majority of Canadians repartner after a divorce or separation. Remarriage, however, is now less common because of the increasing propensity to cohabit after divorce (Beaupré, 2008). With higher rates of divorce and repartnering, stepfamilies are now more common in Canadian society. The definition of **stepfamilies** includes unions based on marriage and cohabitation, whereas in the US the term refers only to remarried families. Almost half of all stepfamilies are **blended families** that include at least one child from a previous relationship plus one created in the current relationship. In 2011, one in ten children were found to be living in stepfamilies in Canada (Statistics Canada, 2011a).

Cohabitation (also known as common-law or consensual unions) has become prevalent in Canada, especially among Canadian youth who commonly cohabit before marrying. Common-law couples are the fastest growing family structure in Canada according to the 2011 Census. The 1981 Census of Population offered the first data on the prevalence of common-law couples. From 1981 to 2001, cohabiting families with children quadrupled in number, and roughly 15 per cent of children were living with their cohabiting parents (Liu, Kerr, and Beaujot, 2006; Wu, Hou, and Schimmele, 2008). By 2011, the proportion of common-law couples increased to 16.7 per cent. Indeed, the 2011 Census showed that for first time the number of common-law couple families in the country surpassed the number of lone-parent families (Statistics Canada, 2011b) (see Figure 3.1). The proportion of children aged 14 and under who lived with common-law parents rose from 12.8 per cent in 2001 to 16.3 per cent in 2011.

While cohabitation rates have grown across Canada, there are some striking regional differences. According to the 2011 Census, fully 31.5 per cent of couples in Quebec were living in common-law relationships (Statistics Canada, 2011a), making Quebec comparable to some Scandinavian countries (Keirnan, 2002). The rates are much lower across all other provinces, such as in Ontario at 10.9 per cent. Kerr, Moyser, and Beaujot (2006) compared cohabitation patterns in Quebec to the rest of Canada, finding that the latter more closely aligns with North America. Individuals with fewer years of education and lower incomes are more likely to cohabit and less likely to marry (Bumpass and Lu, 2000; Smock and Manning, 2004). In contrast, in Quebec those who cohabit are not necessarily economically more vulnerable, and the differences between people who marry and cohabit are less distinct than in the rest of Canada (Kerr, Moyser, and Beaujot, 2006). Quebec also differs from the rest of Canada in that cohabitation has become more accepted as a family form in which to become a parent. For the rest of Canada, cohabitation is seen as a probationary relationship before marriage but not as an acceptable environment to raise a child (Le Bourdais and Lapierre-Adamcyk, 2004).

Why the divergence in patterns of cohabitation in Quebec compared with other (Anglo) provinces? Demographers Le Bourdais and Lapierre-Adamcyk (2004) argue that a partial answer can be found in the different religious and cultural backgrounds of the two societies. The Catholic Church played a vigorous role in shaping Quebec society until the 1960s, when the culture shifted towards secularization—known as the Quiet Revolution—that was central to the development of modernity. Most Quebeckers embraced this revolution, abandoning the Church and its doctrines. Paralleling other Catholic societies such as Spain and Italy, women embraced the pill as a contraceptive method, and the fertility and marriage rate plummeted. In contrast, the Protestant Church exerted less control in other parts of Canada, and non-Catholic Canadians did not feel the same need to separate themselves from religious institutions. Transformations in gender ideologies and practices may also play a role in the difference. The feminist movement has had a stronger history in Quebec than other parts of Canada, pushing a culture of greater equality between women and men. Studies of the differences between cohabitation and marriage show that the former tends to be more egalitarian. Cohabitation leads to more sharing of domestic work than does marriage, and cohabiting women are more likely to participate in the labour market (Le Bourdais and Sauriol, 1998; Shelton and John, 1993).

Finally, family change is tied to greater ethnic and racial diversity in Canada. On average, 225,000 individuals have immigrated to Canada each year since the early 1990s (Statistics Canada, 2007l). There has also been substantial growth among Canada's Aboriginal population. In 2006, there were 1.2 million self-identified Aboriginals—North American Indian/ First Nation, Métis, or Inuit (Statistics Canada, 2008n). In thinking about these significant demographic changes, family life has emerged as a key focus of discussion. In the next section, we will look at the ways scholars theorize family transformation.

Intimacy: Meanings and Theories

Family demographers tell us about *how* families are configured, but social theorists help us think about the reasons *why* family change occurs. One of the key transformations in family life that theorists have addressed is the increasing separation of sexuality from the constraints of reproduction, a process that has gathered great speed with the rapid innovation in reproductive technologies and contraception.

New reproductive technologies encompass a broad range of technologies that seek to facilitate, mediate, or disrupt the process of reproduction, including conceptive technologies such as in vitro fertilization (a procedure in which eggs from a woman's ovary are removed and fertilized with sperm in a laboratory), antenatal testing (diagnostic procedures performed before the birth of a baby), contraception, and abortion. New reproductive technologies have helped to produce novel family structures and facilitate redefinitions of sexual and intimate relationships (Eichler, 1997).

For more on new reproductive technologies, see "New Reproductive and Genetic Technologies" in Chapter 16, p. 326.

What are the social circumstances enabling contemporary transformations of sexuality, marriage, and childbearing? Sociologist Anthony Giddens (1992: 28) theorizes the emergence of "plastic sexuality" as enabling the transformation of intimacy, especially for women who are experiencing a "revolution in female sexual autonomy." Malleable eroticism offers a form of self-expression at the individual level and within the realm of social norms. Sexuality is not only increasingly detached from reproduction, but it has also been largely freed from the constraints of patriarchy (a social system structured by male headship), religion, and other means of social control. Giddens argues that individuals today shape their erotic needs according to individual identity and on pleasure and performance. Plastic sexuality results not only from the sexual freedom made possible by contraceptive and new reproductive technologies, but by the increasing economic and social independence of women. Emancipatory social movements—such as the women's and lesbian and gay movements—have called into question traditional gender norms.

This emancipatory potential is also present in the emergence of the **pure relationship**, which Giddens (1992: 2) defines in terms of "confluent love," a "relationship of sexual and emotional equality" between men and women. In contrast to romantic love, usually thought to require a lifetime commitment, confluent love is more contingent on the emotional satisfaction and pleasure that a relationship offers at any particular moment. Compared to times past when women had few options outside of marriage and family life, women and men are now free to participate in the pure relationship as long as it offers satisfaction. Thus, the domestic norms of getting married, staying together, and raising children no longer constitute a pressing moral obligation.

Similar to Giddens, sociologists Beck and Beck-Gernsheim (2002: 22) argue that "the ethic of individual self-fulfilment and achievement is the most powerful current in modern society." For them, membership in family life has become more contingent as a matter of choice. Individualization or the idea that the individual is becoming the central unit of social life has changed the nature of social ties within and between families to create the "post-familial family," which offers a new understanding of family based on its diverse manifestations (Beck-Gernsheim, 1998).

Many theorists place lesbian and gay relationships at the forefront of these cultural shifts that are transforming intimacy. Giddens (1992) argues that lesbians and gay men are forging new pathways for heterosexuals as well as for themselves. Research on same-sex relationships has illuminated the ways that lesbians and gay men are recouping the values of care and intimacy, against the grain of competitive individualism (Adam, 2004). Weeks, Donovan, and Heaphy (1999: 85) state that "one of the most remarkable features of domestic change over recent years is . . . the emergence of common patterns in both homosexual and heterosexual ways of life as a result of these long-term shifts in relationship patterns." Thus, social change in the way that intimacy is organized influences the wider organization and structure of sexuality.

Theories on the democratization of intimacy offer a broadly optimistic account of the changing nature of family life, and some empirical research confirms the move towards the pure relationship among certain populations. Demographer David Hall, for example, used data from the 1995 Canadian General Social Survey to examine how Canadian couples living in what he operationalized as egalitarian "pure relationships" (married and cohabiting) desired fewer or no children. He concluded that childbearing and the ideal of the pure relationship often work at cross-purposes. Kate Hughes (2005) conducted a qualitative study of adult children of divorce from Generation X—the generation following after the postwar baby boomers—who no longer felt pressure to stay married. She found that these Gen Xers connected their sense of personal growth with the formation and termination of intimate relationships. These studies confirmed the importance of the ideal of the pure relationship to family change.

Scholars have criticized the tendency in some of this literature to overstate the degree of family transformation that is occurring in society. Others point to a lack of attention to pervasive gender inequalities and class differences in intimate life (Jamieson, 1998). One approach that does attend to inequality has come out of an interactionist tradition to examine the links between intimate relationships and gender stratification (Dozier and Schwartz, 2001). This growing literature studies the ongoing interactions that both create and sustain difference and inequality. Sociologist Barbara Risman (1998), for example, has examined the ways that ongoing interactions perpetuate an unequal division of labour in the home and the workplace. She shines light on how gender structures work, family, and community to perpetuate dominant gender norms that support men's economic and social superiority.

Sociologist Neil Gross (2005) critiques the idea that romantic/sexual intimacy is fuelling what social theorists have called "detraditionalization"—the decline or reconfiguration of tradition—in the late modern era. Gross argues that there has been a decline in "regulative traditions," which in the past worked to exclude those who failed to participate in the culturally dominant nuclear, heterosexual, married family. This decline has not necessarily meant, however, the replacement of ultimate fluidity and agency in relationships. Instead, "meaning-constitutive traditions"—commonsense understandings passed down from one generation to the next—still reinforce the regulative tradition of heterosexual marriage as the dominant ideal.

Marriage Debates: Legal Structures and Cultural Privilege

There is general agreement among sociologists and demographers regarding changes to family life in the past five decades. Widespread debate, however, exists over how to interpret these transformations. Much of the debate concerns the relationship between marriage and children's well-being. Is the married, nuclear family consisting of wife/mother, husband/father, and their children the essential form of family—the only configuration for carrying out the vital function of rearing the next generation? Can other family patterns (e.g., single mothers, single fathers, two women, or two men) be as successful?

The current state of the research on these questions has offered mixed conclusions. On the one hand, scholars find evidence that children raised in two-biological-parent married families tend to have better educational, social, cognitive, and behavioural outcomes than children from married step, cohabiting, and single-parent families. The differences in these family types are modest, however, and there are mediating factors in the relationship between marriage and better outcomes, including economic resources, parents' own socialization, and family conflict/stress (Brown, 2010). Moreover, some of the advantages scholars measure are due to selection factors rather than marriage itself. In other words, it is not marriage that causes financial success and happiness; rather, individuals who are happier and financially secure are more likely to marry. In addition, growing evidence finds that children raised by lesbian parents fare as well as those raised by heterosexual married parents; less is known at this stage about children of gay male parents (Biblarz and Stacey, 2010; Stacey and Biblarz, 2001).

CASE IN POINT
The Changing Legal Path of Marriage and Cohabitation

Laws and attitudes concerning marriage have changed substantially since the 1960s, and the state of marriage and the family is now contested terrain among scholars, policy-makers and politicians in North America. Many view its fate as in such dire straits as to necessitate greater restrictions on access to divorce, and to call for more narrowly legislating access to marriage's benefits and responsibilities. In the United States, research showing that children who live with their married biological parents fare better has led to specific policy interventions through federal and state "marriage promotion" programs. A dominant focus of the U.S. welfare reform law of 1996 was the need for policies to promote and maintain two-parent, married families. In the last decade, the federal government and individual states have allocated welfare funds to support initiatives and research to promote marriage, especially among low-income couples who have some of the lowest marriage rates. While the goal of these policies is to reduce poverty by encouraging marriage, there is evidence that many of these programs may actually create more inequality among families by siphoning funds earmarked for needy single mothers to offer free marriage workshops to the general population, where more privileged families tend to participate (Heath, 2012).

There is no equivalent to the U.S. model of marriage promotion in Canada. For a time, in fact, Canada appeared to be moving in a contrary policy direction. Beginning in the 1970s, unmarried couples and children born outside of marriage began to receive an increasing number of rights and obligations. First, legislation at the provincial level in the 1970s introduced spousal support for unmarried couples. Following judgments of the Supreme Court of Canada, several provinces have amended their statutes in the past decade to offer unmarried couples property rights, and in many provinces couples can sign a cohabitation agreement that allows them to opt into matrimonial property rights.

In 2002, the legal path of marriage and unmarried cohabitation, once on its way towards convergence, parted ways. The Supreme Court of Canada decided that it is constitutional to exclude unmarried cohabiting individuals from family property laws, a decision that effectively revives the legal significance of marriage (Bailey, 2004). Will Canada move in the direction of the United States to shore up and promote the legal significance of heterosexual marriage? There are organizations in Canada that mobilize to create laws and policies in this direction. Focus on the Family Canada—a Canadian affiliate of the American evangelical Christian organization Focus on the Family—founded the Institute of Marriage and Family Canada (IMFC) to conduct and compile social policy research on marriage and family. This organization defines marriage as an institution created by God to be a permanent, lifelong relationship between a man and a woman, a definition that excludes same-sex couples. It is unlikely, however, that the Canadian arm of these organizations will have the same impact as they have had in the United States, since same-sex marriage has been legal in Canada since 2005, and Canadians tend to be more tolerant of diverse family forms.

The marriage debate concerns what role law and public policy should play in supporting and regulating the family. Historically, there have been diverse arrangements for societal recognition of marriage in Canada. From the late seventeenth to the early nineteen century, fur traders of the Hudson's Bay Company contracted marriages "à la façon du pays (or according to the custom of the country)" (Eichler, 1997: 44). Diverse forms of marriage could also be found among Aboriginal people, including polygamy and same-sex marriage (Carter, 2008). As a British colony, colonial politicians in Canada distinguished the "civilized" tradition of marriage as the only legally and socially accepted form of intimate relationship from the "ancient barbarians, "heathens," and other peoples they characterized as uncivilized" (Bradbury, 2005: 105).

The Canadian state promoted marriage rights as a way to build the nation (Carter, 2008). It did this by encouraging marriage among desirable white Europeans and by preventing family formation among non-white populations. An early example involves roughly 700 impoverished women, called the *filles du roi*, who were sent from France to Quebec between 1663 and 1673 to marry men they had never met and raise families in New France. In the 1800s, thousands of Chinese men immigrated to work on the Canadian Pacific Railroad. When it was completed in 1885, the Canadian state began instituting policies to obstruct Chinese migration and nuclear family reunification. Federal legislation imposed an expensive head tax on Chinese wage labourers and on the spouses and children of Chinese men already in Canada. In this way, authorities sought to control the migration of Chinese women and thwart procreation among Chinese families that could eventually displace white people's labour power (Satzewich, 1993).

Regulating families was also a tool used to control the Aboriginal populations of Canada. The Indian Act of 1876 defined Indian identity and established

For more on The Indian Act, see "Aboriginal Peoples" in Chapter 12, pp. 231–4.

legal and non-legal categories that had bearing on the rights of Aboriginal people (Bourassa, McKay-McNabb, and Hampton, 2004). Under the Act, Indian women who married non-Indian men were denied their Indian status, their band membership, education and treaty rights, and the right to pass on status to their children. In comparison, an Indian man who married a non-Indian woman kept his Indian status, and the non-Indian woman and her children received status. The Act imposed a patriarchal model on Aboriginal families by making legal status and citizenship rights depend on the husband.

Thus, marriage at the turn of the nineteenth century was considered so central as to be "the bulwark of the social order" (Snell, 1991: 2). It remained largely patriarchal, with most married women economically dependent on their husbands. Obtaining a divorce was very difficult, and children born outside of marriage were thought of as "illegitimate," subject to social stigma and holding fewer rights than children born in wedlock. Laws and attitudes concerning marriage have changed substantially over time. The Divorce Act made divorce more common and easier to obtain, and further revisions occurred in 1985 to ease the adversarial aspects by introducing "no fault" provisions. The stigma surrounding cohabitation and unwed childbearing has also declined. Another major change has been the recognition of the constitutional right for lesbians and gay men to legally marry in Canada.

Canada became the fourth country in the world to legalize same-sex marriage with the ratification of the Civil Marriage Act in 2005. Lesbian and gay rights movements in Canada and Quebec successfully framed the issue in terms of Canada's national political culture that should tolerate sexual diversity (Smith, 2007). The legalization of same-sex marriage in Canada has been accompanied by significant shifts in attitudes towards lesbians and gay men. Anderson and Fetner (2008) found a noteworthy degree of change in attitudes among all age groups in Canada and the United States. Their study offers evidence against the claim that ideas on controversial social issues are fully formed by early adulthood, and change little with age.

In Canada, there are varying cultural practices of marriage that pose a challenge to Canadian laws and norms involved in regulating family life. Despite the growing dominance of the "love-marriage," arranged marriages—marriages in which parents or extended kin determine the choice of spouse—are still prevalent in many societies, including in South Asia. South Asian women who migrate to Canada through marriage—often through an arranged marriage—represent a vulnerable population due to their tenuous legal status, and immigration policy can intensify this vulnerability by granting the resident spouse control of the process (Walton-Roberts, 2004).

Many South Asian women in arranged marriages come to Canada with very little knowledge of their spouses. Before policy changes set forth in the new Immigration and Refugee Protection Act of 2002, there were numerous reports of women who, after experiencing intense emotional and physical abuse from resident husbands and extended kin, were abandoned. The new family sponsorship policies seek to reduce the risk of women being mistreated by considering the men's criminal record or history of domestic violence, reducing the number of years of required sponsorship, and adding language to sponsorship contracts outlining women's rights. A qualitative study that examined understandings of sponsorship among South Asian brides who entered Canada after the new immigration policy found that English-proficient women were cognizant of their rights and reported significant support. In contrast, non-English-proficient women did not fully understand the conditions of sponsorship and were subject to more severe abuse and neglect (Merali, 2009). This research points to the need for further changes to immigration policy to support non-English-proficient women.

Children of immigrants who grow up in Canada tend to view marriage very differently from their parents. Many studies of South Asian families find evidence of serious intergenerational conflict over marriage customs, with the second generation demanding more say in decisions to marry and desiring more gender egalitarian relationships (Zaidi and Shuraydi, 2002). One qualitative study found that youth and their parents were making compromises to reduce such tensions (Netting, 2006). Indo-Canadian youth who chose their own mate would pick someone in their own caste or at least religion to make the choice more acceptable to their parents. Parents often begrudgingly accepted these choices, showing the importance of the intergenerational bond to these families. If parents did find something seriously wrong with the partner, the young adults expressed their willingness to reconsider their choice.

The issue of polygamy has posed a particular challenge to the role of the state in recognizing relationships in Canada. Polygamy is a global phenomenon, most commonly practised as polygyny in which one man has several wives. The practice is illegal in Canada, raising the question of whether individuals should have the right to participate in this family form without it being criminal. The BC Supreme Court has recently addressed this question.

Mormons openly practised polygamy (or plural marriage) in North America, until 1890 when it was banned by the mainstream Mormon Church. Since then, groups of fundamentalist Mormons have continued the practice often in isolated areas, one of which is Bountiful in southern British Columbia. In 2010, the BC Supreme Court began an unprecedented reference case to determine the constitutional validity of polygamy's criminal prohibition in Canada. In his ruling, Justice Bauman found that while the law does infringe on religious freedom, it is warranted by the harm polygamy causes to children, women, and society. For now, the ruling is definitive. However, given the family transformations discussed in this chapter, society will continue to grapple with the question of why, if marriage is about love and commitment, the number of marriage partners should be limited to two. In the next section, we will consider the changing landscape of dating, marriage, and commitment among youth.

The Changing Landscape of Young Adult Relationships: Dating and Hooking Up

While marriage rates have dropped in Canada, the median age at first marriage has risen substantially. In 2008, the average age for men to marry was 31.1 years—a six year increase from its record low in 1970, and the average age for women was 29.1 years—a 6.5 year increase from its record low in the 1960s (Vanier Institute, 2010). The rising age of first marriage has meant that most young adults experience a period in their life course called the independent life stage, which encompasses a period of relative social independence (Rosenfeld, 2007). The rise of the independent life stage has reduced parental control over the dating and mate selection choices of their children. How do youth today form sexual and romantic relationships?

Historically in North America, romantic relationships among heterosexual unmarried youth shifted from courtship—a defined period preceding engagement and marriage—to dating, which took many forms and had less focus on commitment. Dating involves social activities between two people over time to discover the possibility of a committed relationship. It arose in the 1920s after the invention of the automobile, which offered youth more mobility and privacy (Bailey, 1989). Until the late 1960s, dating was the dominant model in which young people found a mate, and it was structured in relation to specific codes for dress and behaviour, including defined gender expectations (Coontz, 1993). Men asked women to go out, paid for the date, and initiated intimacy and sex.

Social historian Beth Bailey asserts that "it has been more than a quarter of a century since the dating system lost its coherence and dominance" (1988: 141). She argues that a "new system of courtship" was established in the mid-1960s in American society. While scholars have acknowledged dramatic changes among youth in their sexual behaviour after 1965, some things have remained the same. In the early twenty-first century, Canadians pursued their first romantic relationships at a similar average age to that of their grandparents (about 16 and 17 years old). On the other hand, there have been numerous changes in attitudes toward premarital sex. In 2004, about 90 per cent of Canadians said they would accept the reality of premarital sex among adults, whereas this figure was quite low before 1965 (Bibby, 2004).

The big change in sexual behaviour came with the Baby Boom generation. The National Health and Social Life Survey documents that Americans born after 1942 were more sexually active at younger ages than those born between 1933 and 1942. This trend, however, appears to stop or reverse among the youngest cohort born between 1963 and 1972 (Armstrong, Hamilton, and England, 2010). One study found that the number of women who have had premarital sex by age 20 (65–76 per cent) is roughly the same for all cohorts born after 1948 (Finer, 2007). The 1990s did witness a brief drop in this number for adolescents between the years 1991 and 2001 (Centers for Disease Control and Prevention, 2002a). Still, nearly one-half of US high school students have had sexual intercourse in their lifetime (Centers for Disease Control and Prevention, 2002b). In the past few decades, there has been an increase in the incidence of oral sex: over one-half of American adolescents have either received or performed oral sex, a sharp rise from mid-century findings (Leichliter, et al., 2007). Laumann, et al. (1994: 102) described this increase as the most "basic change in the script for sex between women and men" in the twentieth century.

Today, adolescents most often begin dating through involvement with mixed-gender friendship groups (Connolly, Furman, and Konarski, 2000). Social and romantic activities are integral to the development of relationships among adolescents, and hanging out with their partner and friends, holding hands, and telling others they are in a relationship generally precedes sexual activity (O'Sullivan et al., 2007). Sexual encounters outside of a relationship are practised by a large number of adolescents for their first and subsequent sexual experiences (Grello, Welsh, and Harper, 2006).

In recent years, studies have begun to explore the phenomenon of "hooking up" among heterosexual university students (Bogle, 2008). Glenn and Marquardt (2001: 4) define a hookup as: "when a girl and a guy get together for a physical encounter and don't necessarily expect anything further." They discovered that hooking up has become quite common in the university environment. One study of undergraduate students in a Northeastern university in the United States found that 78.3 per cent of men and women sampled hooked up (Paul et al., 2000). Yet, this high number can be a bit deceiving. Another study found that on average 80 per cent of students hookup less than once per semester over their entire university experience, and many of these hookup involve relatively light sexual activity—one-third included sexual intercourse, and the other two-thirds involved other activities like oral sex or just kissing and non-genital touching (Armstrong, Hamilton, and England, 2010).

Some researchers assess casual sexual encounters as detrimental for heterosexual young women (Bogle, 2008); others frame them as offering women sexual agency apart from time-consuming relationships (Hamilton and Armstrong, 2009). In the past, studies of adolescent girls found a stronger emphasis on personal relationships and romance in contrast to adolescent boys who can be less emotionally engaged and who focus on sexual competition and scoring (e.g., Gilligan, 1982; Martin, 1996). One study of high-school adolescent boys found them to be relatively less confident in initiating physical sex and more emotionally engaged in romantic relationships than these previous characterizations (Giordano, Longmore, and Manning, 2006). Yet, research suggests that as boys gain more social maturity, dominant gender dynamics of male confidence in initiating dating and sexual encounters prevail.

Researchers have assessed patterns of dating in terms of dominant scripts—the cognitive schema people use to organize the world around them (Ginsburg, 1988). **Sexual scripts** refer to the cognitive models that individuals draw on to assess and choose sexual activities and behaviour (Simon and Gagnon, 1986). A prevalent sexual script bolsters the "sexual double standard"—the idea that women should limit their sexual activities to committed relationships while men have the liberty to pursue sex within or outside of a relationship. The sexual double standard labels women who have casual sex as "sluts," whereas men who hookup are just doing what guys do (Crawford and Popp, 2003). This double standard contributes to broader patterns of gender inequality by privileging men's desires and needs over women's.

The phenomenon of hookups has not necessarily challenged dominant sexual scripts, and heterosexual dating remains highly gender-typed (Eaton and Rose, 2011). In their study of 273 undergraduate students in a large public university in the southern United States, Reid, Elliott, and Webber (2011) studied student responses to a vignette that described a heterosexual hookup followed by a first date that did not involve sex. They found that students viewed both women and men as sexual beings with desires that could be fulfilled through hookups, a "semianonymous, casual, and mutually pleasurable affair that carries few long-term consequences" (Reid, et al., 2011: 564). This non-stereotypical assessment changed, however, when discussing the first date. Students described the need for the woman, but not the man, to engage in impression management as a way to ensure her potential as "dating material." Thus, the sexual double standard, reduced in the party setting, was reaffirmed in a dating situation where the woman must reframe her behaviour according to the sexual script of the "good" girl who doesn't "put out" on the first date.

Most of the literature on dating and hookups has concentrated on the heterosexual world. Thus, there is limited research on the relationship patterns of young lesbian, gay, bisexual, and transgender (LGBT) youth. Past research found many similarities in dating scripts between white, middle-class heterosexual and lesbian and gay youth (Klinkenberg and Rose, 1994). Dating among same-sex youth conformed to dominant cultural scripts. For example, lesbians often focused on emotional connections, whereas gay male youth were more likely to participate in sexual activity. On the other hand, there were differences in other cultural scripts between lesbian/gay male and heterosexual youth, including the ways they planned a date and initiated sexual activity.

Same-sex romantic relationships still face the challenge of developing in the face of factors associated with being part of a stigmatized minority. LGBT youth often feel isolated and experience verbal and physical abuse in high school (Elze, 2003). One small-scale study of lesbian and gay youth found that internalized homonegativity—anti-LGBT beliefs applied to oneself—brings a decrease in how satisfied youth are with their relationship and in their feelings of mutual attraction (Mohr and Daly, 2008). Another small-scale study of gay/bisexual male adolescents in the Castro district of San Francisco found a tension between a desire for love and monogamy and a lack of community support for such relationships (Eyre et al., 2007). With the improving climate for LGBT youth, facilitated by the increasing presence of gay–straight alliances—student organizations that provide a safe and supportive environment for LGBT students and their straight allies—it will be important to conduct more research on LGBT sexual behaviour and romantic relationships to uncover beliefs about sex, love, and compatibility.

Techno Transformations: Internet Dating and Cybersex

High rates of union instability and movement mean many people searching for a new mate have been involved in previous marriages and/or cohabitations. With a large pool of individuals in the relationship market, new pathways are available to meet potential partners. Personal ads have flourished in the past decades as a way to facilitate dating or sexual encounters. The Internet offers an easily available outlet for personal ads. A nascent body of research examines how new technologies, including the Internet and speed dating, reassert and challenge dominant ideas about what men and women search for in mates.

Recent research indicates that between 3 and 6 per cent of current marriages or long-term partnerships begin over the Internet (Sprecher, 2009). Studies of targeted segments of Internet users offer evidence of its common use to develop personal relationships, but only a small proportion of these actually progress into romantic relationships. Representative surveys further indicate that only a small percentage of existing relationships were initiated following online communications. Instead, it is still more common to meet someone through more traditional networks, such as school or work. However, as the current popularity of "online dating" continues to increase, it is becoming an important avenue for meeting romantic and/or sexual partners.

Internet users report high levels of personal control over the process of electronically mediated communications to initiate relationships (Ben-Ze'ev, 2004). Researchers are finding the effects of online technology to both transform and reproduce dominant cultural practices associated with the initiation and development of intimacy between adults (Barraket and Henry-Waring, 2008). **Social exchange theory** understands interpersonal relationships according to the social psychological principle of minimizing costs and maximizing rewards (Myers, 1993). For example, relationships that offer more than they take are the ones people tend to sustain. To gain maximum reward, individuals advertise their best traits and seek an exchange for what they view as socially desirable (Phua and Kaufman, 2003). This perspective applies to both face-to-face and electronically mediated interactions (Merkle and Richardson, 2000). Interactions that take place face to face or in cyberspace involve interpersonal exchanges that seek positive rewards, but differences in online forms of communications do exist, including less need for spatial proximity, greater anonymity, and more emphasis on self-disclosure (Cooper and Sportolari, 1997).

Researchers have found that, when choosing a prospective partner, Internet daters tend to make decisions based on racial preferences. Feliciano et al. (2009) sampled profiles from an online dating site to find that whites exclude blacks, Latinos, Asians, Middle Easterners, East Indians, and Native Americans as potential dating partners. On average, white men are more willing than white women to date non-whites; however, among those with stated racial preferences, white men are more likely to exclude blacks as possible dates. In contrast, white women are more likely to exclude Asians. The researchers point to the ways that these preferences relate to racialized images of masculinity and femininity that shape who dates, cohabits, and marries. For example, white men who exclude dating black women may rely on stereotypes that place black women outside of idealized perceptions of femininity (Collins, 2004). Likewise, white women who exclude Asian men draw on stereotypes of Asian men as asexual and lacking masculinity (Espiritu, 1997).

Many of the early, more high profile Internet newsgroups, websites, and e-mail discussion lists targeted a gay and lesbian audience (Wakeford, 2000). Computer-mediated communication has opened new doors for lesbians and gay men to find relationships and sexual partners, especially in geographically isolated areas. In his analysis of personal advertisements from the online gay and lesbian global Web portal PlanetOut, Gudelunas (2005) found that postings differed mainly by gendered identities, and by whether the user came from an urban or rural area. Women in small towns were more likely to identify as butch or femme (masculine or feminine identity), but men and women in large cities mostly failed to answer this question. Overall, Gudelunas found that users maintained their local identities even while they participated in the more global cyberspace of PlanetOut.

Cybersex has also come of age with the advent of the Internet. It involves two or more people engaging in online sexual talk and may include masturbation and orgasm (Daneback, Cooper, and Mansson, 2005). There has been very little research on cybersex to date. In their study of cybersex using a sample collected from a Swedish web portal (N = 1828), Daneback et al. (2005) found that almost one-third of men and women said they had engaged in cybersex. Women between 35 and 49 years reported significantly more cybersex activity than did men in that age group. Both men and women between the ages of 50 and 65 were not interested in cybersex, likely due to the fact that this age group has had less exposure to the Internet. Gay men were over four times more likely to have participated in cybersex compared to heterosexual men.

Another study explored the mechanics and perceptions of cybersex interactions in "massively multiplayer online role playing games." Valkyrie (2011) found that cybersex in the context of online gaming both draws on and expands the original understandings of "cybersex." Players participate in virtual worlds that involve specific tools to augment their practices, including erotic texting accompanied by "emotes" that simulate "virtuophysical touch to heighten the pleasure and intimacy of cybersex" (Valkyrie 2011: 91). Players also used eroticized (gendered) avatars as a visual tool to enhance their fantasies and to express themselves erotically. The phenomenon of cybersex blurs the boundaries of the body, sex, and of what counts as being sexual.

Online and electronic communication is shaping the global marketplace of buying sexual services. Sex workers increasingly advertise online and set up appointments with prospective clients via the Internet, no longer requiring middlemen (Bernstein, 2007). Sociologist Elizabeth Bernstein has studied the ways that electronic communication offers new avenues for intimate encounters; the Internet has actually transformed the geographic space and practice of sexual labour, offering greater opportunity to perform sexual labour without the reliance on red light districts and walking the streets.

Living Alone, Families of Choice, and Living Together Apart

The twentieth and twenty-first centuries have witnessed a steady decline in larger household sizes. In recent years, the number of single-person households has increased steadily. According to the 2011 Census, overall household size has decreased in recent decades due to increased shares of one- and two-person households and to decreases in the proportion of large households comprised of five or more people (see Figure 3.2).

For the first time in 2011, the Census counted more one-person households than couple households with children. Between 2001 and 2011, the number of one-person households increased from 25.7 per cent to 27.6 per cent. This trend is not unique to Canada. In fact,

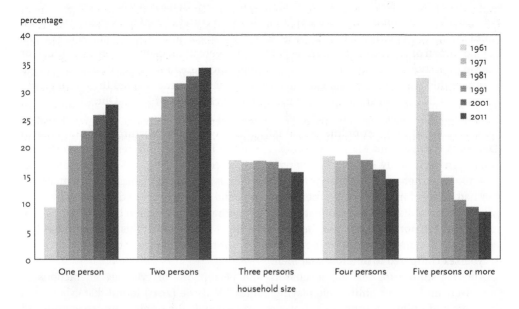

Figure 3.2 **Distribution (in percentage) of Private Households by Household Size, Canada, 1961–2011**

SOURCE: Statistics Canada, Censuses of Population, 1961 to 2011.

about four in ten households in Finland (2010), Norway (2011), and the Netherlands (2011) were one-person. Canada's proportion of single-household families is comparable to the United States and the United Kingdom (Statistics Canada, 2011c).

Qualitative research indicates that while the number of people who are single has increased, the prevailing meanings regarding singleness are still fairly negative (DePaulo and Morris, 2005). Being single is generally thought of as being "selfish, deviant, immature, irresponsible, lonely, unfulfilled, emotionally challenged, lacking interpersonal ties and strong social bonds" (Budgeon, 2008: 309). The stigma of being single comes from being an outsider to the idealized norm of coupledom in popular culture and in how societal benefits and social policy are distributed.

Shelley Budgeon (2008) conducted in-depth interviews with 51 people aged 24–60 who either were not in a sexual relationship or had a non-cohabiting sexual partnership. She found that participants tended to describe their singleness in a way that distanced them from the couple ideal, bridging a discrepancy between their positive self-identity of being single and their social identity shaped by the negative stereotypes of singleness. Friendships were an important mechanism that participants said they relied on to reduce the stigmatization they faced. By shifting their meaningful relationships towards friendships and away from sexual relationships, the participants embraced an ideology concerning the value of being single as part of social belonging.

Friendships have also been an important component of **families of choice**. Weeks, Heaphy, and Donovan (2001: 9) define families of choice as "kin-like networks of relationships, based on friendship and commitment beyond blood." These family configurations can include blood relatives, but the importance of these relationships is based on choice rather than just on blood or legal ties. The concept of families of choice emerged out of the historical exclusion of lesbians and gay men from the heterosexual nuclear family. Acknowledging the importance of particular values of family to everyday life, such as continuity, commitment, and material and emotional support, non-heterosexuals created their own families based on these values. Over time, the concept of families of choice has been applied to heterosexual family relationships, as well.

What do sociologists mean by friendship? Pahl and Spencer (2004) note the failure of many sociologists to operationalize the concept in empirical research, instead using an assumed definition. To rectify this, they offer a typology of friendship to clarify the boundaries between relationships that are given (mostly through kinship ties) and the ones that are chosen (both kin and non-kin). They further designate the strength of relationships based on high or low commitment. By elucidating kin and friendship patterns, they find involvement in highly complex sets of relationships within and between generations. Jamieson (1998: 88) confirms the importance of strong boundaries in friendship, saying that "actual friendships are often closer to stereotypes of kin and community relationships (for example, based on mutual obligation, kept within careful predefined boundaries) than to the ideal of friendship." People's friendship patterns also change over time (Pahl and Pevalin, 2005). Younger people choose their closest friends outside the family, but this tendency changes as people age, and the proportion of individuals who name their relatives as a friend increases.

Another emergent family form that has been characterized as placing more importance on friendship is the phenomenon of "living apart together" (LAT), an intimate relationship with a partner who lives somewhere else. LATs are becoming increasingly accepted as a specific way of being in a couple. Studies have found that LATs do not only live apart due to necessity in terms of housing or labour market constraints, but rather that many choose not to live together even when it would be possible for them to do so.

Analyzing a representative sample of 320 British people who were living apart together, Duncan and Phillips (2010) found that LATs have diverse origins and motivations. About one-third of the sample felt that the relationship was not ready to take the step of living together. Another substantial proportion had external constraints on living together, including affordability or the job and education market. Some people who connected emotionally and intimately still chose to live apart as a more desirable solution to the complexity of modern life. Another qualitative study of individuals living apart together found that those interviewed offered positive remarks on aspects of not living with their partner, and they portrayed LATs as a valid way of being in a relationship, not as a move in a progression towards a "proper" relationship (Roseneil, 2006). Thus, some individuals are able to make specific choices around the specific configuration of living patterns.

Conclusion

Long-term transformations in marriage, family, and intimacy involve a move away from institutional factors, although these still remain important, towards more relationship fluidity. Women's entry into the labour force in the past 60 years has transformed family structures and marital relationships. Marriage and family, once solidly grounded in familial ties and kinship obligations, now offer a range of options—from relationships embedded in traditional gender roles to those based on individual choice and personal satisfaction. Choice includes the possibility of who to include as part of one's kinship network, whether to marry or remain single, when and how to participate in reproductive relationships, whether to cohabit or live apart together, among others.

Along with transformations of intimacy have come strains in family life in North America and Europe, marked by high rates of relationship dissolution and concerns over how to balance family and work life. Even though heterosexual relationships have become more gender egalitarian, there are still persistent gendered inequalities, especially within heterosexual marriages where research has found unequal participation between men and women in household and parental tasks. The sources of these persisting differences include institutional barriers for women in entry and earning power in the labour market, the tenacity of deeply held assumptions about the fundamental nature of men and women, and continuing inequalities in power within the household. The growth of income inequality between countries in the global north and south is also generating a hierarchy of families with those at the top retaining economic and social capital to live and work more securely, and those at the bottom experiencing insecure living conditions that force them to uproot to seek the means to survive.

These transformations represent particular challenges to instituting policies and law to support the numerous manifestations of the family unit in the future. How do we best protect children's interests to secure the support of adults who have formally expressed their commitment to rearing children? How do we strengthen interdependency and personal commitment among adults? The answers will likely depend on finding ways to support the variety of situations with respect to family, to diminish inequality within and among families, and to allow people to form, revise, and pursue the conception of the "good relationship" that is most suitable to their circumstances.

STUDY QUESTIONS

1. In this chapter, you learned about the changes in family formation, the decline in the number of people getting married, and the rise in cohabitation rates. Do you think that marriage is becoming less socially significant in Canada? Why or why not?

2. How has the transformation of intimacy impacted family life in Canada? What is meant by the term "plastic sexuality," and why is it important to the study of intimacy?

3. How has the legal structure of marriage in Canada worked to exclude people based on their gender, sexual orientation, and race and ethnicity?

4. Studies of youth sexual practices over time show that "hooking up" does not represent a sudden change in youth sexual culture. Apply what you have learned about social exchange theory in this chapter to assess the costs and benefits of the hookup culture for university students.

5. How has electronically mediated communications technology changed dating practices in North America? Think about this in terms of sexual practices, geographic distance, and various relationship forms, such as LAT.

6. Friendship is an important intimate and social connection for many people. What role does friendship play in changing family forms, including singleness, "families of choice," and LAT? What is friendship's significance across the life course?

Further Readings

Armstrong, Elizabeth A., Laura Hamilton, and Paula England. 2010. "Is hooking up bad for young women"?, *Contexts* 9: 22–7. The research finds that women's hookup experiences vary from uniformly negative to offering some benefits.

Carpenter, Laura, and John DeLamate, eds. 2012. *Sex for Life From Virginity to Viagra, How Sexuality Changes Throughout Our Lives.* New York: New York University Press. This collection critically examines sexuality and intimacy across the entire lifespan, including the topics of puberty, sexual initiation, hooking up, coming out, sexual assault, marriage/life partnering, disability onset, immigration, divorce, menopause, and widowhood.

Gabb, Jacqui. 2008. *Researching Intimacy in Families.* Palgrave Macmillan Studies in Family and Intimate Life. Basingstoke, UK: Palgrave Macmillan. Using original data, this book sets out the theoretical debates on intimacy and demonstrates the potential of qualitative mixed-methods to examine the complexity of family life.

Heath, Melanie. 2012. *One Marriage under God: The Campaign to Promote Marriage in America.* New York: New York University Press. This book is the first ethnography to assess the discriminatory consequences of marriage promotion policies as they are practised on the ground.

Whitty, Monica, Andrea Baker, and James Inman, eds. 2007. *Online Matchmaking.* New York: Palgrave Macmillan. This collection covers various online relationship issues including different internet communication spaces, cybersex and body theories, online subgroups, and cyberstalking.

Wu, Zheng. 2000. *Cohabitation: An Alternative Form of Family.* Toronto: Oxford University Press. Using data from the Canadian census, the General Social Survey, and the Canadian Fertility Survey, this book covers issues concerning the rise in cohabitation in Canada, including shifting attitudes towards cohabitation, why people choose cohabitation over marriage, childbearing within cohabiting relationships, and the legal and public policy implications of this trend.

Websites

www.unmarried.org

The Alternatives to Marriage Project (AtMP) advocates for equality and fairness for unmarried people, including people who are single, choose not to marry, cannot marry, or live together before marriage. The Project provides information to the unmarried, fights discrimination on the basis of marital status, and educates the public and policy-makers about relevant social and economic issues.

www.cwhn.ca

The Canadian Women's Health Network site has articles about the links to sites on sexuality, sexual health, and relationship issues from a feminist perspective.

www.stepinstitute.ca

The Step and Blended Family Institute is a counselling service that focuses on step and blended family issues. The Toronto-based Institute provides information, group counselling, couple counselling, and workshops in person and by telephone.

www.vanierinstitute.ca

The Vanier Institute of the Family is an advocacy organization that conducts research on the structural, demographic, and economic challenges for Canadian families.

4

Parenting Young Children: Decisions and Realities

AMBER GAZSO

LEARNING OBJECTIVES

- To introduce students to the life course perspective and how it helps them understand the decision to parent and the everyday activities of parenting young children

- To demonstrate how the experience of parenting today is contextualized by changes in Canadian family life over time

- To help students see the decision to become a parent as a major life course transition that is connected to gender socialization

- To teach students that the everyday practices or events of parenting are intimately connected to and textured by ideological discourses, culture, individuals' participation in other social spheres (e.g., the labour market), and relationships with others and social policy (e.g., child care)

- To introduce students to how differences in family structure and the sexuality of parents informs the performance of parenting

Introduction

Having and raising children involves parents' constant management and negotiation of their emotions, mental fortitude, and physical energy. At all stages of their growth and development, children can provide parents with feelings of wonderment, accomplishment, and affection, whether it is concerning their first steps or their graduation from high school. Children can also present parents with many, even limitless, challenges that range from sleepless nights and trouble finding child care, to partners who do not equally participate in housework, workplaces that fail to grant days off for caring for sick children, and weak economic support from governments during hard times. Parenting in Canadian society today is, not surprisingly, a fruitful topic of sociological interest.

In this chapter, I adopt a life course perspective to focus on an important stage in some people's lives—the decision to become a parent and the subsequent everyday realities of parenting infants and/or young children. The life course perspective emphasizes transitions, pathways, and trajectories that develop over the course of an individual's life (Elder, 1994); becoming a parent is a transition in a person's family trajectory. People are perceived to have agency but the choices they make over their life, such as the choice to raise a child, are understood to be shaped by social structures such as the economy or social policy. Additionally, the choices and opportunities available to any individual are culturally and ideologically mediated and temporally and historically situated; earlier decisions will shape later outcomes (Mitchell, 2009). A final principle of this theoretical perspective important in the study of parenting is that of linked lives: the behaviour of one family member shapes and is shaped by the behaviour of other family members, including parents and children (McDaniel and Bernard, 2011). The everyday events or practices of parenting are connected to people's relationships in social domains such as paid work and child care, and with others too, including family and friends in networks of support. Through the lens of the life course, we can see the interconnectedness among everyday parenting activities as they are experienced within particular social contexts.

This chapter is organized as follows: the first section begins with a general overview of changes in Canadian families in order to situate the experience of parenting today; the second section considers the factors, including one's gendered sense of self that underpin the decision to have a child and raise a family;[1] and the third section highlights everyday parenting of young children as linked to other dimensions of social life.

General Overview: Parenting and Social Change

Popular media and rhetoric tends to suggest that parenting occurs most often in nuclear families. In fact, people are parenting in arrangements that are more diverse than nuclear families made up of a wife, husband, and children, are doing so at later ages, and are parenting fewer children today than in the past. According to the 20011 Census the majority of Canadians over the age of 15 live in family households consisting of more than two people. However, whereas nuclear families were the most prevalent family structure from 1901 to 2001, the year 2006 marked the first time that unmarried couples without children outnumbered married couples with children (Milan, Vézina, and Wells, 2007). The 2011 Census revealed that the number of couples living with children has continued to decline (Statistics Canada, 2012a). The number of individuals parenting children with a partner in a common-law union or on their own increased between 2001 and 2011. During this same period, there was an 13.9 per cent increase in cohabiting same-sex couples (Statistics Canada, 2012a). According to 2006 Census data, married same-sex couples were more likely to be raising children than cohabiting or common-law same-sex couples; 24.5 per cent of women in married same-sex couples were parenting children compared to 14.6 per cent of women in same-sex common-law couples. For male same-sex couples, parenting is not as common. Nine per cent of married same-sex couples versus 1.7 per cent of common-law same sex couples were raising children (Milan, Vezina, and Wells, 2007). The 2011 Census reveals that parenting continues to be more popular among female same-sex couples than male same-sex couples; 16.5 per cent of female same-sex couples have children at home versus 3.4 per cent of male same-sex couples. As well, there has been an increase in the number of children under 14 years of age living with grandparents (4.8 per cent in 2011 versus 3.3 per cent in 2001) (Statistics Canada, 2012a).

Parents are older and rearing fewer children than in the past. In 2008 the average age of mothers at childbirth was 29.3, a 2.6 year increase since 1975; 49.6 per cent of mothers who gave birth in 2008 were over the age of 30 (Human Resources and Skills Development Canada, 2012a). In 1959, women had 3.93 children. By 2007, this number had dropped to 1.7 (Human Resources and Skills Development Canada, 2012b). Considering census families, defined as couples with children, married couples had more children than common law couples in 2006 and 2011 (Statistics Canada, 2007i; 2012a). While lone-mother families continue to be more prevalent in Canadian society, lone-father families are growing. Census data shows that between 2006 and 2011, lone-father families rose by 16.2 per cent whereas lone-mother families increased by 6.0 per cent (Statistics Canada, 2012a). In light of these trends, the popular idea that children are commonly raised by one mother and one father is certainly less than accurate.

Today's parents also raise children in a social climate characterized by fewer or leaner supports for parents. Waves of **welfare state** restructuring have weakened federal income supports designed to assist parents with the daily cost of family life. From 1944 to the mid-1980s, all mothers in Canada were entitled to Family Allowances until their child reached the age of 18. This program provided all mothers with a monthly benefit amount that was to assist them in their raising of their children regardless of mothers' attachment to the paid labour force or their total household income. In the 1980s, Family Allowances were reformed and targeted at mothers with incomes below a certain threshold. The Canada Child Tax Benefit and National Child Benefit, Family Allowances' modern-day replacements, continue to be income-tested programs and so are available to only some parents. Although all parents are entitled to the Universal Child Care Benefit introduced by the Harper government in 2006, it is only $100 a month; for families with child care costs over $1,000 a month and who do not qualify for child tax benefits, this benefit may be of little help. Between 1940 and 1996, Unemployment Insurance (UI) provided parents with financial support during times in which they were unemployed. With the replacement of UI with Employment Insurance (EI) in 1996, the federal government introduced new eligibility criteria. Whereas people qualified for UI on the basis of weeks worked for pay, EI eligibility is assessed by hours of work. Parents who work part-time or seasonally are often ineligible for income support from the government if they become unemployed.

Provincial governments have also participated in creating greater financial and care burdens on parents. Although social assistance programs provide economic relief in times of economic need, such as when a person is unemployed or providing care to young children, restructuring from especially the 1990s onward has resulted in total monthly benefits that are well below Statistics Canada's **Low-Income Cut-offs**. According to widespread rhetoric, social assistance is a program of "last resort." As a program for parents, however, it can result in them not having enough money for basic needs like adequate housing or nutritious meals (Gazso, 2007a). Low-income parents also struggle to find suitable child care arrangements should they desire to return to paid work or education. It can be a long wait to receive a subsidy and a space in a licensed childcare centre. For two-parent families, even when both parents are engaged in paid work a good portion of one parent's paycheque goes toward the purchase of outside child care, a topic returned to later in this chapter.

Deciding to Parent

There are many pathways that result in the event of parenthood. Parenthood is no longer the given and natural condition of solely heterosexual and legally married couples (Stacey, 2006). Besides a woman conceiving a child with her male partner, straight and queer individuals can become parents of children through, among other avenues: adoption, artificial insemination, surrogacy, foster care, In-Vitro Fertilization (IVF), and/or partnering with someone who has children from an earlier union (Foster, 2005). For example, IVF technology can enable a woman to receive a donated ovum so that she may conceive and bear a child and have full legal and social obligations in raising the child; the genetic mother does not share these rights. Or, two gay men may become parents through adoption or surrogacy, where a woman has agreed to conceive a child by being artificially inseminated with one or both of the men's sperm. In her qualitative study, Dempsey (2010: 1152–4) explains that lesbian women and gay men can negotiate still more complex reproductive relationships with others through three approaches. In "standard donor" relationships, a male donates sperm to a woman but has no familial relationship with the woman or child. Unlike the "standard donor" relationship, a "social solidarity" relationship involves a donor who could be acknowledged as the child's family member but primary social and legal obligation rest with the woman inseminated. Finally, "co-parenting" relationships can involve two people agreeing to parent a child, conceived by artificial insemination, but do not have to share a residence nor be in a sexually intimate couple relationship. As Farrell, VandeVusse, and Ocobock (2012) observe, conventional conceptions of childbearing and formal, legal definitions of family have been transformed with the advent of such assisted reproductive technologies. In essence, contemporary pathways to parenthood are "reflexive, uncertain, self-fashioning, plural, and politically embattled" (Stacey, 2006: 29).

Sociologically, the decision to parent is an interesting one. Stacey (2006) argues that an emotional impetus underlies the decision to parent today, more so than the economic one of the past when children were sources of labour and family financial security. Children promise an emotional intimacy that can be grounding in the midst of a society that can sometimes feel unsafe because of challenges such as economic turbulence, crime, and social exclusion. Prior to an adult's perception of the emotional gain associated with children, the development of gender identity and gender socialization over the early life course can underpin the decision of whether to raise a child. From childhood and into later life, women and men interact with others and multiple discourses that ascribe gender identity and roles such as mother or father according to dominant masculine and feminine stereotypes. The development or achievement of a gendered self, in line or in opposition to this ascription, is a life-long process and one that is connected to the decision to parent.

The family can be a primary site in which boys and girls are taught to view their biological sex as essentially determining their life choices. Boys and girls grow older in a society characterized by **institutionalized heterosexuality**. The family and other socialization agents such as school and media teach sexuality and reproduction as naturally concomitant (see also

Valverde, 2009). That is, children are taught that opposites attract and when one partners, one should partner with the opposite sex in order to reach fulfillment of their biological destiny—reproduction. Through these socialization agents, boys learn to view fatherhood as associated with particular masculine characteristics: aggression, leadership authority, power and control, and detached rationality. Girls learn to understand motherhood as assuming characteristics of passivity, submission, and emotional intimacy. Moving along the life course, from adolescence into adulthood, women and men continue to be socialized to understand children as a normal and essential outcome of sexual intimacy. In particular, women are taught to desire children and see the act of mothering as inevitable and natural. According to Nelson (2006), the idea that a woman only reaches her full potential through motherhood is historically rooted, emerging as a social discourse in the eighteenth century, coupled with the idea that all "normal" women have a deep-rooted instinct to mother.

To place attention on gender socialization in the decision to parent is not to deny individual agency. Most people would vehemently argue that they choose to parent at a particular optimal moment in their lives. However, sociologically, we must understand the choice to parent as linked to earlier experiences of gender socialization, particularly the social construction of parenting as a natural event in one's life. Moreover, pressures to parent according to heteronormative configurations of the family are experienced regardless of one's sexuality (Epstein, 2009). Individuals who identify as LGBTIQ[2] are also exposed to discourses about parenting as a natural outcome of heterosexual coupling. They must navigate gendered constructions of masculinity and femininity in different ways than straight individuals by working against assumptions about their sexuality and prospective child rearing given their perceived biological bodies. In some circles within the queer community, to be queer is to be opposed to constructing families that fit the monolithic **nuclear family** model. In their study of American gay men who adopted children, Armesto and Shapiro (2011) found that the choice to parent had to be made in opposition to dominant beliefs that fathering and gay identity cannot coexist. In choosing to parent through adoption, gay men had to consciously challenge heterosexual privilege associated with parenting and be willing to establish parenting roles that did not conform to traditional gender roles.

CASE IN POINT
"Dykes Planning Tykes": Excerpt from an Interview with Rachel Epstein

Rachel Epstein is an educator, activist, researcher, writer, service provider, and a parent. She is the recipient of awards for LGBT community activism. In this interview she compels us to take a closer look at queer parents who are choosing to have and are raising children in Canada.

Tipper: Are there particular issues that lesbian mothers need to contend with that maybe heterosexual mothers don't, bearing in mind that there is huge diversity within both groups?

(Continued)

Epstein: In answer to your question, I immediately think about "Dykes Planning Tykes," a course for lesbian/bi/queer women who are considering parenthood. Kathie Duncan and I developed the course in 1997 and it's been running for 11 years in Toronto. It is currently being offered as a partnership between the LGBTQ parenting Network and The 519 Community Centre. Since 1997, over 400 people have taken that course. You might ask, why a course? One of the things that is true for most lesbian/bi/queer women is that we usually don't wake up pregnant. For us, the process of bringing kids into our lives usually involves a lot of thought, planning, time, energy and, sometimes, money. We have to think through our options. If we are interested in getting pregnant, we have to think about known versus anonymous sperm donors. These are not easy decisions. We have to think about the involvement of known donors, legal concerns, questions of children's right to know their biological origins. Making these decisions, one is confronted with deeply-held ideas about blood, biology, family, kinship, race, and culture. A lot of reflection goes into this process. For others, adoption is a consideration. Then you have to become familiar with the difference between private, public and international adoption, you have to understand the adoption process, and you have to think about your level of "outness" in that process.

LGBT people who are thinking of becoming parents also have to look at their support networks and relationships with their families of origin. On the first night of Dykes Planning Tykes we ask the question "How supportive or not supportive is your family of origin of you becoming a parent?" There are always some people who don't have that support and this can be really painful. At the same time, many of us have developed large networks of support and extended "families of choice," sometimes because of rejection from our biological kin. Sometimes adoption workers, and others, don't fully understand the ways that we make family. Because we have been put in the position of defending our right to parent for so long, it is still an issue for many queer people that they don't feel fully entitled to become parents or fully confident that, really, the kids will be okay—even though so many of us are having kids and creating families and, CLEARLY, our kids are turning out fine. And, of course, the research supports this. In fact, the research demonstrates some unique benefits for kids growing up in queer families. And yet, despite these findings, given our history, many people still carry the idea that it is not okay or that it is not going to be fair to kids.

In all of our courses—Dykes Planning Tykes, Daddies and Papas 2B, and Trans Fathers 2B—we spend a good deal of time helping people develop a sense of confidence in themselves as parents and the knowledge that the kids will be fine. Lately we've been bringing in a panel of teenagers who have grown up with queer parents. Hearing from these delightful young people goes a long way in assuaging people's fears.

SOURCE: Vanier Institute of the Family. 2009. "In Other Words: An Interview with Rachel Epstein" *Transition*. Ottawa: VIF. Available at http://30645.vws.magma.ca/media/node/286/attachments/In_Other_Words.pdf; accessed 10 October 2012.

The life course transitions of deciding to parent and becoming a parent must also be connected to societal institutions other than the family. According to Ranson (1998), a woman's decision to have a child is connected to the meeting of educational and career goals and available opportunities within the Canadian labour market. Indeed, one of the reasons women are having children at later ages is because of their relationships with education. As Beaujot (2004) observes, young adults are increasingly aware of their needs to invest in themselves in order to be competitive in the current labour market. The achievement of income security through labour market attachment is increasingly prioritized before childbirth. In her qualitative research with mothers, Ranson (1998) also found that the organization of paid work was important to a woman's sense of the "right time" to have children. The Canadian labour market is characterized by occupations that facilitate parenting and those that inhibit it. For example, the profession of teaching at elementary or post-secondary levels may be organized in such a way that parents have up to two months off from paid work each year. Depending on one's field of paid work, a person may have more autonomy in scheduling their paid work time in balance with their child caring responsibilities. Other jobs that are long in hours and high in responsibility can make the raising of a child seem challenging or even impossible.

For more on fathers taking parental leave see "Child Care" in Chapter 9, pp. 171–3.

Finally, the decision to parent can also be understood as linked to women's and men's relationships with social policy and/or workplace policy. For example, many prospective parents consider whether or not they will be entitled to parental leave, paid by the federal government and/or their employer, should they take time off from their occupations for the birth or adoption of their child. Should they be eligible for Employment Insurance, monthly benefits from the federal government cover 55 per cent of their average insurable wages for them to take up to 35 weeks off of paid work; mothers are also entitled up to 15 weeks of maternity leave. Depending on their place of employment, prospective parents may also be entitled to a top-up of their monthly benefits from their employer for a portion or all of their time away from their job. Other available workplace policies can also inform a person's decision to parent such as provisions for absenteeism if a child is ill.

Several factors underpin a person's decision to rear a child in today's society. Personal choices intersect with the opportunities within and barriers of other institutions and social structures. The interaction between choice and structure partially underlie some of the wider trends observed earlier, such as having children at later ages and having smaller families. Nonetheless, people are still having children and are parenting. In the next section, we turn to the "hows" and "doings" of parenting and how it is connected to other everyday activities.

The Performance of Everyday Parenting

The performance of parenting dramatically changes women's and men's lifestyles. Women's and men's independence and autonomy are reconfigured by the presence of an infant or young child who is wholly dependent on them for the meeting of most basic needs including food, shelter, clothing, affection, protection, and socialization. Sleepless nights associated with the parenting of infants are replaced by busy days managing young children's schooling and recreational needs. Parenting practices must be re-imagined again when navigating relationships with young adolescents who become increasingly independent, or when children become adults themselves and need support surrounding life-altering decisions about post-secondary education and/or employment. This section focuses on the everyday practices of parenting infants or young school-aged children (i.e., under the age of 12). Whereas the decision to parent was linked to both identity and institutions as per the life course perspective, I focus here on how the activities of parenting young children are performed in connection to activities and transitions in other domains of social life, including micro-interactions within the family home and with others and relationships with institutions and structures, such as the workplace and social policy. Parenting young children is influenced by and performed in constant negotiation with one's sense of gender identity, discourses about the practice of parenting, cultural background, attachment to the paid labour market, the division of housework and childcare, relationships with social policy, and social support systems, all factors that additionally shape one's overall life course.

Gendered Discourses on Parenting

Just as gender socialization influences the decision to parent, the actual activities of everyday parenting are intimately tied to dominant ideas about masculinity and femininity. Mothers and fathers, regardless of their sexuality, experience powerful Westernized discourses about moral mothering and fathering. In terms of the performance of mothering, a "good" mother is selfless, devotes considerable time and energy to the caregiving of her children including the provision of education, is emotionally available, and prioritizes caring above paid work (Beck-Gernsheim, 2002; Hayes, 1996).

According to Hayes (1996), mothers daily experience pressure for their mothering to conform to the ideology of intensive mothering. Gaining traction from the 1900s onward, this ideological discourse prescribes mothering as necessarily involving incredible amounts of time, devotion to the child's well-being first and foremost and regardless of cost, and reliance on expert knowledge. Transforming in tune with mothers' realities over time, the contemporary manifestation of this ideology places great importance on mothers' paid work attachment for children's well-being and the subsequent need to find the best expert child care to replace mothers' own care (Hayes, 1996). "Good" mothers are ideal role models and creators of an environment for their children that provides for excellent social, physical, and emotional development (Gorman and Fritzsche, 2002, as cited in Nelson, 2006). Indeed, Fox (2001) reminds us that society is still organized around the assumption that women will want to be fully responsible for an infant's care. Mothers tend to be overwhelmingly represented in both culture and expert discourse as "naturally" suited to caring for infants compared to fathers (Wall and Arnold, 2007).

According to Nelson (2006), qualities of "good" fathering are narrowly conceived. The longstanding perception is that fathering is associated with economic provision. Historically, "good" fathers were first and foremost constructed as economic providers to their children, a quality befitting the **patriarchy** associated with a nuclear family model. Today, economic provisioning is still considered central to a father's role in most segments of society (Featherstone, 2003). Others' perceptions of fathers' masculinity are tied to their apparent status and power associated with earning. Fathers additionally experience pressure to conform to a particular and masculine style of fathering, such as rational authority figures or as disciplinarians. Hegemonic masculinity predominantly shapes the culturally available ways of performing fathering in contemporary society (Connell, 1987). Cultural discourses tend to position fathers as part-time or secondary parents, with their parenting fitting around their paid work attachment (Wall and Arnold, 2007).

Some scholars do observe slight changes in the perception and practices of fathering, linked to an increased attention to fathers in the past decade (Este and Tachable, 2009; O'Donnell, Johnson, D'Aunno, and Thorton, 2005). Compared to mothers, fathers seem to be permitted more choices in terms of their care responsibilities; fathers are mothers' helpers or playmates (Fox, 2001). Chuang and Su (2009) find that fathers are active participants within families, not just mere helpers, when they engage in increased levels of caregiving, playing with children, and the doing of household chores.

In a qualitative longitudinal study, Brannen and Nilsen (2006) discovered that there is both change and continuity in the performance of fathering. They studied fathering by different generations of British men born between 1911 and 1931, 1937 and 1953, and 1962 and 1980, and discovered three models. "Work-focused" fathers were fathers whose lifestyles were primarily shaped by their paid work attachment; work-focused fathers were from all three generations. "Family men" were fathers from the two older generations and split their time between paid work and child care. "Hands-on" fathers were only those fathers of the youngest generation. Few of them had been main earners in their lives and were a low-skilled group in terms of education and paid work experience. Brannen and Nilsen conclude that the apparent growth in hands-on fathering by the younger fathers reflects cultural change and societal context. Weak labour market prospects for these men meant fathering could be understood as caregiving, and caregiving was no longer thought as the exclusive domain of women. Younger generations of men in their study saw fathering more in terms of relational and caring involvement with children, and of sharing the responsibility for children's everyday needs (Brannen and Nilsen, 2006).

Sociologist Andrea Doucet has conducted extensive qualitative research on fathering in Canada. Her own study of heterosexual fathers who are primary caregivers revealed these fathers as openly affectionate with their children (Doucet, 2006; 2009). Doucet and Merla (2007) additionally discovered that stay-at-home fathers see important differences between their work as fathers and the work of mothers. Fathers did not strive to be a mother or to replace mothers but rather prioritized the promotion of children's physical, emotional, and intellectual independence and risk-taking, involved children in housework, and encouraged independent play. While fathers stressed positive traits of their fathering that matched hegemonic masculinity, they also fathered in ways that successfully integrated feminine psychological traits and skills such as softness and emotional literacy (Doucet, 2009; Doucet and Merla, 2007). According to Wall and Arnold (2007), there is considerable consensus that "new fathers" are fathers who are nurturing, develop close emotional relationships with children, and share the joy and work of caregiving with mothers. However, there is also considerable academic debate around the extent to which cultural expectations match with conduct of fathers (see also, LaRossa, 1988), something that will become quite clear in the below section on paid and unpaid work.

Some mothers and fathers would maintain that they are simply parenting in ways that make common sense to them. However, according to psychologist Diana Baumrind's research, there are particularly styles of parenting. *Authoritarian* parenting refers to parents who shape, control, and evaluate their children on the basis of a set of criteria or rules or behaviour. Parents know what is "right" and children are to obey them or experience punitive responses. *Authoritative* parenting emphasizes the use of rational, issue-oriented discussion to direct and guide children. Parents performing this style of parenting perceive children as capable of engaging in reasoning and encourage them to participate in discussions about how their behaviour may be changed. Finally, *permissive* parenting refers to parents who permit children to follow their own impulses and desires and actions and offer little punitive intervention. Children are perceived to be capable of regulating their behaviour and though parents intervene, this is often in an accepting and affirmative manner; they are a child's resource rather than regulator (Baumrind, 1966). Within psychological studies, authoritative parenting has been found to positively impact children's psychosocial maturity, social relationships with peers and adults, autonomy and academic achievement (Robinson, Mandleco, Frost Olsen, and Hart, 1995). Relatively speaking, attachment parenting is a newer style of parenting. Coined by pediatrician William Sears, this style of parenting stresses the development of strong emotional intimacy with infants through baby-wearing, breastfeeding on demand and for at least one year or more, and co-sleeping (Sears and Sears, 2001).

The everyday "hows" and "doings" of parenting are discursively mediated. Women and men who parent do so in the face of prescriptive discourses about "good" mothering and fathering. Whether parenting with someone else or alone, parenting involves consciously acting and behaving with an awareness that activities and behaviours will be perceived as conforming or not conforming to these ideas and the consequences of these perceptions. For example, the social construction of "good" mothering has become so extreme that mothers, especially those that engage in paid work, seem to be destined to be found wanting in some way. This is despite the fact that considerable research does not find paid employment negatively impacts children's development (Nelson, 2006: 344). Gendered ideas about "good" mothering and "bad" fathering dovetail with actual practices or styles of parenting. In her qualitative study of mothers who breastfed children to "full-term" (approximately three to four years of age), Faircloth (2010) found that mothers' choices to breastfeed in this manner were shaped by expert, scientific discourses that promulgated "good" mothering by equating it with attachment parenting. According to Faircloth, the contemporary ideology of intensive mothering rests on assumption of mothering performed in the style of attachment parenting. As historically conceptualized, "good" fathering, by contrast, may require parenting as per an authoritarian style. However, there are exceptions to these discursive constructions since newer practices of fathering seem more varied.

Culture and Diversity

Assuming all social groups equally practice parenting according to Westernized gendered discourses can result in overlooking cultural nuances and differences in parenting (Ochocka and Janzen, 2008). For example, Ochocka and Janzen (2008) observe that immigrant Chinese and Chinese-American parents practised authoritarian parenting to a greater extent than Euro-American parents. However, while authoritarian parenting was found to predict poor school achievement among Euro-Americans, Chinese children were high achievers under this style. In this section, we focus on a sample of Canadian research that reveals how cultural values and behaviours are tied to "good" parenting in particular racial/ethnic groups.

From a life course perspective, the parenting practices of Aboriginal families today are historically contextualized by past cultural genocide, including dispossession of land, mandatory placement of children in residential schools, and the removal of children from their families of origin through foster care or adoption (Fuller-Thomson, 2005). Despite, or because of, these enduring troubles, Aboriginal communities continue to practise parenting according to deeply engrained traditions and values. Among Aboriginal families in Canada, a great deal of importance is placed upon the role of community (Macdougall, 2010). While children are recognized as having biological parents, social parents, including extended family members, elders, and neighbours play a prominent role in raising and rearing children (Anderson, 2001). According to Anderson (2001), the idea that children are welcome is a persistent and traditional value among Aboriginal cultures. In my own qualitative research with Aboriginal lone mothers, I found that parenting continued to be performed in embracement of this value even in Westernized communities. Georgia, a lone mother of four children, explained: "Having four kids drives you nuts but, hey, what can you do? You brought them into this world, it's your responsibility. I've got to look after them. . . . They have no choice. So it's up to me to look after them, how I see fit for their safety, health and well being. That's part of the, uh, *traditionalism*, let's say . . . (Gazso, 2009b: 156, italics in original). Other research shows that Aboriginal fathers may hold the same traditional values but may face a number of challenges to their involvement in parenting. Compared to other men, Aboriginal men are more geographically mobile and nine times more likely to be incarcerated (Ball, 2009: 30). When adult parents are incapable of parenting because of mental health problems or drug addictions, grandparents can play important instrumental roles. In raising their grandchildren, they are responsible for their mental and physical care and especially to socialize them to cultural traditions and teaching (Fuller-Thomson, 2005).

The experience of immigration is a major life course event and one that is especially revealing of how cultural norms and values impact the everyday performance of parenting young children. Newcomers to Canada experience a social context with cultural norms about child rearing that may be very different than those in one's country of origin, as well as stereotypes about their culture and family practices (see, for example, Walton-Roberts and Pratt, 2005). Settling into life in Canada can be made difficult if economic hardship accompanies the first few years of residence and subsequently creates family troubles like marital instability (Liu and Kerr, 2003).[3] Often new immigrant parents must negotiate their children's desires to integrate into broader culture with their own desires to transmit cultural values according to their past styles of parenting (Mitchell, 2009). This can lead to family and parent–child conflict (Hassan, Rousseau, Measham, and Lashley, 2008). Alternatively, values and practices associated with parenting may change in accordance to new social surroundings of a host country (Chao, 1994 as cited in Ochocka and Janzen, 2008).

Este and Tachble (2009) explored the meaning of fatherhood among refugee Sudanese men in Canada. Fatherhood was understood as care, commitment, and responsibility with the majority of men maintaining that providing for their family in general was their main priority. Fathers also held strong beliefs that their roles were to instruct their children about the difference between right and wrong and to pass on Sudanese customs and traditions. Because of changes in their family lives as a result of immigration, some fathers assumed a greater role in raising their children in Canada than in their country of origin. Hassan et al. (2008) observed that Caribbean immigrant families are often headed by women who assume both economic and child care responsibilities. For immigrant Caribbean families, the family unit can often be perceived as a source of protection against danger. Generally speaking, transmission of filial respect is emphasized and physical punishment is considered to be an appropriate child discipline tool by some Caribbean parents (Hassan et al., 2008).

Within South Asian families, familial obligations are commonly expected to supersede personal desires. Familial obligations may be framed within the dharma and karma among Hindu South Asians and these sentiments may also be shared by South Asians of other religious backgrounds (George, 1998, as cited in Spitzer, Neufold, Harrison, Hughes, and Stewart, 2003). Caregiving is also expected to be necessarily multi-generational, involving loyalty to kin beyond one's immediate family of origin, and primarily the purview of women. For example, Spitzer et al.'s (2003: 277) study of migrant Chinese and South Asian women revealed that all respondents shared the perception that women were the "most appropriate caregivers for the elderly and children." Daughters and daughters-in-law, in particular, were the preferred caregivers for the respondents' households. Additionally, most respondents rejected the idea of caregiving as a burden despite its association with their exhaustion, ill-health, or anxiety. Caregiving was crucial to women's role within the family and the community.

Among Chinese families, parenting may be performed in line with generational assumptions about power and responsibility. For Ho (1981, cited in Chuang and Su, 2008), Confucianism values of social harmony, clear lines of authority, and the meeting of collective rather than individual needs are historically embedded in familial relationships including specific gender roles and expectations such as the idea that fathers hold power and authority within the family. Some researchers support the notion of "strict father, warm mother" but other studies reveal higher levels of father involvement in children's lives (Chuang and Su 2008). Fathers are now adopting a more Westernized parenting approach where parenting practices are more child-centred. Chuang and Su (2008) compared the fathering of immigrant Chinese-Canadians and mainland Chinese fathers. They found that mainland Chinese and immigrant Chinese-Canadian fathers were actively involved in making everyday decisions about their children's needs. However, mothers' authority over children's needs was found to be more prominent among families in China than in Canada. In contrast, the balance between mothers' authority and joint decision-making was more balanced in Canada. While fathering practices seem to be shifting, other generational dynamics of support, such as filial responsibility and respect for aging parents, have remained fairly constant. Mainland Chinese and Chinese-Canadian parents both relied on their own adult parents for advice and support. Indeed, traditional Confucian teachings on family solidarity and respect for one's elders means grandparents play a significant role in family life (Chuang and Su, 2008).

Besides Westernized gendered discourses, rich traditions and values associated with particular cultural groups also inform the performance of parenting. Not surprisingly, clashes can emerge when mothers and fathers have to reconcile competing cultural claims about parenting. Indeed, migration often results in the reconfiguration or renegotiation of familial and gender roles as immigrants encounter different values and new challenges (Spitzer et al., 2003).

Paid and Unpaid Work

The parenting of young children involves engagement in paid or unpaid work including household work and child care. Women's and men's workforce and family trajectories have become more similar over time; few couples are able to make ends meet through the earning of one partner alone. Between 1976 and 1997 the percentage of dual earner families with a child under the age of 16 increased from 34 per cent to 56 per cent (Marshall, 1998). Canadian Census data further reveals that between 2000 and 2005, the number of economic families[4] with two earners working full-time full-year increased from 21.5 per cent to 38.4 per cent (Statistics Canada, 2008). Although men are still the primary earners, the number of women who are single-earners within two-parent families (where their partners did not work) has increased, from 4 per cent in 1976 to 16 per cent in 1997.

Paid work provides the main source of income for the majority of family households. Engaging in paid labour permits parents to feed, clothe, and shelter their children as well as facilitate children's engagement in recreational or leisure activities or purchase child care services. Although the median income of economic families with children has increased by 20.6 per cent between 1980 and 2005, an increase attributed to women's greater involvement in the labour market (Statistics Canada, 2008), differences emerge in regard to how sufficiently paid work enables parents to achieve these necessities of family life. Dividing families into five income quintiles, Statistics Canada (2008) finds that families at the bottom one-fifth of the distribution experienced only a 0.7 per cent increase in their median earnings. In contrast, the one-fifth of families at the top of the income distribution experienced a 7.0 per cent increase in their median earnings between 2000 and 2005 (Statistics Canada, 2008). Many parents are working for pay full-time full-year in a societal context increasingly characterized by growing income security for some and little change in income security for others.

Indeed, having a job is not a guarantee that parents will be able to adequately care for children and other family members. Some parents are already experiencing or risk experiencing worse economic conditions and the challenges associated with these. According to Fleury and Fortin (2006), 1 in 10 adults were among the working poor[5] for at least one year between 1996 and 2001, a finding partially attributed to family characteristics, including number of earners and children. Workers who were the sole earner in their family were at greater risk of financial difficulty and this risk increased with the number of children in their care.

Parents' incomes from paid work are connected to child poverty. In 2005, just over 2 per cent of children in couple families with two full-time full-year earners experienced low income. In couple families with one earner, 5.6 per cent of children experienced low income. Female lone-parent families with one full-time full-year earner fared worse than male lone-parent families, with 9.9 per cent of children versus 5.9 per cent of children experiencing low income (Statistics Canada, 2008). When parents cannot provide their children with adequate economic resources, children's health and well-being is affected. Fleury and Fortin (2006) find that children who live in poor families experience more than twice the incidence of chronic illness and physical and developmental disabilities than children living in non-poor families. Poor children are more likely to have problems with their vision, hearing, speech, and mobility than non-poor children. Poverty is also connected to children's educational development and opportunities. Poor children score lower on measures of cognition and school achievement and are twice as likely to drop out of school as their non-poor peers (Fleury and Fortin, 2006).

Income inequality additionally characterizes the paid work performed by mothers and fathers. Women's increased engagement in paid labour does not change their unequal earnings comparative to men. Although women's tendency to engage in more part-time work, because of caregiving responsibilities, does partially account for their lower earnings,[6] even when both women and men worked full-time full-year in 2006 women's yearly salaries were less than those of men (Statistics Canada, 2010a). In 2005, young women aged 25–29 and employed full-time full-year earned 85 cents for each dollar earned by men (Statistics Canada, 2009). Mothers may be committed to paid work in the same way as fathers but reap fewer economic rewards associated with this commitment. Moreover, today's mothers are more likely to be balancing the caring of their very young children with paid work. According to Statistics Canada (2007j), 65 per cent of mothers with children under the age of three years worked for pay in 2005 compared to 28 per cent in 1976. In 2005 the majority of mothers with at least one child under the age of 16 worked 30 or more hours per week. Mothers' time spent in paid work lessens if they have two children or more. Focusing on generational cohorts of women aged 25 to 64, Pacaut, Le Bourdais, and Laplante (2011) observe that mothers of two or more children, born between 1937 and 1946, re-engaged with the labour market to a greater extent than mothers born between 1967 and 1976. They speculate that this difference by cohort is linked to the greater availability of parental leave today (Pacaut, Le Bourdais, and Laplante, 2011). Compared to fathers, mothers still engage in stay-at-home parenting for longer periods of time and to a greater degree.

Even if they are engaged in paid work, women perform the bulk of caregiving for infants and toddlers within families. Within two-parent families where heterosexual couples are married or cohabitating, women spend more time engaged in domestic labour and child care than men (Beaujot and Ravanera, 2009; Gazso, 2009a). Time-use data from the 1986 and 2005 General Social Surveys reveals the number of hours in which women and men perform paid and unpaid work and other activities. Women have increased their daily time spent in paid work, from 3.3 hours in 1986 to 4.4 hours in 2005. Women's time spent doing housework remained unchanged and their time spent providing primary care slightly decreased, a decrease attributed to their increase in paid work. Compared to men, however, women still performed more hours of primary care for children. They spent 2.8 hours in 1986 and 2.4 hours in 2005. Men spent only 1.0 hours in 1986 and 1.4 hours in 2005 (Marshall, 2006).

There have been some changes in fathers' time spent in paid and unpaid work. More fathers are doing more unpaid work within the home (McMullin, 2005). Using time-use data from the General Social Surveys conducted in 1992, 1998, and 2005, Beaujot and Ravanera (2009) find increases in the numbers of husbands who perform more unpaid work than their wives (from 1.7 per cent to 3.0 per cent) and the numbers of couples who equally perform the same amount of time of paid and unpaid work. However, others observe that the experience of providing care is different in kind and quality for fathers. Whereas women spend a greater proportion of their care time in physical care activities (bathing, feeding), research has shown that fathers may engage in play, talking, educational, and recreational activities (Craig, 2006). Nonetheless, more fathers are choosing to

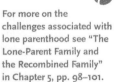

exit paid work and take on full responsibility for their young children's care. Marshall (1998) finds that the numbers of men who were stay-at-home dads increased between 1976 and 1997, from 1 per cent to 6 per cent. According to Doucet and Merla (2007: 462) fathers choose to stay at home for a number of reasons, including their partner's employment and/or encouragement from their partner to share caregiving work, preference of home care over daycare, and lack of affordable childcare facilities.

For more on the challenges associated with lone parenthood see "The Lone-Parent Family and the Recombined Family" in Chapter 5, pp. 98–101.

Balancing paid and unpaid work is particularly challenging for lone parents. The number of lone mothers engaged in paid work has increased over time (Ferrao, 2010) but not all mothers earn wages that sufficiently raise them above Low Income Cut Offs (LICOs). Some lone parents receive social assistance to top up their monthly pay. However, the overall conditions of receiving welfare can further limit their ability to become fully self-sufficient. When lone mothers on social assistance are perceived as employable, they are subject to mandatory education, programming, or job searches in order to remain eligible for monthly benefits (Gazso, 2007b). They are also expected to exit social assistance as soon as they find paid work. It is often the case that family care responsibilities hinder their employability efforts and vice versa. For example, Breikreuz, Williamson, and Raine (2010) find that parents cannot always access suitable daycare for their children and so cannot participate in paid work as they may wish. Should they not participate in paid work in the ways dictated by the conditions of their social assistance receipt, they risk being expelled from the caseload. Parenting alone and on social assistance is made more challenging because this parenting is performed in circumstances of poverty, regulated by the government, and without adequate social support, a point discussed further in the next section.

Among gay and lesbian couples who parent young children, researchers find that the conventional gendered division of paid and unpaid work is largely irrelevant. Parents in these families engage in a sharing of paid and unpaid work in different ways. Dunne (2000a) finds that that lesbian relations are based on mutual dependence and seem to be characterized by an equal division of paid and unpaid labour. Rather than attempting to conform to traditional gender roles, partners negotiate the division of paid and unpaid work by accounting for such things as personal aptitude and desire (Sullivan, 2004). The same has been found for gay couples. In their study of new gay fathers, Schacher, Auerbach, and Silverstein (2005) discovered that gay couples experienced conflict or role strain when deciding who would relinquish engagement in full-time paid work in order to be the primary caregiver of children. Fathers' shared commitment to "hands-on" fathering was what enabled them to resolve this conflict and "de-gender parenting" or resist seeing roles and duties as ascribed by gender. Gay and lesbian parents seem to more fairly navigate the timing and division of paid labour market attachment and/or full-time responsibility for child care.

Engaging in paid and unpaid work are major responsibilities of parents of young children. The everyday practice of parenting involves a constant act of juggling paid work with other time demands associated with raising young children, such as household labour (e.g., laundry, preparing meals, cleaning) and caregiving (e.g., bathing, feeding). This juggling can prove more difficult when income earned from paid work is insufficient for the meeting of family needs or when parents do not equally participate in housework and child care responsibilities.

For more on child care, see "Child Care" in Chapter 9, pp. 171–3.

Social Policy and Other Supports for Child Care

From a life course perspective, the everyday performance of parenting is interlinked with the caregiving provided by others. Whether a lone parent or partnered with someone else, most parents are supported in their provisions of child care by other people or government programs. Although there is diversity in terms of how families manage caregiving for children and other dependents depending on family members' culture and race/ethnicity, conventional kinship ties are still incredibly important to provisions of child care in the early years of parenting (Lashewicz, Manning, Hall, and Keating, 2007). Family members across generations provide important sources of physical, financial, and emotional support, ranging from grandparents providing child care relief for a few hours a week to adult children receiving financial aid from their parents to purchase clothing and shoes for children. Grandparents, particularly grandmothers, are likely to be more involved in raising grandchildren if their child is absent from the household; often, grandparent involvement in parenting a grandchild occurs as an alternative to foster care (Pearson et al. 1997, as cited in Gladstone, Brown, and Fitzgerald, 2009). Support structures can include others not part of conventional kinship ties, as is common with LGBTIQ individuals creating "chosen families" (Sullivan, 2004).

Currently, there is no national child care program in Canada. Responsibility is often split between federal and provincial or territorial jurisdictions, which produces significant variation in the cost, quality, and source of child care (Albanese, 2009). Parents rely on a range of paid services in their communities. Care outside of the home can include licensed care within daycare centres or home care, or unlicensed care within someone else's home. According to Beaujot and Ravanera (2009), children most often received care in the home of a non-relative or from a daycare centre in 2002–03. Fifty-four per cent of children ages six months to five years were in some form of non-parental care compared to 42 per cent in 1994–95 (Bushnik, 2006). Compared to two-parent families, lone parents make greater use of licensed, regulated daycare centres, regardless of their employment status (Beaujot and Ravanera, 2009). This is partially explained by lone parents' economic situations. Lone parents are more likely to have lower incomes than two-parent families and so are more likely to be eligible to have the cost of their child's licensed daycare subsidized by the government.

Differences emerge when the child care accessed by parents within the province of Quebec is compared to other Canadian provinces. Unlike other provinces, Quebec regulates affordable child care to all parents regardless of their incomes; parents pay $7 a day for child care (Albanese, 2006). More Quebec parents who work full-time for pay rely on some form of child care than other parents, 83.7 per cent versus 70.1 per cent, respectively; 42.2 per cent of Quebec children are in daycare versus 21.2 per cent of other Canadian children (Beaujot and Ravanera, 2009). Moreover, while other provincial governments are becoming less involved in the provision of child care services, Quebec is the exception as it has been revamping policies to "reflect the increased need and desire to assist families, and women in particular, with the mounting challenges associated with juggling paid and unpaid work" (Albanese 2009: 120).

Excluding the unique situation of child care in Quebec, affordable and high quality child care, especially that which is provided by licensed providers such as Early Childhood

Educators, is scarce and expensive across Canada. As well, there is a shortage of subsidized child care in Canada, which creates a barrier for those seeking employment and compromises family budgets. Subsidies may not cover the full cost of child care. For example, in Ontario, subsidies are paid by municipal service managers to regulated (both non-profit and for-profit) child care providers on behalf of eligible parents (Canadian Council of Social Development, 2009). Municipal service managers are able to set their maximum subsidy below full cost and do so in many communities. According to Albanese (2009), the need for non-parental care has increased along with child care fees but the number of government-regulated and licensed daycare spaces do not meet this demand. Only 15.5 per cent of Canadian children aged 0–12 years could be accommodated by licensed child care centres in 2003–04 (Canadian Council of Social Development, n.d.).

Parents may qualify for other tax benefits that support their caregiving of young children. As noted earlier, all parents with children under the age of six are currently entitled to the Universal Child Care Benefit of $1,200 a year. The UCCB is intended to support families with the costs of their child care choices. Low-income parents may be eligible for the Canada Child Tax Benefit (CCTB) and National Child Benefit Supplement (NBS) but even this eligibility may not profoundly change their ability to afford child care. Lone parents' receipt of these child benefits is considered additional income by social assistance ministries and is deducted from total social assistance monthly benefits each month. Parents who are struggling to make ends meet and provide care to their children may be entitled to policy supports but the interaction of these supports often results in them being no further ahead in the achievement of income security.

Even without an immediate, physical connection with children, parents may be caring for young children from afar. This is perhaps best illustrated by the experiences of migrant workers who maintain a constant emotional connection with their children despite the impossibility of physical connection. Canadian immigration policy provides opportunities for persons from developing countries to migrate to Canada for paid work in agriculture and/or as domestic workers. Migrant workers who are mothers or fathers are often separated from their young children for lengthy periods of time. The everyday parenting of young children is then performed most often by other family members. However, migrant workers also parent transnationally. Remittances sent home to families provide for children and are of benefit to the wider economy of a migrant worker's country of origin. Mothers and fathers also provide emotional support to children through telephone or Internet communication (e.g., Skype). Bernhard, Landolt, and Goldring (2008) find that this performance of transnational parenting by Latin American mothers is often associated with guilt, tension, shame, and isolation. In her research on Filipina domestic workers, Cohen (2000) also finds that transnational mothering creates stress within families, particularly when mothers' time spent working for pay in Canada leads to estrangement from their own children. Transnational parenting can produce short-term benefits for families in economic need but can have long-term consequences of fragmenting family ties.

The caring of young children involves more than parent–child interactions. Several people assist in the raising of Canada's children today. Not all parents can easily find or afford child care, and this suggests that our policy system for child care is woefully inadequate.

Conclusion

Deciding to parent and then raising young children constitutes an important period in some people's life courses. Choosing to parent a young child today is a major decision in one's life that is shaped by and linked to gender socialization and interactions with others, educational decisions and pathways, opportunities in the labour market and workforce trajectories, and available supports from the government. The choice to parent must be understood as a choice made in view of other opportunities or constraints. For example, as we have seen, some women and men may reportedly desire to parent but place this choice on hold for the time it takes them to gain particular educational credentials and achieve a semblance of income security—other important stages in their life course.

Once a person becomes a mother or father, no matter how this is achieved, their own identities and life courses change, particularly because of the newfound reality of dependent children. Parenting also requires re-imagining one's identity as a parent in the midst of powerful messages about how one should parent. For some parents, dominant Western images of and ideas about parenting must be reconciled with their other specific cultural norms and values. Different cultural groups within Canada have their own historical traditions and practices associated with caring for and raising children. And families migrate to Canada with their own cultural capital on parenting. Ideas about parenting and the actual practice of parenting can be culturally diverse. No matter their race or ethnicity, individuals' parenting practices are shaped by past cultural conventions and new ideas about parenting (e.g., attachment parenting) that are popularized in media.

Parenting has also been shown to be interconnected with the meeting of daily needs, for food, shelter, and clothing. The majority of parents engage in paid work in order to care for their children. A mother or father's paid labour informs the child care choices they make. One parent usually stays at home for a period of time in order to provide full-time care sometimes, as in the case of women, at the risk of gendered power imbalances. In nuclear families, fathers do still spend more time in paid work than mothers. In two-parent families where both parents engage in paid work, most need affordable and adequate child care services during their children's younger years. For many parents, finding good child care is a major source of stress.

To conclude, this chapter has employed a life course perspective to highlight the performance and act(s) of parenting in our current Canadian context. Choosing to parent is a major life course decision, one that has implications for parents' lives—everyday.

STUDY QUESTIONS

1. Why is a life course perspective useful to understand parenting?
2. From a life course perspective, how can we see the birth of a child as a major transition in one's life but also see parenting as a series of everyday events or activities?
3. How does gender socialization impact decisions to parent?

4. In what ways have changes to social policies made it more difficult for people to parent today?

5. How is transnational caregiving both similar and different to the caregiving performed by mothers and fathers who live with their children in the same residence?

6. How are the paid work and child care experiences of lone-parent families different from two-parent families?

Further Readings

Baker, M. (2006). *Restructuring Family Policies: Convergences and Divergences.* Toronto: University of Toronto Press. This book offers an interesting comparative analysis of transformations in social policies for families, and their impacts, over time.

Doucet, Andrea. (2006). *Do Men Mother?* Toronto: University of Toronto Press. This intriguing and exciting book offers a glimpse into the world of stay-at-home fathers.

Epstein, Rachel. Ed. (2009). *Who's Your Daddy? And Other Writings on Queer Parenting.* Toronto: Sumach Press. This edited collection explores what it means to parent from a queer perspective.

Fox, B. (2009). *When Couples Become Parents: The Creation of Gender in the Transition to Parenthood.* Toronto: University of Toronto Press. This thought-provoking book analyzes the gendered division of labour as it emerges or does not in couples as they move from late pregnancy into early parenthood.

Ranson, Gillian. 2010. *Against the Grain: Couples, Gender, and the Reframing of Parenting.* Toronto: University of Toronto Press. This exciting book explores how parents work against structural and conventional understandings of mothering and fathering in rearing and caring for their children.

Silvia, E.B. Ed. (1996). *Good Enough Mothering: Feminist Perspectives on Lone Mothering.* London: Routledge. This edited collection explores ideas about moral mothering and how they are experienced by lone mothers.

Websites

www.cfc-efc.ca/
The Child and Family Canada public education website houses 50 non-profit organizations that provide resources on children and families.

www12.statcan.gc.ca/census-recensement/2011/rt-td/index-eng.cfm
Statistics Canada provides recent Census information on families, households, and marital status.

www.vanierinstitute.ca/
The Vanier Institute of the Family provides research, consultation, and policy development on Canadian families, respecting their diversity while doing so.

Notes

1. This chapter focuses on persons who have chosen to deliberately change their life course by having and raising children rather than those who become parents through an unexpected and unplanned pregnancy.

2. LGBTIQ refers to individuals who self-identify as lesbian, gay, bi-sexual, transgender, intersex, questioning, or queer.

3. Prejudice and discrimination and/or devaluation of foreign education credentials can contribute to immigrants' greater initial earnings deficiency when compared to other Canadians. For example, immigrant women are often concentrated in lower-wage positions in the sales and service industry despite the fact that they are overqualified for these positions (Spitzer et al., 2003). However, as immigrants become familiar with the requirements of their new country's labour markets, this economic hardship can wane (Liu and Kerr, 2003).

4. Economic families include all persons related by blood, marriage, or adoption and living in the same dwelling.

5. The working poor are defined as people aged 18 to 64 who engage in paid work for a minimum of 910 hours per year and experience low income according to the Market Basket Measure (MBM).

6. Other structural factors like occupational segregation by gender and/or glass ceilings inhibit women's advancement to higher levels of management and impact their earnings.

5

Separation and Divorce: Fragmentation and Renewal of Families

CRAIG MCKIE

LEARNING OBJECTIVES

- To understand that family breakdown and divorce are separate processes
- To appreciate that Canadians may choose the family context in which they live with few restrictions, and that many are choosing not to marry and thus do not require divorce if their relationships dissolve
- To learn that divorce has become increasingly easily available since 1968
- To discover that family breakdown has unfavourable consequences for the previous partners and any children they may have, and that these consequences may be made more difficult by a bitter divorce
- To recognize that families that break down often experience a substantial and persistent decline in their standard of living
- To understand that members of some religious communities may require additional religious divorce processes in addition to civil divorce in order for a person to remarry within those religious communities
- To recognize that forming new families from remnants of old families brings a new range of adjustment problems for parents and children

Introduction

It is remarkable how rapidly the personal rights and freedoms of individual Canadians emerged in family matters and became established in law in the second half of the twentieth century. Canadians are now free in the main to live, love, and cohabit as they wish, and comparatively easily freed of previous spousal relationships should they so choose. In less than 60 years, for instance, we have gone from a rigid and uncongenial divorce regime, which denied divorce with dignity to most Canadians, to the present era in which child-less couples can jointly apply for an uncontested divorce by simple written assertion of marriage breakdown and can be certain of receiving one in short order without further complications.

For the first 100 years of its existence, Canadian law in the fields of marriage and of divorce was largely a direct continuation of English law inherited in colonial times prior to Confederation and subject to only minor refinements. Received English law itself was the product of hundreds of years of judicial decisions and occasional legislation and should be understood in the context of the doctrine of the established Church of England. It held to the view that marriage was an indissoluble contract as a general rule. The core principle was that marital breakdown was simultaneously a violation of the terms of a legal contract and of a divinely blessed union as well. Violations (understood as at-fault marital offences) would give rise to valid claims for money restitution and damages, to community disapproval, not to mention the impairment of the ability to remarry. Nevertheless, some latitude or leeway was left such that marriages could, with much difficulty, be legally dissolved in certain circumstances, and with church annulments repairing the moral blight of failed marriages in similarly strictly limited circumstances of flawed marriage process, real or contrived. In other words, in the English legal tradition, dissolution of a marriage would be made infrequent, difficult, and time consuming but neither the state nor the Church was categorical in its rejection of undoing faulty marriages.[1] And how could it have been otherwise since the Church of England owed its very existence to King Henry VIII's repeated requirements for marital dissolution and remarriage denied him by the Pope in Rome?

In the present era since the passage of the Divorce Act in 1968, Canada has in large measure abandoned both the legal and ideological bases of inherited English law. In addition, provincial family legislation, which covers most separating couples whether married or not, was completely overhauled, and Canadians acquired a Charter of Rights and Freedoms that explicitly guaranteed freedoms of association, religious belief, and other fundamental freedoms, which pertain indirectly to the right to live in almost any family context one desires and which cannot be easily overridden by legislation. But divorce, and the allied provincial family law processes, nevertheless remains potentially litigious and adversarial in nature to this day. In operation, divorce is not often about reaching a civil and peaceful redefinition of future interests. The objective is still a binding, written, and enforceable contract between former marital partners that redefines their obligations to each other in perpetuity.

The fundamental changes in Canadian divorce and provincial family law which occurred in the twentieth century went hand-in-hand with the rapid secularization of Canadian society and diminution both of religious ideologies of all types and of theocratic social control of much mating behaviour that used to attract religious admonition. The arrival of same-sex marriage (and divorce) in the early twenty-first century is but one more step in the same direction. Few impediments now exist for any Canadian to cohabit however and wherever and with whomever he or she wishes, and to subsequently dissolve any such household without fear of legal prosecution. Residual restrictions are confined to bigamy and polygamy where multiple formal marriages are involved, and situations involving the sexual exploitation of minor children and close relatives, always provided these come to the attention of law enforcement authorities.

The social imperative to clarify and re-label a broken family arrangement (whether based on a marriage or more commonly, as time goes by, not so based) remains strong. Clarity is required in sexual access issues, in support obligations, and in the child access rights that inevitably arise when families fragment, through separation or death, to become lone-parent families, then often to reformulate themselves within the context of a new marital union. While the English language lacks complex naming conventions for ex-kin and for step-kin, the law helps to clarify the obligations if not the exact nature of complex multiple-family arrangements that have become very common in the recombined families of the present era. They are more common in large part because we typically live much longer lives and, as a result, relationships have much more time at risk than was the case just a few generations ago. This felt necessity to rectify relationships and renew the nature of obligations seems very widespread, though the substance of the rules-making systems differs widely around the world.

For more on religious and state disapproval of marital dissolution in the past, see Chapter 2, p. 30.

The nature of those codes of practice, some being rules of practical application and some based in theological beliefs, is still in flux. Theological conflict concerning separation and divorce still often derives from the medieval dispute within Christianity over whether marriage is a sacrament (and thus permanent) or not a sacrament and thus dissolvable by the judicial organs of the state alone. There is much nuance in this argument as it has developed over the last 500 years, but contemporary Canadian practice clearly is informed by the latter, more liberal and permissive interpretation. The influence of religious views may still be seen, though, in the prohibition of multiple concurrent marriages (which are permitted under certain circumstances in the Islamic tradition—bigamy is criminalized in Canada by Section 290 and polygamy by Section 293 of the Criminal Code), and in the requirement for an authoritative legal process to divorce (in contrast to the much more informal Islamic divorce process or the requirement for a religious divorce process in some other cultures and religious traditions).

While the force of religious injunctions on mating behaviour in Canadian society has now considerably abated, its residue can still be seen in the laws of the land and, of course, in the culture-based behaviour of members of other cultures who have made a new life for themselves in Canada. Customs such as arranged marriages persist in this country though seldom seen or discussed openly. In the end, the personal freedoms conferred by the Charter of Rights and Freedoms and the accumulated jurisprudence of the common-law system have allowed Canadians to be innovative in forming and dissolving their social relationships with little or no fear of ecclesiastical retribution for their departures from expectations.

No better example of incremental liberalization of family law can be cited than the contemporary extension of marriage rights and obligations, and the inevitable extension of divorce rights and the potential for child custody disputes to same-sex couples. The first Canadian divorce of a former same-sex married couple was awarded in Ontario in September 2004. The unhappy couple, whose marriage lasted only five days, wished to remain anonymous.

The Legal Environment for Divorce in Canada

The terms and conditions for granting a divorce or a family law settlement in any given era are a direct reflection of the positive values attributed to an intact marriage (the contract being ended by divorce) or a non-marriage-based family (which is being dissolved and its assets distributed under provincial family law). Dissolution of either cannot seem to be too easy or costless lest offence be given to the ideals of the institution of the **family**. The way in which these values are expressed, however, is very much bound up in the conventional rhetoric of a particular era.

Until comparatively recently, roughly to the end of the nineteenth century, a marriage in essence was the transfer of chattel (a woman) from one owner (the father) to a new owner (the father of the prospective husband) in return for or together with tangible and intangible valuables such as a dowry, mutual enjoyment and protection, and the production of heirs to the family fortunes. Assent by the actual marrying couple was most often a formal requirement for marriage but coercion was by no means unknown. Indeed, some aspects of the traditional wedding in Canada still mirror this practice in ritual, as in the giving away of the bride by the father or a stand-in for the father. If, for the moment, one sees a marriage in this historical context as a commercial transaction between one male as a seller and another male as purchaser, then it stands to reason that the premature end of a marriage was the occasion for the reassessment of the terms of the initial transaction. If, after a marriage, adultery took place, a male (but not a female) third party could be sued for money damages for what was termed "criminal conversation." This arrangement gave rise to the still common expression "a double standard" since husbands and wives were bound by different standards of behaviour.

A marriage was thus not only a relationship between partners but also a contractual building block of society, somewhat akin to a diplomatic agreement between clans, in which the state had a continuing and vital interest. A married couple had in some sense a capital value, which could be damaged through misbehaviour, and sanctions against offenders were called for.

But in the early twentieth century this view began to change. Looked at in this new fashion, the interests of the state and of the parties to a failed marriage came to lie in the peaceful simplification of the contractual tangle. Resolution lay in affixing new and continuing financial obligations, assessing damages, and apportioning the assets of the dissolving union in an orderly and predictable fashion. Once these matters had been resolved, then the marriage contract itself could be dissolved (though the process was costly, tedious, and often involved perjury), in much the same way a business corporation is wound up and its charter surrendered.

Prior to 1968 in Canada, the availability of divorce was a provincial patchwork. Some provinces (for example, Nova Scotia) had their own divorce legislation and others (such as Quebec and Ontario) did not. This situation arose because divorce is a federal power under the Constitution, but successive Canadian governments failed to legislate in this area, leaving pre-Confederation statutes and practices still in place in some provinces. Persons living in provinces without divorce legislation who wished to obtain a divorce had to file a petition with the Senate of Canada alleging and providing proof of a marital offence (adultery, desertion, etc.) as grounds. A special committee of the Senate reviewed these petitions and, if it found that the evidence provided was sufficient, the marriage would be ended by an Act of Parliament. This system was unfair on its face since it required the financial means to secure evidence and to file the petition, and also because it led to the falsification of grounds (such as trumped-up adultery with confirming photos). Almost all of this unseemly and duplicitous political theatre, a legacy of centuries of English legal practice that Canada had inherited, ended in 1968, though adultery remains a ground for divorce to this day.

Modern divorce legislation, which dates from the Divorce Act in 1968, has removed from the mix all vestiges of the financial interests of parents as injured parties and changed the conflict to one strictly between the divorcing partners themselves. It also lessens the impor-tance of the notion of marital offences (though many, such as bestiality, remained listed as causes for a divorce action from 1968 to 1985) and moved to a predominantly "no fault" basis of settlement that abandons the notion of assessment of damages. But the core of the process remains the same. The parties are obliged to demonstrate marriage breakdown, settle their financial obligations in some fashion, settle custody and residency arrangements for any minor children of the marriage, and divide the assets and future income according to guidelines set out by the state. If the partners are unable to reach a settlement on these issues, a court will do it for them in a judgment. In other words, and in spite of extensive reform, divorce is still treated in many respects as the dissolution of a failed corporation.

The Ebb and Flow of Marital Unions

Most, but not all, Canadians find themselves in a marriage-like relationship at one time or another in their lives. A small proportion of people remain single and apart for their entire lives but this is surely atypical in present times. Figure 5.1 shows in rough detail some of the more prominent pathways. A newly formed couple has a number of choices. The part-ners may choose to cohabit on a short-term trial basis (the dissolution of which does not typically give rise to any legal process at all); they may form a durable common-law union (perhaps out of a preference or perhaps out of necessity if there is an impediment such as a previous undissolved marriage) so as to present themselves to the world as the equivalent of married. This latter status does give rise to legal consequences under provincial family law if the union dissolves and was of considerable duration. And, of course, the couple can marry, in which case both family law and divorce law apply if the marriage ends in a separation. Finally, members of any of these three types of unions can, if they are agreeable, ignore the law altogether and proceed to the formation of new unions (always provided that, if married, they cannot legally remarry with impunity). It goes without saying that many couples remain in one stage or another, perhaps for the life of one of the married couple, then perhaps to enter the cycle again as a widow or widower with a remarriage late in her or his own personal life cycle. The death of a mate in a sense is similar to separation since it demands another kind of family law action, namely the distribution of the assets of the departed spouse, sometimes with probate. When a separated spouse dies, the two types of legal action can become intertwined.

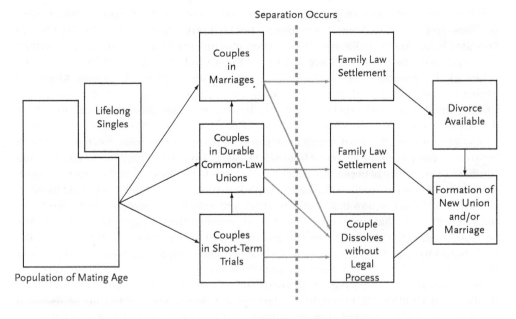

Figure 5.1 **The Life Cycle of Marital Union Formation and Dissolution**

In the present era of divorce in Canada, which dates from the passage of the Divorce Act (1968), the number of divorces granted in Canada increased dramatically as an initial wave of people who could not obtain divorces easily under the previous divorce regime took advantage of the new liberalized legislation to obtain divorces. Between 1971 and 1982, the annual total number of final decrees awarded rose from 29,684 to 70,430. A further revision of the Act in 1985 made marriage breakdown the sole grounds for divorce and eased the evidentiary standard to the demonstration of breakdown. Marriage breakdown is now indicated either by (1) separation of one year's duration; (2) adultery that can be proven; or (3) demonstration of intolerable mental or physical cruelty. Once again, after this revision the number of divorces increased, reaching a peak in 1987 at 96,200. Thereafter, total numbers levelled off and then declined as the backlog was cleared.

From the summary of divorces granted for the years 1998–2008 (Table 5.1) we can see that the number awarded in Canada in recent years has held steady at approximately 70,000 (down from the all-time peak in 1987). This represented a rate of 211 divorces for every 100,000 persons in Canada in 2008. The risk of married couples in Canada divorcing now reaches a peak after the third anniversary (Kelly, 2012: 8) and thereafter declines rapidly. In about two-thirds of cases, child custody decisions were privately settled without judicial intervention. Of the minority of cases that were decided by a court, about 45 per cent of decisions in 2004 were in favour of mothers. A further 46.5 per cent of the decisions involved joint custody, leaving a small minority of cases in which a father was awarded sole custody (about 8 per cent). Paternal sole custody remains unusual, as it always has been. Typically, paternal sole custody is awarded where older children close to the age of majority have expressed a preference (Statistics Canada, 2008: 73).

Table 5.1 **Divorces Granted in Canada 1998–2008**

	1998	1999	2000	2001	2002	2003	2004	2005	2006	2007	2008
Canada	69,088	70,910	71,144	71,110	70,155	70,828	69,644	71,269	74,681	73,167	70,226
NFLD and Labrador	944	892	913	755	842	662	837	789	831	969	907
Prince Edward Island	279	291	272	246	258	281	293	283	287	278	306
Nova Scotia	1,933	1,954	2,054	1,945	1,990	1,907	2,000	1,961	2,161	2,006	1,902
New Brunswick	1,473	1,671	1,717	1,570	1,461	1,450	1,415	1,444	1,527	1,499	1,458
Quebec	16,916	17,144	17,054	17,094	16,499	16,738	15,999	15,423	14,965	14,336	13,899
Ontario	25,149	26,088	26,148	26,516	26,170	27,513	26,374	28,805	31,983	31,242	29,692
Manitoba	2,443	2,572	2,430	2.480	2,396	2,352	2,333	2,429	2,221	2,279	2,241
Saskatchewan	2,246	2,237	2,194	1,955	1,959	1,992	1,875	1,922	1,983	1,850	1,858
Alberta	7,668	7,931	8,176	1,955	1,959	1,992	1,875	1,922	1,983	1,850	1,858
British Columbia	9,827	9,935	10,017	10,115	10,125	9,820	10,049	9,954	10,235	10,071	8,903
NWT including Nunavut	93	85	..	..	..	..	..	..	..	..	..
Northwest Territories	..	..	94	83	68	62	71	65	54	64	58
Nunavut*	..	..	7	8	6	4	15	10	21	12	26

*Nunavut totals are included under NWT for 1998 and 1999.

SOURCES: Adapted from Statistics Canada. *Report on the Demographic Situation in Canada 2005 and 2006, 2008*, Table A-6.3, Catalogue no. 91-209-X, p. 75. 2005 data from http://www.statcan.gc.ca/tables-tableaux/sum-som/l01/cst01/famil02-eng.htm. Unpublished data for the years 2006–2008 provided by Statistics Canada, Health Statistics Division Client Services, April 2012.

Publication of the annual data series on divorces by Statistics Canada has now ceased with the completion of processing of the 2008 records. The data from the final years of 2006 to 2008 were collected from the Central Registry of Divorce Proceedings (CRDP) at the Department of Justice Canada but tabulations have not yet been published. They are available to scholars only on special request. Henceforth, the only source of information on the divorces of Canada will be the Civil Court Survey of administrative files. It covers only seven provinces and territories and the results are somewhat non-comparable, jurisdiction to jurisdiction (see Kelly, 2012).

As to the probability of the marriages of Canadians ending in divorce, Statistics Canada has reported that the proportion of marriages expected to end in divorce by the 30th wedding anniversary was 40.7 per cent in 2008, 41.9 per cent in 2006, and 37.9 per cent in 2004 (Kelly, 2012: 8). These rates are marginally higher than in the previous decade, being well above a recent low of 34.8 per cent in 1997 (Statistics Canada, 2002c), but much below the all-time high of 50.6 per cent established in 1987. The variability of these proportions reflects many factors, such as the extrapolation of the then-current annual divorce totals—but to be clear, the calculation does *not* predict the probability of divorce for any particular married couple.

The average age of those divorcing has gradually increased. By 2004, the average age at divorce was 43.0 years for men and 40.0 years for women (Statistics Canada, 2008: 72). Preliminary figures for 2008 suggest that the average age for divorcing men continues to rise (44.5 years) and also for women (41.9 years). This gradual increase reflects both the more advanced age at marriage and the increasing number of younger Canadians whose unions are not based on a marriage. For instance, Statistics Canada (2002b) reported that by 2001, a clear majority of young Canadians aged 20 to 29 years had chosen *not* to base their first union on a marriage. Later, in the results of the 2006 General Social Survey, Statistics Canada reported that there were approximately equal numbers of persons who terminated a marriage or a common-law union between 2001 and 2006, with approximately one million persons in each category (Statistics Canada, 2008: 72).

Within the total of about 70,000 divorces annually, the proportions in each province and territory are roughly the same year after year even though some provincial populations are growing rapidly as a result of immigration (for example, Ontario) and some have lost population as a result of out-migration (such as Newfoundland and Labrador). Since the overall number of Canadians has increased during the period (and more importantly, since the number of Canadians in the marriageable years has increased even more as a result of the general aging of the population), the rate of occurrence might seem to be going down. However, as we have seen, a rapidly increasing number of Canadians do not marry when they form their unions and are thus never in need of a divorce. In each of the years 2001, 2002, and 2003, for instance, the crude marriage rate in Canada (4.7 marriages for every 1,000 people) was at the lowest level ever recorded (Statistics Canada, 2008: 74).[2]

Another part of the reason for this apparent decline in the incidence of divorce is to be found in the marked decrease in a type of marriage that was entered into in previous eras as a direct result of extramarital pregnancy. More than a few of our parents and grandparents married at an early age and in a great hurry because of just such a predicament. Today, the ready availability of medical abortions (in 2006, there were 91,377 performed in Canada resulting in a ratio of 28.3 abortions for every 100 live births in the previous year of 2005: Statistics Canada, 2008p) and the generally liberal access to contraceptives of all sorts help limit the number of panic marriages. Such hasty marriages would have been at great risk of a subsequent separation and divorce because of the youthfulness of the new partners, the tensions of having a young baby in the new household, and the improbability of such partners spending the next 65 years together, as life expectancy figures suggest they might. On the other side of the ledger, Statistics Canada reports that by the time of the Census of 2006 almost 1.4 million Canadian couples were living in a common-law relationship (or about 10.8 per cent of the population aged 15 and above, up sharply since 1981 when the proportion was only 3.8 per cent). The proportion of all couples in Quebec living together without marriage was particularly high at 34.6 per cent (Statistics Canada, 2008: 70).

It is important in this context, and in the discussions which follow, to keep in mind that with the cancellation of the mandatory long form Census for 2011, the only definitive Census-derived information from 2011 onward will be household headcounts, basic age/gender information, and current marital status. Data from the mandatory Census 2a questionnaire on household family composition will not be available until after this volume goes to press. The loss of the data from the mandatory Census 2b long form questionnaire in 2011 means little, if any, detail will henceforth be authoritatively known about Canadian families because the discontinued obligatory long form Census was the primary source of much of what is known about family income, education, and a host of other important

Box 5.1
Rules of Marital Dissolution

The rules pertaining to ending marriages can take two major forms: those embodied in religious assertions and those embedded in law. The two sets of imperatives can exist, as they often do in Canadian society, in fundamental conflict. In Canadian society, individuals are free to ignore both sets of rules in their own private lives, providing they are willing to live with the consequences of their failure to act, as in declining to file for a divorce, for instance. Today, the individual Canadian is free to form and to dissolve whatever alternative mating arrangements he or she might choose to adopt (with perhaps the sole exceptions that actual polygamy is forbidden by law when a person enters into multiple formalized marriages, though prosecutions are rare in the extreme, and where sex with minors is involved and prosecutions are common).

Rules of marital union dissolution do several things:

- They define the circumstances under which marital pair bonds can be formally dissolved.
- They make adjudication of disputes systematic.
- They define which public figures are entitled to adjudicate marital disputes.
- They attach the obligations for familial support systematically and if necessary unilaterally, and they provide for enforcement of support orders.
- They define the obligations of ex-partners to each other.
- They redivide social space into realms of those eligible for permissible new pair bonds, define those who are disallowed candidates, and criminalize violations of these boundaries, such as occur, for example, with incest.
- They create permissive space for future intimate behaviour and also define its limits.

social measures. It also means that the cross-assessment of the quality of other datasets will be seriously impaired, given the absence of benchmark Census data.

The possible inference that fewer relationships are being dissolved today is not called for.[3] Indeed, the opposite is probably the case; however, many separations today have no statistical or legal consequences. Further, the current divorce totals for a given year do not reflect the separation reality for that year. This is because of a considerable delay in obtaining a divorce from first filing—and first filing on separation grounds alone can only occur when a year has elapsed following the separation. Part of this delay is the result of satisfying the requirements of the legal process, part is a function of court capacity, and part is the general economic condition that affects the ability of the parties to pay the not inconsiderable costs for the process to proceed to conclusion. And it is certain that many of the persons in Canada who will be awarded divorces in Canada this year are already firmly locked into new relationships when the final decree is granted. For instance, for a decade, approximately 35 per cent of new marriages have included at least one previously married spouse.[4] These provisos and qualifications all highlight the importance of considering relationship formation and dissolution (a process in social behaviour) separately from the divorce process (a process in law).

The Emergence of Shariah Law in Canadian Legal Institutions

Because Canadian society now consists of individuals from many places and cultures, it is not possible to generalize about how Canadians actually live out their pair bonding and dissolution experiences. What we all experience in common is the law. Whether or not religious rules apply is now strictly a matter of individual choice, in striking contrast to earlier periods when the demands of religious edicts were sometimes harsh and imposed with considerable force. Some cultural practices that newcomers to Canada might otherwise be inclined to follow are ruled out by law, as is multiple marriage, or are granted no standing in law, as is religious divorce. One striking departure from this pattern has begun to emerge, however.

The gradual and subtle introduction of Islamic law (shariah) in Canada has raised some difficult and troubling questions. In the normal course of events, countries have one universal system of civil and criminal codes. Indeed, it is one of the elemental aspects of democracy that all citizens be accorded the same rights and privileges under law. Canada has always been an exception to this rule by the acceptance of the Civil Code system in Quebec, an integral part of the historic bargain that brought Quebec into Confederation. Other slight departures of a purely optional nature have existed for some time. Among these are the orthodox Jewish requirement for a religious *get*[5] or divorce before remarriage can occur, and a similar Roman Catholic requirement for a religious **annulment**. The *get* has been an especially vexing problem for some divorcing wives because it is granted (or not) exclusively by the husband of the failed marriage. Lawsuits of the common civil variety to compel the delivery of a *get* are not unknown.

But the introduction of shariah principles in recent years is a qualitatively different initiative. In reflection of the growing diversity of cultural origins present in Canadian society, disputes involving Muslim women's dowries, divorce, inheritance, and property ownership have been arriving in civil court.

In Ontario until 2006, judges might choose to refer such cases to an Islamic tribunal for binding arbitration, provided the parties were willing.[6] However, the matter of parallel justice systems in Ontario came to a head in early 2006 when the government of Ontario ultimately decided against continuing this practice. The Family Statute Law Amendment Act, passed 14 February 2006, ensures that only Ontario family law can be used in binding arbitrations in Ontario. According to Attorney General Michael Bryant, "the bill reaffirms the principle that there ought to be one law for all Ontarians" (Gillespie, 2006). In the previous May, members of the Quebec National Assembly had voted unanimously to reject the use of Islamic tribunals in the Quebec legal system.

But in British Columbia, courts have on occasion upheld a Muslim woman's *maher*, a form of prenuptial agreement that defines in advance the amount of payment to be made upon subsequent marriage termination. Acknowledging that a *maher* has force and effect in Canadian courts as a contract (even though it has purely religious legitimacy) is a step in the direction of parallel legal systems, which is completely alien to the Canadian legal context. Although it does have some resonance with sentencing circles and restorative justice initiatives carried out in Aboriginal communities across Canada with the blessing of the courts, the fact remains that some few separation and divorce proceedings in Canada are now taking place in a purely religious context, with judgments only subsequently confirmed (as in "rubber-stamped") in a conventional civil court document. Actions such as that of the province of Ontario in disallowing the use of religion-based tribunals in the settlement of civil disputes may simply drive these activities underground with judgments officially registered with an Islamic court in another country for instance.

The Emotional, Social, and Economic Fallout of Marital Discord, Separation, and Divorce

The effects of separation of a previous couple occur independent of any subsequent divorce process. Separation is a social fact, as are the factors that most often give rise to it. Divorce remains an *ex post facto* legal recognition of that social fact; it merely confirms the obvious, though it may have incidental stigmatizing effects on self-identity for those affected.

In no sense, then, does the legal act of divorce cause suffering and hardship. There is no denying that these often arise in the process of ending marital households, and, in particular, economic stress and emotional trauma impinge on the lives of any children of the household. Nevertheless, it would be a mistake to see these as arising from actions in the civil legal system, though that suffering and hardship can undoubtedly become more bitter there. Rather, the operations of provincial family law and the federal Divorce Act seek to bring both accountability and renewal of social futures to the separated couple, together with counsel and advice on reducing disharmony and fostering a positive environment for the fragments of any previously united family. Admittedly, the extent of the success of those efforts is mixed.

Box 5.2
Divorce Canadian Style

- To be divorced, you must first be married—but to be separated and/or have support orders and custodial judgments entered against you, you need not first be married. **Separation** is a social process of relationship dissolution; divorce is a legal process of marriage dissolution. One can be separated from more than one other person at a time. Some separated Canadians never divorce and simply cohabit with a new partner, as is their right.
- A couple in Canada may live together without legal marriage. In the fullness of time (a period that differs from province to province) they will be considered to be a social unit and thus exposed upon separation to family law in respect of property divisions, and to support obligations and custody arrangements for any minor children. Likewise, they are considered as an economic unit under the Income Tax Act after the passage of a certain amount of time. Consensual unconventional couple arrangements not based on a marriage are seldom if ever the subject of legal censure; their subsequent dissolution

(Continued)

does not result in a divorce or come to public attention at all (except possibly in regard to how they have declared their income for tax purposes).

- If you marry in violation of the legal consanguinity ("shared blood") provisions or bigamously, the marriage is invalid. It can be annulled and if you committed bigamy you can be charged. But, if your marriage was invalid at the outset, you cannot obtain a divorce. Where this leaves children of such a non-marriage is anybody's guess, but in general the marital status of one's parents is now irrelevant for most if not all legal purposes.
- Children of dissolved marriages or marriage-like unions most often reside with a female parent by well-entrenched habit. This is the result of decades of court decisions and custom both in Canada and elsewhere, which have held custody of and residence with the mother to be preferable. Joint custody now figures prominently in the Canadian picture, though not necessarily joint residence. Access and residential arrangements for dependent children are different from custody. Joint parenting arrangements may exist in the presence of a custody award to one parent.
- Foreign divorces may or may not be recognized in a Canadian province for the purposes of remarrying. As with the status of foreign marriages, out-of-country divorces are honoured out of courtesy most of the time, but an application for recognition in a Canadian province is required. The principle involved is referred to as judicial **comity** or the accommodation of foreign legal decisions. It might not extend to arranged marriages of minor children or to sham divorces obtained in a foreign country, however. Recent judgments also suggest that same-sex couples who live in another country in which such marriages are not permissible but who marry in Canada may not be able to secure a Canadian divorce. The government has announced the intention to amend the Civil Marriage Act to allow divorces upon mutual application in such cases. This would establish a second channel to divorce designed exclusively for same-sex, non-citizen, Canada-married couples with much narrower grounds than are available to Canadians.
- In Canada, contact with religious authority is not at all necessary for divorce or for the definition of support obligations that arise from dissolved relationships. Nevertheless, some religious communities maintain tradition-based non-legal parallel processes for divorce and for the adjudication of private domestic disputes. Religious divorces and annulments have, in general, no applicability or standing in the civil courts.

Recent literature tends to combine the effects of separation and divorce as if they were a single package—inappropriately, if only for the reason that many separations cannot give rise to a divorce because no marriage has been contracted. For instance, a recent study based on results from the 2001 British census asserts that about three-quarters of current British family separations involving children in the United Kingdom today involve unmarried partners (Frean, 2005). In conceptually consolidating the consequences of separation and divorce, much literature tends to attribute to divorce effects that might more appropriately be seen as the effects of relationship breakdown, or even results of the prior dysfunctionality of families that ultimately dissolve. In this admittedly complex situation, it cannot be easily established that many observed effects might not have occurred even if the couples in conflict had stayed together.

Keeping in mind this important caveat, what are the observed effects of family separations? Reginald Bibby has recently addressed this question with published results from a large survey of Canadians in 2003 (Bibby, 2005: 65–70). Bibby finds a large number of impacts, among them (1) social strain with relatives who often disapprove; (2) decreased quality of school and workplace performance of the former spouses and of their children; (3) negative emotional impacts; and (4) financial hardship. But close to nine in ten of Bibby's separated/divorced respondents reported being happier on balance after the separation than before it, though many are hesitant to cohabit again in light of their experiences. For the children of separation/divorce, Bibby reports a number of negative effects. For instance, he reports that two-thirds of such children later in life report that family dissolution made life "harder for us," more than 50 per cent said they "didn't have enough money," and significant proportions reported feelings of inferiority, embarrassment, and weaker school performance, particularly for male children. Again, it is necessary to restate that implicit comparisons to intact families rather than to a hypothetical situation had their own conflicted families persisted are shaky.

In an earlier review of the literature, Anne-Marie Ambert noted the following measurable consequences of divorce: poverty (especially for women); higher incidence of depression, anxiety, and other emotional disorders; and increased risk of problems for children of divorced parents including such behaviour problems as fighting and hostility, lower educational attainment, adolescent pregnancies, and long-term risk for further marital problems (Ambert, 2002: 17–19).

For more on violence during separation, see "Homicide Data" in Chapter 14, pp. 281–2.

What is the cause and what is effect? Looking at the precursors of family dissolution, for instance, one obvious dimension of family breakdown involves a tense and potentially violent style of relating between spouses in chronic conflict, a situation that might be one of the more important reasons why one spouse leaves the other. The tension and violence do not arise in isolation. Each might stem from well-founded anger at the behaviour of the other, or for oft-cited reasons of financial stress, medical condition, misuse of drugs and alcohol, or infidelity—the list of possible triggering behaviours would be very long indeed. If nothing else, domestic assault figures indicate that the marital household in conflict is one of the primary locations in which Canadian crimes of violence occur. In light of this fact, accounts of post-separation hardships must be weighed against the real risks of physical and emotional trauma, which are greatly diminished by separation.

For the balance of family breakdowns, including those unions that never involved a marriage or overt violence, there are as many reasons for discord as there are partners. Unhappiness, frustration, and the "gradual growing apart" prominently mentioned by Bibby as a pre-eminent "cause" are persistent features of the human pair-bonding condition, as is perhaps the resolve to do better the next time. Though there could be no accounting of these causes and effects (and many are both causes and effects), it is certain that all spousal unions of whatever form are subject to such pressures from time to time.

Many children experience at least one episode of living in a lone-parent family at some time during their early years and they tend to experience such interludes as negative. While such periods of time may relieve them of the burden of living in the harsh environment of marital discord, the long-term consequences of the insecurities such episodes may produce cannot but have an effect later in their adult years. Myles Corak has shown that "parental divorce seems to influence the marital and fertility decisions of children. . . . Adolescents whose parents divorced tend to put off marriage, and once married suffer a greater likelihood of marital instability" (Corak, 1999: 5). Again, though, it is better to read "divorce" as "permanent separation" in these conclusions. Typically, separation brings with it a decline in standard of living as the expenses of maintaining two households instead of one are absorbed. This must also have effects in constraining what is financially feasible for the children of a dissolved union, and, of course, for the separated partners as well.[7]

The Lone-Parent Family and the Recombined Family

According to the present census classification, families in Canada may be divided into families of now-married couples with or without children, common-law (unmarried) couples with or without children, and lone-parent families. Married couples form the largest of the three categories, although they represent a gradually declining proportion of the total. However, the statistical snapshot of Canada's families taken every five years disguises the fact that many of today's families (or fragments therefrom) were once to be found in one of the other categories. For many, family structure is episodic over the long life course typical of today's Canadians: spells of coupledom are interspersed with periods of lone parenthood or being single.

Data from Statistics Canada's Family History Survey showed that by 1984 about 18 per cent of Canadian women aged 18 years and over had been at one time lone parents. In that survey, the typical duration of lone-parenthood for Canadian women was just over five years on average (Moore, 1989: 342). For many years, and continuously since 1991, there have been at least one million lone-parent families in Canada at any given time (and about 1.4 million at the time of the 2006 Census), more than 80 per cent headed by a woman. At the time of each five-year census, however, this group is not composed of all or even of predominantly the same people as in the previous census. By any standard single mothers with dependent children are among the poorest of Canadians (by either asset or income measures).

The major difficulties for lone parents relate to child care (expenses, availability, hours of operation, and transport to and from), lack of skills and training (as a result of time spent out of school and/or the labour force), the employment practices of Canadian employers (inflexibility and lack of concern), adequacy and affordability of housing, the continuing effects of elevated stress, and, perhaps most importantly, the unfulfilled need for social and emotional support. Over the long run, low incomes produce low pension entitlements, fewer household and personal assets, and sparse interpersonal networks, all giving rise to the prospect of a potentially troublesome old age.[8]

Many millions of Canadians have experienced episodes of living as children in a lone-parent family. In earlier decades, this was most likely the result of the premature death of a parent, especially during wartime when in addition to mortality there may have been very prolonged absences of a parent without any certainty that he might someday return. Today, life as a child in a lone-parent family is most likely the result of the separation of parents, whether or not they were ever married. With the passage of time, many lone parents establish new relationships—indeed, that may be the only way out of the lone-parenthood wilderness for many. A relatively small proportion of Canadian two-parent families with children now contain a step-parent, most often a step father who occupies the position by virtue of establishing a residential marital relationship with a separated mother and her child or children.[9] Sometimes, newly arrived biological or adoptive children of the current union partners are blended into the family. In addition, one or both partners may have other children who are not living with them. Some may reside with the new couple sporadically and some may live elsewhere but visit the household. These combinations take so many forms, all arising out of the need to satisfy the many conflicting demands on time and money of parents, that neat summation is difficult. In contemporary Canadian family life, innovation is a keyword.

Stepfamilies and Blended Families

When remnants of previously dissolved families combine in a new relationship they tend to become unremarkable in their communities because, for most purposes, they are indistinguishable from their always-intact family counterparts. Their household income levels are on average much closer to those of **intact families** than they are to those of lone-parent families headed either by a man or by a woman (Juby et al., 2003: 6, Figure 1). This parity is attributable almost entirely to having two adult earners in the labour force, a pivotal marker for potential prosperity in Canadian society today.

While immediate friends and family members may know of previous marital dissolutions the newly combining family members may have experienced, for outsiders the cues are subtle. Perhaps there are differing surnames, physical dissimilarities among children of the family, patterns of periodic visits by other adults, or other distinguishing signals. These might give vague clues to outsiders of a non-traditional family history. But even these aspects cannot be taken as decisive for identification purposes. Enough variation exists in the population of Canadian families now that most outsiders have learned not to press questions in the forward manner their grandparents might once have followed. Today's typically high levels of residential mobility—in a society where 80 per cent of the population reside in urban areas—have disrupted the dense web of community knowledge about family genealogy that characterized nineteenth- and early twentieth-century Canadian agrarian society.

Combined families' unremarkable social status also is aided by treatment under the law in much the same manner as their more traditional counterparts and significantly also by the Census of Canada, in that no questioning is directed to family history, only to the family present. This means that the considerable data resources generated by the Census remain mute on the question of lifetime exposure of individuals to episodes of life in **stepfamilies** in general and in **blended families** in particular. It is only when surveys specifically ask about the family history of current household members that information may emerge. In Canada, the General Social Survey, conducted annually by Statistics Canada, gathers information on such families, and but not on every cycle nor in exhaustive detail. Likewise, commercial survey firms seldom venture onto this ground. In the future, the relatively new National Longitudinal Survey of Children and Youth from

Statistics Canada promises to provide much of the missing detail.[10] For now we lack data about the long-term dynamics of combined families. One suspects that many combined families appreciate this anonymity and welcome their integration into society as conventional families that appear stable, traditional, and unproblematic for their surrounding communities. If for no other reason, publicly accepted integration means that they can leave behind the derogatory cultural stereotyping that step-parents have attracted over the millennia.

As one would expect in a society in which minor children of a dissolved family overwhelmingly reside with the mother, one large category of stepfamilies contains a mother with her biological child or children, joined in the new domestic relationship with a man who has assumed the role of step father to her children. The 2006 Census results reported a total of 512,000 stepfamilies in Canada, almost identical to the figure five years prior. In 2001, the General Social Survey had reported that about 50 per cent of current stepfamilies (then estimated to total 503,000 in 2001, in contrast to 3,768,000 "intact" families reported) contained only the mother's children, only 10 per cent had solely the father's children, and the remaining 40 per cent contained a blend of the new couple's children (either from two or more previous relationships or jointly in the current one). In about 80 per cent of the blended cases, the new couple had children by birth or adoption (Statistics Canada, 2002b). Note that because of the present orientation of the question asked, today's "combined families" will cease to be "combined" as soon as older children leave the household. When all the adult children born of only one current parent have left, what remains is simply a childless couple unless all of the children were born of the couple or unless all children born of either parent were adopted by the complementary partner. The question not asked is whether or not the respondent has *ever* lived in a combined and/or blended family setting. We simply do not know how many Canadians have experienced a combined family episode at some time in their lives or much about what happened in it.

When questioned in the Reginald Bibby survey mentioned previously, respondents who had entered a new marital relationship that involved step-parenting reported very positively on their experience. About 80 per cent characterized their new relationships as being much happier than their earlier ones. About the same proportion said that they had adjusted very or fairly well to their new partner's children and that the children had adjusted well to them. Men were slightly more positive than women, and those who had been previously married were more positive than those who had never previously married before entering a new combined family with a previously attached spouse and children. However, only about 56 per cent of stepchildren, when asked to look back on their childhoods, reported they got on well with step-parents while 65 per cent reported similarly about relations with step-siblings. Significant numbers of grown stepchildren are thus indicating strain in the combined family, though it is not clear that this strain is inherently worse than in intact families (Bibby, 2005: Tables 6.9–6.11).

A combined family may change the surnames of some members in favour of a single last name, a legal process that is quite easily and inexpensively done. A cost in lost identity may ensue, however, as surnames continue to convey origins and expectations, albeit to a much lesser extent than in the past when surname often conveyed membership in a mythic kinship collective centred on a particular place on earth.

One may speculate as to the nature of the special strains of the combined family setting, all the more so if the separation and combination cycle happens more than once. There may be non-custodial parental visits, conflicts among parental practices and expectations, awkwardness in formal introductions, and some degree of financial "fallout" from previous failed relationships. Often there also will be new "kin" and kinship relations to be learned for a larger-than-normal number of extended families, titles for which the language often fails. These exceptional relationships form a more complex kinship puzzle than usual for the children of a combined family, one that does not fade with maturity but becomes more complex as time goes by. For the mature children of some families this ultimately adds extensive obligations to a multiplicity of aging parents along with their other responsibilities as adults. Children of combined families may well find themselves in late middle age with four or more parents to assist in their declining years, parents who may have experienced financial reversals in their lives due to family dissolution and who may have remained the poorer for it.

Recent Developments in Divorce and Family Law

A series of court decisions in the early years of the twenty-first century made same-sex marriages not only legal but also easily available in most parts of Canada. These judgments had a set of quite predictable consequences outside of the obvious one that same-sex marriages might now be conducted. It was immediately evident that married same-sex couples would require access to divorce and family law financial settlements, access that necessitated the rewriting of much of the existing family legislation. Since some same-sex couples facing divorce in the future will have minor children—whether from a previous relationship, conceived through some technical means, or adopted—new paradigms of child custody and shared parenting will also be required since traditional preference for custody to the mother is still overwhelmingly followed in social practice (it is probably declining very slowly with time) but is not particularly relevant in the same-sex context.[11]

In addition, a slight but significant movement has appeared in the direction of rehabilitating "fault" or marital misconduct as a factor in financial settlements attendant to divorce. For instance, the British Columbia Appeals Court held in a judgment in 2004 that a Vancouver woman, Sherry Leskun, whose husband Gary left her for a remarriage to another woman, should continue to receive support payments (Schmitz, 2004: A2). In the normal course of events this woman might reasonably have expected that her $2,250 monthly support payment would be terminated with the passage of some few years after divorce as the Act intends. There is in Canada a general expectation under the legislation that former spouses must begin to support themselves after a transitional period normally limited to just a few years (recently specified as eight years in an Alberta decision) and without regard to marital offences committed by the other party. But in this case, the Court ruled that "emotional devastation" caused by adultery had undermined her ability to work. This judgment was subsequently upheld by the Supreme Court of Canada on the narrow grounds that while spousal misconduct cannot be considered, its emotional consequences can be. But the British Columbia Appeals Court ruling does raise an important question outside the bounds of law. Why should serious misconduct be subject to sanction in virtually all arenas of social life *except* in marriages?

Other evidence of a slight hardening of attitude towards former spouses in the throes of a marital dissolution can be found. For instance, in 2007 Ontario increased the maximum debtor prison sentence from 90 to 180 days (served without the normal recourse to early release provisions) for failure to pay child support established under court orders. Each year in Ontario, a few hundred non-compliant parents spend time behind bars and may also lose their drivers' licences. But for whatever reason, defaulting spouses in Ontario still owed at least $1.2 billion by early 2005. Much of this debt is not recoverable, either because the defaulter's whereabouts are unknown or because the defaulter has no funds to attach (as in the old lawyer's adage, "you can't get blood out of a stone"), or even because the defaulter is in jail and is therefore unable to be employed.[12] In a somewhat similar vein, in a Manitoba case (*Schreyer v. Schreyer*) reviewed by the Supreme Court of Canada in 2011, a divorced husband managed to evade a matrimonial property settlement debt by declaring bankruptcy which protected the husband's principal asset, a farm, from division.

In another decision, the Supreme Court of Ontario has ruled that a woman who left her common-law husband of more than 20 years some few months before he died is not entitled to the survivor pension she would have received were she to have been married to or still living with the deceased at the time of his death. This ruling has the effect of asserting that *a common-law relationship is over in law at the time of separation*. Continued cohabitation (as signified by the intent of both parties to be together) is required to establish a claim to survivor benefits. Thus, a common-law partner who leaves a relationship immediately acquires the status of divorced spouse no matter the conditions under which he or she left the household. This judgment effectively diminishes the emergent parity between married and common-law couples and holds that married couples have a higher degree of obligation to each other than their unmarried counterparts (Paraskevas, 2004: A2).

Finally, in another important decision of the Supreme Court of Canada, in 2008 the Court ruled that divorcing couples should be made to share debts as well as assets, debts such as the unrealized tax liabilities for tax shelter assets not yet liquidated in this case (*Stein v. Stein*). This case arose because current family legislation in the provinces is largely silent on the question of contingent debts such as postponed capital gains taxation (Tibbetts, 2008: A5).

In a few cases divorce settlements have been reopened well after the fact to take into account new realities, such as a big lottery win that was hidden and then cashed in only after the family law settlement was signed, or the permanent incapacitation of an ex-spouse occurring after an agreement was reached. These reopenings are very uncommon, as are support awards made against former wives in favour of former husbands. In the future, though, they may become more common. In a recent case (*Rick v. Brandsema*) the Supreme Court of Canada ruled that additional payments over and above the original settlement had to be paid by Mr Brandsema on the basis that he had provided false financial information before the agreement was signed. Additionally, the Ontario Court of Appeal ruled in 2009 that deteriorating economic conditions which have seriously diminished the value of matrimonial assets from that at the date of separation (heretofore the standard valuation point) should be reflected in final settlements of equalization payments (*Serra v. Serra*). Should economic conditions become really grim at some point in the future, it is likely that some former spouses may seek to have their support payments varied downward for the same underlying reason, involuntary impoverishment. One other important issue, the question of whether common-law spouses have the same rights as married couples to support and division of property upon separation, is now before the Supreme Court of Canada in 2012 (*"Eric" v. "Lola"* [surnames under a publication ban]).

In practice, support payments and the post-separation splitting of assets seem intended to work as parts of a capital redistribution system meant to enhance the economic status of ex-wives and their minor children. In creating such a system, governments hoped that the necessity for large state transfer payments to otherwise bereft ex-spouses would decline. Ex-spouses are additionally instructed (if not already employed) to get a job as soon as possible. Overall, this system, in place for more than 30 years, has been remarkably unsuccessful in addressing the continuing problem of lone-parent poverty, defined either in terms of asset ownership or of income levels. Inadequate enforcement of support payment orders remains a largely unresolved issue, as is the meagre supply of assets and income to attach or divide in very many cases. Poor couples who divide their incomes and assets simply get poorer separately. While this insight should not be startling, it is apparently lost on many Canadians. A study completed for BMO Financial Group in 2011 suggests that potential money woes were well down the list of concerns of Canadians contemplating separation and/or divorce. "Disruption of family life" was listed first by 41 per cent of respondents in contrast to those listing "standard of living" at 14 per cent.[13]

Conclusion

Major changes in social practice and in the legal environment have gone hand-in-hand with demographic changes to greatly enhance the episodic nature of spousal unions in Canada in the last half-century. On the demographic side, the rapid extension of life expectancies and widespread immigration/migration, with consequent dispersal and mixing of previously static populations, have produced a greater awareness of alternatives among people who are experiencing unsatisfactory domestic arrangements. The effect of perceived alternatives has raised the importance accorded to choice in marital matters, or more broadly, to an entitlement to happiness. These and other related factors have in turn contributed to the loosening of once-strict legal regimes for social control in family matters as they applied historically both to cohabitation and to its termination in separation. Likewise, newcomers to Canadian society, who often have become adherents to somewhat unfamiliar religious credos and modes of family life, are free to continue in their beliefs and practices when they are not in fundamental conflict with Canadian law.

There are few indications that Canadians are now less likely to cohabit in a marriage or marriage-like union at some point in their lives than they were in the past. Likewise, there is little indication that present unions are now more durable or less conflict-prone than they were in the past. Certainly, the emotional and economic consequences of separation on cohabiting partners and on their children are no easier to endure now than formerly. Often, the result of separation continues to be a descent into a period of intense poverty and personal turmoil.

Looked at in a purely legal context, however, proportionately fewer separating partners are in need of a divorce because fewer cohabiting couples are married. Thus, both marriage and divorce have been to some extent pushed towards the margins of social life in the years since the federal Divorce Act was enacted in 1968. On the other hand, provincial family law settlements have become much more central as separating couples unwind their financial entanglements and define the overhang of future support obligations, particularly where minor children are involved. In view of the substantial number of combined families in Canadian society, there seems no slackening in the willingness to try cohabitation again for a second or subsequent time. Each recombinant union contributes in its own unique way to the dense thicket of contemporary kinship charts and support obligations defined with the assistance of the ever-present legal profession.

STUDY QUESTIONS

1. Is lessening the incidence of separation and divorce in Canada a desirable social goal? In your view, what mechanisms might be useful to decrease the incidence of separation and divorce in Canada? Which would be most likely to succeed?

2. Should Canadian law take religious beliefs and practices into account by making the divorce process specific to the various belief communities? Would that expansion include the few small polygamous communities in western Canada such as that at Bountiful, BC? How does the Charter of Rights and Freedoms affect prosecutions against those claiming religious freedom from polygamy charges under the Criminal Code of Canada?

3. How do Canadian rates of separation and divorce compare to those in other countries? Is there anything Canadians can learn from the experience in other countries? Can you detect similar trends in the data over time in several countries or are there distinct groups of countries? If there are groupings, is grouping related to the religious environment or level of education in each?

4. What proportion of Canadian children will experience an episode of living in a lone-parent family in the years to come? Is that proportion likely to rise or fall in the future? How great a handicap is a period of living in a lone-parent family? Personal interviews may throw interesting light on the lived experience.

5. Why has the role of step-parent been portrayed so negatively in the past? This role is a staple of standard story telling, Cinderella's step mother being but one example. Can you find any studies which deal with this relationship? Can you find any evil step fathers in this lore?

6. How many same-sex divorces can Canadians expect to see in the years to come? Can you find current data and extrapolate to the future? What special problems might arise in same-sex divorces uniquely?

7. What public policies might be enacted to address and remedy the poverty of post-separation lone-parent families in Canada? Other than enforcement of support orders,

what changes could be made to Canadian legislation to make things easier for lone parents? Public daycare schemes, financially assisted retraining plans, subsidized housing, and public transit are just of few of the many policy levers which could be considered. Which would offer the best prospect for success and/or value for money spent?

Further Readings

Brownstone, Harvey. 2009. *Tug of War: A Judge's Verdict on Separation, Custody Battles, and the Bitter Realities of Family Court.* Toronto: ECW Press. This book is an informed insider's view of family court actions in Ontario, including a discussion of reopening and variance of concluded settlements.

Clark, Warren, and Susan Crompton. 2006. "Till death do us part? The risk of first and second marriage dissolution," *Canadian Social Trends*, Summer, Catalogue no. 11–008, 23–33. This article is a short treatment of assessed risk of termination of two main types of marriages.

Debrett's. 2012. *Guide to Civilised Separation: In Association with Mishcon de Reya.* London: Debrett's. This selection provides a fairly detailed guide to conflict reduction in failing British marriages.

Gentleman, Jane F., and Evelyn Park. 1997. "Divorce in the 1990s," *Health Reports* 9, 2 (Statistics Canada Catalogue no. 82–003–XPB). This report provides a numerical review of trends in Canadian divorce in the 1990s.

Gillis, John R. 1985. *For Better or Worse: British Marriages 1600 to the Present.* Oxford: Oxford University Press. This detailed scholarly volume documents the various changes and practices in British marriages in the last 400 years.

Grossberg, Michael. 1985. *Governing the Hearth: Law and the Family in Nineteenth-Century America.* Chapel Hill: University of North Carolina Press. This is a detailed scholarly volume on the various changes and practices in America in the nineteenth century.

Hudson, Joe, and Burt Galaway, eds. 1993. *Single Parent Families: Perspectives on Research and Policy.* Toronto: Thompson Educational Publishing. Hudson and Galaway have edited an insightful book of readings on lone-parent families in Canada.

Lochhead, Clarence, and David Hubka. 1994. *The Extent, Composition and Economic Characteristics of Blended, Common-Law and Single-Parent Families in Canada, and Family Expenditure on Child Care.* Ottawa: Department of Justice Canada, Working Document 1994–12e. This is a comprehensive account of the characteristics of such families in Canada.

McKie, D.C., B. Prentice, and P. Reed. 1983. *Divorce: Law and the Family in Canada.* Ottawa: Statistics Canada. This text provides an overall view of marriage, divorce, and family law in Canada from early settlement times to approximately 1982. It contains tabular data from the Central Divorce Registry at the Department of Justice and from the Office of the Official Guardian in Ontario, and a life table indicating the probability of divorce in each single year of marriage based on then-available data.

Rotermann, Michelle. 2007. "Marital breakdown and subsequent depression," *Health Reports*, Vol. 18, No. 2, Statistics Canada, Catalogue 82–003, 33–44. This short article discusses the possible connection between marital breakdown and the later occurrence of clinical depression.

Statistics Canada. 2002. *Changing Conjugal Life in Canada*. General Social Survey—Cycle 15, Catalogue no. 89–576–XIE, July. This is an account of the emergent types of cohabitation in Canadian society, including an overview of how separation and divorce have changed the nature of Canadian family life.

Zukewich, Nancy, and Melissa Cooke-Reynolds. 2003. *Transitions to Union Formation 1998, no. 2*, Statistics Canada Research Paper, Catalogue no. 89–584–MIE– no. 2, July. This is a brief assessment of the avenues Canadians employ in their journeys towards marital union formation.

Websites

www.vifamily.ca/about/about.html
The Vanier Institute of the Family provides a great deal of information on all aspects of contemporary family life, including separation and divorce and their consequences. Many of the publications are free to download from the site, most often in Acrobat format.

http://laws-lois.justice.gc.ca/eng/
Various essential documents can found at this government of Canada site, including the current Divorce Act and the current provincial family law for Ontario.

www.e-laws.gov.on.ca/navigation?file=home&lang=en
This site features a legislative history overview for Ontario.

www.mcss.gov.on.ca/mcss/english/pillars/familyResponsibility/
The Family Responsibility Office for Ontario has many free publications to download. Each of the provinces and territories has its own legislation and usually a copy is available online.

www.justice.gc.ca/eng/pi/fcy-fea/
Information on a number of topics related to divorce and separation can be found at this federal Justice Department site.

www.duhaime.org/LegalResources/FamilyLaw.aspx
Duhaime's Canadian Family Law Centre provides a wealth of information on separations and divorce in Canada and has even more information specific to British Columbia, including links to BC family legislation. It has an excellent section on the treatment of matrimonial property and spousal support in Canada.

www.international-divorce.com/canadian_family_law
This page contains a brief summary of the Canadian family law regime, as well as links to the comparable family legislation in dozens of other countries around the world.

http://canada.justice.gc.ca/eng/az.asp
This site presents studies under the headings of divorce and of family law (also available as a downloadable PDF files) that, for the first time in Canada, analyze data based on the situation "before" and "after" certain family transitions, such as parents' separation or family recomposition, thereby providing new insight into the relationship among family change, income, and labour force participation.

Notes

1. Pre-Christian marriage arrangements persisted in Scottish law until 1939. "Handfasting" provided a one-year trial marriage (August to August) to demonstrate fertility. At the end of the year, this ancient form of trial marriage could be dissolved by either party without consequence (Moffat and Wilson, 2011: 116–17).

2. The preliminary counts of marriages in Canada in the years 2004 through 2007 were 148,585, 148,439, 149,792, and 151,695 respectively, indicating a continuation of the stable observed pattern (Statistics Canada, CANSIM, table 0530001). This is not an isolated Canadian phenomenon. Current marriage totals in 2007 in the United Kingdom were the lowest seen since 1895 when the population was little more than half what it is now. On another not unrelated measure, UK divorce rates are also at their lowest level in 26 years.

3. The data from the 2001 General Social Survey conducted by Statistics Canada clearly show a "growing instability in the unions of today's women. The probability of seeing their first unions dissolve is increasing: women ranging in age from 30–39 are expected to be twice as likely to see their unions end in separation or divorce as women ranging in age from 60 to 69." Statistics Canada, *Changing Conjugal Life in Canada*, July 2002, Catalogue no. 89–576–XIE, 5.

4. Vanier Institute of the Family, Chart 21, "Proportion of marriages in which at least one spouse has been previously married (1970–1996)." Available at http://www.vifamily.ca/library/profiling2/chart21.html.

5. A *get* is a Jewish religious document purported to be necessary to separate the combined soul of a married man and woman. Without a proper *get*, even though the man and woman have physically separated, they are still bound together in some mystical fashion—and considered to be still fully married. The great difficulty for contemporary life is that the wife *cannot* initiate the process. Note as well that under Jewish law, divorced women are prohibited from marrying a Cohen.

6. The Arbitration Act (1991) in Ontario allowed faith-based arbitration (for Muslims, Jews, and members of other established faiths) in matters of divorce, custody, and property disputes such as inheritance outside the formal court system. Participation was supposed to be voluntary but as sociologists know well, informal social pressure to comply can be intensely coercive. That part of shariah law that pertains to criminal events is clearly contrary to the Charter of Rights and Freedoms, but this does not mean that Canadian Muslims might not someday challenge this aspect as well. The orthodox Jewish arbitration system (*Beth Din*) provides rabbinical decisions, the substance of which are then embodied in a conventional court document of settlement. Rabbinical decisions now deal with separation, division of assets, and other civil matters involving business disputes. This avenue is available in large Canadian cities only where community numbers warrant it.

7. For a graphic view of the economic impacts of being in a lone-parent family, see Chart 4, "Real Median Disposable Income," in Garnet Picot and John Myles, *Social Transfers, Changing Family Structure and Low Income among Children*, Statistics Canada Research Paper Series, no. 82, 1995, Catalogue no. 11F0019MIE, 10.

8. Michelle Rotermann (2007) discusses findings from the now cancelled National Population Health Survey on associations between marital dissolution and subsequent depression among people aged 20 to 64. She concludes that "Marital dissolution often sets in motion a series of stressful disruptions that create further personal and financial difficulties, which themselves may contribute to depression."

9. Vanier Institute of the Family, *Profiling Canada's Families II*, Section 28, "Mine, yours and ours—Canada's 'blended' families." Available at http://www.vifamily.ca/library/profiling2/part28.html.

10. Data from the 1994–5 cycle of the NLSCY suggest that Canadian families by type are as follows: 75.7 per cent intact, 14.5 per cent lone mother, 1.1 per cent lone father, 0.1 per cent lone step-parent, 6.1 per cent blended stepfamily, and 2.5 per cent non-blended stepfamily (where "blended" means a family in which at least one of the children does not have the same biological or adoptive parent as the others) (Marcil-Gratton, 1999: 1).

11. Custody disputes between former same-sex spouses are not unknown. In a case in Ontario in 2008 for instance, an Ontario Superior Court judge ordered Connie Springfield to return to northern England with her two adopted daughters to honour the provisions of a shared custody agreement with her former same-sex partner, Sarah Courtney. The judge referred to the deliberate spiriting away of the children in violation of a standing joint custody agreement in the judgment (Wattie, 2008: A3). In another more recent case, an Alberta court granted custody of a young girl to a gay man over a claim by his former partner and the biological father of the child (Slade, 2011: A7).

12. For a discussion of the various provincial spousal and child support programs, see Chantal Steeves, "Interjurisdictional Cases of Spousal and Child Support," Statistics Canada, *Juristat*, 28 March 2012, Catalogue 85–002–X.

13. The survey was done for BMO Financial Group by Leger Marketing between 15–18 August 2011 and sampled 1,504 Canadian adults. A press account of the results can be found in Bradley Bouzane, "Majority of Canadians underestimate financial burden of divorce: BMO," *Vancouver Sun*, 5 October 2011. While the dataset has not been released, an extended discussion of the results is available as "BMO Financial Group Divorce Panel Conference Call, Thursday, October 6, 2011" upon request to BMO.

6

"Mid-Life Crises": Understanding the Changing Nature of Relationships in Middle-Age Canadian Families

KAREN M. KOBAYASHI

LEARNING OBJECTIVES

- To understand the nature of intergenerational co-residence in mid-life families
- To appreciate the nature of support/care given to older parents by mid-life adults, usually daughters
- To learn about the nature of intergenerational ambivalence in mid-life families
- To discover emergent research about diversity and the intersection of diversity markers in mid-life families
- To be able to discuss the relationship between mid-life families and social policy

Introduction

The application of a **life-course perspective** to the study of families has resulted in a partitioning of family time into stages. This allows researchers to isolate and examine the changing nature of relationships at different periods of the family life course. Given this life-course focus on the interplay between "aging, social change, and family dynamics" (Moen, 1991: 135), researchers have applied a synchronous theoretical framework to examine family change over time at both the micro and macro levels.

This chapter focuses on the mid-life stage in families, often referred to in the literature as the "sandwich stage" because of its chronological placement between young adulthood and later life along the family life-course trajectory. Recently, however, with the increasing demographic complexity of North American families, it has become even more difficult to assign distinct structural markers, such as age, to entrance and exit from life-course stages. The age range of 45–64 years, previously used to define middle age, is no longer seen as valid or appropriate. As Allen et al. (2000: 913) point out in their review of the literature on families in the middle and later years, "there is no agreed upon chronological or processual definition of middle age." Indeed, it is the transitions to various stages (e.g., the return to work, the "empty nest," caregiving) triggered by the occurrence of life events in the domains of work and the family (e.g., re-entry into the paid labour force, adult children leaving home, care for aging parents), and not age markers per se, that seem to define the parameters of mid-life in the family literature. In the family domain, "demographic changes highlight the evolving nature of mid-life" (Antonucci and Akiyama, 1997: 147). For example, with the increasing age at first marriage for both men and women in Canada over the past few decades, the transition to parenthood has inevitably been delayed into the thirties for many couples.[1] With the mean age at first birth for women at just under 30 years of age (29.3 years) in 2006 (Statistics Canada, 2008a) and average life expectancy at 81 years (80.7 years) (Human Resources and Skills Development Canada, 2010), Canadians are more likely to be well into their forties and fifties—at one time the definition of a middle-age family—while being "sandwiched" between the needs of growing children and aging parents (Allen et al., 2000; Statistics Canada, 2004). This trend is likely to continue well into the future as the pursuit of career trajectories (i.e., post-secondary education and full-time employment) and of family interests and responsibilities becomes increasingly "normative" for Canadian women.

What are the implications of these changing demographic trends for middle-age families? This chapter explores the impact of such changes in the broad contexts of living arrangements and intergenerational relationships, two of the main areas of sociological research on mid-life families in Canada and the United States, and concludes with a discussion on social policy issues.

Co-residence and Home-Leaving

Recent statistics from the 2006 census indicate that over one-half (60 per cent) of young adults aged 20–24 years and over one-quarter (26 per cent) aged 25–29 years still co-reside with their parents, supporting the contention that "mid-life parenthood often comprises prolonged periods of co-residence with grown adults" (Mitchell, 1998a: 2). The provinces with the highest proportion of **intergenerational co-residence** (young adults 20–29 years with their parents) are Newfoundland and Labrador and Ontario at 52.2 per cent and 51.5 per cent, respectively, but all provinces (see Figure 6.1) and the majority of census metropolitan areas (see Figure 6.2) have seen substantial increases in co-residence over the past five to 20 years. This new family arrangement, coupled with an increase in the average age at first birth, means that mid-life parents may be well into their fifties before experiencing an "**empty nest**," if ever. Such a delay in the transition to a one-generation household has implications for parent–child relationships in the latter years of middle age as it is likely to coincide with the timing of parents' retirement planning or, in cases of prolonged co-residence, the passage into retirement. This intersection of key transition points along family and work trajectories in mid-life reflects the multiple linkages of roles in these two domains over the adult life course.

Why is it taking longer for recent cohorts of young adult children to leave the parental home to establish residential independence? There are a number of reasons for the postponement of this life course transition. Research indicates that children's economic/

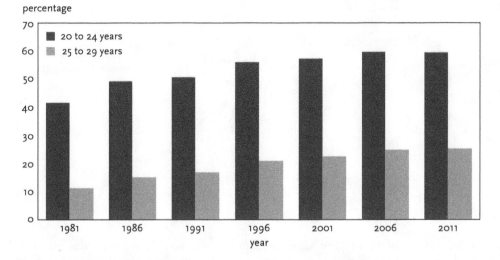

percentage

Figure 6.1 **Percentage of Young Adults Aged 20 to 24 and 25 to 29 Living in the Parental Home, Canada, 1981 to 2011**

SOURCE: Statistics Canada, 2011. "Census in Brief: Living Arrangements of Young Adults Aged 20 to 29," *Families, households and marital status, 2011 Census of Population.* Ottawa: Statistics Canada, p. 3, available at http://www12.statcan.gc.ca/census-recensement/2011/as-sa/98-312-x/98-312-x2011003_3-eng.pdf.

financial needs are a key factor influencing the home-leaving behaviour of young adult children (Shehan and Dwyer, 1989; White, 1994; Mitchell and Gee, 1996; Cohen and Kaspar, 2002; Carr, 2005; Mitchell, 2006; De Marco and Berzin, 2008). Mid-life parents, who presumably are in their peak earning years, provide a significant amount of financial and instrumental support to co-resident children at this stage in the family life course. Assistance takes multiple forms, including the payment of tuition and other fees for post-secondary education and/or vocational training, and, most importantly, the continued provision of housing, utilities, meals, and transportation. Given increases in unemployment and underemployment rates, declines in affordable housing, and the trend towards extensions in schooling for young adults over the past few decades, parents may continue to be, as noted earlier, the primary resource for adult children well into later life (Mitchell, 1998b, 2006; Sage and Kirkpatrick Johnson, 2012; Settersten Jr., 1999, 2007).

The shift in the timing of home-leaving among young adults can also be attributed to the continuation of a long-term trend towards the postponement of marriage. The most recent statistics available indicate that the average age at first marriage is currently 29.1 years for women and 31.1 years for men, up from 22.0 and 24.4 years, respectively, in 1975 (Human Resources and Skills Development Canada, 2012). The increasing age at first marriage coupled with the propensity of young adults for leaving home just prior to marriage, for a number of different reasons ranging from economic to cultural, has resulted in prolonged periods of intergenerational co-residence in mid-life Canadian families (Mitchell and Gee, 1996; Mitchell and Lovegreen, 2009). In addition to ethno-cultural factors, the timing of parents' transition to an "empty nest," then, can be seen as directly linked to the

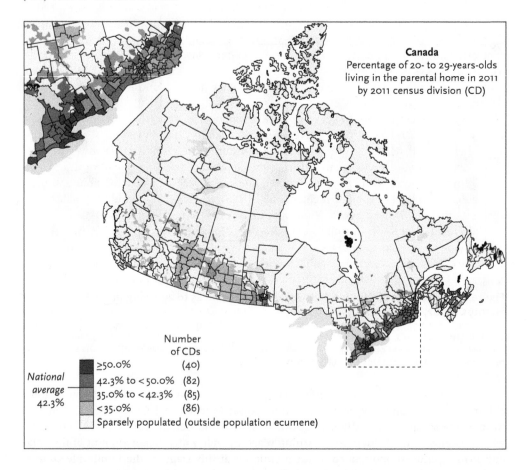

Canada
Percentage of 20- to 29-years-olds
living in the parental home in 2011
by 2011 census division (CD)

Number
of CDs

≥50.0%	(40)
42.3% to < 50.0%	(82)
35.0% to < 42.3%	(85)
< 35.0%	(86)

*National
average
42.3%*

Sparsely populated (outside population ecumene)

Figure 6.2 **Percentage of 20- to 29-year-olds Living in the Parental Home in 2011 by 2011 Census Division**

SOURCE: Statistics Canada, 2011. "Census in Brief: Living Arrangements of Young Adults Aged 20 to 29," *Families, households and marital status, 2011 Census of Population.* Ottawa: Statistics Canada, p. 7, available at http://www12.statcan. gc.ca/census-recensement/2011/as-sa/98-312-x/98-312-x2011003_3-eng.pdf.

inter-relationship between economic and marital status characteristics of adult children (Mitchell, 2010).

In addition to the economic and marital characteristics of adult children, family struc-ture plays an important role in determining home-leaving behaviour. Young adults living in blended or stepfamilies are more likely to leave home early than those who reside in either single- or two-parent biological families (Mitchell, 1994, 2006; Eshleman and Wilson, 2001). Premature home-leaving by adult stepchildren is related to a weakened sense of mutual obligation as family members in step-parent–stepchild relationships and related conflict over power relations within these families (Eshleman and Wilson, 2001; Aquilino, 2005). Divorce and widowhood also influence co-residence patterns in mid-life

Canadian families: there is a decreased likelihood that adult children will live at home if parents are divorced or a parent is widowed (Boyd and Norris, 1995). This may be due to the custodial or widowed parent's decreased ability to provide financial support to adult children in co-resident families, an impetus for the child to seek residential independence (Aquilino, 2005).

Although intergenerational co-residence is regarded in the literature primarily as a reflection of adult children's needs, Ward and Spitze (1996: 537) note that children do not always express satisfaction with this living arrangement. In fact, they maintain that "coresidence [actually] violates the child's norms and expectations about adulthood and independence, and [that] children may experience greater strain over exchanges in shared households." The recognition of a tension between co-resident parents and adult children and its relationship to living arrangements has been a focus of research on the quality of intergenerational relationships in mid-life families (Shehan and Dwyer, 1989; Ward and Spitze, 1996; Mitchell and Gee, 2003; Mitchell, 2006). In many cases, incongruence between parents and young adult children over expectations for support may lead to intergenerational disputes within the family (see "Case in Point" box). Within more traditional immigrant cultures, parent–child incongruence on adherence to core family and religious values (e.g., filial obligation, family shame) can be the source of extreme conflict leading to the eventual breakdown of the nuclear family unit.

CASE IN POINT

Intergenerational Conflict in a Cluttered Nest: The Voice of a Young Male, Indo-Canadian Adult Child

I personally feel my father is not living up to that obligation of taking care, of being supportive, and fulfilling his roles, for example, tuition fees. Every time I have asked for money, he's refused. [This son does not contribute to the household finances.] Me and my father don't speak to each other, so that is kind of rough. I've laid down the foundation of the dynamic in my family. Now, there's problems. There's that implicit assumption that the younger, the kids, will take care of the parents, right? Now my grandparents are also feeling like my parents are not living up to their obligations.

SOURCE: Mitchell and Gee (2003). Reprinted with permission of authors.

The intersection of ethnicity and immigrant status has implications for continuing co-residence in mid-life families. North American research indicates a stronger sense of obligation to support young adult children in Asian immigrant families (Kamo, 2000; Mitchell and Gee, 2003). Mitchell and Gee (2003), in a study of multi-generational households, include an exploration of the co-residential experiences of South Asian and Chinese immigrant families, currently the two largest visible minority populations in Canada (Statistics Canada, 2008b). Their findings, although limited by a small sample size, highlight the salience of cultural preferences (for example, mid-life parents' complete assumption of all financial responsibilities for their young adult children as an expression of their parental obligation to take responsibility for their children) and not economic needs as the key determinants of living arrangements over the family life course. Results from Pacey's (2002) comparative study between Canadian and Chinese-Canadian immigrants support these findings in a sample of older adults.

The importance of cultural exigencies can be seen even in the context of post-immigrant visible minority families. In a study on parent–child relationships in Japanese-Canadian families, third-generation mid-life children recalled that both cultural and socio-economic factors shaped their preferences to co-reside with parents as young adults (Kobayashi, 1999). Despite the Canadian-born status of the mid-life parents, there was an enduring expectation that the nuclear family would stay intact until children, particularly daughters, made the transition to marriage. This cultural "pull factor," combined with the economic necessity, in many cases, on the part of adult children to remain at home, formed the basis for intergenerational co-residence in mid-life families.

Returning Home

The return of adult children to the parental home in young adulthood is becoming an increasingly common experience in contemporary middle-age families. These young adults, referred to in the literature as "boomerang kids" (Mitchell and Gee, 1996; Mitchell, 1998b, 2006) due to their pattern of leaving the family "nest" and returning again at some point(s) over the family life course, have been the focus of a number of recent studies on parent–adult child co-residence (White, 1994; Ward and Spitze, 1996; Mitchell, 1998b; Mitchell et al., 2002). This literature has examined the antecedents and consequences of a "cluttered nest" both for home-returning children and for their parents.

The experience of home-returning is shaped mainly by adult children's needs and social situations, particularly economic necessity and/or marital status transitions. The antecedents of return co-residence are, in fact, remarkably similar to those for continuing co-residence. Ward and Spitze (1996: 537), in a comparative study on living arrangements in the United States, find that co-residence by parents and adult children—whether continuing or return—is largely a "response to the circumstances of children." Indeed, the return of adult children to the parental home is often precipitated by marital disruption (i.e., separation, divorce, or the breakup of a common-law relationship) and/or economic difficulties (i.e., transition from full-time employment to unemployment or underemployment, single parenthood). This finding is supported by the results of studies undertaken by Mitchell and Gee (1996) and Mitchell (1998b, 2006) in the Canadian context.

How does the return of children to the "empty nest" affect mid-life family relationships? Although much has been written on the consequences of the "cluttered nest" in mid-life, research findings in this area have often been contradictory. The effects of **boomerang children** on family relationships have ranged from positive to negative. On the positive side, the overall marital satisfaction of mid-life parents has been found to be quite high among those who are living with returning children as parents may receive additional support (emotional, instrumental, financial) from pooled resources (Mitchell and Gee, 1996; Ward and Spitze, 1998). Thus, returning children may actually act as the antidote to "empty nest syndrome" for parents. Of negative consequence, however, is the decrease in self-reported relationship satisfaction between parents and adult children in the post-return home period due to conflicts over power relations in the home (Kobayashi, 1999). Returning adult children may not adapt well to the reassertion of authority by parents within the household, particularly if the "ground rules" are not open for negotiation. The negative effects of home-returning are multiplied even further in families of children who are "serial home leavers," those who leave and return multiple times (i.e., three or more) over the family life course (Mitchell and Gee, 1996; Mitchell, 2006).

Support for Older Parents

Cutbacks to health care and social services over the past decade in Canada have precipitated an increased reliance on the family by governments at all levels for the care of older adults. This issue is particularly salient for mid-life families—Michelson and Tepperman (2003: 56) point out that almost one-half of caregivers are between the ages of 35 and 54 years, with an average age of 51. And, according to Cranswick and Dosman, in 2007, most eldercare (75 per cent) was provided by those between 45 and 64 years of age. What will be the consequences of changes to public policy and programs then for mid-life families? This is an important and timely question as Canada faces the challenges of aging in an unusually high proportion of the population early this century.

For more on caregiving and the health of older Canadians see "Families: The Mainstay of Care" in Chapter 7, pp. 134–7.

For the first time in our history, it is estimated that Canadian adults will spend a longer time caring for their aging parents than they spent in raising their children (McDaniel, 2005). Given the gendered nature of caregiving in our society, this means that the burden of care will continue to fall on women in mid-life (Dentinger and Clarkberg, 2002; McDaniel, 2005). Although the compression of morbidity to the latter years of old age (80 +) has resulted in a greater number of disability-free years for older parents, the need for social support from middle-aged children (daughters, in particular) remains fairly constant over time. This is because **social support** is comprised of three main domains—financial, instrumental, and emotional—and need for assistance in each of these areas is influenced by the timing of a number of later life-course transitions, namely widowhood, retirement, and the onset of chronic illness. As older parents experience these transitions in later life, their reliance on middle-aged adult children increases either temporarily or long term. The extent to which support is provided (the adult child's response) is dictated both by parents' assistance needs and by the quality of the parent–child relationship. For some mid-life adult children, being "sandwiched" between the competing demands of caregiving for young adult children and older parents can be extremely stressful, leading to negative financial and health outcomes (Gee and Mitchell, 2003).

An older parent's experience of widowhood, an often unexpected transition, has consequences for support ranging from temporary assistance with some activities of daily living like bill payments or grocery shopping (instrumental support) to permanent reliance on children for financial help and/or companionship to combat depression (emotional support). Of course, in the latter situation, the long-term need for assistance may require a complete restructuring of children's lives as they try to negotiate caregiving with full-time work and parenting roles and responsibilities. Although multi-generational co-residence may be the best solution, it may cause considerable strain on the relationship between parent and child.

It is less likely that retirement, a transition that older parents are expected to have planned for during their working lives, will have such an onerous effect on middle-aged children's lives. In fact, if healthy, financially secure, and married, retired parents may end up providing financial or instrumental assistance to children in the form of child care and domestic and yard work. Nevertheless, there is great diversity in the older adult population, and a large proportion of Canadians have a difficult time adjusting financially and emotionally to retirement. Older parents in this group require the most support from children to help them adjust to the truncation of their work trajectory.

Perhaps the transition that gives rise to the most significant alteration in the family trajectory of middle-aged children is the onset of chronic disease or disability in an older parent(s). Support is transformed into caregiving when a parent becomes ill; this transformation is salient because it requires a great deal of sacrifice (temporal, emotional, financial) on the part of middle-aged children, mainly daughters, who often are forced to make life-altering decisions regarding work and family in a very short period of time.

Intergenerational Ambivalence

Despite increases in continued and return co-residence of adult children in mid-life families over the past few decades, these experiences are still considered non-normative by Canadian society. An expectation persists that adult children will leave the parental home, which also is regarded as an indicator of the success of parents' child-raising skills or abilities. The launch of children from the nest is perceived as parents' "raison d'être," a key transition point along the family life course trajectory. Given the salience of this event, it is not surprising that incompatibility between parents' expectations and children's behaviour in this regard may often lead to ambivalence in intergenerational relationships (Fingerman et al., 2004).

A recent concept in the sociological literature on the family, **intergenerational ambivalence** has been used to describe mid-life parent–child relationships. To date, it has been used to examine relationships between adult children and their aging parents and in-laws (Pillemer and Suitor, 2002; Willson et al., 2003; Rappoport and Lowenstein, 2007), and to explore the nature of social ties—with both family and friends—in a diverse age sample of adolescents and adults (Fingerman et al., 2004). Findings from Willson et al.'s study point to the significance of gender in ambivalent social relationships. Mid-life women are more likely to experience ambivalence in their relationships with each other and in their roles as caregivers to older parents and in-laws, suggesting that "structural arrangements give rise to ambivalence and the relationship experience is shaped by gender within the context of socially defined demands and obligations" (Willson et al., 2003: 1068). The exception, it seems, is in mid- to later-life sibling relationships, where women (positively) report close ties and the most social contact with their sisters (Connidis and Campbell, 1995; Connidis, 2001).

Diversity in Mid-life Families

Studies of satisfaction in marital and parent–child relationships in mid-life have tended to examine relationship quality as it is impacted by intergenerational living and/or social support arrangements with children (e.g., Marks, 1995; Mitchell and Gee, 1996; Carr, 2005), only occasionally highlighting the actual relationship between or well-being of members of the dyad. This myopic view of mid-life families is problematic in that it fails to recognize the experiences of separated/divorced, remarried, childless, parentless, gay and lesbian, and long-term or permanent "empty nest" families, groups of emerging importance in the mid-life Canadian population. We will focus on a few of these groups in this chapter.

Separated/Divorced

The topic of divorce has recently been the focus of research examining the impact of marital status transitions on spousal and children's well-being over the life course (Montenegro, 2004; Williams and Umberson, 2004). In an American Association of Retired Persons (AARP)-funded study based on 1,147 interviews with men and women who had been divorced at least once during their forties, fifties, or sixties, the effects of divorce are profound; that is, the findings indicate that the divorce experience is "more emotionally devastating than losing a job, about equal to experiencing a major illness, and somewhat less devastating than a spouse's death" (Montenegro, 2004: 7) (see Box 6.1). Clearly, divorce is perceived as a disruptive and stressful event when it occurs in mid-life, potentially leading to a number of negative life-course consequences.

Box 6.1
After 40, It's Wives Who Divorce the Husbands

Two-thirds of divorces after age 40 are initiated by wives, debunking the myth of an older man divorcing his wife for a younger woman, a new survey shows.

"That obviously happens, but mostly it's women who are asking for the divorce," said Steve Slon, editor of AARP *the Magazine*. . . . The magazine will publish the results Thursday in its July–August issue.

"The Divorce Experience: A Study of Divorce at Mid-life and Beyond" surveyed 1,147 people ages 40 to 79 who had divorced in their forties, fifties, or sixties. The questionnaire survey, completed in December, had a margin of sampling error of plus or minus 3 percentage points.

The survey found that women over age 40 seemed more aware of problems in their marriages, while men were more likely to be caught off-guard by their divorces. Twenty-six per cent of men said they "never saw it coming," compared with 14 per cent of women.

"The increase in women initiating a divorce reflects the empowerment of women to leave bad marriages," said Linda Fisher, AARP's director of national member research. "Thirty

(Continued)

years ago, many of these women might not have been able to (divorce) because of lack of self-confidence and financial means," she said. "Women are more likely to have more self-confidence and the means to leave a marriage when the circumstances are untenable."

The AARP study found that most women said they filed for divorces because of physical or emotional abuse, infidelity, or drug and alcohol abuse. Men said they sought divorces because they fell out of love, they had different values or lifestyles, or infidelity. The report also found that most older divorced people move on to other serious relationships.

Seventy-five per cent of women in their fifties reported enjoying serious, exclusive relationships after their divorces, often within two years. Eighty-one per cent of men in their fifties did the same.

SOURCE: Chaka Ferguson, Associated Press Writer, Yahoo! News, 26 May 2004.

Perhaps the most significant consequences of divorce in mid-life are its effects on parent–child relationships and the well-being of children. Indeed, the primary reason for partners remaining in an unhappy marital union and delaying separation is concern over the welfare of their children (McDaniel and Tepperman, 2007; Montenegro, 2004). With the experience of divorce increasingly becoming a mid-life phenomenon,[2] children who are most likely to be affected by parental divorce are in their late adolescent to young adult years. At this stage in the life course, children are in the process of forming attitudes about marriage and family themselves and may be more vulnerable to the negative impact of parental disagreement or conflict (Kozuch and Cooney, 1995). Despite concerns over the long-term effects of divorce on children's attitudes and behaviours, there is little evidence to suggest that exposure to the marital disruption of mid-life parents negatively affects the quality of parent–child relationships, children's ability to cope with challenging life events such as moving, or their overall optimism about marriage (Dunlop and Burns, 1995; Landis-Kleine et al., 1995; Taylor et al., 1995).

How do mid-life parents themselves fare in the aftermath of divorce? The ability to cope varies greatly according to gender. In the financial domain, middle-aged women, particularly those with sole or majority custody of adolescent or young adult children, are more likely than their male counterparts to fear (and to actually experience) economic instability (Finnie, 1993; Montenegro, 2004). Emotionally, although both men and women experience loneliness and depression following marital dissolution, women have greater rates of depression and distress than do men in the post-divorce period (Wu and Hart, 2002). This is not surprising in view of women's distress being largely tied to their feelings of anxiety over their children's well-being as well as the uncertainty surrounding their financial status (Montenegro, 2004). Loss of spousal support, however, appears to have a significant impact on men's overall health; that is, separation/divorce results in both poorer physical and mental health for men (Wu and Hart, 2002), suggesting that the instrumental and emotional support wives provide in marital unions is an important determinant of health for husbands. This is not the case for women, who tend to have stronger informal support networks (friends and family) outside of marriage and, thus, do not suffer such notable declines in their physical well-being.

Remarried

According to the most recent statistics on marriage in Canada, remarriage, like divorce, is a mid-life transition, with the average age of remarriage for previously divorced women being 41.4 years and the average age for men, 45.0 years (Statistics Canada, 2003). Remarriage in mid-life is also a gendered transition: men are more likely than women to remarry, a pattern that holds well into later life (Ambert, 2005). There may be a number of reasons for this, including the idea that divorced or widowed women in middle to older age groups greatly value their new-found independence and thus prefer to remain single (Baker, 2001). For men, it may be the case that they find it difficult to make the transition to being "on their own" without the emotional and instrumental support of a partner and subsequently seek out companionship soon after a divorce to fill that void. Although research on remarriages in general indicates that these couples are at an increased risk of divorce compared to first marriages, it has been suggested that remarriages in mid-to-later life may actually have a lower likelihood of marital disruption. This is especially the case when both partners have previously been married (Wu and Penning, 1997).

The remarriage of two previously married individuals in mid-life often involves the "blending" of two families, referred to in the literature as a "complex stepfamily." This reconstitution, that is, the integration of adolescent and/or young adult stepchildren into a new family form, brings with it a number of challenges at this stage of the life course (Sweeney, 2007). In mid-life families, the adaptation process for stepchildren is influenced by a number of factors, including children's age at their parent's remarriage, their residential status (co-resident or not), and the quality of the parent–child relationship prior to the remarriage. For example, the difficult period of adjustment that many co-resident children undergo soon after a parent's remarriage may be attributed, in part, to their resentment at the introduction of another authority figure into the home. Depending on the child's age, this may coincide directly with the development of his/her desire to establish a sense of independence from the family, with the step-parent perceived as yet another barrier to the achievement of this goal (Hetherington and Kelly, 2002). Of course, the degree of closeness between parents and their children prior to remarriage has a significant impact on the adaptation of children to their new family structure. Children who have close relationships with their custodial parent in the pre-remarriage period are likely to adjust better to a stepfamily arrangement than those who have a history of conflicted or strained relations (Ahrons and Tanner, 2003).

Gays and Lesbians

Gay and lesbian families in mid-life are becoming increasingly diverse as more and more same-sex partners in middle age are making efforts to "blend" existing families or to have children together either via medical technology or through adoption (Epstein, 2003; Miller, 2003). Such emergent family forms may be referred to as "new nuclear" or "new blended," with same-sex dyads forming the nucleus of the family unit. Often the result of the end of a heterosexual union(s), the "new blended" family is part of a mid-life phenomenon in Canadian families. As once-married partners "come out" after years of marriage and child-rearing, they find themselves trying to negotiate both a divorced and a new sexual identity in middle age. For custodial parents, in particular, this may be a difficult period of adjustment for themselves and their adolescent and/or young adult children. Bringing together families who have not yet made their own transitions to a gay- or lesbian-headed single-parent unit may result in conflicted relations early on in the "new blended" family (Epstein, 2003).

Recently, the caregiving relationships of mid-life gays and lesbians have been recognized as important topics in the literature on social support in families. One of the key exploratory studies to emerge in this area focuses on the experiences of mid-life and older gays caring for chronically ill partners (Hash, 2001). The findings highlight a number of important similarities and differences between the experiences of gays and lesbians and heterosexual caregivers. Not surprisingly, homophobic attitudes of informal (family and friends) and formal (health-care and human services professionals) resources are a major barrier to providing care for chronically ill loved ones. Beyond that, on a structural level, unsupportive policies and practices serve to exacerbate the problem of discrimination and/or non-recognition of same-sex partnerships in the context of caregiving.

Childlessness

Childlessness in mid-life can be either by choice or due to **involuntary infertility**, the inability to conceive despite the wish to conceive (Ambert, 2006). As the average age at marriage continues to increase in Canadian society, one of the principal reasons for involuntary childlessness has become delayed child-bearing. A woman's decision to put off starting a family until her mid-to-late thirties and forties may have profound implications for her ability to conceive, given that significant fertility declines take place from the age of 35 years onward (Heaton et al., 1999). For mid-life women with fertility issues, one of the most often sought options for child-bearing is assisted reproductive technology (i.e., in vitro fertilization).

Despite their higher propensity for divorce (controlling for number of years married), childless couples report greater marital satisfaction on a number of relationship dimensions than those who are parenting (Twenge et al., 2003). In another study comparing parents and childless couples, Koropeckyj-Cox (2002) tests a typology of parental status from Connidis and McMullin (1993) in her exploration of the factors influencing subjective well-being among mid- to later-life individuals in these two groups. The findings indicate that parental status in mid-life is linked to psychosocial well-being; good-quality relationships between parents and adult children are associated with a sense of positive well-being among parents in mid-life to later life. Further, the relationship between childlessness and well-being is gendered: women who are childless report higher levels of distress than their male counterparts and have, overall, lower subjective well-being than mothers in close parent–child relationships.

Mid-life Families and Health

With increasing life expectancies for men and women in Canada and the compression of morbidity to the latter years of the life course, health issues in midlife families have not been widely studied by sociologists. An exception to this has been recent American research on health and marital quality over the life course. Using growth curve evidence from a national longitudinal survey, Umberson and her colleagues (2006) conclude that marital strain, i.e., poor perceived marital quality, has a negative impact on self-rated health status for both men and women as they age. Thus, from a life course perspective, negative marital interactions in early life, if they persist, may have a cumulative deleterious effect on the physical and mental health of mid-life family members.

Interestingly, in exploring health disparities across the life course in American families, researchers have found that single mothers in mid-life report poorer health than their married counterparts, indicating that perhaps the stress and financial strain that accompanies lone parenthood may indeed be related to a number of health issues over time (Williams and Dunne-Bryant, 2006; Williams, 2008; Williams et al., 2011). Indeed, in a sample of mothers who participated in a 30-year study, those who had children outside of marriage reported being less healthy when they reached their 40s than those who had postponed motherhood until after marriage (Williams et al., 2011). Further, the transition to marriage for single mothers, even when it occurred after motherhood, did not appear to have a positive effect on their health. The authors suggest that public health campaigns in the US to promote marriage, which were started by the government in 1996 and aimed at single, low-income mothers, may not actually have any positive effect on women's health. These findings underscore the need for longitudinal research on the consequences of marriage promotion in the Canadian context given the significant rise in common law unions over the past three decades.

Social Policy

This chapter would not be complete without a discussion of the relationship between mid-life families and social policy in Canada. Three central issues need to be highlighted in this regard: (1) mid-life parent–young adult co-residence; (2) social support in mid-life child–older parent relationships; and (3) diversity in mid-life families.

With young adults finding it increasingly difficult to leave the parental nest (and increasingly necessary to return) for financial reasons, parents have become the social safety net for their children regardless of their own socio-economic position (Mitchell and Gee, 1996). Since research in this area has, for the most part, focused on middle- to upper-class parents (those with the financial means to assist adult children through co-resident living arrangements), the experiences of low-income families have been all but ignored. In Canada, the consequences for young adult children are most dire for those whose parents lack the financial means to provide assistance by allowing them to stay at (or return) home. Cuts to social welfare programs over time have weakened the "knots of the net" in low-income families, increasing the likelihood of earlier than expected launches and the posting of "no re-entry" signs for children wanting to return home. As a result, young adult children may be forced into a cycle of poverty, living out on the streets, suffering from chronic unemployment or underemployment, and subsequently engaging in high-risk behaviours like drug and alcohol abuse.

The issue of social support to older parents has been of primary interest to governments in light of reductions to health-care spending in this country. At one time, a shared responsibility existed between government and family; now, the provision of social support and **caregiving** to older adults has been pushed further and further away from the public into the family domain. Responsibility for support has become more "informalized" as hospital and community support service budgets have been cut. Who bears the brunt of this excess burden for care? The onus falls squarely on the shoulders of mid-life women—the **sandwich generation**—who are the primary caregivers to older parents and parents-in-law in addition to co-resident adolescent and/or young adult children. As a result of this "caregiving squeeze," middle-aged women have a higher likelihood of transitioning from full-time to part-time employment or of leaving the paid workforce altogether. To date, despite the findings from numerous research studies and reports (e.g., Fast et al., 1997; Keating et al., 1999), neither government nor employer-supported policy has adequately addressed the issue of paid leave for **elder care** for mid-life women.

Recognition of the diversity in mid-life Canadian families in the policy domain has been limited for the most part to issues of class, gender, and family structure. For example, governments have focused their efforts on the development of social welfare policy and programs for young to middle-age single mothers (female-headed lone-parent families) living at or below the low-income cut-off line (LICO), a group characterized by intersecting identity markers of diversity. With the continuing emergence of diverse family forms in mid-life, such as gay- and lesbian-headed families and childless (by choice or not) couples, it is imperative that governments develop and institute policies that address and attempt to break down systemic barriers (e.g., definitions of "parent" in maternity/paternity leave policy, definitions of "family" for caregiving leave) that have, to date, served to marginalize these groups in Canadian society.

Conclusion

This chapter has provided an overview of the key research areas in the study of mid-life families in North America. Wherever possible, connections to the Canadian literature have been made. It is important to note that Statistics Canada, through the collection of detailed family data in the census and General Social Surveys (i.e., Cycles 5.0, 10.0, 15.0, 20.0, and most recently 25.0), is a valuable resource for information on changing patterns of family life over time. Co-residence, social support, caregiving, work-life balance, and

For more on work–life balance see "Studying Paid and Unpaid Work" in Chapter 9, pp. 175–6.

marital transitions are but a few of the broad topic areas relevant to mid-life families that can be explored using national data sets. The door is also now wide open to pursuing new research projects on such emergent topics as intergenerational ambivalence in mid-life parent–young adult relationships, the ethnocultural dimensions of parent–child co-residence in mid-life, and partnership satisfaction in mid-life gay and lesbian unions.

As contemporary family researchers, we need to expand our definitions of family life-course stages and recognize the linkages between lives at individual and structural levels. In addition, in a field that has long been dominated by quantitative research, greater acknowledgment and appreciation are needed of the contributions that qualitative and mixed-method studies have made and have yet to make to the growing body of literature on the family life course. Although this has been an uphill battle for many years, recent published exploratory work by Mitchell and Gee (2003), Mitchell (2006), and Carr (2005) on mid-life families have fuelled our optimism for change. Mid-life family researchers can learn much from family gerontologists, who have for some time recognized the value and importance of narrative research (see the work of Bill Randall, Gary Kenyon, Phillip Clark, Brian DeVries, and Jay Gubrium, for examples) in understanding the lived experiences of older adults and their family members.

Finally, research and policy must inform one another in the family domain. Given the increasing diversity of the Canadian population in terms of age, class, ethnicity, immigrant status, sexual orientation, and family structure, it is clear that a broader mandate for family research in this country must be developed. Such an initiative is needed to address some of the critical policy issues for mid-life families and the implications for their aging in the coming decades.

STUDY QUESTIONS

1. Discuss the term "boomerang children." What factors have contributed to the emergence of this phenomenon in mid-life Canadian families?
2. What are some of the consequences of divorce in mid-life? Of remarriage?
3. What is "intergenerational ambivalence"? How has this concept been used to examine older parent–adult child relationships?
4. Discuss why the life course perspective is an appropriate conceptual framework for exploring the nature of intergenerational relationships in mid-life families.
5. Identify some of the key policy issues related to social support in mid-life families. How might you design a study to explore the intersections of identity markers of diversity (e.g., age, ethnicity, immigration status, sexual orientation) vis-à-vis (a) living arrangements and (b) intergenerational relationships in mid-life families?

Further Readings

Connidis, Ingrid Arnet. 2001. *Family Ties and Aging*. Thousand Oaks, Calif.: Sage. This Canadian book effectively integrates theory and current research about contemporary mid- to later-life family relationships. Connidis's inclusion of discussions on the relationships of emergent family types (e.g., childless older adults, common-law partnerships, gay and lesbian partnerships) that have often been neglected or ignored in the social policy and research domains makes this a timely and important contribution to the literature on aging and families.

Donaldson, Christa. 2000. *Midlife Lesbian Parenting*. Binghamton, NY: Haworth Press. This innovative and important book focuses on the experiences of nine mid-life lesbian mothers parenting young children. The findings highlight the structural and individual (personal) challenges that face these middle-aged mothers on a day-to-day basis.

Fast, Janet E., and Norah C. Keating. 2000. *Family Caregiving and Consequences for Carers: Toward a Policy Research Agenda*. Ottawa: Canadian Policy Research Network. Commissioned by the CPRN, this is one of the first reports to outline a research agenda to examine the social policy implications of family caregiving work. Focusing on the consequences in a number of domains (e.g., work, family) for the care provider, the report highlights the need for government and employer-initiated policies and programs that are sensitive to the diverse challenges facing caregivers.

Mitchell, Barbara A., 2006. *The Boomerang Age: Transitions to Adulthood in Families*, Edison, NJ: Aldine. Focusing on families in mid-life, it is the first Canadian book to explore the complex structural and personal dimensions of family relationships and their implications during the transition to adulthood stage of the family life course.

Settersten, Richard A., Jr. 1999. *Lives in Time and Place: The Problems and Promises of Developmental Science.* Amityville, NY: Baywood. Integrating life-course concepts, theory, and research from sociology, psychology, and anthropology, this book breaks new ground in the aging and life-course literature. It successfully argues for the adoption of a more integrated, interdisciplinary approach to the study of human lives over time that more fully explores the relationship between social structure and agency in such domains as work, education, and the family. Policy-relevant discussions are highlighted throughout.

Websites

http://olderwomensnetwork.org/fightfor/
This website provides a listing and outline of the advocacy issues that the Older Women's Network (Ontario Inc.) focus on for women in mid- to later life.

www.swc-cfc.gc.ca/rc-cr/pub/index-eng.html
A comprehensive listing of Status of Women Canada's policy research publications, this list includes publications on the integration into policy research, development, and analysis of identity markers of diversity for women.

http://assets.aarp.org/rgcenter/general/divorce_1.pdf
Featuring links to the both the executive summary and the full report, this website provides a discussion of the key findings from a groundbreaking American Association of Retired Persons (AARP) study (2004) on divorce in mid- and later life.

www.vanierinstitute.ca/research_and_publications
The Vanier Institute website provides a comprehensive collection of research topics and publications on families over the life course in Canada, including a presentation of research findings on families in mid-life.

www.asaging.org/lain
The Lesbian and Gay Aging Issues Network (LAIN), a constituent unit of the American Society on Aging, brings together professionals and academics from all disciplines in the field of aging to address the unique concerns of older lesbians and gay men (also relevant to mid-life lesbians and gays). The organization's home pages include a selection of useful articles from the group's quarterly newsletter, *OutWord*.

Notes

1. It should also be noted here that a growing number of Canadian adults are opting not to have children, thereby increasing the number of childless couples in mid-life.
2. According to Statistics Canada (2008), the age profile of separated and divorced Canadians is changing: from 1986 to 2002, the median age at divorce increased to 44 for men and 41 for women.

7

Aging in Canadian Families Today

NEENA L. CHAPPELL

LEARNING OBJECTIVES

- To gain an overview of some of the characteristics of Canada's older adults now and in the future
- To learn the central role families continue to play in the lives of older adults and that older adults continue play in the lives of their families
- To understand how the different facets of our health change as we age
- To understand what family caregiving entails
- To recognize how the formal health care system can assist family caregivers
- To learn how families and the health care system interface and could do so differently

Introduction

It is only recently that, for the first time in history, virtually everyone is living to old age (barring wars, accidents, etc.). This has a profound effect on families, of whatever form. It matters not whether one is in a heterosexual, homosexual, lesbian, single parent, or blended family—its members can now expect to live to old age and within old age, to live for approximately another 20 years. And one can expect to live with more generations alive than was true in the past (referred to as **vertical extension**) but with fewer siblings (referred to as **horizontal shrinkage**). These changes in the structure of the family have implications for all generations, including older adults. In this chapter we examine family life in old age with a focus on older adults themselves, although the implications for younger adults (older adults' children) and youth (older adults' grandchildren) are also discussed.

The chapter begins with a discussion of lengthening life expectancy that is resulting in a growing older population and then proceeds to profile the diversity that characterizes older adults in Canada today. Both the central role of families in the lives of older adults and the declines in physical health but not overall well-being that characterize this population are described. Attention then turns to family caregiving, the dominant care system for older adults and their first resort for care. Part of this discussion includes an examination of how other countries are supporting family caregivers but, at the present time, Canada is not. The role the health care system could play in supporting families is considered in light of the complementary relationship between family caregiving and formal services.

Canadians Are Living Longer

The first of Canada's Baby Boom Generation turned 65 years old in 2011, drawing attention to gerontological issues. The fact that we tend to define old age as beginning at age 65 is a social definition associated with the age of eligibility for Old Age Security payments and pensions. Interestingly, it is not related to the age at which people actually retire. Kapteyn (2010) compared legal retirement ages with the actual age of retirement in 18 countries around the world between 2002 and 2007. There was little relationship between the two; nor was there a relationship between average life expectancy in the country and actual age of retirement. This was true of both men and women and is characteristic of Canada. Age 65 is also unrelated to declines in health. For example, our eyesight begins declining before this age; our hair typically turns grey before this age; and there is no sudden deterioration simply because we turn 65. Importantly, with the end of mandatory retirement and the upcoming increase in the age of eligibility for the Old Age Security payment, the age of eligibility for full pension benefits is also likely to rise. In time, old age will come to be seen as an age older than the current 65 years, probably 67 initially, and then perhaps 70 within the foreseeable future.

Canada, like other countries, is aging. How long we can expect to live (our **life expectancy**) has been rising since the early 1900s; in 1981 life expectancy was 76 years; in 2006 it was 81 years. However, those who reached 65 years of age could expect to live even longer, with a life expectancy at that age of another 20 years, i.e., they could expect to live to 85 (Statistics Canada, 2010b). The impending size of the old age cohort when all of the baby boomers are 65 or older has lead to the labelling of this generation as the "grey tsunami." It is true that both the numbers and proportions of older adults within the Canadian population is increasing. In 2010, 15.3 per cent of Canada's population was 65 years of age or older; in 2030 the proportion will be 24.1 per cent (representing 4,386,969 and 7,844,309 individuals respectively) (Denton and Spencer, 2010). By 2015 it is expected that the proportion of older adults will be greater than the proportion of youth, those less than 15 years of age (CIHI, 2011) (see Figure 7.1). Many European countries have life expectancies at the present time that are higher than Canada's. The highest life expectancy is found in Japan (23.1 per cent of their population was 65 or older in 2010, comprised of 29.29 million people) (Statistics Bureau, 2008).

As the baby boomers age so too does the elderly population become older. For example, in 2010, 13 per cent of seniors were 85 and older. In 2052, 24 per cent of seniors will be in this age group (2 and 6 per cent of all Canadians respectively). After 2031 the percentage of older adults age 65 to 74 (the **young elderly**) will begin to decrease as the post-baby boom generation enters the ranks of older old citizens (CIHI, 2011). Living longer translates into

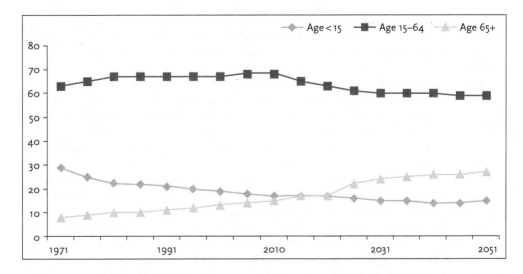

Figure 7.1 **Composition of the Population by Age, Canada, 1971 to 2051**

SOURCE: Statistics Canada, 2010b, population estimates, 1971 to 2010, and population projections, 2009 to 2036

most young children knowing their grandparents, both grandmothers and grandfathers sharing these experiences much longer, indeed into young adulthood; adult children will have their parents alive much longer; and older adults will have extended families of three, four, and sometimes five generations alive at one time.

While we have come to expect that each generation will live longer than the preceding one, there are concerns that this may not hold for those who are college students today. Rising rates of obesity suggest they could have a shorter life span than their parents—the baby boomers. The dramatic decrease in the life expectancy of men in Russia, down to 58 in the early 1990s after the collapse of the former Soviet Union, demonstrates how quickly trends can reverse (Magnus, 2009). Feshbach (2001) attributes this to decades of environmentally destructive practices including but not restricted to conventional air and water pollution and contamination around nuclear and chemical sites throughout the country, including in densely populated areas. Diseases such as heart disease, tuberculosis, hepatitis B, and HIV/AIDS are confounded with social problems including poverty, alcoholism, and drug abuse. At the same time, fertility dropped so dramatically that, by the early 1980s, Russian women were bearing little more than half the number of children required to maintain population size.

Older Canadians: A Profile

Canada's older adults are diverse, not surprising given that they span over 20 years. More older adults today are women than men and the differential grows the older the age that is examined. In 2010, 52 per cent of those aged 65 to 74 were women while 60 per cent of those aged 75 and older were women. The income of older adults has been increasing over time, with fewer falling below the low income cut-off set by the government of Canada. Nevertheless, the income gap during retirement between elderly men and elderly women is still evident. In 2008, elderly women's mean after-tax income was only 65 per cent of that of men; this was no different from the mid-2000s (a $13,300 gap) (CIHI, 2011).

For more on immigrants to Canada, see "Immigrants" in Chapter 12, pp. 229–31.

Most seniors were born in Canada, although 28 per cent in 2006 were immigrants (Public Health Agency of Canada, 2010). Most of these immigrants moved to Canada when they were young, which means that they spent most of their adult lives in Canada. Not all immigrants are **visible minorities** (persons, other than Aboriginal people, not white in race or colour) and not all visible minorities are immigrants. The situation is different still when examining Aboriginals who constitute only 1.4 per cent of Canadian seniors, due to their lower life expectancy (Turcotte and Schellenberg, 2007).

Not all seniors are retired; as noted above, legal retirement age and actual retirement age are unrelated. This is likely to continue with the abolition of mandatory retirement. Although in the mid-1970s to the mid-1980s it was normal to retire around 65, this has subsequently changed, dropping to around 60 by the late 1990s. A lowering of the minimum age for drawing benefits from the Canada Pension Plan (albeit with reduced benefits) and widespread government cutbacks, corporate downsizing, and incentives to retire early were all likely contributing factors. By 2005 the age of retirement had risen slightly to 61. Most people retire voluntarily (three-quarters) but just over one-quarter do so involuntarily due to mandatory retirement at the time, becoming unemployed and being unable to find another job, downsizing, and the number one reason—ill health. Those with less education are more likely to be forced into retirement. The vast majority of retirees enjoy life just as much or more than prior to retirement (almost 90 per cent).

Retirement typically affords time for leisure that we did not have before. Older adults spend more time than previously on sleep and rest, as well as personal care; domestic chores; and shopping, reading, and watching television. Turcotte and Schellenberg (2007) report on four types of leisure activity engaged in by Canadian seniors: passive, cognitive, social, and physical leisure. Passive leisure includes activities such as watching TV, listening to the radio, and driving for pleasure. Cognitive leisure refers to things such as reading, educational pursuits, entertainment events, hobbies, playing cards, and using the computer. Social leisure refers to spending time with friends and relatives and talking on the phone. Physical leisure refers to physical activity. Combining cognitive, social, and physical leisure into an active leisure category, they find that older adult men spend more time in active leisure than passive leisure until after 75 years of age; older adult women spend more time in active than in passive leisure even beyond age 75.

Among older adults today, most are married, especially men: 44.1 per cent of women and 73.9 per cent of men in 2006 (Statistics Canada, 2006). Among women almost as many are widowed (42.7 per cent of women; 12.7 per cent of men). This gender differential is due to the fact that women have a longer life expectancy than men and also marry men a few years older than themselves, a combination that results in husbands typically dying first (with consequences for caregiving, discussed later on). While widowhood increases with age, the gender gap also increases the older one becomes (see Figure 7.2).

Because of this marital status difference, older women are more likely to live alone than are older men. In 2006, 17.5 per cent of older men lived alone whereas 37.6 per cent

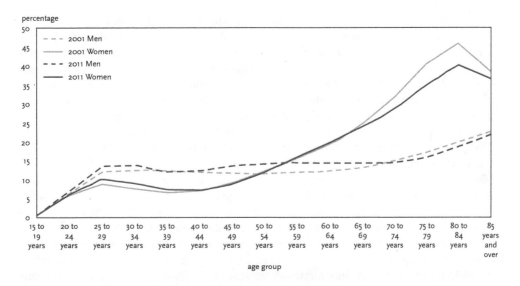

percentage

Figure 7.2 **Percentage of the Population Aged 15 and Over Living Alone by Age Group, Canada, 2001 and 2011**

SOURCE: Statistics Canada, 2012e, http://www12.statcan.gc.ca/census-recensement/2011/as-sa/98-312-x/2011003/fig/fig3_4-2-eng.cfm, p. 2.

of older women lived alone (Statistics Canada, 2006b). Most men live only with their spouse (61.4 per cent) while the proportion for women is about the same as those living alone (35.4 per cent) (Statistics Canada, 2006b). These gender differences mean that older women are much more likely to change their living arrangements in later life and there are implications for the care they receive (discussed later). Whether this is desirable or not is unresolved in the literature; it likely varies depending on the person and their circumstances. For some it will be a welcome independence, for others it can mean loneliness and lack of support.

Fewer older Canadians live in multigenerational households or with their children although this is more common among immigrant families than non-immigrant families. For example, in 2001, fewer than 3 per cent of those who were Canadian-born lived in multigenerational households but 7 per cent of those born outside of Canada did so (Milan and Hamm, 2003). And some groups, such as the Chinese, tend to live with both their spouse and their adult children when they are older rather than only their spouse as is common in Canada. Among Chinese seniors living in Canada, Chappell and Kusch (2007) find that 13.5 per cent live with only their spouse, 8.7 per cent live alone, and the remainder live with both their spouse and their children. They live with children often before their own or their spouses' health declines.

Older adults today have less formal education than baby boomers or younger adults, not surprising given that access to post-secondary education did not open up until the 1960s. As each cohort enters old age, therefore, more and more seniors will be characterized by higher levels of education. As society has transformed with knowledge intensity and complexity, literacy and numeracy become increasingly important to understand and seek out information related to life matters including finances, health, and housing. In 2003, over 80 per cent of Canadian seniors possessed prose literacy skills considered insufficient to cope in our complex society; similar figures are evident for document literacy and numeracy (Turcotte and Schellenberg, 2007). This will change as the baby boomers grow old but it is especially important to recognize for older adults today in terms of how society makes information available. Relatedly, computer use is lower in older adult households than those younger. Among those 65 and over, households with Internet access increased from 3.4 per cent to 22.7 per cent between 1990 and 2003. In 2010, 51 per cent of those 65 to 74 years old used the Internet and 27 per cent of those 75 years and older used it (Statistics Canada, 2011).

Older adults, like younger adults, often participate in organizations. In fact, just over half (54 per cent) were members of at least one organization in 2003, the same as for those aged 25 to 54. The figure decreases, but not substantially for those 75 and over (to 46 per cent). Frequency of participation is also similar among younger and older adults with 43 per cent saying they participate at least once a week. However, seniors are more likely to participate in religious organizations and senior men in service clubs, and they are less likely to participate in sports, health, school, neighbourhood, civic, or community organizations than are those who are younger (Turcotte and Schellenberg, 2007). This represents differences in both life stages and interests. Both higher levels of education and having been involved in the organizations when younger predict involvement in the later years.

Over one-third of older adults volunteer their time to charities and other non-profit organizations (39 per cent in 2004) and those between 65 and 74 contributed an average of 250 hours each of volunteering in 2004. Health often prevents older adults from volunteering; again those with more education and those who volunteered in the past are more likely to volunteer in their later years. Volunteering helps not only the community, but older adults as well. Volunteering brings social connectedness, and volunteers report having more friends and more close friends than do non-volunteers (Hall, et al., 2006).

Older adults are interested in current affairs, with the vast majority (89 per cent) following the news daily; this is substantially more than the 68 per cent of 25-to-54-year-olds who do so. While those who have more education are more likely to do so, even among those aged 65 to 74 with less than high school education, more (85 per cent) are up-to-date with the news than are 25-to-64-year-olds with a university degree (74 per cent) (Turcotte and Schellenberg, 2007). Older adults are more likely to vote in municipal, provincial, and federal elections than are younger adults and, overall, voter turn-out increases with age. In the 2008 federal election in Canada, 37.4 per cent of those who voted were 18 to 24 and 68.4 per cent 65 to 74 (Elections Canada, 2008).

Families Are Alive and Well

Despite the fact that we hear much about changes taking place in today's society, families—and the function of families as we age—appear to be intact regardless of the form those families take. Women now are often employed, grown children sometimes move to geographically distant places, and we live in an individually oriented and self-preoccupied society. The older and middle generations, that is, are independent and separate. Research, however, does not verify claims of the demise of the family. Rather, immediate family members constitute the largest proportion of older adults' social networks. Fully 98 per cent of older adults say they have a family member or friend they feel close to (Turcotte and Schellenberg, 2007), with 89 per cent identifying relatives they are close to and 83 per cent identifying friends (Schellenberg, 2004). The death of a spouse, other family member, or friends, as well as living alone and childlessness can place an individual more at risk of social isolation and also loneliness (Koybashi et al., 2009; Sykorova, 2008).

The flow of interaction and assistance between the generations is bidirectional and reciprocal. Frequent and affectionate interaction across the generations is the norm and the interactions are stable over several decades (Roberts and Bengston, 1996). Furthermore, the older adult generation gives more to their children than their children give to them, at least until, and sometimes continuing into, very old age. The older parent generation helps with in-kind support such as baby-sitting and, notably in the early stages of their grown children's lives, with finances when able. Adult children tend to assist their parents more when the parent's health fails (more about this later).

Because of increased longevity and vertical extension of the generations, most children now have grandparents. In 2001 there were 5.7 million grandparents who had, on average, 4.7 grandchildren. Most first become grandparents in their late 40s or early 50s; as a result, not all grandparents are retired (53 per cent were retired in 2001) (BC Council for Families, 2011). Today, grandparents and grandchildren can expect to have 20 years together and for some, especially grandmothers, 30 years. Grandparents play an important role in the lives of their children and their grandchildren. They babysit; they transmit family history, traditions, and values; and they can be confidants and role models. How grandparents feel about their relationships with their grandchildren varies depending on how often they see each other; the quality and amount of time spent alone with their grandchildren; whether they give advice to their own children about raising the grandchildren; whether they give advice to their grandchildren; the quality and amount of time they spend with their grandchildren when the parents are not at work; whether they talk to their grandchildren about day-to-day issues such as household chores, homework, school, etc.; how often they send "traditional" mail to their grandchildren, that is, letters and cards; and how important each of these things is to the grandparent (AARP, 2002).

Several provinces have laws in their child welfare legislation that give rights to grandparents to have access to their grandchildren and some give priority to grandparents and other family members as caregivers when the parents cannot provide care (Devine and Earle, 2011). In the decade between 1991 and 2001, the number of Canadian children under 18 years of age living with their grandparents without a parent in the home increased by 20 per cent, especially among First Nations peoples. Despite high rates of poverty among First Nations peoples, they were nevertheless more likely to be raising grandchildren, to be raising two or more grandchildren, and to also be caring for a senior (Fuller-Thomson, 2005). However, as MacKenzie and colleagues (2005) note, when governments make it more difficult for the service system to accept children and pressure families to provide the care, grandparents can become the only option families have. They often accept the responsibility at great personal sacrifice and can do so either continuously or sporadically depending on the parent's situation.

In 2006, 65,000 children in Canada were being raised by their grandparents without a parent in the household (Snell, 2008). These **skip-generation** households (i.e., those with grandparents and grandchildren but no middle [parental] generation living in the household) typically arise because the parents are unable or unwilling to care for their own children due to substance abuse, mental health problems, teen pregnancy, child abuse or neglect, or death. Most skip-generation grandparents are women (67 per cent) and are married (57 per cent) (Milan and Hamm, 2003). In 2006, similar to 2001 (Statistics Canada, 2009a), 0.5 per cent of children in Canada aged 14 and younger lived in skip-generation households.

Health in Old Age

It is deteriorating health in old age that causes so much concern over the affordability of our health care system. A common refrain is that the swell of older adults that will occur when all of the baby boomers become elderly will bankrupt the system. However, declines in health will not necessarily lead to such dire consequences (the oversimplified idea that a demographic trend, in this case population aging, will lead to catastrophic consequences for society is known as **apocalyptic demography**). First, we look at their health needs. Provision of care is discussed in the next section. While it is true that our physical health declines as we age, not everyone declines in the same way, at the same rate, or with the same severity. There is great heterogeneity among those 65 and older.

Declines are most evident when examining chronic conditions and disability. Prevalence rates vary by condition but overall, 81 per cent of older adults living in the community in Canada have some chronic conditions with the average number rising with age. Those aged 65 to 74 have an average of 1.9 chronic conditions; among those aged 85 and older the rate is 2.5 (Gilmour and Park, 2006). Cardiovascular disease and cancer are common chronic conditions causing death. Other common chronic conditions include arthritis, diabetes, heart disease, high blood pressure, and mood disorders not including depression (CIHI, 2009). The overall prevalence of chronic conditions is higher among elderly women than elderly men, although the prevalence for specific conditions varies. It is often said in gerontology that "men die quicker but women are sicker" to capture the fact that women have a longer life expectancy but they also experience more poor health.

Although dementia (Alzheimer's disease is one type of dementia accounting for more than half of all cases) is a common fear among middle-aged and older adults, it afflicts only a minority in old age. The prevalence does increase the older we become. Canada's only national study examining the prevalence of dementia was the Canadian Study on Health and Aging (1994). It established the rate at between 7 per cent and 8 per cent among those aged 65 and older, with women more likely to have dementia than men; this fact could change if men achieve the same life expectancy as women. The prevalence increases to fully 35 per cent among those aged 85 and over, and the figure is 65 per cent when milder forms of cognitive impairment are added in (Graham et al., 1997; National Advisory Council on Aging, 2004).

Unlike dementia, rates of depression appear to decrease as we age, with those aged 15 to 24 the most likely to suffer from this condition. In 2002, only 1.9 per cent of elderly women and 2.1 per cent of elderly men suffered from depression; women appear less likely than men to suffer from it in this age group (Government of Canada, 2006). A recent report from CIHI (2010) claims a high rate among those living in nursing homes—fully 44 per cent—with clinically significant symptoms. It is unknown whether overall rates are low, as concerns have been expressed for some time that depression tends to go unreported. On the other hand, with the recent rise in the use of pharmaceuticals, especially for mental and mood fluctuations, we may find an over-diagnosis in the future.

The good news is that having a chronic condition does not necessarily mean that one becomes functionally disabled. Fully 80 per cent of Canadians age 65 and over are function-ally able to live independently (Canadian Encyclopedia, 2009). However, the rate of activity restriction increases with age from 12 per cent among those aged 15 to 64 to 43 per cent among those aged 65 and over (to 56 per cent among those aged 75 and over) (Statistics Canada, Turcotte and Schellenberg, 2007). The fact that, within old age, functioning disability increases, has led the World Health Organization (WHO) to claim old age starts at 75 in terms of disability (Heikkinen, 2003b). Women experience more disability than do men; they live longer with more disability (Chappell and Cooke, 2010).

For a definition of disability, see "Defining Disability" in Chapter 13, pp. 250–2.

When it comes to older Canadians' perceptions of their physical health, they accurately rate it as lower than do younger adults (among those aged 55 to 64, 48.8 per cent of men and 53.2 per cent of women rate it as excellent or very good; among those aged 65+ 39.3 per cent of men and 38.9 per cent of women do so).

We do not know whether the baby-boomers will have better, worse, or similar health to those currently elderly. The rates of some chronic conditions (such as cardiovascular disease, arthritis/rheumatism, hypertension and bronchitis/emphysema) have declined between the 1970s and 1990s but, for other conditions such as diabetes, asthma, migraine headaches, and the total number of chronic conditions, the rates have increased (Wister, 2005). In terms of disability, a decreasing trend in some countries has led to optimism for the future but this trend does not characterize many countries and it does not characterize Canada. In fact, a recent study by Keefe and colleagues (2012) reports the overall rate of disability among Canadian older adults has decreased but it is accounted for by a decrease in mild disability. Those with moderate and severe disability have increased from 1996 to 2001 (by 4 per cent and 2 per cent respectively).

The Public Health Agency of Canada (PHAC) defines mental health (as opposed to mental illness) as:

> the capacity of each and all of us to feel, think, and act in ways that enhance our ability to enjoy life and deal with the challenges we face. It is a positive sense of emotional and spiritual well-being that respects the importance of culture, equity, social justice, interconnections and personal dignity. (CIHI, 2009: 3)

In Canada, most older adults rate mental health as good and the difference with younger adult groups is slight (70.1 per cent of elderly men and 69.4 per cent of elderly women say their mental health is excellent or very good while the figures are 72.5 per cent and 73.3 per cent respectively for those aged 55 to 64) (Penning and Chappell, 2010; Statistics Canada, 2010b; 2010c). The same high perceptions are found when examining overall well-being, happiness, and life satisfaction. Older adults are at least as happy as younger adults, perhaps even happier (Statistics Canada, 2006b). Fully 79 per cent of older women and 77 per cent of older men say they are happy with another 19 per cent of older women and 19 per cent of older men saying they are somewhat happy (Milan and Vézina, 2011).

All of this is to say that yes, our physical health declines as we age and continues to do so within old age. However, not all chronic conditions lead to functioning difficulties and older adults, while having realistic views of their health, nevertheless reveal high levels of overall well-being. Furthermore, we each age individually, so while these statistics refer to the group as a whole, each older person ages differently. And, in fact, severe poor health tends to occur in old-old age (defined variously in the literature as 75+, 80+, 85+, 90+) and happens to only a proportion of us. **Frailty** does not happen to all older adults but the term refers to something broader than disability alone or disease state alone, even though it is difficult to distinguish from both. There is no consensus on a definition of frailty, but it generally refers to a vulnerability to adverse outcomes resulting from the interaction of the simultaneous deterioration of many organ systems (Hogan et al., 2003; Rockwood and Mitnitski, 2007). The proportion who are frail varies depending on how it is measured and, as yet, there is no consensus on the best way to do that (Song et al., 2010).

Interest in identifying those who are frail is reflective of the longstanding gerontological interest in distinguishing between those elderly persons who maintain their independence in their later years and those who become dependent. This effort is evident in the gerontological literature since the 1970s with many terms emerging to mark the distinction including young-old, middle-old, and old-old as well as successful aging, productive aging, active aging, and robust aging. The definitions vary, typically embracing physical aging but also sometimes including quality of life. What they have in common is an attempt to distinguish "good" aging from less desirable aging and implicitly denigrate and redefine those who are "old" as undesirable (Chappell and Penning, 2012).

We grow old within families, irrespective of whether we live in the same household with them. Families become especially important when our health fails; this continues to be true as we age. This is the topic of the next section.

Families: The Mainstay of Care

When the health of older adults has deteriorated such that they can no longer function independently, they require care. **Informal care** is a type of social support that comes from family and friends and is referred to as caring, caregiving, assistance, support, and interaction, among other terms. It can be instrumental (tangible) and/or emotional (intangible). It is the major form of care in old age accounting for between 75 per cent and 90 per cent of the total personal care provided to older adults (Kane et al., 1990; RAPP, 2010). The four activities most related to **long-term home support** from family and friends (primarily family) are housework, shopping, meal preparation, and personal care. Furthermore, over one-third of elderly women and just under one-half of elderly men receive all of their care from family and friends with no assistance from formal services (Lafrenière et al., 2003).

We distinguish between informal (family and friend) and formal caregiving and typically characterize the former as not being paid and as involving an emotional aspect. We consider formal care as involving pay and tasks without a major emotional component.

That distinction is, though, often blurred. Family caregivers usually also perform skilled tasks and formal care providers will often refer to emotional relationships with their clients, sometimes referring to them as family-like (Chappell, 2008; Ward-Griffin and Marshall, 2003). Sometimes older adults pay informal caregivers monetarily or in-kind; sometimes older adults receive assistance from formally organized but unpaid volunteer agencies.

Because a family member is providing care, it does not mean that they identify themselves as a caregiver. It also does not mean that they perceive what they do as work (O'Connor, 2007). When and how an individual comes to view themselves as a caregiver—and not all do—is not understood. However, assistance within reciprocal interdependencies or exchanges where the persons involved are capable of performing the activities even though they do not, would not be considered caregiving. An example is the gendered division of labour often found within households where women prepare the meals and do the housework and men look after the yard and the cars; each is capable of doing the others' tasks but does not; this is not caregiving.

Most (but certainly not all) caregivers are women (56.5 per cent in 2007), typically wives because women tend to marry men older than themselves and they have a longer life expectancy than their husbands. When the husband's health begins to decline, the wife is there to assist him. However, by the time the wife's health begins to fail, she is widowed. Then it is typically her daughter who assists her. Most caregivers are aged 45 to 65 although one-quarter are themselves seniors. Within the gendered division of labour, women tend to provide the equivalent of 1.5 days per week of care while men provide on average 1 work day per week; women tend to assist with homemaking, personal care, and emotional support whereas men tend to assist with instrumental tasks such as home repair. Women are also more likely to organize the overall care. However, when there is no female available, sons step in and care. Most are providing care to someone living in the community (just under 85 per cent) with the remainder caring for someone living in a residential care facility or supportive housing (Cranswick and Dosman, 2008; RAPP, 2010). That is, the care continues when the older adult enters a long-term care institution but there is often a shift from more direct care to more indirect (overseeing) care; emotional support continues (Keefe and Fancey, 2000).

Social class differences can affect caregiving. Those in disadvantaged positions in society are more likely to experience poorer health than those in more advantaged positions (i.e., social class is a social determinant of health); in consequence, they require more care and place heavier demands on family members. However, family members also have fewer resources to assist them in their caregiving roles. Interestingly, Glaser and Grundy (2002), when comparing care provision among manual compared with non-manual groups, found that the greater likelihood of co-resident care among manual groups was accounted for by the fact that spouses in the manual group were more likely to have worse health and therefore needed care. Furthermore, among unmarried persons, women in the non-manual groups were more likely to be providing co-resident care for a parent than women among manual workers, resulting from the fact that more women among non-manual workers are unmarried. That is, the long-standing finding that the unmarried, especially the never married, are more likely to be the caregiver to a parent in old age than are children who are married, still holds.

Perhaps unexpectedly, partnership dissolution (separation, divorce) does not necessarily translate into a lack of support in later life. Ex-family still often provide assistance in old age when the individual needs it (Glaser et al., 2008), although divorced men see their children less and receive less assistance from them than do divorced women (DeJong Gierveld et al., 1997; Lin, 2008). Similarly, geographically mobile families, both across and within countries, also maintain connections with older family members and strive to meet their needs (Antonucci et al., 2007).

The relevance of ethnicity or subcultural group is related to their history of disadvantage similar to class-based inequalities and includes socio-economic, physical environment, and formal social network disadvantages. These hardships of a lifetime, including discrimination and prejudice, can accumulate so that in old age poor health is the result (Bajekal et al., 2004; Nazroo et al., 2004). The assumption that these groups are characterized by high **familism** that includes care of their older members, especially care by adult children of their older parents, receives very mixed support in the literature.

What we do know is that social support varies depending on the group and this includes variation among different ethnic groups. For example, Nazroo and colleagues (2004) report in Great Britain that South Asians have intense routine support systems among family members; black-Caribbean and mixed white- and black-Caribbean older adults tend to live close to one child but not to other children. Moriarty and Butt (2004) find that Indians, Pakistanis, and Bangladeshis live close to many members of their families and to each other; Chinese, blacks, and black-Caribbeans live further apart, sometimes in different countries. The Chinese in Canada historically lived in ethnic enclaves but currently they are younger, better educated, have well-paying jobs, and live outside of Chinatowns among other Canadians (Li, 1998). Furthermore, virtually all families support one another, irrespective of ethnic origin or social class, although how they do so can vary. The extent to which ethnic group provision of care emanates from their normative culture or out of necessity (they cannot afford to hire help) is unknown because of the confounding of low social class with many ethnic groups. It could well be related to both.

One of the major concerns for family caregivers is the stress and **burden** that can accompany this role. Family caregiving can result in depression, guilt, worry, anxiety, loneliness, worse health for the caregiver, social inactivity, and isolation (Ho et al., 2009; Vitaliano et al., 2003). Those at higher risk of experiencing stress and burden include those providing more extensive assistance, with lower income, lower formal educational levels, women, and those who are younger, typically non-spouses (Navaie-Waliser et al., 2002; Pinquart and Sorenson, 2003; Robison et al., 2009). A poorer quality relationship between the two family members and not receiving help from formal services have also been related to greater burden (Lyonette and Yardley, 2003).

The extent to which being employed adds to the burden of the adult child caregiver is unresolved. For some, it provides respite from the demands of caregiving. Research findings are inconsistent (Kemp and Rosenthal, 2001; Penning, 1998) but most of these studies examine whether the caregiver is employed or not. They study employment status, not the effects of caregiving on employment. When Reid and colleagues (2010) examined the perceived effects of caregiving on working outside the home, they found the status of employment (working or not) unrelated to well-being, self-esteem, or burden. However, among those who are employed, they also studied the total number of work interruptions. Those reporting their performance at work is affected due to their caregiving are more likely to feel greater burden and lower levels of both self-esteem and well-being.

Despite the interest in stress and burden, we also know that family caregivers are coping. Health Canada (2002) finds that 43 per cent say they are coping very well and 49 per cent say they are coping generally well; less than 5 per cent report they are not coping well. Nevertheless, fully 70 per cent also say that caregiving has been stressful, close to 80 per cent say they experience emotional stress, 54 per cent say they have some difficulties with finances, and 70 per cent say they need a break either frequently or occasionally. That is, families are there for one another and help one another during old age, even with the stresses and demands of the role. Furthermore, being burdened as a caregiver does not mean overall well-being is lowered. Burden and overall well-being are two distinct concepts even though caregiver burden affects overall well-being (Chappell and Reid, 2002). This occurs because being a caregiver is only part of our lives, albeit for some it can be a majority part. Among those who are burdened, most are not burdened all of the time and most nevertheless want to continue in this role.

We also know that family caregivers express many satisfactions emanating from the care they provide. Self-affirmation, self-confidence, learning about oneself and about aging, a sense of satisfaction, enjoyment, a closer relationship with the care recipient, improved well-being, and greater tolerance of others are among the satisfactions mentioned (Tarlow et al., 2004; Braithwaite, 1998). Spouses derive satisfaction from fulfilling their marital vows and adult children from fulfilling filial obligations and giving back (Pinquart and Sorenson, 2003). Both negative and positive aspects of caregiving co-exist as is true of most roles and relationships (Andren and Elhmstahl, 2005).

Furthermore, despite the popularity of the terms **sandwich generation, generation in the middle,** and "hidden victims" to refer to adult children in the baby boom generation who are caring for their parents and still raising their own children and sometimes also being employed, the terms are misnomers. This situation refers to no more than one-quarter of middle-aged caregivers (Penning, 1998; Williams, 2005) with at least three-quarters not sandwiched. Rather, the adult child usually provides care to a parent after their own children have grown and left the home and prior to caring for a spouse, usually a wife caring for her husband. **Serial caregiving** more aptly captures the situation of most caregivers. It is not known which situation is more stressful, performing all or most of one's caregiving at once or doing it serially over a longer period of time, or for whom. (See the "Case in Point" box for a discussion of current issues regarding caregiving.)

And in the Future?

What will family care for older adults look like in the future? To a large extent we do not know. What we do know is that for the time being we are living longer with more complex health problems. That is, those who live to old age are no longer only the healthy survivors but rather virtually all of us, with many health problems. We do not know whether families can provide much, if any, more care than they currently provide or whether families in the future will be capable of the complex care that will be required by many. And the baby boomers will have fewer surviving children to provide care than is true of the older adults preceding them.

CASE IN POINT
Who Will Care for Canada's Older Population?

This issue is in the forefront of many public discussions hosted by different levels of government, health care organizations, think tanks, and "the public." Possible solutions range from privatizing Canada's health care system, allowing both the public and private systems to co-exist, to revamping the public system. Within the latter, suggestions abound: fund only proven interventions, include pharmaceuticals of proven value, incorporate home care, support caregivers. There are also suggestions that we promote better family cohesion (suggesting families are not sufficiently cohesive now and are not doing enough)! Calls for federal leadership have been heard for well over two decades.

Despite the popularity of "evidence-based" and "evidence-informed" decision making within government circles, the lack of action is striking. Much science exists to inform this area, some of which has been reviewed in this chapter. Yet debate continues, science remains largely ignored, and governments do little to protect public health care in this country.

Why do you think we have this situation?

What solutions are possible?

Drawing on the fact that the main family caregivers today are spouses and adult children, and knowing much about marriage, divorce, and fertility rates among baby boomers, it is possible to somewhat project availability of informal caregivers. Gaymu and colleagues (2007) project a decrease in widowhood that will primarily affect women. This will result from an increase in male life expectancy that is larger than for women so more women will be married longer within old age. As a consequence, Keefe and colleagues (2007) expect the proportion of older adults living alone will not increase, and may slightly decrease depending on the specific years being examined. Those with at least one surviving child will also increase. These projections refer to the proportion of older adults in intact marriages and with surviving children, both of which will increase from what we know today.

When we look at *numbers*, rather than percentages, the size of the baby boom generation will result in more older adults not in a marriage and without surviving children than was true in 2001. That is, those most likely to require the most help—those living alone and those without children—will increase in numbers, although this change will not be dramatic until after 2020. When the baby boomers start to turn 75, their health will deteriorate most (Gaymu et al., 2007). It is estimated that the older population in need of care will increase by 2.5 per cent between 2026 and 2051 (Keefe et al., 2007).

These projections do not tell us whether old-old couples, possibly both members having complex health problems, will be able to care for one another. We do know that men caring for wives are more likely to seek assistance than are women caring for husbands; they are also more likely to institutionalize their wives (Martel and Légaré, 2001; Delbès and Gaymu, 2006). Whether rates of divorce and marriage dissolution will increase is also unknown; we know that at present those who live alone and need care are more likely to receive formal services than are those living with someone, usually a spouse (Grundy, 2006). We do not know how willing new partners who have been together a short time will be to provide extensive care. Also unknown are the ways in which adult children will change their views on care provision for their parents. In Quebec, Guberman and colleagues (2012) find that baby boomers currently caring for their parents are setting limits to their caregiving. They expect services through public support to assist in this role and to do so while also adhering to the norms of family responsibility. However, the baby boomers have more siblings than their parents: a potential source of care.

Baby boomers are distinctive in other ways. They are more highly educated as a group than their parents and therefore more likely to have worked in professional and managerial positions, and they are more ethnically diverse. They also have fewer children (today's college-age children) than their parents, are more likely to have separated and divorced, and have developed different family forms. Their life histories are more varied, likely with more transitions in their employment careers and more transitions in and out of the labour force. Their parents, those who are elderly today, tended to have less fluid life courses wherein they remained married, transitioned into employment and stayed there until they retired, had less formal education, and had more children. The baby boomers are the generation of feminist and gay rights, of the sexual and drug revolutions, and of unprecedented consumerism (Pruchno, 2012). They are though, like their parents, embedded in families.

Formal Care to Assist Families

It is accepted in virtually all societies that families bear some responsibility to care for their members and generally, families do so willingly and often prefer to do so rather than bringing formal services into the home. It might be concluded that an obvious policy choice is, therefore, to support caregivers but currently no national policy exists. Policies and programs that support caregivers are important for a variety of reasons. We need family caregivers; the formal care system could never replace all that caregivers do; caregivers want to provide care for family members; many caregivers make great sacrifices in order to provide the care that they do; and without assistance in this role, caregivers' own health can deteriorate and result in greater demands on the formal health care system at much greater cost.

Federally, there are a few modest tax measures, such as compassionate care leave, available through the employment insurance program and the Federal Family Caregiver Tax Credit. There are many calls for greater financial support through tax initiatives, more adequate compassionate care leave provisions, flexible workplace arrangements, greater pension security and other income support measures, direct payment to caregivers reimbursing their expenses, compensation and indirect financial support, pension credits and dropouts from pensions, as well as calls for the federal government to take a lead role ensuring family caregiving is recognized in legislation, policy, and practice (British Columbia Law Institute and the Canadian Centre for Elder Law, 2010; Canadian Cancer Society, 2011; Canadian Caregiver Coalition, 2008; Special Senate Committee on Aging, 2009). To date, little action has been forthcoming.

Other services, also few in number, fall under provincial jurisdiction. Limited **respite** services are the only services for caregivers per se (i.e., rather than the older adult, although services for the older adult can certainly assist the family caregiver). Three forms of respite are typically offered: sitter attendant services giving short breaks to caregivers; adult daycare where the older adult leaves the home for a few hours a week; and short-term respite beds in nursing homes. Manitoba (News Release, 2011) recently proclaimed an annual Caregiver Recognition Day to recognize and acknowledge the work of caregivers.

Despite Canada's scarcity of formal assistance for family caregivers, several other countries provide much more. For example, since the 1980s Denmark has given home help free of charge to older adults based on a needs assessment, not means-tested, and also provides financial incentives for caregivers (Leeson, 2004). In addition, family caregivers are entitled to lost earnings if they are caring for a dying relative and a medical assessment reveals that hospital treatment is futile. Families, including the older adult(s) involved, decide whether care is to be provided by the local authority, a private person, or an authorized private service. The local authority pays irrespective of which is chosen. Finland provides allowances for the caregiver, whether a relative or another person, and the family caregiver has the right to two days off per month at which time the municipality arranges for the care and insures the family caregiver against injury and provides pension benefits (Ministry of Social Affairs and Health, 2006; Parkatti, 2004).

Australia's Home and Community Care Program recognizes caregivers both as clients and as integral to care for older adults. This program provides respite care options, general community support services, information and counselling, employment-related benefits, and cash benefits for the extra costs of co-residence with the care recipient (20 per cent of the single-rate retirement pension; it is not means-tested or taxable). If a caregiver is unable to work due to caregiving, they can apply for a means-tested payment that is equivalent to the retirement pension (Goodhead and McDonald, 2007).

We do, furthermore, know something about the types of interventions that are good for the health of family caregivers to older adults. Chappell and Pridham (2010) conducted a review of the international literature on such interventions and note that the ones that are successful include an assessment by trained assessors; an assessment of caregivers early and on an ongoing basis; sufficient resources to adequately address the needs identified; the active involvement of the caregiver in developing multidimensional and flexible programs tailored for them; caregivers being viewed as partners as well as clients who have needs and are treated accordingly; the facilitation of caregivers' self-identification and recognition of their own needs; options that are culturally sensitive; and the implementation being evaluated and outcomes being monitored.

Support for family caregivers can also include, with or without support from the formal care system, sectors outside of the formal health care system such as voluntary organizations, churches and other not-for-profit agencies, service and neighbourhood agencies, as well as informal groupings of friends and neighbours. At present, there is no co-ordination role to bring these different organizations within different sectors together. Nevertheless, stakeholders helping older adults often include members of several different groups and sectors, often some outside of the formal health care system. Reporting on an experiment funded by the McConnell Foundation of Montreal to do precisely this in meeting rural caregivers' needs, Chappell and colleagues (2008) note the success of the three projects examined was based on embracing caregivers as partners; raising awareness of caregiving issues among caregivers themselves, their family, friends, and the general public; networking and engaging stakeholders including those outside of the formal health care system; creating advocacy structures including key stakeholders; caregiver leadership; and building community capacity that encourages creativity and individualizing support.

The Informal/Formal Care Interface

From a government's point of view, there is concern that the provision of services to caregivers in addition to those targeted to older adults themselves will replace the care currently provided by the family. That is, family members will no longer care for their older members. At the present time, Canada's health care system acts as a safety valve when family care cannot cope with all the care required or when there are no family members and, as such, has policies that sustain the primacy of the family. However, several studies examining the effect of informal care on the use of formal services typically report that informal care substitutes for formal services but this is truer for lower skill services, such as house cleaning and grocery shopping, than for higher skill services such as nursing, personal care, and physician services (Van Houtven and Norton, 2004; 2008; Bolin et al., 2008). Drawing on data from 11 European countries, Bonsang (2009) reports similar findings and, in addition, that the substitution effect of informal for formal care disappears when older adults have heavy disability and require care that is beyond the skill level of family caregivers. Daatland and Lowenstein (2005), studying five European countries, also find that greater provision of care by the state does not **crowd-out** family care but instead increases the total level of care to older adults. And the availability of services from the state allows older adults to establish more independent relationships with their family members.

Conclusions

This chapter has examined older adult members of families, a status virtually all of us can expect to fulfill now that life expectancy is into the 80s. As the baby boomers become elderly, both the numbers and proportions of older adults in the population will increase. Older adults, however, are a heterogeneous group spanning some 20+ years. Nevertheless, women outnumber men and gender differences in the aging experiences are evident, as are social class and ethnic variations. We spend most of our time after retiring in a variety of both active and passive leisure pursuits. And, we virtually all age within families, now within families of two, three, and even four generations involving various exchanges and interactions. The diversity that characterizes older adults is also evident when examining health in old age; even though our physical health declines with age, not all aspects of health decline and those that do decline will do so at varying rates among different individuals.

When our health does fail, it is families who are the first to provide care and they provide the vast majority of care. This has continued despite changes in family form and in a society in which many women are employed, children are often geographically mobile, and family dissolution is not uncommon. We expect family caring will continue into the future but what it will look like is not certain. While we can expect a greater proportion of older couples and seniors with surviving children when the baby boomers are elderly, we also know there will be a greater number of seniors, a greater number without any children, and more with complex health problems. Given the work family caregivers now undertake, it is not clear that they can do more in the future. However, new forms of informal care could arise, such as siblings helping siblings.

Formal services are received when the family can no longer cope or is not available; formal services and family care are complementary to one another, irrespective of the type or extent of state involvement in the provision of services. This, however, does not mean that families can do everything, that they can undertake complex care needs, or that their own health will not suffer resulting in more demands on the formal care system. There are good reasons for Canada to provide more and better support to family caregivers so they can continue to provide the care that they willingly do. And there are several countries around the world from which Canada can learn in this respect.

STUDY QUESTIONS

1. What role do families play in the lives of older adults?
2. What role do older adults play in the lives of families?
3. Why do we refer to family caregiving as the dominant care system of older adults?
4. How can the formal health care system better support older adults and their family caregivers?
5. What might the future look like for older adults in terms of their health?
6. What might the future look like for older adults in terms of the care they receive?

Further Readings

Chappell, N.L., and M.J. Hollander. 2011. "Evidence-Based Policy Prescription for an Aging Population. Invited Essay." *HealthcarePapers* 11 (1): 8–18. This paper provides an argument for a type of health care system that would be appropriate and cost-effective for an aging society in Canada.

Crimmins, E.M. 2004. "Trends in the Health of the Elderly," *Annual Review of Public Health* 25: 79–98. This article is American, so not all facts and figures translate exactly to Canada, but most do. It provides an excellent overall of health of older adults.

Jönsson, I. 2003. "Policy perspectives on changing intergenerational relations," *Social Policy and Society* 2 (3): 241–8. This article presents a comparison of 11 European countries that differ in terms of their state provision of services for seniors. It reveals how state involvement in care for seniors does not lead to the withdrawal of family care.

Keefe, J., J. Légaré, and Y. Carrière. 2007. "Older Canadians with disabilities: Projections of need and their policy implications," *Canadian Public Policy*, January, 33(special supplement on health human resources), S65–S80. This article uses Canadian data to provide projections of older adults in the future with and without surviving spouses and children.

Wilson, K., M.W. Rosenberg, and S. Abonyi. 2011. "Aboriginal peoples, health and healing approaches: The effects of age and place on health," *Social Science and Medicine* 72(3): 355–64. This article focuses on Aboriginal peoples and their distinctive situation in relation to health.

Websites

www.statcan.gc.ca/ads-annonces/89-519-x/index-eng.htm
This site provides the Statistics Canada report on the latest statistics describing Canada's older population. From this site a wealth of information on seniors can be accessed through numerous reports and other publications made available from Statistics Canada.

www.ccc-ccan.ca/
The Canadian Caregiver Coalition website contains numerous reports on basic facts about family and friend caregivers, advocacy papers, and information on relevant groups concerned with informal caregiving.

http://canadadementiacrisis.ca/
The Alzheimer Society of Canada is an advocacy, funding, and support agency for those with Alzheimer's and other forms of dementia, their family members, researchers, and others interested in the area. It contains much information on dementia, caregiving, and support for families.

www.cagacg.ca
The Canadian Association on Gerontology is Canada's national scientific and educational association, established to provide leadership in matters related to the aging population. It promotes research, education, and practice related to aging. It hosts an interdisciplinary scientific and educational meeting annually and publishes the *Canadian Journal on Aging*, both of which are important sources of information on aging, especially in Canada.

http://search.who.int/search?q=elderly&ie=utf8&site=default_collection&client=_en&proxy stylesheet=_en&output=xml_no_dtd&oe=utf8
This link will take you to the World Health Organization's many studies, reports, etc. on older adults across the world. Topics include specific studies on disability, dementia, health care, the social determinants of health, various diseases, age friendly communities, environmental issues, and financing.

FAMILY ISSUES

Families face many challenges, make many decisions, and develop diverse strategies as they face shifts in social, economic, and political contexts. That said, the challenges that they face and the strategies they adopt inevitably vary between different types of families. One issue that all family members face is that of giving meaning to their lives together. This is done, in part, by family rituals such as wedding ceremonies. Beyond the symbolic meaning of relationships, families also serve as an economic base for most Canadians. In order to meet the material needs of family members, at least one, but increasingly more than one family member must earn an income so that family members can purchase the goods and services that they need to survive. On top of that, there is a great deal of unpaid labour that is essential to a family's well-being.

Families whose members earn low incomes may end up living in poverty and so must cope with the consequences of this. How families cope with the consequences of their situations depends on a number of characteristics. We must therefore pay attention to characteristics such as sexual orientation, minority status, and the presence of disabilities in family members to better understand how Canadian families work.

Chapter 8 takes up the issue of family rituals. Deborah K. van den Hoonaard focuses special attention on the rituals associated with marriage and death. She begins by looking at pre-marriage rituals and weddings and considers how they have evolved over time. Finally, she discusses rituals of separation, such as funerals, which mark the end of a life together. Important themes in this chapter include the gendered nature of family rituals, and the ways in which family rituals have changed under the influence of conspicuous consumption and individualization. In North America, rituals associated with marriage have come to be defined as women's business, and women tend to be regarded as the proper experts on rituals. At the same time, individuals now exercise greater individuality in their choices about how to conduct rituals. This reflects a long-term trend toward greater individual autonomy in our society.

In Chapter 9, Andrea Doucet describes patterns of paid and unpaid work in families, first by looking at what has been an important topic in sociology: the relationship between gender and paid work. She considers how paid work has been dominated by a male model of employment and then discusses the changes that have occurred to that model in recent years. Historically and even today, unpaid work, like paid work, has been and is gendered. Doucet examines the gender division of labour with respect to the connections between paid and unpaid work, the relationship between paid and unpaid work and state policies, and the differences and inequalities in paid and unpaid work.

Don Kerr and Joseph H. Michalski demonstrate in Chapter 10 the relevance of family and demographic changes to recent poverty trends, while also considering some of the broader structural shifts in the Canadian economy and in government policies. For example, changes in family structures alone have generated some degree of economic uncertainty, especially for women and children. The authors review poverty trends over time and consider the relationship of low income to family type and number of earners. They also examine the high rates of poverty among female-headed lone-parent families and recent immigrants, and contrast that to family poverty later in life, which has declined substantially in recent years. They show that unlike older Canadians, young families with children have fared less well. The authors discuss the coping strategies that poor families use to survive and consider the evidence on the consequences of poverty for poor people's lives.

Doreen M. Fumia, in Chapter 11, examines the issue of same-sex marriage in Canada, how debates have both unsettled and reproduced mainstream notions of national identity, and changes in marriage law in Canada in the form of Bill C-38—the Civil Marriages Act—which shifted the definitions about which couples could legally say "I do." Central to Fumia's analysis is an understanding of Canada as a "heterosexual nation" and what this means in light of changes in law and practice. She explores how concepts of "normal" and "abnormal" sexuality, of meaning and identity, demarcate heterosexual from homosexual relationships, and thus how lesbian and gay human rights claims to same-sex marriage limit the possibility for confronting a heterosexual nation where sexual orientation still leaves many people as "others," outside the nation looking in.

In Chapter 12, Frideres and Madibbo discuss family patterns among ethnic minorities. They present a socio-demographic overview of three broad groups—Aboriginal peoples, immigrants, and visible minorities—by looking at such factors as age distribution. They then explore socio-economic factors, including labour force participation and unemployment. Frideres and Madibbo examine family structure, organization, and conflict among racialized families. Data are presented on lone-parent families and fertility to show that many new immigrants and Aboriginal people live in households that are different from the standard nuclear organization usually treated as typical of Canadian-born, non-visible minority families.

Michelle Owen, in Chapter 13, seeks to understand the impact that disability has on families. She begins by discussing the problem of defining disability, with a special focus on the social model of disability. The chapter aims to show that disabled Canadians and their families are marginalized in our society. Owen finds fault with the general lack of support services for caregivers, and describes often onerous caregiving responsibilities within families. Owen explores the economic implications of parental disability in regard to employment and learning, and domestic labour. She also reviews issues pertaining to violence and abuse against disabled women and children. She concludes, among other things, that social perceptions regarding families and disabilities must be radically altered.

8

Marriage and Death Rituals

DEBORAH K. VAN DEN HOONAARD

LEARNING OBJECTIVES

- To understand the role of ritual societal norms in marriage
- To learn about the historical development of rituals associated with marriage
- To understand how rituals reinforce the evolution of the social meaning of marriage
- To discover how rituals associated with marriage reinforce traditional gender stereotypes
- To learn about the role of consumerism in the evolution of marriage and death rituals

Introduction

Ritual plays a significant role in promoting and maintaining the social norms associated with marriage. Perhaps one thinks of weddings first, but there are other rituals that are linked with marriage: bridal showers, bachelor parties, honeymoons, anniversary celebrations, vow renewals, and funerals and mourning practices. How have these rituals changed over time and how do those changes reflect changes in society?

While marriage rituals reinforce gender norms and stereotypes, they also reflect the hyper-individualism that increasingly characterizes society. When we think of rituals, many of us conjure up images of practices related to religious worship. We may also think of the pageantry of weddings or the somber dress and music of traditional funerals. Rituals often identify the sacred in society and always involve symbolism and predictable practices. Rituals bind people to the society in which they live by mediating between their individual experiences and the social structure (Cheal, 1988a).

The rituals that we associate with marriage, particularly weddings and funerals for spouses, are often religious observances. These milestones of marital life demonstrate the religious *ethos* associated with marriage in particular religions, that is, the "codes of behavior [which are] to be lived out in everyday life" (Swenson et al., 2005: 535). As fewer people attend religious services on a regular basis—21 per cent in 2005, a decrease from 30 per cent in the 1980s (Lindsay 2008)—marriage ceremonies and funerals may be the only connection that many Canadians have with a religious community.

Rites of passage mark one's movement from one status to another. For example, a graduation celebrates an individual's transition from being a student to being a non-student. These rites almost always accompany status elevation (Turner in Cheal, 1988b). Van Gennep (1960, cited in Cheal, 1988a) provided the most well-known description of rites of passage. He explained that these rituals have three parts. The first consists of separation from one's previous status. The second and most interesting step involves liminality, or transitional rites. Finally, the third involves rites of incorporation into the new status. The liminal phase associated with marriage—beginning with the engagement through the wedding ceremony—includes a number of rituals. Van Gennep believed that the number of rites of transition reflects the importance of marriage as well as its impact on the community and numbers of social groups. The rituals we associate with marriage are rites, rituals that are accorded public legitimation (Cheal, 1988a). Rites of passage that we associate with marriage include bridal showers, weddings, and honeymoons.

Rites of progression, in contrast, celebrate continuity. Erving Goffman referred these practices as "maintenance rites" which we use to "guarantee the well-being of a relationship . . . as if the strength of a bond deteriorates if nothing is done to celebrate it" (Goffman, 1971: 73). Rites of progression include anniversary celebrations as well as renewal of marriage vow ceremonies.

Rituals associated with marriage occur before, during, and after marriage. Pre-wedding rituals, such as bridal showers, bachelor parties, and bachelorette parties, take place while a couple is engaged. During the marriage itself, the honeymoon is a rite of passage. Anniversary rituals and the renewal of vows are rites of progression. Rituals associated with the end of marriage traditionally include funerals but also, more recently, divorce rituals. These rituals reflect the norms and moral sentiments current in society (Montemurro, 2002: 68).

Pre-wedding Rituals

During pre-wedding rituals, engaged individuals are in the liminal state—they are not quite single but not yet married. The most widespread of these, at least in North America, is the bridal shower which Beth Montemurro refers to as an "early ritual" that precedes the final stop in the bride's status passage. Through participation in this ritual, the engaged woman demonstrates a commitment to her new status while the women in the community establish their solidarity with her (Montemurro, 2002).

Beth Montemurro (2002: 13) traces the origins of bridal showers to sixteenth-century Holland, where wealthy, urban women who had access to shops that provided items "suitable to setting up a household" organized events with a ritualized format that bear a very strong resemblance to today's bridal showers. Like today's bridal showers, gathering, eating, socializing, and watching the bride open gifts characterized these early events.

Traditional bridal showers, planned and attended exclusively by women, provide the bride with items she will need in her new status as a wife (Cheal, 1988a). The appropriate gifts—pots and pans, dishes, linens, small appliances, and others—reflect traditional gender roles and underscore the wife's primary responsibility for cooking and cleaning.

These occasions include a ritual order and ritual expectations of events (Montemurro, 2002). The participants know what will happen and in what order. Each woman, from the bride-to-be to the hostess to the guest, knows her obligations. The bride is the guest of honour and takes centre stage during the entire event. She may feel awkward as the object of intense scrutiny but knows that, particularly during the gift-opening stage, she must act "delighted and grateful" (Montemurro, 2002: 76).

The hostess is often the maid of honour. Her job is to plan, host, and orchestrate the shower (Goffman, 1963, cited in Montemurro, 2002: 79). For the hostess, this means inviting the right people and organizing the shower as the bride expects and/or approves of.

Women feel an obligation to participate in bridal showers although Montemurro reports that many guests find them boring. Nonetheless, their attendance demonstrates social solidarity and symbolizes support for the coming marriage and acknowledgment of the bride's new status. Women's attendance fulfills their obligation as members of their gender community (Montemurro, 2005: 87).

There is no male equivalent of bridal showers. Rather, bachelor or stag parties mark men's departure from their single life. In contrast to the domestic tone of bridal showers, men's parties involve drinking, carousing, and lamenting the end of the groom's sexual freedom (Montemurro, 2005).

There have been some adaptations within the last 30 years that suggest a diminution in the conventionally gendered nature of bridal showers. These include the groomal shower and the co-ed shower. Superficially, these invented rituals appear to be evidence of **gender convergence** but they serve to reinforce conventional gender roles.

Co-ed showers have become quite common. They resemble cocktail parties rather than traditional bridal showers and do not manifest the ritualized format that characterizes bridal showers. Although co-ed showers involve gift giving, the presents are not usually domestic gifts. The gifts appear to be peripheral to the event and gift themes are masculine, for example, "stock-the-bar" motifs directly focused on alcohol (Montemurro, 2005: 25).

The gift-opening stage of the co-ed shower is a time for joking more than gratitude and emphasizes the masculine. Co-ed showers often include ritualized embarrassment of the groom (Braithwaite, 1995; Montemurro, 2005), which reinforces men's role of incompetence in shower rituals. The men might not know that they are supposed to pass the gifts around after looking at them, and the women tease them about their incompetence. Moreover, men are not supposed to be knowledgeable about wedding tasks (Montemurro, 2005). Co-ed showers, rather than leading to gender convergence, reinforce conventional gender expectations of brides and grooms.

Felix Berrardo and Hernan Vera (1981) report on a groomal shower. He was the only man in attendance; his bride-to-be was not present. Berrardo and Vera interpret this shower as an indicator of possible societal and matrimonial changes. The shower symbolized solidarity among friends and a promise that their friendship would not be interrupted—regardless of gender or marital status. Significantly, unlike for brides, there were no domestic gifts. Rather, there were sexual gag gifts that imitated a stag party. Berrardo and Vera (1981: 398) describe an atmosphere of "sexual innuendos cast within a friendly atmosphere." Berrardo's women friends understood that cross-gender friendship is unusual and difficult to maintain once the groom-to-be marries. The groomal shower is not common, and it has not presaged fundamental social change.

The other adaptation of pre-wedding rituals which seems to challenge traditional gender scripts are bachelorette or "stagette" parties. These parties arose in direct response to bachelor parties and include elements appropriated from the male model. The symbolic meanings are, however, quite different as they challenge the patriarchal definition of the place of women (Tye and Powers, 1998; Montemurro, 2003). Bachelorette parties have a ritualized format that includes starting at home where the bride-to-be is dressed up in sexualized gear. The party then moves to a bar, where the bride engages in hyper-sexualized behaviour with men who are strangers to her (sometimes male strippers), and often returns home in a cab. The components of the bachelor party are present but in a way that reflects parody and trivialization. The rituals of the bachelorette allow the woman to be sexualized as the subject rather than the object. She is dressed up, sometimes as a bride, and decorated with sexual items. Tye and Powers (1998) describe bachelorettes in Atlantic Canada where the brides wear tee shirts with hard candy attached to the outside; when the women are at a bar, they invite men to suck the candies. The gifts of the bachelorette are highly sexualized gag gifts, and the conversation is a light-hearted sexual talk.

Montemurro (2003) explains that the symbols of the bachelorette party suggest that the participants use elements from bachelor parties in order to "get even" with the men. The novelty of male strippers is greeted with humour rather than arousal. The bachelorette mimics and mocks the bachelor party by interpreting the sexual elements as comical rather than sensual.

The sexual character of the bachelorette recognizes that contemporary women are not necessarily virgins, but it does not supplant the bridal shower, which treats the bride as if she is inexperienced. Bachelorette parties suggest increasing equality but are not wholly a sign of social change. Women are still ambivalent about their sexuality and recognize that even though they are not expected to be naive, sexual innocents, a "good woman" likes sex, but not too much. She conforms to long-term monogamy rather than having many superficial relationships. Nonetheless, the bachelorette symbolically celebrates and ritually laments the bride's "last days of freedom" (Montemurro 2006: 33) as the bachelor party does for men. It implies that marriage for women has become a choice, as it has always been for men. Montemurro (2006: 147) notes that bachelorette parties' popularity has increased along with the emphasis on lavish weddings.

The bachelorette has a subversive quality that men recognize. In Atlantic Canada their feeling of threat has resulted in the development of "Jack and Jill" or "stag and stagette" parties. This new form reflects the resilience of traditional gender dynamics (Tye and Powers, 1998). It may also reflect the women's success at challenging the hegemony of the gendered constructions of "early" marriage rituals.

The centerpiece of the rituals associated with marriage is the wedding. Traditionally, weddings were religious ceremonies that "enhance[d] the sense of family cohesion and identity and connection to the religious collective" (Chatters and Taylor, 2005: 520). Clergy members performed weddings that included guidelines that reinforced religious beliefs about marital roles, particularly in the wording of wedding vows. Some traditional Christian wedding vows include the husband's promise to "guide" the wife and the woman's promise to "obey" her husband. As society has moved towards a more equal ideal of marriage, the vows have evolved to become equivalent. The husband and wife make identical promises to one another.

In traditional weddings, one is struck by the symbolic nature of the standard wedding props. Weddings, however, have changed in the twentieth and early twenty-first centuries, pointing to rising individualism in society.

Weddings in the Past

Marriage has always entailed public recognition. In Jewish and Christian traditions, this public recognition originated with biblical stories. As far back as *Genesis*, we witness the marriage of Isaac and Rebekah, during which Isaac led his bride from her family to reside with his. Significantly, although the marriage was arranged by the two families, Rebekah was asked to give her consent before the marriage took place. Biblical accounts of marriage include matchmaking and the union of two families rather than of two individuals. This model of marriage still exists in some parts of the world and continued until the twentieth century in the West (Marcus, 2004).

Weddings are necessary for marriage because a social institution "requires public affirmation [and] knowledge." The public nature of weddings and the community's recognition and support of the couple's reciprocal bond explain the need for witnesses to the vows (Cott, 2002: 1–2). Even when couples elope, a witness is part of the ceremony, as seen in many humorous portrayals of elopements in Hollywood films.

Historically, in North America, weddings were "communal celebrations embedded in a system of reciprocity." They were informal events at which "sociability" strengthened both family and community ties. Early weddings were the "loving product of family labor" (Howard, 2006: 1–2, 11, 14). This type of wedding still exists in small communities. For example, in the Atlantic Provinces, I attended wedding receptions held in public halls for which friends and family of the bride and groom provided large, pot-luck feasts. In large part, however, this type of wedding has disappeared, particularly in urban areas.

For more on early marriages and family formation in the past, see Chapter 2, pp. 22–42.

Although contemporary weddings still use the props of earlier times, their meaning has changed. In nineteenth-century North America, the bride dressed in a white gown that symbolized virginity and "True Womanhood" (Howard, 2006: 13). Flowers worn as garlands were also symbols of the bride's virtue (Chesser, 1980). Giving away the bride originated in the idea that the father "owned" his daughter. Once a woman married, her husband took over ownership. Carrying the bride over the threshold, which has romantic connotations today, also symbolized the husband's ownership of his wife (Sanders, cited in Chesser, 1980: 206).

One wedding ritual that has almost disappeared is **charivari** which entailed forcible separation of the bride from the groom after the marriage and tying old shoes or cans to the rear of their car. Charivari was meant to frighten away the devil (Chesser, 1980: 208). Some small communities still retain forms of this tradition although it is likely that the participants do not know its original meaning. In some parts of the Maritimes, male relatives and friends may "kidnap" the bride from her husband for a few hours, ostensibly to prepare the couple for the unexpected. Today, we are more likely to see a car with a "just married" sign on the back.

Contemporary wedding rituals still use heavily gendered symbols that the wedding industry has co-opted as it has commercialized the wedding ceremonies.

Evolution of Weddings through the Twentieth Century

Weddings before the twentieth century were public events with predictable symbols. Everyone knew exactly what to expect as one generation passed down traditions to the next. As the twentieth century got underway weddings became more individualized and increasingly included "consumer rites" which involved "invented traditions or elaborations of older customs" (Howard, 2006: 2). As the century wore on, the "symbiosis between consumer culture and romantic love" developed (Shissler, 2006: 118). Wedding vows became more flexible, moving to vows that the couple wrote rather than those a religious or civil authority provided. The epitome of the association of romantic love with consumer culture was the 2011 wedding of Kate Middleton and Prince William. People all over the world watched their wedding, which provided the fantasy of a woman's dream of romance and a storybook wedding come true.

Let us look at two components of contemporary weddings and examine how their use and meaning has evolved: wedding rings and wedding dresses.

The wedding ring is the "oldest and most universal marriage symbol." It originally represented trust and power. Men originally wore the ring until it became associated with obedience. From then on, women began wearing it (Chesser, 1980: 205). In the 1920s, the jewelry industry began to portray marriage as a consumer rite. Stores introduced bridal sets which included matching engagement and wedding rings and constructed them as tokens of romantic love (Howard, 2006). At about the same time, jewellers introduced a "male engagement ring campaign" using very masculine images of knights going into jousting tournaments. These images attempted to establish the male engagement ring as a heterosexual tradition and to overcome the link of jewellery with femininity. The time, however, was not right; the woman's engagement ring was a sign of a man's ability to pay for it and a symbol of his love. An engagement ring for men did not fit this story (Howard, 2003: 840–3).

The mid-century attempt to introduce a wedding ring for men was successful because the social context had changed, and jewellers were able to provide a symbolic understanding of wedding rings for men that fit with the times. After the Second World War, middle-class men's identity became more associated with marriage and with personal concerns. A man's wedding ring became a symbol of his maturity. Jewellers promoted a double-ring ceremony that "naturalized this conservative version of masculinity, making it seem 'traditional'" (Howard, 2003: 850). By 1956, the Catholic Church had introduced official double-ring ceremonies.

The success of jewellers' attempts to introduce matrimonial rings for men depended on the social context. The 1920s' engagement ring for men failed because it was not consistent with the concept of masculinity of the day. The groom's ring later succeeded because there were new conceptions of the family and of gender roles. By the 1950s, it had become desirable for a man to "look married." The postwar era and the growth of suburbs put women and men on a more equal plane and encouraged marriages characterized by togetherness (Howard, 2006: 67). As a result, men adopted the groomal wedding band.

The white wedding dress that we think of as standard originated with Queen Victoria in 1840. However, it was not until the 1940s that one could simply expect a bride to be dressed in white. As the century progressed, the once-worn gown began to achieve a special ritual significance as it preserved the individuality of the bride (Howard, 2006: 175). At this time, the belief that the wedding should reflect the personality of the bride began to supplant the standardized wedding ritual.

The irony, of course, is that women spend hundreds—sometimes thousands—of dollars on a dress that they will wear once while men usually rent a tuxedo, to avoid spending money on something that they might never use again. The wedding gown, for women, has achieved a romantic aura while men's wedding clothes have not. The clothing of Kate Middleton and Prince William at their "romantic and regal nuptials" reflects this contrast:

> Kate . . . emerged from a Rolls-Royce wearing a classic fitted white V-neck gown, with a long-sleeved lace overlay and nearly three-metre train. . . . The elegant number was designed by Sarah Burton. . . . Kate also wore a 1936 Cartier "halo" tiara. . . . William, 28, wore the red uniform of the Colonel of the Irish Guards. (CBC, 2011)

"Trashing the dress" is a fad that underlines both the romantic nature of the wedding dress and the increasingly extreme gestures of **conspicuous consumption** (Veblen, 1994). To commemorate this practice, wedding photographers take pictures of brides' ruining their dresses by, for example, standing in the ocean while wearing them. This provides a "fairy-tale appeal" that includes the notion that the woman has found the right person, and will not need a wedding dress again. Ironically, couples see trashing the dress as taking a stand against tradition (King, 2008).

During the twentieth century, department stores began to take over the role of female relatives in the wedding-planning process. In 1938, Eaton's established its Wedding Bureau. It promoted a service that included all aspects of the wedding ceremony, and its staff ensured that the wedding would go smoothly. As Vicki Howard (2006: 132) explains, the Wedding Bureau "standardized the physical outlines of nuptial rites [including] a wider array of ritual props . . . lamps, white ropes, [etc.]." This development presaged the establishment of new professionals—bridal consultants, now called wedding planners—whose presence implied that female members of the family were no longer qualified to plan a wedding (Howard, 2006: 154).

The evolution of the department-store wedding bureau to the wedding consultant to today's wedding planner has moved weddings even farther away from being communal rites to becoming consumer rites and has reinforced the notion that weddings really belong to the bride. Weddings have become more lavish and have incorporated the symbol of the perfect wedding that fulfills the bride's notion of a dream wedding.

Weddings in the Twenty-First Century

In the twenty-first century, the wedding industry has explicitly adopted the "language of commodity and commerce" (Howard, 2006: 221). It has eschewed the traditional and become a consumer "spectacle" that focuses on the creation of a perfect day that fulfills each bride's fantasy. The emergence of professionals who do most of the work of planning the wedding echoes the outsourcing of tasks that used to be part of the wife's role in marriage (e.g., cooking and childcare). These "wifely chores" have been transformed into consumer services in the process of the commercialization of intimate life (Hochschild, 2003, cited in Blakely, 2008: 639–40).

Outsourcing the task of wedding planning does little to change gendered responsibility. It is the bride who works with the wedding planner; the groom remains inconsequential. Wedding planners reinforce the ideology of the wedding as the achievement of the bride's dream, allowing her to "'have it all': the job, the husband, and the perfect wedding" (Blakely, 2008: 657–9).

Media coverage of celebrity weddings also contributes to the consumer culture of weddings. In this coverage, the bride is the main character who is both project manager and "emotional childish fantasizer." Sharon Boden (2003) interviewed 15 couples about the planning of their wedding. The couples reported strict gender segregation which constructed the brides as the main character "in the creation of her perfect day" and the groom as incompetent. This segregation intensified on the wedding day which symbolically started with the bride's donning the wedding dress which turned her into a "fantasy object" and the centre of attention (Boden 2003). Humble, Zvonkovic, and Walker (2008) and Humble (2009) report that couples approach wedding planning in one of three ways: traditional, transitional, or egalitarian. Brides in traditional couples plan the wedding and agree with the ideology that weddings are for the bride rather than the couple. Traditional grooms describe their brides as "natural planners" (2009: 11). In contrast, egalitarian couples shared the planning and responsibility, resisted others' gendered expectations, and rejected the ideology that weddings are for brides. Transitional couples expressed a desire to share the planning work, but in actuality, the bride did most of it. Both members of the couple describe the men's work as if they did more than they actually did.

Weddings are big business in North America with estimates of an average cost of $23,330 in Canada in 2011 (Institute of Marriage and Family, 2012). Websites such as Weddingchannel.com showcase weddings in which couples establish their individuality as they throw elegant receptions for over 100 of their "family and closest friends." The site includes slide shows of weddings with descriptors that emphasize the uniqueness of each wedding as well as its success:

> a very personal affair [with] elements that symbolize [the couple's] relationship and individual achievements. . . . They even included their dogs. . . . The wedding was truly gorgeous, and the details came together so nicely that the wedding was selected as a finalist for Wedding of the Year . . . [while another couple's wedding] reflected their style of modern elegance. . . . [The couple] personalize[d] every detail. . . . Their most important goal was achieved—they both had so much fun and zero regrets! (www .weddingchannel.com)

Very lavish weddings often contribute to a couple's indebtedness, a characteristic of modern marriage. *Money* magazine provides an illustrative example (Chatzky and Gengler, 2005) of a couple whose wedding cost $41,000. It included a dress that was "deeply discounted" at $1,100 and a bachelorette party that involved flying the bridesmaids to Las Vegas. Examples of extravagance are fodder for the media, particularly for critics of contemporary weddings. A commentary in *U.S. Catholic* magazine (Conway, 2006: 26) describes over-the-top weddings that verge on the ridiculous. One marriage ceremony took place in a kick-boxing ring. This extreme illustration is an example of extravagant weddings that emphasize the personalities and affluence of couples rather than solidarity with the community.

One new incarnation is the "destination wedding." This type of wedding has increased 400 per cent since 1998 and now makes up about 7 per cent of all Canadian weddings (Palmer, 2008, Nelson, 2010). They are so popular that Martha Stewart is partnering with a resort chain in the Caribbean to sell destination wedding packages (Nelson, 2011). Couples who embrace destination weddings are attracted to exotic places where they will experience "100% romance" (Johnston, 2006: 192). Some destination weddings involve the movement of whole wedding parties to locales far from home and require significant financial investments for all who attend. In others, the bride and groom go off by themselves, emphasizing the isolation of the couple and the elevation of marriage bonds above all others. The privatization of marriage is complete. Lynda Johnston explored "wedding tourism" in New Zealand. She concludes:

> Wedding tourism separates the couple from their previous social networks, glorifies their relationship . . . over their ties to parents, extended family, friends. . . . In their place, nature steps in . . . a tourist wedding in New Zealand romanticizes both nature and heterosexuality. The couples, like the landscapes, are deemed to be pure, natural, exciting and romantically "meant to be." (Johnston, 2006: 203)

Another development of the twenty-first century is the wedding website, often referred to as "**wedsites.**" Couples create these wedsites to communicate details of their wedding ceremony. In a study of wedsites, Laura Beth Daws (2009) discovered that, although they look like joint efforts, brides usually construct wedsites using the term "we" to suggest both members of the couple were involved. Wedsites emphasize a romantic proposal story and manage the change in the couple's identity from single to married. Daws concluded that that media messages about fantasy and celebrity weddings were prominent in brides' minds as they developed their wedsites.

One cannot but think of sociologist Émile Durkheim, who introduced the concept of the cult of the individual (1964, cited in Cheal, 1988b: 102) to emphasize features of modern culture that make one feel special and unique. The irony is that individualism is rampant in twenty-first century society, but individuals think that they are rebelling against culture by buying into practices like destination weddings and wedsites that celebrate the uniqueness of a couple rather than its integration into social life. I recently ran into a friend in New Brunswick whose daughter was heading to South America for her wedding. She had decided to go an exotic location rather than have a church wedding where she and her family lived because she did not like to conform. My friend was very surprised to find out that destination weddings, rather than unique, are the latest thing.

Alternative Approaches

Sometimes we can learn a great deal about mainstream rituals by looking at whom they exclude and by examining different models. To look at whom wedding rituals exclude, we will look at the experience of gay, lesbian, bi-sexual, and transsexual (GLBT) individuals as participants in wedding rituals. The relatively recent legal recognition of "gay marriage" allows us to examine weddings of GLBT couples. We will then discuss what wedding ceremonies look like in the Bahá'í Faith, a religion founded by Bahá'u'lláh in nineteenth-century Iran.

Finally, we will see how Inuit weddings attempt to incorporate some aspects of Western weddings without focusing on the origins of these aspects.

For more on legal changes to same-sex marriage in Canada, see "Chain of Events in Canada: Bill C-38 Confronts Heteronationalism" in Chapter 11, pp. 214–15.

Ramona Faith Oswald (2000, 2001; Oswald and Suter, 2004) has demonstrated the force of heterosexuality as a component of marriage by exploring the experience of GLBT research participants as family members or guests at weddings. She argues that wedding rituals implicate GLBT family members as "others" or outsiders (2000: 350). The exclusion of GLBT partners, the need to appear heterosexual in one's dress, the omission of a GLBT partner in family portraits, the pressure to participate in the rituals of catching the bouquet and garter, the pressure to dance in heterosexual pairings, and being treated as single women and men who desire heterosexual marriage communicate the sense of not belonging. The marginalizing of GLBT participants in wedding ceremonies and receptions reinforces the heterosexual nature of marriage.

One of the outstanding debates of the last 20 years concerns the recognition and legitimation of GLBT marriage. Although the debate still rages on, gay marriage has been legally recognized in Canada since June 2005. Prior to that point, GLBT couples publicly announced their relationships through **commitment ceremonies**. This invented ceremony incorporates some aspects of marriage, such as a lifelong commitment, at the same time as it intends to escape the gendered messages of traditional wedding ceremonies. Civil Ceremonies Ltd., for example, defines a commitment ceremony as:

> A meaningful and dignified ceremony for adult couples . . . to make a public declaration of life-long commitment, love, and dedication between two people.

The wording of this definition avoids any mention of gender or sexual orientation. The ceremony upholds the cult of the individual and promotes this invented ritual as a consumer rite. Many GLBT websites advertise services and products, including white gowns and flowers that approximate traditional wedding dress.

As soon as gay marriage became legal in Canada, GLBT couples started marrying and a wedding industry burst into existence. This industry came complete with wedding planners, photographers, and wedding ceremonies that use many traditional wedding symbols (for example, the company IDoinToronto.com). Similar to wedding planners who market to heterosexual couples, IDoinToronto.com promises that:

> All of our packages are meant to be customized, so that we come up with exactly the wedding that . . . want. We're here to assist you in making your dream day come true.

Canadian scholars have begun to study how GLBT couples are planning their weddings which, as rituals, lead to their being "'more out' . . . as a result of their public declaration of marriage" (MacIntosh, Reissing, and Andruff, 2010: 79). Shari R. Lash (2007) and Áine M. Humble (2013) have carried out research into how GLBT couples approach their weddings. Lash (2007) interviewed lesbian couples in Toronto who planned their weddings in a liberal Jewish context. She found that, for these women, legal entitlement diminished the need for ritual innovation. Their weddings resembled egalitarian ceremonies for opposite-sex couples. Lash concluded that these couples' Jewish weddings were "meant to assert sameness [with other weddings] rather than difference." By using traditional Jewish wedding symbols, such as a **chuppah**, the canopy under which couples stand during the ceremony, the women stressed the "equivalency of same-sex love" (Lash, 2007: 88).

In contrast, Humble (2013) interviewed couples who were over 40 years old when they married and who lived in Nova Scotia. "Intentionality permeated" the planning for these weddings. Couples made carefully thought-out decisions about whom to invite, where they would get married, the incorporation of gay symbols and avoidance of features associated with heterosexuality, and the importance of making a good impression on their hetero-sexual guests that would "represent same-sex marriages well" (2013). Couples' life course experiences of heterosexism and homophobia influenced their decisions.

We can also see a different approach by looking at weddings in the Bahá'í Faith, a reli-gion that emphasizes lack of ritual in everyday life. The Bahá'í Faith has no clergy. No one officiates a Bahá'í wedding; however, two witnesses must be present.

The Bahá'í wedding can be as simple or as elaborate as the couple wishes it to be. In terms of what to wear, what readings or prayers are to be read or sung, what guests to invite, where it will be held, what food is to be served, or what music is to be played (if any), there are only a few requirements for a Bahá'í wedding to take place. First, the bride and groom must consent to their own marriage (to forestall the practice of arranged marriage). Second, the couple must acquire consent from each of their parents for marriage (such consent does not imply membership in the Bahá'í community).

During the wedding ceremony itself, the only requirement is that the bride and groom each recite the phrase "We will all, verily, abide by the Will of God" as an expression to obey God rather than each other. The Bahá'í local governing body appoints two people to witness the wedding. Bahá'í weddings are legally recognized throughout Canada. Interestingly, New Brunswick requires the local Bahá'í governing body to register a "marriage officer." This person represents the province but does not perform the wedding as a clergy person would.

CASE IN POINT
The Marriage of Inuit and Southern Marriage Practices

The following is an account of Jeff and Lisa-Jo van den Scott, who lived in Nunavut for five years. It illustrates how contemporary, commercial props have been added to traditional Inuit weddings without the participants' distinguishing between what we would consider necessary or extra. This mirrors the wholesale continuation of traditional props, like carry-ing the bride over the threshold, that we include today without much thought.

Tingmihuqaviq (a pseudonym, as are the names below) is a small, remote, Inuit community with a population of roughly 2,200 located in the Kivalliq region of Nunavut, Canada, along the west coast of Hudson Bay. Extremely isolated, Tingmihuqaviq was settled in the late 1950s although there has been a Hudson's Bay Company settlement of *qablunaaq* (people from the South, usually white) since the mid-1920s, when contact with

(Continued)

"the South" began in earnest. Prior to the 1920s, contact with white people was nearly non-existent.

Preparations for the marriage often consist of sewing the bridal clothing. This is becoming more difficult as fewer people know how to sew traditional clothing. When someone from a traditional family gets married, this is not a problem. When Patricia got married, she really wanted to do it right by *qablunaaq* standards so she did not even consider traditional clothing. Katherine wanted to wear the traditional *amoutik*, but she could not get anyone to help her or make a wedding *amoutik* for her. I don't know if the contemporary wedding *amoutik* would be beaded. I think generally not, now, although it was in the past. It used to be a big thing for a bride (with her family) to make her wedding *amoutik*, a very traditional, fancy *amoutik*. Now women get married in an *amoutik* that is half-way between traditional, ceremonial and everyday use *amoutik*.

Many brides now order items for their weddings from catalogues with the help of their *qablunaaq* friends who have credit cards. Some are connected enough to the South to do it themselves. I have done this twice for friends.

Both times, my friends ordered things I would consider frills at weddings, unimportant items or things associated with the kind of revelry at weddings that is mostly on television. For example, they ordered champagne flutes for the entire bridal party, themselves, and each set of parents. Each one had to be engraved. (Try spelling twelve Inuit names, first and last, over the phone and yes, I was on the phone while my friend sat by since my English was better).

Champagne flutes seemed to be treated as vital to the wedding. Pens were also ordered for the book that people sign. Dresses, a roll-out red carpet, invitations, matchbooks (embossed) . . . this sort of thing. My Inuit friends seem unable to figure out which rituals in the South are "necessary" for the wedding to be defined as a wedding, and which are variations or less integral to the weddingness of a wedding. The dress can be swapped out for a traditional *amoutik*, but the flutes were an absolute necessity for Patricia and Katherine.

When it comes to the wedding itself, the bridal party is dressed up, as are the parents (sometimes traditionally, but often in *qablunaaq* finery). This finery is particularly notable because you can't wear it outside. It is too cold. I have only ever seen women in dresses at their graduation and at weddings. The audience for the wedding is all over the board. A few are dressed up, several are in clean jeans, that are sort of dressed up, and some are still in their ripped sweats and sweatshirts. I have even seen an audience member wearing pajama bottoms. The whole gamut is represented. The average, I would say is to dress normally. People often keep their parkas on, unzipped, but not always. The real show is with the wedding party.

I have a theory that weddings in movies and on TV are so focused on the bride and groom and immediate party that this carries over into what residents think they "should" be focusing on here for a wedding to fulfill all the requirements according to *qablunaaq* standards. The odd part is that often times no *qablunaaq* are even present. Jeff and I were the only ones at one wedding! The preacher immediately came over to us afterwards and apologized for its not having been in English for us. We told him we were very happy that we had the honour of hearing it all in Inuktitut, as indeed we were.

SOURCE: Lisa-Jo van den Scott, personal communication, 2008.

Honeymoons

The last rite of passage to take place during the establishment of a newly married couple—a "late" rite—is the honeymoon. Just like weddings, honeymoons have become both more individualized and more routinized during the twentieth century. Women have taken over responsibility for planning the honeymoon, thus emphasizing a more feminized script and further entrenching women's place in the emotional sphere of marriage and family life. Like weddings, honeymoons of the nineteenth-century were community events during which family and friends might accompany the couple, and later became privatized as individuals began to seek fulfillment within the marital relationship rather than in the larger social group.

The honeymoon, as the last rite of passage into marriage, provides the first opportunity for each member of the couple to "discover" the "self" as a marital partner. Even though a couple may have lived together for years, the honeymoon provides their first set of memories as a married couple. Today's honeymoon has a cultural script that includes:

images of secluded beaches, tropical nights, and sexual passion. If one cannot afford to go to exotic, tropical places, one can always rent the Tropical Room at the Edmonton Mall. (Bulcroft et al., 1997: 471)

We, therefore, have seen the development of destinations where one can purchase an escape as well as the romance that contemporary couples crave. Like weddings, honeymoons have come to symbolize the "bride's 'dream' experience" and the couple as "passionate consumers" (ibid., 483).

For the most part, rites of passage associated with marriage reinforce conventional gender norms and reflect increasing individualism and consumerism as they have become entrenched in late twentieth- and early twenty-first-century cultures. As Nancy Cott (2002: 225) has commented:

Love is exalted in our society—it is the food and drink of our imaginations. Sexual love [has] even more of a halo. . . . But where does marriage stand, when there is widespread awareness that half of all marriages end in divorce? . . . Splendid, elaborately detailed weddings have swelled in popularity, as though money spent on a wedding is ballast designed to keep the marriage afloat.

If spending a lot of money on engagement rituals, weddings, and honeymoons seems like the way to get the right start on a marriage, then rites of progression may help maintain marriage by celebrating the accomplishment of remaining married.

Renewing Vows: A Rite of Progression

Couples have always had private anniversary traditions or routines. In addition, there are socially defined, traditional gifts for each anniversary that symbolize the strength of marriage as it endures. Thus, according to the tradition, the ephemeral quality of paper makes it appropriate for a first anniversary while the 75th anniversary calls for diamonds. Recently, jewellers and others have developed a more contemporary list that reflects the increased consumerism of contemporary society. Today, clocks have replaced paper for the first anniversary and diamond jewellery replaces tin or aluminum for the 10th (Rose Floral and Greenhouse, 2008). Today's jewellers equate a husband's expression of love for his wife on their anniversary with a very expensive diamond ring (*Sun Sentinel*, 2008).

The practice of renewing marriage vows gained popularity during the 1990s and received wide media coverage. In addition to individual couples' having renewal ceremonies, churches put on mass events. For example, a Catholic Church held a renewal ceremony for 720 couples while a Baptist minister had a special service on Valentine's Day for 75 couples. The rite has become so established that "Dear Abby" had a column in 1992 that included a "protocol of formal vow renewal ceremonies" (Braithwaite and Baxter, 1995: 117–18).

The vow renewal event, like other marriage rites, has both public and private meanings. The public aspect recognizes the social embeddedness of the marriage relationship as well as the uniqueness of each private relationship. Vow renewals often take place in association with a special, landmark anniversary such as the 25th or 50th anniversary. Other reasons for renewing wedding vows include an opportunity to give thanks after a hardship, an opportunity to have a lavish event when one was not possible at the time of one's wedding, and emerging from a rocky period in one's marriage (Braithwaite and Baxter, 1995; Guth, 1999).

Marital rites of progression may have become more important in response to high rates of divorce. As maintenance rites, they "pay homage" to the institution of marriage as well as to their "unique marital bond" (Braithwaite and Baxter, 1995: 179).

As with other rites associated with marriage, anniversary rituals and vows of renewal belong more to the bride or wife than to the husband or man. This is evident in the many jokes revolving around husbands' forgetting their anniversaries. An article in *Esquire* provides humorous advice about how a husband can avoid the vow-renewal event that his wife wants:

> SHE WANTS TO DO IT. That's okay, that's good. . . . But trust me, You do not want to do this to your [male] friends. . . . It's a spectacle, it's invariably tacky, and it tends to breed resentment. Still, you love her; you want to make her happy. . . . You might propose . . . a second honeymoon if you wish. . . . And your friends will be cheering you on—from a safe and appropriate distance. (Hamilton, 2007)

Even when marriages are successful and last a very long time, they eventually come to an end through the death of one of the spouses or through divorce. Rituals of separation mark the status passage from being a spouse to being single.

Rites of Separation

The rites of separation associated with death include a funeral or memorial service and the activities and props of mourning, which serve both "integrative and regulatory goals." For the widow or widower, they provide a transformation of the sense of self, the transition to a new social status, and a connection to that which is lost (i.e., the status of wife or husband and the person who has died) (Neimeyer et al., 2002: 237).

The social context dictates the degree to which the widowed person must retain or give up the connection to their deceased spouse. In traditional Indian culture, the widow was expected to participate in **suttee**, a practice that required her to jump onto the funeral pyre and be cremated with her husband. This practice, which has been illegal for many years, constructed the wife so that she would have no legitimate status after the death of her husband.

The Catholic Church provides a model of widowhood that communicates the belief that a woman should only marry once. The Church has religious orders of widows who vow celibacy and offer their love completely to God (Rees, 1995). Some see this practice as "remain[ing] united in faith with our husbands" (ibid., 399). Thus, for women, widowhood, rather than moving a woman to a single status, is a component of marriage. This move into a religious order is not widespread today, but contemporary Canadian widows often continue to wear their wedding rings for the rest of their lives to symbolize their continuing connection to their husbands (van den Hoonaard, 2001). In contrast, people encourage today's Canadian woman to let go of her husband and to recognize that "life goes on." This practice insists that the marital relationship has ended at death, perhaps before the widow is ready to see herself as someone other than a wife.

When funerals are celebrated in a recognizable fashion by the community, they communicate its support for the bereaved individual. With the advent of secularization and individualism, these practices have become more fluid and private. As well, secularization has led to funerals becoming more commercialized as professional funeral directors have taken over from family and clergy.

Before the 1970s, funerals were "fixed events" that offered the widowed person a strong sense of **symbolic communitas**, (Turner, 1995 [1967], cited in Wouters, 2002: 2) a feeling of connectedness to the whole community. They offered the mourner a sense of "we-feeling" to the community and gave friends and family a concrete way to support the bereaved spouse (Wouters, 2002).

Late in the twentieth century, as a culture of individuality increased, people complained that traditional funerals were "stiff" and impersonal. New funeral rituals began to focus on "personalization," that is, funerals focusing on the "unique qualities of the deceased emerged" (Emke, 2002; Wouters, 2002). In the twenty-first century, options for funerals are broad, and widows and widowers can decide what kind of commemoration they want to arrange. Often the bereaved tries to follow the wishes of the spouse. Thus, the widowed person continues the marital relationship even after death.

With the freedom to make choices about death rituals, some people request that there be no funeral. Some spouses, widowers, in particular, go against the wishes of the deceased spouse (van den Hoonaard, 2010) because they, like many people, believe that funerals are really for the living (Emke, 2002). Also associated with secularization is the move to defining the funeral or memorial meeting as a mechanism to "celebrate the life" rather than "mourn the death" (Emke, 2002: 272). Recently, funeral homes have become "corporatized" resulting in the disappearance of funeral directors who are embedded in the community. Corporate funeral companies encourage funeral directors to behave more like salesmen than counsellors and work within a consumer model that includes replacing traditional funeral rites with "celebrations of life" that involve personalized items that symbolically represent the person who will be remembered (Sanders, 2009).

Mourning rituals accompany funerals in giving meaning to the end of marriage. They were much more set in the past than today. Queen Victoria had a great impact on what was considered appropriate mourning dress in England and Canada. She was in "full mourning" for three years, and established mourning fashion during the Victorian era (Hell, 2001). Mourning customs served both social and personal needs (Pike, 1980).

Mourning fashion reflected both the gendered understanding of being a wife or husband and social class. There were rigid guidelines for widows' dress, but widowers had more latitude and mourned for a shorter period of time (*Harper's Bazaar*, 2005 [1886]). Widows' clothes, however, were not only black, including the distinctive mourning veil, but also made from expensive material. One could identify a widow of lower economic standing because she would dye a dress black rather than buy a new dress. Thus, Victorian widowhood was "another sphere in which women figured as the pillar of home and society" (Pike, 1980: 656).

Today there are no rules about how widowed people should dress or how family and community members should support them as they move out of marriage into a new status, an anomic situation. The stigma of widowhood is still there, but there are no norms to tell the members of the community how to act, particularly once the funeral has passed. In some ways, the liminal period, in which the mourner is between being married and single, has almost disappeared. This problem also affects people who have lost other members of their family. With no concrete norms, bereaved family members may find themselves ostracized by others who have no ritual way to handle an encounter.

There are some vestiges of liminality left. In Jewish culture, for example, many people still sit **Shiva**. During this week of confinement from routine duties, the widow or widower allows her- or himself to be cared for by family and close friends (Marcus, 2004: 216). At the end of the mourning period, the person rejoins society with the new status. Similarly, in Newfoundland, there were several external signs of mourning that were traditional, for example, keeping one's window blinds lowered (Emke, 2002: 271). These props of liminality allow the community to acknowledge the loss.

Becoming widowed is not the only way to leave marriage. As divorce has become more common and socially acceptable, rituals to mark this status passage have appeared. Phil and Barbara Pennington (2001) are proponents of what they call a "parting ceremony" during which "the past relationship is carefully honored, difficult feelings are truthfully shared and the future is gracefully accepted." The Penningtons suggest that friends be present to witness the ceremony, which includes vows and commitments made by the members of the parting couple. If parting ceremonies were to become widely recognized, they would establish the status of a divorced person as legitimate and potentially reduce the stigma.

Conclusion

Our examination of rituals associated with marriage and death shows that secularization, individualization, and commercialization of rituals in society have increased. Nonetheless, these rites, whether of passage, progression, or separation, continue to promote a gendered view of marriage that puts much of the responsibility for their planning in the hands of women. The symbolism and the implicit meanings maintain the belief that issues about the family are really "women's issues." If you are a student in a class on Sociology of the Family, there are likely far more women in the class than men, significantly exceeding the proportion one might expect based on the female to male ratio at your university.

At the same time, Andrew Cherlin (2004) suggests that we are experiencing a "deinstitutionalization of marriage." This trend is partly the result of the huge growth and acceptability of cohabitation and having children outside of marriage. In Canada, one-half of all stepfamilies are formed by cohabitation rather than by marriage. This trend is even more pronounced in Quebec where 84 per cent of unmarried women who had children were cohabiting (Statistics Canada, 2002, cited in Cherlin, 2004: 849–50). Overall, common-law couples made up 17.9 per cent of all couples in Canada in 2006 and 22.6 per cent of people aged 25–29 were in common-law unions (Institute of Marriage and Family Canada, 2009).

Cherlin suggests that the place of marriage has changed from a social institution with which one associated oneself early in adult life, to an accomplishment, a "capstone" (2004: 855). At the same time, the rites of passage, particularly the wedding, which once provided the legal and social approval for having children, has become an event "centred on and controlled by the couple, themselves, having less to do with family approval or having children" (ibid., 856). Contemporary lavish weddings, rather than demonstrating the affluence of families of those getting married, "display the attainment of a prestigious, comfortable, stable style of life" of the couple (ibid., 857). We might say that weddings now straddle the boundary between rites of passage and rites of progression. Although the couple moves into the new status of married people, many have already lived together for some time and plan weddings that underline the success of their lives together so far.

In sum, it appears that couples are depending more on their own resources for marriage and family formation. This move towards privatization means that people cannot or do not depend on their community in times of joy or sorrow. Only the future will tell whether the pendulum may, at some time, swing the other way.

STUDY QUESTIONS

1. What expectations do you have of rites of passage regarding marriage and family for your own life (or what experiences have you had, if you have already married)? To what extent do they fit with the ideas of commercialization and individualization of family rituals that this chapter presents?

2. How do rites of passage, progression, and separation associated with marriage reinforce traditional gendered conceptions of married life?

3. Why does Andrew Cherlin think that marriage has become deinstitutionalized? To what extent do you agree?

4. How has secularization affected rituals associated with marriage and death?

Further Readings

Emke, Ivan. 2002. "Why the Sad Face?: Secularization and the Changing Function of Funerals in Newfoundland," *Mortality* 7, 3: 269–84. Emke charts changes in funeral practices in Newfoundland and demonstrates the impact of secularization on how funerals are planned and on the disappearance of socially defined mourning rituals.

Goffman, Erving. 1967. *Interaction Ritual.* New York Pantheon Books; Goffman, Erving. 1971. *Relations in Public.* New York: Harper Colophon Books. A brilliant observer of social interaction, Goffman's descriptions shed light on "small," face-to-face situations that characterize marriage and family rituals.

Howard, Vicki. 2006. *Brides, Inc.: American Weddings and the Business of Tradition.* Philadelphia: University of Pennsylvania Press. This is a fascinating book that looks at the evolution of the commercialization of weddings of North America through the twentieth and early twenty-first century. Of special interest is the impact of Eaton's Wedding Bureau.

Humble, Á, M. 2009. "The Second Time 'Round: Gender Construction in Remarried Couples' Wedding Planning," *Journal of Divorce and Remarriage* 50: 260–81. This article describes how couples plan their weddings. The author interviewed couples in Nova Scotia who were getting married for the second time to demonstrate how the three categories of traditional, transitional, and egalitarian approaches to gender influence wedding planning.

Tye, Diane, and Ann Marie Powers. 1998. "Gender, Resistance and Play: Bachelorette Parties in Atlantic Canada," *Women's Studies International Forum* 21, 5: 551–61. This article discusses the subversive nature of bachelorette parties in response to bachelor parties and the success of the challenge to gendered, pre-wedding ritual scripts.

Websites

www.weddingchannel.com

This site provides an example of the commercialization of wedding rituals. If you look closely and critically at the language and promises it includes, you can see how profit-making industries are shaping contemporary marriage rituals.

www.idointoronto.com
This service provides advice and services for GLBT couples who want to get married. If you take a look at the photos and services it offers, you will see that it supports conventional, elaborate weddings. Note the presence of white wedding dresses and tuxedos.

www.civilceremonies.co.uk
This website illustrates the trend of having "commitment ceremonies" that avoid traditional marriage vows and that attempt to escape traditional, gendered messages. Ironically, these ceremonies seem to have many of the trappings of conventional weddings.

www.healingdivorce.com
The information on this website represents the move to "invent" ceremonies of separation for couples to plan and participate in when they get divorced. It includes video clips as well as the story of the divorced "couple."

9

Families and Work: Connecting Households, Workplaces, State Policies, and Communities

ANDREA DOUCET

LEARNING OBJECTIVES

- To find out about the changing forms of paid work which contest the simplicity of one single model of paid work (i.e., the standard employment model)
- To recognize the wide and diverse category of unpaid work
- To learn about key issues in the study of paid and unpaid work, including connections between paid and unpaid work, links between paid and unpaid work and the state, complexities involved in measuring unpaid work, and detailing the costs of care and why gender differences in paid and unpaid work do matter
- To appreciate the strong gender divisions of labour in both paid and unpaid work, as well as the intricate links between gender, class, and ethnicity
- To understand how paid and unpaid work are configured in our own lives as well as in those of our parents' and grandparents' generations

Introduction

When I was growing up in a small town in northern New Brunswick in the 1960s and 1970s, my days usually began with the shrill call of the 8 AM whistle at the local paper mill calling the men to their work shifts. My father was one of those men. Along with hundreds of others, he would enter the mill through a front gate that was usually staffed by the mill's only female employee, have his work card punched, and then work 8–12 hours in the paper-making plant. My father worked at the paper mill for nearly 40 years. He received about five weeks of holidays each year, and we were well treated with a generous dental plan and university scholarships, as well as with lobsters in the summer and a large fir tree each Christmas.

Meanwhile, my mother cared for six children. Piecing together a life out of a labourer's salary, she sewed most of our clothes, pickled summer vegetables from my grandmother's garden for the winter, and served beef and fish in an infinite variety of ways from cows reared by my grandfather and fish caught by friends of my father who were seasonal fishermen. My mother's days were filled with the regular family chores of cooking all meals "from scratch," housecleaning, washing clothes in an old-fashioned wringer washer in our basement, hanging out loads and loads of laundry, and driving us to various activities when required. She also volunteered at church and school events, diligently brought our old clothes to what were called the "low-rental houses" just down the street from the paper mill, and worked tirelessly to accommodate the countless relatives who drove down from Ontario to visit their New Brunswick homestead each summer.

Through all my growing up years until I took my first course in feminism at York University in the late 1970s, my belief was this: *My father worked. My mother did not work.* The simplicity of that belief and the way in which I did not challenge it still astound me now. Yet, I was not alone. For decades, sociology was concerned only with paid work and with men's work. In Canada in the mid-1970s, a major survey of sociological research on Canadian women pointed out that women's unpaid domestic work in the home had been almost completely ignored (Eichler, 1975). Eight years later, the same author concluded again that "by and large housework is excluded from consideration in the social sciences" (Eichler, 1983). Thus, housework, as a key form of unpaid work, was neither seen as "work" nor viewed as worthy of study. Since the 1980s, however, all of that has changed and there has been tremendous interest in the study of paid and unpaid work, women's work and men's work, and an ever-expanding area of research and study that falls under the umbrella term of "**gender divisions of labour**" in paid and unpaid work.

Paid Work

The above description of my father's working life is what researchers have identified as the **standard employment relationship** wherein a worker has continuous full-time employment with the same on-site employer for all or most of his/her working life (Fudge and Vosko, 2001; Vosko, 2010). This model of work has also been described as one of "48 hours for 48 weeks for 48 years" (Coote et al., 1990) or a "male model of employment" (Brannen and Moss, 1991). The word "male" is inserted here for several reasons. First, this model of work has been described as "male" because the continuous unbroken commitment to the labour market has been available mainly to men. Second, the financial remuneration given to women for their paid work has consistently been less than that accorded to men. Third, women's employment has been marked by a dominant pattern of part-time employment while males have consistently worked full-time. Finally, the standard employment relationship has gradually given way to what researchers refer to as non-standard employment.

Gender and Paid Work

The past several decades have witnessed dramatic international growth in the share of women who are part of the paid workforce. In 2009, 58 per cent of all Canadian women aged 15 and over had jobs, up from 42 per cent in 1976. There have been particularly sharp increases in the employment rate of women with children. In 2009, 73 per cent of all women with children under age 16 living at home were part of the employed work force, up from 39 per cent in 1976. Women with children are still less likely to be employed than women without children; that is, 80 per cent of women under age 55 without children had jobs while 64 per cent of women with children under age three were employed (Statistics Canada, 2010d). Table 9.1 shows the employment rates of women by the age of the youngest child at home for the years 1976–2009.

Gender and Wages for Paid Work

A second reason for the argument that employment is characterized by a male model of work is that women's participation in the labour market, while increasing, has never been on an equal footing to that of men. This is best indicated in the fact that women's earnings continue to be less than those of men. According to a recent report from The Library of Parliament, women's average hourly wages remain lower than men's in all occupations. The greatest male–female wage gap, however, occurs in blue-collar occupations where women earn 70 to 71 cents for every dollar earned by men. On the other hand, women's earnings are more comparable to their male counterparts (98 to 99 cents for every dollar earned by men) in the following occupations: art, culture, health, and recreation and sport (Cool, 2010). While women earn less than men in paid employment, the situation is even more aggravated for women who are both visible minorities and recently arrived immigrants (i.e., in Canada for less than seven years) (Palameta, 2004).

For more on the history of changes to paid work, see Chapter 2, p. 26.

Gender and Part-Time Work

The labour market has male connotations because it is mainly men who work in full-time continuous work. Women of all ages are more heavily concentrated in part-time work. Many women, between the ages of 24–44 and between 45–64, are attracted to part-time service-sector jobs because of their responsibility for children as well as care of the elderly. For women ages 25–44, one in five worked part-time in 2009 while only a small minority of adult men (less than six per cent) did so. Women in the **sandwich generation** who are caring for young children as well as the elderly are also likely to work part-time in comparison to men. Table 9.2 shows the percentages of part-time workers in the labour force in 2009, by age and sex.

The Rise of Non-standard Employment

A fourth and final point about standard employment, or a male model of work, is how a contrasting model has grown up rapidly alongside it. That is, while my father's work pattern was consistent with the dominant norm of (white) male employment in Canada after the Second World War, this model of paid work began to wane in the late 1970s when other forms of employment, largely filled by women as well as particular groups of men (i.e., men under 25, recent immigrants, and visible minorities), became common (Fudge and Vosko, 2001; Vosko, 2010). Such employment has been variably termed as **non-standard**

Table 9.1 **Percentage of Women with Children Employed, by Age of Youngest Child, 1976 to 2009**

	Youngest child < 3	Youngest child aged 3 to 5	Total with youngest child < 6	Youngest child aged 6 to 15	Total with children < 16	Total < 55 without children < 16 at home
1976	27.6	36.8	31.4	46.4	39.1	60.9
1977	29.3	37.9	32.7	47.5	40.4	61.2
1978	32.0	40.6	35.4	49.2	42.6	62.3
1979	34.6	42.9	37.8	50.9	44.6	64.1
1980	36.9	45.2	40.1	53.5	47.1	65.2
1981	39.3	46.7	42.1	56.2	49.3	66.0
1982	39.4	46.5	42.1	55.3	48.8	64.9
1983	42.2	47.9	44.4	55.0	49.8	65.7
1984	44.1	49.1	46.1	57.0	51.6	66.1
1985	46.7	52.0	48.7	59.1	53.9	67.7
1986	49.3	54.4	51.3	61.8	56.6	69.1
1987	50.2	56.1	52.5	63.8	58.2	69.8
1988	51.8	58.2	54.3	66.5	60.4	71.7
1989	52.9	59.2	55.4	69.0	62.3	72.7
1990	53.4	59.5	55.8	70.1	63.0	73.5
1991	54.4	60.1	56.5	69.0	62.8	72.6
1992	54.0	59.4	56.0	68.0	62.1	71.6
1993	54.4	59.4	56.3	68.5	62.4	71.6
1994	55.6	59.1	57.0	68.5	62.8	72.1
1995	56.0	60.2	57.7	69.8	63.8	73.0
1996	57.8	60.5	58.9	69.8	64.5	72.4
1997	58.8	62.1	60.1	71.1	65.9	73.4
1998	59.2	63.9	61.2	72.1	67.0	74.8
1999	60.1	66.0	62.6	73.4	68.4	76.0
2000	60.3	67.3	63.2	74.4	69.2	76.3
2001	61.3	67.0	63.7	75.3	70.1	76.8
2002	61.9	68.1	64.5	77.0	71.4	77.9
2003	62.7	68.5	65.1	76.7	71.6	79.0
2004	64.5	69.4	66.6	77.0	72.4	79.3
2005	64.7	70.6	67.2	77.4	72.8	78.7
2006	64.3	69.4	66.4	78.2	72.9	79.9
2007	65.1	72.6	68.1	79.4	74.3	80.9
2008	64.6	70.3	66.8	80.0	73.8	81.2
2009	64.4	69.7	66.5	78.5	72.9	80.4

SOURCE: Adapted from Statistics Canada, 2010d. "Paid Work," in *Women in Canada: A Gender-Based Statistical Report*, catalogue 89-503-X, p. 9.

Table 9.2 **Employed Persons Working Part-time, by Age and Sex, 2009**

Age	% Working Part-time	
	Women	Men
15–24	54.8	38.7
25–44	19.5	5.8
45–54	20.0	5.1
55–64	28.3	11.0
Total	30.65	15.15

SOURCE: Adapted from Statistics Canada, 2010d. "Paid Work," in *Women in Canada: A Gender-Based Statistical Report*, catalogue 89-503-X, p. 14.

employment (Krahn, 1991, 1995), contingent employment (Polivka and Nardone, 1989), precarious employment (Vosko, 2000, 2010; Vosko et al., 2003), or temporary employment (Galarneau, 2005). Whatever its name, this employment is heavily characterized as part-time, temporary (e.g., short contracts, casual or seasonal work), or self-employment. Such jobs increased almost twice as rapidly as permanent employment in recent years and accounted for almost one-fifth of overall growth in paid employment between 1997 and 2003. What all of these jobs share are low wages, insecure working conditions, and limited access to social benefits and statutory entitlements (i.e., Employment Insurance, maternity leave, and parental leave). Notable as well is the marked distribution along gender lines. For example, in 2007 women accounted for 7 in 10 of those employed in part-time temporary jobs or part-time self-employment and for over three-quarters of part-time permanent employees (Vosko and Clark, 2009).

Unpaid Work

Unlike paid work, the definitions and meanings of unpaid work are difficult to pin down. Unpaid work is largely invisible or unnoticed, difficult to measure, and has many subjective meanings that vary according to context. While there are many ways of categorizing unpaid work, most sociologists agree on several dominant types. These include housework, child care, community and inter-household work, subsistence work, informal caregiving, and volunteer work. The first three categories are explored below.

Housework

Several general points can be made about the first category of unpaid work. For one thing, housework is not a universal and homogeneous category. Its detailed composition varies between countries, regions, and classes, and according to such factors as available technologies, number of children, and income level. Second, housework has changed greatly during this century (Luxton, 1980; Cohen, 1983): while labour-saving devices have made some aspects of housework less onerous (i.e., laundering and dishwashing), growing consumption patterns within households and greater activity levels of children have led to new kinds of housework that entail household management, organization, and planning (Taylor et al., 2004; Doucet, 2006). Third, as Olivia Harris pointed out over three decades ago, the degree to which housework is oppressive or burdensome differs greatly and will be influenced by income level as well as by the various forms of co-operation and collectivity between households (Harris, 1981).

Child Care

In households with children, the care and upbringing of these children constitute a large part of parents' daily lives. While I am conceiving of housework and child care as two separate categories of unpaid work (see also Fox, 1998, 2001), they are obviously closely linked. Both kinds of work are usually performed for other household members and thus may be viewed as "familial" work (Delphy, 1984). Moreover, some tasks (e.g., cooking for children) may constitute *both* housework and child-care activities. Finally, it is important to recognize that both housework and caring activities may have monotonous and routine aspects as well as rewarding and creative dimensions.

Several noteworthy distinctions can, however, be drawn between housework and child care. First, improved technology may have had an impact on household tasks (e.g., cooking and clothes washing) but it has had little impact on caring activities, which are heavily reliant on human input. That is, while the majority of Canadian women do not, in comparison to women in the 1960s and 1970s, wash clothes by hand or with a time-consuming wringer washer, and while most households often buy pre-packaged or takeout food to relieve the demands of cooking every night, the care of children cannot be replaced by technology. While parents may joke or complain that the television and computer have become technological babysitters, the fact is that an adult must still supervise their children regardless of what activities they are doing. Infants still require the same amount of time and attention as they have for generations, while many school-aged children have high levels of homework and varied levels of participation in extracurricular activities that require time, planning, and organization.

For more on child-care policy see, "Social Policy and Other Supports for Child Care" in Chapter 4, p. 80.

A second distinction between housework and child care is that housework allows for greater flexibility than child care; this is particularly the case with infants and young children where continuous care must be undertaken by household members or must be arranged and organized to be undertaken by others. When children are ill or emotionally troubled, parents often find that they are the ones who need to be with their child. Similarly, while certain aspects of housework can be put on hold, child care cannot. This was beautifully expressed by one particular woman, "Laura," whom I interviewed in Britain in the early 1990s as part of a study on couples attempting to share housework and child care (Doucet, 1995, 2000, 2001). Laura made the point that every five years she went on strike over issues of housework. Quite simply, she stopped vacuuming, dusting, doing her husband's laundry, and cooking meals on the weekend. As she put it:

> Every five years I went on strike. I stopped doing certain things so that Richard would start doing more. And sure enough, he started doing more. But I never went on strike around the children. That would have been very unwise. I just would never take those risks with my children. But with housework? Absolutely!

CASE IN POINT
Who Pays for Housework Help?

Women more than men have become "time poor" as their participation in paid work has gone up while their responsibility for housework has not decreased. Statistics Canada's analysis of the 2005 General Social Survey reveals that in families where both spouses work full-time, the woman is still responsible for most of the daily housework, such as meal preparation and cleanup, house cleaning, and laundry (Marshall, 2006). Furthermore, while Canadian households are increasingly paying for household cleaning services (10 per cent of husband and wife households in 2000), a key factor that determines the decision to hire domestic help is not only the household income but, even more important, the wife's share of the household income. According to a report from Statistics Canada:

> Buying domestic help is not just a matter of having sufficient household income. It is also matters whose income it is. Consider two husband and wife households, identical in every respect except that the husband makes 75 per cent of the income in one household while the wife makes 75 per cent in the other. . . the second household will be roughly twice as likely to pay for home services. (Palameta, 2003: 15)

What these Canadian data reveal most poignantly is how a woman's greater financial contribution to the household provides her with a greater rationale for easing her unusually large share of domestic labour. In 1989, American sociologist Arlie Hochschild wrote that working women are coming home to take on a second shift of work. Canadian women with good income levels are demonstrating that they are now attempting to avoid this second shift by putting some of their income towards housework relief.

Like Laura, historically and cross-culturally, women overwhelmingly have taken on the work and responsibility of caring for children. Indeed, many researchers have argued that, more than any other single life event, the arrival of children most profoundly marks long-term systemic inequalities between women and men (Brannen and Moss, 1991; Fox, 1998, 2001; Dowd, 2000). This is not to say that fathering and mothering have been static over time. Yet, while women have become secondary workers and wage earners for the household, and sometimes the principal breadwinners, they still remain as primary carers, or shared primary caregivers. Men, on the other hand, have moved from being primary breadwinners but have retained a secondary role in caregiving (Chesley, 2011; Doucet, 2006; Haas and O'Brien, 2010).

While the overwhelming majority of men have not come to share equally in the responsibilities for raising children, there has nevertheless been somewhat of a revolutionary change in father involvement, in Canada as well as in other Western countries. A good indication of Canadian men's increasing involvement in child care is perhaps best revealed in two sets of statistics. The first has to do with fathers at home on a long-term basis while the second has to do with fathers taking parental leave. With regard to the former, the most recent statistics from Statistics Canada suggest that stay-at-home fathers (about 54,000 of them in 2010) have increased 25 per cent since 1976 while stay-at-home mothers have decreased by approximately the same figure (Statistics Canada, 2010d). The second indication of fathers increasing participation in the care of children relates to the extension of parental leave in Canada (from six months to one year) and the increased use of parental leave by fathers to care for infants. A recent study by Statistics Canada reported that in 2006, 20 per cent of eligible fathers took paid parental leave, compared to just 3 per cent in 2000 (cf. Pérusse, 2003; Marshall, 2008).

Community and Inter-household Work

An extension of both housework and child care is found in a category of work that has only recently come to be considered in sociological studies on unpaid work. In my own work (Doucet, 2000, 2001, 2004, 2006, 2011), I have used the term "community responsibility" to refer to the extra-domestic, community-based responsibility for children. This work of parents *and others* appears in varied guises in a wide body of feminist and sociological research. Terms such as "kin work" (Stack, 1974; Di Leonardo, 1987), "servicing work" (Balbo, 1987), "motherwork" (Collins, 1994, 2000), and "household service work" (Sharma, 1986) describe domestic work as much wider—spatially, theoretically, and practically—than simply housework and child care. This idea of community responsibility is also explored in the work of scholars working in developing countries, who point to complex webs of social relations within which domestic labour and parenting occur (Scheper-Hughes, 1992; Moser, 1993; Goetz, 1995, 1997). Moreover, black feminist scholars highlight how community networks and inter-household relations are integral elements of black motherhood (see Collins, 1991, 1994). Canadian author and filmmaker Sylvia Hamilton has illuminated community responsibility and inter-household work in the lives of African-Canadian women living in Nova Scotia (Hamilton, 1989).

In summary, both Canadian women and men engage in a considerable amount of unpaid work. But what is the gender divide in unpaid work? It is now a well-recognized cross-cultural and historical fact that women take on the lion's share of unpaid work—whether housework, child care, inter-household work, subsistence work, informal caring, or volunteer work (Bianchi et al., 2000; Coltrane and Adams, 2001; O'Brien, 2005; Miranda, 2011). In 2001 in Canada, about 21 per cent of women aged 15 and over devoted 30 hours or more to unpaid household work a week, compared with 8 per cent for men (Statistics Canada, 2003e). Moreover, Canadian statistics from the 2005 General Social Survey (released in 2006) indicated that while women and men averaged just under 9 hours a day on paid and unpaid work combined, there was a distinct gender division of labour, with women spending an average of 4.4 hours a day on paid work and 4.3 hours on unpaid work, and men spending 6.3 hours on paid work and only 2.5 on unpaid work (see Figure 9.1). It is important to note, however, that paid work has increased for both men and women,

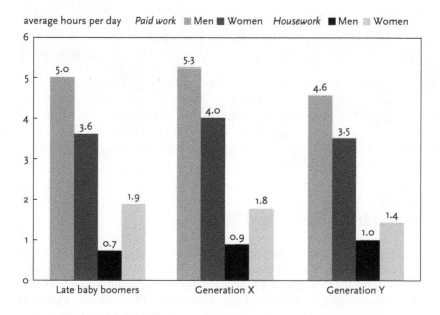

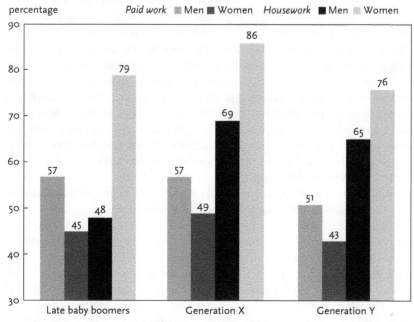

Figure 9.1 Paid Work and Housework

NOTE: Numbers may not add due to rounding. "Other unpaid housework" includes primary child care and shopping for goods and services.

SOURCE: Adapted from Marshall, K. 2011. "Generational change in paid and unpaid work." *Canadian Social Trends*. No. 73. Statistics Canada Catalogue no. 11-008-X. p. 13–24. http://www.statcan.gc.ca/pub/11-008-x/2011002/article/11520-eng.pdf (accessed 1 November 2012).

and while women's unpaid work has decreased (by a half hour), men's unpaid work has increased from 2.1 to 2.5 hours per day.

Studying Paid and Unpaid Work

As noted earlier, it was not until the 1970s that unpaid work was accorded mention within academic studies, and more specifically within sociology. Three of the "classic" empirical studies of housework (including child care) documented women's "occupation" as domestic labourers within their own homes (Oakley, 1974; Luxton, 1980; Lopata, 1981) and emphasized the isolating and monotonous nature of most housework tasks as well as the fact that housework is overwhelmingly women's work. While these early studies, and the many more that followed, concluded that men did little unpaid domestic work, one criticism of early studies on housework and child care was that they did not fully investigate men's roles in domestic work. In contrast to Ann Oakley's early definition of housework as "an activity performed by housewives within their own homes" (Oakley, 1974), many studies have sought to challenge the idea that only housewives do housework. Indeed, the past three decades have produced an astonishing number of case studies on gender divisions of labour, that is, on *who* does *what* in relation to unpaid and paid work. These studies generally fall under the rubric of "gender divisions of labour," "work–life balance" (Duxbury et al., 2004) or "work–life integration" (Johnson et al., 2001).

Beginning in the 1970s, Canadian academic studies of gender divisions of labour within the household have collected basically three major types of data on the division of domestic work: *time* (Meissner et al., 1975; Zuzanek, 2001), *tasks* (Marshall, 1993; Blain, 1994), and *responsibility* (Luxton, 1980; Doucet, 2004a, 2006). All three of these areas of study have revealed constant movement and change. For example, Statistics Canada data from 2010 shows that gender differences in the time spent in paid and unpaid work have narrowed over three generations. In young "Generation Y" couples (aged 20–29), the gender differences in the time spent in paid and unpaid work are smaller than they were for couples the same age in 1986 (Marshall, 2011). Still, the data consistently show women putting in more time, taking on more tasks, and, most importantly, having the greatest responsibility for housework and child care. In focusing on work–life balance issues, Canadian researchers have employed a combination of large-scale surveys as well as in-depth interviews (Fast and Keating, 2001; Duxbury et al., 2004). These studies have pointed to how, although men have increasingly come to appreciate the importance of work–family balance, most of the balancing or juggling of home and work continues to fall on women.

In pointing out the persistent connection between women and the time, tasks, and responsibilities associated with caring for children and with domestic life more widely, and their holding the weight of balancing work and family life, many researchers have also considered *why* gender differences persist in paid and unpaid work and why the progress towards gender equality or symmetry has been slow. Several explanations have repeatedly been put forth, including differing gendered expectations of women and men in relation to earning and caring (Pleck, 1985; Deutsch, 1999; Dowd, 2000; Williams, 2010); **gender ideologies** (Hochschild, 1989; Deutsch, 1999; Williams, 2010; Gaunt, 2012); discourses of motherhood and fatherhood (Lupton and Barclay, 1997; Dienhart, 1998; Mandell, 2002; Miller, 2011); and the role of class and social networks in influencing women's and men's choices and decisions, particularly with regard to earning and caring (Bott, 1957; Morris, 1985; Barker, 1994; Doucet, 2000, 2001; Shows and Gerstel, 2009).

In addition to these findings on gender equality and gender differences, four key areas of study have been emphasized: the connections between paid and unpaid work; the relationship between paid and unpaid work and state policies; the differences and inequalities in paid and unpaid work; and, finally, the overarching question, "What difference does difference make?"

Connections between Paid and Unpaid Work

Talcott Parsons most famously promoted within sociology the notion of complementary spheres of home and work and corresponding gender divisions of labour, with women taking on unpaid work in the "private" sphere and men taking on paid work in the "public" sphere (Parsons and Bales, 1955; Parsons, 1967). This dichotomy between home and work, paid and unpaid work, and a household model with men as breadwinners and women as homemakers, characterized to some extent the early stages of industrial capitalism where the reorganization of production physically separated the home from the workplace. As described earlier, it was a time when men left the home each morning to go to work while women stayed at home. Spatially, practically, and ideologically, the spheres seemed to be separate.

There are, however, several problems with this dichotomy between home and work and between paid and unpaid work. First, women, especially women in low-income households as well as African-Canadian women, have always worked outside the home (Carty, 1994). Cross-cultural research has clearly demonstrated that many working-class households have always required more than the male wage; thus, women have contributed to the maintenance of the household either by intensifying domestic and self-provisioning work inside the home, by earning money through the informal economy, or by earning a wage themselves (Bradbury, 1984, 1993; Tilly and Scott, 1987).

A second problem specific to the home/work distinction is the debatable extent to which a clear line of demarcation existed between home and work. This thesis is challenged by the fact that a considerable number of women, as well as men, have always been employed as outworkers or homeworkers. This false distinction between home and work is well captured in the concept of the "household work strategy," which, as defined by Ray Pahl, is "how households allocate their collective effort to getting all the work that they define has, or feel needs, to be done" (Pahl, 1984: 113). The household work strategy of each household blurs the distinction between home and work because it combines basically three kinds of work that can be done at various sites, including the household, the workplace, and within other households: (1) domestic work; (2) various forms of work in the informal or voluntary economy; and (3) paid employment in the formal economy. While Pahl developed his concept of the household work strategy within a British context, similar ideas have been developed in Canada by Meg Luxton and Bonnie Fox, through the articulation of family

CASE IN POINT
The Evolution of the Stay-at-Home Dad

Twenty years ago, the stay-at-home father was a curiosity, a spectacle, viewed with a mixture of suspicion and praise. I know this because I began to conduct research on these men two decades ago. They were hard to find and reluctant to speak about being the odd man out in a sea of mothers or what one father called "estrogen-filled worlds."

Today, stay-at-home dads are everywhere. They walk proudly with their babies in slings; they're daddy bloggers creating online and community dad groups; and they're injecting a male presence at library story time and infant play groups. Television programs, such as *Modern Family*, *Up All Night*, and *Parenthood*, portray stay-at-home dads as smart, handsome, willing, and content. And high-profile women such as Meryl Streep, Angelina Jolie, Christiane Amanpour, and Sarah Palin all live with men who have been called, or call themselves, stay-at-home dads.

The term "stay-at-home dad" (SAHD) is part of our twenty-first century discourse and is used in a taken-for-granted manner by academics, journalists, and bloggers. The term is important. It signals a radical shift in traditional gendered forms of breadwinning and caregiving. Yet I think it's time to re-think the stay-at-home dad label.

First, it is difficult to know to whom it refers. According to Statistics Canada, a stay-at-home dad is part of a husband–wife couple who have dependent children at home (at least one under 16) and where the wife is employed and the dad is not employed; they also note that this means dad is "not going to school and not looking for work, but able to work—meaning not disabled." Using this definition, in 2011, there were 60,875 Canadian stay-at-home dads (13 per cent of all stay-at-home parents).

While these numbers indicate a three-fold increase since 1986, they also seriously underestimate the numbers of fathers who provide much of the daily care of children.

Excluded from these numbers are secondary, irregular, flexible, or part-time earners; part-time students; work-at-home dads (WAHDS); unemployed job-seekers, the underemployed, and discouraged workers. Moreover, statistics that follow only husband–wife families exclude a growing number of single, divorced, and gay fathers.

A second problem with the SAHD label is the now out-dated distinction between work and home. This distinction, rooted in the early stages of industrialization when there was a physical separation between factory and home, led to a mythologized view of home as a separate world—a refuge behind a white picket fence, or as historian Christopher Lasch called it, a "haven in a heartless world."

This image was reinforced in TV and magazine images of the 1950s North American housewife standing at the door of her suburban home, waving her husband off to work.

This separation still pervades our understandings of work and care. We assume that the worker goes off to work while the caregiver stays at home. In today's world, however, these lines are blurred. Employed parents may work via their smartphones while they are at school events and take on some parenting duties while at work. Stay-at-home parents, on the other hand, may take on paid work while infants are napping, while kids are at

(Continued)

school, or when another parent or caregiver is available. As I argued in my book *Do Men Mother?*, while most stay-at-home dads are the home-based, flexible, or secondary earner, they nevertheless maintain some connection to the labour market.

Finally, the stay-at-home label assumes that care is not work. Many feminist scholars have sought to correct this assumption by arguing for the economic value of unpaid work. The argument that care is work also appeared in the recent exchange, rehashed for days in the American media, between Hilary Rosen and Anne Romney. When Democrat Rosen quipped in an interview that Romney "actually never worked a day in her life," the wife of the Republican presidential candidate replied, "I made a choice to stay home and raise five boys. Believe me, it was hard work." In my research, I have heard many stay-at-home dads use similar words to describe "the hardest job I've ever done."

In the past few years, the meanings and daily practices of work and care have radically shifted. Careers have become more fragmented, and, notably, the shame of working intermittently has faded in step with any of the earlier embarrassment of being a stay-at-home dad.

In the midst of a global recession, families have come up with innovative ways of paying the bills and caring for children.

This may mean that mom stays late at work and dad makes dinner, or that mom works downtown and dad works at home—but both are still working to put food on the table.

Instead of stay-at-home dads, should we think instead of work-at-home dads (as well as work-at-home moms)? This would connect to a large body of research on how women have long created lives composed of a patchwork of paid work and unpaid work.

More and more men are now living such lives. No longer confined to one job—48 hours a week, 48 weeks a year, for 48 years—men now combine working and caring, at work and at home, paid and unpaid. Perhaps the most compelling story of fatherhood in 2012 is not about the rise of stay-at-home dads (SAHDs) but about the richly nuanced lives of work-at home dads (WAHDs).

Read more: http://www.ottawacitizen.com/life/evolution+stay+home/6790417/story .html#ixzz246ZqnGAp

SOURCE: Doucet (2012).

households as sites of "social reproduction" (Fox and Luxton, 2001), which refers to "the activities required to ensure day-to-day and generational survival" (Luxton, 1998).

Since the 1980s, numerous books have appeared with titles including the words "women, work, and family" wherein scholars have investigated the impact of women's labour force participation on gender roles within the household, as well as the inter-relationship between the spheres of home and work (Lamphere, 1987; Zavella, 1987; J. Lewis et al., 1988). All of these studies have argued in varied ways that women's experiences of paid and unpaid work cannot be treated as entirely separate things. By the late 1980s and early 1990s it became clear that the issue was not simply a woman's issue and that leaving men out was further solidifying the binary distinction between paid and unpaid work that these analyses were seeking to dissolve. While a few scholars picked up on the importance of examining men, work, and family in the early 1980s (C. Lewis, 1986; O'Brien, 1987), this crucial focus came to be part of mainstream sociological research on work and family in the 1990s and in the new millennium. Indeed, research on men as fathers, as domestic partners, and as carers has created a burgeoning literature (Unger, 2010; Williams, 2010; Hoffmann, 2011; Marsiglio and Roy, 2012).

The issue of fatherhood as a burgeoning area of research and public attention is addressed in the "Case in Point" box. This material is an Op Ed that I wrote for Father's Day in June 2012. Drawing on my two decades of research on stay-at-home fathers, I reflect on what the category "stay-at-home" father means, the evolution of the concept and the lives of men who inhabit the concept, and the issue of the need to re-think how we understand paid and unpaid work.

Connections between Paid and Unpaid Work and State Policies

While connections need to be emphasized between home and work, they also need to be drawn between home, work, and state policy. That is, in examining the "choices" and actions of women and men as they negotiate paid and unpaid work—who stays home and who works, how housework is divided, and who takes responsibility for varied aspects of domestic life, caring, and earning—we are reminded, as sociologists, that such actions, decisions, and "strategies" must be situated in a wide set of social relations where women's and men's lives are structured differently. In this vein, state policies in relation to paid and unpaid work do matter. If we take the example of formal child care, Canada's report card has been mixed. In terms of the early years of child-rearing, Canada's approach to child care has come under heavy scrutiny in recent years. According to a study by the Organisation for Economic Co-operation and Development (OECD), Canada's approach to child care provides "basic babysitting, but not much else for working parents, and disregards the importance of early education" (Doherty et al., 2003; OECD, 2004). As a nation, Canada also invests less than half of what other developed nations devote to early-childhood education and has enough regulated child-care spaces for less than 20 per cent of children under six with working parents. This compares to the United Kingdom where 60 per cent of young children are in regulated care while in Denmark the figure is 78 per cent. The exception is the province of Quebec, which has a public child-care system, based on daycare centres and private home care and at a cost of only $7 a day. Quebec currently accounts for about 40 per cent of regulated child-care centres in Canada (see Chapter 15).

One positive aspect of state support for parenting is Canada's generous parental leave policy, which ranks as one of the best in the world. Also, according to the OECD, one of Canada's strengths is its Employment Insurance Act of 2001, providing paid parental leave for almost a year as a "very important contribution to both equal opportunity for women and infant well-being and development" (OECD, 2004). While excellent, it nevertheless has its weaknesses in that its connection with Employment Insurance (EI) means that self-employed and part-time workers, who are a growing proportion of the workforce, are largely excluded from both maternity benefits and parental leave (Deven and Moss, 2005).

Gender Differences in Paid and Unpaid Work: What Difference Does Difference Make?

In examining gender differences in paid and unpaid work as well as how ethnicity and class intersect with gender, the question "Why does this matter?" can often arise. Indeed, this question is invariably asked by at least one student each year when I teach the sociology of gender: *What difference does it make that women do most of the unpaid work in society?* Another way to frame this question is to ask a question that I have often raised in my work: *What difference does difference make?* Drawing particularly on the work of feminist legal scholar Deborah Rhode, we can see that the issue of concern is not that of difference per se, but rather "the disadvantages that follow from it" (Rhode, 1990). As phrased by Rhode: "The critical issue should not be difference, *but the difference difference makes*" (Rhode, 1989).

Thus, what difference does difference make? It matters in several ways. First, ample scholarship has highlighted the economic, social, political, and personal costs to women of the gender imbalance in the "costs of caring" (Folbre, 1994, 2001; Ruddick, 1995) for the very young, the very old, the sick, and the disabled in all societies. American journalist Ann Crittenden describes the gender disparity in care and the costs to women particularly well in her best-selling book, *The Price of Motherhood: Why the Most Important Job in the World Is Still the Least Valued.* She writes:

> The entire society benefits from well-raised children, without sharing more than a fraction of the costs of producing them. And that free ride on female labor is enforced by every major institution, starting with the workplace. (Crittenden, 2010)

In addition to this "free ride" of unpaid labour that society reaps from women, this weighting of the balance of unpaid labour on the side of women has been very costly to the paid work opportunities for many women (Bianchi et al., 2000; Coltrane, 2000; Crittenden, 2010; Folbre, 2001; Adams and Coltrane, 2004; Cohen, 2004). These costs can include occupational downgrading; loss of earnings, pensions, and benefits; economic vulnerability in cases of divorce; and long-term poverty for women (Brannen and Moss, 1991; Folbre, 1994, 2001; Ginn and Arber, 2002; James et al., 2003; Arber and Ginn, 2004).

A third point about the difference is that we must ask *which* women and *which* men are most affected. Aboriginal men, and men of ethnic minorities, particularly recent immigrants, are disadvantaged in paid work in comparison to males and females who are white and middle-class. Yet Aboriginal women and ethnic minority women are doubly disadvantaged because they are faced with inequalities in the labour market while still taking on extra shifts of unpaid work.

A further, conceptual problem entails teasing apart the intersecting inequalities between women and men of different ethnic, citizenship, and socio-economic backgrounds. Specifically, there is an increasing pattern whereby middle-class families with ample economic resources rely on other lesser-paid women (e.g., nannies and housekeepers) for domestic work and child care (Bakan and Stasiulis, 1997; Coltrane, 2003; Stasiulis and Bakan, 2005). Paying others to perform domestic services such as child care and housework ultimately passes on women's traditional domain from one group of women to another, thus complicating and hardening the boundaries that exist around gender and caring. A good example of this trend has been Canada's Live-In Caregiver program, whereby thousands of women have come to Canada, mainly from the Philippines. Working as nannies with low pay and high levels of stress, these women highlight the tremendous inequalities between women based on ethnicity and citizenship rights (Spitzer et al., 2003). The end result is that work and homemaking remain as devalued "women's work" wherein an ever-broadening lower tier of women are paid meager wages to perform a "modified housewife" role while other women do work that is more socially "valuable." As phrased eloquently by one author, this model seems to trap us into "endlessly remaking the world in the same image: some people in the public sphere, the world of power, of importance, and some people in the private sphere, rocking the cradle but never really ruling the world" (Rothman, 1989).

Finally, it is important to point out that gender differences in unpaid work can also make a difference to men. While feminists have been calling for men's involvement in housework, child care, and informal caring partly to ease the gendered costs of caring and as one of the routes towards greater gender equality, men have also been busy documenting the personal and relational losses that they incur from not being fully involved in caring. Most of these claims are found in the burgeoning literature on fatherhood, which has drawn attention to the costs of stress and work–family conflict, the burden of being breadwinners, and the lack of opportunities to develop close emotional and relational attachments for men who are distant or absent fathers (Kvande, 2009; Smith, 2009; Haas and O'Brien, 2010). Alternatively, scholars have pointed to the important generative effects for fathers who are highly involved with their children (Lamb, 2004; Allen and Daly, 2007; Daly, Ashbourne, and Brown, 2009; Ashbourne, Daly, and Brown, 2011). As summarized in a Canadian overview of fathering research a decade ago, "[i]t is clear from the research that father involvement has enormous implications for men on their own path of adult development, for their wives and partners in the co-parenting relationship and, most importantly, for their children in terms of social, emotional and cognitive development" (Allen and Daly, 2002).

Conclusion

My household today has dramatically different configurations of paid and unpaid work to those undertaken by my parents in the 1960s and 1970s. Much of my unpaid work is invested in child care and the community responsibility for my three children as well as in housework and small bits of informal caregiving. My paid work consists of being a professor at a Canadian university. My paid and unpaid work occurs in relation to that of my husband, who, as a self-employed naturopathic doctor, varies his hours between full-time and part-time paid work. In addition to the housework, child care, and some parts of community responsibility that my husband takes on, he also takes on a fair bit of subsistence work in our household (painting, household repair, gardening, landscaping, and baking).

Moreover, our paid and unpaid work have to be considered in relation to the larger structural and ideological changes that have occurred in Canadian society with regard to norms and practices for women and men at work and at home over the past four decades. Unlike my mother, I have used varied private services over the years to assist me with both child care and housework. Unlike my father, I have not been with only one employer but have worked in several different jobs and two careers over the past 28 years. The sites of where my paid work is done are multiple: university classrooms, my university office, my home office, and coffee shops where I read and write. My division of unpaid labour with my husband has been symmetrical, intertwining both equality and differences, with varying contributions from each of us at differing times depending on the ages of our children, the pressures from our respective jobs, our backgrounds, and personal inclinations. Our paid and unpaid work opportunities are also structured by class and ethnicity.

As detailed throughout this chapter, the dramatic changes in the paid and unpaid work patterns in my household are directly related to the tremendous changes in ideologies and family forms, as well as the varied types of paid and unpaid work that have proliferated in the past few decades. Families continue to change and evolve and it could well be argued that the traditional family model, which characterized the household where I grew up (with a breadwinner father and child-rearing mother), has been replaced by multiple new family forms (Gerson, 2009). These new forms, which American sociologist Judith Stacey (1990) named the "postmodern family," include single-parent families (both single-father and single-mother families), blended families, two-household families with joint custody of children, cohabiting couples, lesbian and gay families, stay-at-home father families, and various sorts of two-income families. This movement towards what David Cheal called a "convergence to diversity" and the "destandardization of the family" (Cheal, 1991) continues to exist alongside a parallel move towards non-standard employment models. This evolving diversity, complexity, and plurality in both paid and unpaid work will continue to pose exciting theoretical and methodological challenges to sociologists engaged in the study of work and family life.

STUDY QUESTIONS

1. Why is the standard employment model often considered to be a "male" work model?
2. What types of unpaid work do you engage in? Do you consider these to be "work"? Why or why not?
3. Why do scholars consider it important that men take on a fair share of society's unpaid work?
4. Look back to the generations of your parents and grandparents and reflect on how they structured their paid and unpaid work. What challenges and opportunities did women and men face? How was paid and unpaid work structured by gender, ethnicity, and class?

Further Readings

Bezanson, Kate, 2006. *Gender, the State, and Social Reproduction: Household Insecurity in Neo-Liberal Times*. Toronto: University of Toronto Press. This book explores how women and men, families, and households coped with the neo-liberal changes introduced through policies implemented by the Ontario Conservative government throughout the 1990s, and the subsequent impacts on and gender divisions of labour and standards of living.

Doucet, Andrea. 2006. *Do Men Mother?* Toronto: University of Toronto Press. This book builds on international literature on fathering and mothering and the narratives of over 100 Canadian fathers who are primary caregivers of children, exploring the interplay between fathering and public policy, gender ideologies, community norms, social networks, and work–family policies.

Fox, Bonnie, 2009. *When Couples become Parents: The Creation of Gender in the Transition to Parenthood*. Toronto: University of Toronto Press. Following 40 heterosexual couples during their first year of parenthood, Fox documents and analyzes the challenges they confront, and the support and personal resources they have to do so. She focuses on the way social and material resources combine in the partners' negotiations around work and care, the resulting divisions of paid and unpaid work in their families, and relationship dynamics.

Gerson, Kathleen, 2009. *The Unfinished Revolution: How a New Generation is Reshaping Family, Work, and Gender in America*. New York, NY: Oxford University Press. Against a popularly held view that pins recent shifts American family life on declining morals, Gerson argues that economic forces are mainly responsible for the "non-traditional" work and care arrangements made by contemporary families. Yet she also shows how many young women and men, in seeking to negotiate the demands of work and home in a gender-equal fashion, still end up in highly gendered relations and patterns of paid and unpaid work.

Macdonald, Cameron Lynne. 2011. *Shadow Mothers: Nannies, Au Pairs, and the Micropolitics of Mothering*. Berkeley, CA: University of California Press, 2011. This book explores both the strength and warmth of the bonds between mothers and their childcare providers, and the "skirmishes" that erupt between the two groups, situating the latter within broader, classed, cultural, and social tensions.

Williams, Joan, 2010. *Reshaping the Work-Family Debate: Why Men and Class Matter*. Cambridge, MA: Harvard University Press. Williams challenges the conventional wisdom that women "decide" to leave work because they would prefer to be stay-at-home mothers—a view that implicitly guides most workplace policy in the US and creates challenges for both women and men.

Websites

www.genderwork.ca

The Gender and Work database at York University in Toronto explores how gender relations shape and are shaped by institutions such as labour markets, trade unions, and immigration. The site also examines the intersections between gender, race, class, age, and disability.

www.worklifecanada.ca

The Guelph Centre for Families, Work, and Well-being at the University of Guelph conducts and disseminates research relevant to individual and family well-being and the interface between work and family.

www.fira.ca

The Father Involvement Research Alliance is a Canadian group of individuals, organizations, and institutions whose aim is to build and share knowledge about fathers' involvement in families. It offers scholarly research, tools for family practitioners, and resources and networking for families, researchers, policy-makers, and activists.

http://workfamily.sas.upenn.edu/

The Work and Family Researchers Network (formerly the Sloan Work and Family Research Network) is an international membership organization of interdisciplinary work and family researchers. The WFRN also includes the participation of policy makers and practitioners as it seeks to promote knowledge and understanding of contemporary work and family issues.

10

Family Poverty in Canada: Correlates, Coping Strategies, and Consequences[1]

DON KERR AND JOSEPH H. MICHALSKI

LEARNING OBJECTIVES

- To understand the nature and extent of family poverty in Canada
- To recognize the demographic characteristics of low-income families and how the face of family poverty has changed in Canada over time
- To be able to identify the main factors contributing to the dynamics of family poverty, including socio-demographic, economic, and political dynamics
- To develop an appreciation for the coping strategies that low-income families use to deal with their relative lack of disposable income
- To understand and be able to identify the most important consequences of family poverty

Introduction

Although a rich country by international standards, Canada has its share of families who clearly experience economic hardships. Social inequality and poverty have long characterized Canadian social life, as families confront the daily struggle of making ends meet. In drawing international comparisons across countries with similar levels of socio-economic development, the research consistently finds that Canada falls somewhere between the United States—where levels of poverty and inequality are relatively high—and much of Continental Europe—where the incidence of poverty is moderated somewhat by more comprehensive welfare states (Congleton and Bose, 2010; Picot and Myles, 2005; Rainwater et al., 2001; Smeeding et al., 2002). Thus, despite Canada's considerable wealth, many families face the challenges, and even the stigma, associated with poverty in a context of relative affluence and economic prosperity (Family Service Toronto, 2011).

The last two decades of the twentieth century were turbulent years for many Canadians, which coincided with some notable ups and downs in the North American economy.

In examining trends in family income security, Torjman (1999) describes the period as involving both good news and bad news, or "both crests and crashes." For example, Canadians experienced two severe recessions, in the early 1980s and then in the early 1990s. After a period of about 15 years of sustained economic growth, Canada again witnessed an economic recession in 2009, although this time, without the same sorts of job losses and double-digit unemployment observed earlier. While the Canadian economy grew relatively rapidly through the latter 1990s and early 2000s, the short-lived Canadian recession in 2009 involved an upturn in the unemployment rate, from just under 6 per cent in early 2008 to about 8.5 per cent by 2009. The most up-to-date information available from Statistics Canada on family income provides us with some indication as to the consequences of this economic downturn for Canadian families, in terms of both average income and the incidence of low income.

In the current chapter, we focus on data available on the economic circumstances facing low-income families, from the early 1980s through to 2010. Although average family income has increased modestly in *real* terms for several decades (i.e., after adjusting for inflation), many families continue to experience major financial setbacks. Picot et al. (1998) highlight three distinctive types of events as potential explanations: (1) "demographic" events that influence the types of families and living arrangements in which Canadians share and pool income; (2) "economic" events that influence the availability of jobs and the sorts of wages available in the labour market; and (3) "political" events that influence the types of transfer payments that Canadians receive from government. The current chapter develops these themes further by demonstrating the relevance of family and **demographic changes** to recent poverty trends, while also considering some of the broader structural shifts both in the Canadian economy and in government policies. For example, changes in family structures alone have generated some degree of economic uncertainty, especially for women and children.

We plan to demonstrate that family poverty tends to be linked to key events—not all of which can necessarily be predicted or controlled. Many low-income families thus struggle to survive and, in some cases, successfully escape poverty. The many potential negative consequences, however, should remind readers that poverty has potential costs not only to the families immediately affected, but for society at large.

Has the Problem of Poverty Worsened in Recent Decades?

In addressing the issue as to whether poverty has worsened in Canada over time, one must choose some form of statistical indicator with which to work. Yet in reviewing the literature, we encounter a multitude of different working definitions of poverty (Canadian Council on Social Development, 2002; Whelan and Maitre, 2007). For instance, some researchers have set poverty thresholds at relatively low levels by considering only the most basic of physical needs necessary for short-term survival in their definitions (Montreal Diet Dispensary, 1998; Fraser Institute, 2001; Sarlo, 2008). Others have set the bar much higher in pointing out that the long-term well-being of families implies much more than merely meeting their barest necessities (Federal–Provincial Working Group on Social Development Research and Information, 1998; Canadian Council on Social Development, 2006).

For our purposes, we work with the most commonly cited poverty line in the Canadian literature: Statistics Canada's **low-income cut-offs (LICOS)** after tax. Owing in part to the credibility of Statistics Canada, many policy analysts, editorialists, and social scientists consider the LICOS to be the preferred indicators. The LICOS are a reasonable compromise insofar as they fall somewhere near the mid-range of the many working definitions currently available. In addition, Statistics Canada's LICOS vary by family size and by five different sized urban and rural communities. For example, in 2010 the after-tax low-income threshold ranged from $23,202 for a family of four living in a rural locale to $35,469 for such families living in one of Canada's largest cities. In developing these LICOS, Statistics Canada has systematically examined spending patterns and disposable income, since families that spend an inordinate percentage of their income on necessities (food, shelter, and clothing) are likely to be experiencing economic difficulties.

Table 10.1 provides information on recent trends in income poverty in Canada (1980–2010). In addition, Table 10.2 presents comparable information on median family income, or the midpoint in the income distribution where one-half of all families falls above and one-half falls below. Thus we can move beyond a narrow focus solely on families at the bottom of the income distribution. The low-income rates and median incomes are further broken down by family type and number of earners per household. This provides us with some indication as to how people are adapting to some rather fundamental changes in family life over the last couple of decades, especially in terms of changing family structure and the manner in which households earn and pool their resources. The information in Tables 10.1 and 10.2 has been adjusted for inflation, with all figures presented in constant 2010 dollars.

In reading Tables 10.1 and 10.2, we can see how both income poverty and **median income** have fluctuated over time, while also varying in a rather pronounced manner by family type and number of earners. As mentioned previously, the last two decades of the twentieth century have been characterized by periodic ups and downs in the North American economy, with two particularly difficult periods during the early 1980s and early 1990s. For example, in considering all **economic families**, income poverty rose during the recession of the 1980s (from 8.7 per cent in 1980 to 10.2 per cent in 1985), whereas median income fell (dropping from about $67,800 to $64,200, expressed in constant dollars). Both of these statistical indicators are influenced by the availability of jobs and wages in the Canadian labour market, i.e., by labour market events and macroeconomic conditions (see Kenworthy and Pontusson, 2005). The increased incidence of low income is not surprising in light of the double-digit unemployment and inflation of the early to mid-1980s, which exacted a heavy toll on many families and, in particular, on families of low or modest means.

The economic upturn of the late 1980s was translated into income gains and reduced poverty, both of which are reflected in Tables 10.1 and 10.2. Unfortunately, these gains were once again washed out during a second **recession** in the early 1990s. Suggestive of the difficulties that many families encountered during this latter period, median income was lower in 1995 ($62,600) than at the beginning of the decade in 1990 ($66,900) and even lower than it was 15 years earlier in 1980 ($67,800). In working with these income data, many social scientists in the mid-1990s highlighted this lack of progress (McFate, 1995; Richardson, 1996; Kazemipur and Halli, 2000). In terms of low income, the incidence was once again somewhat higher in 1995 (11.4 per cent) than it was at the beginning of the 1980s (8.7 per cent in 1980).

Table 10.1 **Incidence of Low Income (after tax) for Selected Family-Unit Types, 1980–2010 (a)**

	1980	1985	1990	1995	2000	2005	2010
Persons in economic families, two persons or more	8.7	10.2	9.0	11.4	9.3	7.5	5.9
Persons in non-elderly families (b)	8.8	10.8	9.7	12.5	9.9	8.1	6.3
Persons in married couples, no earners	30.0	31.3	28.8	29.0	33.6	31.9	24.4
Persons in married couples, one earner	7.6	9.0	9.5	10.4	10.2	7.4	8.1
Persons in married couples, two earners	1.2	1.8	2.7	2.8	2.2	2.9	2.2
Persons in two-parent families with children (c)	7.2	9.2	7.5	10.9	8.7	6.9	5.1
Persons in two-parent families with children, no earners	68.1	84.1	75.3	81.2	84.1	84.2	66.4
Persons in two-parent families with children, one earner	13.0	17.6	17.1	22.1	23.1	17.1	14.2
Persons in two-parent families with children, two earners	4.1	5.9	4.9	6.0	4.6	3.9	3.0
Persons in lone-parent families	42.1	48.6	43.7	44.1	32.4	26.5	18.7
Persons in male lone-parent families	17.9	18.5	18.4	21.9	12.3	11.6	8.6
Persons in female lone-parent families	45.5	52.5	48.2	47.5	36.2	29.7	20.6
Persons in female lone-parent families, no earners	89.2	90.4	86.1	82.2	89.2	80.8	74.4
Persons in female lone-parent families, one earner	38.3	45.6	40.6	34.5	27.6	23.5	11.5
Persons in elderly families (d)	7.6	5.2	2.8	2.6	3.5	2.0	3.2
Unattached individuals	37.2	34.9	31.3	35.0	32.9	30.5	26.9

a. After-tax low income cut-offs (1992 base) were determined from an analysis of the 1992 Family Expenditure Survey data. These income limits were selected on the basis that families with incomes below these limits usually spent 63.6% or more of their income on food, shelter and clothing. Low income cut-offs were differentiated by community size of residence and family size.

b. Families in which the major income earner is 65 years or older.

c. With single children less than 18 years of age. Children 18 years+ and/or other relatives may be present

d. Oldest adult 65+ years

SOURCES: Statistics Canada. Table 202-0804 - Persons in low income, by economic family type, annual (accessed: June 26, 2012); Income Statistics Division, Statistics Canada, Table 202-0411 Survey of Consumer Finances & Survey of Labour and Income Dynamics

In the early 1990s, as with the earlier recession, persistently high rates of unemployment and a decline in real earnings characterized the North American economy. In addition, the political context shifted with the election of more fiscally conservative governments, both

Table 10.2 **Median Income, by Selected Family Types, 2010 constant dollars, annual 1980–2010**

	Median 2010 constant dollars						
	1980	1985	1990	1995	2000	2005	2010
Economic families, two persons or more	$67,800	$64,200	$66,900	$62,600	$68,100	$70,700	$74,400
Non-elderly families (a)	$70,700	$67,900	$70,900	$66,600	$72,900	$75,900	$81,100
Married couples, no earners	$25,100	$28,500	$31,400	$28,300	$33,600	$31,200	$36,500
Married couples, one earner	$54,300	$54,900	$52,700	$51,000	$52,900	$60,600	$57,300
Married couples, two earners	$78,200	$72,100	$74,800	$73,100	$77,200	$81,300	$85,000
Two-parent families with children (b)	$73,100	$72,400	$76,900	$73,600	$81,000	$84,600	$91,300
Two-parent families with children, no earners	$22,300	$20,500	$19,700	$21,300	$22,500	$19,700	$32,400
Two-parent families with children, one earner	$57,000	$56,800	$54,200	$52,500	$53,300	$55,900	$54,600
Two-parent families with children, two earners	$76,500	$75,100	$77,300	$77,600	$83,700	$86,100	$92,200
Lone-parent families	$29,000	$26,400	$27,100	$28,400	$35,400	$38,100	$41,800
Male lone-parent families	$50,200	$48,400	$49,900	$41,300	$51,500	$54,000	$56,600
Female lone-parent families	$27,200	$24,500	$24,300	$26,800	$31,500	$34,500	$39,600
Female lone-parent families, no earners	$15,200	$16,000	$17,600	$19,300	$16,600	$18,500	$17,700
Female lone-parent families, one earner	$29,000	$27,700	$28,500	$32,000	$34,100	$34,900	$39,600
Elderly families (c)	$37,100	$38,000	$45,100	$43,500	$44,000	$47,600	$48,800
Unattached individuals	$23,500	$22,900	$24,200	$22,500	$24,000	$25,400	$28,500

a. Oldest adult less than 65 years
b. With single children less than 18 years of age. Children 18 years+ and/or other relatives may be present
c. Oldest adult 65+ years
SOURCE: Income Statistics Division, Statistics Canada, Table 202-0411, Survey of Consumer Finances & Survey of Labour and Income Dynamics

federally and across many provinces. Unemployment insurance and income assistance programs became more restrictive, and this had a direct impact on the economic well-being of lower-income Canadians (Meyers and Cancian, 1996). Federal and provincial budgetary constraints compounded difficulties in the economy because governments that had hitherto run large fiscal deficits reduced their direct transfers to families (Picot et al., 1998).

The economic situation in Canada improved, with declining rates of unemployment and poverty. In 2000, the unemployment rate fell below 7 per cent (something it had not done since 1976), in stark contrast to the 12 per cent peak only seven years earlier. The unemployment rate declined even further into the first decade of the current century, dipping below 6 per cent by early 2008. Macroeconomic conditions improved, especially in terms of Canada's record high labour force **participation rate** of just over 67 per cent. In other words, by 2008 this meant that roughly two-thirds of all Canadians aged 15 and older were involved in the labour force, either working on a full-time or part-time basis or actively searching out employment (Statistics Canada, 2008i). Furthermore, data on income and unemployment show that a smaller proportion of Canadians relied on government transfers as their primary means of support.

Following a period of sustained economic growth and job creation, Canadians made up the ground they lost during the two previous recessions. By 2005, median family income had risen to $70,700 relative to only $62,600 ten years earlier. The most recent economic downturn that began in 2009 has not been enough to offset these gains, with median income up to $74,400 by 2010. While not reported in Table 10.2, this is down only slightly from a high of $75,300 in 2008. In terms of the low income, Statistics Canada reports that 5.9 per cent of all families had an income below its after tax LICOS as of 2010, which is again lower than five years earlier.

With respect to household earnings, the norm these days consists of two wage earners per family rather than one. Through 2008, Canadians across the income distribution enjoyed gains, such that both upper-income and lower-income families witnessed some improvement in their economic circumstances. While the unemployment rate shot up to over 8.5 per cent in latter 2009, overall the first decade of the twenty-first century appears to be characterized by higher family incomes and a reduced incidence of low income. It is far from certain as to whether this trend will continue into the second decade of the current century.

Low Income, Family Type, and Number of Earners

Despite the most recent gains suggested in Statistics Canada's income statistics, certain types of families clearly continue to be at a much higher risk of experiencing economic hardship. For example, evidence from the Canadian Survey of Labour and Income Dynamics (SLID) indicates that in the year following divorce or separation, women are far more likely to end up in a low-income household as compared with their male counterparts. In addition, these women (especially those under the age of 40) are much more likely to remain in low-income situations for longer periods than men (Gadalla, 2008).

For more on poverty in lone-parent families, see "Recent Developments in Divorce and Family Law" in Chapter 5, pp. 101–3.

Table 10.1 documents how the likelihood of low income has long been much higher for female-headed, lone-parent families. In 2010, the likelihood of a female-headed, **lone-parent family** being classified as poor was more than three times that of all families (at 20.6 per cent in contrast to 5.9 per cent) and four times that for two-parent families with children (at 5.1 per cent). Similarly, median income varied quite dramatically across family types as well. For instance, the median income of female-headed, lone-parent families ($39,600) was only 43.4 per cent of the median income of two-parent families with children ($91,300).

Many lone-parent families, the overwhelming majority of which involve mothers rather than fathers, continue to experience great economic hardship and are seriously over-represented among the poor. This observation is especially consequential in light of some of the remarkable changes in patterns of family formation that have characterized Canada (and most other Western countries) over the last few decades. Sociologists have come to appreciate the importance of residential living arrangements for the well-being of adults and children alike, and, in particular, with respect to how individuals earn and pool resources (Beaujot, 1999; Cheal, 1999; Kenney, 2004). High rates of divorce, union instability, and non-marital fertility have contributed to a rapid increase in the proportion of families headed by a lone parent—which often implies little or no economic contribution coming from a non-resident parent. Although lone-parent families now comprise more than one in five families with children (or 23 per cent according to the 2006 census), among families with children classified as income poor, over half (52.4 per cent) are single-parent families (Statistics Canada, 2007b; authors' calculations).

Recent trends in family structure therefore have important implications for the economic vitality of families. By their very nature, single-parent families are at a disadvantage in a society where the dual-earner family has now become the norm. The traditional breadwinner family, with a clear gender division of labour, no longer exists in majority form. For example, in considering dual-parent families with children, about nine out of 10 men and eight out of 10 women are in the labour force. Most dual-parent families currently have two earners, which confers upon them a clear economic advantage. The median income of two-earner families with a child was $92,200 in 2010, as compared to a median income of $54,600 among such families with only one earner (see Table 10.2).

Even among families with particularly young children, there has been a major shift in the labour force participation of their parents. The majority of new mothers return to paid employment after a short respite to care for their newborns. Survey data have revealed that upon giving birth to a child, an overwhelming majority of Canadian women (well over 80 per cent) indicate that they plan to return to the labour force within two years (Marshall, 2003). While many women (and increasingly, some men) take advantage of parental leave, in most instances the absence from the labour force is temporary. On the other hand, lone-parent families obviously face disadvantages that dual-parent families do not regarding their ability to re-establish themselves in the labour market. For example, single parents often cannot easily share child-care responsibilities with a partner (see Wooley, 2004). The age of the children has a particularly important impact on labour force participation of lone parents due to the difficulties of simultaneously raising very young children and maintaining a full-time job. Thus, employment rates for female lone parents tend to rise sharply as their children age and depending on the availability of other caregivers or social supports (Woolley, 1998). These difficulties are often compounded by the shortage of suitable and affordable child-care spaces for preschool children as parents seek to re-enter the labour force (Cleveland et al., 1996; Friendly et al., 2007).

Recent statistics indicate that about one in five female lone-parents reports no involvement in the labour force, which almost guarantees economic hardship (Statistics Canada, 2008i). Regardless of individual or family circumstances, welfare payments across Canadian provinces fall well below what most Canadians consider adequate for a reasonable standard of living. These programs have complex rules relating to eligibility for assistance. Yet in reviewing these different programs, we find that one generalization certainly applies across jurisdictions: Canadian welfare

For more on shortage of suitable child-care, see Chapter 4, p. 67.

Box 10.1

Economic Mobility and Family Background: How Does Canada compare with other wealthy countries?

Being raised in a poor family does not necessarily imply a lifetime of poverty. By the same token, being raised in a wealthy family does not correspondingly guarantee prosperity. "Economic mobility" is the extent to which individuals or families improve (or worsen) their economic circumstances over time. For example, a child raised in a working-class family could obtain a professional degree and high-paying job in adulthood. This mobility can be thought of as either "intra-generational" (within a person's lifetime) or "inter-generational" (across generations).

The extent of economic mobility varies considerably across different societies, as influenced by local labour market conditions, government policy, and the direct day-to-day experiences and decisions of families and individuals. In a recent study comparing the "intergenerational" economic mobility of several countries, Corak et al. (2010) suggest that Canada's mobility compares favourably with other wealthy countries, including two countries with which it shares much, both culturally and economically: the United States and the United Kingdom. After examining earnings across generations, Corak et al. (2010) provide evidence to suggest that a poor child in America or the United Kingdom is far more likely to remain poor as an adult than is true of the typical Canadian child. In fact, the degree of economic mobility documented for Canada even compares relatively well with some of the more social democratic countries of Western Europe, including the Scandinavian countries Finland, Norway, Sweden, and Denmark.

Figure 10.1 summarizes this research using a statistic called the index of intergenerational elasticity (see Corak, 2004). Without getting into technical detail, this index works with data on individual earnings for persons in young adulthood (latter 20s) relative to the earnings of their parents at a similar stage of the life cycle (i.e. across two generations). The index provides us with evidence on the extent to which disadvantage is passed on from one generation to the next. A score of 1.0 on this index would theoretically imply absolutely no economic mobility, whereas a score of 0 implies that neither advantage nor disadvantage is passed on from one generation to the next (a completely level playing field for all young adults in establishing themselves in the labour market). In reading Figure 10.1, the degree of intergenerational mobility appears to be more than twice as high in Canada than in the United States, Italy, and the United Kingdom, among other Western European countries.

In recent studies, Corak et al. (2010) and Corak (2009) have highlighted several factors that are relevant in explaining Canada's advantage, while making systematic comparisons with the United States. One important factor is the reality that the poor in the United States are on average far poorer than those with low incomes in Canada, as public income transfers have long played a more important role in Canada. For example, many Canadian families receive some form of public support, including a federal child tax benefit, which is a progressive system of income transfers as delivered through the income tax system. The generosity of this benefit varies according to the family's market income as well as its number of children under the age of 18. While this benefit has played a rather limited role in reducing the incidence of low income, it has significantly reduced the severity of poverty among those households that are in fact classified in this manner.

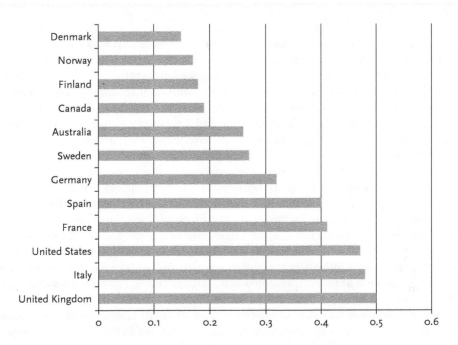

Figure 10.1 **Estimates of Intergenerational Elasticity of Earnings between Generations for Selected Rich Countries**

SOURCE: Corak et al. (2010), Corak (2009).

Similarly, the wealthiest American households (top 1 per cent) are particularly affluent, to a greater extent than its northern neighbour. The overall level of economic inequality is greater in the first place relative to Canada. Taxation and public policies have been described as less "progressive" in the United States, failing to compensate to the same degree for family background and labour market inequalities. In other words, because of the difference in the extremes of their earnings distributions, there appears to be notably less mobility at the very top and very bottom of the United States' income distribution.

Finally, children in the United States are more likely to be raised in a challenging family context, including being born to young or teenage mothers, and/or being raised in a lone-parent family. American parents work longer hours than Canadian parents, while at the same time having fewer benefits, childcare opportunities, and job security. In terms of education, there is greater variation in the quality of public education in the United States too, with a smaller proportion achieving at least some post-secondary education. As a quality education is among the most important predictors of economic success in establishing oneself in the workplace, this directly translates into less upward mobility for the most disadvantaged of American families and communities.

programs are not particularly generous. The reality is that families that rely on social assistance to make ends meet usually experience severe economic hardship. For example, in 2009, the total welfare income for a lone-parent family with one child across provinces ranged from an average of only $14,829 in Manitoba to a high of $19,297 in Newfoundland and Labrador (National Council of Welfare, 2011).

Lone parents frequently have fewer alternative sources of income to compensate for their lower incomes, as many receive either no child support from former partners or often highly limited support (Marcil-Gratton and Le Bourdais, 1999; Stewart, 2010). While Canadian law has attempted to enforce the idea that absent parents should maintain financial responsibility for their children, the rates of default on child payments remain high. Among children whose parents have separated or divorced, about one in three of all custodial parents has absolutely no agreement on child support. For those separated parents who have such an agreement, a significant proportion (approaching one-half) regularly faces default (Marcil-Gratton et al., 2000). In addition, most non-marital births (i.e., children born to women not in a marital relationship) involve little or no contact with the biological father after the birth, which obviously translates into an absence of child support payments. And those who are poorer, unemployed, with less education, and from minority backgrounds are overrepresented among those prosecuted for child support debt (Millar, 2010).

Moreover, women as lone parents share the same disadvantages that other women face in the Canadian labour market in general (Caragata, 2003; see Breitkreuz, 2005). Women continue to face obstacles in obtaining equal pay for work of equal value, although younger cohorts appear to have been making some significant gains as of late. If one further considers the intersection of visible minority status and Aboriginal status with gender, the labour market access and earnings differentials become especially pronounced (Lee, 2000; Smith and Jackson, 2002). Beyond issues of race and ethnicity, part of the gender-based disadvantage reflects the incidence of low-income families headed by males and females: 8.6 per cent among male lone parents and 20.6 per cent among female lone parents in 2010. On average, male lone parents tend to be older than their female counterparts, much more likely to be employed, and, when working, earn a significantly higher wage.

Poverty among Families in Later Life

Older Canadians can be characterized by their diversity in terms of life history, family characteristics, and economic statuses (Weeks, 2012). With several additional decades of life experience, it is logical that older people tend to be less alike than younger people. In documenting the life history of the elderly, we observe considerable diversity of their life courses, work histories, and patterns of social interaction over a more extended length of time. As an example, some older people have managed to accumulate considerable wealth and property over their lifetimes, whereas others have relatively little. Although some older Canadians benefit from a high income relating to their past investments and/or private pension plans, others are completely reliant on government transfers as they move into later life—which places them at much greater risk for being unable to meet their basic needs (Green et al., 2008).

While acknowledging such diversity, we can also draw a few generalizations as to the living arrangements and relative economic status of older Canadians. Most of those aged 65 and older currently live in small households, either with their spouse, sometimes by themselves, and occasionally with an adult child. Whereas older men are more likely to be living with a spouse in later life, older women are far more likely to be living on their own. Widowhood is much more common for women than for men, as women outlive men by about five years on average and tend to marry men slightly their senior. Although women are more likely to outlive their husbands, men are more likely to marry on the event of their spouse's death. Thus women are much more likely to spend the last several years of their lives living by themselves—a reality that has direct ramifications for their economic well-being.

The expansion of the welfare state in Canada during the second half of the twentieth century had a dramatic impact on the economic well-being of elderly Canadians (Myles, 2000). Various programs were introduced and expanded, and these programs—including Old Age Security, the Guaranteed Income Supplement, the Canada Pension Plan, and the Quebec Pension Plan (among other benefits)—significantly reduced the risk of sliding into poverty. When the Dominion Bureau of Statistics first started reporting information on the incidence of low income in Canada in the 1960s, Canadians aged 65 and older were more likely to be classified as income poor than any other age group. In fact, more than 40 per cent of elderly families were classified as having low income at that time (Podoluk, 1968). Since then, however, the rates of low income have declined substantially and have fallen to levels below that of other age groups (Statistics Canada, 2009).

Many of the income support programs that were expanded during the 1970s and 1980s were highly successful in reducing the likelihood of economic hardship among the elderly (Myles, 2000). Picot and Myles (2005) report that as recently as the late 1970s, the rate of low income (defined as less than half the median family income) among elderly households was just under 35 per cent. Two decades later, the elderly low-income rate had declined to less than five per cent—a more dramatic decline than for any other group in Canada. As there has been far less support to subsidize families at earlier stages of the life course, the incidence of poverty is now lower among families with at least one person over the age of 65 than it is among any other family or household types. Although the median income of elderly families (at $48,800 in 2010) is lower than across all families, so too is average family size and the likelihood of income poverty. According to Statistics Canada, the incidence of low income in 2010 after taxes plummets to only 3.2 per cent among elderly families (Tables 10.1 and 10.2).

While most families in later life can avoid poverty by pooling government transfers, even without savings or private pension plans, this option is not possible for the elderly who live alone. Just as older women are more likely to outlive their husbands, so too are they more likely to slip into poverty on the death of their spouse. About 15.6 per cent of unattached women aged 65 years or older who lived alone were classified as being in the low-income bracket in 2010, while 11.5 per cent of unattached older men were classified in this manner. Clearly, a great many unattached Canadian seniors remain vulnerable, as some have insufficient assets and pension plans to retire in comfort. Fundamental in this context is whether or not the elderly live in families, which again hints at the importance of family living arrangements and the manner in which individuals share resources in predicting low income and economic hardship (Cheal, 1999).

Low Income, Family Change, and Child Poverty

For more on child poverty see "Impact of Measures on Child Poverty" in Chapter 15, pp. 300–3.

Public policy in Canada has been far less generous towards families at earlier stages of their life course than in subsidizing families at latter stages. The expansion of income support programs for the elderly has not been accompanied by anything comparable for young families with children. If anything, as governments expanded income support programs for older Canadians in recent decades, income support programs directed at younger families have become less generous. For example, during the 1990s, unemployment insurance and income assistance programs became more restrictive, which obviously had a greater impact on younger families (with or without children) than on elderly families. Moreover, the federal government also abandoned its universal Family Allowance program, further reducing the institutional support available for families with children. The net impacts of more limited social transfers for low-income families can be seen in a variety of ways. The evidence from Canada's National Longitudinal Study of Children and Youth, for example, reveals that the welfare reform programs of the 1990s failed to improve the well-being (school readiness) of those youngsters living in poverty (Williamson and Salkie, 2005).

In short, there has been a major shift in the age distribution of the poor in Canada. While in the 1960s elderly Canadians were about twice as likely as children to be classified as income poor, the situation these days has nearly reversed itself. The shift in the age distribution of poverty is arguably one of the most striking changes to characterize the distribution of family income over the last several decades (Cheal, 1999). This raises troubling questions relating to public policy and generational equity (Preston, 1984). Many of the aforementioned changes in the structure of the Canadian family—including the increased incidence of lone parenthood—have had a much greater impact on the economic well-being of children than on older age groups.

Poverty among Canadian children deserves special mention for a variety of reasons. First, children are particularly vulnerable because of their dependency on parents or caregivers for their economic well-being. Most research on income poverty, however, completely neglects the manner in which resources are shared within families, such as between spouses and between adults and children. The implicit assumption of an equal sharing of financial resources can potentially obscure important differences in the actual level of economic hardship experienced by individual family members (Phipps and Burton, 1995; Woolley, 1998). Yet the well-being of children ultimately depends on the judgment and goodwill of their parents, as well as the adults' decisions and options regarding family composition, work opportunities, and housing and community locations. Children have far less influence in these areas, despite the significance of such factors in shaping their economic well-being.

While poverty or low-income rates may appear to be somewhat stable in drawing comparisons over time, the actual distribution of individuals and families classified as poor will vary somewhat in response to different life events and especially in terms of changing family characteristics. In Canada, Finnie (2000) has shown that roughly half of those defined as "poor" early in the 1990s escaped poverty within four years, even though a substantial minority remained poor for four consecutive years. Those at greatest risk for such "persistent poverty" were single mothers with children. In addition, Picot et al. (1999) have concluded from their analysis of the Survey of Labour and Income Dynamics that divorces, separations, and remarriages have as great an impact on children entering or leaving poverty as does the changing labour market situation of their parents.

Economic Well-Being among Visible Minority Communities

In Canada, Aboriginal peoples are far more likely to be living in low-income situations as compared with the non-Aboriginal population. For starters, the median income for Aboriginal people tends to be roughly 30 per cent lower than that of non-Aboriginals (Wilson and Macdonald, 2010). Although the information remains incomplete in assessing low income among Aboriginal peoples, the data indicate that nearly one in five self-identified Aboriginals living in private households and almost 43 per cent of unattached individuals lived in low-income situations in 2005 (Collin and Jensen, 2009). In comparison, roughly 8.4 per cent and 28 per cent of the respective non-Aboriginal populations experienced low income that year. Aboriginal women tend to fare even worse than their male counterparts. By extension, nearly 28 per cent of Aboriginal children 15 years and younger experienced low income as compared with about 13 per cent of the non-Aboriginal population: 33.7 per cent of First Nations children, 20.8 per cent of Inuit children, and 20.1 per cent of Métis children.

As with Aboriginal peoples, those who identified themselves as visible minorities for the 2006 Census were more than twice as likely to be living in poverty or below the after tax, low-income cutoffs (22 per cent) as compared with the white or caucasian majority (9 per cent). The visible minorities or "racialized" members of Canadian society living in poverty tend to be rather different in terms of key demographic information in comparison with the non-racialized majority. In particular, racialized individuals living in poverty tend to be younger, married, more educated, immigrants, and unemployed (National Council of Welfare, 2012). For example, 32 per cent of racialized persons between the ages of 25–64 with university degrees lived in poverty. Even more dramatically, approximately 90 per cent of racialized individuals living in poverty are newcomers to Canada, or first-generation immigrants (National Council of Welfare, 2012). The historical evidence points to a more general decline in the economic well-being of recent immigrants spanning at least three decades (Picot, 2004). The economic struggles of many newcomer families tend to produce other outcomes, such as an exodus of young immigrants from secondary schools, which may serve to perpetuate poverty across generations (Anisef et al., 2010).

Shortcomings of Income-Based Measures of Poverty

Income-based indicators of economic well-being have many well-known limitations, most of which have been discussed in detail elsewhere (Cotton et al., 1999; Collins, 2005; Head, 2008; Hulchanski and Michalski, 1994). These measures tend to systematically under-report or exclude various types of in-kind public assistance, the sharing of resources and services across households and generations, the impact of exchanges in the informal economy, the bartering of goods and services, and various types of employment benefits such as extended medical insurance and drug plans. This is particularly problematic in documenting the economic well-being of Canadians because these resources and entitlements can vary considerably across individuals and households.

For example, merely consider the economic situation of a college or university student temporarily earning a relatively low income, yet receiving generous non-declared income support from a parent or relative. This is a dramatically different situation from a young adult working full-time at a minimum wage job without any such aid from a family member. Similarly, a young adult living precariously close to the poverty line in a low-wage and insecure job is in a vastly different situation from a young university graduate setting out in a career-type job with perhaps a temporarily low wage but with generous benefits, a pension plan, job security, and the promise of higher income. The aforementioned income statistics do not directly provide us with this sort of detailed information necessary to delineate such differences across individuals and households. In fact, there is currently a scarcity of comprehensive data at the national level that would allow us to carefully consider many of these issues, both cross-sectionally and over time.

Most income-based measures of income poverty also exclude information on wealth, which again varies in an important manner across households. Economists typically define wealth to mean the stock of assets held by a household or individual that either yields or has the potential to yield income. Wealth can take on a variety of forms and is typically defined as the difference between total assets and total debts. Total assets include all deposits, investments in mutual funds, bonds, and stock holdings, as well as registered retirement savings plans, locked-in retirement accounts, homeownership, vehicles, etc. Total debts include mortgage debts, outstanding balances on credit cards, student loans, vehicle loans, lines of credit, and other money owed. While there is considerable income inequality in Canada, there is an even greater level of wealth inequality—which actually appears to have worsened somewhat over recent years (Statistics Canada, 2002e, 2006a). For example, in 1984 the top decile of all family households in Canada controlled 51.8 per cent of wealth, but by 2005 this had risen to 58.2 per cent (Morissette and Zhang, 2006).

While households classified as income poor are considerably more likely to have little wealth or property, clearly there is not a perfect association between income and wealth. For example, consider the economic situation of someone who has paid off his or her mortgage, has major investments in terms of securities and the stock market, and yet for whatever reason chooses to live on a relatively low income. Alternatively, consider a new immigrant to Toronto or to some other large city in Canada trying to establish herself in the labour market for the first time, without any property or investments. Rising housing costs also work against the interests of many, including new labour force entrants, whether they are newly arrived to Canada or have recently completed their education (Zhang, 2003). Once more, these sorts of disparities are not obvious when restricting ourselves exclusively to the distribution of income across families.

Just as wealth differs enormously across households and individuals, it tends to vary systematically by life cycle stage as well. In working with Statistics Canada's 2005 Survey on Financial Security, Morissette and Zhang (2006) demonstrate major discrepancies by age group. Among families whose major income recipient was aged 35–44, median wealth in 2005 dollars was about $84,200, as compared to a median of over $200,000 for families whose major income recipient was aged 55–64. Everything else being the same, younger people not only tend to have lower incomes, but also typically have less overall wealth. Similarly, Morissette and Zhang (2006) have documented that median wealth varies in an important manner by education, immigration status, and number of years residing in Canada. There are also important differences in wealth as documented across family types, in comparing lone-parent families with dual-parent families, elderly with non-elderly families, or households with or without children (see Figure 10.2).

Lone-parent families reported a negligible median wealth of only a few thousand dollars, which contrasts sharply with dual-parent families with children aged 18 and over, who reported a median wealth of almost $260,000 in 2005. In fact, when we systematically examine differences in wealth across individuals and family types, the inequalities documented in terms of income largely become accentuated. The precariousness of certain types of households and families (e.g., lone-parent families or non-elderly individuals living alone) appears to be even more obvious when we consider differences in terms of assets and wealth. To the extent that those who left income poverty in recent years continue to work in low-wage, insecure jobs with relatively little wealth or property, they are clearly more vulnerable to economic downturns. Many Canadians could easily fall back into poverty with the loss of a low-income job and, in turn, have relatively little wealth to draw from in getting through the worst of economic times.

How Do Low-Income Families Cope With and Survive Poverty?

How do low-income families survive, particularly those with limited market incomes and/or meagre state transfers, such as social assistance? Several commentators have observed that economic factors, globalization, and the subsequent restructuring of the Canadian welfare state have increased the vulnerability of large segments of the population (McMullin et al., 2002; Caragata, 2003; Lightman et al., 2008). Social assistance rates declined and eligibility requirements tightened across Canada during the 1990s, as the proportion of unemployed workers eligible for Employment Insurance benefits fell significantly—and the overall size of the Canadian safety net continued to shrink over the next decade (Krahn et al., 2007; Cooke and Gazso, 2009; Mendelson et al., 2009). Despite these changes, research reveals that women, in particular, continue to weigh several advantages (e.g., increased income, self-esteem, independence) and disadvantages (e.g., overload, exhaustion, less supervision of children) in evaluating their welfare experiences (Duck, 2012; London et al., 2004). The evidence in the North American context further suggests that many of those who move from welfare to employment do not necessarily improve their income situations or family well-being due to the unstable, low-income jobs that they were able to obtain (Scott et al., 2004; Lightman et al., 2010).

As welfare supports tightened up during the 1990s, a variety of community support services developed and in-kind contributions grew. Both Chekki (1999) and Capponi (1999) argued that many agencies—soup kitchens, church and school programs, community centres, Salvation Army centres, and other charitable organizations—expanded their operations in the face of growing demands. In addition, Michalski (2003b) has demonstrated the importance of food banks as a supplemental source of support for low-income families

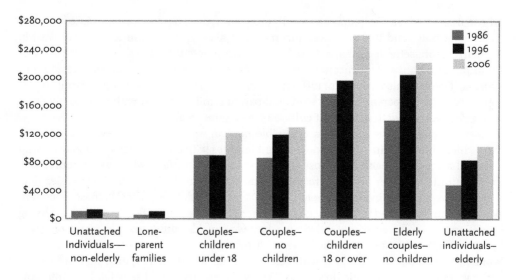

Figure 10.2 **Median Wealth by Family Type, 1984–2005**

SOURCE: Morissette and Zhang, (2006); Statistics Canada, *Assets and Debts Survey*, 1984; *Survey of Financial Security*, 1999 and 2005.

that has expanded dramatically over the past two decades, but especially in the 1990s. In the decade from 1999–2009, food bank usage in Canada remained relatively stable as compared with the overall growth in population. The short-term impact of the 2009 recession, however, produced a nearly 10 per cent spike in food bank usage, reaching an all-time high in 2012 as more than 880,000 Canadians accessed food bank programs across the country (Pegg and Stapleton, 2012). Thus food banks continue to be an important coping strategy for about 2.5 per cent of Canadians monthly (see "Case in Point" box).

Indeed, low-income families typically rely on a broad range of economic survival strategies. The available research demonstrates that these strategies vary in part in response to the degree of urbanization and, more specifically, the resource infrastructures and support networks available in different locales (Harvey, 2011; DeVerteuil, 2005). The labour market represents one key structural dimension, with the commercial infrastructure providing a variable range of options for low-income households in their efforts to meet their basic needs (Iyenda, 2001). In addition, different locales provide distinct opportunities for exchanges, including a variety of non-market and non-governmental economic options such as household production, self-provisioning, and other forms of unpaid work in the informal economy (Felt and Sinclair, 1992; Reimer, 2006), as well as community-based exchanges (Engler-Stringer and Berenbaum, 2007; Raddon, 2003), access to social supports and networking (Barnes, 2003; Letkemann, 2004), and the many non-profit organizations associated with the voluntary sector (Small, 2006). Further evidence suggests that women in particular expand their access to resources by engaging in volunteer service and mobilizing to establish greater organizational ties and connections with others (Messias et al., 2005).

Where job loss occurs and in high unemployment areas, material hardships such as food insufficiency, an inability to meet housing costs, or even the affordability of telephone services routinely crop up (Lovell and Oh, 2005). Families with limited resources compensate by reducing their expenses in general, receiving public assistance, retaining a stable residence, and cutting food expenditures (Yeung and Hofferth, 1998). Most heads of household, though, prefer to return to the paid labour force. Under Canada's revised "Employment Insurance" program, the evidence reveals that many individuals accept less than optimal jobs and the prospects of additional training in order to recover lost income more quickly (Martel et al., 2005).

Edin and Lein (1997) studied the importance of three additional strategies above and beyond employment income and welfare supports for sustaining low-income households among women: (1) informal network supports from friends, family, and absentee fathers; (2) side work in the formal, informal, and underground economies; and (3) agency-based strategies from community groups and charitable organizations. Since neither welfare nor low-wage work provided adequate income for living for the families in their study, Edin and Lein (1997: 6) reported that "all but one of the 379 mothers spoken to were engaged in other income-generating strategies to supplement their income and ensure their economic survival."

CASE IN POINT
What Role Do Food Banks Play in Helping to Sustain Low-Income Families?

The first food bank in Canada opened in Edmonton in 1981 as a stopgap measure to assist poor individuals and families on an emergency basis. Throughout the 1980s, the number of food banks continued to grow across Canada, such that by 1989 there were nearly 160 located across the ten provinces (Oderkirk, 1992). The number of food banks doubled over the next two years and expanded quite rapidly through the 1990s. In just two decades, the total number had grown to roughly 600 food banks working with more than 2,000 agencies dispensing groceries and/or serving meals in every province and territory in Canada (Wilson, with Tsoa, 2001). Figure 10.3 summarizes the trend in food bank usage over the last decade, which fluctuated slightly, before a recent surge on the heels of the 2008–9 economic recession. The relative consistency of these numbers suggest that food banks have become well entrenched as a common response to hunger in Canada (Michalski, 2003b).

More generally, food banks and emergency food programs are part of the bundle of coping strategies that many low-income individuals and families use to survive (Tarasuk, 2001; Tarasuk and Dachner, 2009; Michalski, 2003a). Kennedy (1995) has demonstrated that in the Greater Toronto Area, the coping strategies for low-income families include a vast array of budgeting and money-saving schemes, including public transit, bulk shopping, selling personal possessions, doing without telephones, forgoing recreation and entertainment, or even simply consuming less food or doing without altogether. While by

(Continued)

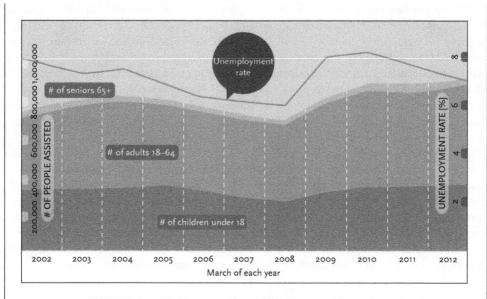

Figure 10.3 **Monthly Food Bank Users in Canada, 2001–2012**

SOURCE: Pegg and Stapleton, 2012; Food Banks Canada.

no means a comprehensive service or welfare supplement, food banks are an additional source of support among a patchwork of low-income survival strategies (Tarasuk, 2001; Tarasak and Eakin, 2003).

The available studies clearly indicate that those who access food banks in urban settings on average tend to have household incomes far below established poverty lines (Michalski, 2003b). Their economic statuses are almost always quite precarious, with housing costs consuming the majority of available monthly income (Pegg and Marshall, 2011; Vozoris et al., 2001). The depth of their need has been measured more formally over time by comparing their disposable income with household needs (shelter costs, food, clothing, transportation, dental or special health needs, recreation, and so forth). In focusing on Toronto, Michalski (2003a) has estimated that the disposable income of food bank users actually declined significantly during the latter 1990s. In this context, it is not surprising that a proportion of Ontario residents became increasingly dependent on public assistance and the voluntary sector to help meet their most basic of needs.

In Ontario, Vozoris et al. (2002) have demonstrated that income from Ontario Works (welfare) alone proved insufficient to cover the core needs for households residing in market rental accommodations on a regular basis. Even if families were fortunate enough to live in rent-geared-to-income housing, a great many expenses beyond the bare necessities (e.g., school expenses, reading materials, gifts) routinely placed them in a deficit-spending position and thus unable to afford regularly a nutritious diet. Herein the importance of relying on informal sources of support or developing a range of alternative coping strategies cannot be overstated.

For example, the majority of food bank users indicated one specific coping mechanism involved simply being hungry once each month or more, while nearly half reported that their children were hungry at least that often as well (Michalski, 2003a). Other coping strategies included not having a telephone, walking rather than owning a vehicle or using public transportation, forgoing recreation, relying on charities, borrowing money or receiving cash advances, and financial or food gifts from extended family or friends in the past year. In summation, the research has confirmed that low-income families employ a range of adaptive strategies—informal support networks, unreported and underground work, self-production, and in-kind supports from voluntary and charitable organizations—in their ongoing struggles to secure the basic necessities of life (Bostock, 2001; Michalski, 2003a; see Jarrett et al., 2010).

What Are the Consequences of Poverty?

Very briefly, we wish to consider an issue that has been examined more extensively than any other aspect of low-income families: What are the consequences of poverty? Many consequences are highly predictable and have been well documented. Others are not especially obvious or well understood. Health consequences, for instance, have long been associated with a relative lack of family resources and poverty in general. Social scientists have established that a direct relationship exists between socio-economic status (whether measured in terms of income levels or other measures of social class) and health status (Kosteniuk and Dickinson, 2003; Phipps, 2003). The groundbreaking Whitehall Study of British civil servants determined that those employed at the highest grades had about one-third the mortality rate of those in the lowest grades (Marmot and Smith, 1997). The study found that death rates were three times higher among junior office support staff as compared with senior administrators, even though these were all white-collar workers in the same offices and living in the same area of the country.

Interestingly, having a sense of control over one's work significantly relates to one's health status—a finding replicated in the second stage of the British research or the Whitehall II Study (Griffin et al., 2002). Higher incomes appear to be linked to improved health not simply as a result of the ability to purchase adequate housing, food, and other necessities, but also because of the enhanced sense of control and mastery that people have over their lives. Even the level of job insecurity or the threat of losing one's job apparently contributes to increased distress and a decreased sense of control—which have negative effects on self-reported health status.

The 1999 *Report on the Health of Canadians* found that Canadians in the highest income bracket were more likely to report their health as excellent and to live longer than those in the lower income brackets. Further, statistical evidence revealed that the poor were at greater risk for most types of illnesses and almost all causes of death (Federal, Provincial, and Territorial Advisory Committee on Population Health, 1999). Income-related disparities affect the nutritional quality of food selection, which has direct implications for health inequalities (Ricciutto and Tarasak, 2007). Indeed, in their review of more than a dozen studies using eight data sets across four countries, Benzeval and Judge (2001: 1379) conclude the following: "All of the studies that include measures of income level find that it is significantly related to health outcomes."

Even more compelling has been the finding that childhood financial circumstances may be linked to adult health outcomes (Duncan and Brooks-Gunn, 1997). Obviously, many other factors may intervene and otherwise affect such long-term outcomes, but the impacts of sustained poverty and the likelihood that children and adolescents may be deprived of various social and economic advantages cannot be denied (Curtis et al., 2004). In fact, the research confirms that the relative disadvantages for children commence even before they are born, as poor children have significantly greater risks of being born prematurely and with lower birth weights, suffer greater intellectual impairment such as mental handicaps, and experience higher infant mortality rates (Wilkins and Sherman, 1998). By the time poor children have entered formal schooling, the evidence indicates that they have already fallen behind in terms of school readiness, cognitive achievements, and early academic performance (Williamson and Salkie, 2005).

Growing up in a poor family has consistently been linked to a variety of negative outcomes, including academic problems, psychosocial morbidity, and, more generally, a range of emotional and behavioural problems (Lipman and Offord, 1997; Kornberger et al., 2001). Adolescents who have experienced persistent poverty tend to have lower self-esteem and poorer school performance and attachment, engage in a range of risky or unhealthy practices (e.g., drugs and alcohol abuse), and commit more acts of delinquency and other forms of anti-social behaviour (McLeod and Shanahan, 1996; Robinson et al., 2005).

Why should poverty have such negative effects on children, who are often quite resilient? Certainly many children *do* survive and even thrive in the long term *despite* their relatively deprived conditions. The main reason for having potentially negative short-term and long-term effects may be more the result of the problems and stressors that parents face in providing adequate financial, physical, and often emotional resources than anything else. Lone-parent mothers, for instance, often experience a high level of stress in meeting the requirements of both child care and income support. This often leads to poorer health outcomes for both parent *and* child, which in turn introduce additional obstacles to securing gainful employment (Baker, 2002). More generally, while the causal connections can be quite complex, research has shown that several home-related or environmental factors such as a difficult physical environment may also mediate the relationship between low income and intellectual development (Guo and Harris, 2000; Brannigan et al., 2002). Neighbourhood and community cohesion can serve to lessen the impact of family poverty, as the potential for additional social supports increases (Jarrett et al., 2010; Klebanov et al., 1994). Low-income families tend to live in poorer neighbourhoods and in lower-quality housing, which introduce additional obstacles as they attempt to provide children with the same types of services that most middle- and upper-income Canadians take for granted.

Conclusion

Despite Canada's considerable wealth, many families with low income remain in poverty and continue to face major challenges—especially in light of the most recent recession in 2009. Many statistical indicators highlight various gains, such as the overall growth in the economy, rising family incomes, and reduced low-income rates. In working with Statistics

Canada's LICOs, we find that the country experienced several years of declining low-income rates and reliance upon social assistance.

A careful appraisal of the available data, however, leads us to emphasize that some issues of considerable concern should not be downplayed or overlooked. The persistently high incidence of low income among recent immigrants (at about 2.5 times the levels observed for non-immigrants), for example, offers one source of concern in a country increasingly dependent on immigration. The high level of income poverty among female lone-parent families should not be overlooked either, particularly in view of the important consequences for the young. In addition, while many Canadian families witnessed income gains during the late 1990s and early 2000s, the evidence suggests that upper-income Canadians experienced the greatest gains. Statistics Canada reports a real upturn in income inequality over this period in terms of family income both "before tax" and, to a lesser extent, "after tax" (Heisz, 2007).

As highlighted in this chapter, family change and demographic events have an impact on income poverty, especially to the extent that they influence the types of families and living arrangements in which Canadians share and pool income. Changing family structures in particular have generated some degree of economic uncertainty, especially for women and children. Whereas lone-parent families comprise about one in five families with children, among families classified as income poor, over half are single-parent families (Statistics Canada, 2005c). Many of these changes observed in the Canadian family, in terms of non-marital fertility and marital instability, have had a greater impact on the economic well-being of women than they have on men.

The consequences for children have been particularly important, as child poverty persists despite political pronouncements such as the House of Commons 1989 resolution to end child poverty by the year 2000. Canada has simultaneously witnessed a shift in the age distribution of the poor over past decades. In the 1960s, elderly Canadians were about twice as likely as children to be classified as income poor, but this situation has nearly reversed itself as the likelihood of poverty stands much higher among families with children. Thus the incidence of low income and poverty varies considerably, depending on family type and number of earners, as well as variations linked to age, life course stage, immigration, visible minority status, labour market conditions, and other factors.

In closing, two observations are worth repeating. First, the evidence suggests that for some families and individuals, an exit from welfare over the past decade has actually led to a worsening of an already bad situation. Second, over this same period, there has been a substantial increase in the number of food banks in Canada, as well as other charities that serve meals and/or provide for other basic necessities. In a sense, food banks have become institutionalized during a period of more restrictive governmental income supports. Thus, while unemployment insurance and welfare payments have been more restrictive since the 1990s, governments have *not* been poised to reinvest in significant ways that might compensate for these policy changes. Finally, still other problems that low-income families face may be more intractable, particularly in regard to dealing with certain unpredictable events and interpersonal decisions that shake families up or leave them vulnerable. Where family poverty cannot be prevented, however, the research points to the significance of a great many negative outcomes linked to living in poverty over a sustained period of time. From a social transfer standpoint, the costs associated with dealing with the long-term consequences of family poverty inevitably exceed the costs associated with reducing or preventing such poverty in the first place.

STUDY QUESTIONS

1. The last two decades were turbulent years for many Canadians, with some noticeable ups and downs in the North American economy. Discuss these trends in terms of median income and income poverty, with particular attention to the economic recessions of the early 1990s and 2009. Since the time of writing this chapter (using Statistics Canada data through to 2010), how do you think the economic conditions of Canadian families has changed (i.e., have we witnessed changes for the better or for the worse)?

2. Picot et al. (1998) highlight three distinctive types of events in the explanation of recent trends in terms of income poverty, including "demographic" events, "economic" events, and "political" events. Discuss the relevance of each in reference to recent trends in the economic well-being and poverty of Canadian families.

3. The number of families living on welfare in Canada declined during the 1990s and early 2000s. What are some of the contributing factors responsible for this decline? Do you think that this trend will continue over the next several years? Why or why not?

4. Evidence suggests that one-third of all persons who left welfare during the late 1990s and the first decade of the twenty-first century saw their household income decline— sometimes dramatically. Why did this occur?

5. What are the most significant effects or consequences of poverty on families? Who, in your view, suffers the most as a result of family poverty?

Further Readings

McKeen, Wendy. 2004. *Money in Their Own Name: The Feminist Voice in Poverty Debate in Canada, 1970–1995*. Toronto: University of Toronto Press. The author presents a feminist perspective on social policy debates regarding poverty over the last three decades of the twentieth century, and also discusses the implications of "women-friendly" social policies.

National Council of Welfare. 2011. *The Dollars and Sense of Solving Poverty*. Ottawa: National Council of Welfare. The monograph outlines the reasons for why poverty persists, despite existing programs in wealthy countries. The authors demonstrate how the direct and especially indirect costs of poverty are far greater than the fiscal requirements of a more comprehensive and effective income support system designed to truly eradicate the problem.

Picot, Garnett, and John Myles. 2005. *Income Inequality and Low Income in Canada: An International Perspective*. Analytical Studies Research Paper Series 11F-0019-MIE-2005-240. Ottawa: Statistics Canada, Analytic Studies Branch. This is an overview of income inequality and low-income trends in Canada from an international perspective, establishing the extent to which Canada can be considered a low-income country as compared with other Western nations.

Statistics Canada. 2009. *Income in Canada*. Ottawa: Statistics Canada, catalogue no. 75-202-X. The definitive annual publication has been the most reliable source of income statistics in Canada, but has been discontinued in the current format. Statistics Canada presents the highlights and summary statistics on income and low income among Canadian families, along with trend data.

Websites

www.ccsd.ca
The Canadian Council on Social Development, a non-profit social policy and research organization, focuses on issues such as poverty, social inclusion, disability, cultural diversity, child well-being, and employment.

www.lisdatacenter.org
The Luxembourg Income Study is a non-profit co-operative research project with a membership of 25 countries, including Canada, on four continents: Europe, America, Asia, and Oceania. This research project regularly publishes comparative and international research on poverty across member countries.

www.campaign2000.ca
Campaign 2000 is a cross-Canada public education movement to build Canadian awareness and support for the 1989 all-party House of Commons resolution to end child poverty in Canada by the year 2000. Campaign 2000 annually releases national and provincial reports cards on the state child and family poverty in Canada.

www.caledoninst.org
The Caledon Institute is an independent social policy think tank established in 1992, offering critical research and policy analysis on a wide range of topics such as pensions, welfare benefits, child benefits, Employment Insurance, taxation, community development, and health and social spending. Their publications are available online at no cost to the general public.

Note

1. The authors would like to thank Marie-Josée Bourgeois, Client Services, for her timely assistance in obtaining up-to-date income data from Income Statistics Division, Statistics Canada.

11

Intellectual Debates, Testimonials, and Changing Social Values: Same-Sex Marriage in Canada

DOREEN M. FUMIA

LEARNING OBJECTIVES

- To be able to distinguish between marriage as a private lived experience of two people and marriage as a relationship between two people and the state
- To learn about key events and debates that led to adoption of the Civil Marriages Act (Bill C-38) in Canada
- To understand how same-sex marriage challenges a heterosexual nation
- To understand why same-sex couples feel compelled to be recognized by the state through marriage
- To understand why supporters of same-sex relationships oppose same-sex marriage

Introduction

Just as Adrienne Rich (1995) claimed that motherhood is both a personal relationship and a public institution, so, too, can it be said of marriage. To view marriage as an institution is to step back from viewing it as a relationship *between* two people and, rather, view it as a relationship between two people and the state. When we focus on marriage as an institution, we are less interested in the specificity of any one couple and more interested in which couples fit into state regulations that define and protect family relations. In addition, it is important to point out that focusing on any relationship between the state and the people is always embedded in a broader discussion about the nation and its citizens.

In this chapter I first ask: What is marriage for? I then examine how same-sex marriage came to be legalized in Canada. I then step back to examine the process the state engaged in when deciding whether or not pursuing same-sex marriage was appropriate for Canadian society using information from the Ontario court challenge in *Halpern v. Canada*, 2003. This case, as other provincial court challenges did, drew on intellectual experts and individual stories from same-sex couples. This first section of the paper emphasizes the focus on legitimizing same-sex relationships through same-sex marriage and includes the views of those who oppose same-sex relationships. In the following section, I focus on debates that assume the legitimacy of same-sex relationships and focus on whether marriage is a useful institution at all. One side of these debates argues that suggesting people operate outside the logic of state institutions, such as family and marriage, means surrendering their right to full citizenship participation. The other side argues that marriage constrains, excludes, and disadvantages a wide range of family forms, and people who live in them, that are not recognized through the institution of marriage. Given this, marriage is not a useful pursuit. I end the paper with a brief discussion about these two sets of debates and think towards broadening our limited concepts of families, marriage, and citizenship.

What Is Marriage For?

One scholar who writes about the historically varied and changing criteria for marriage and family relationships in the West is E.J. Graff (2004). Graff provides a historical overview of marriage and notes its changing status based on changing economic and social needs. She explains that in earlier historical periods, marriage was viewed as a contractual business relationship based on money matters for the family unit, such as income earning and property acquisition and preservation for income including farms, dowries, and the status of wives and servants. According to Graff, in later periods of industrial and post-industrial capitalism, less emphasis was placed on money and property for the basis for marriage and an increased emphasis was placed on psychological relationships and the importance of feelings. She does note, however, that even with the emphasis on matters of the heart there continues to be economic interdependence.

The formalized regulation of "coupledom" concerns local communities and the state. Acceptable norms about how to recognize who is and who is not married have varied from simply declaring a commitment before God to signing documentation that is legally binding. More recently, there has been a departure from religious and legally formalized marriage and an increase in unmarried couples cohabiting in common-law relationships. Cohabitation and common-law relationships are similar to, but not exactly like, marriage. Marriage is taken more seriously—in ways that have both legal and social ramifications—by banks, insurers, courts, employers, schools, hospitals, cemeteries, rental car companies, frequent-flyer programs, and more. Graff (2004: 49) remarks that "marriage is a word that is understood to mean that you share not only your bedroom but the rest of the house as well . . . [it] is the marker that allows the courts to assume that you two wanted your relationship to be respected after death."

Different couple relationships are marked by a citizen's relationship to the state and to each other. For example, in common-law relationships, unlike marriage, there is no presumption that assets should be divided equally at the end of such a relationship upon separation or death. One aspect underpinning the same-sex debates that will be discussed in more depth later is the significance that access to state-recognized marriages makes, given that marriage and common law are so similar. While there are few differences, some say the devil is in the details.

The de-emphasis on money as the central factor in the institution of marriage has been followed by the erosion of other historical underpinnings that have been viewed as immoral practices, such as premarital sex and child-bearing outside marriage. One of the most significant shifts has been that of the heterosexual presumption that has defined marriage, "one man + one woman = marriage," as a placard against same-sex marriage proclaimed at a March 2005 protest in Ottawa. What these shifts signal is a redefinition of the moral underpinnings of state-recognized relationships and families. The question that Graff asks in the title of her book is apt here: What is marriage for?

> [O]nce society got rid of the ideas that sex without babies is bad . . . once our philosophy and laws protect sex for pleasure and love, how can same-sex marriage be barred? (Graff, 2004: 84)

This quote is a good place to begin to think about the legal and moral shifts that have led us to debating whether or not to legitimate same-sex relationships and marriage.

Same-Sex Marriage and Sexual Others

While people in different parts of the globe continue to be persecuted, tortured, and/or murdered if caught in a same-sex relationship,[1] in other parts of the world laws have supported such relationships. Canada became the fourth country in the world to legalize same-sex marriage following Spain (June 2005), the Netherlands (2001), and Belgium (2003). The United Kingdom (2005), South Africa (2006), Norway (2008), Sweden (2009), Portugal (2010), Iceland (2010), Argentina (2010), and New Zealand (2013) have also legalized some form of same-sex unions. Lesbian, gay, bisexual, trans, and queer identified (hereafter LGBTQ) groups in many parts of the world are still fighting for legalizing same-sex relationships; at the time of writing 6 of the United States' 50 states (and the District of Columbia) had passed laws legalizing same-sex marriage: Connecticut, Iowa, Massachusetts, New Hampshire, and New York. Other states continue to debate the same-sex marriage issue, California being most notable (*Wall Street Journal*, 14 June 2012). California passed a same-sex marriage law in 2008 and just months later lost the legal right in a referendum, Proposition 8, during the presidential election in November of that year. In 2010, the ban on same-sex marriage was overturned. The legal right to marry in California was challenged again in 2012 but the earlier ruling was upheld. According to BBC News' website (31 July 2012) it is believed that same-sex marriage will be challenged again, next time in the Supreme Court.

It is imperative that we keep our eyes on same-sex marriage laws that tap into hotly contested moral territory. Even in Canada, since same-sex marriage was legalized, debates have arisen that have the potential to undermine it, especially given that the federal government at the time did not systematically review all the laws and policies that might need adjustment. The result is that legal problems for married same-sex couples have persisted in administrative areas, such as immigration. For instance, in the last year a Canadian citizen has claimed the right to have his civil partnership, which was performed in Britain, equivalent to same-sex marriage in Canada. While the Ontario government was not opposed to this, the federal government has intervened to oppose the claim. There is a long history that precedes the fights to legalize same-sex marriage and many of those fights happen more than once.

Struggles over who has the right to marry are embedded in social constructions of how we are located in society. Identities are key to those constructions and in the case of marriage, the focus is on sexual identities. Sexual identities are multiple and marked as different and marginal through notions of racialization and sexual difference. As sexual Others, we are identified not by who we are (for instance, professors, students, sales clerks, lawyers, union representatives) but, rather, by what we do (for instance, sexual acts). Therefore, when non-heterosexual relations are considered for legitimacy within the institution of marriage, **normalization**, that is, the ways in which identities are constituted within social norms, needs to be discussed. It is important to say a word about the terms used to identify non-heterosexual identities: lesbian, gay, bisexual, transgendered, transsexual, two-spirit, intersexed, and queer, hereafter referred to as LGBT2SIQ. While this acronym aims to identify multiple identities that constitute non-heterosexual orientations, it is not meant to conflate the varying political and social struggles embedded in each identity. This chapter, because it addresses state-sanctioned same-sex relationships, focuses on identities represented in **human rights claims** within the frame of the Charter of Rights and Freedoms. For this reason, the subjects of the category "same-sex marriage" are predominantly those who can fit into a normative notion of "lesbian" or "gay," which, like other normative identities, are assumed to share white middle-class values. When the terms "lesbian" and "gay" are unmarked and most often used without any qualifying signifiers to mark race, class, or specific sexual orientation such as transsexual, then mainstream identities of **whiteness**, middle-class status, and able-bodiedness are assumed (Bérubé, 2001). While important earlier work theorizes sexual identities and refuses fixed categories of sex and/or gender (for instance, Beauvoir, 1989; Butler, 1990; Grosz, 1993; Wittig, 1993), the reference in this chapter to lesbians and gays is not meant to assume fixed identities as ontological truths. Rather, referring to "lesbians and gays" is meant to note how these essentialized identities have monopolized the debates around same-sex relationships in ways that exclude other and more marginalized groups from the discussion.

Lauren Berlant (1997) contends that identity is marketed in national capitalism as a property. That is, identity is something you can purchase a relation to or something you already own that you can express—"my masculinity," "my sexual differences." According to Berlant, identity is fundamentally sexual (17). Further, Foucault (1990), Butler (1990), and Katz (1995) have argued that sexuality is the modern form of self-intelligibility. It is this very notion of identity being fundamentally sexual that creates the conditions of possibility for national identity to be viewed as heterosexual. And, in response to perceived threats to national identity amid public debates about same-sex relationships, a renewed urgency to protect heterosexual norms is presented by opponents to same-sex marriage. Berlant (1997: 17), writing from the perspective of a scholar living in the United States has this to say:

> [A] virulent form of revitalized national heterosexuality has been invented, a form that is complexly white and middle class. . . . I simply do not see why the nation has to have an official sexuality . . . that uses cruel and mundane strategies both to promote shame for non-normative populations and to deny them state, federal, and juridical supports because they are deemed morally incompetent to their own citizenship.

Berlant here pointedly asks a very important question: Why must a nation have an "official sexuality"? This question is aptly applied to debates around same-sex marriage, though national threats to identity are not limited to debates on this one issue. Normalized heterosexual images regularly make their way into the public sphere. Take, for instance, the familiar heterosexual image of a politician posing with his or her opposite-sex spouse, or of a soldier kissing his or her opposite-sex spouse or partner farewell when heading off to battle on behalf of the nation. A nation that has a heterosexual identity is deeply troubled when such images are disrupted by non-heterosexual images that emerge to represent "the family," "the soldier," and "the politician." It is in this way that we can understand how private issues of sexual identity are indeed public issues of national identity, in this case, identities represented by heteronationalism. This is apparent when we examine how same-sex marriage was raised as a troubling spectre for Canadian heteronationalism.

Box 11.1
Key Events in Sexual Minorities Movements in Canada, 1980s–2012

- 1981   Sexual minorities confront police as they raid the bathhouses in Toronto and over 300 people are arrested. This is sometimes referred to as Canada's "Stonewall."
- 1985   The Parliamentary Committee on Equality Rights recommends that the Canadian Human Rights Act be changed to make it illegal to discriminate based on sexual orientation.*
- 1996   Bill C-33 is passed. It adds "sexual orientation" to the Canadian Human Rights Act.
- 2000   Bill C-23 (Modernization of Benefits & Obligations Act) is passed. It recognizes same-sex couples as common-law partners and provides equality in over 68 federal statutes. Marriage, however, remains the lawful union of one man and one woman to the exclusion of all others and is reserved for heterosexual couples.
- 2001   The Canadian census includes the category common-law same-sex relationships. There were 34,200 same-sex couples enumerated.
- 2003   The Ontario Court of Appeal rules that, effective immediately, same-sex couples should be entitled to marry; denying them wedding licences, the Court determines, would be unconstitutional. Michael Leshner and Michael Stark become first couple to marry.
- 2004   On 9 December the Supreme Court of Canada decides that the federal government, not the provinces, has the authority to legislate the definition of marriage.
- 2005   Seven provinces (Ontario, Quebec, British Columbia, Manitoba, Saskatchewan, Nova Scotia, and Newfoundland and Labrador) and one territory (Yukon) deliver court decisions that provide equal marriage rights to same-sex couples.
- 2005   Since the legalization of same-sex marriages in seven provinces and one territory, 3,000 same-sex weddings have been registered. It is announced that the 2006 census will include a category, "same-sex married spouse."
- 2005   1 February: Legislation to make same-sex marriage legal in Canada is introduced (Bill C-38).** The Act is cited as the Civil Marriage Act.
- 2005   29 June: Bill C-38 passes final reading in the House of Commons with a vote of 158 to 133.

- 2005   19 July: Bill C-38 passes in the Senate with a vote of 47–21 (3 abstentions).
- 2005   20 July: Bill C-38 receives royal assent and becomes the law of the land.
- 2006   The first census that collected data on same-sex married spouses takes place. There were 45,300 same-sex couples enumerated and of these, about 7,500 (16.5 per cent) were married and 37,900 (83.5 per cent) were common law.
- 2006   The ruling Conservatives attempted to reopen the same-sex marriage debate; however, it was defeated in the House of Commons by a vote of 175–123. Minsters on both sides broke rank: 12 Tories voted against the motion and 13 Liberals supported for it.
- 2012***   An unidentified lesbian couple, neither of who are Canadian residents, married in Canada in 2005 and sought a divorce in 2009. One woman is now living in Florida and one in Britain. Since legal same-sex marriage is not recognized where they live they appealed to Canada for a divorce. However, they were denied their request on the grounds that they did not meet the residency requirements stated in the Divorce Act (one year). Bill C-32 has been introduced to amend the Civil Marriage Act in order to close this gap and allow non-resident same-sex couples who were married in Canada to divorce in Canada. It received first reading on 17 February 2012 (Library of Parliament Publication number 41-1-C32E).
- 2012   Prime Minister Stephen Harper reiterated that his government will not reopen debates over whether or not same-sex marriage should be legal in Canada.
- 2012   The 2011 Census information posted 19 September 2012 counted 64,575 same-sex couple families, up 42.4 per cent from 2006. Of these couples, 21,015 were same-sex married couples and 43,560 were same-sex common-law couples. The number of same-sex married couples nearly tripled between 2006 and 2011, reflecting the first five-year period for which same-sex marriage has been legal across the country. Same-sex common-law couples rose 15.0 per cent, slightly higher than the 13.8 per cent increase for opposite-sex common-law couples.**** (Statistics Canada, 2012a)

* The provinces and territories changed their human rights laws to include sexual orientation as follows: Quebec, 1977; Ontario, 1986; Manitoba, Yukon, 1987; Nova Scotia, 1991; British Columbia, New Brunswick, 1992; Saskatchewan, 1993; Newfoundland and Labrador, Alberta, and Prince Edward Island, 1998 (Canadian Lesbian and Gay Rights Organization Archives).

** This enactment extended the legal capacity for marriage for civil purposes to same-sex couples in order to reflect values of tolerance, respect, and equality consistent with the Canadian Charter of Rights and Freedoms. It also made consequential amendments to other Acts to ensure equal access for same-sex couples to the civil effects of marriage and divorce. All parliamentary publications can be found at www.parl.gc.ca.

*** Since same-sex marriage was made legal in Canada there has been little public debate about this topic since 2006.

**** These numbers have been challenged and are thought to be high. Census Manager, Marc Hamel, reported that an automatic algorithm might have overestimated (by up to 4,500 couples) the number of same-sex married unions across the country. The error is thought to have occurred because people who live and marry in one province move to another temporarily for work and often move in with a person of the same sex (as a roommate). Thus, reporting they are married and living with a person of the same sex confused the data (Smith, 2012).

Chain of Events in Canada: Bill C-38 Confronts Heteronationalism

There was a specific historical-political moment that led to Canada legalizing same-sex marriage (Bill C-38, The Civil Marriage Act). Initially, it looked as though Bill C-38 would easily become law in 2005 under the federal Liberal party led by Paul Martin. Then there was a sharp turn and all of a sudden it seemed such a law was highly improbable. The turn occurred when the Liberal party was under attack for their alleged culpability in a scandal created by the misappropriation of public funds (this became known formally as the "Gomery Inquiry" and informally as the "sponsorship scandal"). The Conservative party, led by Stephen Harper, threatened to call a vote of no confidence, generating talk that the Liberals would fall. The Conservatives capitalized on this vulnerability to attack the Liberal's move to unsettle a heterosexual nation with legalized same-sex marriages. The Liberals had to confront two possibilities of public shaming. On the one hand, there was the public shame arising from the charge against them of moral corruption in the sponsorship scandal. In this instance, they might have been able to downplay the scandal if they bartered for political credibility with the Conservatives by backing down on Bill C-38, an Act that troubled the family values of Conservative party members. On the other hand, there was the public shame arising from backing down on Bill C-38, a promise that many of their Liberal party members supported and a promise that carried sway with the third and smaller party, the New Democrats (NDP). Could Bill C-38 save or sink the Liberals? At the eleventh hour, Prime Minister Paul Martin and NDP leader Jack Layton were conjured up as queer bedfellows when the Liberals agreed to barter political power with the left and continued to support Bill C-38, thus enabling the Prime Minister to maintain a tenuous hold on Liberal power.

In this confusion, Martin's former placating move in response to the pressure from the Conservative party—to strike a committee to hear public consultations on Bill C-38 which would have delayed its passing into law or possibly endangered it altogether—was reversed. The result was Bill C-38 passed without delay in the House of Commons by a vote of 158 to 133, and came into force 20 July 2005 making same-sex marriage legal in all of Canada. It reads: "Marriage, for civil purposes, is the lawful union of two persons to the exclusion of all others" (SC, 2005, c33).

As these events unfolded, it was a reminder of two things. First, rights-based claims from the margins are always tenuous. And second, while Graff's question—"How can same-sex marriage be barred?"—follows a compelling logic, it ignores the fierce opposition based on traditional family values and conservative religious beliefs, an opposition that continues to be given space in public debates. Even when there is a clear commitment to keep church and state separate, once a social issue arises that generates strong moral opposition *and* is viewed as a threat to the moral fabric of national identity, religion becomes the vocal gate-keeper. Controversy over Bill C-38 was no exception. Yet, unlike previous religious debates that have only opposed legalizing same-sex relationships in the past, the religious debate this time both rejected and supported same-sex marriage. The following quotation opposed to Bill C-38 represents a common expression of opposition to same-sex marriage based on a Biblical interpretation of one man + one woman = marriage.

We've never believed the State can issue or declare a right that people can be married. . . . [Homosexuality] is a choice of form of relationship people want to live in. They make their choice but they have no right to call that marriage. (Brian Rushfeldt, executive director of Canada Family Action Coalition)

Not all religious leaders opposed same-sex marriage. Many participated in nationwide rallies on 10 April 2005 to support gay marriage. In Toronto, a statement of support was issued by the Religious Coalition for Equal Marriage Rights, a multi-faith coalition that stated it wants to dispel the myth that people of faith must be opposed to same-sex marriage (Canada Press online, 11 April 2005). The multi-faith coalition includes representatives from liberal and traditional faith communities across Canada, including the United Church of Canada, the Canadian Unitarian Council, the Muslim Canadian Congress, the Canadian Friends Service Committee of the Religious Society of Friends (Quakers), the World Sikh Organization, Canadian Rabbis for Equal Marriage, Metropolitan Community Church, Ahavat Olam Synagogue (Vancouver), Church of the Holy Trinity (Anglican) in Toronto, Apostolic Society of Franciscan Communities—Canada, Saint Padre Pio Congregational Catholic Community (Toronto), and liberal and progressive members of the Buddhist, Catholic, First Nations, Hindu, Mennonite, and Muslim communities (www.canadianchristianity.com).

On 9 April 2005, thousands of people opposed to same-sex marriage gathered on the Parliament Hill lawn in Ottawa. This protest was sanctioned by Stephen Harper (currently Prime Minister of Canada), who "denounced the federal plan to legalize same-sex marriage, telling the crowd that a Tory government would bring in legislation defining marriage as the union of one man and one woman" (Canada Press online, 11 April 2005). Those in opposition to Bill C-38 further argued that marriage is not and never has been considered a human right, while religion is. Harper's aim was to keep the nation heterosexual by ensuring that marriage would be limited to one man and one woman.

Over 100 Canadian lawyers wrote an open letter opposing Harper's political views based on legal grounds (www.law.utoronto.ca/samesexletter.html). While Harper was unsuccessful at this time in his attempt to prevent any challenge to the heterosexual nation, his position demonstrates the unstable relationship between the state and sexual citizens. Same-sex debates indeed have not dwindled with the passing of Bill C-38. Even when the disruption of the heterosexual nation is legal, those who are socially conservative continue to call for a return to traditional heterosexual family values. While the call to re-visit Bill C-38 has been voted down a number of times now and same-sex marriage continues to be law, the assumption of citizenship for sexual citizens is never a secure assumption. Laws may change, yet social stigmas are slow to fade. And as we know, social stigma acts as a powerful counterforce to legal rights.

Experts and Experience: Changing Canadian's Views

Same-sex marriage did not simply appear as a good idea out of the blue. Years of political struggle led up to it. For example, archived at Equality for Gays and Lesbians Everywhere (EGALE) is a wide array of testimonial affidavits collected prior to the passage of Bill C-38.

These testimonials are from expert witnesses[2] and individuals living in same-sex partnerships. They attest to the strong support, desires, and rationales for legalizing same-sex marriage in Canada (see www.equalmarriage.ca). The three general themes expressed in these documents found on the website above can be summarized as follows. One is immigration, that is, to bring a non-Canadian partner to live in Canada. Another is full citizenship participation, that is, to have same-sex relationships and families legally acknowledged in every way that heterosexual relationships are. The third is for social legitimacy, in the eyes of family members, friends, and colleagues. There were several court challenges to provincial laws regulating marriage. The following is a selection of affidavits and statements that were generated during Ontario's fight to legalize same-sex marriage.[3] These statements shift the epistemological lens from the activist stance of radical transformation to the very "ordinary" experiences of people. They bring to voice some of the reasons people fight for marriage rights.

The following is from Alison Kemper and Joyce Barrett's testimonial affidavits. These lesbian mothers have two children born and raised within their relationship that began in 1984.

> AK: The reality is that same-sex couples have kids, love them, and want more than anything the best possible lives for our children. Our lives together have been spent overcoming those who would wish us to be apart or invisible. We are committed to ensuring that our children have as secure and rich a life as possible. Marriage is one more step.

> JB: Instead of being recognized as an equal family, we are considered to have an "alternative lifestyle." We're not very alternative. We're very ordinary. We'd like to be married because it's the ordinary thing to do with the feelings and commitments we share.

Reflecting the symbolic and cultural meanings of marriage, Biddy Martin (1994: 47) holds that many queer folk are just ordinary people, and this is something we must acknowledge. While pursuing radical queer politics that rightfully strive to deconstruct categories that feed discourses of homophobia, "queer deconstructions of gender cannot do all the earth-shattering work they seem to promise." LGBTQ-identified people who are "just ordinary" want the right to marry without waiting for radical changes required in order to be considered legitimate outside the logic of family and marriage.

Michelle Bradshaw and Rebekah Rooney's affidavit follows. Michelle is a student, black lesbian, 28-years-old, and hearing-impaired.[4] Rebekah Rooney is white, 24-years-old, a student with a learning disability.

> MS: I am not afraid, dismayed or ashamed of my relationship with Rebekah, as some people feel I should be. I am ecstatic, happy, content, calm all in one. But mostly I am proud. I want the world to know! . . . Because in the end, same-sex couples should have the same rights as heterosexual couples to choose if they want to tell, express, yell it to the world and to have the law congratulate/validate/support through legal means *all* who form that special bond of marriage/family.

> RR: If the government refuses to validate our relationship, why should the citizens of this country? Homophobia is rampant in our society, in large measure because it continues to be sanctioned by government.

Michael Leshner works as a Crown attorney for the Government of Ontario. Originally from Halifax, Michael Stark is the eldest of five children. They are known as "the Michaels" and have been together for 20 years.

> ML: It should not be necessary for me to justify my application for a marriage licence and requiring me to do so would be discriminatory, humiliating and upsetting. Being denied a marriage licence suggests that Mike and I do not love each other, and that our hopes, our dreams, our life together do not exist. Mike and I, while supposedly equal citizens of this great country, are deemed non-persons, because we are gay.

> MS: My brothers and my sister have all been legally married. We have the same parents and upbringing; we all work and pay taxes; and we have all fallen in love and settled down with our partners. Although my relationship is longer than that of any of my siblings, I find myself deposing my first affidavit, and commencing a court proceeding, to seek a marriage licence—simply because I am gay. It is unfair that I have to justify my marriage licence application to anyone, or that I have to convince anyone of my love of Michael. I should not have to ask permission to marry Michael from anyone other than him. I look forward to the day when I can call each of my siblings and invite them to my wedding as they each have done for me.

These accounts of three same-sex couples reflect the reasoning provided by "experts" and at the same time provide experience of such reasoning. It is clear that the people writing these submissions are educated, some are professionals and represent themselves as deserving to be included in the citizenship body, in other words they present as respectable "good" lesbians and gay men. The themes the affidavits elicit are many. Alison and Joyce want same-sex marriage to help them validate their family, confront homophobia, stabilize family life for children, and transform the notion of "alternate" family units into a more visible, common and accepted form. Michelle and Rebekah feel that same-sex marriage will allow them to publicly celebrate their love with pride. Pride is a strong theme that underpins all lesbian and gay rights movements as demonstrated in Pride celebrations around the globe. They also believe, as do the Michaels, that equal rights with heterosexual counterparts are an important factor. Finally, Michelle and Rebekah, as an acknowledgement of the relationship citizens have with the state, implore their government to take responsibility for the harm they experience in their lives.

The Michaels' full affidavit not quoted here ties the acceptance of their 20-year love relationship to the state's approval and without it, they believe, their love does not exist within a legal context. This tie redefines emotional attachments to love and marriage that Graff referred to as a legal imperative. They also suggest there is an infantilizing aspect when being compelled to ask permission for a right that should be automatically granted. The affidavit strategically positions Stark as the male head of a large family, the eldest of five siblings, the one who should be able to set a good example. He is paradoxically prevented from fulfilling his heteronormative patriarchal responsibilities by a government that on the one hand supports traditional family roles yet, on the other, denies him access to one such role by denying him the right to marry.

The following excerpts from the affidavits of three lesbian mothers and one child of a lesbian mother explicate some of the worries and tensions that same-sex headed families, at best designated "alternate" and at worst rendered invisible, experience when denied marriage rights.[5] The first affidavit is from Robin Roberts, who is in a lesbian relationship. Both women are lesbian mothers and have been together for 17 years. Together they raised four children from previous marriages.

> RR: Had we been able to marry, . . . we believe that having the recognition of Canadian law behind us would have made it easier for our children to deal with their peers, and it would have freed our energy to be totally out of the closet, with the safety and comfort of the backing of the law behind us, as it is for heterosexual families who are able to take their status for granted.

The following affidavits are from a family of two lesbian mothers, Jane (birth mother) and Joy (who adopted Jane's children) and one of their two children, Sarah.

> Jane: Adoption could not give us all that I want and have a right to enjoy. I also want to be married. I want society to witness our covenant and understand that ours is a vital, entrenched union. If we win the right to marry, we will still be marginalized in public opinion, but eventually the legislation will trickle down and have a salutary effect. I get hurt when heterosexuals friends get married after knowing each other six months or a year or two years. Joy and I have been partners for eight years—how long do we have to wait?

> Sarah: By the fifth grade my queer family had become an unmentionable. My best friend and I spent every day together for three years before we "came out" that both our mothers were gay. It had always been understood, but to speak it made it the potential property of schoolyard taunts. How can marriage be sacred when it doesn't even sanctify my own family?

In the first excerpt Jane positions her partner and herself as worthy citizens and makes national claims about how Canadian families should be constituted to include them. Further above, Robin invokes two tropes associated with women—the "best interest" of the child and women's safety—when she identifies marriage as a tool that would enable her children to deal with their homophobic peers and provide safety and comfort to mothers. Finally, the one voice from a child of lesbians expresses the need for the silence to be broken so that same-sex headed families can be acknowledged and legitimated thereby dismantling the stigma cast upon children of lesbians.

As I read through the volumes of testimonies in support of same-sex marriage generated by court challenges across Canada, I think about how people try to makes their lives more livable. As problematic as any toehold on respectable marriage is, it is also hard to think outside the logic of marriage relationships (Bell and Binnie, 2000). Further, as Bell and Binnie (2000) point out, advocates insist that far from assimilationist strategies, same-sex marriage is "held as capable of undermining the most solid of social structure ('the family') by infiltrating it and exposing its contradictory logics from within" (57).

Similar to the personal testimonies, the expert witnesses who participated in court challenges (fn 2) articulate intellectual rationales for legalizing same-sex marriage. Taken together, the testimonies and affidavits demonstrate how very political the personal is.

In addition to the personal and expert witness accounts in court cases, that make a strong case for legalizing same-sex marriage, there are bodies of literature that both support and oppose it. The literature that supports same-sex marriage stems from an equal rights perspective, that is, the same rights for heterosexuals are due to same-sex couples. This stance focuses on freedoms and inclusion and echoes much of what has been said in the affidavits. For instance, Evan Wolfson (1996) suggests, there is no reason to forego the benefits of same-sex marriage since these help us to counter the real harm done to real-life same-sex couples every day. Wolfson further argues that unless marriage is abolished and replaced by a single system to which everyone has access, an ideological and moral distinction will continue to value one relationship form over another. Nan D. Hunter (1995) believes that same-sex marriage could potentially transform the institution of marriage. Part of Hunter's argument rests with the notion that by its unconventional gender structures, same-sex marriage could destabilize the gendered structure of marriage and its concomitant discourses of dependency and authority. Barbara Findlay, QC, says, "Lesbians and homosexual men in Canada have almost the same rights and responsibilities as heterosexual Canadians in family law. But the devil is in the details: 'Almost' equal can mean big problems for same-sex families in Canada. . . . [I]t means that for lesbians and gay men, rights in Canada under family law depend on where they live."[6] It also depends on the law being interpreted in favour of same-sex relationships, especially when the "best interest" of the child is invoked.

Even if the institution of marriage is less popular, it remains the operative logic that underpins family and nation, a logic that is difficult to think outside. As Barbara Smith says, "[a]s long as we live under this system, all people should have access to the same benefits regardless of sexual orientation" (1997: 201). There are many reasons that lesbians and gay men and their allies oppose or support same-sex marriage. These are powerful debates that must include people's lived experiences when we challenge how we think about same-sex marriage. Nobody expects same-sex marriage to undo all the harm inflicted by homophobia. Cheshire Calhoun poses an important question when she asks if it is fair to put the onus on lesbians and gay men to "transform gender relations, to remedy class-related inequities and to end the privileging of long-term, monogamous relations" (2000: 138–9). Same-sex marriage just makes it easier for some families.

As noted previously, not all who support same-sex relationships support same-sex marriage. In the next section I turn to arguments from supporters of same-sex relationships who nonetheless oppose same-sex marriage.

Intellectual Debates: For Same-Sex Relationships and against Same-Sex Marriage

The reason for identifying the "sides" of the debates is to keep visible the multiple voices and claims to marginal sexual identity and the divergent strategies for making lives more livable (Butler, 1997).[7] A central critique of same-sex marriage from supporters of same-sex relationships is that rights-claims serve to simultaneously include some and exclude others and thus cannot be relied on to fundamentally shift the dominant centre of heteronormativity. This is a very different intellectual landscape from the one where it is argued that same-sex relationships are morally wrong. Susan Boyd and Claire Young (2005), Lauren Berlant and Michael Warner (1998), Diane Richardson (2005), Mariana Valverde (2006) and others strongly support same-sex relationship but oppose same-sex marriage on the basis that such political gains are limited, reinforce individualism in the current neo-liberal climate, and rather than destabilize the patriarchal and oppressive institution of marriage, same-sex marriage reaffirms it. Further, those opposed to same-sex marriage posit that it depends on state-sanctioned conjugal relations that cast aside relationships that do not conform to such arrangements (Baird, 2007; Boyd and Young, 2005; Brownworth, 1996, Card, 1996; Eichler, 1997). Thus, sexual minorities who can be viewed as being closer to the heteronormative centre, those who assimilate to heterosexual married couples, have a greater chance of being socially accepted. More marginal sexual minorities—people of colour, people with disabilities, and trans-identified people—not only remain outside, as "different," but they are further kept from moving into spaces that might have included them if the system of marriage were to be dismantled.

For more on "remaining outside", being labelled different and "othering", see "The Social Model of Disability" in Chapter 13, pp. 251–2.

Brenda Cossman (1996) argues that family as a social construct is not the problem; rather, the problem lies in the legal and political system that demand people either fit into a presumed heterosexual unit or be excluded from the benefits of a legal family unit. This argument directly parallels discussions on marriages. Nancy Polikoff's (2008) work insists that we abandon the compulsion to arrange familial units based on conjugal relations and think more broadly of valuing all families as economic units, the units Kath Weston discussed in her 1992 book, *Families We Choose*. Martha Fineman (2000) and Carol Smart (1984) concur and advocate for legal families to be based on caregiving units between inevitable dependents and their caretakers.

Many have argued that marriage is underpinned by gender and biases. For instance Clair F.L. Young (2006) points to class and gender in her work on tax implications for

CASE IN POINT
Tracking Conjugal Relationships

The Canadian state has been interested enough in its citizens' conjugal relationships to track them in census polls: marriage data from 1921, divorce data from 1972, marriage stats that included common law since 1981, common-law as a separate category since 199, and same-sex marriage from 2006. The terms "cohabitation" and "common-law relationship" are formally sanctioned by the state and now include the category of two non-related same-sex adults living together.

Statistics Canada data from the 2011 census indicate that married couples accounted for 67 per cent per cent of all families, down from 68 per cent in 2006 and 83 per cent in 1981. At the same time, the proportion of common-law couples has increased by 13.9 per cent since 2006, more than four times the increase for married couples (Statistic Canada, 2011). The 2011 census also reported a total of 6,272,935 married couples in Canada (down 1.7 per cent since 2006) and 1,524,345 common-law couples (up 1.5 per cent over the same period).

married same-sex partners in Canada. She states that income splitting for wealthier married couples is a tax advantage and one that is not available to those couples in lower income brackets. In fact she points out that class and gender operate to expressly disadvantage those with lower incomes since married or legal common-law couples' income is aggregated thus often placing them in a higher tax bracket. Two individual, low incomes of $20,000 when combined are viewed as $40,000 and taxed at a higher rate. Women commonly earn less (recent figures published by the Canadian Labour Congress state that in Canada the women's earning power is 68 cents to the male dollar). Young's work on the tax implications for same-sex marriage includes an analysis that accuses the government of using the legalization of common law and same-sex marriage as a cash grab (there were increased tax revenues over a five-year period of $9.85 billion). The financial disadvantage demonstrated by comparing two female wages or a single female breadwinner to the data available for middle class heterosexual couples, shows that same-sex lesbian couples are additionally disadvantaged. Along with Young's class and gender analysis is that of Victoria Brownworth (1996). Brownworth writes about the class biases in marriage. She reminds us of the lack of formal marriage rites in populations where the expense of a wedding is prohibitive. Brownworth notes that marriage reflects inherently middle class values since low-income couples often just "shack up" (1996: 96). Further, Suzanne Lenon (2008) draws on critical race scholar Darren L. Hutchinson (1997) to explicitly point to the racial politics of same-sex marriage. The starting point for such a critique is colonial histories that have never served black people or their relationships and marriage in particular has been used to racialize legitimate and illegitimate families and relationships.

Lenon contends,

> because most lesbians and gay men of colour remain invisible and marginalized within larger gay and lesbian mainstream organizations, it is unlikely that a marriage license will "close much of the gulf between them and the centre of a heterosexual society that is stratified by race, class, gender and sexuality." Instead, many (or most) of the benefits from same-sex marriage will accrue to white and upper class individuals. (Lenon, 2008:48)

The arguments advanced to oppose same-sex marriage focus on opposition to marriage as a state-imposed institution on our personal relationships. As such, these debates call into question all marriage relationships. It is important to continue to fight against state regulations that construct as many exclusions as they do inclusions. It is also important to question how same-sex couples can be expected to change the institution of marriage without the co-operation of opposite-sex couples. That is, unless we all agree to dismantle the institution of marriage, we are all caught in its grip. Whose relationships will the state legitimate and respect, even after death? More marginal sexual minorities are in the shadow of human rights claims made by white middle-class (mostly) lesbians and gays. Recognizing a modern form of self-intelligibility as a sexual self does not secure a place in the national imaginary. There are always overlapping and contradictory national imaginaries that take shape within very particular historical, social, and political contexts. That is, national representations carry with them the weight of cultural, economic, and political dominance of certain groups.

Coming a Long Way or Maintaining the Status Quo?

Currently, there is no national family policy in Canada. There is a decentralized system with two levels of government: federal and provincial. Marriage comes under the purview of federal family law (definitions of marriage) while the solemnization of marriage comes under provincial legislation (who can apply and age requirements). The different provincial legislations regarding marriage, divorce, and custody lead to a claim that a "patchwork of entitlements" has been created (Hurley, 2005: 3). Despite this, in Canada, same-sex couples have the legal right to live together, be married, and raise their children created by donor insemination, adoption, or in the context of (former) heterosexual relations. Increased visibility of sexual minorities and changing laws make it impossible to ignore the fact that there have been significant changes in the social struggle to re-imagine family units. A recent Angus Reid Poll reports that in Canada, three in five respondents (59 per cent) support same-sex marriage (Angus Reid, n.d).

For more on lack of unified, cohesive family policies in Canada, see "Introduction" in Chapter 15, pp. 292–4.

So, we have come a long way in law and in changing views about who are considered legitimate citizens based on their intimate relationships. Same-sex marriage has destabilized the assumed heteronationalism of Canada and this cannot be underestimated, nor can the ongoing resistance to it. Young and Boyd (2006: 214) explain that "many lesbians and gays from other countries have looked to Canada as a model for their own jurisdictions, while others have come to Canada to marry" (Kitzinger and Wilkinson, 2004).

The calls by social conservatives for protecting the opposite-sex definition of marriage have "exposed the fragility of marriage as an historically specific social institution, as opposed to a naturalised, timeless one" (Young and Boyd, 2006: 214). Further, traditional female and male roles, as they relate to childrearing, have also been interrupted. Yet, social stigmas hold strong well after laws change the meanings of those stigmas. I offer an example from my teaching.

I ask students in the university classes I teach if there is any such thing as a nuclear family norm in Canada today. Most often the question is pushed back at me. "No. Just look around." Their answer is that the face of families has changed so drastically that there is no one norm. Support for their beliefs arises from their view of marriage as a personal reflection of their own individual, moral, tolerant, and inclusive perspective. These views are articulated by students saying "it doesn't matter what people do as long as they don't hurt anybody else," and by their references to the influx of LGBTQ characters on television programs such as *Glee*, *Modern Family*, *Smash*, and *The New Normal* and in movies such as *Brokeback Mountain*, *The Kids Are All Right*, *Easy A*, and *Because I'm a Cheerleader*.[8] They argue that this reflects more tolerant societal attitudes, and remind me there is same-sex human rights legislation that additionally proves Canada no longer views the traditional heterosexual nuclear family model as the only acceptable family unit. Before I launch into my argument that family and marriage are both a private experience and a public institution and that social stigmas are hard to shift, I ask students to reflect on their personal experience of heteronationalism. I ask them to test whether their relatives—parents, siblings, aunts, uncles, grandparents—accept same-sex relationships or marriage by asking them if their relatives would be accepting if they were to go home and announce that they were involved in such a relationship.

Being invited to reflect on personal experiences, their answers become more elaborate, qualified, and less assured. When I ask them to consider their response if a child of theirs announced that he, she, or gender-neutral child was identified with any of the following sexual or gendered identities—lesbian, gay, bisexual, transgendered, transsexual, two-spirit, intersexed, or queer—they struggle much more as they examine the penalties that come with discrimination based on the differential social positioning each of these identities carries. The ambivalences created by the disjuncture between same-sex marriage as a public institution and as a personal experience confuse the landscape of sexual citizenship and belonging. Same-sex couples can now say "I do" in Canada. Yet what this exercise demonstrates to students is that there are conditions placed on the meaning of a legal document (in this case a marriage licence) that is procured within a heavily coded frame of heterosexist presumptions. To belong to mainstream communities requires more than the legal right to have access, it requires that people meet the criteria tacitly agreed upon by strictly guarded community standards.

Conclusion

This chapter has introduced an earlier time when the foundation for marriage was based on preserving property and economic stability. I argued that the shift from money matters to matters of the heart has created an opening for asking: What is marriage for? Once the role of marriage was no longer solely linked to economic and biological reproduction, and sex without marriage entered into acceptable social relations, denying same-sex relationships and marriage lost its broad appeal. Canada has its own very specific moment when the longstanding law that upheld marriage as a relationship between opposite-sex couples was struck down. Yet, social stigmas that cling to former times remain lodged in cultural and social understandings within individual families and communities and among friends, making the gap between law and social practice hard to close. I have presented debates argued from the perspective that same-sex relationships are unquestioningly legitimate. One side argues for the necessity of legal rights claims to marriage while the other side argues for the dissolution of this state institution. The opposition to same-sex relationships seems to be waning. Indeed, according to Statistics Canada people's attachment to the institution of any kind of marriage is in decline. Given this and the exclusions that marriage creates, "What is marriage for?" continues to be a compelling question.

STUDY QUESTIONS

1. Do you think "What is marriage for?" is a useful question to ask? Why or why not?
2. What does it mean to be legally declared married yet not experience social belonging?
3. What is the difference between common-law and same-sex relationships?
4. Why is the right to marry so important to some people and not others?
5. What is the difference between a personal relationship between two married people and a legal relationship between married people and the state?

Further Readings

Foster, Deborah. 2005. "The Formation and Continuance of Lesbian Families in Canada," *Canadian Bulletin of Medical History* 3, 22 (2): 281–97. Foster begins with the history of lesbian and gay rights in Canada from 1969–2002 and discusses issues such as what a lesbian mother is; how she reproduces; and what rights she, her partner, and her children may or may not have. She refers to studies that conclude the children of lesbian mothers do as well or better than those mothered by heterosexuals.

Foucault, Michel. 1990. *The History of Sexuality*. New York: Vintage Books. This account of sexuality, and the identification of "the homosexual" as a (sub)species of "man," covers long and complex histories. One of the many arguments advanced by Foucault is that censorship of sexuality increases rather than decreases people's desire to discuss and practice it.

Graff, E.J. 2004. *What Is Marriage For? The Strange Social History of Our Most Intimate Institution*. Boston: Beacon Press. Graff argues that marriage in Western societies has changed so much over the years that it challenges us to think about its social purpose. Building on a history of marriage, she asserts that there is no longer a reason to deny same-sex couples the right to marry.

MacDougall, Brian. 2000. *Queer Judgments: Homosexuality, Expression, and the Courts in Canada*. Toronto: University of Toronto Press, 2000. This book documents human rights-based court challenges that contribute to the rich and diverse history of the struggle for recognition of same-sex relationships in Canada. Along with this history, MacDougall also provides thought-provoking and critical analysis of seeking sexual minority legal status.

Smith, Miriam. 2008. *Political Institutions and Lesbian and Gay Rights in the United States and Canada*. New York and London: Routledge. This book is written by a scholar who has followed the legal and social struggles in the fight for equal rights for LGTBQ people in Canada and the United States. Her research is thorough, informative, and current.

Websites

www.egale.ca

EGALE (Equal Rights for Gays and Lesbians Everywhere) seeks to advance equality and justice for lesbian, gay, bisexual, and trans-identified people and their families. It posts both current and archival materials about LGBT issues in Canada.

www.clga.ca

The Canadian Lesbian and Gay Archives, established in 1973, documents and preserves lesbian and gay history in Canada (and beyond). It offers public access to collected histories, personal records, photographic collections, moving images, posters, audiotapes, and artifacts.

http://samesexmarriage.ca

This website of the organization Equal Marriage for Same Sex Couples includes contemporary, historical, and legal information about same-sex marriages, as well as reporting about events in queer communities, for example, a photo documentary of the first same-sex wedding in Canada.

http://religioustolerance.org

This website of Ontario Consultants on Religious Tolerance discusses religious, moral, and political debates in Canada and elsewhere.

Notes

1. One example is Uganda where a law was proposed (October 2009) that not only outlawed same-sex relationships, it states that it will be a punishable crime for anyone to neglect to report people known to them to be in a same-sex relationship for more than 24 hours (*Globe and Mail*, 25 November 2009, A1).

2. Below is a selection of expert witness affidavits from *Halpern v Canada*, June 2003 found at http://www.sgmlaw.com/en/about/Halpernv.CanadaAttorneyGeneral.cfm:

   - Affidavit of Barry Adam, http://www.sgmlaw.com/media/PDFs/Adam.pdf [on the cross-cultural evidence of same-sex partnerships and marriage and the evolution of cultural conceptions of homosexuality]
   - Affidavit of Bettina Bradbury, http://www.sgmlaw.com/media/PDFs/Bradbury.pdf [on the history and evolution of the institution of marriage in Canada]
   - Reply Affidavit of Bettina Bradbury, http://www.sgmlaw.com/media/PDFs/BradburyReply.pdf [responding to a government affidavit, sworn by Edward Shorter, which suggested that the recognition of same-sex marriage would threaten the continued existence of heterosexual marriage]
   - Affidavit of Margrit Eichler, http://www.sgmlaw.com/media/PDFs/Eichler.pdf [on the evolution of the family in Canada]
   - Affidavit of Katherine Arnup, http://www.sgmlaw.com/media/PDFs/Arnup.pdf [on the history and evolution of the family in Canada, and how previous changes, now considered innocuous or progressive, were thought to be a threat to the continued existence of marriage, the family and civilization]
   - Affidavit of Andrew Koppelman, http://www.sgmlaw.com/media/PDFs/Koppleman.pdf [demonstrates the relevance and applicability of the miscegenation analogy to denying gays and lesbians the right to marry and refuting the claim that a registered domestic partnership regime would be an adequate alternative to marriage]
   - Affidavit of Susan Ehrlich, http://www.sgmlaw.com/media/PDFs/Ehrlich.pdf [on the social construction of meaning and whether the term "marriage" could include same-sex couples]
   - Affidavit of Adele Mercier, http://www.sgmlaw.com/media/PDFs/Mercier.pdf [responding to a government affidavit, sworn by Robert Stainton, that claimed the term "marriage" could refer only to heterosexual unions]
   - Affidavit of Jerry Bigner, http://www.sgmlaw.com/media/PDFs/Bigner.pdf [reviews the social science evidence relating to lesbian and gay parenting, showing that lesbians and gays have equal parenting skills to their heterosexual counterparts and that children raised by lesbians and gays are just as healthy and well-adjusted as children with heterosexual parents]
   - Affidavit of Judith Stacey and Timothy Biblarz, http://www.sgmlaw.com/media/PDFs/Stacy.pdf [responding to a government affidavit, sworn by Steven Nock, which suggested that all of the social science evidence on lesbian and gay parenting was worthless, and to an affidavit filed by an intervener coalition of right wing groups, sworn by Craig Hart, which claimed that social science research shows that "natural"—i.e., heterosexual—family structures provide greater security and stability for raising children]

3. On 5 November 2001 an Ontario Court heard the case of eight same-sex couples seeking the right to marry, together with a companion case brought by the Metropolitan Community Church of Toronto. The national lesbian, gay, bisexual, and transgendered rights organization EGALE had intervenor status (http://www.egale.ca/index .asp?menu=22&item=288).

4. The rare race- and disabled-identity markers in one affidavit accentuate the dominance of white able-bodied subjects of same-sex marriage.

5. http://www.samesexmarriage.ca/legal/bc_couple.html.

6. www.Canadian-Lawyers.ca

7. David Bell and Jon Binnie (2000) cogently assemble the views on all sides of the same-sex marriage debates and challenge readers to think to the future for a politics that moves beyond these debates. They highlight much of the leading work on critical sexuality including Lauren Berlant, Judith Butler, Davina Cooper, Eva Pendleton, Yasemin Soysal, Michael Warner, Jeffery Weeks, Kath Weston, and many others.

8. While television programming is important to LGBTIQ history (see Gay and Lesbian Milestones in the Media at http://religioustolerance.org/hom_medi.htm for an overview of lesbians and gays on television and in film), you should keep a critical eye on the fact that often the roles are played by people who are straight and the script and plot reflect heterosexual presumptions about what it means to be lesbian or gay.

12

Building Bridges: Immigrant, Visible Minority, and Aboriginal Families in the Twenty-First Century

JAMES S. FRIDERES AND AMAL MADIBBO

LEARNING OBJECTIVES

- To understand the social and economic position of immigrant, Aboriginal, and visible minority families in Canadian society
- To identify the social structure and organization of different types of families
- To learn about the challenges facing Aboriginal, immigrant, and visible minority youth
- To find out why people intermarry
- To understand the role of gender in minority families
- To discover patterns of conflict in minority families

Introduction

This chapter highlights Canadian diversity and the changing experiences of immigrant, visible minority, and Aboriginal families. Census data shows that since the 1970s, Canada has been one of the primary destination points of immigrants from around the world. Over the past four decades, people of South Asian origin, Africans, and Latin American immigrants have settled in Canada. In the end, it is estimated that by 2031 nearly one-quarter of the population will be foreign-born and one-third will consist of visible minorities (Malenfant, Lebel and Martel, 2010). As such, since the 1970s scholarship on families has been influenced by the increasing ethnic diversity in Canadian society. Segmented assimilation has been the primary explanation as to the divergent trajectories exhibited by various ethnic families and reflect the social and human capital they bring as well as the modes of incorporation offered them by the host society (Gratton, Gutmann, and Skop, 2007). As a result of such a dramatic change in the population makeup, Mann (2009) points out the traditional framework of class and community has been replaced by the framework of ethnicity and multiculturalism in understanding the role of family. He goes on to argue that ethnic diversification has now become a major feature of social structure and personal relationships in society.

Over the past half-century there have been major changes in family life and the increasing number of ethnic and religious groups that make up Canada added to the complexity of family structure. These changes also have impacted minority families in that family adjustment is particularly difficult for individuals whose language, customs, and values are different from those of native-born Canadians. Prior to immigrating to Canada, immigrants have experienced family life, and these experiences from their homeland have forged their core values and ideologies. These values and ideologies are supported by their family, kinship ties, and social location in the community as well as by the values embedded in their home culture. However, as immigrants enter Canada, individuals are required to adapt to a new cultural environment that generates a high level of uncertainty and stress. Immigrants must quickly learn different aspects of the host culture in order to manage their daily activities (Sharlin and Voin, 2001). Moreover, many immigrants left their home culture with different conceptions as to what a family is and the roles individuals play in the family; these conceptions may be different from how Canadians view the family. Adaptation to Canadian culture may require fundamental adjustments in the relationship between husband and wife, parents and children, adults and their elderly parents, and even in-laws (Laaroussi, 2006). Additionally, immigrating can amputate long-standing social networks and secondary ties from the immigrant's relational world (Ebaugh and Curry, 2000). Aboriginal people have held family "core values" that have not always been congruent with mainstream society and they also have had to incorporate new views about family as they come into contact with the larger societal values.

Since the social and demographic attributes of people have direct and indirect implications for the study of the family, we will first offer a brief socio-demographic overview of each of the three groups, focusing on the availability of marriage partners, the age distribution of the group, the number of children born to families, along with the residential patterns of these families. We will then examine how these families are organized and structured through the analysis of the roles each family member plays, parental arrangements, child care, elder care, types of households, and the new forms of family that emerge. These are important considerations for researchers and policy-makers to take into account when looking at families, perhaps especially those of marginal groups within society. The chapter ascertains that sources of conflict within the family include the willingness to hold traditional cultural values or resistance to new and alternative values, intergenerational tensions, changing gender roles that may result in downward social mobility, particularly that of the husband, along with the issues of "astronaut" families, empty-nester divorces, the postponement of parenthood, and shrinking household sizes that impact on the functioning of the family. Even though these families face the challenges of family violence, discrimination, and alienation of youth within society and institutions, arrangements such as various types of social networks, multiple strategies of identification, and intermarriages and mixed unions enable minority families to better cope with the changing dynamics and structure of families and facilitate incorporation into the host society.

The Diverse Canadian Family: Demographic Profile

Immigrants

The ethnic mix of Canadian society continues to increase in diversity in terms of ethnicity, nationality, race, language, and religion. Early immigrants to Canada were from the United States, the United Kingdom, and Western Europe and nearly all were white and held Judeo-Christian religious beliefs.

For more on immigration waves see the section on chain migrations in Chapter 2, p. 28.

Even with the massive immigration in the late nineteenth and early twentieth centuries, most of the immigrants to this country fit this profile because Canada's immigration policy prioritized immigrants from Europe. However, with the passage of new immigration rules in the 1960s, overt **discrimination** against non-white source countries was eliminated. As a result, immigrants from around the world have come to Canada to find a better life for themselves and their children. Table 12.1 clearly shows this change. Before 1961 over 40 per cent of immigrants came from two source countries and over 80 per cent came from only 10 countries. However, by the early twenty-first century, just over half of all immigrants came from 10 countries, and no single country was among the primary source countries for all periods under consideration. Moreover, nearly half of the immigrants coming to Canada since 1991 are from three locations—all representing visible minorities (China, India, Philippines). Over the past decade, over 2.2 million immigrants were admitted to Canada and recent statistics show that one in 10 families in Canada is comprised of recent

Table 12.1 **Top 10 Countries of Birth for Immigrants to Canada, before 1961, 1991, 2006, and 2010**

Before 1961	1991	2006	2010
UK (24.3%)	China (10.8%)	China (12.2%)	Philippines (13%)
Italy (16.5%)	India (8.5%)	India (12%)	India (10.8%)
Germany (10.8%)	Philippines (6.7%)	Philippines (8.3%)	China (10.7)
Netherlands (8.9%)	Hong Kong (6.5%)	Hong Kong (5.5%)	United Kingdom (3.4%)
Poland (5.0%)	Sri Lanka (3.4%)	Sri Lanka (2.0%)	United States (3.3%)
United States (3.9%)	Pakistan (3.2%)	Pakistan (4.1%)	France (2.3%)
Hungary (3.1%)	Taiwan (2.9%)	Taiwan (1.1%)	Iran (2.4%)
Ukraine (2.4%)	United States (2.8%)	United States (3.7%)	United Arab Emirates (2.3%)
Greece (2.3%)	Iran (2.6%)	Iran (3.0%)	Morocco (2.1%)
China (1.8%)	Poland (2.4%)	Poland (<1.0%)	Republic of Korea (2.0%)
South Korea (2.5%)			Pakistan (1.8%)
Africa (12 %)			Colombia (1.7%)
Latin America (9.8%)			

SOURCES: Adapted from 2001 Census, Analysis Series, *Canada's Ethnocultural Portrait: The Changing Mosaic*, Catalogue no.96F0030XIE2001008 (Ottawa: Statistics Canada), 39; J. Reitz, ed., *Host Societies and the Reception of Immigrants* (San Diego, University of California, 2003), *Report on the Demographic Situation in Canada*, Catalogue No. 91-209-X,2008), (http://www.cic.gc.ca/english/resources/statistics/fact2010/permanent/10.asp),http://www.statcan.gc.ca/pub/91-209-x/2011001/article/11526/tbl/tb;-eng.htm#a3

immigrants. Today, from an international perspective, the immigration rate in Canada is twice as high as in the United States and higher than any other G8 country.

In regard to recognizing diversity, Canada officially adopted a **multiculturalism** policy in 1971; the Multiculturalism Act was proclaimed in 1988. In 2006, the proportion of Canada's population born outside the country reached 19.8 per cent—its highest level in 70 years. Canada's immigration policy is guided by three objectives—in order of preference: development of a strong economy, family reunification, and support for our international obligations and humanitarian goals with respect to refugees.

The age distribution of recent immigrants is very different from that of the Canadian-born population, with two-thirds of the immigrants of ages 15–44 and only 14 per cent under the age of 15. Overall, foreign-born persons are under-represented at younger ages and over-represented at older ages. This contrasts to an overall Canadian-born population with a median age of 37 while the foreign-born population has a median age of 47. The proportion of women in the immigrant population is similar to that of the Canadian-born population. However, when comparing specific ethnic groups, there are wide variations. For example, among recent immigrants from the Philippines, 62 per cent are women. At the opposite end of the spectrum, immigrant women from Iraq (41 per cent) and Ethiopia (46 per cent) make up a smaller proportion of total immigration from those countries. These figures have implications for potential mate selection and the propensity for inter-ethnic/religious marriages.

The fertility rate of Canadian women has varied over time but the overall trend has been towards significantly lower birth rates—reaching a low of 1.47 in 2010. However, for new immigrant women, the fertility rate in the past 10 years has been 3.1 children per woman, significantly higher than the rate of Canadian-born. For immigrant women who arrived in Canada 15 years ago the rate is 1.5. These numbers show that fertility rates among immigrant women decline after they arrive in Canada, eventually reaching a rate equal to women who are native-born Canadians. The fastest fertility rate decline is among women from Southern Europe. While Asian women have shown a steep decline in the number of children they have, the number of children per woman is still much higher than the overall population—1.89 compared to 1.47 for native-born Canadian women. On the other hand, women from other countries, such as South Asia (2.5), Africa (2.4), and Central/West Asia and the Middle East (2.2), far exceed this rate (Belanger and Gilbert, 2005).

These figures are important for both government policy and planning (e.g., pension, activities). The low fertility rate of Canadian women has resulted in a 60 per cent decline in the rate of natural increase in our population over the past two decades. If this low fertility rate continues for another 20 years, the number of deaths will exceed the number of births. Thus, the population of Canada will begin to decrease unless other measures, such as increasing the number of immigrants or implementing policies to encourage women to have more children, are undertaken.

Recent immigrants are similar to Canadian-born individuals in that most live in nuclear families with no relatives other than parent(s) and children. However, recent immigrants are still more likely to live in extended families. One reason may be cultural, although a substantial portion of this may also be a result of financial necessity. Recent immigrants are poorer than the Canadian-born and many elderly immigrants are "sponsored" by their families. Consequently, many of them choose to live with their relatives or sponsors. Overall, the propensity for immigrants to live in households of three or more generations is about four times that of their Canadian-born counterparts. However, immigrants from different countries of origin vary significantly in this regard (e.g., 40 per cent of South Asians live in three-generation households compared to 2 per cent of Canadian-born).

Visible Minorities

One key demographic trend in Canada has been the rapid growth in both the number and proportion of people belonging to a **visible minority** group (Belanger and Malenfant, 2005). The term "visible minority" represents a subset of both native-born and immigrant Canadians.

From 1996 to 2010 the Canadian population grew by 7.9 per cent while the visible minority population grew by 28 per cent, and 73 per cent of all immigrants coming to Canada in this period were members of visible minority groups. Over the past two decades, this population has increased substantially, reaching 13.4 per cent of the total population by 2001 and contributing 17 per cent of all live births in Canada. Projections are that visible minority members will make up 31 per cent of the Canadian population by 2031. South Asians are the largest visible minority group today and when combined with Chinese, they make up one-half of the visible minority population (see Table 12.2). The majority of the growth in the visible minority population within Canada is through immigration (e.g., Chinese, 75 per cent; South Asian, 70 per cent), while for groups such as Japanese (35 per cent) and blacks (58 per cent), who have long histories in Canada, growth is based to a greater extent on natural increase (i.e., they are more likely to be Canadian-born) and less on immigration. Today, the majority of visible minorities live in Ontario or British Columbia. As is the case with immigrants, visible minorities are linguistically diverse; speaking Canada's two official languages—English and French, in addition to other languages such as Mandarin, Arabic, and Urdu. This new "rainbow" population in Canada has led to new conceptions about how Canadians view themselves and how others are defined within our society (Pendakur, 2000).

Since the concept was created, it has taken on both legal and social significance, and visible minority status is now one of the four designations (women, disabled, visible minority, Aboriginal) that must be taken into consideration by government and the private sector in regard to employment practices such as hiring and promotions. The political justification for such a classification is that all these groups are seen to experience similar types of barriers to employment and other services.

Aboriginal Peoples

Aboriginal peoples, as identified in the Constitution Act, 1982 (Section 35), are comprised of three separate groups: Indians (sometimes called First Nations), Métis, and Inuit. All of these groups have been subjected to a variety of policies and programs of the government since well before Confederation. For Indians, the Indian Act was first enacted in 1876 and brought together many pieces of legislation dating prior to Confederation that

Table 12.2 Population by Visible Minority Group and Projection Scenario, Canada, 2006 and 2031

| Visible minority groups | 2006 | | Reference Scenario 2031 | | | | | |
| | | | Low growth | | Medium growth | | High growth | |
	Thousands	Per cent	Thousands	Per cent	Thousands	Per cent	Thousands	Per cent
Total	32,522	100	39,251	100	42,072	100	45,008	100
Total—visible minority	5,285	16.3	11,377	29.0	12,855	30.6	14,434	32.1
Chinese	1,269	3.9	2,408	6.1	2,714	6.4	3,038	6.7
South Asian	1,320	4.1	3,181	8.1	3,640	8.7	4,136	9.2
Black	815	2.5	1,620	4.1	1,809	4.3	2,012	4.5
Filipino	427	1.3	908	2.3	1,020	2.4	1,139	2.5
Latin American	317	1.0	657	1.7	733	1.7	814	1.8
Southeast Asian	250	0.8	409	1.0	449	1.1	491	1.1
Arab	276	0.8	806	2.1	930	2.2	1,062	2.4
West Asian	164	0.5	457	1.2	523	1.2	592	1.3
Korean	148	0.5	361	0.9	407	1.0	455	1.0
Japanese	85	0.3	131	0.3	142	0.3	153	0.3
Other visible minorities	213	0.7	439	1.1	489	1.2	541	1.2
Rest of the population	27,237	83.7	27,875	71	29,222	69.4	30,575	67.9

SOURCE: Éric Caron Malenfant, André Lebel, and Laurent Martel, 2010. *Projections of the Diversity of the Canadian Population, 2006 to 2031.* Ottawa: Statistics Canada, Demography Division, p. 23

impacted Indian people. The Indian Act also created new powers for the federal government (e.g., the reserve system—a complex and evolving control mechanism that still exists). The Act affects Indians from birth to death and from bedroom to boardroom; its contents control almost every behaviour of Aboriginal peoples.

Today, nearly 1.4 million individuals identify themselves as Aboriginal with a projected population of 1.6 million by 2026 (see Table 12.3). This accounts for just over 3 per cent of the total Canadian population. When compared to the numbers 20 years ago, this represents an increase of over 25 per cent. Such an increase is the result of decreased death rates, continued high birth rates, legal changes as to who can be a "registered Indian," and more individuals being willing to identify themselves as Aboriginal. While there are differences among the three subgroups on a number of demographic and social factors overall, Aboriginal people remain remarkably homogeneous with regard to their marginal position in Canadian society.

The Aboriginal population is young. Nearly one-third of all Aboriginal people in Canada are under the age of 14, and the median age is 24.7. This reflects a fertility rate of well in excess of 3.4—over twice the national rate. The rate of natural increase for Aboriginals is about 20 per 1,000 people, while the comparable rate for the Canadian population is 5.1. At the same time, the death rate for Aboriginals is almost half of that for the general population, in part due to the higher average age of the general Canadian population. Life expectancy among Aboriginal people is about five years less—for both women and men—than for the total Canadian population, a result of relatively poor living conditions and high suicide rates, among other factors.

Overall, the Aboriginal peoples of Canada occupy the lowest levels of education, occupation, labour force participation, and income. Moreover, their participation in almost every institutional order of Canadian society is marginal and they continue to struggle to maintain their culture and traditions (Frideres and Gadacz, 2008).

Table 12.3 **Size and Growth of Aboriginal Ancestry and Aboriginal Identity Population, Canada**

	2006	% growth (1996–2006)	Projected population 2026	Average annual growth rate 2006–2026 (%)
Total Aboriginal ancestry	1,389,560	26.1	1,566,900	1.5
Total Aboriginal identity	1,172,786	44.9	1,325,300	1.3
North American Indian	698,025	29.1	871,000	1.4
Métis	389,780	90.9	376,000	1.3
Inuit	50,480	25.5	75,000	1.9
Multiple response	58,300	127.3	196,000	1.4

SOURCES: Adapted from 2001 and 2006 Canadian Census. *Analysis Series, Aboriginal Peoples of Canada: A Demographic Profile*, Ottawa, Statistics Canada; J. Frideres and R. Gadacz, *Aboriginal People in Canada*, Toronto, Pearson Education, 2008; *Aboriginal Demography*, INAC: Strategic Research and analysis Directorate, Policy and Research Division, Ottawa, ND; *Registered Indian Demography—Population and Family Projections, 2004–2029*. INAC Strategic and Analysis Directorate—CMHC Policy and Research Division, Ottawa, ND.

Aboriginal people have a long history of their family organization and structure being under attack from the dominant society. For example, long before signing the numbered treaties, residential schools were established and Aboriginal children were forced to attend and live apart from their families (immediate and extended). During this time, intense assimilation procedures were enforced: young people were not allowed to speak their native language at the schools, the cultural and spiritual practices of their people were banned, and many young Native people were exploited economically and/or sexually. Nearly five generations of Aboriginal people were subjected to programs that systematically destroyed the structure and functioning of Aboriginal families, climaxed by the "Sixties Scoop," when thousands of children from dysfunctional (according to Euro-Canadian norms) Aboriginal families were removed from their homes and sent to distant foster homes and for adoption. However, in 2008 the Government of Canada issued an apology for its residential school policy and provided financial compensation for people attending residential schools as well as establishing a Truth and Reconciliation Commission to address the residential school impacts.

This short review of the three groups sheds light on the diversity within minority families (Walters et al., 2002) and provides a "snapshot" of their position in Canadian society. It shows different histories, demographic profiles, and different strategies to deal with the new post-colonial efforts of the Canadian government. We now turn to specific issues that are germane to family and present a comparative assessment with regard to these issues. We begin with the issue of how family is linked to the structure and organization of Canada.

Socio-economic Location in Canadian Society

For more on poverty among immigrants and racialized groups, see "Economic Well-Being among Visible Minority Communities" in Chapter 10, p. 197.

The socio-economic status of individuals has a great impact on the structure and functioning of the family. Those individuals who have a reasonable income can obtain adequate housing, provide social amenities for family members, achieve higher educational goals, and develop interpersonal skills. On the other hand, for those families who live in poverty, family quality of life is marginal in almost every dimension (e.g., type of housing, crowding).

Morissette, Zhang, and Drolet (2002) show that wealth inequality has increased over the past two decades with substantial declining median wealth for recent immigrants. Zhang (2003) found that for immigrants in the 40–90th percentile of wealth, their incomes were greater than native-born Canadians. However, for those below the 40th percentile, immigrant wealth was much lower than native-born Canadians.

In reviewing the three target groups included in this chapter, we find that for recent immigrants and Aboriginals, the labour force participation rate is about 50 per cent. The unemployment rate for these two groups is about 20 per cent (triple the overall Canadian rate), although in some areas it may be as high as 60 per cent (Teelucksingh and Galabuzi, 2005). Thus, it is no surprise that about one-third of Aboriginals live in poverty, 30 per cent graduate from high school, and less than 2 per cent go on to university. Visible minorities experience a median after-tax income gap of over 13 per cent compared to the overall Canadian income. Data show that the proportion of recent immigrants with family incomes below the poverty line rose to nearly 34 per cent by 2001 (Frenette and Morissette, 2003).

Overall, recent immigrants have low-income rates 2.5 times those of Canadian-born residents (Pendakur, 2000; Li, 2001). Only four out of 10 highly educated immigrants will find a job within one year that uses their skills, resulting in a poverty rate for visible minority persons between 40 and 50 per cent. Employed visible minority members earn about 81 cents for every dollar earned by a Canadian-born, non-visible person, and one in every five visible minority immigrants with a university education is in the poorest 20 per cent of Canadians.

Socio-economic factors in a child's family can have major impacts on the child's well-being and future development, including their future employment possibilities, income, and success in functioning in families of their own. Statistics Canada shows that in 2005, one-third of the children who had at least one parent immigrating to Canada in the past decade were living in poverty.

On virtually every measure of hardship, children from immigrant, visible minority, and Aboriginal families fare less well than children in families of white, Canadian-born parents (James, 2010). Children of immigrants are more than four times as likely to live in crowded housing while Aboriginals are nearly 10 times more likely. Immigrant and Aboriginal children are more likely to have poorer health and to live in families that are worried about being able to afford food for their children. At the same time, Houle and Schellenberg (2008) found that family is important to immigrants—nearly half of them sent remittances to their source countries ranging from $500 to $3,000 per year.

Residence

Where families reside has important consequences for their employment, development of networks (social capital), and ability to draw on community support. The residential patterns of immigrants in Canada are clear. Over 80 per cent of all immigrants reside in British Columbia, Quebec, and Ontario, and within these provinces over 75 per cent live in Vancouver, Montreal, and Toronto. Immigrants cited two principal reasons for choosing major urban centres: (1) a family member or close friend was already living in the area and (2) the perception of greater employment opportunities. As a result of this pattern, immigrants now make up a significant percentage of the populations of major urban centres. Toronto is a good example: nearly 50 per cent of the city's total population is foreign-born.

Today, nearly half of the Aboriginal population lives in urban areas, with more than one-quarter living in 10 metropolitan areas across Canada. This population is much more mobile than the non-Aboriginal population and statistics show that nearly one-quarter of the Aboriginal population relocate in the span of one year (compared to about 10 per cent for non-Aboriginals). This high level of mobility creates many challenges for Aboriginal families in the areas of education, social services, housing, and health care.

With the increase in the number of visible minorities comes an expansion of visible minority neighbourhoods in urban centres (Hou, 2004). The number of ethnic/racial neighbourhoods that can be defined as "concentrated" has increased from six in 1981 to nearly 350 in 2006. This ethnic concentration has both short- and long-term implications for selecting marriage partners, job opportunities, and socialization techniques. Many of these neighbourhoods are poor, have a high percentage of recent immigrants, and contain a high proportion of visible minorities. However, these concentrations are not "ghettos," such as are common to cities in Europe and the United States. Many people choose to remain in the community because of their networks/friendships within the community even though they could afford to leave (Murdie, 2008). For example, in Vancouver large concentrations of Chinese are a result of voluntary decisions to reside within the newly formed Chinese community. These concentrations create social networks in the neighbourhood, develop social capital, and produce high levels of **institutional completeness**. Plans are underway in Toronto and Calgary to build Muslim residential enclaves. Compared to the Canadian-born population, visible minorities are 20 times more likely to live in extended family units. In addition, because of this and their high poverty rates, they also tend to have the highest rates of crowding in housing units of any group, with the exception of Aboriginal peoples.

These types of ethnic communities allow the groups to develop a hybrid type of identity and maintain social control mechanisms over family and community members. Second, these neighbourhoods can provide social capital for families and build dense networks to support their social and economic goals. The emergence of ethnic enclaves transforms the physical and social attributes of the neighbourhood, challenges the way of life established by previous residents, and generates tension in local space. However, the long-term implications of such segregated ethnic enclaves are yet to be determined.

Family Issues

Family Structure and Organization

It is estimated that nearly half of the children born since 1980 will spend at least part of their childhood with fewer than two parents in the home and among those with two parents, frequently one is a step-parent. In 2006, for the first time ever, there were more census families comprised of couples without children than with children. The census also shows that a growing proportion of young children have a mother in her 40s as women delay childbearing. The number of young adults aged 20–29 living at home has increased from 32 per cent (1986) to 44 per cent in 2006. Since the 1950s, when less than 10 per cent of the children were living with only one parent, the rate has now doubled. For the period of 1985–2004 nearly 22 per cent of all the children born had "unstated paternity." Nearly half of the Aboriginal children born to Aboriginal women under 15 during this period had an unstated paternity while 30 percent of children born to mothers in the age group 15–19 had unstated paternity. Children born from older mothers had unstated paternity ranging from 12–19 per cent (Mann, 2009). These are major changes in family structure over the past quarter-century.

Most European and Asian families follow a patrilineal kinship structure, meaning that kinship is traced through the father's line. On the other hand, for many Aboriginal groups a matrilineal (tracing kinship through the mother's line) kinship structure is the norm. Over the years, the dominant Euro-Canadian group has sought to impose its own policies onto Aboriginal peoples; however, people in many First Nations communities still recognize the importance and power of women and respect "powerful women" who support the community.

According to the 2006 census, 81 per cent of Aboriginal families consist of husband and wife, compared to 86 per cent for non-Aboriginals and 87 per cent for immigrants. Just over 17 per cent of Aboriginal families were female lone-parent while 12 per cent of non-Aboriginal families were headed by female single parents (see Table 12.4). Table 12.4 identifies the growth as well as the residence of Aboriginal families. In terms of marital status, over half of the total Aboriginal population has never married, while over one-third are married. For non-Aboriginals, 38 per cent have never married and just less than half are married. The separation and divorce rates of Aboriginal and non-Aboriginal Canadians are similarly comparable, although the percentage of Aboriginal people who are widowed is much lower than that for the non-Aboriginal population (3.2 per cent versus 7.5 per cent).

Birth and fertility rates for Aboriginal people are much higher than for the non-Aboriginal population (25 live births annually versus 12 per 1,000 women, and 3.2 children per woman ages 15–45 versus 1.6). Young children—those under the age of 14—of Aboriginal origin tend to live in family structures different from those of non-Aboriginal Canadians. For example, 83 per cent of non-Aboriginal young children live with two parents. However, in the case of Aboriginal peoples on reserves, less than two-thirds of young children resided in a two-parent family, and in an urban setting the numbers decline to less than half. Conversely, twice as many Aboriginal children lived with a lone parent as did non-Aboriginal children. In urban areas, over five per cent of young Aboriginal children lived away from their parents, compared to 0.6 per cent for non-Aboriginals. At the same time, many Aboriginal children reside with their grandparents as part of their traditional culture. However, an increasing number of Aboriginal children are being placed under institutional care. For Aboriginals, there has been an increase from 4 to 6 per cent in terms of institutional care over the past decade, while for non-Aboriginals the institutional care rate is less than 1 per cent.

Has the organization of families changed over time? The organization of the Aboriginal family was profoundly changed during the twentieth century in two separate actions. First was the establishment of residential schools, where young Aboriginal children (estimated at 125,000) were forcibly removed from their families and sent to live in boarding schools. This led to the underdevelopment of parenting skills for several generations. The large-scale

Table 12.4 Size and Growth of Aboriginal Families and Lone-Parent Families, Canada, 2001 and 2026

	All	On reserve	Rural (off reserve)	Urban (off reserve)
Total Aboriginal families				
2001	337,700	39,700	69,700	178,300
2026	615,100	192,300	104,000	318,700
Total lone-parent families				
2001	88,800	30,900	15,500	42,300
2026	161,600	66,500	22,300	72,800

SOURCES: Adapted from *Aboriginal Demography*, INAC: Strategic Research and Analysis Directorate, Policy and Research Division, Ottawa, ND, *Registered Indian Demography—Population and Family Projections, 2004–2029*. INAC Strategic and Analysis Directorate—CMHC Policy and Research Division, Ottawa, ND.

involvement of the provincial governments in social services for Aboriginal people in the 1960s and 1970s meant that Aboriginal children were once again forcibly removed from their families and sent to non-Aboriginal families. Steckley and Cummins (2001) show that, in 1964 alone, over one-third of the young Aboriginal population in BC was removed from Aboriginal homes.

In terms of household activity, Aboriginal and non-Aboriginal Canadians reveal similar patterns for such activities as housework, child care, and elder care. For example, nearly 80 per cent reported no care for seniors, nearly 50 per cent had no children under their care, and about 10 per cent did not involve themselves with household work. For those who did engage in these activities, the patterns for Aboriginal and non-Aboriginal were similar.

When immigrants come to Canada, they are faced with a decision as to how they will cope with their new social environment. They can try to preserve the culture of their origin, they can try to become "Canadian" as quickly as possible, or they can try to develop a hybrid that incorporates both the "old" and the "new." Regardless of the strategy they choose, immigrant families find ways to cope with the new norms, values, and behaviours of Canadian society (Beck and Beck-Gernsheim, 2002). Rer-Strier (1996) identified three coping strategies employed by immigrants: (1) unicultural, (2) rapid assimilation, and (3) bicultural. The first strategy involves the parents remaining as the primary socializing agents. The second strategy is for parents to withdraw as the chief socializing agent and defer to other agents in the new country (e.g., teachers, social service professionals). A third strategy involves encouraging the child to live in a bicultural world, whereby in the home and for family-related activities the parents are the chief socializing agents but outside the home the children are expected to conform to the culture of their new environment (Anisef and Kilbride, 2003). Each strategy involves risks and benefits, although the traditional unicul-ture strategy has the highest risk for immigrant families. This is primarily because retaining one's "home" culture while residing in Canada can result in a lack of integration and reduce social and economic opportunities. In addition, new forms of family have emerged over time. One new form of family—the "split household"—is somewhat unique to Asian immigrants (particularly natives of Hong Kong, Singapore, South Korea, and Taiwan). The split-household family is organized according to time and space so that over time a family is distributed over a long distance or wider expanse of space (Liu, 2012; Man, 2007).

Box 12.1
Transnational Familial Arrangements

Transnational familial arrangements are strategies of transnationalism by which immigrants build social networks that link the country of origin with the country of settlement. They are triggered by structural barriers such as the lack of recognition of international credentials and the nature of the part-time and low-paying jobs that are mostly available to new immigrants. Transnational familial networks such as the "split household," "astronaut family," "transnational mothering," "satellite children," or "sandwich generation" allow immigrant parents to maintain employment while raising children in separate geographical spaces but can also result in conflict and other adverse impacts on these families.

Many new immigrants and Aboriginals live in households that are different from the standard nuclear organization that is typical of Canadian-born, non-visible minority families. Our research supports the segmented assimilation process and has identified three different types of extended family. First, in the "upward extended" family, parents or older relatives of the head of household also live in the household. "Downward extended" families occur where the children and/or grandchildren of the head of household live in the same residence. Finally, there are those extended households that are called "horizontal extended" families, in which, for example, the sibling or close relatives (e.g., cousins) of the head of household live in the same house. Immigrant and refugee families use all three forms of extended families while Canadian-born families tend to use only the upward extended family structure. In addition to these extended families there are households of refugee and immigrant youth who lost their nuclear families in conflicts and immigrated to Canada on their own. As is the case with the Lost Boys and Girls of Sudan, these youth share houses with their peers who become their new families.

Family Conflict

Prior research has identified three conflict patterns in families. One pattern emerges when the husband takes on the instrumental role and the wife takes on the emotional role. Over time, if one becomes more isolated, lonely, or dependent on the other, the other person will see the second as "ignorant and a burden" and this will lead to spousal conflict. A second scenario is when women get new opportunities after marriage and this new situation (e.g., a job outside the home) gives her self-confidence to challenge the traditional power distribution and role allocation (Darvishpour, 2003). Alternatively, if the man experiences a status change that decreases his power in the family, he may try to maintain dominance by, among other things, referring to old norms and rules that legitimize relations as they were before. A third pattern of conflict arises between generations within a family. Generational conflicts are endemic to all families, regardless of their ethnicity. The general basis for such conflict is the fact that the children are growing up in a different social milieu from that in which their parents were raised. In the case of Canadian-born families, the discontinuity is minimal but nevertheless evident. However, immigrants and Aboriginal people may find that they are living in a society that has many different cultural rules from those during their own childhoods, for example, the shift from an age-graded society in which respect for one's elders was a given to the contemporary twenty-first-century Canadian society that stresses individual equality and glorifies youth. In addition, young immigrants and Aboriginals tend to assimilate rapidly. As such, cultural gaps between the generations become more pronounced and visible. For example, some Hispanic traditions promote family co-operation that is the antithesis of Canadian values of individualism. Young immigrants are then faced with making a decision about living in a unicultural or bicultural world. At the same time, older immigrants have similar problems to deal with. In Vietnamese and Aboriginal cultures, for example, where elders are important family members, they may find themselves marginalized because they don't speak an official language and/or are not consulted on important family decisions.

Economic necessity for many immigrant and Aboriginal families requires that women and/or children enter the labour market. This tends to reverse the "provider" role that may be expected in their homeland. Immigrant women and children are able to enter the labour market more quickly than men because of the availability of low-paying jobs for females/youth, and thus they become the principal breadwinners for the family. In turn, they take on the status and power that accompanies the "provider" role. This inversion of roles, if not dealt with skillfully and with sensitivity, can create hostility and resentment within families and create stress and health problems (e.g., depression, violence, alcoholism) for all members of the family.

None of the above situations may create more than minor episodic bouts of conflict, each of which can be resolved in a short time and with minimal resources. However, when conditions escalate or become chronic, the conflict may turn to physical or emotional abuse inflicted on family members by other family members. One of the results of such conflict is marital/family dissolution which impacts all family members.

Raj and Silverman (2002) found a paucity of research on the prevalence of intimate partner violence in immigrant communities but suggest community organizations feel that violence against immigrant women has reached "epidemic proportions." Qualitative studies by Husaini (2001), and Dosanjh, Deo, and Sidhu (1994) looked at family violence in the South Asian community and found that it was a serious concern. Moreover, they found that battered immigrant women are less likely than non-immigrant women to seek both informal and formal help for intimate partner violence. In cases where spouses have been sponsored, many experience what is called "sponsorship debt" (Cote et al., 2001). Others have found that cultural barriers to receiving help often come from community or religious leaders who compel women to stay in abusive relationships and not to speak publicly (Smith, 2004; Saris and Potvin, 2008). They fear that disclosure to outsiders promotes criticism of their culture or ethnicity. Finally, immigrant women are less likely to seek help because of isolation, lack of language skills, fear of deportation, lack of information with respect to available services, and lack of culturally sensitive or safe services available to them. Values implicit in existing mainstream services often clash with the values of many immigrant women. For example, services offered by mainstream service organizations focus on individual rights and empowerment while immigrant women may come from a cultural system that believes the values of the community should be of central concern. Finally, mainstream service agencies have few connections with immigrant communities and thus are ineffective in dealing with ethnocultural community issues. On the other hand, research done by Brownridge and Halli (2003) shows that the pattern is not universal. They found that immigrant families from "developed" nations have a lower prevalence of violence than Canadian-born families.

Elder care is one of the greatest challenges facing an aging Canadian population (particularly for immigrants) and families play an important role in providing this care. The demand for elder care services is currently being met through three different types of organizational arrangements. Informal support, the most common, consists of uncompensated services provided by family members and friends. Medical health-care workers funded by the state provide the second type of service. Finally, there is independent living within long-term care. Under this type of care, health-care workers provide services either in an institutional setting or at the aging individual's home. Immigrants and Aboriginal peoples are more likely to engage in informal support while native-born Canadians tend to use long-term care facilities. Immigrants and Aboriginals argue that there are few culturally sensitive care facilities and thus only they understand the cultural significance of certain types of care. This is changing, though, as some cities are opening ethnic elder care facilities. All three of our target groups use state-funded health services when the aging relative requires major health care. Nevertheless, providing care for the elderly causes psychological, emotional, and economic burdens for families and thus places seniors at an increased risk of being victims of abuse. Like family assaults against children and youth, rates of elder abuse have escalated 35 per cent over the past five years.

Elder abuse by ethnicity is rarely mentioned in the literature on family, but an Ontario Native Women's Association study carried out in 1989 found that abuse of older adults was identified as a serious problem in some First Nation communities (Ontario Advisory Council on Senior Citizens, 1993). The Family Violence Initiative Report (2002) shows that Aboriginal women and men experience higher levels of spousal violence compared with non-Aboriginal peoples (20 per cent compared with 7 per cent). Aboriginal women were three times more likely than non-Aboriginal women to report having been assaulted by a current or former spouse and spousal homicide is more than eight times higher than for non-Aboriginal women. This study also found that nearly half of the children in these communities have been physically abused by a family member.

Familial violence seems to increase when factors such as economic and social deprivation, alcohol and substance abuse, the intergenerational cycle of violence, and overcrowding and substandard housing are evident. For Aboriginal families, the breakdown of healthy family life is linked to residential school upbringing and the loss of traditional values, and family violence is a partial consequence of colonization, forced assimilation, and cultural genocide—the learned negative cumulative multi-generational actions as well as the behavioural patterns practised by the dominant group to weaken and destroy the harmony and well-being of the Aboriginal community.

The Role of Gender in Family

The role of women in the family is an important issue that has short- and long-term consequences for all involved. However, men and women immigrants are treated differently as they settle into Canada, and how well each immigrant is able to integrate depends on a number of factors such as entry status (defined as being "independent" or "dependant"), involvement in the labour market, and involvement in social networks (Boyd and Grieco, 2003). An independent immigrant has access to language-training programs, job-training programs, and a host of other programs that support **immigrant integration** into Canadian society; dependants have no access to these services. In Canada, most women enter as dependants and this consequently places barriers for them to integrate (e.g., they do not have access to language programs). It also impedes their involvement in the labour market, leaves them subject to abuse with no avenue of escape, and limits access to resources. Canadian-born women are more likely to be active participants in the labour market than immigrant women. In addition, their participation does not involve taking on low-paying jobs and learning one of the official languages in addition to specific technical or social skills.

As noted earlier, participation in the labour market by females can bring about an increase in social mobility, economic independence, and relative autonomy. This in turn may change the distribution of power in the family, leading to greater authority and participation in household decision-making by family members that have not traditionally had that role. At the same time, labour force participation by women may increase the burden they must carry (e.g., caregiving and housework).

Previous research pictures immigrant women as passive victims of their culture (men being the oppressors) and their surroundings. While this stereotype is common for specific ethnocultural groups, it is an oversimplified view that reflects the **ethnocentrism** of the researchers. First, Canadian women are equally oppressed in various ways. Second, it ignores the fact that women and men have their own centres of power and competence and the stereotypes underestimate women as an active agent. Third, this stereotype ignores the fact that people from the same country or ethnocultural group do not constitute a homogeneous group and that within some immigrant families there are conditions for an equal relationship. Finally, this stereotype often leads to a focus on the problems of "women" and seldom on their possibilities and freedom of action. In general, immigration to Canada has led to a dramatic increase in power resources for many immigrant women.

In Aboriginal communities there has been and continues to be a gender split on a number of community issues. Men occupy major economic and political positions in the community even though they generally have less education and training than women. As Aboriginal women have taken on more and more responsibility on the reserves, legal and social issues have taken on a "gender" perspective. Over time these gendered views of the world have become public and major conflicts have pitted men against women.

Youth

Overall, young people from all ethnic groups engage in similar activities—watching television, listening to music, and spending time with their friends. At the same time, youth from the groups we have studied in this chapter have different experiences in growing up. For example, nearly three-quarters of immigrant youth are involved in the labour force in order to support their families and they are expected to participate in family enterprises when required. This affects their ability to spend time on social and extracurricular activities as well as on academic pursuits. In other cases female youth will be treated very differently from their Canadian-born counterparts.

In 2006, over one-quarter of all Canadian children under the age of 18 were recent immigrants or were born in Canada to immigrant parents. These youth face diverse linguistic, psychological, and socio-economic challenges in their lives. Their complex needs with respect to health, education, social services, and the justice system are linked and are played out in the home, at school, and in the community (Ngo, 2009). They want to be accepted by the mainstream culture but at the same time they want to maintain and affirm their own personal identity. In their cultural adjustment, they often experience cognitive and emotional changes. In addition, immigrant youth have to struggle with the changing dynamics within their own families. Issues such as a clash of cultures, changing roles in the family, and changes in family relationships have been identified as problematic for youth. For example, because young people tend to learn English/French and understand Canadian culture earlier than their parents, they become aware of Canadian expectations much earlier than their parents.

Linguistic and cultural barriers pose challenges for youth to understand school routines, educational rights, and responsibilities. Moreover, parents are unaware of social support services and their imagined role in the education process may differ from the expectations of the schools. Data from the National Longitudinal Survey of Children and Youth reveal that children of immigrant parents start school with low achievement levels in reading, writing, and mathematics. However, their performance generally reaches or exceeds the performance of children of Canadian-born parents before they complete elementary school. Children whose mother tongue was neither English nor French have higher dropout rates as they move from elementary to middle school. Nevertheless, the academic performance of immigrant youth who achieve Grade 10 is equal to that of Canadian-born students.

Visible minority youth encounter barriers to full integration and thus remain within the confines of their group. Within the education system, practices such as the underrepresentation of material pertaining to minority history and culture in the school curriculum, high suspension and drop-out rates, absence of minority teachers, and enrollment in the Basic and General levels alienates these youth (Madibbo, 2010). This differential treatment results in a clear spatial division (segregation) of groups in a variety of contexts in schools, such as in the cafeteria and in school activities. In addition, when outside the school and within the larger community, visible minority and Aboriginal youth must confront other issues. For example, their arrests by the police based on **racial profiling** are ongoing, and their detention rate is seven times higher than for other Canadians. Moreover, the incarceration rates for visible minorities are twice as high as for non-visible minorities (Derouin, 2004). Despite the official rhetoric and Canada's long history of receiving immigrants, young immigrants to the country often perceive a general non-acceptance of immigrants (or visible minorities) by people within their community and the media (Arthur et al., 2008). They see systemic social barriers that face them and their parents in securing employment or in gaining recognition of their professional qualifications, which often results in **underemployment**.

Intermarriage/Mixed Unions

Research by Parkin and Mendelsohn (2003) notes that Canadians work, date, and socialize with people from different ethnic and religious backgrounds. Their results show that although most people feel that ethnicity is important for establishing personal identity, they did not think it was important for choosing a spouse. However, census data reveals there is a discrepancy between attitudes and behaviour: most marriages are ethnically/religiously homogenous. While this pattern is slowly changing, today we find that the incidence has tripled over the past quarter century and today nearly 4 per cent of all unions in Canada involve a visible minority and a non-visible minority (or a different visible minority) partner (Milan and Hamm 2004). While these absolute numbers are low, they represent a 55 per cent increase since 1981 and our overall intermarriage rate is one of the highest in the world (Rodriguez-Garcia 2007). Of mixed unions in Canada, just over half were non–visible minority men and visible minority women. However the actual rate of intermarriage varies by ethnic group (Milan and Hamm, 2004). As Table 12.5 shows, Japanese have the highest rate of intermarriage, followed by Latin Americans and blacks. At the other end of the scale, South Asians have the lowest rate of mixed unions, followed by Chinese and Koreans.

Table 12.5 **Persons in Couples and in Mixed Unions by Visible Minority Group, 2006**

	Total	In a couple		In a mixed union	
	Number	Number	Percentage	Number	Percentage
Visible minority group					
All persons belonging to visible minority groups	3,922,700	2,181,200	55.6	331,300	15.2
Chinese	1,005,600	587,500	58.4	56,000	9.5
Black	562,100	216,800	38.6	55,200	25.5
South Asian	957,600	612,800	64.0	41,500	6.8
Latin American	244,300	130,300	53.3	40,000	30.7
Filipino	320,900	179,200	55.9	35,600	19.8
Arab/West Asian	321,800	185,000	57.5	26,500	14.3
Japanese	66,400	37,200	56.0	22,200	59.7
Southeast Asian	184,600	98,200	53.2	18,100	18.4
Korean	114,600	62,800	54.8	6,800	10.8
Multiple groups or n.i.e.[1]	144,700	71,400	49.3	29,400	41.3

1. Less common visible minority groups are reported in the visible minority N.I.E. (not included elsewhere) category. This category includes respondents who reported a write-in response such as Guyanese, West Indian, Kurd, Tibetan, Polynesian, and Pacific Islander. Belonging to multiple visible minority groups means that respondents reported more than one visible minority group by checking two or more mark-in circles, e.g., black and South Asian.

SOURCE: Milan, Maheux, and Chui. 2010. p. 72. Available at http://www.statcan.gc.ca/pub/11-008-x/2010001/article/11143-eng.pdf.

Another form of intermarriage focuses on the native/foreign-born status of the individual spouses. Over half of marriages involving immigrants reveal that both partners are recent immigrants, 13 per cent consist of one recent immigrant and one earlier immigrant, and in 16 per cent one recent immigrant and one Canadian-born spouse are joined. On the other hand, 40 per cent of immigrants who came to Canada prior to 1981 are married to a Canadian-born spouse. Today, 7 per cent of foreign-born couples are mixed racial unions, while only 2 per cent of Canadian-born couples are mixed. Canadian-born visible minority couples are more likely to be a mixed union than with the same visible minority. However, the longer foreign-born visible minorities are in Canada, the more likely they are to be in a mixed union. We also find that no matter which group we compare, mixed unions are much more likely to be common-law rather than formal marriages.

There also is the issue of interreligious marriages (Clark, 2006). Today we find that nearly one in five Canadian couples is in an interreligious union. The groups with the largest per cent of interreligious unions are Protestants and Catholics (21 and 16 per cent respectively). Those with the smallest rate of interreligious unions are Sikh (3 per cent), Hindu, and Muslim (9 per cent each). While the rate of interreligious unions has increased over the past two decades for Protestants and Catholics, it has decreased for the other three groups identified above. As with interethnic unions, most of interreligious unions are by young, well-educated urban dwellers that are foreign-born.

There are a number of reasons for the increase in intermarriages. First, the social and geographical mobility of people means more opportunity to meet people from different backgrounds. Second, because of the increased diversity in Canada, people have greater opportunities in school, work, and other social places to meet individuals from diverse backgrounds. Third, with the increasing numbers of immigrants from across the world, residents have a larger pool to draw upon for potential marriage partners. In the case of Aboriginal people, females tend to move from rural to urban settings with their children and enter the labour force, thereby increasing their chances of bonding with non-Aboriginal persons. Fourth, a multicultural society such as Canada has reduced the level of prejudice, discrimination, and social distance of immigrants, visible minorities, and Aboriginals in Canada. However, intermarriage rates vary between men and women. For example, more Arab men than women tend to marry outside their group, while Asian women have higher exogamous rates than Asian men.

While the majority (86 per cent) of Canadians has not experienced discrimination, well over one-third of visible minorities have encountered discrimination in Canada (Arthur et al., 2008). Nevertheless, Canadians demonstrate a growing openness to other cultures. Still, many in Canadian society would not feel comfortable if their son or daughter married someone from certain other groups. For example, two-thirds of Canadians would feel very comfortable if their child married a Euro-Canadian while only 52 per cent would feel that way if their child married a black or Chinese and 37 per cent if they married a Muslim. There are significant generational differences in views on mixed unions. While one-quarter of Canadians between the ages of 18 and 29 expressed some discomfort with marriage to Muslims, this figure increases to over 50 per cent for those over the age of 60. In the case of Chinese, 20 per cent of those over 60 years of age would feel "uncomfortable" if their child married a Muslim, whereas less than 10 per cent of those in the 18–29 group responded that way (Jedwab, 2004). In the end, Rodriguez-Garcia (2007) points out that the process of partner choice and family formation is a multidimensional phenomenon contingent on a number of personal and social factors.

Conclusion

The easing of divorce law, the changing economy, and other social changes in Canadian society has brought about a major shift in how marriage and the family are viewed. In addition, changes in immigration policy have opened the door to immigrants from around the world and created a racial, ethnic, and religious diversity in our society. This diversity has led to different organizations of family as well as to various processes of socialization. Communities and schools have been overwhelmed by this diversity and only recently are developing strategies for integrating families from diverse backgrounds. Over time more Aboriginal people have moved off reserves and are now a major force in the urban centres. In all these cases, families have had to adapt and integrate into Canadian society. As such, parents still interpret the world to their children and in turn the children learn how to cope with the dynamics of integration and adaptation to Canadian culture. Relatives and kinship relations (real or fictive) form networks of social and economic care and interdependence. In some cases these systems span three or four generations. At the same time, the nature and structure of communities provide more or less support for families. Institutions such as health and social services and the court system also are trying to adapt to incorporate Canada's growing diversity while maintaining equality and justice.

Finally, the backgrounds (human capital) of parent(s) are important in establishing the level of functionality for families. For example, immigrant families with high education attainment and secure jobs, and who are not visible minorities, find the adjustment less problematic than those without this human capital. Nevertheless, families develop the structure of their children's basic values, and this schema is part of a group's "culture." As such, it becomes the basis by which family and individual experiences are processed and evaluated. It is, in short, a world view that serves as a framework for evaluating experiences and gives stability and order to family life. Unfortunately, these structures do not converge across cultural groups and allow all to apply the same schema to each of life's challenges.

STUDY QUESTIONS

1. Compare the social attributes of the three groups examined in this chapter with the general Canadian population. What are the main similarities?
2. How do families differ among the three groups under consideration?
3. How does the socio-economic status of a family impact its role and function?
4. How does domestic violence impact a family?
5. What are the social factors that create a mixed union family?
6. How could one counter the barriers that the youth face?

Further Readings

Belkhodja, C. 2008. "Immigration and Diversity in Francophone Minority Communities," *Canadian Issues* (Spring). This issue of *Canadian Issues* explores schooling, official bilingualism, discrimination, and social services along with their implications for francophone immigrants including families.

Frideres, J., and R. Gadacz. 2012. *Aboriginal People in Canada*, 9th edn. Toronto: Prentice-Hall Canada. This book provides a comprehensive assessment of both the history and current status of Aboriginal people in Canadian society, with "facts and figures" on a number of topics (e.g., health, language, crime, and demography).

McQuillan, K., and Z. Ravenera. 2006. *Canada's Changing Families: Implications for Individuals and Society.* Toronto: University of Toronto Press. Using data from Statistics Canada, the contributors to this volume illustrate how families have altered their routines and the division of labour within the family. The changing economy's impact on alternative family arrangements, divorce, and fertility are investigated.

Mandell, N. and A. Duffy, eds. 2010. *Canadian Families: Diversity, Conflict and Change*, 4th edn. Toronto: Nelson and Thompson. The authors offer progressive feminist theoretical and methodological approaches in studying the family. Issues such as gender, race, class, same-sex couples, violence, and discriminatory policy affecting Aboriginal peoples and visible minority families are discussed in historical and contemporary contexts.

Ward, M. 2006. *The Family Dynamic: A Canadian Perspective*, 4th edn. Toronto: Thomson Nelson. The author presents the current status and the future of the family in Canada, and discusses a range of topics relevant to the family and its future.

Websites

www.statcan.ca/start.html

The Statistics Canada website provides information on Canada's people, economy, and government. Up-to-date information on families is available and new publications on the topic are presented. The site also includes official Canadian census data on families.

www.canada.justice.gc.ca/eng/pi/fv-vf/index.html

The Department of Justice has a "family violence initiative." This includes any form of abuse, mistreatment, or neglect that children or adults experience with other member of their family. A series of publications and statistics are available on the topic of family violence. There is also a family violence youth site.

www.cic.gc.ca

Immigration and Citizenship Canada sheds light on the various categories of immigrants, including the family class, and provides publications dealing with citizenship, settlement, and integration.

www.aadnc-aandc.gc.ca

This is the official site for Aboriginal Affairs and Northern Development Canada. Historical, statistical, and legal aspects of Aboriginal people are part of this federal government website.

www.ofa.gov.on.ca

L'Office des affaires francophones de l'Ontario points out a range of aspects concerning Francophone immigrants such as their demographics, language policy, education, and services in French.

13

Lack of Support: Canadian Families and Disabilities

MICHELLE OWEN

LEARNING OBJECTIVES

- To understand the impact disability has on Canadian families
- To be able to distinguish between the medical and social models of disability
- To recognize the role gender plays in the lives of disabled people
- To describe the relationship(s) between poverty and disability
- To identify the factors that put people with disabilities at increased risk of violence and abuse

---

Introduction

Too many Canadian children and families face inordinate difficulties because they live with the stresses, the acquired poverty, the health issues, the exclusion, and the other markers of disability, even though these issues are becoming more widely recognized in Canada (Roeher Institute, 2000b: vii). In this chapter we will examine disability in Canadian families. As the title suggests, the argument being presented is that disabled Canadians and their families are marginalized in our society. The chapter begins by providing background information regarding definitions, models, and frameworks. It is then divided into three sections: Children and Youth with Disabilities, Parents with Disabilities, and Violence and Abuse.

Disability affects many Canadians and their families. In 2006, 4.4 million people in this country (14.3 per cent of the 2006 census population, or one in seven) reported that they had a disability (Statistics Canada, 2007g). This represents an increase of over three-quarters of a million people, or 1.9 per cent since 2001 (Statistics Canada, 2007g). This rise may be attributed to both an aging population and less stigma attached to reporting a disability

(Statistics Canada, 2007e). Moreover, approximately 11 million people (35.6 per cent) have a family member with a disability (Environics Research Group, 2004; see Figure 13.1). Unfortunately, despite the widespread and growing impact of disability, disabled Canadians and Canadian families continue to experience a lack of support.

Aging accounts for some 40 per cent of the increase in disabilities in Canada and we are an aging society (Statistics Canada, 2007g). In this sense, all people without disabilities can be considered TABS **(temporarily able-bodied)**. While 11.5 per cent of working-age adults (aged 15–64) report having a disability, seniors (aged 65 and over) have a rate almost four times higher at 43.4 per cent (Statistics Canada, 2007g). This number increases to 56.3 per cent for Canadians aged 75 and over (Statistics Canada, 2007g).

Canada has one of the highest life expectancies in the world, and women live longer than men (82.2 years versus 77.1) and are thus more apt to experience disabilities (Des Meules et al., 2003) concurrent chronic health problems (Statistics Canada and Status of Women Canada, 2012: 360). In 2006, 15.2 per cent of females in Canada reported having disabilities, compared to 13.4 per cent of males (Statistics Canada, 2007g). Figure 13.2 shows the rates of disability for females and males in Canada. Disabled women are more likely than disabled men to be single, have lower incomes than men with disabilities, and "less tangible social support" (Des Meules et al., 2004). Furthermore, women and girls with disabilities are oppressed by sexism and **ableism** (and in some cases racism, classism, homophobia, etc.). Demas, for example, argues that Aboriginal women with disabilities face "triple jeopardy" (1993a: 89).

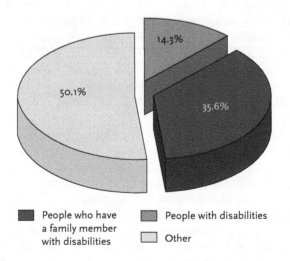

14.3%

50.1%

35.6%

| People who have a family member with disabilities | People with disabilities |
| Other |

Figure 13.1 **People with Disabilities and People with Family Members with Disabilities, Canada**

SOURCES: *Participation and Activity Limitation Survey 2006*; Environics Research Group 2004.

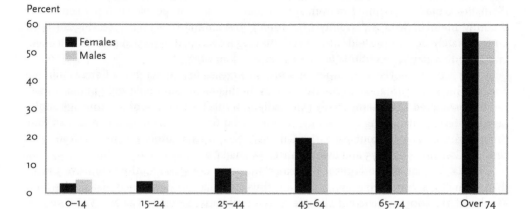

Figure 13.2 **Rates of Disability in Canada**

SOURCE: Statistics Canada: *Participation and Activity Limitation Survey, 2006.*

Defining Disability

There are no easy definitions of "disability," and the terminology used in disability activism and studies has been hotly debated. Defining words is a political act, as feminist and critical race theorists have struggled to highlight. Some people use a wheelchair or a cane and are noticeably disabled, while others have chronic illnesses or mental health issues that are not so readily apparent. These are sometimes referred to as **visible and invisible disabilities**, a distinction that of course only makes sense if one is sighted. Some disabilities are permanent (paraplegia), while others are temporary (broken limbs) or they come and go (relapsing/remitting multiple sclerosis). Who is disabled and what counts as disability is constantly changing.

The 2006 **Participation and Activity Limitation Survey (PALS)** considered people to have a disability if they reported "difficulties with daily living activities, or who indicated that a physical or mental condition, or health problem reduced the kind or amount of activities they could do" (Statistics Canada, 2007f). A national post-censal survey on people with disabilities, PALS includes information on children (aged 14 and under) and adults (aged 15 and over) who reported having a disability according to the above definition. The 2006 study added territorial and Aboriginal data missing in 2001, and modified the definition of "collective household" (Statistics Canada, 2007f). However, people living on First Nations reserves and in institutions were excluded, as they were in 2001. Unfortunately the Conservative government cancelled PALS in 2011, replacing it with the less comprehensive Canadian Survey on Disability. Results from this survey are due to be released in 2013. Thus PALS 2006 is still the most current national resource on disability, and it was used to update this chapter for the third edition of *Canadian Families Today*.

The federal government acknowledges that the concept of disability is always shifting and thus "defining disability is not an easy task" (Government of Canada, 2002: 10). Although national survey data rely on self-identification for a broader range of individuals, much like many community-based organizations and activists, benefits and disability-oriented programs use a far more limiting definition. Neither the Charter of Rights and Freedoms nor the Canadian Human Rights Act unequivocally define disability, although they do prohibit discrimination against persons with physical and/or mental disabilities.

Whenever a definition is not explicitly given by a piece of legislation, it is up to the courts to determine scope and limitations. For example, a 2001 Quebec Supreme Court decision was that "various ailments such as congenital physical malformations, asthma, speech impediments, obesity, acne and, more recently, being HIV positive, constitute grounds of discrimination" (Office for Disability Issues, 2003: 14–15). The focus of this ruling is on how society treats (or mistreats) people with non-conformist bodies, which is an example of social model theorizing.

The Social Model of Disability

The **social model of disability** can be understood as "the relationship between a person with impairment and the environment, including attitudes, beliefs, climate, architecture, systems and services" (Hurst, 2005: 65). This is in contrast to the earlier models such as the bio-medical or individual which centred disability firmly in bodies (Oliver, 1996a). This served to reinforce disability as a personal tragedy and fuelled feelings of pity in non-disabled people. A good example is the Jerry Lewis telethons, which many people with disabilities find demeaning. It is useful to distinguish between two social models: the materialist or radical, and the idealist or rights interpretation (Sheldon, 2005: 118–19). According to Alison Sheldon, while a radical social model focuses on capitalism as "the root cause of disablement," rights-based analyses lead to "short-term policy reforms and sticking-plaster solutions" (ibid., 118, 121). From her perspective, the impact of globalization must be taken into account as we theorize disability.

The Union of Physically Impaired Against Segregation (UPIAS) (1976) in Britain was perhaps the first to make an unambiguous distinction between personalized physical **impairments** and the social experience of disability: "In our view it is society which disables physically impaired people. Disability is something imposed on top of our impairments by the way we are unnecessarily isolated and excluded from full participation in society. Disabled people are therefore an oppressed group in society" (cited in Oliver, 1996a: 33).

Hence, since the 1970s, disability activists and theorists have put forth a social model of disability that identifies barriers as being systemically rather than biologically based (Crowe, 1996). As Jenny Morris (2001: 2) writes, citing a definition used by the British Council of Disabled People:

> Disability is the disadvantage or restriction of activity caused by a society which takes little or no account of people who have impairments and thus excludes them from mainstream activity (therefore, disability, like racism or sexism, is discrimination and social oppression).

Thus, the social model of disability has much in common with analyses that theorize race and gender as social constructions and not as biological or "natural." The emphasis in defining "disability," as a result, has shifted from a medical model of (ab)normality (Malec, 1993) to a focus on social structures. This has been a significant move in the rethinking of disability and the beginning of political action. Previously, the concept of disability was centred on individual impairments and people with disabilities were "othered" because of their difference from the ableist norm. Within the social model external obstacles, as opposed to individual characteristics, are viewed as disabling (Block and Keys, 2002). For example, the lack of a ramp is the problem, not the fact that someone uses a wheelchair.

Despite the progressive thrust of the social model of disability, gender differences have been an ongoing source of tension. However, as Thomas (1999) maintains, experiences of disability are always shaped by gender. A number of academics and activists have struggled for recognition of the double discrimination faced by people who are marked as both "women" and "disabled" (see Wendell, 1996). The concept of **gendered disablism** (Thomas, 1999: 28) is increasingly receiving recognition. Unfortunately, other differences, such as race (ibid.) and sexuality (Tremain, 1996), have received far less attention.

Theoretical/Methodological Frameworks

Although this chapter is based in the social model of disability, it is important to acknowledge some of the critiques of this mode of theorizing, such as the denial of bodies and pain (Wendell, 1996). Not all disabling experiences can be fixed by altering the environment. A cross-disability perspective has been employed, rather than focusing on any one disability or type of disability. This encompasses "visible" and "invisible disabilities," including so-called physical disabilities (mobility, vision, hearing), mental health issues, chronic illnesses, intellectual disabilities, and learning disabilities. Self-identification is critical in this context because it shifts the power of naming away from those in authority and contributes to our cultural identity. Finally, the terms "persons with disabilities" and "disabled persons" are alternated. The former is derived from "people first" language and is more common in the Canadian context though by no means standard. The intent is to signal that people have many identities in addition to disability. The latter phrase is used more in Britain and fits better with the social model of disability. It is increasing used by Canadians who want to highlight the disabling features of the social environment.

Children and Youth with Disabilities

Statistics Canada (2007h) reported that in 2006 there were approximately 5.5 million Canadian children aged 14 and under. Of this total, 202,350 (3.7 per cent) had disabilities, representing 2.7 per cent of girls and 4.6 per cent of boys. Boys 14 or younger are more likely than their female counterparts to have disabilities that limit activity, but once they move into the next age category (15–24) this prevalence disappears (Cossette and Duclos, 2002). Overall the incidence of disability increases with age of the child—this was found to be true regardless of gender (Statistics Canada, 2007g; see Table 13.1).

Table 13.1 **Disability Rates for Canadian Children Under the Age of 15, By Sex and Age Groups, Per cent, 2006**

Age	Child disability rates	Disability rates among boys	Disability rates among girls
0–14	3.7	4.6	2.7
0–4	1.7	2.1	1.2
5–9	4.2	5.3	3.0
10–14	4.9	6.0	3.7

SOURCE: Statistics Canada, *Participation and Activity Limitation Survey, 2008.*

Demographics

Over half (55.1 per cent) of disabled children in Canada are considered to have "mild to moderate disabilities," with Quebec and Ontario having the highest incidences of children with severe to very severe disabilities (48.8 per cent and 39.7 per cent of children with disabilities, respectively) (Statistics Canada, 2007h). Of the population of children with disabilities in Canada, 13.6 per cent (27,540) are preschoolers (0–4 years) (Statistics Canada, 2007h). The most common type of disability among preschoolers are chronic health conditions such as asthma, severe allergies, heart conditions or disease, kidney conditions or disease, cancer, epilepsy, cerebral palsy, spina bifida, cystic fibrosis, muscular dystrophy, fetal alcohol syndrome, etc. (69.8 per cent) (Statistics Canada, 2007h). Developmental delay (62 per cent), including delays in intellectual and/or physical development, and other delays such as speech impairment were the next most prevalent type of disability causing activity limitations for this age group (Statistics Canada, 2007h).

The majority (86.4 per cent, or 174,810) of all disabled children are school age (5–14 years) (Statistics Canada, 2007h). The most common types of disabilities reported for this age group in 2006 were learning disabilities (69.3 per cent) and chronic health conditions (66.6 per cent) (Statistics Canada, 2007g). Boys reported experiencing learning disabilities (4.1 per cent) and chronic disabilities (3.8 per cent) at a higher rate than girls (2.2 per cent for each) (ibid.). That same year a disability related to learning affected 121,080 school-age children, or 3.2 per cent of all children aged 5 to 14 in Canada (ibid.). Learning disabilities are often not diagnosed until children start school, and parents continue to struggle to obtain special education for their children with disabilities (Statistics Canada, 2008h). Over 40 per cent of parents with children with disabilities reported in 2006 that they had a difficult time accessing special education, regardless of the type or severity of their child's disability (ibid.). Emotional, behavioural, and psychological conditions such as autism were the most difficult to accommodate (ibid.).

Impact of Children with Disabilities on Families

Many parents of children with disabilities experience considerable frustration, largely stemming from a lack of supports rather than from dealing with their child's disability (Roeher Institute, 2000b). While in the past many disabled children were institutionalized, they are increasingly likely to live at home with their families rather than in institutions (Roeher Institute, 2000a). However, in some cases, children are placed in residential or foster care because of inadequate family supports (Howlett, 2005). Family breakdown is not uncommon, and children with disabilities are over-represented in female-headed lone-parent families (Fawcett, 1996) compared with other children (18.1 and 14.1 per cent, respectively) (NPHS, 1996, as cited in Roeher Institute, 2000b).

Family Income, Employment, and Poverty

The average household income for preschool and school-age children with disabilities is lower than the household incomes of their peers without disabilities (Table 13.2). In 2006 the average household income for families with disabled children was $69,440, compared to $85,294 for families without children with disabilities (Human Resources and Skills Development Canada, 2011a). Further, there is a correlation between the presence of a child with a disability in the household with the likelihood of a family's income falling below the Low Income Cut-Off (LICO) (Statistics Canada, 2008j). Currently one in five families with children having activity-related disabilities reported falling below the LICO, as compared to one in 10 families without children with disabilities (ibid.). Having a disabled child does not only influence income, but it can also impact the employment situation of families. Many families of children with disabilities (nearly 62 per cent of families with preschool children and 54 per cent of those with school-age children) report that their child's condition has impacted the family's employment situation (Government of Canada, 2004).

For information on the negative impact of poverty on health, see "What Are the Consequences of Poverty?" in Chapter 10, pp. 203–4.

The impact was found to be positively correlated to the severity of the child's disability—while 40 per cent of families of children with mild to moderate disabilities reported an impact on their employment, this proportion almost doubled to 73 per cent in families having children with severe to very severe disabilities (Benhia and Duclos, 2003).

Having a child with a disability can thus force families to rethink the way they organize work and family life. In almost half the cases one or more family members make changes to their employment (Human Resources and Skills Development Canada, 2011a). Compared to fathers, mothers are most likely to be responsible for providing, arranging, and advocating for care for their disabled children (Roeher Institute, 2000a). Hence, women are more likely than men to experience an impact on their employment due to their child's disability. Mothers' employment is affected almost 90 per cent of the time while fathers' employment is affected about 33 per cent of the time (Human Resources and Skills Development Canada, 2011a).

For more on women's employment, see section on the cost of caring under the heading "Gender Differences in Paid and Unpaid Work: What Difference Does Difference Make?" in Chapter 9, pp. 180–1.

So children with disabilities are more likely to be poor than other children (Human Resources and Skills Development Canada, 2011a; Roeher

Table 13.2 **Average Household Income of Canadian Children, 2001**

Age	Children with disabilities	Children without disabilities
0–4	$54,660	$66,138
5–14	$63,366	$72,069

SOURCE: Statistics Canada, *Participation and Activity Limitation Survey, 2001*, as cited by Office for Disability Issues, 2003.

Institute, 2000b). This trend also goes in the opposite direction: "Children living in poverty are 2.5 times more likely than children in high-income families to have a problem with vision, hearing, speech or mobility" (Ross and Roberts 1999, as cited in Roeher Institute, 2000b: 5). According to the Roeher Institute, *poverty can lead to disability* in a number of ways. People living in impoverished conditions have little access to nutritious foods, both during pregnancy and as children grow. Poor people tend to live in areas or circumstances that may increase the risk of injury and also tend to have less access to health services, as well as lower literacy levels, all of which have been linked to increased rates of disability and/or ill health (ibid.). Labelling is a concern for these children, as well: "Poor children, like children who are from visible minorities, are also more likely to be labelled as having a disability than children from more privileged families" (ibid., 6).

The Roeher Institute also suggests that *disability can lead to poverty*. Families with disabled children are more likely to experience "family breakdown" and the corresponding reduced family income. Parents of children with disabilities also experience increased barriers to participation in the paid labour force and must contend with costs that families without disabilities do not face. These expenses include those related to "tutors, special diet, special clothing, transportation, babysitting, medications, supplies and equipment, and home adaptations" (ibid.).

Some parents have no other alternative than to care for their children full-time rather than participating in the paid labour force (Hanvey, 2002: 11). According to the 1996 National Population Health Survey, young people with disabilities are more than twice as likely as young people without disabilities to live in familial environments that depend on government, not employment, for their main source of income (16.9 per cent compared with 8.1 per cent) (ibid.). "For many families of children with disabilities it makes more sense to use social assistance than to take a job with low wages, since they are entitled to receive more disability-related supports when on welfare" (ibid., 6). Because social assistance can provide these disability supports, many parents of children with disabilities simply cannot "afford" to work (see Table 13.3).

Aboriginal families with disabled children living on reserves experience unique problems related to support and social assistance. Because of federal guidelines for support, social assistance on reserves tends to be lower than elsewhere. And since the mid-2000s

Table 13.3 **Employment Impact for Parents of Canadian Children with Disabilities by Severity, 2006**

Employment impact	Total	Mild to moderate	Severe to very severe
Not taken a job	26.4	16.4	39.8
Quit working	21.6	13.2	32.9
Changed work hours	36.5	26.9	49.4
Turned down promotion	19.7	10.5	31.9
Worked fewer hours	38.4	29.1	50.8
Worked more hours	9.7	6.4	14.2

SOURCE: Statistics Canada, *Participation and Active Living Survey*, 2008.

money is dispersed to First Nations who in turn distribute funds to band members (Aboriginal Affairs and Northern Development Canada, 2010). Aboriginal families caring for a child with disabilities do not receive any disability supports, and often subsequently move off reserve to access these supports, or else go without or have to pay for these supports themselves (National Population Health Survey, 1996: 6).

According to Roeher Institute (2000a), 50 to 60 hours of a parent's week is spent providing disability-related supports to their child(ren). Employers are not required to accommodate people caring for their children with disabilities, so parents are forced to alter their commitments to their jobs or leave the paid workforce entirely, with very little government assistance (Roeher Institute, 2000b). In Canada, a monthly supplement called the Child Disability Benefit (CDB) is available to parents of children with disabilities. It has a maximum amount per child, as well restrictions based on the age of the child, the length of time received, the type of disability, and the severity of the child's disability. The CDB is a tax-free benefit of no more than $2,000 per year, which is only available for "low- and modest-income families, who care for a child under age 18 with a severe and prolonged mental or physical impairment" (Canada Revenue Agency, 2005: para. 2).

The Dearth of Supports for Disabled Children

Housework, Family Responsibilities, and Personal Activities

Although having a child with a disability creates additional demands for parents, nearly 60 per cent of parents of preschool children and almost 80 per cent of school-age children with disabilities report not needing additional help with housework and family responsibilities (Government of Canada, 2004). Parents of preschool children with disabilities are more likely than parents of school-age children with disabilities to report needing additional help with housework and family responsibilities. Parents of children with severe to very severe disabilities were more likely than parents of children with mild to moderate disabilities to report unmet needs (29.7 per cent versus 10.7 per cent) (Statistics Canada, 2008k).

Cost is a major factor preventing parents of disabled school-age children from getting the assistance they require—73.5 per cent cited cost as a reason for not receiving the help they need (Statistics Canada, 2008k). Usually, parents (56 per cent of those reporting) resort to "free" help that comes from family members outside the home though more than a third (36.7 per cent) reported "out-of-pocket" expenses for required assistance (ibid.). As one parent of a child with a disability describes this frustration: "I want them to have a life. They need opportunities to develop. This is not possible for me to do without needed supports and services" (Roeher Institute, 2000b: 1).

Family access to disability-related supports can be difficult and fraught with problems. According to the Roeher Institute, families report that eligibility screening is too rigid and does not sufficiently take individual family circumstance and disability-related costs into consideration. As a result, families living with disabilities face multiple barriers to gaining access to need supports. Not just cost, many families report a lack of local resources and a lack of information about local services (Statistics Canada, 2008k). In addition, access to services seems to vary between families and regions: "Fewer than four in ten (37.5 per cent) parents reported that special services were not available locally, while 39.5 per cent of parents reported not knowing where to go to find help" (Statistics Canada, 2008k). Families also report being discouraged by long waiting lists and not being able to afford short-term relief care, transportation, and equipment.

Since the late 1990s, the disparity of supports in Canada has left some families caring for disabled children with no option other than to temporarily relinquish guardianship over their children. According to the report of the Ontario ombudsperson, up to 150 families in Ontario signed temporary custody agreements with the Children's Aid Society in order to obtain supports needed by their children with severe disabilities. Douglas Elliott, a lawyer representing many of these families in a class-action lawsuit, argued that "many parents were concerned their children would not continue receiving care once legal custody was restored. Parents had turned to a children's aid society because that was the only way to obtain treatment" (Howlett, 2005: A13).

Parental Caregiving Responsibilities

Due to the inadequacy of support services, parents and other familial caregivers are often forced to fill the gap themselves. This can result in what a 2003 Canadian study has termed "caregiver strain" (Duxbury and Higgins, 2003, cited in Pappone, 2005). People in the workforce who are caring for aging parents or children with disabilities are vulnerable to a variety of problems, including depression, fatigue, family conflict, and financial problems. Research illustrates the multiple responsibilities of parents of children with disabilities: nurses, advocates, trainers and educators, and service co-ordinators (Haverstock, 1992, cited in Roeher Institute, 2000b). One parent interviewed encapsulates this sentiment: "I'm everything—I'm the playmate, storyteller, therapist, disciplinarian, advocate, cook, and parent" (ibid., 10).

Parenting does not end when a child grows up and/or leaves home, particularly for some disabled children. And, as Heather Hewett's story emphasizes (see Box 12.1), a number of people besides parents are included in the "networks of support" for a person with a disability (Hewett, 2004). Heather's sister's situation highlights the fact that all of us, people with and without disabilities, are ultimately interdependent. Her family is not unlike other families except that the interdependence is widespread and hence more obvious. While Hewett is writing in the American context, her description of the "intricate web" that allows her sister to live interdependently is relevant for Canadians.

Home and Respite Care

Access to **home care** varies across Canada and even within provinces and territories. There is no "consistent or coherent home care coverage, nor standards defining access to basic services" (Roeher Institute, 2000b: 9). A 2005 report by the Council of Canadians with Disabilities identifies these jurisdictional issues as problematic (Krogh and Ennis, 2005).

Families also report needing more **respite care**—those services that give parents/guardians a break from their caregiving responsibilities. The Roeher Institute (2000a), in a study of 50 families of children with disabilities, found that 90 per cent identified respite care as one of the most crucial supports needed for them and their children but this need was not being met. Access to respite care is particularly difficult for families in rural areas, as well as

Box 13.1
A Sister's Story

My 31-year-old sister has Down syndrome. She lives in her own house, three miles away from my 70-something parents, and she works part-time busing tables at a local café. An extended network of people help her live on her own: my mother, her full-time advocate and teacher; my father, her biggest fan and supporter; her caseworker, Alicia, who oversees the coordination of her social services; her live-in house companion, Eleanor; her habilitation training specialist, Delores, who helps teach her skills such as balancing her checkbook; her speech pathologist, Judy; her boss, David; her 80-something best friend, Ellen, who gives her rides around town; and finally, her close friends Laurie and Elizabeth, two middle-aged dance therapists who listen to her and provide her with an endless supply of hugs. Then, of course, there's me, but I live thousands of miles away.

From my vantage point, it is particularly evident how much of my sister's daily existence depends on this extended family of friends and professional caregivers. In this respect, her life is not so different from that of other families in our country. Many families rely on similar (though not always as extensive) networks of support; it is just that in my sister's case, the intricate web holding her up cannot be ignored. It is there, in plain view, for all who look.

SOURCE: Hewett, 2004.

for children with exceptional support needs. Demand for in-home respite is high and there are not enough public resources to assist everyone (Dunbrack, 2003).

Child Care

Many parents rely on child care services to help meet their family needs. While the majority still rely on a family member in the home, 24.4 per cent (one in five) used after school programs and another 20.7 per cent (one in four) used the child care service of a non-relative outside of the home (Statistics Canada, 2008k). Location and transportation to child care services however, makes choosing facilities more complex because the facilities must be able to meet the child's special needs (ibid.). The federal Office for Disability Issues (2001) reported that approximately 20 per cent of parents of disabled preschool children were refused child care or babysitting services due to their child's impairment. This percentage was not found to vary significantly based on severity of disability.

Although the deficiency of child care in Canada is a concern for all Canadians, for parents of children with disabilities accessing child care can be even more difficult. Child-care facilities are not required to include children with disabilities, although some do. When child-care centres accept children with disabilities, it is usually done on a child-by-child basis, with some disabled children accepted and others not (Roeher Institute, 2000b). In 2006, 25 per cent of parents reported that a daycare centre had refused their child with a disability (Statistics Canada, 2008k).

According to the Roeher Institute, the problem is inadequate funding—centres would be more inclusive if there were enough money. Getting their children into daycare is not the only problem. Even when they have managed to secure child care, parents may encounter difficulties in getting their child to the centre and back home again, rigid hours of operation, inflexible curricula, and a lack of training among staff about disability (Roeher Institute, 14).

Parents with Disabilities

There is far more information available about disabled children in this country than about disabled parents. Neither PALS nor the Canadian Census have collected data pertaining to parents with disabilities. So all we can do is speculate: how might the experiences of disabled people shape the lives of those who are actively engaged in parenting? What we do know is that working age adults with disabilities are not doing as well at forming or maintaining families as their counterparts without disabilities. In 2006, 56.2 per cent of disabled people aged 25–54 were married or in a common-law relationship compared to 71.4 per cent of non-disabled Canadians. People with disabilities are also more likely to be separated or divorced (24.2 per cent) than people without disabilities. Furthermore, the average household income for a single disabled person in this age group is only 67.0 per cent of the average household income for a single non-disabled adult (Human Resources and Skills Development Canada, 2011a).

In addition to structural barriers, social stigma and moral regulation surround parenting by disabled people, especially women, who are most affected by medical procedures designed to control fertility and reproduction. In the past, women with disabilities have been denied the right to have children through forced sterilization and chemical birth control (Malacrida, 2009a, 184; Ridington, 1989). Increasingly, women's lives are subject to a process of "geneticization," with common conditions being labelled genetic diseases (Lippman, 1993: 40). The assumption is that no one would want to raise a disabled child given the choice. A case in point—abortion is currently prohibited for sex selection in Canada but not for the elimination of disability (ibid., 62). Prenatal screening and testing have in fact become routine, opening the doors to a new type of eugenics (Peters and Lawson, 2002).

Mothering Challenges

"Mothering or even fathering with a disability is assumed to be potentially 'damaging' for children ... [and] family 'dysfunction' is presumed to be inevitable" (Blackford, 1999: 281). It is not uncommon for mothers with disabilities to face disbelief and discrimination regarding pregnancy and parenting, to have their custody challenged, or their children taken away. For example, adaptive measures such as lifting babies by clothing and harnesses on wheelchairs are not always understood or well received by the non-disabled public (Auliff, 2001). Kuttai documents many of the challenges women with disabilities face as they become parents including encounters with medical professionals and social judgment (Kuttai, 2010).

Blackford (1999: 280) argues, however, that "through the intimate experience of caring for and knowing a person with a disability, and through feeling cared-for and understood by a person with a disability, oppression associated with disability prejudice and with **familialism** [restrictive ideas about what constitutes the 'family'] is reduced." In addition, children of disabled parents learn to respect difference and are exposed to a more egalitarian family environment, as well as gain a profound awareness and recognition of the lived experience of space and the body (ibid.).

Canadian women with disabilities over 45 years of age are less likely to be married than disabled men (Des Meules et al., 2003). In the 25–44 age range, women with disabilities are more likely than women without disabilities to be single, divorced, separated, or widowed (Des Meules et al., 2003). Overall disabled women are much more likely to live alone (26 per cent) than non-disabled women (14 per cent) (Statistics Canada and Status of Women Canada, 2012: 361). Adult Canadian women (15 years of age and over) with disabilities are more likely than similarly aged men with disabilities to live outside their family and to be lone parents (Fournier-Savard, 2006). As Fournier-Savard reports, in 2001 36 per cent of disabled women lived alone, with another relative, or with an unrelated person, compared with 24 per cent of men with disabilities (ibid., 292–3). For seniors the figures rise to 53 per cent for women with disabilities versus 24 per cent men with disabilities (ibid., 293). In 2001, 13 per cent of women with disabilities in this country were lone parents, compared with just 3 per cent of their male counterparts (ibid., 293) (see Table 13.4).

Despite the challenges, the number of disabled Canadian women who are mothers is increasing (Blackford et al., 2000). But according to Blackford et al., the needs of expectant mothers with chronic illnesses and/or disabilities are not being met by current models of prenatal care and education. The authors suggest, "If prenatal education is individualized and culturally respectful, education can be a medium to address the empowerment needs of marginalized expectant mothers" (ibid., 899).

In their research, Blackford and her colleagues interviewed disabled mothers who had given birth to a child within the past two years about their maternity experiences. They found that the women noted six areas of prenatal care that needed improvement: learning resources for self-care, opportunities to voice anxiety, supportive relationships, communication within the family, information pertaining to postnatal care, and special circumstances (ibid.).

Informal Caregiving

In 2006 63.7 per cent of PALS respondents reported that they needed assistance with at least one daily activity such as getting dressed. That year 53.1 per cent of disabled adults indicated that all their needs were met, down from 62.3 per cent in 2001. Severity of disability and cost were the main factors influencing whether or not a person could get the help they needed (Human Resources and Skills Development Canada, 2009).

Although the most common source of assistance in everyday activities is family (1.9 million Canadians with a disability report receiving assistance from a family member), more than one-quarter of disabled people say that their friends and families are unable to provide these informal care services (ibid.). Usually one family member, typically a woman, provides the majority of informal care services: "The role of informal caregiver can be challenging, especially since many caregivers are also employed, are lone parents or have responsibilities besides helping a person with a disability. Caregivers may need support to keep providing quality care to people with disabilities" (Government of Canada, 2004: 19).

Table 13.4 **Family Status of Men and Women 15 and Over with Disabilities, 2001**

	Lived alone, with another relative or unrelated person (%)	Lone parent (%)
Women with disabilities	36	13
Men with disabilities	24	3

SOURCE: Fournier-Savard, 2006.

Working-age adults with disabilities are more likely to receive informal care from family members who live with them than from any other resource. According to Government of Canada, "Informal caregivers often face long-term financial repercussions in the form of, for instance, turning down career opportunities, being unable to update skills, saving less for retirement and experiencing reduced working hours, pay and pension benefits" (ibid., 20). Re-entering the workforce after a period of full-time caregiving has also proven to be difficult for these caregivers, and the 2004 government report suggests improved access to respite care, as well as better workplace accommodations for caregivers, to better support these familial caregivers.

For Aboriginal Canadians with disabilities, supports to family caregivers are even more limited. Insufficient reimbursement and/or respite care services exist for family caregivers of disabled Aboriginal people, even when the caregivers themselves have disabilities. The Aboriginal Reference Group on Disability Issues (1997) cautions: "In many rural and remote communities there are no respite service providers at all. Lack of respite services is likely to lead to family deterioration and by extension to community deterioration" (ibid., 23).

Employment and Learning

Working-age adults with disabilities are only half as likely as other Canadians to find viable employment (Statistics Canada, 2008j). Moreover, disabled workers earn less than non-disabled workers, and women with disabilities in Canada continue to earn less than men without disabilities. In 2006 Canadian women with disabilities had an average income of $20,236, compared to $30,638 for men with disabilities (Statistics Canada, 2008l). Moreover, persons with disabilities "can be doubly disadvantaged by extra costs related to disability" (Government of Canada, 2002: 44).

Disabled people who are parents of young children experience even more difficulty in finding paid employment opportunities because of their child-care responsibilities (Office for Disability Issues, 2003). This issue is particularly prevalent among disabled mothers. Fawcett (1996: 163) explains, "The greater likelihood of being a lone parent, coupled with lower participation rates among lone parents, contributed to the lower likelihood of labour force participation among women with disabilities." This contributes to "less access to the more generous income support programs, and higher rates of poverty overall" (1996: 151). A 2002 discussion paper sums the situation up in this way:

> Canadian research has made it clear that major roadblocks to labour force participation of parents with disabilities exist in the workplace. While there is a need for additional investment in accessible child care, there is also a need for greater awareness on the part of employers about the particular situation of parents with children with

disabilities. Flexibility in hours and location of work, recognition of particular needs in benefits packages, and awareness on the part of managers and co-workers are essential. (Harvey, 2002: 11)

Post-secondary education narrows the gender gap in labour force participation, as well as the wage gap, for persons with disabilities:

> Among persons with disabilities whose highest level of education was primary school, or less, the participation rate for women was about 53 per cent that of men (25.3 per cent participation rate for women, compared to 48.2 per cent participation rate for men). [However], women's participation rates as a proportion of men's rose to about 92 per cent for those with either a non-university post-secondary diploma (67.6 per cent participation rate for women, compared to 73.4 per cent participation rate for men) or a university degree (69.8 per cent participation rate for women, compared to 76 per cent participation rate for men). (ibid., 153–4)

According to more recent figures, working-age women with disabilities are now surpassing their male counterparts in regard to completing high school (27 per cent vs 23 per cent) and college (24 per cent vs 17 per cent). Disabled men are more likely to attain a trade certificate than disabled women (18 per cent vs 10 per cent). In terms of university degrees, the gap is narrow between women and men with disabilities (13 per cent vs. 12 per cent) (Human Resources and Skills Development Canada, 2011b).

Impact of Dependent Children on Labour Force Participation

Similar to other Canadian women, the labour force participation of disabled women is largely influenced by their (unpaid) domestic labour responsibilities, including the care of dependent children. The age of dependent children is often a factor:

> Women with disabilities who had children under the age of six were less likely to be in the paid labour force than those who had no dependent children or had school-aged children. Among women aged 25 to 34 with disabilities, for example, 68.2 per cent of those who had no dependent children were in the paid labour force; for those with children under age six, the figure dipped to 59.8 per cent, and for those with children over age five, it was 62.9 per cent. (Fawcett, 1996: 158)

Employed women aged 15–64 with disabilities who had children were more likely than other women with disabilities to require some form of job redesign or accommodation (ibid.). In addition, parents of young children with disabilities reported turning down advancement opportunities, working fewer hours, not taking a job, altering their working hours, or having to resign (Government of Canada, 2003, Statistics Canada, 2008k). This suggests, according to Fawcett, that the interaction of child-care responsibilities with employment responsibilities affected the higher rate of job accommodation.

Domestic Labour

Disabled women are more likely than disabled men to perform most of the basic household chores. This was found to be true, regardless of severity of disability or living arrangements. In this vein, "men with disabilities were much more likely to have assistance with household chores—whether it was required for the disability or not" (Fawcett, 1996: 165). Men with disabilities were also more likely than women with disabilities to report needing assistance with meal preparation, even if it was not required as the result of their disability.

In Fawcett's words, "While the majority of both women and men with disabilities did not require assistance with basic household chores strictly because of their disability, the majority of men were likely to receive assistance anyway; the majority of women were not" (ibid., 167). The assistance received by men with disabilities may have been from a family member inside or outside of the household, a friend outside the household, or hired help through a service or agency.

Assistance with household chores was very much related to whether or not the individual lived alone or with others. Those who lived with others received much more assistance than those who lived alone (ibid.). Disabled women who live with other people were more likely to perform their own meal preparation.

Blackford (1999: 279) found that although oppression in families where a parent has a disability certainly exists, strengths can be gained from the experience: "In organizing the social relations of family life when a parent has a chronic illness like multiple sclerosis, family members often learn to do it differently."

Violence and Abuse

While all people with disabilities are more likely than people without disabilities to experience abuse (The Roeher Institute, 1994: v–vi), family violence impacts more on disabled women than on any other group in our society. According to the National Clearinghouse on Family Violence (1993a: 3), women and children with disabilities are "one of the most highly victimized groups in our society" and violence and/or fear of violence are "the most critical issues facing women with disabilities." They are "particularly vulnerable to threats to their physical safety, and to psychological and verbal abuse and neglect" (Government of Canada, 2002: 54). According to a 2012 international review of two decades of studies pertaining to violence against disabled children, a quarter of young people with disabilities aged 2 to 18 years have experienced violence. Overall the researchers estimate that "disabled children are at nearly four times greater risk of experiencing violence than those without a disability" (Bellis et al., 2012).

Children

It has been estimated that, in Canada, disabled children are the victims of abuse up to 10 times more frequently than children without disabilities (Sobsey, 1994, cited in NCFV, 2000). "Among children with disabilities . . . research has found that 39 to 68 per cent of girls, and 16 to 30 per cent of boys are subjected to sexual abuse before the age of 18" (Bunch and Crawford, 2000: 18). Children with mental or developmental disabilities are especially vulnerable (BC Institute against Family Violence, 1996; Government of Canada, 2004).

Although they are more likely than other children to be victims of abuse, violence against children with disabilities has received little attention. For disabled children, some forms of abuse are so subtle that they are not easily recognized by the law. The Roeher Institute (2000b: 18) reports that "abuse may come in the form of restricted movement, invasive 'therapy' or rough handling while receiving personal care (e.g., for washing, feeding, grooming, using the toilet) . . . abuse could come at the hands of parents, teachers, health professionals and others."

Violence against children with disabilities varies by gender, as well as by type of disability. While girls are at particular risk for sexual assault, boys are more likely to be physically abused and neglected (Canadian Mental Health Association, 1993, cited in Roeher Institute, 1995). "Girls with intellectual disabilities are twice as likely as boys to be sexually abused before the age of 18 years" (ibid., 19). Children who are deaf also experience higher levels of abuse than other children, as do children with physical disabilities.

Where disabled children are most vulnerable is debatable. DAWN Toronto's (1995: 32) research concluded: "The most dangerous place for her [girl with a disability] to be is in her own home. . . . If a girl with a disability is sent to foster homes or institutions, she still faces a high risk of sexual and physical assault." However, other sources maintain that Canadian children who have been institutionalized due to physical and/or intellectual impairments have an increased risk of maltreatment (NCFV, 2000). And although protective measures are now in place to prevent this from recurring, children living in institutions continue to be victimized more often than other Canadian children (Doe, 1999).

Children with disabilities are at an elevated risk for abuse, in part because of the difficult circumstances common to their families (Roeher Institute, 2000b). According to the Roeher Institute's 1994 report for the National Clearinghouse on Family Violence (cited ibid., 18):

> Children with disabilities are more likely to be abused within their families when their families experience isolation (which may be increased by demands of caregiving), are overwhelmed by the demands of caregiving, lack opportunity to develop effective coping skills, or engage in difficult caring activities while lacking respite and other supports.

The report goes on to state that additional stresses such as unemployment, as well as a family history of abuse, use of corporal punishment, or substance abuse, can all contribute to the risk of abuse. The authors suggest that this kind of abuse is more prevalent where negative social attitudes towards disability are prominent (Roeher Institute, 1994).

Child abuse is an issue of power. The risk of disabled children experiencing abuse is often intensified because of their increased levels of dependency and vulnerability (NCFV, 2000). Their vulnerability is heightened because of social stereotypes about their impairments. For instance, children with disabilities may experience social isolation within their own families or peer groups due to a family member or friend's negative attitudes towards disability. For example, a child may be left out of a family game, without any accommodations being made to include the child, because of assumptions of the child's inability to participate successfully. Social isolation can lead to an increased vulnerability to abuse (NCFV, 2000).

The murder of Tracy Latimer is one of the most high-profile cases involving a child with a disability (see "Case in Point" box). On 24 October 1993, Robert Latimer, a Saskatchewan farmer, killed his 12-year-old daughter Tracy by using a hose to feed carbon monoxide from his truck's exhaust pipe into the cab where he had placed her. She was born with cerebral palsy and was unable to perform many of the so-called activities of daily living without assistance. It is important to read about Tracy's life because so much media attention has been focused on her father and his quality of life. The murder of any child is horrific, but because Tracy was disabled her murder was framed as a type of "mercy-killing."

Women

DAWN Toronto (1995: 32) characterizes violence against women and girls with disabilities as a crisis, estimating that over two-thirds of women with disabilities experience physical or sexual assault before they reach puberty. The Canadian Research Institute for the Advancement of Women (CRIAW) states that "Violence is a major cause of injury to women, ranging from cuts and bruises to permanent disability and death" (CRIAW, 2002: 6). Women who are physically or sexually abused as adults or children are at greater risk of a variety of health problems, including chronic pain, anxiety, and clinical depression (ibid., 7).

As for children with disabilities, violence against women with disabilities often comes in the form of family violence. This can include "physical, psychological or sexual

---

CASE IN POINT
Tracy Latimer

It was true that Tracy had cerebral palsy, that she experienced pain and would have encountered more but it was not true that it was constant or excruciating as [her mother] Laura's testimony said. Like other children disabled at birth, Tracy knew no other life. This was the life she had been given, and she enjoyed it, valued it and fought to keep it, just as most able-bodied people value their lives.

The communication book entries written by Laura and read for the Crown during the second trial showed Tracy relished these simple pleasures at least until Tuesday, October 19, the date of the last entry, five days before her life was taken from her. Laura's entry that day read, "Tracy was good, ate and drank fine [sic] Tracy was good, ate really well, had a bath, Bob [Tracy's father] bathed her." It was the day Robert Latimer decided on using exhaust fumes to kill her.

In able-bodied people pain is a symptom, but in Tracy it was a death sentence carried out by her father and condoned by her mother, the defence attorney, the judges and juries and most media and their audiences. It was not her intermittent pain that was the predominant issue in either trial. It was her disability. Because she couldn't speak, the assumption was that she couldn't comprehend and, if she couldn't comprehend, her death really wasn't as monstrous as the killing of someone who could.

SOURCE: Enns, 1999: 46–7.

maltreatment, abuse or neglect of a woman with disabilities by a relative or caregiver. It is a violation of trust and an abuse of power in a relationship where a woman should have the right to absolute safety" (NCFV, 1993: 1). Disabled women who live in institutions (who are more dependent on a higher number of people) may be at an even greater risk.

Like women without disabilities, violence against women with disabilities is usually per-petrated by someone known to the victim, someone in their inner circle, their "family." Women with disabilities are particularly vulnerable, however, because they often depend on a variety of people to help them in carrying out their everyday lives—"attendants, inter-preters, homemakers, drivers, doctors, nurses, teachers, social workers, psychiatrists, ther-apists, counsellors, and workers in hospitals and other institutions" (ibid., 2). Thus the "family" of a woman with a disability includes "not only parents, husbands, boyfriends and other relatives, but also friends, neighbours and caregivers" (ibid.).

Barriers to Obtaining Help

It can be exceedingly difficult for a disabled woman to leave an abusive relationship. In addition to reduced self-esteem, a woman with disabilities who reports violence may risk poverty or loss of housing, fear that she will not be believed, face further violence or institu-tionalization, and could lose her children (ibid.). Research suggests that up to 90 per cent of incidents of abuse against disabled people do not get reported (BC Institute against Family Violence, 2003). Social attitudes about disability, not the individual's impairment, are the largest contributor to the increased vulnerability to abuse experienced by women with dis-abilities (NCFV, 1993a).

Summary

There is a real lack of support for Canadian families living with disabilities. Disability affects many Canadians and their families: some 4.4 million people have disabilities and approxi-mately 11 million people without disabilities have a family member with disabilities. And the rate of disability is higher for women and Aboriginal people than for other Canadians. Moreover, we are an aging society, and rates of disability increase with age.

Disability and poverty are inextricably intertwined: disability leads to poverty and poverty leads to disability. The average household income for families with preschool and school-age children with disabilities is lower than the household incomes of their peers with-out disabilities. Family breakdown is not uncommon, and children with disabilities are over-represented in lone-parent families. Disabled children, especially those with mental or developmental disabilities, are at increased risk of violence. Cost is a major factor prevent-ing parents from getting the assistance they require. Working-age adults with disabilities are only half as likely as other Canadians to find viable employment, and they have lower average incomes than people without disabilities.

Disabled women are more likely than disabled men to perform most of the basic house-hold chores. Compared with fathers, mothers are most likely to be responsible for provid-ing, arranging, and advocating for care for their children with disabilities. Child care is the primary barrier to participation in the paid workforce for parents (especially mothers) of children with disabilities. Women with disabilities are more likely than women without disabilities to be single, divorced, separated, widowed, and lone parents of dependent children. Parenting, especially mothering, with a disability is surrounded by social barriers and stigma. Violence against disabled women often comes in the form of family violence.

The social model of disability identifies obstacles as being systemically rather than biologically based. From this perspective, the barriers that prevent a full life are the problem, not disabilities themselves. Disabled Canadians clearly need increased support in order to thrive as family members. For example, increased public funds are needed for social assistance, disability supports, health needs, home care, respite care, child care, accessible transportation, adequate housing, education and training, etc. One of the difficulties, as outlined in this chapter, is inconsistency across jurisdictions. This matter needs to be addressed by all levels of government immediately.

In addition, social perceptions regarding families and disabilities must be radically altered. Despite progress in many areas, modern Canadian society is still marked by a strong sense of what is (and is not) "normal." This is most evident when it comes to ideals of the perfect body. Ask yourself, What would you think if you saw a child with cerebral palsy in a classroom full of non-disabled children? Or two young people with intellectual disabilities holding hands and kissing? What about a mother breast-feeding a baby while using her wheelchair? These are images that are not yet common, but hopefully will be one day.

STUDY QUESTIONS

1. Do you consider yourself a disabled person? Do you have family members and/or friends with disabilities? Reflect on the ways in which disability impacts on your life.
2. How is disability defined in Canada? What are the implications of the social model of disability?
3. In what sense are many people "TABS" (temporarily able-bodied)? Have you ever thought about yourself in this way? What about your family or friends?
4. What ableist assumptions underpin the organization of paid and unpaid labour?
5. How does sexism (ageism/racism/heterosexism, etc.) intersect with ableism?
6. What barriers are faced by people with visible disabilities versus so-called invisible disabilities?
7. Why are disabled people so vulnerable to violence? Who is particularly at risk?

Further Readings

Enns, Ruth. 1999. *A Voice Unheard: The Latimer Case and People with Disabilities*. Halifax: Fernwood. Enns uses the disability perspective to discuss the much-debated murder of Tracy Latimer by her father. Included are accounts by other Canadians with disabilities and an examination of the legal case through court documents. The book also presents an overview of the history of disabled people and their efforts in advocacy.

Kuttai, Heather. 2010. *Maternity Rolls: Pregnancy, Childbirth and Disability*. Nova Scotia and Winnipeg: Fernwood Publishing. Kuttai employs theory and personal narrative to tell her story about being a woman with a spinal cord injury who becomes a mother. She describes her accident, meeting her current partner, being pregnant, giving birth, and parenting. Significantly, Kuttai maintains that the social stigma around mothering with a disability comes from the belief that disabled women are asexual.

Malacrida, Claudia. 2010. "Discipline and Dehumanization in a Total Institution: Institutional Survivors' Descriptions of Time-out Rooms," in *Rethinking Normalcy: A Disability Studies Reader*, Tanya Titchkosky and Rod Michalko, eds. Toronto: Canadian Scholars' Press Inc., pp. 181–95. In this chapter Malacrida draws on her interviews with 29 survivors of an institution for "moral defectives" in Alberta. The interviewees, 12 women and 9 men, describe the "Time-out Rooms" used for disciplinary purposes. Although the focus is on one Canadian institution up to the 1980s, the discussion of eugenics and sterilization has broader implications.

Oliver, Michael. 1996. "The Social Model in Context," in *Understanding Disability: From Theory to Practice*. Hampshire and New York: Palgrave, 1996, pp. 30–42. Oliver is one of the first people to write about disability models in general, and the social model in particular. In this piece he traces the development of disability theorizing and calls for the expansion of models. In the 1980s Oliver posited a binary opposition between what he termed the "individual" (which included medicalization and personal tragedy models) and the social models.

Wendell, Susan. 1996. *The Rejected Body: Feminist Philosophical Reflections on Disability*. New York: Routledge. Wendell criticizes past feminist theorizing about the body for favouring the able-bodied experience and, for the most part, ignoring the experience of disability. The book sets out to teach feminist scholars why disability is of importance to their work by pointing to disability studies as a significant but often overlooked feminist ally.

Websites

www.abilities.ca

The Canadian Abilities Foundation publishes *Abilities*, Canada's Lifestyle Magazine for People with Disabilities. Topics covered on the website include "Family Life," "Social Policy," and "Health and Activity." A digital issue of the magazine is available at no cost. There are also blogs, a Canadian access guide, and a directory of Canadian disability organizations.

www.ccdonline.ca

This bilingual website provides information on the issues at the forefront of the agenda of the Council of Canadians with Disabilities (CCD). CCD advocates at the federal level for the elimination of inequality and discrimination in the lives of men and women with disabilities. Members include national, regional, and local advocacy organizations controlled by disabled persons.

www.dawncanada.net

DisAbled Women's Network (DAWN) Canada is a national feminist organization controlled by and comprised of women who self-identify as women with disabilities. This website includes profiles of disabled women, special initiatives, related links, and an e-mail discussion group.

www.disabilitystudies.ca
This site is sponsored by Canadian Centre on Disability Studies, a consumer-directed, university-affiliated centre dedicated to research, education, and information dissemination on disability issues.

www.phac-aspc.gc.ca/chn-rcs/ld-vi-eng.php
The Living with Disabilities page is part of a larger Public Health Agency of Canada website. There is a guide to services for disabled people, a seniors' section, and resources pertaining to violence and abuse.

www.pwd-online.ca
Persons with Disabilities Online is an accessible, bilingual Government of Canada website. The purpose of the website is to provide integrated access to information, programs, and services for persons with disabilities, their families, their caregivers, service providers, and all Canadians.

Note

1. Thanks to Gary Annable, Carly Johnston, and Levi Labelle for their assistance.

PROBLEMS, POLICIES, AND PREDICTIONS

The final section of this book considers a diverse selection of topics—family violence, family policies in Canada, and the future of the Canadian family.

In Chapter 14, Aysan Sev'er discusses the various definitions of violence and abuse in families and reviews a number of theories that have been used to explain family violence and abuse, including individual pathology models, social learning theories, stress and crisis theories, and feminist explanations of violence. Sev'er examines the available data on violence against women and spousal homicide, and discusses problems inherent in the collection of such data. The chapter then examines the consequences of abuse for women and children, and Sev'er suggests that perhaps the most enduring consequences of abuse are psychological. She argues that the powerlessness and dependency cycles in families that make children, women, and aged persons vulnerable to maltreatment can be broken. Awareness must be translated into programs for educating and promoting non-violent solutions in social relationships, as well as into social policies that can break the cycle of abuse.

Social policies concerning families have a central importance in Canadian life. They determine how families are defined and formed, which family members are entitled to governmental support, and the amount and type of support that families receive. In Chapter 15, Catherine Krull examines family policy in Canada with a special focus on those measures that relate to families with children under the age of 18 years. Examples of such policies include arrangements for children in state care, paid maternity and parental leaves, and child and family benefits. She points out that Canada lacks a comprehensive national family policy, unlike some other countries around the world. Rather, family policies in Canada consist of a piecemeal set of programs and policies that either directly or indirectly have an impact on families, often leaving gaps and "cracks" through which some families fall. She demonstrates this through a discussion of the patchwork of child and family benefits aimed at reducing poverty that continue to result in large disparities in poverty rates across family types. Krull notes that Quebec has taken the lead in Canada in terms of implementing policies geared towards supporting families and reducing poverty. She concludes that the rest of Canada has an opportunity to use and build on Quebec's example in the future.

The final chapter in this edition of *Canadian Families Today* offers a view to the future. In the closing chapter, Margrit Eichler discusses issues involved in making predictions about the future of family life, examines past predictions by family sociologists and other experts about the future of the family and how successful they were, and considers the basis on which such predictions are made. Eichler explores which bases for prediction seem to yield more solid results. She concludes that overall there have been a number of spectacular misprognoses—that the family is a dying institution and that gender roles within the family are unchanging and unchangeable—as well as some surprisingly accurate predictions on such matters as the nature of sexual relations inside and outside of marriage, cohabitation, fertility, and new reproductive technologies. She draws the conclusion that identifying societal changes and reflecting on their importance for the family are the most useful predictive analyses for family studies but they are also the most difficult. Eichler concludes her chapter by making some predictions of her own.

14

All in the Family: Violence Against Women, Children, and the Aged

AYSAN SEV'ER

LEARNING OBJECTIVES

- To debunk some common "myths" about families
- To understand and be able to define different types of abuse
- To distinguish the strengths and weaknesses of existing theories of abuse
- To understand the difficulties of measurement of abuse
- To develop an awareness about the incidence and consequences of wife/partner, child, and elder abuse
- To think about possible interventions at the social and structural levels of society

Introduction

Families come in many configurations. Yet, myths make families appear to be more homogenous than they really are. For example, people think about families as heterosexual couples with children, although some families are same-sex (with or without children), and some other families are child-free. Families are assumed to reside all together, whereas many families are headed by mothers, some families live apart, and yet others commute. The most entrenched myth about families is that they are loving and caring groups of related people. Folk wisdom, religions, conservative politicians, movies, the media, the music industry, and children's stories intentionally or unintentionally contribute to this myth. The vision is so potent that we even project "traditional family" characteristics onto imaginary worlds where Bambi, the Lion King, Shrek, etc., live within familial love. Many families are indeed close and loving. Nevertheless, it is also true that positive myths often hide the severe power differences among family members due to gender and age (Katz, 2006). Since early 1980s, the "dark side of the family" has been recognized (Straus et al., 1986; Gelles, 1987, 1994) where power differences sometimes translate into mental, physical, and/or sexual abuse. In extreme cases, many women and children and some men lose their lives at the hand of a family member (Pottie-Bunge, 2002; Statistics Canada, 2011e).

In this chapter, I will review the basic definitions of intimate forms of abuse. Then, I will introduce theories that explain violence. I will then focus on the most frequent types of violence: the abuse of female partners, child abuse, and elder abuse. Violence within families extends to dating relationships, same-sex couples, and caregiving institutions (Ristock, 2002). Rarely, male partners are also victimized by their partners. However, this chapter will focus on the most frequently and most seriously targeted members of families—women, children, and the elderly. Overall, the discussion will concentrate on Canadian patterns, and will conclude with some suggestions to stop the violence.

Defining Violence

United Nations (UN) Definition

The Declaration on the Elimination of Violence Against Women (UN, 1993) defines violence as "any act of gender-based violence that results in, or is likely to result in, physical, sexual, or psychological harm or suffering to women, including threats of such acts, coercion, or arbitrary deprivation of liberty, whether occurring in public or in private life." Moreover, "physical, sexual, and psychological violence in the family, including battering, sexual abuse of female children in the household, [and] marital rape," are considered a violation of human rights (UN, 1993, Articles 1 and 2).

Legal Definitions

In the Canadian Criminal Code (CCC), violence within the family is subsumed under sections 265–268 (assault, assault with a weapon, aggravated assault, and sexual assault) or under homicide (section 229). The Criminal Code requires both an "intent" and an "act" for an incident to be considered a crime. The single exception to the CCC rule is treason, where intent is sufficient even without the "act" component. Criminal neglect (section 219) is another area which blurs the requirement of an act.

General Definitions

Abuse, **violence**, **spousal violence**, and **neglect** are generally defined in the following ways.

- *Abuse.* Definitions of abuse include bad practices or customs and using harsh and insulting language. By referring to customs, the definition hints at the relationship between the abuser and the abused. By reference to insults, there is recognition that the induced hurt can be psychological.
- *Violence.* Definitions of violence include rough force in action, rough treatment, harm or injury, and unlawful use of force. Like the CCC definition of assault, the definition of violence emphasizes both the act itself and the outcome (harm or injury). Yet, it does not presuppose intention.

- *Spousal violence.* Statistics Canada defines spousal violence as "cases of murder, attempted murder, sexual and physical assault, threats, criminal harassment, and other violent offences in which the accused person is a spouse, ex-spouse, or common-law partner of the victim" (Statistics Canada, 2005d).
- *Neglect.* Neglect includes commissions (acts that put others at risk/injury) or omissions (failing to prevent risk/injury). Examples of neglect are abandonment, failure to provide food, medical care, and the emotional well-being of children. Neglect is the most common form of abuse, especially when the relationship is a one-sided dependency (child on parent, or elder parent upon adult child), when it is repeated, and when the consequences are (or could have been) severe (Rose and Meezan, 1995). Although difficult to prove and prosecute, CCC recognizes criminal neglect.

Feminist research questions the generic terms of abuse. For example, rather than "domestic abuse" or "family violence," which fails to identify the most likely perpetrators or targets, they insist on such terms as "woman abuse," "wife abuse," "violence against female partners," and "child abuse" or "elder abuse." They also insist that violence within families (1) is not random; (2) is not one-time, but cyclical; (3) is often severe; and (4) in general, perpetrators of violence are men and victims are women, children, and the aged (DeKeseredy, 2011; Sev'er, 2002a).

In this chapter, I will use "abuse" and "violence" interchangeably. Unless otherwise stated (e.g., child or elder abuse), "violence" means intimate partner abuse against women. As in the Statistics Canada (2005d) definition, intimate partners may include married or common-law spouses or ex-spouses. Same-sex partners may also perpetrate violence, but our knowledge on that type of violence is still sketchy (Renzetti, 1998; Ristock, 2002). Violence also mars dating relationships, but I will leave that topic outside of the current focus (DeKeseredy and Schwartz, 1997).

Types of Violence

Physical violence approximates the CCC definition of assault, where one person (usually a man) intentionally and repeatedly hurts another (usually a woman, a child, or an elder). At the extreme, murder (intimate **femicide**, infanticide, filicide) is the outcome (Schwartz and DeKeseredy, 2007; Sev'er, 2002a; Statistics Canada, 2011e).

Intimate sexual violence occurs when someone forces another (most likely a woman) to engage in sexual activity or intercourse against her/his consent or will (Mahoney and Williams, 1998). It can also take the form of inflicting pain or exposing the partner to unwanted pregnancy or sexually transmitted diseases. Sexual violence against children ranges from sexual touching, molestation, and incestuous rape to participation in the making of child pornography (Bergen, 1998b; Kendall-Tackett and Marshall, 1998; Sev'er, 2002a). A child is less likely to understand "consent" in reference to sexual abuse and may indeed come to erroneously associate the inappropriate sexual attention with "love." Therefore, the responsibility of molestation must always be placed on the adult, not the child (Transken, 2011). Elder women and disabled members of the family are also prime targets for sexual assault (Sev'er, 2009).

Psychological or emotional abuse is very common, but also very controversial. Some scholars argue that hurtful name-calling, put-downs, and constantly dismissing a woman/child/elder can be just as devastating as hits or punches (Sev'er, 1996, 2002a; DeKeseredy, 2011; DeKeseredy and MacLeod, 1997). Others prefer concepts such as **"controlling behaviours"** (Dobash and Dobash, 1998; Stark, 2007). Some fear that expanding the boundaries of violence to include psychological abuse will dilute the concept (Fox, 1993). Moreover, men may attempt to legitimize their physical violence by claiming they were verbally "victimized."

The literature also includes economic abuse and spiritual abuse as types of abuse. The first refers to one partner's (most likely a woman) lack of access to resources and opportunity to partake in the family's financial decisions. Elders, especially those who may have forms of dementia, are also prime targets of economic abuse. Spiritual abuse occurs when one partner (or parent) forces another to practise a different belief system (Canada's Aging Population, 2002; APA-Online, 2008).

Theories about Interpersonal Violence

Theories are logically interrelated statements that order, describe, explain, and predict the causes and consequences of personal or social problems. Micro theories seek the causes of events within the person, interactionist theories focus on social interaction, and macro theories concentrate on the structural domains and inequalities. To understand the complex phenomenon of intimate violence, we have to consult a range of theoretical orientations.

Individual Pathology Models

Theories of psychopathology are capable of explaining violence perpetrated by a few, troubled individuals (e.g., notorious killers like Ted Bundy, "Son of Sam," and Jeffrey Dahmer), but they are weak in explaining violence within families. Pathology models also propose single-trait explanations such as alcohol/drug dependencies. Indeed, statistics show a close link between addictions and violence against women (Dugan and Hock, 2000: 21; Jacobson and Gottman, 2001). Some findings suggest that men who were heavy drinkers were six times more likely to assault their female partners than a comparative group of non-drinking men (see Rodgers, 1994; Johnson, 1996). Yet, despite the high correlation, alcohol consumption cannot be considered the cause of intimate abuse for the following reasons:

- Not all men who drink, abuse. Some men who are non-drinkers also abuse.
- Abusive men do not abuse their partners or children each time they drink.
- Abusive men do batter their partners or children when they are not drinking.
- Some alcoholics who stop drinking continue to abuse (Gelles, 1993; Gelles and Straus, 1988).

Another intrapersonal theory of violence classifies the victimizers as "cobras" or "pit bulls" (Jacobson and Gottman, 2001). Cobras are defined as anti-social, cruel, egotistical men who enjoy hurting a variety of people, including their partners. They lack empathy and thus hurt people without remorse. Cobras generally have charismatic personalities but are also capable of murder. Pit bulls, on the other hand, confine their violence to their family/ spouse. They are jealous, possessive, and they fear abandonment. Once pit bulls sink their teeth into their partners, it is extremely difficult to get them to let go (ibid.). Yet, typologies such as these help little in understanding the wide variation in abusers and the circumstances in which they inflict abuse.

Freud (1974 [1920]) also proposed a typology by focusing on the victims of violence. Freud perceived women as masochistic, emotionally immature, and deviant. Women were seen as "deficient men," both biologically (lacking a penis) and morally (never successfully completing their identification process). Ironically, Freud also saw strong women as maladjusted, and as taunting and "castrating" the men in their lives. Thus, whether women were strong or weak, Freud saw them as the engineers of their own demise, and there is a disturbing resurrection of some of these damaging stereotypes (Steed, 1994; Kelly and Radford, 1998; Russell and Bolen, 2000). When the music-diva Rihanna's badly beaten and bruised face appeared in the mass media (Rush and Dillon, 2009), I was teaching a gender course. The class consisted of about 50 women and five men. Since our topic happened to be violence against women, I asked for my students' views on the highly publicized violence. In different ways, almost all expressed displeasure with Rihanna for turning a "personal matter" into a media circus. Some (female) students claimed that Rihanna was jealous of Chris Brown's popularity and fame, and was trying to "sabotage" his career. Although I have always encouraged my students to engage in candid discussions, I must admit that I was totally taken aback by the victim-blaming that went on, especially within the context of a feminist course.

In reality, intrapersonal theories have little explanatory power in understanding a widespread phenomenon like men's violence against women, children, and elders. Only about 10 per cent of intimate violence can be attributable to some kind of clinical pathology (Gelles and Straus, 1988). No violence could or should be explained by attributing pathology to the victims. This leaves most intra-family abuse to be explained through factors other than individual pathology (Sev'er, 2002a). Moreover, personalizing violence fails to challenge the social-structural context of violence, such as poverty, inequality, and patriarchy (DeKeseredy and MacLeod, 1997; DeKeseredy, Alvi, and Schwartz, 2006; Sev'er, 2002b).

Social Learning Theories

Social learning theories see aggression as a learned behaviour through interaction with significant others and through the rewards and punishments for behaviour (Bandura, 1973). Learning may be gender-specific. For example, girls who experience violence may be more likely to tolerate partner violence in their adult lives whereas male witnesses/victims of violence may become abusers themselves (Levinson, 1989; Scully, 1990).

Intergenerational transmission is extremely important when one considers the fact that children witness violence against their mothers in about 40 per cent of violent marriages (Wolfe, Zak and Wilson, 1986; Ney, 1992; Rodgers, 1994; Lehmann, 1997; Fantuzzo and Mohr, 1999). Moreover, many children (especially girls) are victims of sexual violence (Kendall-Tackett and Marshall, 1998; Statistics Canada, 2008m; Transken, 2011). To understand child abuse, Finkelhor (1986, 1988) extended the learning theory to what he calls the **dysfunctional learning model (DLM)**. The components of DLM are traumatic sexualization and feelings of betrayal, powerlessness, and stigmatization. All of these dimensions may have serious consequences for child victims.

A branch of learning theories focuses on male peer support (Godenzi et al., 2000) and highlights the impact of violent peers, and subcultures of violence. In highly masculinized circles, male peers may reward misogynist acts and punish those who deviate from macho expectations (DeKeseredy, 2011; Godenzi et al., 2000). There is substantial support for male peer support models, especially among college students (DeKeseredy and Kelly, 1993; Schwartz and DeKeseredy, 1997; Schwartz et al., 2001).

Yet, Kaufman and Zigler (1993) show that transmission of violence is not absolute, but mediated by biological, socio-economic, and cultural factors. For example, although some abusive men may have been witness to or victims of violence in their childhood, a larger proportion of abused children do *not* become abusers. In contrast, some boys who were never abused do become abusive men. Although some form of learning takes place in almost all situations, what exactly is learned—aversion to or acceptance of what is being modelled by the significant other—will vary. Moreover, learning theories in general are inadequate in explaining child sexual abuse, because even in macho subcultures, there are strong taboos against child molestation. Therefore, some forms of intimate violence require an explanation other than early socialization.

Stress and Crisis Theories

A version of the frustration/aggression theory proposes that family violence is the outcome of stress. Yet, families differ in how they deal with stressful events. In what is called the ABCX **model**, Hill (1958) proposed that events (a), mediated by family's resources (b) and the meanings associated with the event (c), will lead to a particular outcome (x). For example, a pregnancy (a) may be seen as a blessing in one family (positive b/c), but a crisis in another (negative b/c). A more current version of the model (double ABCX) purports that the history of the family's ability to deal with the same or a similar event/crisis will also affect the outcome, sometimes exacerbating, other times cushioning, the impact (McCubbin and Patterson, 1983).

Dependency theory is also a stress model. It asserts that violence against an aging parent results from stress, especially when the elder's debility escalates. Scarcity of resources and the increasing needs of the elderly also tax the caregivers. Interestingly, Pillemer (1993) has transposed the causal direction suggested by the dependency theory. He contends that the abusive adult children are the ones who are dependent on their aging parents: they abuse to usurp parental resources. Either way, stress from the incongruence in the relationship (dependent parent or dependent adult child) is seen as the cause of abuse.

Stress theories of violence are intuitive and alluring. There is no doubt that skills, resources, past experiences, and emotional or economic dependencies of families affect coping skills. However, there are major problems with stress theories. First, by failing to identify violence as a moral wrong regardless of the conditions that engender it, they appear to resign to the unavoidability of violence. Second, stress theories de-genderize (and sometimes, de-age) interpersonal abuse. For example, mothers under stress may physically abuse their children, but it is extremely rare that they sexually abuse them. Father figures may do both, with or without stress (Crull, 2008; Transken, 2011). Young children do not abuse their parents, but some older children do. Older women are still most likely to be abused by their male partners, whereas both older men and older women are equally likely to be abused by their sons (Statistics Canada, 2012; Sev'er, 2009). Third, stress theories are blind to cultural variations. In patriarchal cultures where age brings status, abuse of elders is rare. In cultures where the aged are marginalized, they easily become scapegoats for other people's frustrations (Sev'er, 2009).

Feminist Explanations of Violence

Feminist explanations of men's violence towards intimate partners are numerous (Dobash and Dobash, 1979; Yllö and Bograd, 1988). Marxist feminism, socialist feminism, and radical feminism form some of the better-known variations. Although details of these theories fall outside of the focus of this chapter, it is important to stress that feminist theories converge on seeking the roots of violence in social structures without disregarding the role of interpersonal or intrapersonal processes.

Feminists criticize the gendered distribution of power and resources, the gendered division of labour, and the role of a patriarchal system that protects these inequalities. In feminist explanations, the triangulation of gender, power, and control determines relations in work, politics, law, health, and education as well as male dominance within coupled relationships (Stark, 2007). Radical feminists claim that even men who do not directly harass, abuse, or otherwise subjugate women benefit from the patriarchal status quo (Russell, 1989; O'Brien, 1981; MacKinnon, 1982; Rubin, 1983; Bart and Moran, 1993). Pence and Paymar's (1993) conceptual model for the interrelated dimensions in the cycle of violence suggests that power-seeking men intimidate, emotionally abuse, and degrade their partners. They also isolate them, minimize their complaints, or blame them as the instigators of their own suffering or use coercion and threats to silence their partners (ibid.).

Others (Johnson, 2008; Laroche, 2005), assert that intimate violence is not a unitary phenomenon. Instead, violence is seen in three, analytically separable categories: **intimate terrorism**, violent resistance, and situational couple violence. The authors suggest that the first is rare in ongoing relationships, but much more common in ex-partner relationships (especially by separated men). They also suggest that surveys are not capable of capturing this type of violence, giving credibility to feminist critiques of surveys (ibid.).

Feminist theories are quite robust in explaining the abuse of female partners, female children, and older women. Their combined assertions on control of resources and control over women's mobility and sexuality explain why men abuse and how they often get away with it. Feminists place violence on a continuum, where personal experiences interrelate with social, educational, political, legal, criminal justice, and economic dimensions. Extended versions also examine social constructions of masculinity, including male sexual socialization (Bowker, 1998; Seymour, 1998). However, feminist assertions are less robust in dealing with men's violence towards male intimates (sons, aged fathers, etc.). With a few exceptions (Sev'er, 2002a; Swan and Snow, 2006), they are also shy in addressing women's own violence. Moreover, only recently have feminist theories started to address race, ethnicity, and culture (Guruge et al., 2010). Table 14.1 summarizes the major assertions of violence theories and their general applicability.

Table 14.1 **Explanatory Power of Theories of Violence**

Type of theory	General assertions	Explanatory power		
		Wife abuse	Child abuse	Elder abuse
Intrapersonal models	Cause: Individual pathology or addictions	Low	Low	Low
– Individual pathology	Creates typologies to predict violence			
– Addictions	See alcohol as the cause			
– Freud's psychoanalytic	Blames women as weak or as domineering			
Social learning	Cause: Modelling, imitation, or exposure	High	High	Low
– General social learning	Evaluates the rewards or punishments			
– Intergenerational transmission	Emphasizes the behaviour of significant others, and emphasizes gendered learning			
– Dysfunctional learning	Stresses traumatic sexualization and feelings of betrayal			
– Male peer support	Emphasizes macho male-peer cultures			
Stress and crisis models	Cause: Inability to deal with stress and inadequate coping	Low	Medium	High
– ABCX model of stress	Emphasizes events, resources, and perceptions			
– Double ABCX model	Emphasizes earlier experience/coping			
Feminist theories	Cause: Power difference between family members	High	High	Medium
– Marxist feminism	Emphasizes structural inequalities and work			
– Social feminism	Emphasizes unequal division of labour and different access to opportunities			
– Radical feminism	Emphasizes patriarchal legitimization and reproductive subjugation of women			
– Power and control model	Emphasizes interrelated aspects of the violence wheel			

Violence against Intimate Partners

Violence against women crosses over boundaries of ethnicity, race, education, income, sexual orientation, marital status, and physical ability (Crawford and Gartner, 1992; Koss and Cook, 1993; DeKeseredy and MacLeod, 1997; DeKeseredy, 2011; Renzetti, 1998). Nevertheless, poor, uneducated, immigrant, or refugee women may be more isolated and thus more vulnerable to social conditions that fuel violence (Richie and Kanuha, 2000) or may come from cultures where male violence is tolerated (Guruge et al., 2010; Sokoloff and Dupont, 2005).

For more on immigration policies and abuse, see Chapter 3, p. 54.

As the first Canada-wide study involving 12,300 women, the Violence Against Women Survey (VAWS, 1993) reported that 29 per cent of women had experienced intimate violence at some point in their lives. The most recent victimization survey was conducted in 2009. Six percent of Canadians with a current or former spouse reported physical or sexual victimization during the past five years (Statistics Canada, 2012). Reported rates of violence in younger age groups (25–34) was three times higher than those reported by 45 and older respondents (ibid.). Reported violence for the past five years among common-law spouses (17 per cent) was much higher than in intact unions (4 per cent). These rates of reported violence are stable since 2004, and lower than those reported in 1999. What is discerning is that there was a sharp decline in reporting to the police. Only 22 percent of the spousal violence victims stated that the incidents came to the attention of police, whereas the comparable percentage of reporting was 28 per cent in 2004 (Statistics Canada, 2012).

There are differences in self-reporting of spousal violence amongst the provinces. For example, in Newfoundland and Labrador and Prince Edward Island, only women have reported violence, whereas in all other provinces, both men and women have done so (Statistics Canada, 2012). Although the proportion of reported violence was similar for women and men in eight of the 10 provinces, the consequences of violence were much more severe for women than men (ibid.). For example, 34 per cent of the assaulted women stated that they were sexually assaulted, beaten, choked, or threatened with a gun or a knife (versus 10 per cent of men). Also, women were twice as likely to be injured during the attacks.

Violence between same-sex partners is included in the general survey (Statistics Canada, 2012). The rate of violence reported by lesbian and gay partners is twice as high as that reported by heterosexual partners. This discrepancy may be due to estimation errors resulting from the small numbers of same-sex versus the much larger numbers of heterosexual couples. Another reason could be that a larger proportion of responding gays/lesbians stated they did not have a current partner. As discussed before, violence amongst estranged couples is generally higher.

Homicide Data

Although homicides in Canada are on an overall decline, between the year 2000 and 2009, there were 738 spousal homicides in Canada (Statistics Canada, 2012). The rate of spousal homicide against women is three times higher than the rate for men (ibid.). For both women and men, spousal homicide rates peak among 15- to 24-year-olds. Also, termination of relationships does not guarantee the termination of violence. Instead, relationships that were not violent can turn violent, or relationships that were already violent may become more violent at the onset of separation (DeKeseredy and Schwartz, 2008; Johnson, 1995; Kurz, 1996; Sev'er, 1997, 1998; Kaufman-Kantor and Jasinski, 1998). Numerous findings attest to the increased risk engendered by separation (Crawford and Gartner, 1992; Wilson and Daly, 1993; Rodgers, 1994; Johnson, 1995; Kurz, 1995, 1996; Fleury et al., 2000; Gartner et al., 2001; Jacobson and Gottman, 2001; Sev'er, 2002a). In the most recent Canadian survey (Statistics Canada, 2012, Chart 4.2), it is observed that the rate of spousal homicides against females has consistently been about three to four times higher than that for males (also see Glass, 1995; Johnson, 2008; Johnson and Dawson, 2011).

An earlier national survey also tabulated homicide/suicide rates amongst spouses (Statistics Canada, 2005d). What was observed was that 76 per cent of all homicide-suicides involved family members. Over half of these were committed by male spouses/ex-spouses,

---

CASE IN POINT
Abuse of Women by Male Partners and Intimate Femicide

Dugald Jamieson (49) was sentenced to 12 years in prison for what the judge called a "callous" killing of his common-law wife Carol-Ann Brunet (54). Although he was on probation for an earlier assault on her, Dugald showed up at Carol-Ann's house, viciously stabbed her in the stomach, asked her to mop the blood off the floor, forced her to have sex with him, then left the house to party with his friends. Although Carol-Ann's situation was getting more dire, Dugald refused to call the police or an ambulance, fearing that he would be in trouble for violating his probation. Carol-Ann died from peritonitis within 24 hours after the stabbing (*Toronto Star*, 24 Feb. 2012: A8).

Guang Hua Liu (41) who was a mother of three, was last seen alive on 10 August 2012. Shortly after her disappearance, her severed head, right foot, and hands were found in a park in Mississauga. The grisly discoveries continued with the finding of two calves, an arm, and a thigh scattered in Highland Creek in Scarborough. In early September, Liu's torso was discovered in a suitcase, floating in Lake Ontario. Police report that parts of Liu's body are still missing. Chun Qi Jiang (40), who is the victim's estranged partner, has been charged with second-degree murder (*Toronto Star*, 7 Sept. 2012: A2).

---

and 97 per cent of the victims were women. Jealousy, arguing, and the dissolution of relationships were the prominent reasons for homicide-suicides (ibid.).

Problems with Numbers

Official Reports

In police reports, homicides almost always find an accurate statistical representation. However, the same cannot be said for official reports about violence statistics. Part of the problem is reporting. Statistics Canada (2012) estimates the total number of victims of spousal violence between 2004 and 2010 to be 1.2 million. However, only 27 per cent of these incidents were reported to the police, and the reporting is down to 22 per cent in more recent years (ibid.). Women are more likely to report spousal violence than men. Yet, even when women report violence, they do so after numerous incidents of victimization (ibid.). From these findings, we can deduce that three-quarters of victims *do not* report the violence they suffer to police. One reason for underreporting is that family relationships are designated to the private sphere. A selective blindness or a desire to hide what goes on behind closed doors leads to the under-reporting of serious crimes like incest, child abuse, elder abuse, and woman abuse. The displeasure expressed by my gender course students with Rihanna's charges against her abuser was mostly governed by the "private sphere" norms they shared. The truth is that shrouding violence with silence never helps to break the cycle of violence.

Fear of the perpetrator, immature age, feelings of shame, lack of social support, family pressure, ignorance about the law, and distrust towards police are also responsible for low rates of reporting. Most women do not call the police; those who call do so only if the attack was severe, if their own or their children's lives were in danger, or only after repeated beatings (Finkelhor, 1988; Kurtz, 1995; Sev'er, 2002a). Language restrictions may make immigrant and minority women even more reluctant to report their experiences (Guruge et al., 2010; Rodgers, 1994; Johnson and Sacco, 1995; Huisman, 1996).

Data from Women's Shelters

In 2010, there were 533 Canadian shelters for women in operation, providing 11,461 bed spaces (Statistics Canada, 2011g). About 300 of the available shelters were transition homes, the remaining being equally divided amongst second-stage housing, women's emergency shelters, and general emergency shelters (ibid.). Shelters routinely compile information on the characteristics of women and children who seek refuge; however, although the reliability of data from shelters is very high, shelter-based findings over-represent some and under-represent other characteristics. For example, shelter clientele in contrast to Canadian women in general are:

For more on abuse in Aboriginal families, see Chapter 12, p. 241.

- preponderantly younger women, with young children;
- often literate, but not highly educated;
- unemployed or employed in low-paying jobs with lower socio-economic status; and
- mostly urban dwellers.

Shelter data also over-represent certain groups (blacks and Aboriginals) but under-represent others (women from the Middle East and Asia) (Huisman, 1996). In sum, although shelters provide extensive information about violence against women and children, these data under-represent older, more affluent, and some immigrant women.

The Standardized Conflict Tactics Scale (CTS)

Measuring abuse is a problem because the person whose experience matters most is often contested (Currie, 1998). So far, the **Conflict Tactics Scale (CTS)** from the New Hampshire school remains the most frequently used tool of measurement (Gelles and Straus, 1988). In its original form, violence was defined in gender-neutral terms as an act carried out with the intention of causing pain or injury to another person (ibid.). The scale items were concerned with acts such as throwing something; pushing, grabbing, or shoving; slapping; kicking, biting, or hitting; trying to hit with something; beating up; threatening with a knife or a gun; and using a knife or a gun. The violent acts were listed under presumed ascendance of severity. Respondents (both sexes) were asked whether any of these events happened to them within an identified span of time (last year, last five years, lifetime). It is not surprising that studies using the original CTS helped to create the myth of symmetry of intimate partner violence. Although recent versions of the CTS (Straus et al., 1996) added items (like sexual attacks) to expand the validity of the instrument, the presumption of ascendancy of severity remains problematic. Moreover, just the belief that violence is "quantifiable" still raises suspicion. In addition, even the revised CTS is insensitive to intent, context (who hit who first, whether the act was offensive or defensive), frequency, sexual forcefulness, or the severity of consequences (a slap may leave a bruise or break a jaw). Thus, studies using the CTS find symmetry between men's and women's violence, but feminists insist that men and women are unequal combatants (Kelly, 1997; Pagelow, 1985; Sev'er, 2002a). Johnson (2008) also argues that quantitative surveys fail to measure "intimate terrorism" (also see Johnson, Leone and Xu, 2008).

Consequences of Abuse of Women

Consequences of violence can be both physical and psychological. Physical consequences can range from cuts, bruises, lacerations, broken bones, induced miscarriages, and muti-lations to death. Repeated violence also leaves emotional scars. Women victims of abuse report chronic pain, sleeping problems, eating disorders, chronic depression, and an increased propensity for attempted suicides (DeKeseredy, 2011; Stark and Flitcraft, 1996). Women victims of violence also are more likely to abuse both legal and illegal drugs (Sev'er, 2002a). The parenting skills of abused women may also be seriously compromised (Orava et al., 1996; Levendosky and Graham-Bermann, 2001). If loss of employment, inability to work, frequent absences, use of medication, use of healthcare services and police and criminal justice systems are factored in, the societal cost of violence against women could be over 4 billion dollars in Canada (Canadianwomen, n.d.; also see Barnett, Miller-Perrin, and Perin, 2005). Even these massive estimates do not include the bruising social costs of witnessing violence by young children.

Child Abuse

Like intimate partner abuse, child abuse can be physical, sexual, psychological, or in the form of neglect. Gender and age hierarchies and privacy norms that shield families from social scrutiny can increase the vulnerability of children. Neglect is very common, and numerous studies suggest that the effects of neglect may be cumulative (Kaufman-Kantor and Little, 2003; English et al., 2005). In 2002, an emaciated five-year-old Jeffrey Baldwin died, covered with sores and weighing only as much as an average 10-month-old baby would weigh. In 2006, his maternal grandparents were convicted of second-degree murder for Jeffrey's starvation death. The little boy had been placed under his grandparents' care following allegations of physical abuse by his natural parents. Unfortunately, rather than finding comfort, he spent his tragic life "in a cold, urine-soaked, feces-coated dungeon," with occasional scraps of food, and water he drank from the toilet (Coyle, 2006). He was so emaciated that he was never able to stand upright or walk. The sentencing judge called Jeffrey's demise the worst case of neglect in the history of Ontario (ibid.). In this case, the parents, grandparents, neighbours, friends, and even the child-protection agencies had failed this boy. The question is how many other children who are still alive also suffer from severe forms of neglect?

Physical, sexual, and/or psychological forms of abuse disproportionately victim-ize female children (Public Health Agency, 2003; Statistics Canada, 2012). Most North American scholars interpret child abuse as a gross violation of Article 19 of the UN

Convention on the Rights of the Child, which Canada ratified in December 1991. Canada also ratified the optional protocol of the same convention in July 2000 (UN Ratifications, n.d.). Article 19 states that all children have a right to protection from all forms of violence (UNICEF, 2000). Ironically, section 43 of the CCC still allows teachers, parents, or parent substitutes to use force in disciplining a child under their care, and most Canadians resist repealing this controversial section.

In Canada, an early national survey brought the issue of child abuse to the forefront when 53 per cent of girls and more than 30 per cent of boys under the age of 21 reported experiencing at least one incident of sexual molestation (Government of Canada, 1984; Duffy and Momirov, 1997). In 2009, police reports include 55,000 child victims of physical or sexual assaults. Of these, close to 15,000 were victimized by a family member (Statistics Canada, 2012). Parents were responsible for 59 per cent of all family-related sexual offences and physical assaults against child victims (ibid.). Female children's likelihood of being victims of sexual assault was four times greater than their male counterparts (ibid.). Moreover, girls' sexual victimization started in early ages and lasted until later ages, peaking at age 14, whereas boy's victimization was highest between the ages of 5–8 (ibid.). Research has also shown that pregnancy is a very vulnerable time for women (Kurz, 1995, 1996; Sev'er, 2002a). This means that via abuse of the mother, some forms of violence start even before the child is born.

Between 2000 and 2009, there were 326 child murders in Canada committed by a family member (Statistics Canada, 2012). Parents committed 84 per cent of family-related homicides (ibid.). Infants were at the highest risk, followed by one-to-three-year-olds (ibid.). Fathers were more likely to kill their children than mothers were (Statistics Canada, 2008m). In six out of every 10 child murders, the accused is between 15–24 years of age (ibid.). Moreover, between 1961 and 2003, 517 Canadian children became victims of a

---

Box 14.1
Child Abuse and Murder

An estranged Alberta couple, Meara McIntosh (27) and Richard Saunders, were caught up in a bitter custody battle. During a court-ordered parental visit, Richard killed his little boy Colton (3) and himself. Rather than returning Colton to his estranged wife, Richard locked the little boy in his car and let the exhaust fumes snuff out both their lives. Previously, Meara had gotten a restraining order against her estranged husband, claiming that he was likely to shoot her to death. However, even Meara had not thought about the mortal danger Richard posed to her little boy (Richards and Zickefoose, 2008).

On 8 September 2012, Noah (6) was killed by his father Wojciech Kosalka, in a father–son homicide–suicide. The neighbours unanimously voiced what they perceived to be an exceptionally close relationship the father–son pair had over the three years the family lived in a plush neighbourhood in Milton, ON (*Toronto Star*, 10 Sept 2012: A1). Although the reasons behind the tragic murder–suicide were not reported, and may never be known for sure, research suggests that men kill their children to get back at their wives, especially if their wives are planning to leave or have left them.

homicide and parental suicide. Boys under one and girls between one and five were at the greatest risk of being homicide–suicide victims (Statistics Canada, 2005d). Unfortunately, no comparable data were gathered for the 2012 Statistics Canada report.

A long list of researchers argue that witnessing violence against their mothers has negative consequences for children (Jaffee et al., 1990; Bagley and King, 1991; Reppucci and Haugaard, 1993; Wolak and Finkelhor, 1998; Fantuzzo and Mohr, 1999; Zima et al., 1999; Russell and Bolen, 2000; Jacobson and Gottman, 2001; Sev'er, 2002a). In light of what can be gleaned from theories of intergenerational transmission of violence, the implications of these findings are sobering (Health Canada, 1996; Graham-Berman and Levendosky, 1998; Turton, 2008).

Child abuse statistics are riddled by measurement and reporting problems. Neglect is difficult to detect unless it reaches extreme proportions such as the one resulted in Jeffrey Baldwin's death. Younger children may not have the language to report abuse and older children may be too frightened to do so. Thus, child abuse remains a grossly under-reported crime, and problems with official reports include:

- Strong taboos exist against talking about children and sexuality, even when children are sexually victimized.
- Young children may be threatened or dissuaded from disclosing the abuse, or they may be blamed or disbelieved.
- Strong positive biases about parent–child relations and social norms regarding family privacy may deter observers (neighbours, teachers) from reporting the abuse.
- Young children's injuries from out-of-the-ordinary sources may be difficult to identify and hard to prove.
- Mothers of abused children may also be victims of spousal violence. This will reduce their ability to intervene on their children's behalf. Sometimes, abused women themselves use violence against their children.

Effects of abuse will vary according to age, severity, duration of abuse, and the relationship of the abuser to his/her victim (Crull, 2008; Finkelhor, 1988; Transken, 2011). Very young children are the most vulnerable. Physical abuse may lead to cuts, bruises, infected sores, malnutrition, broken bones, and death. Since many more girls than boys are sexually victimized, abuse may produce genital tears, infections, sexually transmitted diseases, and/or unwanted pregnancies. Perhaps the most enduring consequences of abuse are psychological—the angst of eating disorders, self-hatred, self-blame, feelings of worthlessness, inability to trust, inability to form relationships, and problems with sexual intimacy as either promiscuity or frigidity, and suicide ideation (Crull, 2008; Kendall-Tackett and Marshall, 1998; Sev'er, 2002a; Transken, 2011).

Elder Abuse

On 16 December 1991, the UN passed resolution 46/91 to encourage the governments of the world to incorporate principles of independence, participation, care, self-fulfillment, and dignity for their aging citizens. The goal was to "add life to the years that have been added to life" as a result of improved hygiene, control of infectious diseases, and reduction of premature deaths (Seniors Resource, 2005). Despite the UN call for dignity for the aged, one of the most perplexing crimes of our time is violence against the elderly. Statistics Canada (2011f) reports more than 2400 victims of abuse over 65 years of age in 2010.

Although definitions of senior abuse may vary, most fall under the categories of physical, emotional, sexual, economic, and neglect (Health Canada, 1999; Department of Justice, 2003; McDonald, Collins, and Dergal, 2006; Sev'er, 2009). Often, victims suffer more than one type of abuse. Although Canadians over 65 are the least likely age group to be victims of violent crimes, those who are victimized by family members are on the rise (Lindsay, 1999; Statistics Canada, 2012). In fact, violence against seniors has increased by 14 per cent since 2004 (Statistics Canada, 2012). Older females are twice as likely to be victimized by a family member (41 per cent) as older men are (23 per cent). Older women are equally likely to be victimized by their spouse and grown children, but older men are most likely to be victimized by adult children (ibid.).

The Hidden Nature of Abuse of Seniors

DeKeseredy (1996) refers to seniors as "hidden victims." Many of them live isolated lives and some may be immobile, or may have reduced physical or mental capacity. Moreover, older adults may be physically, emotionally, and/or economically dependent on their abusers. Elderly victims may remain silent, especially if the abuser is a spouse, son, or daughter. Moreover, disbelief, shame, or fear of further victimization may prevent older victims from reporting the violence they experience (Sev'er, 2009). Some researchers have explored the negative effects of co-dependency of seniors. **Co-dependency** occurs when a person who does not have a problem him- or herself is seriously affected by someone who does have a problem such as addictions to drugs, alcohol, or gambling. A co-dependent person may try to cover up, rationalize, or minimize the negative effects of the other person's behaviour on his/her life (Alcohol and Seniors, 2005). In the case of the aged, co-dependency may also take on the form of minimizing the abusive behaviour of a son or a spouse.

Box 14.2
Elder Abuse and Murder

In March 2007, Donald Noseworthy (55) was sentenced to three-and-a-half years of imprisonment for manslaughter. This was the first time in Canadian history that neglecting to provide the necessities of life had led to a conviction of manslaughter. As the judge noted, Donald's mother Mary (78), who suffered from Alzheimer's, was repeatedly abused both mentally and physically. Mary was also kept tied to a filthy bed, and near starvation (CTV, 2007).

In March 2008, Aaron Howard (19) brutally killed his mother Frankel (61). Neighbours testified that Aaron was always verbally abusive to his mother. At the end, he bludgeoned her to death with a lead gas pipe. Then, he carried her blood-soaked body to a refrigerated room in the basement and left her there for a week. When his girlfriend inquired about the blood stains in the home, he said the family dog killed an animal and dragged it to the basement (Lofaro, 2008).

In Canada, reported cases of elder abuse range from 4 to 7 per cent of the 65+ population (Canada's Aging Population, 2002). The rates for the 85+ group is much higher. Yet, given the strength of factors that suppress reporting, this may be the peak of an iceberg (Neysmith, 1995; Patterson and Podnieks, 1995; Canada's Aging Population, 2002). Moreover, 65+ portion of the population is on the rise, and is expected to reach over 22 per cent of the population by 2030. Thus, violence against seniors will become a much larger problem than it already is (Canada's Aging Population, 2002; McDonald, Collins, and Dergal, 2006; Sev'er, 2009). As mentioned, older women victims of abuse are not well served by the shelters and transition houses, which are geared towards younger victims with dependent children (Patterson and Podnieks, 1995; Sev'er, 2002b). Institutionalized elders may also be subjected to abuse by their care providers (Canada's Aging Population, 2002). Recently, the *Toronto Star* published a series of articles on violence in old-age institutions, including over-medication, beatings, and even sexual assault towards women. The Ontario government ment promised to toughen the regulations that govern old-age homes (Goar, 2012).

Consequences of Elder Abuse

In societies like China and the Middle East, and amongst many Aboriginal groups, age often confers status. The younger generations are routinely socialized into showing respect and deference for their elders. Abuse may still occur, but the communal sanctions against it are likely to be strong. In contrast, North America reveres wealth, power, mobility, and physical perfection, and often marginalizes people weakened through age. A preoccupation with individuality and the emphasis on nuclear versus extended forms of family also contribute to the alienation of the elders from the younger generations. Thus, isolation may increase abuse, and in turn, abuse may increase isolation, creating a vicious cycle (Neysmith, 1995; Patterson and Podnieks, 1995).

Injuries often have more serious consequences for seniors. They may take longer to heal or may precipitate death—a broken hip can be a cause of death in an elder person. Statistics Canada (2012) underscores that one-third of older adults who suffer family-related violence have suffered minor or major injuries (also see National Centre, 2005). Psychological feelings of despair may also push a senior into taking his or her life. Still, the largest proportion, and the hardest to detect form of violence towards the elderly is through neglect.

Discussion and Conclusions

What can be done at the personal, social, and structural levels to combat intimate abuse? Social theories provide some clues about prevention and intervention.

Individual pathology theories are generally ineffective since few offenders have clinical pathologies. It is also erroneous to attribute pathology to the victims. What is true is that jealous, highly controlling, and abusive partners in the early stages of relationships are likely to escalate their abuse in the future. Parents or partners who are young or substance-dependent are also more likely to revert to violence. Yet none of these factors, in isolation, accurately predicts violence.

The social dynamics of violence are promising. Attitudes, perceptions, prejudices, and behaviour develop throughout one's life, but learning is most crucial in early childhood. Unfortunately, the media and other symbolic socializers often blur the boundaries of acceptable and unacceptable behaviours. When children see violent significant others, the propensity for them to use violence increases (Hatty, 2000). Children may learn to dismiss violence when their abusive fathers, or sports or music world heroes avoid condemnation for their unacceptable behaviour. Let me re-focus on Rihanna's and Chris Brown's turbulent relationship. After suffering a vicious attack involving punching, biting, putting her in a head-lock, and threats on her life, Rihanna eventually got back together with Brown (Menon, 2012). Experts are wary about what kind of message these idols are sending to their young fans (ibid.). We live in an information-saturated world. Parents, educators, mentors in sports and entertainment industries, and public leaders alike must act in non-violent ways, in both words and deeds.

The power model suggests that abuse finds a fertile ground in imbalances of power. Protecting historically powerless groups (children, women, and the elderly) transcends family boundaries and may require political and judicial interventions. The UN decrees and conventions underscore the responsibility for the states to proactively end both systemic and family forms of violence. The agents of intervention may include police forces, prosecutors, and judges sensitized to gender, ethnicity, and race issues. Availability of shelters, short- and long-term affordable housing, skills-training, provision of quality child care, and access to counselling may help the victims. The rebuilding of the welfare state to ensure guaranteed income/affordable housing would also reduce economic dependencies of women on men. The criminal justice system should be the last resort, albeit an important one, in dealing with interpersonal violence (Pence and Paymar, 1993; Dobash et al., 1995). Johnson and Dawson (2011) remind us that policies to protect the vulnerable must be carefully crafted to avoid infantilizing the poor, women, or the aged.

Elder abuse will likely escalate through the demographic increase in 65+ population (Sev'er, 2009). Aging Canadians are often considered obsolete in our youth-oriented culture. Children who grow up in nuclear families lack positive older role models while adult women are often sandwiched between caring for the old and the young. Intergenerational stress may be exacerbating both structural and gendered problems in later stages of life. Canadians must devise ways to combat negative stereotypes about aging while decreasing the care-giver burden on women.

STUDY QUESTIONS

1. Define and compare different types of abuse.
2. Discuss the problems with reporting of abuse and measurement of abuse. Discuss the similarities and differences in reporting violence against women, children, and the aged.
3. Why do some feminists object to the concept of psychological abuse?
4. What are some consequences of child abuse? Why are younger children more vulnerable for abuse?
5. Why is elder abuse one of the most under-reported crimes?
6. Can you imagine a society where there is no intimate partner violence? Why or why not?

Further Readings

Crull, Marie C. 2008. *Following Sexual Abuse: A Sociological Interpretation of Identity Re-formation in Reflexive Therapy.* Toronto: University of Toronto. The book is a reflexive analysis of therapeutic accounts gathered from four sexually abused girls/women. Readers are provided with selected windows into the harrowing recollections of abuse, the shattered selves of girls/women, and their journey (through dreams, symbols, written accounts, and narration), towards a more integrated self.

DeKeseredy, W.S. 2012. *Violence Against Women: Myths, Facts, Controversies.* Toronto: University of Toronto Press. This book succinctly summaries violence related research and theories.

Johnson, Holly, and Myrna Dawson. 2011. *Violence Against Women in Canada: Research and Policy Perspectives.* Toronto: Oxford. This book presents one of the most noteworthy syntheses of violence research and findings in Canada.

Sev'er, Aysan. 2002. *Fleeing the House of Horrors: Women Who Have Left Their Abusive Partners.* Toronto: University of Toronto Press. Sev'er's book analyzes the struggles of 39 women who have left their abusive partners and proposes a model of post-violence adjustment.

Sev'er, Aysan. 2012. *Mothers, Daughters and Untamed Dragons.* Bradford, ON: Demeter Press. This is a novel about the love and conflict that simultaneously exist between four generations of mothers and daughters. Although the characters are fictitious, the author brings into focus the dynamics of family conflict.

Statistics Canada. 2011. "Family Violence in Canada: A Statistical Profile," *The Daily,* 27 January. This document contains the latest and the most comprehensive statistical information on intimate partner violence in Canada.

Transken, Si. 2011. "Noises and unwanted odours in old closets," in *Skeletons in the Closet: A Sociological Analysis of Family Conflicts,* A. Sev'er and J. Trost, eds. Toronto: Wilfrid Laurier University Press, pp. 139–55. This book provides a collection of real-life narratives of family conflict written by 10 academics. The editors provide an in-depth review of the family conflict literature in the introduction and conclusion chapters.

Websites

www.unhcr.ch/huridocda/huridoca.nsf/(Symbol)/A.RES.48.104.En?Opendocument
This UN site includes the Declaration on the Elimination of Violence Against Women, as well as information on all kinds of violence in work, health care, and family life.

http://canada.justice.gc.ca/en/ps/fm
The federal Justice Department offers strategies to eliminate violence within the family as well as detailed statistical information and provincial comparisons.

www.citizenship.gov.on.ca/owd/english/facts/preventing.htm
The Ontario Women's Directorate, an agency within the provincial government, presents detailed statistical information on violence against women in Ontario and facts on women's stays in shelters.

www.statcan.gc.ca/pub/85-224-x/85-224-x2000010-eng.pdf
Statistics Canada's *The Daily* publishes detailed statistical reports on various issues, and
this site allows searches by topic and date. It also includes excellent yearly reports on intimate violence, especially for the years 2009–2011.

www.statcan.gc.ca/pub/85-002-x/2011001/article/11495-eng.pdf
This Statistics Canada site provides the latest information on Canadian shelters and the
characteristics and experiences of women who use them.

www.un.org/womanwatch
Woman Watch, a UN research arm and website, tracks reproductive, health, and violence
issues that the world's women face.

15

Investing in Families and Children: Family Policies in Canada

CATHERINE KRULL

LEARNING OBJECTIVES

- To understand the development of Canada's family policies within a liberal welfare state
- To understand the ideology and implications of a universal approach versus a targeted approach to family policies
- To become aware of Quebec's progressive family policies and how they might serve as a model for the rest of Canada
- To get a better comprehension as to why Canada's targeted family policies have not yet eradicated child poverty as promised by Parliament in 1989
- To become conscious of the reasons why state intervention is necessary if parents, especially mothers, are to successfully integrate employment and family responsibilities, and to recognize how barriers to such integration impact gender equity
- To appreciate the challenges that governments, family policy-makers, and advocacy groups face in Canada in developing the new child-care measures

Introduction

Canadian governments have always influenced families: determining who marries, marital age, and how unions end. Generally, governments ask family members to care for and support one another and the adults reproduce—perpetuating Canadian culture and adequate numbers of taxpayers, consumers, and workers (Baker, 1994, 2010). Conversely, Canadians rely on state economic and social support in "balancing" child-care with paid work. **Family policy**, therefore, is central for Canadians—defining families, their form, which family members are entitled to government support, and amounts and type of support.

Family policy comprises rules and programs. In this chapter, that policy, narrowly defined, comprises measures affecting families with children under age 18. It includes direct and indirect cash transfers like family allowances and tax relief; benefits for workers with family responsibilities such as maternity–paternity leave; services, including daycare, pre- and after-school care, and early childhood education programs; other benefits affecting housing, education, and health; and legislation affecting abortion and child alimony (Gauthier, 2010).

Nonetheless, Canada lacks a comprehensive national policy. State intervention is generally minimal: restricted primarily to child abuse, child neglect, and limited financial support. It varies by gender and different income and cultural groups (Baker, 2001a, 2008). A governmental "hierarchy of help" exists in assisting families: the labour market first, the family second; if either fails to meet family needs, state involvement occurs in limited, targeted ways (Beauvais and Dufour, 2003). However, this system obstructs parents' full participation in family care and paid work, especially women's progress for equality and independence (Krull, 2011, 2012).

Explaining the lack of a cohesive national family policy is complex. Like other countries, an aging population and increasing globalization challenge Canada. Governments must consider the conflicting viewpoints of family-oriented public interest groups—electors of the left and right who put them in office (Evans and Wekerle, 1997: 13); their debates encumber cohesive policy. Canada's federal nature also provides constitutional impediments. Ottawa focuses more on income support; emphasizing child protection, provincial and territorial governments concentrate on welfare assistance and other services (Tézli and Gauthier, 2009).

Moreover, families have undergone considerable change (Krull, 2011, 2012). As the 2011 Census indicates, Canadian families are in a state of flux. This census data shows that 39.2 per cent of census families were couples with children, with married couples still accounting for the majority of all census families. However, while married couples account for two-thirds of families, this is a marked decline, with the proportion of lone-parent families and common-law couples increasing, to 16.3 per cent and 16.7 per cent of total census families respectively. The increase in lone-parent families is important: 19.3 per cent of all children live in households with a single parent, an increase of more than 1 per cent over a decade, with women accounting for 80 per cent of lone parents. The percentage of children living in common-law households has also increased to 16.3 per cent. Stepfamilies—counted for the first time in the 2011 Census—comprise 10 per cent of all census families in which children are present, and 12.6 per cent of all couples with children. At the same time, 0.5 per cent of children under age 14 live in foster homes (Statistics Canada, 2012a). Clearly, the traditional nuclear family is a social institution facing stiff competition. Indeed, in addition to the increases in single-parent families, blended families, and common-law families, the 2011 Census showed increases in multi-generational families—4.8 per cent of children live in a household with at least one grandparent—skip-generation families, which account for 0.5 per cent of all households with children, and same-sex households. In whatever form, families constitute the basis of Canadian society and government policy must account for these changes, particularly as they pertain to families raising children. Accordingly, the role of government and the changing requirements of parents, children, grandparents, and other family members in the shape and purpose of family policies are decidedly important.

Canadian family policy falls between Western European and American models. Mirroring Western Europe in health and education investments—but at a lower level—and in some federal benefits, they exceed those enjoyed by Americans. In one crucial area, however, Canada joins its southern neighbour: a shameful history of high child poverty rates and low public family expenditures (Chen and Corak, 2008: 540; Brusentsev and Vroman, 2007: 28).

To understand present Canadian family policy, four questions arise: (1) How have recent policies developed? (2) How have they responded or not responded to changes in Canadian families? (3) What are their strengths and weaknesses? and, responding to criticism, (4) Has the state produced more effective policy? Here, one point needs emphasis. Quebec provides a stellar example of government initiatives that prioritize the family, offering a potential model for developing the rest of Canada's cohesive national policy. Despite constraints on public finance, but confronting increasing family needs, Canada's various levels of government began serious and promising discussions toward a national policy in the late 1990s. But the process remains arduous as Canadian governments oscillate over understanding their role versus that of parents in raising healthy, educated, and well-adjusted children.

Canada's Family and Child-Related Policies

Maternity and Parental/Adoption Leave Benefits

Paid maternity and parental leaves occupy a central place in Canada's **liberal welfare state**. In specific terms, these policies are meant to assist Canadians in balancing family and employment. However, Canada has not had the best track record in this regard. Although all of Western Europe, Australia, New Zealand, and Japan adopted some form of paid maternity leave legislation by 1939, it took Canada until 1971 to offer women such assistance. The reason was that "the responsibility of protecting pregnant women at work and compensating them for the loss of earnings was not seen as a governmental responsibility" (Gauthier, 1998: 197).

When the legislation was finally passed, the responsibility for **maternity benefits** (and later parental/adoption leave) was divided between the federal and provincial/territorial governments. The provinces and territories were obligated to determine the length and conditions of maternity leave, while financial replacement fell under the jurisdiction of the federal government's Unemployment Insurance (UI) program. If they had been paying UI premiums, working mothers were initially given 15 weeks of paid leave and received approximately 67 per cent of their regular salary as unemployment benefits. And if they so chose, these women had the option of taking two additional weeks of unpaid leave. Women adopting a child were finally made eligible to receive benefits in 1984. The provinces also offered unpaid maternity leave and, although unpaid, it nevertheless was beneficial because these mothers were guaranteed the right to return to the same or an equivalent job (Jensen and Thompson, 1999: 13).

Bowing to pressure from women's groups, the federal government introduced 10 weeks of **parental leave** in 1990, which could be taken by either parent or shared between them; the parent who took leave received unemployment benefits equalling 60 per cent of her/his regular salary. In 1996, two changes were made to maternity benefits: (1) eligibility for maternity benefits were now to be based on the number of hours worked rather than the number of weeks; and (2) the amount women received was reduced from 60 per cent to a maximum of 55 per cent of their regular salary with a ceiling of $413 per week (Baker, 2001a; OECD, 2004). Gauthier (1998) conducted an international comparative study shortly after these changes took place in Canada and found that when both the duration of the leave and maternity pay were taken into consideration, Canada was among the lowest of 22 industrialized countries.

In January 2001, the federal government doubled the amount of time that new parents could receive benefits, from 25 to a maximum of 50 weeks (Government of Canada, 2005). While maternity leave remained the same (15 weeks at 55 per cent of insurable earnings), parental leave increased from 10 to 35 weeks at 55 per cent of insurable earnings up to a maximum amount, as of 1 January 2012, of $45,900. To be eligible for the maximum, parents had to have worked a minimum of 600 hours of insurable employment in the previous 12 months. At present, a mother can add the parental leave to her maternity leave—giving her 50 weeks of paid leave—or she can take maternity leave (15 weeks), return to her employment, and the father could then take the 35-week parental leave (Government of Canada, 2012a). Although women cannot work while on maternity benefits without having their earnings deducted from their benefits, parents can earn up to $50 per week or 25 per cent of their weekly benefits in part-time work without being penalized (ibid.). Moreover, a pilot project ran between 11 December 2005 and 4 August 2012 that allowed individuals receiving parental benefits to earn up to $75 or 40 per cent of their weekly benefits, whichever was higher (ibid.). On 5 August 2012, a new working-while-on-claim pilot project was implemented that allows claimants to keep 50 cents for every dollar they earn and has no cap on earnings. Both pilot programs have been successful and, since 6 January 2013, eligible EI claimants have the option of reverting to the provisions of the pilot project if it is the more beneficial option. This option pertains to any claims during the period of 5 August 2012 and 1 August 2015 (Government of Canada, 2011c, 2013).

In its October 2004 report card on Canada's child-care system, the Organisation for Economic Co-operation and Development (OECD) praised Canada for its enhanced parental leave, stating that "this has been a tremendous breakthrough for Canadian parents and infants," a finding reaffirmed in the OECD's 2011 Better Life Index (OECD, 2004: 55, OECD, 2011). Canada's birth benefits are also superior to those offered in the United States (Brusentsev and Vroman, 2007). However, Canada's birth benefits can certainly be criticized for restricting eligibility to employed women who have worked for a minimum of 600 hours—this means that many Canadians are excluded. And despite the changes to parental leave, the majority of Canadian fathers still do not take it, citing as their reasons (1) family choice, (2) difficulty taking time off work, and (3) financial issues (Dube, 2008). Despite studies that indicate that greater father involvement positively impacts on a child's cognitive development, educational attainment, and social functioning (ibid.), it seems that cultural expectations of men and insufficient benefits continue to be issues that impede fathers' full involvement in child-care. Even so, between 2001 and 2010 there has been a nine-fold increase in the percentage of recent fathers taking parental leave, from 3 per cent to 29.7 per cent (Government of Canada, 2011a).

From Universal to Targeted Child and Family Benefits

The federal government has been financially supporting Canadian families in some way or another since 1918, when it introduced the Child Tax Exemption, which allowed breadwinners with dependent children an annual fiscal deduction on their income tax (Baker, 2001a; Lefebvre and Merrigan, 2003). In 1945, a monthly Family Allowance was paid to women with children at home. These two contributions were important because they were universal. In other words, they offered financial assistance to all families with dependent children. Family Allowance was also significant because it was paid directly to mothers, which for many women at this time was the only source of income that was theirs alone. These two universal contributions, the Child Tax Exemption and Family Allowance, became known as "child and family benefits" (Baker, 2001a) and developed as the pillars of Canadian family policy (Lefebvre and Merrigan, 2003).

For more on the history of Family Allowance in Canada see Chapter 2, p. 32.

By the late 1980s, Ottawa had become quite concerned about the country's high child poverty rates. Throughout that decade, child poverty rates in Canada ranged from 15.7 to 20.6 per cent—rates that were among the highest in the industrial world and second only to the United States (O'Hara, 1998). In 1989, a resolution was unanimously passed in the House of Commons to achieve the goal of eradicating child poverty by the year 2000. The next year, Canada signed the United Nations Convention on the Rights of the Child, a treaty that committed all signatories to protect and ensure children's rights and to hold themselves accountable for this commitment before the international community.

Between 1988 and 1993, the Conservative government of Brian Mulroney took measures that completely transformed family benefits with the goal of reducing child poverty. "Discussions of poverty focused almost exclusively on 'child poverty,' as children were always seen as the deserving poor, whereas adults drawing social benefits were often suspected of defrauding the welfare system" (Baker, 2001a: 276; also see Stasiulis, 2005). The child tax deduction was cancelled in 1988 and replaced with a non-refundable child tax credit, a device that minimized significantly the amount received by wealthier families. In 1993, the Conservative government abolished both Family Allowance and the non-refundable tax credit and introduced the Child Tax Benefit (CTB). The CTB paid low-income families an annual amount for each child, an additional supplement for each subsequent child under seven years of age, and a Working Income Supplement (WIS). These changes marked a monumental change in Canada's approach to family policy—universal benefits (designed to assist all families with dependent children) were substituted with targeted benefits (designed to assist low-income families).

In 1998, the Liberal government of Jean Chrétien developed the National Child Benefit (NCB). The NCB included the Canada Child Tax Benefit (CCTB)—just a new name for the previous CTB—and the National Child Benefit Supplement (NCBS), which replaced the WIS. In adhering to the parliamentary commitment to reduce poverty, only low-income families can receive the maximum annual basic amount. As of 2012 and after several amendments, the CCTB pays an annual maximum of $1,405 per child to families whose net income does not exceed $42,707. An additional supplement of $249 was paid annually for each additional child under the age of seven years but this payment was replaced in July 2007 with the Universal Child Care Benefit (UCCB), a monthly payment of $100 per child under six years of age. In terms of the NCBS benefit, families whose net income does not exceed $24,863 receive $2,177 for the first child, $1,926 for the second child, and $1,832 for each additional child (Government of Canada, 2012c).

It is also important to note that the NCBS may be fully or partially clawed back by provincial and territorial governments if families are receiving provincial social assistance (welfare). Therefore, while New Brunswick, Newfoundland and Labrador, Nova Scotia, and Manitoba have always allowed or now allow welfare families to collect the full amount allotted by the NCBS, the supplement is fully or partially clawed back in British Columbia, Saskatchewan, Ontario, Prince Edward Island, Nunavut, and the Northwest Territories. Quebec, meanwhile, does not formally participate in the NCB, but has adopted a similar approach to those provinces allowing families to collect the full amount (National Council of Welfare, 2008:142).

The irony is that the federal government increases child benefits but allows provinces to reduce or deny them altogether for families on social assistance, the families most in need given that the welfare rates are well below the poverty line in every province in Canada. Indeed, as of 2007, the last year for which a comprehensive report on NCB was compiled, approximately 320,620 Canadian families continue to have their welfare or child benefits reduced by all or part of the NCBS. While a recent cursory analysis of NCBS by the Treasury Board of Canada Secretariat notes that provincial and territorial governments are beginning to reduce the clawback so that "the vast majority of children living in low-income families, including those on social assistance, are currently receiving some or all of the [NCBS]," the continued existence of a clawback nevertheless reinforces the idea of the deserving and undeserving poor (Government of Canada, 2011b). "Those working for low pay—the deserving poor—get to keep all the NCBS. Those on welfare—the undeserving poor—don't get to keep the NCBS" (National Council of Welfare, 2008: 86). It also discriminates against single mothers, since they constitute the majority of those who collect welfare and who also have their payments clawed back. Not surprisingly, the National Council of Welfare could find no evidence that the NCBS has assisted welfare families to move to paid employment or obtain employment experience (National Council of Welfare, 2008: 87–8).

Children in State Care

Due to differing ways in which provincial governments classify "out-of-home" care, Canada-wide statistics have historically been difficult to calculate (Mulcahy and Trocmé, 2010). According to Peter Dudding, executive director of the Child Welfare League of Canada, "the best estimate from two compilation studies is that between 76,000 and 85,000 kids are in foster care. The lack of data means there's no way the provinces, which fund foster care and often stake decisions on statistics and outcomes, can compare themselves against each other for best practices, . . .

For more on what leads to children in state care, see "Child Abuse" in Chapter 14, pp. 284–6.

It's impossible to create good policy without good numbers" (CBC News, 2012a). However, the latest census release from Statistics Canada indicates that this number is much lower—according to the 2011 Census, which counted foster children for the first time,[1] 47,885 Canadian children are living in foster care (Statistics Canada, 2012d). Despite the variance in definition of foster children and numbers, there is agreement that the majority of foster children are under the age of 14 years. Moreover, although the Census did not count how many foster children were Aboriginal, they did find that the provinces that have the highest proportion of foster children are also the provinces with the largest numbers of Aboriginal peoples; namely Manitoba, followed by the Northwest Territories, Nunavut, and Yukon (ibid.). Other surveys report that approximately 40 per cent of foster children are Aboriginal; and of these children, the majority are placed in non-Aboriginal foster homes (Bokma, 2008; Canadian Press, 2008, Ponti, 2008, Federation of Aboriginal Foster Parents, 2012) and as of 2009 more than 8,000 Aboriginal children (about five per cent of all Aboriginal children) have been removed from their homes across Canada (Government of Canada, 2010). About one-third of foster children have parents whose parental rights have been legally terminated and, as such, are adoptable; yet less than 13 per cent of these children are actually adopted by their foster parents (Bokma, 2008). Aboriginal groups are challenging the federal government on this overrepresentation of their children in state foster care, arguing that the grossly underfunded child welfare on reserves is a continuation of Canada's colonial history.

Foster parents receive a monthly basic maintenance fee or per diem from the provincial government to help with the costs of caring for foster children. These costs include food, clothing, personal care items (toiletries and hair care products), general household costs (e.g., wear and tear, cleaning, paper supplies, insurance), spending allowance (minor recreation toys, magazines, and musical recordings), and gifts to and from the foster child. Foster parents can also collect skill fees, which are meant to compensate them for their level of expertise in caring for a child. Specialized rates are also available for children with specialized needs. The amounts that foster parents receive vary considerably depending on the province in which they live (for details on provincial benefits, see Government of Canada, 2008). The Federal government also pays provincial jurisdictions a Children's Special Allowance (CSA), which is based on the number of children living in that jurisdiction who are under the age of 18 and in state care. This monthly allowance of $298.50 per child in state care is equivalent to the Child Tax Benefit (CCTB) and the National Child Benefit Supplement (NCBS). However, this money does not necessarily get passed on to foster parents. The province determines the allocation of the CSA, and, as such, jurisdictions either pass on the full amount to foster parents, partial amounts, or none at all because they consider it part of their operating revenue (Government of Canada, 2008; 2012b).

However, current benefits are often seen as inadequate. Many existing foster parents are struggling and even deciding to quit because of the lack of state support (MacGregor, 2006; CBC News, 2012a). Canada's foster care system has been fraught with other problems as well. There are not nearly enough foster homes in which to place all children, and foster children often experience an average of seven foster home placements over the course of their childhood (Bokma, 2008). Moreover, because of lack of resources and the sheer number of foster children, it is impossible to scrutinize every home on a regular basis. As such, foster children are more vulnerable to neglect and even abuse (Montgomery, 2008; CBC News, 2012a). It also remains a contested issue as to whether legal responsibility for foster children lies with their foster parents or with the state (Cradock, 2007). There exists significant variability in policies, legislation, definitions, and services, largely because foster care operates solely under provincial and territorial jurisdictions—the federal government is responsible only for Aboriginal foster children. Foster families are also often excluded from other government benefits that most parents receive. For example, the recent new plan of the Ontario government to alleviate poverty excluded foster children living in the province from the new child benefit, denying foster families a total of approximately 5 million dollars (Talaga and Monsebraaten, 2008). Most provinces also terminate benefits once a foster child is adopted, which often deters or hampers successful adoptions (Simmons, 2008). Also troubling is that only 21 per cent of foster children pursue post-secondary education compared to 40 per cent in the general population, while in Ontario children in foster care have a high school graduation rate of 44 per cent compared to a rate amongst the general populace of 81 per cent (CTV News, 2008a; OACAS, 2011).

Despite these tremendous difficulties, there have also been noteworthy successes. For example, the Alberta provincial government recently introduced new innovative amendments to their Child, Youth, and Family Enhancement Act. Under Bill 40, parents who adopt a child who has been a permanent ward of the provincial government will receive the same benefits given to foster parents until the child turns 18 years of age, a measure still in effect as of early 2012. This includes a travel allowance for those adopting an Aboriginal child so that the child can visit their family reserve and stay connected with their cultural heritage. The rationale for these benefits is that "all children who have been in government care have special needs—not because all foster children have physical or psychological problems but because any child who's been made a permanent ward of the government, for whatever reason, will inevitably have gone through rough times" (Simons, 2008). Likewise, the Ontario government has implemented a progressive plan that is meant to increase the enrolment of foster children in post-secondary education. The province is investing the $100 monthly Universal Childcare Benefit allocated for foster children under the age of six years into a RESP fund. The RESP is being supplemented with other federal funds such as the Canada Learning Bond payments and an annual payment from a Canada educational savings grant. This will translate into $23,000 for a child who is 18 years of age and who entered the foster care system as an infant (CTV News, 2008a). Most importantly, it will allow foster children the same possibilities that most Canadian children enjoy. Alongside tuition support, the Ontario government is mulling plans to allow foster children to increase the existing extended care and maintenance age for foster children from 21 to 25, thus providing youths in foster care with the long-term support enjoyed by many of their peers (CBC News, 2012b). However, given the looming fiscal crisis in Ontario, the long-term viability of these measures is questionable. Still, as Reid (2007) argues, "No longer is impersonal and minimal the best approach [to care for foster children]; rather, the most successful programs aim at giving youth the support that any other peer would expect from a parent" (2007: 47).

Assessment of Canada's Child and Family Benefits

Impact of Measures on Child Poverty

Canada's current child benefits have come under a great deal of criticism. Feminists have long argued that they represent a step backward for women in terms of their full and equal participation in the labour force. McKeen (2001: 187) pointed out more than a decade ago that "the move from universal entitlement to means testing on the basis of family income limits women's access to benefits, encourages familial dependency, and turns back progress in the effort to make the recognition of individual autonomy an important policy objective." In essence, Canada's efforts since 1989, when Parliament promised to work towards eliminating child poverty by the year 2000, have failed dismally. In 1989, when the resolution passed, the child poverty rate was 15.1 per cent. Yet, until 2008 poverty rates for children were higher than the 1989 rate for every single year, not lower as promised. As Figure 15.1 indicates, child poverty rates increased after 1989 until they reached a high of 23.5 per cent in 1996 (based on before tax income). They decreased to 15 per cent in 2009, a rate only slightly below the 1989 rate when Canada promised to eradicate child poverty. It also means that 639,000 children, approximately 1 in every 10 children in Canada, continues to live in poverty (calculated by figures reported in Campaign 2000, 2011: 4). According to a 2012 United Nations report, when child-poverty rates are compared with overall poverty rates, Canada ranks 18 out of 35 industrialized countries and is in the bottom third in terms of the percentage of children in poverty (UNICEF, 2012). In response to the report, UNICEF Canada's executive director David Morley stated that "The face of poverty in Canada is a child's face—this is unacceptable. It is clearly time for Canada to make children a priority when planning budgets and spending our nation's resources, even in tough economic times" (UNICEF Canada, 2012).

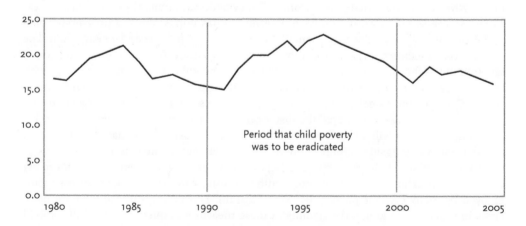

Figure 15.1 **Poverty Rates for Children under 18, Canada, 1980–2006**

SOURCE: Statistics Canada. *Table 202-0802 - Persons in low income (before tax), annual, 1980–2006*, CANSIM (database).

Critics of Canada's current NCB program have argued for over a decade that focusing on impoverished children rather than on impoverished families relieve governments from the responsibility to alleviate the causes of poverty (see, for example, ibid.; Jensen, 2003; O'Hara, 1998; Lefebvre and Merrigan, 2003). It is important to realize that children are poor because their parents are poor. Moreover, when we focus solely on children, the rights and concerns of adults become marginalized; their voices unheard. Once children have left the nest, poor parents are no longer entitled to benefits and risk falling into deeper poverty. This is not to say that governments should not invest in children but rather that governments also need to focus on alleviating the factors that aggravate adult poverty such as: (1) declining welfare incomes; (2) the low-wage wall (jobs with long hours, no or few benefits, and no opportunities for advancement or wage increases); (3) inadequate minimum wages; (4) reduced access to employment insurance; (5) shortages of affordable housing and help for the homeless; and (6) lack of quality, affordable child-care spaces (National Council of Welfare, 2006b: 5–7). Governments need to develop policies tailored to the specific segments of the population who are most likely to suffer from these hardships that exacerbate poverty. Single mothers are a case in point.

Large disparities in poverty rates exist between family types. Poverty rates are approximately 10 per cent for two-parent families, 22.2 per cent for families headed by single-parent fathers, but 52.1 per cent for families with children under six headed by single-parent mothers (National Council of Welfare, 2007a; Campaign 2000, 2011: 7). Moreover, almost half of Aboriginal children under the age of six (not living in First Nation communities) live in a low income family, while one in four Aboriginal youths lives in poverty. Further, amongst racialized Canadians, especially immigrants, who make up a disproportionate percentage of those living in poverty relative to their overall size within the general population, youths comprise almost half (46 per cent) of those who live in poverty (National Council on Welfare 2011b, Campaign 2000, 2011). Despite decreasing over the past two decades, poverty rates for single-parent families headed by mothers remain twice that of such families headed by fathers and account for more than 90 per cent of poor single-parent households. Not surprisingly, there is also a fair amount of provincial variability in these rates. British Columbia and Saskatchewan have the highest poverty rates (16.1 per cent and 14.4 per cent, respectively), whereas Prince Edward Island and Alberta report the lowest (4 per cent and 6.9 per cent, respectively) (ibid., 1).

Quebec has taken the lead in Canada in terms of implementing policies geared towards supporting families and reducing poverty. Since the implementation of its universal child-care program and the 2004 Act to Combat Poverty and Social Exclusion was put into place, Quebec's child poverty rates have decreased dramatically, from 16.1 per cent in 2004 to 7.7 per cent in 2009 (Campaign 2000, 2011: 4), the province now boasts the highest percentage of mothers who are in the workforce (CCSD, 2008; Monsebraaten, 2008), and funds have been allocated to promote the development of children living in poverty (Conference Board of Canada, 2009). The province's objective is to attain one of the lowest poverty rates in the industrial world by 2013. The provincial government's own assessments of where Quebec stands in comparison to other provinces are indeed quite glowing (Ministère de la Famille et des Aînés, 2011). Following Quebec's lead, Ontario and Newfoundland and Labrador have recently taken poverty reduction initiatives. While it is too early to assess the total impact of these measures, Campaign 2000 has praised the progress shown in Newfoundland and Labrador (Campaign 2000, 2011: 2). Unfortunately, Canada has yet to develop a comprehensive poverty reduction plan.

Although being employed offsets poverty to some degree, having only one earner in a family is not adequate for most families. As Campaign 2000's recent report card (2011: 7) has highlighted, 63 per cent of low-income children live in two-parent families. Further, one in three of all children in poverty live in families where at least one parent is employed full-time all year (ibid., 2). As a similar report by the Canadian Council on Social Development (2007) noted, even though the number of parents who are working has recently increased, "working poor parents are stuck behind a 'low wage wall' in poorly paid jobs with few, if any, benefits or opportunities for education, training and advancement" (ibid., 3). As such, it is unlikely that they will rise above the poverty line without some form of assistance.

Of course, the poverty rate, which measures the risk of poverty within any given group, is important in judging policy. But so, too, is the number or percentage of poor families that exist in Canada. According to the National Council of Welfare (2004: 110):

> One of the myths about child poverty is that since single-parent families have high poverty rates, most poor children must live in single-parent families. That has never been the case for any of the years on record. The largest number of poor children has always been the number living in two-parent families.

For example, although two-parent families have a relatively low poverty rate (10 per cent), children living in two-parent families accounted for 54 per cent of all poor children in Canada. In terms of non-two-parent families, 4 per cent of low-income children lived in families headed by single fathers, 40 per cent lived in families headed by single mothers, and 4 per cent were in other living arrangements (Child Care Advocacy Association of Canada, 2011: 10–11). Also telling are the more than 851,000 Canadians who relied on Canadian food banks in 2010, an increase over the 2007 level of 720,000 persons, thus showing the impact of the 2008–2009 recession. Moreover, approximately 38 per cent of food bank users are children (Food Banks Canada, 2011: 2). Contrary to the Canadian government's resolution in 1989 to eradicate poverty by the year 2000, the number of Canadians using food banks in 2007—that is, prior to the recession—had increased by 86 per cent (Canadian Council on Social Development, 2008: 6). The recession has only worsened the matter. Furthermore, most food banks in this country continue to operate with little government assistance, with about a third of them operating with no paid staff (ibid.). Of importance too, is that a year before the recession, almost 40 per cent of Canadians believed that they were only one to two paycheques away from living in poverty (CCSD, 2008: 6).

In May 2002, Canada participated in the United Nations General Assembly Special Session on Children and, along with many other countries, signed the UN Declaration on "A World Fit for Children." In ratifying this document, the federal government promised to develop a national plan of action based on Canada's unique circumstances that took into consideration four priority areas: promoting healthy lives; providing quality education; protecting children against abuse, exploitation, and violence; and combating HIV/AIDS. In 2004, Ottawa released its plan, "A Canada Fit for Children," that reaffirmed the federal government's commitment to make children and families a national priority (see full report online at www.sdc.gc.ca).

Despite these efforts, critics have long claimed that the government is still not doing enough. For example, the Canadian Council on Social Development has estimated that although the government's social investment has had some impact in that it kept 570,000 children out of poverty, CCTB benefits would need to be increased to $5,100 per child for real progress on child poverty (CCSD, 2007: 4). The National Council of Welfare (2004, 2007a, 2007b, 2007c) echoes these concerns, charging that despite government promises to give priority to child poverty and work towards eliminating it, it has done little outside of gradually increasing child benefits. According to the Council,

> It is not by chance that poverty will be resolved—it is by good design. . . . [However, Canada has] no long-term vision, no plan, no one accountable for carrying out the plan, no resources assigned and no accepted measure of results, [and as such], we will continue to be mired in poverty for generations. (2007c: 15, 17)

In its latest Report Card on Child Poverty in Canada, the Conference Board of Canada gave the country a "C," noting that one in seven Canadian children lives in poverty, meaning that the rate of child poverty had increased between the mid-1990s and the mid-2000s (Conference Board of Canada, 2009). Government policies have obviously been inadequate—while poverty rates in the mid-2000s declined gradually, the 2009 rate of 9.6 per cent—very similar to the 2007 pre-recession rate of 9.1 per cent—means that more than 3.2 million Canadians, including 1 million children live in poverty; one-third of all Canadian children experience poverty for at least one year; one in four workers (2 million adults) are in low-wage employment; low-income two-parent families remain, on average, $7,300 below the poverty line; lone mothers and their children remain the most vulnerable to poverty; the poverty rates for Aboriginals, immigrants, and visible minority groups are more than double the average for non-racialized groups (National Council on Welfare, 2011a, 2011b).

Following the Conservative Party victory in the 2011 federal election, fears amongst anti-poverty groups of a deepening morass were acute (Maki, 2013). The 2012 budget, which included numerous cuts to government services, only deepened fears about increasing poverty (*Toronto Star*, 2012). Among these cuts was the closure of the National Council on Welfare, a federal advisory board with a mandate devoted exclusively to fight poverty and cutbacks to the welfare system and with no private sector equivalent. Advocating for families on welfare, the council was a forerunner in fighting against provincial and territorial governments clawing back part of the federal Canada Child Tax Benefit (Kerstetter, 2012). Current welfare reforms have particularly had an adverse impact on single mothers (Maki, 2011, 2013). As Campaign 2000 warned:

> The federal budget not only ignores the current needs of Canada's children . . . but downloads much of today's costs onto them. The 639,000 children living in poverty will be joined by many more because of a budget that concentrates on business and global markets, while failing to address the critical need for universal childcare and affordable housing, public supports that assist families in realizing their economic potential, (Campaign 2000, 2012)

The critics have a point. Canadian families need better policy from their government.

Impact of Measures on Child Care

One area where better policy can be helpful concerns childcare. Despite all political discourse and efforts to this end over the past four decades, little has been done to provide affordable quality child-care. Women have constituted a large part of the workforce for several decades, yet for countless working women the challenge of balancing work and family responsibilities remains daunting (see "Case in Point" box). Many are *forced out of the labour force* to care for young children because they cannot afford to pay for child-care or they do not have sufficient guarantees of return to employment. Conversely, others are virtually *forced back into employment* because they cannot sustain the income loss, even when receiving the limited unpaid parental leave benefits. Today, fathers have taken on more child-care and domestic responsibilities than in the past and, as a consequence, they, too, can find the act of balancing work and family overwhelming. Parents often feel that it is their responsibility to overcome the challenges and problems associated with balancing family life, household work, and market work (Krull and Sempruch, 2011). This message is reinforced by society—one just has to look at the numerous self-help books in any bookstore that offer advice on how to be more creative with time management so to better balance family and work.

CASE IN POINT
Can We (or Should We) Balance Family and Paid Work?

Is it possible to balance family work (caregiving and household work) with paid work (employment)? This issue has challenged feminists, feminist scholars, children's activist organizations, and other family policy advocacy groups, not to mention fathers, mothers, their employers, and all levels of Canadian government. Most of the literature on this subject advocates for better, healthier, and equitable balance between family work and market work. However, others argue that we need to focus on integrating paid work/ family work, not balancing the two as if they are in opposition to one another. Paid work and family have been set against each other, as if they are components in a zero sum game: to not achieve "balance" between the two is equated with failing at our jobs or failing our families (Krull and Sempruch, 2011). Most parents experience the stress of trying to reconcile the demands of their employment with their responsibilities towards—and desire to spend time with—their families. And it's not unusual that parents internalize their difficulty at achieving "balance," often seeing such time crunches as personal failure rather than the failure of our system.

For Maureen Baker, the problem is simple: "Canada and the liberal welfare states offer various programs to assist employed parents, but fathers still earn considerably more than mothers, women still perform more unpaid household work than men, most children remain with their mothers after parental separation, and welfare programs tend to push beneficiaries into low-paid jobs." It follows that existing policy needs to change. Margrit Eichler argues: "In terms of a policy effect, making household workers themselves aware of skills they may possess is only one aspect of a broader issue. Employers, particularly those in positions directly involved in hiring people, need not only to be aware of the skills that may be acquired through unpaid household work, but need to have tools with which to assess them." Margaret Hillyard Little offers a feminist approach: "as feminists, we need to demand increased state support of mothering. While we have been quick to see the limitations of the maternalist discourse of the nineteenth century, we need to make room for a political argument that embraces motherhood and all its demands and duties." Susan McDaniel proposes that "a shared work-valued care model would recognize the value of care as work and redistribute more equitably the costs and benefits of caring for both young and old, both of which, after all, are public 'goods'."

Quebec's family policies, admittedly expensive, offer a model for the rest of the country. Patrizia Albanese explains: "Even with limitations, including long waiting lists, the need to improve quality, and the need for more flexible options, Quebec's model of childcare, coupled with its large and generous package of reforms, is unprecedented in North America. . . . at a time when women's work—paid and unpaid—has been central to the international drive for cheap and productive labour, it is high time that the Canadian state contribute, following the Quebec model, to assisting mothers in bearing their disproportionate share of the cost of social reproduction."

The traditional wife–husband/woman–man-based family is only one of a plethora of family forms; government and the private sector employment policies need to be shaped to meet the Canadian reality where more than sole male breadwinners are responsible for their families. As Susan McDaniel argues, it is time "we move beyond the trapeze image of a balancing act between paid work and the rest of our lives."

SOURCE: Catherine Krull and Justyne Sempruch, eds. *A Life in Balance? Reopening the Family-Work Debate* (Vancouver, Toronto: UBC Press, 2011), pp. 62, 95, 143, 204, 218.

Regulated child-care has always been a provincial and territorial jurisdiction. It follows that policy, child-care services, and funding for childcare vary considerably across jurisdictions. And with the exception of Quebec, subsidies are targeted to low-income families, leaving all other families to face exorbitant costs without help. Many parents cannot afford high-quality care, yet the effect that child-care has on children ultimately depends on the quality of that care.

While feminists and advocacy groups have long recognized the urgent need for a government-supported quality child-care program based on universality, it has remained elusive. As early as 1970, the Royal Commission on the Status of Women stressed the importance of a subsidized national childcare program: "the time is past when society can refuse to provide community child-care services in the hope of dissuading mothers from leaving their children and going to work" (in Jensen and Thompson, 1999: 12). The Royal Commission on Equality in Employment raised the subject again in 1984: "Child care is not a luxury, it is a necessity. Unless government policy responds to this urgency, we put women, children and the economy of the future at risk. . . . policy should not be permitted to remain so greatly behind the times" (Armitage, 2003: 119). In 1982, a federally funded National Daycare Conference was held. The Katie Cooke Task Force, an outcome of the Conference, pushed for a universal daycare system over the next few years.

In 1988, the Canada Child Care Act was introduced in Parliament; it proposed an additional 200,000 subsidized child-care spaces, doubling the number of existing spaces, which accommodated only 13 per cent of children needing care. The bill was not passed by the House of Commons (Armitage, 2003). The issue became politicized, especially given the supposed desire of each federal party in Parliament to end child poverty by 2000. Therefore, in 1993, the opposition Liberals provided a detailed proposal for a national child-care program in their party manifesto, the so-called "Red Book"; but nothing came of it after they won the general election that year. The reason was simple. Daycare remained expensive—"while child care makes for good electioneering, delivering child-care is a somewhat daunting enterprise" due to its enormous expense (Krashinsky, 2001: 3). For instance, full-time employed mothers living outside of Quebec pay an annual average of $6,900 for childcare fees, which amounts to more than 20 per cent of their annual earnings, while for most families, childcare spending tends to average between 5 and 10 per cent (Cleveland et al., 2008: 15). Overall, 33 per cent of the cost of raising a child is due to childcare costs compared to 23 per cent to provide shelter to a child (Child Care Advocacy Association of Canada, 2007).

There also are not enough child-care centres in Canada. Despite the fact that mothers comprise 70 per cent of the Canadian labour force, there are only enough regulated spaces for 20 per cent of young children (Child Care Advocacy Association of Canada, 2011: 3). In its recent Better Life Index, the OECD, which ranked Canada highly in almost all indicators, singled out low childcare enrolment as a major issue, citing problems with "affordability and quality" (OECD, 2011). As the OECD report went on to emphasize, the problem became especially acute amongst sole parents, thus necessitating greater governmental investment in childcare.

By the late 1990s, talks on this matter resumed between the federal and provincial governments, culminating in a series of agreements that moved forward a national agenda for a universal child-care package. In 2003, the Multilateral Framework on Early Learning and Child Care underscored an emerging federal–provincial consensus on the necessity of such a program (CCSD, 2004: 7). However, costs remained an issue for Paul Martin's Liberal government.

Little progress had been made by the autumn of 2004 when the OECD published its study of Canada's child-care system, part of an overall review of such systems in 21 leading industrialized countries. Although the OECD lauded Canada's enhanced parental leave program, it found the country's child-care system severely underfunded with no overarching goals, the training of many child-care workers to be poor, and the problem of high staff turnover at many centres. Canadian parents were also expected to pay more for childcare than in other countries, and despite Canada having one of the highest percentages of employed mothers, the Canadian government contributed half of what other developed countries in Europe did on child-care. Less than 20 per cent of Canadian children under the age of seven had a space in a regulated centre, an extremely low figure compared to other industrialized countries such as Belgium (63 per cent), Denmark (78 per cent), France

(69 per cent), Portugal (40 per cent), and the UK (60 per cent) (OECD, 2004: 7). The OECD report concluded:

> During the 90s, growth in early childhood services slowed significantly in Canada. . . . The result is a patchwork of economic, fragmented services. . . . In the same period, other OECD countries have been progressing toward publicly managed, universal services focused on the development of young children . . . [which are] expected to play a significant role with respect to social cohesion, the alleviation of the effects of child poverty, improved child health and screening, better parenting and family engagement in education. (ibid., 6)

Among its many recommendations, the OECD suggested that Canada double its child-care spending to the average of other OECD countries and that the federal and provincial governments each pay 40 per cent of daycare costs, leaving parents responsible for the remaining 20 per cent. It was also strongly recommended that child-care workers be given better training and that child-care be integrated with kindergarten.

Many Canadians were shocked by these findings. The Child Care Advocacy Association of Canada and the Coalition of Child Care Advocates of British Columbia together recommended that the federal government increase funding for child-care from the current level of 0.25 per cent of GDP to 1 per cent (Child Care Advocacy Association of Canada, 2011: 7). For its part, the Canadian Council on Social Development argued earlier for substantially increased funding from the federal government and a commitment that a developmentally focused child-care system be implemented that achieved the principles of universality, quality, accessibility, and inclusion (CCSD, 2004: 9). Many critics of the current system have suggested that the rest of Canada should look at Quebec as a model to build a national cohesive family policy (Albanese 2006, 2007, 2011; Canadian Policy Research Networks, 2003; Krull, 2003, 2011; OECD, 2004).

Quebec's Family Policies: An Example to Follow

In this context, Quebec's family policies have been distinct from those in the rest of the country in both their evolution and their success. There are several reasons for this. Until 1997, Quebec's family policies had been geared towards promoting population growth: a pro-natal strategy of "strength in numbers" (often referred to as *"la revanche des berceaux"*— "the revenge of the cradle") as a means of overcoming Quebec's subordination to English Canada and safeguarding Québécois culture. Second, there has been more government intervention and a stronger focus on universal support for families than in the rest of Canada. In this way, Quebec has moved beyond being a "liberal" welfare society, like Canada and the United States, and is moving towards a more heavily state interventionist model—similar to those in **social democratic states** such as Scandinavian countries—but with its own distinctive characteristics. Finally, Quebec is unique in that, since 1997, it has had a comprehensive family policy directed at strengthening families, assisting parents in balancing paid work and family responsibilities, and promoting parental employability—all of which are still lacking in the rest of Canada.

Quebec's Pro-Natal Policies

In the past two decades, there have been two major strategies to Quebec's family policy—pro-natalism (1988–97) and strengthening families (1997–present). Its **pro-natal policies** were in part a reaction to the many changes that occurred to family life as a result of the province's Quiet Revolution during the premiership of Jean Lesage (1960–1966). Quebec's new nationalism, often referred to as the "Quiet Revolution" because it "quietly" but radically transformed and secularized Québécois society, generated liberal values, advanced the French language and education for both sexes, and provided an environment conducive to feminist reform (Behiels, 1986; Comeau, 1989; Thomson, 1984). Consequently, beginning in the 1960s, Quebec society witnessed historic changes to family life and to the status of women, including sharp increases in cohabitation, divorce, and births to unmarried women, as well as substantial declines in religiosity, marriages, and births (Albanese 2006, 2007, 2007a, 2009a, 2011; Baker, 1994; Baril, Lefebvre, and Merrigan, 2000; Krull, 2003, 2007, 2011, 2012; Langlois et al., 1992). The sharp decrease in births—from an average of five children per woman in 1959 to 1.37 in 1987—was particularly alarming to Quebec nationalists, who were concerned that Québécois culture would be in jeopardy if the population continued to decline (Krull, 2003; Maroney, 1992; Maximova, 2004: 3).

Advocating direct government intervention, politicians and demographers proposed a monetary incentive program to elevate fertility levels. In a population-engineering effort unprecedented in North America, the Quebec government implemented three programs of direct financial assistance in 1988: allowances for newborns that, after amendments, paid women $500 for a first birth, $1,000 for a second, and $8,000 for third and subsequent births; a family allowance for all children under 18 years; and additional allowances for children under six years. Three rules underscored these programs: universality; monetary increases according to the rank—first, second, and so on—of the child; and more money for young children.

Reactions to the policies varied (Baker, 1994; Gavreau, 1991; Hamilton, 1995; Krull, 2003; Lavigne, 1986). Non-interventionists argued that fertility decisions were individual, not governmental, responsibilities. Feminists charged that Quebec's pro-natal policies marginalized women, reducing them to objects of demographic policy (Maroney, 1992). Social interventionists supported government action, not through pro-natalist intervention but through social policies to improve female equity and assist families. Of particular importance were policies to decrease tensions between employment and family responsibilities. These critiques coincided with a growing awareness that Quebec's incentive policies were not producing expected birth increases—families with three or more children remained atypical. Importantly, policies favouring third and subsequent children were viewed increasingly as contrary to the needs of most families.

From Pro-Natalism to Pro-Family

Quebec radically transformed its family and child support programs in 1997. It created the Ministère de la Famille et de l'Enfance (Ministry of Families and Children) and gave it a budget of $500 million. The new ministry's agenda was threefold (Ministère de la Famille et de l'Enfance, 1999). The first objective was to establish a unified child allowance program for low-income families—the amount of allowances would depend on the number of dependent children under 18 years, family type (single-parent, two-parent), and income (a threshold of $15,332 for single-parent families; $21,825 for two-parent families). This allowance was meant to supplement the CCTB, which Quebec found to be insufficient for a family to survive. The second objective was to implement a maternity–parental leave insurance plan whereby parental remuneration increased during and following pregnancy. The third objective was to provide a network of government-regulated, highly subsidized ($5 per day) child-care facilities that offered a quality educational program to children from birth to kindergarten age. Parents who qualified for an income supplement program had only to pay $2 per day. By September 1997, all but the parental insurance plan had been implemented.

These three policy initiatives demonstrate the Quebec government's efforts at strengthening families and distinguish Quebec's strategy from those in the rest of Canada, the United States, and many European countries. Presently, Quebec is the only province to have universal subsidized daycare. Although the amount that parents pay increased from $5 per day to $7 per day in January 2004, the amount is negligible compared to the amounts paid in other provinces (Albanese, 2006, 2007a, 2009a; Ministère de l'Emploi, de la Solidarité sociale et de la Famille, 2005). The average monthly cost of daycare in Ontario is about $960 compared to $140–$200 in Quebec (Peacock 2012). And in this equation, the portion of cost assumed by the Quebec government is approximately 82 per cent of the overall cost (Hamilton, 2004). Parents on social assistance are not charged for the first 23.5 hours per week and, if they enroll in an employability program, they are not charged for additional hours. To facilitate child-care, employees can also take an annual maximum of 10 days away from work for family reasons.

In developing universal policy initiatives like low-cost child-care services, a range of tax credits, and full-day kindergarten for five-year-olds, Quebec can no longer be classified as a liberal welfare state (Dandurand and Kempeners, 2002; Jensen, 2002). Policy initiatives in liberal welfare states, such as the rest of Canada and the United States, favour targeting specific kinds of families, such as those with low incomes, rather than supporting all of them. Moreover, liberal welfare states are reluctant to involve themselves in the day-to-day activities of family life, including the problems involved with balancing paid work and family life. In this way, based on its child-care and family policy initiatives, Quebec is moving towards the more heavily state interventionist model—social democracy—of the Scandinavian countries (Beauvais and Dufour, 2003).

Quebec's existing family allowance is also innovative. While it targets low-income families with children under 18, the amount paid out is inversely related to the number of adults living in the house: the more adults in the household, the less received in benefits. Thus, single-parent families receive the most in benefits and tax breaks. The design decisions "reflect nothing of the 'moral panic' about lone mothers characterizing some liberal welfare states in the years of welfare reform. Nor do they reproduce the neutrality of programs that do not take into account the particular difficulties faced by lone parents" (Jensen, 2002: 310). In 2002, the province passed Bill 112, a law that committed the Quebec government to develop an anti-poverty action plan with the goal of cutting poverty rates in half by 2012. It also required the provincial government to make public a progress report every three years.

Critics charge that these new initiatives fall short of a universal, non-gender-specific program that assists all types of parenting. The family allowance program provides targeted assistance aimed almost exclusively at working low-income families rather than universal assistance. Moreover, the programs are also expensive and consequently taxes have increased—40 per cent of Quebec's program is now paid for by tax revenues (CUPE Ontario, 2008). Some critics charge that although the new policies promote the financial incentive for parents to work, they have inadvertently limited women's choices by offering more assistance to families with employed mothers than to those in which the mother stays at home (Vincent, 2000: 3). And although not overt, pronatal objectives continue to impinge on policy. Quebec's Family Minister in 2005, Michelle Courchesne, said of the proposed parental leave plan: "We feel that this sort of program will encourage . . . families to give birth, and maybe to have more children" (in Wyatt, 2005: A5). And according to Stéphane Le Bouyonnec, President of the policy commission for the Action Démocratique du Québec (ADQ), "If we have more babies, it would bring a lot more prosperity to this nation. It's a key factor for investors to invest in Quebec . . . . We have to have a nation that will be strong and survive in 20 years. . . . If we don't change our approach, we will decline as a nation" (Séguin, 2008).

Yet, despite these limitations, Quebec continues its efforts to strengthen families and increase the employability of parents. For the Ministère de la Famille et des Aînés, the successor to the Ministère de la Famille et de l'Enfance: "the family is at the heart of its priorities" (Ministère de la Famille et des Aînés, 2012). Since March 2004, Quebecers no longer pay provincial sales tax on diapers, baby bottles, and nursing items, and a new child assistance program replaced family allowances, the non-refundable tax credit for dependent children, and the tax reduction for families (Ministère de l'Emploi, de la Solidarité sociale et de la Famille, 2005; Régie des rentes du Québec, 2012a).While in the 1990s Quebec daycares were frequently overcrowded, had long waiting lists and were characterized by high teacher to child ratios (Thompson, 1999: F7; see also Government of Quebec, 1999: Sections 4.4–4.7), the situation in the province is currently quite different. In Quebec, regulated child-care spaces provided by the province—all of which are subsidized—increased from 78,388 in 1992 to 368,909 in 2008, the highest such increase in Canada (Childcare Resource and Research Unit, Canada, 2007: 15; Ministère de la Famille et des Aînés, 2011: 20). Most recently, the September 2012 provincial elections provided an opportunity for the Parti Québécois to roll out an election platform promising 15,000 additional daycare spots—a place for every child in Quebec—family leave to permit parents to care for children and other family members who are "vulnerable, disabled or elderly," plus, for families that earn $130,000 or less, a $500 tax credit for children aged 5 to 16 who enrol in sports or arts (Beaudin, 2012; Government of Quebec 2012). Forming a minority government after this election, the Parti Québécois is now in the midst of delivering on these expensive promises in a moment of fiscal constraint.

This new family assistance program, paying out more than the three previous ones together, disburses funds every three months to families with children under the age of 18. The payments are dependent upon the number of children, the family income, and the family situation. The monthly maximum for child assistance is $2,263 for the first child, $1,131 for the second and third children, and $1,696 for each additional child, with an additional $793 for single-parent families. Monthly minimum amounts are $635 for the first child with $586 for each additional child and $317 awarded to single-parent families (Régie des rentes du Québec, 2012a). In both cases, the amount paid decreases in a ratio determined by a family's net income exceeding the thresholds. In some circumstances, single-parent families can obtain an additional $700 per year; and in one special case, regardless of parental income, families qualify for a monthly supplement of $179 for each child with a disability (Régie des rentes du Québec, 2012b).

Efforts were also stepped up in 2005 to ensure the employability of parents. A work premium was introduced to encourage low-income parents to remain employed. As with the new child assistance program, the amount of the premium depends on net income and family type to an annual maximum of $2,929 per year for two-parent families and $2,272 for single-parent families (Ministère de la Famille et des Aînés, 2011:12). In 2006, Quebec withdrew from the federal parental leave program and established its own comprehensive program, which was expected to cost $1.6 billion in 2009, an increase from the 2007 rate of $1.45 billion (Ministère des Finances, 2009: 2; Dube, 2008; Krull, 2007). To date, it is the most generous and flexible parental leave program in Canada. The federal program pays new mothers 55 per cent of their insurable earnings for 15 weeks and now covers self-employed women (Government of Canada, 2011c). In contrast, the Quebec program offers new mothers, including self-employed mothers, two options: (1) 75 per cent of their insurable earnings for 15 weeks or (2) 70 per cent of insurable earnings for 18 weeks. While both programs offer new parents 35 weeks of shared leave, the Quebec program offers an additional five weeks of paid leave for just fathers. It is not surprising then that 77.6 per cent of Quebec men took paternity leave in 2010 compared to only 11.1 per cent of men in the rest of Canada (Government of Canada, 2011a). It is also telling that while child-care initiatives dominated Quebec's 2008 provincial election, little attention was given to child-care in the federal election campaign that same year, and while the Liberal Party proposed a billion-dollar child-care fund in the 2011 federal campaign, the issue was marginal (CTV News, 2011).

Quebec's family policies remain the most innovative and ambitious in Canada (Albanese, 2011; CPRN/RCPPP, 2003; Krull, 2011a, 2012; Lefebvre and Merrigan, 2003; OECD, 2004; Ross, 2006). In fact, the Canadian Policy Research Networks (CPRN/RCPPP) claims that "Quebec provides North America's only example of an integrated approach to family policy. It stands as proof that there is room in market-oriented countries for progressive public policies designed specifically for families" (2003: 2). And their policy initiatives are paying off. The universal childcare program has contributed to decreasing Quebec's child poverty by 50 per cent and children's test scores have increased. Overall, Quebec's poverty rate fell by 40 per cent, while incomes for single-parent families headed by women increased by 30 per cent (CUPE Ontario, 2008; Goar, 2009).

The rest of Canada can take some lessons from Quebec in designing effective national policy directed at strengthening families. Perhaps the strongest lesson that can be learned is the benefit of assisting *all* families to better balance employment and family responsibilities, and that families are strengthened not simply by supplementing incomes with small amounts of money but by increasing employability. For the Quebec government: "Poverty is less present in families with full-time jobs. This is why the government has chosen to fight against it not only through providing financial support to the poorest families but also in the field of employment by offering parents conditions making it easier to balance family and job responsibilities" (quoted in Jensen, 2002: 311). Quebec's progress is recognized internationally. In its otherwise unfavourable report card on child-care in Canada, the OECD praised the "extraordinary advance made by Quebec, which has launched one of the most ambitious and interesting early education and care policies in North America" (OECD, 2004: 55).

On the Horizon: New Initiatives

With a policy modelled on Quebec's subsidized daycare program, the Liberal Party led by Paul Martin promised during the 2004 federal election campaign to create 250,000 child-care spaces by 2009. On 5 October 2004, just as the OECD findings were being made public, the Martin government used the occasion of the Speech from the Throne to tell Canadians: "For a decade, all governments have understood that the most important invest-ment that can be made is in our children. . . . Parents must have real choices: children must have real opportunities to learn" (Office of the Prime Minister, 2004). The next day, Prime Minister Martin laid out his government's commitment to "a strong, Canada-wide program of early learning and care for our children, which is the single best investment we can make in their future and in ours" (ibid.).

By November 2004 the federal and provincial governments agreed on a series of principles for a national child-care program: quality, universal inclusion, accessibility, and a developmental focus (Galloway, 2004). Reaching agreement was actually not difficult, as these principles were essentially the same as those proffered consistently for 35 years: from the proposals of the 1970 Royal Commission on the Status of Women, to those of advocacy groups and the Quebec government in the 1980s and after, to the Liberal "Red Book". The problem lay in the details. Even before the principles were agreed, the Quebec government made public its position that it wanted "the right to opt out of any national daycare program with full compensation" since it already had an established child-care system and it only needed additional federal funds to make its own improvements (Séguin and Galloway, 2004).

In their 2005 budget, the federal Liberal government allocated $5 billion over five years to develop a national system of early learning and child-care, adding the proviso that "federal support will need to be ongoing beyond these initial years" (Galloway, 2005b). But desirous of wanting to get a country-wide system into place, the federal government declared that the "provinces will have access to $700 million [the first year's disbursement] in child-care funds to spend virtually as they please."

By the fall of 2005, all 10 provinces finally entered into agreement with the federal government—although the conditions for receiving federal funding varied from province to province. However, the national child-care program re-emerged as a divisive yet central political issue during the federal election campaign of December 2005–January 2006. Paul Martin again stressed the importance of a national system of regulated daycare, promising to more than double his government's $5 billion commitment if the Liberals remained in power. Stephen Harper and the Conservative Party, on the other hand, promoted a policy of paying parents $1,200 annually per preschool child, arguing that this would enable parents the freedom of choosing their own child-care options. Interestingly, men and women were divided over these competing visions of child-care. According to a survey by the Strategic Council, women tended to favour the Liberal policy of a national child-care program whereas men typically preferred the Conservative proposal for parents receiving federal funds directly (Laghi, 2005: A4).

Having won the 2006, 2008, and 2011 elections, the Conservative Party has upheld its family allowance program, the Universal Child Care Benefit, which pays $1,200 annually per preschool child (Canada Revenue Agency, 2012). From its inception, the policy has been heavily criticized. Early critics view it as a step backwards, comparing it to that of Mackenzie King's 1945 Family Allowance (*Globe and Mail*, 2005). The Child Care Advocacy Association of Canada (CCAAC) "continues to call for public policy development and public invest-ment in a quality, inclusive, publicly funded, non-profit early childhood education and care (ECEC) system. This is the right thing to do for children, families and communities, and a powerful booster for the Canadian economy . . . child care in Canada is in a state of crisis. It is a fragmented patchwork that demonstrates the failure of a market-based approach to the development of child care services" (Child Care Canada, 2012).

The Caledon Institute, a think tank that focuses on Canadian child-care, has also chas-tised the Conservatives for its child-care allowance policy, particularly because it eliminated the young-child supplement of the Canada Child Tax Benefit. In 2006, Ken Battle, the Institute's president, argued that the elimination of the young-child supplement, which is approximately $249 annually, "makes the inequality gap between the child-care allow-ance benefits for low- and modest-income families and high-income families all the wider, because the low-income families are losing that $249 annually whereas higher-income families never got it" (Galloway, 2006: A1). Six years later, Caledon made the same criticism: "The federal government touted its new Universal Child Care Benefit (UCCB) as a child care initiative, but such a modest cash benefit cannot provide a substitute for the availability of quality child care. They also revived the non-refundable child tax credit, which excludes poor families. These two programs have needlessly complicated federal child benefits, made them less effective, and confused many parents" (Maytree Conversations, 2012).

On 20 September 2011, the Harper government tabled the "Helping Families in Need Act" (Press Release, 2012). In essence, it will modify the existing Employment Insurance Act [EI] to give new foster parents speedier parental benefits; allow the self-employed to receive EI maternity, parental, sickness, and compassionate care benefits; improve EI parental benefits for military families; extend compassionate care benefits for families of the "gravely ill"; and adjust in an as-yet-undetermined way both the CCTB and UCCB. Additionally, a change to the Canada Labour Code will allow unpaid parental leave in the cases of both "critically ill" children and where children die or disappear as a result of a criminal act. Yet, while certainly an advance, this bill primarily constitutes a refinement of fiscal policy—tinkering with EI legislation—rather than formulating any kind of all-inclusive social policy. Despite her obvious partisanship, a member of the Opposition has pointed out correctly: "This bill is certainly a step in the right direction, but we must not lose sight of the forest for the trees. Since the Conservatives came to power, they have attacked unemployed people on several fronts. The effect of the most recent employment insurance reform they put through will be to further limit access to this scheme—one to which, we must remember, the government does not contribute" (Openparliament.ca, 2012). This bill's purpose is limited, helping important, but select groups: foster parents, the self-employed, military families, and families with children who are either severely ill or have suffered criminal acts. Despite its name, however, which might be better expressed as the "Helping Some Families Act," this legislation runs parallel to but is not integrated with family policy. It came into effect on 14 December 2012. As Philip Toone, NDP MP for Gaspésie–Îles-de-la-Madeleine (Québec) said just before its passage, "This will make it possible for parents to extend their parental leave by the number of sick days taken during that period. The same goes for time spent serving in the Canadian Forces Reserves. This and many other aspects of the bill are quite worthwhile" (Openparliament.ca, 2012a).

Budgetary concerns have left the other provinces eyeing austerity measures, with the likely result that Quebec will continue to outpace its provincial peers in the realm of family policy for the foreseeable future. Stasis in the making of family policy by federal and provincial governments comes just as action is needed to address the rapid changes that continue to shape the country's bedrock social institution. As the 2011 Census showed, Canadian families are now as diverse as they have ever been. In turn, such diversity necessitates active policy-making by government. As one columnist remarked, the 2011 census data suggests "there is room now for new policy specifically designed to address the needs of non-conventional families, and sold as such" (Den Tandt, 2012). "The new Canada," another writer has noted, "is a land of immigrants, where multiple families and generations are more likely to mingle beneath the same roof. Politicians and business leaders should take note" (Ibbitson, 2012). Yet the hurdles that must be overcome for those seeking a proactive and progressive approach to family policy in Canada are significant.

Conclusion

Effective family policies must reflect modern Canada, whose policies have not responded to dramatic changes within families: the **individual responsibility family model** needs abandoning (Eichler, 1997). It views fathers and mothers as equally responsible for family economic well-being and providing care to family members. State responsibilities arise only when husbands/fathers or wives/mothers are absent or cannot fulfil their responsibilities.

More efficient is the **social responsibility model**: minimizing gender stratification without privileging legal marriage over other relationships. Parents bear responsibility for their children's economic well-being whether residing with them or not. With residency not determining responsibility, caring for children is also society's obligation. Accordingly, the state would not distinguish between same-sex and heterosexual couples/parents entitled to the same state benefits.

Comprehensive child-care would integrate family and market employment. Policy-makers often view the home and work place as distinct spheres in "conflict" or in need of "balance" (Krull and Sempruch, 2011a). In the male breadwinner model, households and paid work are incompatible. Women labour at home out of love and concern for their families. Market work, conversely, is "real" work, its value determined by wages. Viewing family and work as irreconcilable creates illusions about careful balance: family pressures not interfering with employment and employment pressures not diminishing family life. Policies helping better balance family and work would reproduce and reinforce the normative heterosexual **"gender contract"**—male breadwinner/female caregiver.

Canada needs to emulate the family-centred child-care policies of Quebec and Scandinavian countries that assume parents' right to employment while caring for their families despite gender, class, sexuality, or marital status. They integrate family and employment responsibilities. Fathers' involvement in childcare is central, breaking hegemonic assumptions about household and childcare work as peripheral to market work. Moreover, the heart of these policies assumes a state integral in supporting all family forms and promoting gender equity.

The essential reason for minimal state involvement in overall family policies resides in Canada being a federal liberal welfare state; different governments have different roles in policy-making. Of course, governments have not abdicated responsibility for families. Paid maternity leave and child and family benefits, plus the plan "A Canada Fit for Children," shows state willingness to help. But for every advance, there are failures—the 2005 Liberal national child-care program is exemplary.

Instead of a comprehensive national policy, Canada possesses piecemeal family programs and policies; and the state has lagged in meeting the socio-economic changes affecting families. Concerning child-care, the rest of Canada has an opportunity to employ Quebec's effective example. Doing so will take more than public money; inter-governmental co-operation and policy require a realistic understanding of contemporary Canadian families. The state and Canadians who give it legitimacy face an immense challenge.

STUDY QUESTIONS

1. What challenges does Canada face in developing a cohesive national family policy?
2. What are the strengths and weaknesses of both targeted and universal family policies?
3. Why have market work and household work been socially construed as distinct spheres? What consequences does this bifurcation have for policy? For gender equity?
4. Discuss why a social responsibility model of the family should improve family policies.
5. Do you think that child poverty can be eradicated by the construction and funding of a comprehensive national childcare policy? Explain.
6. In what ways do Canada's current family policies privilege and reinforce the hegemonic nuclear family and traditional gender roles?

Further Readings

Albanese, Patrizia. 2009. *Child Poverty in Canada*. Toronto: Oxford University Press. Focusing on child poverty in Canada, especially since 1989, Patrizia Albanese discusses why children, especially certain children, are vulnerable. She also examines the consequences of child poverty and assesses why Canada has done so poorly in comparison to other countries. She also discusses possible means to obviate child poverty.

Baker, Maureen. 2006. *Restructuring Family Policies: Convergences and Divergences*. Toronto: University of Toronto Press. Adopting a feminist political economy approach and drawing on national and international research, Maureen Baker demonstrates that nation states with the best outcomes for families offer a variety of social supports. She provides a very extensive treatment of the literature on families.

Blake, Raymond. 2008. *From Rights to Needs: A History of Family Allowances in Canada, 1929–92*. Vancouver, BC: UBC Press. Raymond Blake focuses on the historical–political question of how policies are made while examining the history of family allowances in Canada from their debut in the House of Commons in 1929 to their demise under the Mulroney Government in 1992.

Doucet, Andrea. 2006. *Do Men Mother?: Fathering, Care and Domestic Responsibility*. Toronto: University of Toronto Press. Based on extensive interviews with over 100 fathers, Andrea Doucet demonstrates how men are transforming traditional parenting models. The book focuses on the following key questions: What leads fathers to trade earning for caring? How do fathers navigate through the "maternal worlds" of mothers and infants? Are men mothering or are they redefining fatherhood?

Eichler, Margrit. 1997. *Family Shifts: Families, Policies and Gender Equality*. Toronto: Oxford University Press. This is a classic source to see how families and family policy have changed over the past century in Canada. Eichler offers policy-makers a more realistic and improved family model from which to build future family policies.

Gambles, Richenda, Suzan Lewis, and Rhona Rapoport. 2006. *The Myth of Work–Life Balance: The Challenge of Our Time for Men, Women and Societies*. New York: Wiley. These authors challenge the idea that it is the individual's responsibility to "balance" paid work with other parts of life. Drawing research from seven diverse countries—India, Japan, the Netherlands, Norway, South Africa, the UK, and the US—this book demonstrates that "work–life balance" cannot be achieved through quick fixes and suggests ways that work and workplace need to be reorganized to that people can integrate family life with their paid work.

Gilbert, Neil. 2008. *A Mother's Work: How Feminism, the Market, and Policy Shape Family Life*. New Haven, CT: Yale University Press. Neil Gilbert challenges the conventional view on how to balance motherhood and employment, and examines at the national and international levels how the choices women make are influenced by the culture of capitalism, feminist expectations, and the social policies of the welfare state.

Krull, Catherine, and Justyna Sempruch. 2011. *A Life in Balance? Reopening the Family-Work Debate*. Vancouver, BC: UBC Press. This book challenges the notion—often offered in support of neo-liberal agendas—that paid work (employment) and unpaid work (caregiving and housework) are separate and competing spheres, rather than overlapping aspects of a single existence. The premise of the book is that alternative approaches to integrating work and family have to be taken into account if we hope to build truly equitable family and childcare policies. Possible means of achieving this are discussed.

Websites

www.vifamily.ca/about/about.html

The Vanier Institute of the Family's website offers a range of research publications, public presentations, media interviews, and speeches on an array of issues that affect families.

www.irpp.org/indexe.htm

The Institute for Research on Public Policy, an "independent, non-partisan think-tank," has as its mission the advancement of new ideas to "help Canadians make more effective policy choices." Its website contains numerous publications that assess existing family policies while offering new policy initiatives for future policy-makers to consider.

www.buildchildcare.ca/

Code Blue is a Canada-wide campaign to build a real pan-Canadian child-care system. The campaign brings together national, provincial, and territorial child-care organizations, labour, women's, and social justice groups along with Canadians from all walks of life. The website contains published reports, news articles, and research papers on child-care.

www.oecd.org/topic/0,2686,en_2649_33933_1_1_1_1_37419,00.html

The Organisation for Economic Co-operation and Development's social policy website offers statistics, publications, and assessments on social and family policies for each of the OECD countries. Their purpose is to identify policies that assist families in reconciling work and family life.

www.cprn.org/en/index.cfm

The Canadian Policy Research Network is one of Canada's leading think tanks. Its website offers access to much of its research on a wide array of policy issues that impact families in Canada, Europe, and developing countries.

Note

1. Foster children are defined by Statistics Canada as "'other relatives' in an economic family, that is, a group of two or more persons who live in the same dwelling and are related to each other by blood, marriage, common-law, adoption or foster relationship" (Statistics Canada, 2012a: 17).

16

The Past of the Future and the Future of the Family

MARGRIT EICHLER

LEARNING OBJECTIVES

- To learn about the various bases on which predictions can be made
- To appreciate the inherent difficulties in making predictions
- To place the family into a societal context
- To appreciate the extent of environmental changes that will confront families in the future
- To consider the implications of such changes for families

Introduction

Making predictions is a risky business—they may come back to haunt one. My first reaction was dismay when I was invited to contribute a chapter to this book on the future of the family—on what basis could I possibly make any sensible predictions? Then a colleague suggested that I look at past predictions.[1] This has turned what might have been a very difficult and ultimately self-defeating undertaking into an instructive and enjoyable exercise.

I decided to restrict my review of old predictions to those published at the latest in 1975, meaning that enough time has passed to judge whether the predictions made came true or not.

Family sociology within Canada is a relatively young subdiscipline. The first monograph on the family in Canada was written by Frederick Elkin and published in 1964 (Elkin, 1964). In her overview of the development of family studies in Canada, Nett identifies the 1970s and 1980s as the "period of Canadianization and policy concerns" (Nett, 1988: 9), but Canadian publishing about families really only took off in the 1980s. My search for older sources therefore netted primarily American and some British authors. The oldest source I found is from 1930.

The search for old predictions turned up some very surprising results. Most prominently, the time at which a prediction was made bore no relation to its accuracy. Some older predictions are much more accurate than some that were made significantly later. This being the case, I discarded the notion of ordering the predictions in terms of the time at which they were formulated.

It did not seem advantageous to group predictions in terms of their accuracy or inaccuracy, since I found some of both on virtually every theme. I finally decided to group predictions by topic to avoid repetition and allow for a comparison between successful, unsuccessful, and partially successful predictions under every heading.

This chapter is therefore organized in three parts. First, I examine past predictions about the future of the family, then I consider the basis on which such predictions are made and attempt to determine which bases seem to yield more solid predictions, and third, I engage—with hesitation and much trepidation—in the risky business of making some predictions myself.

Past Predictions about the Family

The observations of Baber (1953) on marriage, from over half a century ago, still seem relevant today:

> There are three types of opinion on marriage: (1) the opinion held by those who consider monogamic, indissoluble [heterosexual] marriage the only divinely sanctioned form and therefore the only one that can ever be tolerated; (2) the opinion held by those few sophisticates at the other extreme that not only is the usefulness of marriage past but also it is now doing a genuine disservice to the family and should be immediately abolished; (3) the opinion held by the vast number of persons in between these extremes that marriage performs valuable service in regularizing sex relations and stabilizing the primary group in which children are reared and that it should be not indissoluble but subject to correction and improvement. The latter are not willing to say that monogamy must always prevail, but only that at present it fits into our total culture pattern better than any other form. It is conceivable that a condition might arise that would call for some other form of marriage (Baber, 1953: 681–2).

Correspondingly, we have a slew of predictions, from sociologists committed to Baber's second opinion concerning marriage, that the family is dead or dying, and opposing views by those who hold to one of the other opinions.

The Future of the Family/Marriage as an Institution

Predictions that the family is about to disintegrate and disappear seem as old as the family itself. Between 1930 and 1970, there was a lot of concern with the "disintegration of the family." Paul wrote in 1930 in Great Britain that "the disintegration of the family is going on, and something will have to take its place" (Paul, 1930: 38). In the United States, Sorokin thought in 1941 that the family had "passed from mere instability into the process of actual disintegration" (cited after Baber, 1953: 678). In 1947, Zimmerman suggested that "the family system will continue headlong its present trend toward nihilism" (Zimmerman, 1947: 808).

In 1949[2] and again in 1959, Anshen commented that in the US "the present collapse of marriage and the family is a perverted triumph of a profaned passion which in truth now largely consists in a reversion to abduction and rape" (Anshen, 1959: 512). This is a particularly interesting comment, since the 1950s are often held up as the golden age of the family in North America.

This negative view of the future of the family could easily be carried forward into modern times. Nimkoff replies to the authors who argue that the family is a dying institution that the same arguments used to demonstrate the collapse of the family can be used to support precisely the opposite. "The issue may be stated thus: Does the individual exist for the family, or does the family exist for the individual?" He suggests that "[t]he totalitarian family organization is as real as the totalitarian state" (Nimkoff, 1947: 603). In his time, family subservience had given way to individualization—which he by and large saw as a positive development, but which authors who subscribe to marriage as a monolithic, indissoluble institution interpret in wholly negative terms.

By the same token, others have argued that marriage and the family are ongoing concerns that have adapted to very different circumstances for a very long period of time and that they would continue to do so. Linton, an American anthropologist, after reflecting on this issue, concluded simply: "The ancient trinity of father, mother, and child has survived more vicissitudes than any other human relationship. It is the bedrock underlying all other family structures" (Linton, 1959: 52). He would probably not insist that the father has to be the biological father of the child.

Cavan concludes her book as follows:

> The exact form of family that will emerge cannot be fully predicted, but present research indicates the need for a family that is flexible, with leeway for individual development; adjustable to external social conditions, keyed to mobility and social change; interdependent with other institutions; and ready to accept important though limited functions, such as meeting personal and sexual needs, giving emotional security, and rearing children for life in an industrialized, urban society. (Cavan, 1963: 533)

Ten years later, Bernard asked rhetorically "does marriage *have* a future?" and answered with an unequivocal "yes," although both its name and form might change. She adds, "I do not see the traditional form of marriage retaining its monopolistic sway. I see, rather, a future of marital options" (Bernard, 1972: 301–2)—which is, of course, what we find today in Canada: legal and common-law marriages, dual-earner couples, traditional breadwinner couples, and some non-traditional breadwinner couples in which the wife is the breadwinner and the husband the stay-at-home parent and spouse, as well as same-sex couples with and without children.

Communal Family Structures/Group Marriages

The authors cited above who are predicting the disappearance of the monogamous, nuclear family see this as a negative, terrible event, threatening the very existence of civilization. In contrast, by the late 1960s and early 1970s a considerable number of intellectuals and authors believed that this form of the family was basically passé and that alternative structures were needed. This was the time of the hippie movement; significant numbers of communes had sprung up in its wake, and various authors had created attractive fictional accounts of communal families (e.g., Skinner, 1948). The women's movement had become a major social force, voicing clear dissatisfaction with the **patriarchal** nuclear **family**: "our American family model, with its emphasis on 'success' on the one hand and 'domesticity' on the other, appears to be actually a model for marital misery" (Howe, 1972: 13). The **zero population movement** had been spawned by the environmental movement, and there were conflicting views on fertility (see below).

This put the family high on the political agenda. A number of symposia and conferences looked at the future of or alternatives to the family and resulted in publications (e.g., Farson et al., 1969; Elliott, 1970; Barbeau, 1971; College of Home Economics, 1972; Goode, 1972; Otto, 1972). In Canada, the report of the **Royal Commission on the Status of Women** was released in 1970. Questioning the role of women inevitably led to a discussion about the future of the family, since until that time women had been largely relegated to and identified with the family.

Monogamous marriage, and the family based on it, was seen as "grim, lifeless, boring, depressing, disillusioning—a potential context for murder, suicide, mental human decay" (Greenwald, 1970: 63). Contemporary marriage was described as "a wretched institution" that turns beautiful romances into a bitter contract and a relationship that "becomes constricting, corrosive, grinding and destructive" (Marvyn Cadwaller, cited in Otto, 1970: 3). In short, the consequences of "continuing family structures as they exist now" are "fearful" (Stoller, 1970: 145).

Having established that it was dangerous to continue to support the nuclear family of their day, a considerable number of authors proposed and some predicted some form of communal or tribal family, or various forms of group marriages (Downing, 1970; Orleans and Wolfson, 1970; Gerson, 1972; Goode, 1972; Hochschild, 1972; Kanter, 1972; Kay, 1972; Platt, 1972; Schulz, 1972).

An interesting feature of these discussions is that they focus primarily on the adults and ignore the raising of the children—certainly one of the reasons why this has not become a significant subform of the family. An exception to this is Levett, who develops a model where every boy has a third parent, "a male figure educated, trained, and equipped to serve the socializing needs of male children" (Levett, 1970: 162). Strangely enough, he does not deal with the socializing needs of female children, who may not have a male figure in their lives at all if they live in female-headed, single-parent families.

Thamm saw the move towards a communal family as the outcome of a linear development: stage 1 was characterized by the consanguine family; stage 2 by the conjugal family, which at his time (1975) was in the process of dissolving; thus leading to stage 3, the communal family, which will have wonderful consequences: "The individual and the collectivity will be merged. Conflict and competition will yield to relations of cooperation, and jealous possessiveness will evolve into a loving concern" (Thamm, 1975: 128–9).

A particular version of some form of communal living was the suggestion of **polygyny** for people over the age of 60. Kassel argued that "the need for polygyny is obvious: there just are not enough men. Therefore, any man over age sixty could marry two, three, four, or five women over sixty" (Kassel, 1970: 138). He listed the benefits of such an arrangement, which included a better diet, better living conditions, help in illness, help with housework, sex, better grooming: "when there is a choice between uninterested, dowdy, foul smelling hags [i.e., widows who did not find a man to remarry], and alert, interested, smartly dressed ladies [the lucky co-wives], the selection is obvious" (ibid., 141).

Since the women in this scenario continue to do all the cooking and other housework, it is not clear why they need a man to achieve all these benefits—they could simply live together. The only activity which is reserved for the man is sex, and here again the women might be content with each other.

By contrast, Rosenberg concludes that while polygyny would make sense, given the "ever growing surfeit of old widows" (Rosenberg, 1970: 181), this is unlikely to actually happen due to the existence of a counter-ideology—the ideology of the nuclear family.

Gender Roles

One of the most important axes of discussion turns around gender roles,[3] specifically, women's roles. Among the more spectacularly wrong predictions we can count those of Parsons and Bales, who argue that the patriarchal family[4] is a *sine qua non* for the welfare of the United States. This includes very specifically that women not be active in the labour force, which, on the one hand, accomplishes the maintenance of the household and child care and, on the other, "shields spouses from competition with each other in the occupational sphere, which, along with attractiveness to women, is above all the most important single focus of feelings of self-respect on the part of American men" (Parsons and Bales, 1955: 264–5).

Given that the labour force participation of women is almost equal to that of men today and that the US and Canada have continued to exist and even flourish, clearly the patriarchal breadwinner family is not necessary to the continued survival of these societies. The fact that Parsons and Bales talk only about the self-respect of men, ignoring what women might desire, lies obviously at the root of some of their misperceptions.

At around the same time, Cavan (1963: 515) suggested that the major contribution of the feminist movement, which "has spent its force," has been the transition from the patriarchal family to "the present-day ideal of the partnership family in which husband and wife share equally in rights and responsibilities." It was, of course, precisely the *failure* of the family to live up to this ideal that generated some of the harshest critiques of the second-wave feminist movement—which at that point was readying itself to re-emerge.

Pollak, reflecting on the consequences of **women's lib**, suggested that "partly due to genetic endowment, partly due to shifts in employment policies, women will prove to be frequently more successful in the role of earner than their husbands. The consequence will be power shifts. Women will gain power, men will lose power, and where power is lost, functions will have to be redefined. Unavoidably under such conditions, fathers will be called upon to assume a greater share in child rearing than in the past" (Pollak, 1972: 71).

This has been borne out to a modest degree. While fathers *do* participate more in rearing their children, the lioness' share is still carried by mothers (South and Spitze, 1994; Haddad, 1996; Shelton and John, 1996; John and Shelton, 1997; Sanchez and Thomson, 1997; Hossain, 2001; des Rivières-Pigeon et al., 2002; Kitterod, 2002).

Winch predicted that husbands would fail to participate more in housework as their wives become more active in the labour force. However, he then also predicted that we would therefore "presently be returning toward a norm that will give increasing emphasis to the differences between the sexes" (Winch, 1970: 14) and that we would hence presumably return to the traditional division of labour—something that has not happened.

In spite of the fact that most men are not at this point doing their fair share of housework, the *norms* have changed. Recently, 99 per cent of respondents of a national Canadian sample agreed with the statement that "Parents need to take equal responsibility for raising children" and 94 per cent agreed that "Couples should share household duties equally" (Bibby, 2005: 6). This suggests that we will continue to move gradually towards a more even balance with respect to housework and care work.

This bears out what Eichler noted in 1975: "there is no equalitarian family in existence in Canada at the present time. . . . It is clear that equality in the family can come neither quickly nor easily, nor in isolation from far-reaching changes in the legal, economic, educational and political systems" (Eichler, 1975: 230). While some of the needed changes have occurred, others are still missing (for instance, a high quality, affordable national daycare system).

Sexuality

Many authors—besides those who argue for alternative family forms—have reflected on the nature of sexual relations within and outside of marriage, although this is almost uniformly restricted to heterosexual relations. Except for one side comment (Schulz, 1972: 420), no one predicted that we would have same-sex marriages in Canada or North America by now. Nonetheless, numerous authors predicted the loosening of restrictions on non-marital sex. Ogburn and Nimkoff predicted that due to technological innovations sexuality would be separated from procreation, and that "the sex act may occur for pleasure rather than for procreation" (Ogburn and Nimkoff, 1955: 308). This, of course, would require "a disappearance of moral and legal sanctions against extra-marital sex" (Winch, 1970: 12). This has certainly happened.

Davids predicted that "the law will accept abortion, all forms of birth control will be seen as medical problems, free of any statutory limitation" (Davids, 1971: 190–1), both of which have happened in Canada.

Divorce and Cohabitation as Alternatives to Permanent Monogamous Marriages

In a 1967 journal article on the future of the family, Edwards argued that:

> Economic overabundance . . . in the long run will have a repressive effect on the rate of marriage. The recognition of alternatives to wedlock, as that concerning alternatives to premarital chastity, will not occasion sudden behavioral consequences. But change is overdue. When women, already imbued with the economic ethos, fully

realize their equality in this sphere, much of the *raison d'etre* of marriage will no longer be present. . . . Women will no longer find economic dependence a virtue and worthy by-product of marriage, for, given the opportunity, they will succeed for themselves as ably as any male might. (Edwards, 1967: 510)

Hobbs notes that *"we are in the process of abandoning the permanence of marriage, while maintaining* (in law and in principle, even if less in reality than ever before) *its sexual exclusiveness"* (Hobbs, 1970: 37, emphasis in original). He then suggests that we should turn this around.

Winch (1970: 15) also predicts a decrease in marriage (which has happened) as well as in birth rates (which has also taken place), as do the Birds: "with fewer mutual responsibilities, these marriages, we can expect, will have less permanence as their goals and interests change, so will their choice of mates" (Bird and Bird, 1971: 6). However, they assume that cohabitation will increase because there will be more free time—in fact the amount of time people with jobs in North America spend on their paid work has increased, not decreased.

Cohabitation has increased, as predicted by a number of people, including the Canadian sociologist Whitehurst who dealt with the topic by calling it "Living Together Unmarried" (LTU). He suggested that LTU "will come to be seen as a kind of period like engagement is today, a trial period in which it becomes (legally or informally) possible to try out one or two live-in situations before making a commitment to long-term marriage" (Whitehurst, 1975: 441). In fact, cohabitation in Canada today exists in three forms: as a premarital arrangement, as Whitehurst suggested, as a permanent alternative to legal marriage, and as a type of post-divorce union. It is particularly prevalent in Quebec and in the northern territories, which have a high proportion of Aboriginal people (Wu, 2000: 53). As can be seen in Table 16.1, in 2006, 16 per cent of all families consisted of common-law couples with or without children.

Table 16.1 **Number of Families in Canada, by Type, Canada 2006**

	Number	%
Total families	8,896,840[1]	100
married couples with children[2] at home	3,443,775	39
married couples without children at home	2,662,135	30
common-law couples with children at home	618,180	7
common-law couples without children at home	758,715	9
lone-parent families	1,414,060	16

1 Refers to the classification of census families into married couples (with or without children of either or both spouses), common-law couples (with or without children of either or both partners), and lone-parent families by sex of parent. A couple may be of opposite or same sex. Children in a census family include grandchildren living with their grandparent(s) but with no parents present.

2 Children refers to never-married children of all ages.

SOURCE: Adapted from Statistics Canada, 2006, *2006 Census of Population*, Statistics Canada catalogue no. 97-553-XCB2006007.

Fertility and Fertility Control

The issues around fertility are particularly interesting. Writing at almost the same time, some authors fear that we are moving towards extinction because women do not have enough babies, while others are concerned about overpopulation and fear that women have too many children. Zimmerman writes about the "sit-down strike on having and rearing children" (Zimmerman, 1947: 793) due to a drop in the birth rate. This, he argues, is particularly problematic because "the sources of immigration (what the Romans called the 'good barbarians')" are now exhausted. "Between 1820 and 1920, the United States imported forty million immigrants from Europe. These are now no longer available." When the surplus population of the Mexicans and French Canadians are exhausted, "almost the only fertile peoples of the western world now available to us—we too will begin the grand finale of the crisis" (ibid.). People from non-Western countries he did apparently not see as a viable source for immigration. Nimkoff went even further in his projections. He worried about "the problem of the mainte-nance of the population"—which could, he feared, lead to the extinction of the human race if it declines over a sufficiently long period of time (Nimkoff, 1947: 604).

For more on pathways to parenthood, see "Deciding to Parent" in Chapter 4, pp. 68–71.

In contradistinction to those who worried about humanity dying out because of the lack of children, others worried about overpopulation. Goode, for instance, noted that the population in the US was still increasing while they were using proportion-ately much more of the world's resources than anyone else. Since most of the children were wanted, he saw no easy solution to this problem, except for one he judged destruc-tive but helpful in the population crisis: "to focus our lives away from the family itself. Totally free abortion, late marriage, all women working, no tax benefits for children, and so on" (Goode, 1972: 123).

Motivated by a similar fear of overpopulation, the Canadian sociologist Davids suggested:

> There will be public control of reproduction—less than 1/3 of marriages will produce children, would-be parents will be strictly screened and rigorously trained in a large number of subject areas, with examinations and a license for parenthood at the end. The age difference between husbands and wives will disappear, childbirth will be delayed into the middle and late thirties. (Davids, 1971: 190–1)

Davids was not alone in proposing/predicting a regulatory approach to population control. Paul E. Ehrlich, Garrett Harding, and Kenneth E. Boulding also put forward this proposition (Blake, 1972: 59), in line with the zero population movement. He was, how-ever, accurate in predicting the postponement of childbirth into the 30s, though certainly not under the conditions he proposed. "Nearly one-half of the women who gave birth in Canada in 2003 were age 30 or older" (Statistics Canada, 2005). Canada's fertility rate has been below replacement (which is calculated as 2.1 children per women) since the early 1970s, (Health Canada, 2008) but Canada's population continues to grow because of immigration. However, worldwide, we are now facing a crisis because of the rapidly increasing human population.

The increase in the global human population and the overconsumption in rich countries, such as Canada, are two of the driving factors in generating environmental problems.

New Reproductive and Genetic Technologies

Ogburn and Nimkoff anticipated in the mid-1950s much of what actually happened with respect to new **reproductive and genetic technologies** in the 1980s and later. On the basis of scrutinizing animal experiments, they predicted the widespread use of birth control pills, increased artificial insemination, in vitro fertilization, use of donor eggs, sex selection of fetuses, Viagra and its female equivalent, hormone replacement therapy, longer life expectancies.[5] Their view is a rare exception compared to that of others, the vast majority of whom ignored evidence pointing in these directions.

On the basis of these predictions, they suggest "when the procreational function is modified by biological research, the effect will be considered revolutionary" (Ogburn and Nimkoff, 1955: 307). Among other things, they argued that the status of women within the family would rise, for one, because women would no longer be blamed for "barrenness," for the other since the various factors would likely result in a decrease of the birth rate, which, in turn, would lead to encouraging child-bearing (fostered by nationalistic–militaristic elements) and hence to an appreciation of motherhood. The latter part, of course, did not materialize—most likely due to the fact that immigration levels have continued to be high in the US (and Canada, as well). They also predicted a refocus on eugenics, which has certainly occurred in the guise of prenatal and pre-implantation diagnoses, although they did not foresee the plotting of the genome and hence assumed that the "hereditary endowment" of an individual would not be easy to establish.

Population (billions)

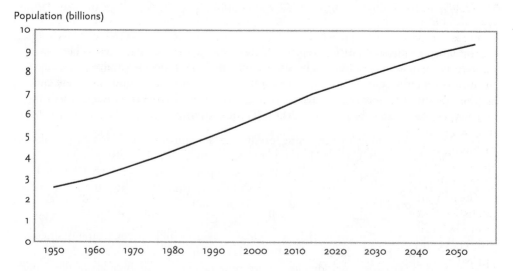

Figure 16.1 **World Population, 1950–2050**

SOURCE: US Census Bureau, International Data Base, July 2007 version.

Unanticipated Trends

Overall, then, there have been a number of spectacular misprognoses as well as some surprisingly accurate predictions. In addition, some trends have taken place that no one predicted. Among these is the return of young people to living with their parents for longer periods of time. In 1981, 27.5 per cent of persons aged 20–29 lived with their parents in Canada (Beaujot, 2000: 15); by 2006 the figure had risen to 42.3 per cent—a tremendous increase in a rather short time (Statistics Canada, 2012e). Even more dramatically, if homosexual relations were dealt with at all, it was under the heading of sexual deviance. No one anticipated same-sex marriages. The 2011 census counted 64,575 same-sex couple families, up from 45,350 in 2006 (Statistics Canada, 2012a). While this constitutes a very small percentage of all Canadian couples, it nevertheless represents a stunning change from the way homosexuality was treated just a few decades ago. It also likely underrepresents the actual number of such couples, since it is highly probable that not all of them declared themselves. Further, with the exception of Ogburn and Nimkoff, sociologists did not foresee the emergence of the new reproductive and genetic technologies and the moral, legal, and social dilemmas they would generate (Basen et al., 1993). No one assumed that people would spend more time working in their paid jobs—if the issue of leisure was considered, the general assumption was that there would be a need to educate people to deal with their ample free time.

The Various Bases for Making Predictions about the Family

In 1964, Reuben Hill identified four methods to predict the future:

1. extrapolation from trends into the future;
2. projection from generational changes;
3. the impact of inventions; and
4. the family specialists' future family.

To this we can add Goode's criterion:

5. identifying societal changes and reflecting on their importance for the family (Goode, 1972).

All of the authors I examined used one or more of these methods to come up with their predictions.

1. Extrapolation from trends into the future. Looking at each of these methods, Hill, along with other authors, realized that extrapolation can only go so far. He judged this "an exciting but dangerous method" (Hill, 1964: 21) because some trends are short-term or not linear, and because assumptions about the social and economic circumstances would need to be crystal clear since predictions were based on them.

2. Projection from generational changes. Hill refers to this method as carrying the same hazards but worth attention. It involves studying three generations of the same family, determining consistent differences that persist through the three generations, and projecting on the basis of trends observed in the youngest married-child generation. In another context, Goode (1972: 125–6) makes a comment that is pertinent to this method of prediction.

Parent–youth conflicts, he suggests, have probably always existed, but parents at least used to know what a child is like at that age because they, too, were once that age. He goes on to note that "when the whole era changes, that similarity no longer exists" (ibid., 125).

The rate of technological and other change has accelerated enormously over the past few decades. Young children today grow up in a world that is in important ways very different from the one their parents and certainly their grandparents grew up in. The Internet shapes their world view; photos on electronic cameras are instantaneous. Most teenagers have cell-phones and are on Facebook, and social media have changed interaction patterns. Children grow up playing video games, surfing the internet, and watching TV and DVDs, and they engage in less physical exercise than a generation earlier, which contributes to higher rates of obesity.

Canadian high school students are growing used to electronic monitors and uniformed police officers in their schools, and youth and parents fear stabbings and murders as well as drug dealers in high schools. Warfare in Afghanistan, Iraq, in various parts of Africa, and in the Middle East is an almost daily fare; millions of people are starving, and the world is currently experiencing its most serious economic crisis since the great depression. Even before that, there have been food riots in a number of countries. Since 9/11, we have grown used to an abrogation of human rights in the name of fighting terrorism. Never in the history of humanity has the gap between the haves and the have-nots been as great as today. In North America, rampant consumerism has to a large degree displaced the values formerly preached by organized religion.

This shrunken and fragile world is qualitatively different from the world even three decades ago. On this basis, it may be very perilous to assume that children today experience the world as similar to the one their parents experienced when they were their age.

Mothers are predominantly in the paid labour force. In Canada, as in the world at large, child poverty is a fact of life. In 2009, 9.5 per cent of Canadian children lived in poverty (Campaign 2000, 2011). Counter to predictions that we would not know how to use our free time, young parents in particular experience a lack of time to accomplish all that must be done. Most children have no or only one biological sibling, although more have stepsiblings.

Given the rapid and far reaching changes, it does not seem particularly promising to use projections from generational changes as a basis for making predictions. There is another problem with doing so: such data are not presently available for Canadian families. Given that I would expect the pace of change not only to continue, but perhaps even to accelerate (see below) the next generation is likely to face conditions very different from those experienced at present by their parents. Hence the behaviour of their parents may not be the best guide for predicting the future behaviours of the next generation.

3. *The impact of inventions.* A number of authors look at technological inventions to predict the future of the family. Hill calls this method "exciting but hazardous" (Hill, 1964: 24) and argues that we have overestimated the speed with which certain inventions would be merchandised. This seems less of an issue today, but he restricts his analysis to household conveniences. If we extend this approach to look at all technological inventions, this is certainly an important part of the world that impacts on the family. Ogburn and Nimkoff's predictions concerning the new reproductive and genetic technologies provide a startling testimony to the efficacy of this approach.

4. The family specialists' future family. This method looks at the type of family advocated by family professionals through their writing and publishing. Hill characterizes this method as novel, interesting, but leading to normative statements rather than predictions. This is very evident in the large spate of predictions and prescriptions around 1970 about communal replacements of marriage and the family.

5. Identifying societal changes and reflecting on their importance for the family. Goode argues that all family issues are structural and what we really need to know if we wish to predict how the family will change is how society will change. This seems to me the most promising but also the most difficult method.

Some Tentative Predictions about the Future of Canadian Families

Given the assessment of the various methods of how to predict what will happen with respect to future families, I am here concentrating on projected societal changes in my attempt to look into the crystal ball.

Worldwide Changes

Unfortunately, the future promises major challenges. At the global level, **climate change** is undoubtedly the single most important issue confronting humanity. The **Intergovernmental Panel on Climate Change** (2007) has pulled together the scientific evidence that climate change is real and is happening, yet so far the world's response has been far below what is needed to prevent further climate change. Canada contributes disproportionately to greenhouse gases (GHG; a major driver of climate change) through its **tar sands development** (Kempf, 2007) and our general way of life.

Already, the rate and severity of natural disasters have increased manifold in the early twenty-first century (see Figure 16.2). Further increases can be expected.

With growing population and tenuous infrastructures the world's exposure to natural hazards is inevitably increasing. This is particularly true as the strongest population growth is located in coastal areas (with greater exposure to floods, cyclones, and tidal waves). To make matters worse any land remaining available for urban growth is generally risk-prone, for instance flood plains or steep slopes subject to landslides. The statistics in this graphic reveal an exponential increase in disasters. This raises several questions. Is the increase due to a significant improvement in access to information? What part does population growth and infrastructure development play? Finally, is climate change behind the increasing frequency of natural hazards?

The severe effects of disasters have much to do with human-generated changes to the environment. For instance, the destruction of much of the mangrove forests on the South Asian coast that was most affected by the tsunami that ravaged this area in December 2004 removed a protective wall that would have greatly diminished the devastating effects of the tsunami. Where the mangroves remained intact, the villages also remained intact (Thekaekara, 2005).

Number of events
per year

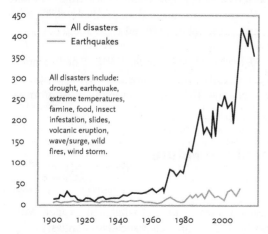

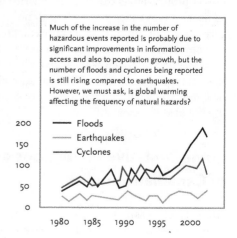

Figure 16.2 **Trends in Natural Disasters**

SOURCE: Centre for Research on the Epidemiology of Disasters (CRED). 2005. Emmanuelle Bournay, UNEP/GRID-Arendal. Available at http://maps.grida.no/go/graphic/trends-in-natural-disasters.

We can thus expect more severe natural disasters, and more sudden swings in climate, with negative effects on the world's crops. In Canada, we have so far not experienced the worst effects of climate change. However, some small island nations are already in the process of preparing for the time in which their countries will be flooded and disappear.[6] On 1 September 2008, Australia, Austria, Canada, Fiji, Maldives, Marshall Islands, Micronesia (Federated States of), Nauru, New Zealand, Palau, Papua New Guinea, Philippines, Samoa, Seychelles, Solomon Islands, Tonga, Turkey, Tuvalu, and Vanuatu put forward a resolution at the UN that the Security Council consider and address the threat posed by climate change to international peace and security. Unfortunately, the world has so far not taken much interest in the fact that several small nations are slated to lose their entire country.

Climate change is a legacy of the exploitation of natural resources by the world's richest countries (which include Canada), of over-consumption, the reckless burning of fossil fuels that, among other things, power an ever-increasing number of cars, exploitation of resources that would have been renewable if they had been used in a sustainable manner (such as fish in Newfoundland), deforestation, the type of meat-rich diet we consume, and other factors that contribute to the emission of greenhouse gases.

At the same time, more topsoil and forest cover are lost every year, while water tables are falling (Brown, 2003). In 2008, there were food riots across the world as a result of sharply rising food prices. Given the current and projected increase in the global human population, we can expect these problems to worsen rather than to improve.

Worldwide, the division of people into haves and have-nots has never been as great as it is today. The personal wealth of a few individuals is almost unimaginable:

The world's 497 billionaires have a combined wealth of $154,000,000,000,000. This is well over the combined gross national products of all sub-Saharan Africa nations ($929,300,000,000) or the oil-rich regions of the Middle East and North Africa ($134,000,000,000,000). It is also greater than the combined incomes of the poorest 50 per cent of humanity. (Nativevillage.org, 2012)

Millions of children in low-income countries grow up malnourished; millions of people die of malnutrition, starvation, and diseases brought on by poverty every year while obesity is recognized as the new epidemic in North America. Even within rich countries, and certainly within Canada, there is a sharp divide between the rich and poor. Homeless people are a common sight today in Canada's big cities.

The production of easily accessible oil has likely peaked,[7] and as it becomes more and more expensive, current differences between rich and poor will be further exacerbated unless governments take decisive actions to prevent this. It is not just transportation that will have to shift, but the vast majority of our food is dependent on cheap oil.

The world economic system is in crisis. In 2007 the global financial crisis started, leading to a severe global recession in 2008. The debt load of many countries is extremely high. As I am writing this, several European countries face extreme austerity measures which may or may not suffice to keep them solvent. Given the interdependence of markets, it is difficult to localize effects of the collapse of any one system.

Climate change has already led to crop failures and food shortages in many parts of the world. The Pentagon is predicting wars due to the consequences of climate change (cf. Dyer, 2009). It is the emissions of the rich countries that disproportionately cause climate change, but the consequences are first suffered by countries in Africa, South Asia, and Latin America. Unless rich countries start almost immediately reducing their GHG emissions up to 80 per cent, the situation will get much worse. If left unchecked, the planet may become uninhabitable for humans.

Canada shamefully has won the "Fossil of the Year Award" five years in a row, from 2007 to 2011, for it obstreperous role in international climate negotiations. As the award ceremony in Durban noted,

> Canada remains the only country in the world to have weakened its emissions targets after returning from COP 15 in Copenhagen and the only country to have signed and ratified the Kyoto protocol and then say that it has no intention of meeting its targets. The Government killed the only major federal renewable energy program in the country while plowing over $1 Billion dollars a year of subsidies into the oil sector. (Climateactionnetwork.ca, 2011)

The cumulative effects of the various trends are likely to result in ever-increasing international turmoil as the countries that have benefited least from the "progress" of the last century pay the highest price.

To this mix we must add the uncertain dangers posed by **genetically modified (GM) crops**. While resistance to GM crops in Europe has been very strong, Canada sees biotechnologies as an important growth area and is committed to develop this sector further.

It is not clear what the long-term effects of these technologies will be. To provide just one example, Monsanto has developed the so-called "terminator seed," which is sterile in the second generation, so that farmers cannot use part of their own crops for replanting but must buy new seed from the company (Kneen, 1999; Shiva, 2000). This is a very troubling situation in its own right. It becomes completely frightening if such genetic traits are able to wander into other crops. Such an effect could have catastrophic consequences for the world's food supply.

The overall effects of these trends are likely to be global economic, social, and political turmoil.

Effects of World Developments on Families

More Three-Generation Families

For more on complex living arrangements see "Co-residence and Home-Leaving" in Chapter 6, pp. 110–14.

Unhappily, if these predictions are right, the pressure on Canadian families is likely to increase significantly. Economic uncertainties may result in people moving together in larger units, thus reversing the trend of shrinking household size. We have already seen that young people live longer with their parents than they used to. We may experience a modest trend to more three-generation families. This might happen partially because of economic uncertainties generated by worldwide political, economic, and environmental instability, as well as by increased immigration from countries in which three-generation families are still the norm.

Decrease in Life Expectancy

I expect life expectancy to decrease. Just as oil production is likely to have peaked, so increases in life expectancy may have peaked. The people whose lifespan has been expanding over the past century grew up in a period where pollution levels and other environmental stressors were considerably lower. Today, many people have compromised immune systems. This means that at a time in which environmental stressors are likely to be greater, the physical capacity of people to deal with them will be lower. There is a constant stream of information about newly identified problems. For instance, flame retardants (PBDs) are now commonplace in the breast milk of Canadian mothers (Picard, 2005a). In addition, lifestyles of both children and older people have resulted in a sharp increase in obesity, which will likely result in more health problems. Furthermore, obese mothers are more likely to give birth to babies with health problems than are non-obese mothers (Picard, 2005b: A15). It may be that the life expectancy of people who are quite old will continue to increase for a while, while that of people born later may be curtailed at the same time. If this were the case, a trend towards lower life expectancies might not show up in general statistics for a while. To check the accuracy of this prediction, we would have to examine cohort-specific mortality rates.

Furthermore, social upheaval can quite literally shorten people's life span. The Russian Federation presents a drastic example of this. By 1989, the Soviet Union, although it still existed, had started to disintegrate. It was the year in which the Berlin Wall fell, and many of the satellite states were moving towards independence. In that year, life expectancy for men in what is now the Russian Federation was 64.2 years. Within the next four years it dropped precipitously to 57.6 years—a stunning drop of 6.6 years! By 2006, life expectancy was 60.4 years. For women, the effects were not as dramatic: female life expectancy was 74.5 years in 1989, 71.9 years in 1993, and 73.2 years in 2006 (UNICEF, 2008).

The Russian example demonstrates that assuming that life expectancy will continue to rise is not a safe assumption. Taking the health issues together with the effects of climate change and other environmental factors which are likely to produce serious social changes, it is likely that life expectancy will also decrease in Canada. If this happens, we will face a combination of lower life expectancy for people who are currently parents of young children. They married later and had children later. When their children grow up and have children themselves, fewer of these children would have all their grandparents alive, and fewer of the parents might receive help from their own parents. For the older people it would, of course, mean that fewer of them would be alive to enjoy their grandchildren.

Low Fertility Coupled with High Immigration Rates

I expect the fertility rate to remain below replacement values, as it is at present. Worldwide, fertility decreases as women attain higher levels of education and take on paying jobs. At present, more Canadian women than men attend university. We will therefore have a highly educated group of women in child-bearing age. At the same time, the pressure for people to immigrate to Canada for political, economic, and, increasingly, environmental reasons is likely to increase. If Canadian immigration policies will admit such immigrants, Canada will significantly increase its proportion of people of colour, since these are the people who will most likely wish to immigrate. Provided Canada manages to overcome its current racism (Henry et al., 2000), this may become its saving grace. People who grew up in countries that have suffered from the economic and environmental policies of past and current times may be more likely to support strict environmental regulations and more just external policies. If a sufficiently large proportion of the population supports stronger environmental protection and more egalitarian social and foreign policies, they might conceivably exert enough pressure on governments to achieve real policy change.

Sexuality

Same-sex marriage is now legal in Canada. This is a major achievement in terms of human rights that should be celebrated. While there is still discrimination on the basis of sexual orientation, and while there is still a significant minority of people who object to same-sex marriage, this is an instance of a rapid evolution of social attitudes and policies.

New Reproductive and Genetic Technologies

The new reproductive and genetic technologies as applied to humans have developed extremely rapidly. They have fundamentally changed, indeed, revolutionized how reproduction is considered within society. Mass media have popularized alternative forms of conception such as in vitro fertilization (IVF). Nevertheless, only a minority of people are directly affected by such techniques, while almost all pregnant women are offered various prenatal diagnostic techniques. Since the intent is usually to abort the fetus if a characteristic perceived as undesirable is detected, this is a form of eugenic gatekeeping. This is being challenged by disability rights activists (Wolbring, 2001). It is unclear what will happen. If religious fundamentalism were to rise in Canada, this practice may diminish. On the other hand, strong economic pressures may keep the practice alive.

Gender Roles

Women in the past 30 years have taken on most of the roles that men used to play, but men have not taken up women's roles to the same degree. Nevertheless, men do contribute a bit more to housework and to child care. I would expect that trend, modest as it has been, to continue into the future, on the basis that normatively almost all Canadians—male and female—agree that housework and child care should be shared (Bibby, 2005). Even though the behaviour lags behind the norms, one would expect that there will be some move to reconcile the two.

Divorce and Cohabitation as Alternatives to Permanent Monogamous Marriage

At present, the trend towards cohabitation as a precursor and alternative to marriage as well as a post-divorce form of union seems strong. The current global financial insecurity is affecting different countries and different groups within countries differently. Canada has so far been sheltered from some of the worst consequences; nevertheless, many people have lost jobs, and the economic future seems uncertain. Given this situation, I would expect cohabitation to become even more popular than it is today, but I would not expect it to displace legal marriage altogether. In times of political and economic turmoil, more people may turn to more fundamentalist forms of religion. For this part of the population, at least, marriage would retain (or regain) its religious value, and therefore I would expect marriage to continue to keep an important place in Canadian culture.

It is possible that my predictions about the future of Canadian families may be as wrong as those of so many eminent sociologists before me. Indeed, I hope so. However, even if the events predicted do occur in their broad outlines, there could potentially be some positive outcomes, if governments and people seize the opportunities (see Table 16.2).

Strangely enough, if oil—and therefore fuel for cars—becomes significantly more expensive, this may have significant positive effects besides the negative effects that it will undoubtedly have. If cars become too expensive to drive for trivial purposes, this may eventually turn suburbs into genuine neighbourhoods. Corner stores would become profitable, more cultural events would likely happen locally, leading to a market for local artists. Local production of produce would receive a boost. Urban agriculture would become a necessity to prevent further loss of farmland and to avoid transportation costs. Population density would need to increase in the suburbs, which would make it possible to introduce better mass transit services. If people started to walk and cycle more, obesity would certainly diminish, thus reducing the importance of one of the factors cited above for lower life expectancy. Pedestrian traffic also increases possibilities for more interaction between neighbours, thus potentially setting the stage for a more robust civil society with more citizen involvement, which, in turn, could result in positive political changes.

Table 16.2 **Household Environmental Practices, by Income Level, 2006**

Household practice	Less than $50,000 (%)	$50,000–$79,000 (%)	$80,000 or more (%)
Uses water-saving showerhead*	53	60	66
Uses water-saving toilet*	30	39	46
Has programmable thermostat**	29	41	55
Uses compact fluorescent light bulb(s)*	49	61	68
Uses chemical fertilizer***	22	32	42
Uses pesticide***	20	30	40
With access to recycling program*	90	96	98
Uses recycling program****	96	97	97

*As a percentage of all households

**As a percentage of households with thermostat

***As a percentage of households with a lawn or garden

****As a percentage of households with access to a recycling program

SOURCE: Prepared by the Vanier Institute of the Family using Statistics Canada's *Households and the Environment Survey*, 2006, public microdata file. Published in *Transitions*, Spring 2008, Vol. 38, 1: 4.

CASE IN POINT
FAMILIES AND THE ENVIRONMENT

In 2008 the Vanier Institute of the Family published an issue of their journal, *Transition*, committed to understanding the relationship between families and the environment. In the introduction of that issue they explained that the Institute's editorial board struggled to find individuals with academic expertise in the two areas. When they could not find anyone, they decided to begin the discussion (and the issue) with an interview with an environmentalist and a family studies expert with an interest in the environment. They invited Margrit Eichler, a sociologist with the University of Toronto's Ontario Institute of Studies in Education—author of this chapter—and David Chernushenko, a sustainability advocate and member of Canada's National Roundtable on the Environment and the Economy to the Vanier Institute to discuss a series of questions on families and the environment. Here is an excerpt from that interview.

LOWE: Let's explore the relationship between families and the environment a little bit further. It seems clear that the short and long-term health of families depends on a healthy and sustainable environment. Does a healthy and sustainable environment depend on healthy families?

CHERNUSHENKO: I like this question because it comes from both directions. Clearly, a healthy environment contributes to a healthier family in all of the pure senses of health. We may define a healthy environment broadly to be one in which people are safe. This will affect levels of stress and mental health. And on the flip side, a healthy family, both

(Continued)

physically and in terms of family dynamic, is more likely to have people discussing things with each other. You may have children coming home and sharing with their parents what they learned at school about recycling.

EICHLER: That's interesting. I have quite a different take on this one. I find this question perplexing, complex, and difficult. We all agree that in order to have healthy families we need a healthy environment because we depend on it. But is it necessary to have healthy families for a healthy planet? I think it depends on the level at which we're putting this discussion. At the global level, I would say yes, because if you look at the environment as a global issue, which of course it is, you cannot try to achieve sustainability without social equity because a lot of environmental problems are generated through poverty and other types of inequity. And you only have families that are healthy when they live in an equitable society, because I would define health as a state of complete wellbeing in physical, mental, social, and spiritual terms. So if you look at it at that level, I would say yes. But if you look at it in terms of Canada, first of all, we do not now have a sustainable society, and the majority of families are probably not healthy; many are poor, many have health problems, many have violence problems, and so on. I do believe these issues need to be addressed jointly. On the other hand, I could imagine a dictator pushing us towards an environmentally more sustainable society. That would then generate unhappy families, as I don't think you have happy families under a dictatorship. The real question, therefore, is how to move toward becoming more sustainable, and whether we need families for that. If we consider this question, I would say the answer is yes.

Source: Except from an Interview with David Chernushenko and Margrit Eichler in Hanchet, Simone (2008) "Families and the Environment: A Discussion," *Transition* (Vanier Institute of the Family), Spring 2008: 4–5 (http://www.vanierinstitute.ca/include/get.php?nodeid=738).

Conclusion

In this chapter, we have looked at a number of predictions that were made about families from 1930 to 1975. Some of these predictions were spectacularly wrong; others were surprisingly accurate. The time at which predictions were made was not a predictor of their accuracy. Instead, the important aspect seemed to be the basis on which they were made: those predictions based on societal or technological changes were more likely to be accurate than those based on extrapolation of trends or predictions of family experts. A fifth method, projection from generational changes, was not employed by enough people to gauge its effectiveness.

Given these findings, I have identified some changes that I anticipate for the future, in particular, climate change and the peaking of oil production. If these two things occur, I expect the future will see a modest trend towards three-generation families as one response to economic uncertainties and political turmoil, a decrease in life expectancy, continuing low fertility with high immigration, less homophobia, a continuing slow erosion of strictly defined gender roles, and a continuing diversity of unions, including common-law and legal marriages and same-sex marriages. The projected increase in natural disasters would mean that families would have to learn to prepare themselves for a variety of disasters.

In other words, families will continue to exist—some will prosper, others less so—and children will continue to be raised within family settings, which will probably be even more diverse than at present.

STUDY QUESTIONS

1. Select a basis on which to make predictions, choose one significant trend (e.g., birth rate, divorce rate, labour force participation of women), and predict how this trend will develop within the next 20 years. Explain why you make this prediction.
2. What are some of the societal factors that affect your own life course and that of one other family member of a different generation?
3. What might the situation of your family be if you were living in another country? Pick a specific country and explain the reasons for your statements.
4. Imagine that it became too expensive for most people to drive cars. How would Canadian cities change? How would this affect your own life and that of your family?
5. The rate of natural disasters has increased greatly in the past decade and will likely increase further. What would be needed to prepare for natural disasters?
6. Canadians are among the worst offenders in terms of contributing to greenhouse gases, which contribute to climate change. How could Canada reduce its greenhouse gas emissions?
7. What could you and your family do to reduce your carbon footprint?

Further Readings

Alternatives Journal. This periodical provides background analyses as well as positive examples of how to deal with environmental problems. The website of the journal is www.alernativesjournal.ca.

CCPA Monitor. As the publication of the Canadian Council for Policy Alternatives, the *CPPA Monitor* provides good up-to-date analyses of current social and environmental issues.

Dyer, Gwynne. 2009. *Climate Wars.* Toronto: Vintage Canada. This is a valuable contribution to the growing body of literature on climate change and the shift in human consciousness around global warming.

Simms, Andrew. 2009. *Ecological Debt. The Health of the Planet and the Wealth of Nations,* 2nd edn. London: Pluto Press. A highly readable book, Simms outlines how the rich countries created climate change, and how poor countries carry the consequences.

Todd, Nancy Jack. 2005. *A Safe and Sustainable World: The Promise of Ecological Design.* Washington: Island Press. Written in a personal style, this is a report of various very impressive successful experiments and projects, using ecological design, to lessen humanity's negative impact on the earth.

Vanier Institute of the Family. 2008. "Families and the Environment," *Transition* 38, 1. This entire issue of the journal of the Vanier Institute of the Family is dedicated to a discussion how environmental issues affect Canadian families.

Websites

www.insnet.org
This is an excellent weekly electronic newsletter with articles on issues of environmental and social justice concern.

www.childcarecanada.org
The Childcare Resource and Research Unit (CRRU) at the University of Toronto is a policy and research-oriented facility that focuses on early childhood education and care.

www.policyalternatives.ca
The *CCPA Monitor* is the monthly newsletter of the Canadian Centre for Policy Alternatives and is available at this site. It takes an integrative social justice/ecological approach to problems and contains thoughtful analyses of current social and environmental issues.

www.gdsourcing.com/works/Vanier.htm
The website of the Vanier Institute of the Family is an up-to-date and reliable source for current and some historical information about family trends.

Notes

1. I owe the idea to Patrizia Albanese, who also lent me some of her old family sociology textbooks and gave me feedback on this paper. Lingqin Feng found a number of old articles and books for me. I would like to thank Gregor Wolbring and David Cheal for helpful comments on the paper. My sincere thanks go to all of them.
2. In the first edition of the book; I am using the second edition.
3. I have consistently opted to use modern terms when discussing phenomena, but it needs to be noted that the term "gender roles" only started to be used in the mid-to-late 1970s.
4. This is not a term they use, but it is certainly an accurate one.
5. I am using modern terms. For the most part this does not reflect the language employed by the authors, but the phenomena under discussion are the same.
6. For the situation in the Maldives, see Agrell, 2008a; for the situation in Tuvalu, see Simms, Chapter 3; for Kiribati, the Marshall Islands, Palau, and Micronesia, see http://www.un.org/apps/news/story.asp?NewsID=28265&Cr=general+assembly&Cr1=debate.
7. This point is made very forcefully in the film *The End of Suburbia: Oil Depletion and the Collapse of the American Dream* (DVD) 2004, *The Electric Wallpaper*. See www.endofsuburbia.com.

Glossary

ABCX model A stress theory that predicts a causal link between events, meanings associated with events, resources, and outcomes.

Ableism The belief that people without disabilities have more worth than people with disabilities. This view may be explicit or implicit.

Abuse A violation of custom, injurious behaviour, or the use of harsh and insulting language.

Active eugenics The sterilization of people, both voluntarily and involuntarily, who were deemed to be undesirable contributors to the common "gene pool." People with intellectual disabilities, physical and sensory disabilities, women, new immigrant groups (particularly eastern Europeans), and First Nations people were particularly targeted in Canada.

Annulment The retroactive finding that an attempted marriage union violated the requirements for a valid marriage from the outset.

Apocalyptic demography The oversimplified idea that a demographic trend, in this case population aging, will lead to catastrophic consequences for society.

Arranged marriage Arranged marriages involve some participation or control in selection of marriage partners by parents, extended family, and, sometimes, community members.

Baby boom The sharp increase in birth rates in industrialized countries in the 1950s and 1960s; a demographic phenomenon that saw a historic jump in the number of births per 1,000 inhabitants (the usual standard of measurement) between 1946 and 1959. This population bulge is explained by a number of historic factors: the Great Depression saw marriage and childbearing postponed, resulting in a low in the gross birthrate of 20.1. After the war, with the economy growing at a healthy pace, a larger proportion of adults married, many at younger ages than the long-term trend, and they had more children than earlier in the twentieth century. By 1946 the birthrate had risen to 27.2 per 1,000 inhabitants, remaining between 27 and 28.5 per 1,000 until 1959, after which it gradually declined. Between 1940 and 1960 the annual number of births rose from 253,000 to 479,000, producing about 8.6 million babies [see **Reconstruction**].

Bi-nuclear family A family consisting of children and their parents who live in two households, usually following a divorce.

Blended family The marital union of two people, at least one of whom was previously in a marriage or marriage-like union and is also a parent. A blended family is created when one parent of an established family marries or cohabits with another such partner, and all their children are considered members of the new family.

Boomerang children The term given to adult children who return to the "empty nest," alone or with a family, subsequently "cluttering" it again. Recent research indicates that young adults, particularly men, are more likely to return for financial reasons and/or instrumental support (i.e., assistance with meals, cleaning, child care).

Brain injuries Brain injuries may occur due to a wide range of conditions, including illness, seizures, infection, alcohol and drug poisoning, neurological illness, stroke, aneurysm, surgery, or physical trauma from sports, accidents, or abuse. Brain injury does not always result in disability. In serious instances, the effects can include intellectual deficits, delusions, speech problems, and personality changes.

Canada's Century Meant to convey optimism about the national and international prospects for the young Dominion at the start of the twentieth century; in effect, an unofficial national slogan offered by the Liberal Prime Minister, Sir Wilfrid Laurier (1841–1919; in office 1896–1911) who presided over the "boom years" at its start. In January 1904, addressing the Canadian Club, an association of business and professional men founded in 1893 to foster patriotism, Laurier happily proclaimed that "The 19th century was the century of the United States. I think we can claim that it is Canada that shall fill the 20th century." [see **Sifton, Clifford**]

Caregiver burden Feelings of physical and emotional stress and depression that caregivers often experience.

Caregiving The social support provided to older adults when they can no longer function independently as a result of deteriorating physical and/or mental health status—i.e., social support that is required by the older adult. Sources can be either informal (i.e., family and friends) or formal (i.e., professional caregivers: doctors, nurses, social workers, rehabilitation therapists, paid home-care workers).

Case study research/case studies A qualitative method of inquiry that investigates a contemporary phenomenon within its real-life context; it helps provide in-depth or detailed contextual analysis of a limited number of events or relationships.

Census family One of the formal and changing definitions of "family" as outlined in the Canadian census. In the 2006 census, it refers to a married couple and the children, if any, of either or both spouses; a couple living common law and the children, if any, of either or both partners; or, a lone parent of any marital status with at least one child living in the same dwelling and that child or those children. All members of a particular census family live in the same dwelling. A couple may be of opposite or same sex. Children may be children by birth, marriage, or adoption regardless of their age or marital status as long as they live in the dwelling and do not have their own spouse or child living in the dwelling. Grandchildren living with their grandparent(s) but with no parents present also constitute a census family.

Century of the Child An objective put forward by Swedish writer, feminist, social reformer and child welfare advocate Ellen Key (1849–1926), who wrote a highly influential international bestseller, *Barnets århundrade* (1900), translated into English as *The Century of the Child* (1909). Key argued that child welfare should be the foremost social cause of the new century. Her proposal resonated with many of the Social Gospel–inspired reform movements in Western Europe, Canada and the United States, and her book became the acknowledged child welfare manifesto of the times [see Social Gospel; maternal feminist].

chain migration A family-based immigration strategy by means of which an individual or small group, usually male and often from the same family and community, leave their country of origin to resettle in another country. After finding work and shelter, these migrants assist other family, kin, and community members to join them. Canadian immigration policy has historically favoured chain migration, with the initial arrivals often serving as legal and economic "sponsors" for later arrivals [see Chinese Immigration Act].

Charivari The set of practices, traditional in some social contexts, that protect a newly married couple from the "evil eye" or the devil by separating the bride and groom or attaching loud items to the back of their departure vehicle.

Child launch Refers to one of the "early adult transitions," the point at which children leave their parental home. This has been increasingly delayed over the past decade or so, resulting in "cluttered" or "crowded" nests rather than the "empty nests" of the past.

Chinese Immigration Act (1923) The culmination of a series of racist federal government policies intended to restrict Chinese immigration to Canada. The Act effectively prohibited Chinese from entering the country, except for merchants, diplomats, and students, thereby also barring the entry of Chinese women since these were male occupations. Because many Chinese immigrants were men intending to bring over wives and children, it also prevented the reunification of families in Canada until it was repealed in 1947 [see chain migration; scientific racism].

Chuppah The canopy under which the couple stands in a Jewish wedding.

Civil unions (registered partnerships) A civil union is a legal procedure through which same-sex and/or heterosexual couples can register their partnerships, thus receiving most of the public and private obligations and rights as married partners.

Climate change The long-term change in the weather pattern of a specific region or for the planet as a whole.

Co-dependency Occurs when a person who does not have a problem him- or herself is seriously affected by someone who does have a problem such as addictions to drugs, alcohol, or gambling. A co-dependent person may try to cover up, excuse, rationalize, or minimize the negative effects of the other person's behaviour on his/her life.

Cohabitation (common-law and consensual unions) An emotional, sexual, and (usually) residential relationship between two people that is not legalized through marriage.

Comity The recognition extended by states in their own territory, courts, and institutions to the legal status and rights of citizens of other countries. Thus, country A would typically recognize marriages and divorces conducted in country B and vice versa. Comity would normally apply between provinces in Canada as well. The word originally meant "courtesy."

Commitment ceremonies Invented rituals through which couples seek to announce to themselves and their family and friends that they intend to stay together for the rest of their lives. They seek to avoid conventional gendered understandings and are used by GBLT couples where gay marriage is not legally recognized.

Community responsibility and inter-household work The extra-domestic, inter-household community-based aspects of being responsible for children.

Conflict Tactics Scale (CTS) A quantitative and gender-neutral instrument which is used to measure acts of violence between intimate partners. It does not measure frequency, intent, premeditation, or consequences.

Conjugal relationship This relationship often includes sharing a household, sexual relations, shared financial support, the raising of children, as well as a social perception of the couple as "a couple." It is assumed that married people are in a conjugal relationship; but a conjugal relationship has to be shown before a couple is seen as being in a common-law relationship.

Conspicuous consumption The lavish and obvious spending on goods and services in order to display one's wealth and accomplishment.

Controlling behaviours As used by feminists, a term that refers to men's psychological domination over women's behaviour, especially language, clothing, social contacts, and work.

Convenience sample Research conducted on readily available or "captive" groups of potential research subjects. Such non-probability sampling means that results cannot be generalized to a broader population.

Crowd out When the provision of care by the state results in less care by family members.

Cultural broker An individual in a position to explain the workings of a new culture to another person.

Dating culture This is a culture where romantic heterosexual relationships between young people are encouraged and expected. Dating culture does not assume that those relationships will lead to marriage or other long-term commitments.

Deficit model Similar to the "medical model" of disability. Disabled people are seen as defined by their impairments, so that their strengths/adaptations are seen as weaknesses/pathologies. This model ignores social aspects of disability such as stigma, poor services, lack of support, and disablism, instead blaming individuals for their challenges.

Demographic changes Population shifts related to their size, distribution, and composition (e.g., ethnicities, age structure, family statuses, etc.), changes in them, and the components of such changes, that is, births, deaths, migration, and social mobility (change of status).

Dependency theory Was developed in the 1950s to refer to the unequal power relations between industrialized and non-industrialized nations. It came to be used in the social theory to explain, among other things, violence against aging parents that results from stress related to scarcity of resources and unequal distribution of power.

Destination wedding A wedding that takes place at a resort or tourist destination where romance and nature are in evidence.

Disablist culture Disablism is a term first used in the UK within the disability rights movement to describe the discriminatory, oppressive, or abusive systems and interactions that arise from the belief that disabled people are inferior to others. Disablist cultures are those that fail to provide accommodations that would permit full participation and citizenship (including the right to parent) to people with disabilities.

Discrimination Negative or positive behaviour towards a person based on attitudes held towards the group to which that person belongs.

Divorce The legal dissolution of a valid marriage.

Dual diagnosis The term used to describe people with physical, mental, or sensory disabilities who also have legal or illegal substance dependencies.

Dysfunctional learning model (DLM) Finkelhor's assertion that child abuse is betrayal that leads to trauma, powerlessness, and stigmatization.

Economic family A group of two or more persons who live in the same dwelling and are related to each other by blood, marriage, common-law relationship, or adoption.

Elder care The care provided to older/later life (i.e., 65+ years) family members and/or friends. The care can range from occasional support with grocery shopping to full-time (24/7) nursing-type assistance requiring caregiver–care recipient co-residence.

Empty nest A family life-course stage when all of the children have transitioned to adulthood and left home to begin their own lives ("flown the nest").

Endogamy/homogamy The tendency for people to partner with or marry someone within their own social group ("endo"—within) or with similar ("homo"—same) characteristics.

Enlightenment The eighteenth-century philosophy emphasizing reason, science, and individualism rather than tradition and religious beliefs.

Ethnocentrism The bias or preference for one's own way of life or culture, as reflected in one's thinking and actions.

Ethnography A detailed field study based on extensive observation and interviews.

Eugenics A term that literally means "well-born." It developed out of Darwinian ideas about adaptation and Mendelian ideas about genetics, becoming a political and social movement to "improve" the race and health status of citizens in North America, the United Kingdom, and Europe in the twentieth century.

Extended family/multigenerational household A family in which two or more generations (e.g., grandparents, aunts, uncles, cousins) share a household.

Extended family Takes in both the household and the wider family circle, including kin such as cousins, aunts, uncles, and grandparents. A combination of these family members may share a household, but the extended family does not necessarily reside together.

Familialism According to functionalists the so-called "traditional" nuclear family remains the ideal. This conservative model is based on rigidly gendered roles, and women are expected to provide physical and emotional care to the rest of the family.

Families of choice Defines family as social networks that include lesbian or gay individuals or other people who become members of a self-defined "family."

Familism Care of older members, especially care by adult children of their older parents.

Family A married couple or common-law couple, with or without children of either or both spouses, or a lone parent, regardless of that parent's marital status, having at least one child living under the same roof.

Family Allowances Act (1944) Proposed by McGill University sociologist Leonard Marsh, research advisor for the federal Committee on Post-War Reconstruction, in his government-mandated *Report on Social Security for Canada* (1943); implemented by the Mackenzie King Liberal government in 1944. Also known as the "Baby Bonus," the Act provided Canada's first universal social welfare program. Starting in 1945, monthly cheques were mailed to every Canadian mother, the amount dependent on the ages and number of children 16 years and under [see reconstruction, Baby Boom].

Family demography A subfield of demography that examines changes in the nature of intergenerational and gender bonds in households and family units.

Family policy An array of policies and programs that directly relate to families with children under the age of 18 years.

Femicide The murder of women by men.

Fertility rate A measure that estimates the average number of children women aged 15 to 49 will have in their lifetime.

Fictive kin Non-related friends/individuals who, because they offer services, support, and goods to a family, come to be considered part of that family.

Filial caregiving Care provided by adult children to older parents.

Fragmented services A common barrier to citizenship and inclusion for disabled people. Services are provided by multiple organizations or by differing providers, information about services and entitlements are difficult to find, rulings change frequently without notice, and information is often in inaccessible formats.

Frailty Severe poor health; something broader than disability alone or disease state alone, even though it is difficult to distinguish from both; a vulnerability to adverse outcomes resulting from the interaction of the simultaneous deterioration of many organ systems.

Friends Friends are neither family nor do they fit a specific status category, like neighbour or colleague. The term "friend" best describes some degree of developed, mutually achieved relationship.

Gender contract The assumption of a male breadwinner/female caregiver exchange.

Gender convergence The process through which traditional gender norms and expectations give way to more equal and less distinct expectations based on gender. The degree to which gender convergence has taken place is uncertain.

Gender divisions of labour The study of how labour is divided by gender in paid and unpaid work.

Gender ideologies A set of social beliefs about men and women's roles and relationships in varied social institutions.

Gendered disablism The notion that gender and disability are interlocking and intersecting sites of oppression. Disability is always gendered. There is no generic experience of disability outside of gender (as well as race, class, sexuality, etc.).

Gender-neutral A term that indicates something is equally applicable to women and men.

Generation gap A concept attesting to the generational differences—at times clashes—in values, mores, and mindset, especially as evidenced in the relationship of parents and children, or, more widely, of elders and youth. While such differences are a historic constant, they have been exacerbated by the rapid sociocultural changes taking place since the mid twentieth century; the term itself gained popularity during the so-called "youthquake" of the 1960s [See Spock, Dr. Benjamin].

Generation in the middle Adult children in the baby boom generation who are caring for their parents and still raising their own children and sometimes also employed.

Genetically modified (GM) crops Plants created for agricultural purposes by humans through the combination of genes from different and frequently entirely unrelated species.

Heterosexism Rather than the term "homophobia," which is suggestive of a fear (phobia), heterosexism aims to target the presumption of heterosexual norms as the main reason that sexual minorities are discriminated against.

Home care The in-home paid or unpaid assistance provided to a person with a chronic disability or illness, allowing the person with the impairment to remain living at home.

Horizontal shrinkage Having fewer siblings.

Household A group of people who occupy the same dwelling or housing unit.

Household work strategy According to Pahl (1984), this is defined as "how households allocate their collective effort to getting all the work that they define has, or feel needs, to be done."

Human rights claims Rights are entitlements to do something without interference from other people. Human rights belong to everyone by virtue of being human, although only some members of society have access to certain rights. When people contend that they are denied entitlements to rights they believe are owed to all humans, they fight for laws and policies to ensure they have access to them.

Ideology A system of connected ideas and beliefs about a subject.

Immigrant integration The extent to which immigrants are able to participate in the social, economic, and political structure of the host country to which they moved.

Impairments Characteristics, features, or attributes that may or may not be the result of illness, disease, or injury, for example: mobility impairments, depression, cancer, being hard of hearing, psychological impairments, etc.

Indian Act (1876) Federal legislation intended to confirm and consolidate all past federal acts to "contain" and assimilate Aboriginals by emphasizing their subordinate position as "wards" of the paternalistic state. They were encouraged to give up their "Indian" status, and all the special treaty provisions that this entailed, in return for enfranchisement, which signified their integration as citizens. The Superintendent General of Indian Affairs was given wide powers over Aboriginal communities and their lands, including the power to decide who could be identified as "status Indian" [see "status Indian"].

Individual responsibility family model A family model premised on gender equality whereby there is no distinction between married and common-law partners, and the state is not responsible for either economic well-being or the provision of care as long as there is a husband/father or wife/mother present.

Informal care A type of social support that is provided by family and friends, typically unpaid, to an older adult who can no longer function independently and requires care.

Institutional completeness The development of many institutions (e.g., banking, shopping, education, religion) to meet the needs of members of a particular ethnic group.

Institutionalized heterosexuality The social world is assumed and understood to be organized and ordered by heterosexuality.

Intact families Families in which all children in the household are the biological and/or adopted offspring of both members of the couple.

Intellectual disabilities Characterized both by a significantly below-average score on a test of mental ability or intelligence and/or by limitations in the ability to function in areas of daily life. There are different degrees of intellectual disability, ranging from mild to profound. Historically, terms such as mental retardation, moron, and idiot, were used to describe intellectual disabilities.

Intergenerational ambivalence In mid-life families, the ambivalent or conflicted feelings that result from the incompatibility between parental expectations and children's behaviour.

Intergenerational co-residence A residential arrangement in mid-life in which at least two generations, most often parents and young adult children, live together.

Intergenerational exchange The exchange of support and assistance between generations, very often between adult children and their parents.

Intergovernmental Panel on Climate Change An organization established by the United Nations to assess the likelihood of climate change. It received the Nobel Peace Prize in 2007 for its work.

Intimate terrorism is one of three categories of partner violence, where the abuser is controlling, dominant, and jealous. M.P. Johnson suggests that this type of violence is perpetrated by more men than women, and also, less likely to be measured by survey research.

Involuntary infertility The inability to conceive a child despite the desire to have a child.

Labour force participation rate The proportion of the population 15 years of age and over that is in the labour force (that is, either employed or looking for work) in a specified reference period.

Liberal welfare state In most areas of political, social, and economic endeavour, individuals have greater responsibilities for their life than government; government intervention and benefits in regard to family policy tend to be minimal since it is thought that individuals bear the responsibility to have and raise children.

Life expectancy How long we can expect to live.

Life-course perspective A paradigm for understanding both continuity and change across time and generations; combines the study of social structure with the experience of individuals over the life course (i.e., history, society, and biography). The key concepts in the study of the life course are life events, transitions, and trajectories (pathways).

Lone-parent family One parent with one or more children who have never married, living in the same dwelling.

Longitudinal studies A study that shows changes over time, usually by tracking a particular group of people or by taking snapshots of different groups at different points in time.

Long-term home support Assistance enabling the person to remain living in their home such as shopping, meal preparation, and personal care.

Low-income cut-offs (LICOs) Income levels at which families or unattached individuals are considered to be living in straitened circumstances. Statistics Canada currently produces LICOs before and after tax, which are periodically revised on the basis of changes in the average standard of living of Canadians. These are essentially "relative measures" of low income that vary by family size and degree of urbanization.

Maternal feminist A sector of the late nineteenth-early twentieth century women's movement that emphasized women's "innate" domesticity as the basis of their public service, and consequently the political power, entailed in the vote, that they needed to perform it effectively. Maternal feminists carried the biologically ordained maternal role out of private homes and into the public sphere. Many middle-class women's organizations were maternal feminist in outlook, participating in Social Gospel reform campaigns on behalf of women, children, and families [see Social Gospel; National Council of Women; Women's Christian Temperance Union; Women's Institutes; second-wave feminism].

Maternal grandparents The mother or wife's parents.

Maternity leave benefits Assistance to women in balancing family and employment through (1) financial support when they take time away from their employment to have and care for their newborn; and (2) protection of their jobs by ensuring that they can return to the same or an equivalent position upon their return to their employment.

Median income That point in the income distribution at which one-half of income units (individuals, families, or households) fall above and one-half fall below.

Mental health diagnoses The range of mental health problems that are diagnosable is broad, from anxiety and eating disorders, to drug and alcohol addictions, depression, and schizophrenia, and the effects vary widely. Some problems are treated with pharmaceuticals, others are managed through therapy, and not all are recognized as disabilities that require support and services.

Modernization A sociological term describing the historical process in which a pre-industrial agrarian society reaches modernity, generally by means of a series of developments driven by industrialization, urbanization, and mass education. In Canada, modernization is associated with the second half of the nineteenth century, and is seen to have intensified with the immigration wave of the pre-World War I years.

Multiculturalism A policy that Canada adopted in 1971 to support the cultural development of ethnocultural groups and to help members of ethnocultural groups overcome barriers to full participation in Canadian society.

National Council of Women of Canada Established in 1893 by Lady Ishbel Aberdeen, wife of Governor-General Lord Aberdeen. It served as a federation of local and provincial women's voluntary organizations and was the largest and most important of the women's reform associations in Canada until well into the twentieth century. Like other such groups, the NCWC emphasized social and political reform to meet the needs of women, children, and families. The organization campaigned for the passage of the Act to Confer the Electoral Franchise upon Women in 1918 [see maternal feminist; Social Gospel; Women's Christian Temperance Union; Women's Institutes].

National heterosexism Western societies are steeped in normative notions that reflect their colonial histories of discovery and conquest (in Canada the history of English and French Christian white settlers is commonly understood). Thus the nation comes to be defined within norms, beliefs, and values that travelled from the homelands to the colony. One of these norms is heterosexuality, a term that defines the national norm and in so doing discriminates against non-heterosexuals.

Neglect Failure to provide care or necessities for someone in need of care; applies both to omissions and commissions.

Neo-liberalism A political philosophy geared to restructuring society (partly by reducing social programs and placing responsibility on individuals to solve social problems) to better meet the demands of the global marketplace.

New Deal A sweeping range of federal programs enacted by American President Franklin Delano Roosevelt in 1933 to address the long-lasting dire repercussions of the New York Stock Exchange crash of 1929 that precipitated an international crisis in capitalism featuring unemployment and widespread destitution. The New Deal standardized "relief" policies, inaugurated massive public works projects, and generally represented the state's responsibility for active intervention to ensure the welfare of its citizens. Similar measures were attempted by Conservative Prime Minister Richard B. Bennett with the "Bennett New Deal" of 1935, but he lost the election that year to Liberal leader Mackenzie King. Most of his proposed measures were ruled unconstitutional due to the federal–provincial division of powers [see social minimum].

New reproductive technologies A broad array of technologies aimed at facilitating or preventing the process of reproduction, such as contraception, abortion, antenatal testing, birth technologies, and conceptive technologies.

Non-standard employment relationship Several types of work that are very different from the norm of a full-time, full-year, permanent paid job, including part-time employment, temporary employment, self-employment, or multiple job holding; also referred to as precarious employment or contingent employment.

Normalization A complex process by which concepts, social practices, identities, or ideas are assumed to be normal. This assumption of "normal" is based on beliefs informed by moral discourses of right and wrong, rather than contextualized through specific political, cultural, and social histories that represent a wide array of values and beliefs.

Nuclear family A family that consists of parent(s) and child(ren); also known as the conjugal family unit, this family type includes at most a mother, father, and their dependent children [see census family].

Parental leave benefits Paid leave that enables fathers to take time away from their employment so that they can participate more fully in their newborn's life.

Participation and Activity Limitation Survey (PALS) The most recent (2006) large-scale survey to collect information on persons in Canada (excluding those in institutions and on First Nations reserves) whose everyday activities are limited due to a physical or mental health problem or illness.

Passive eugenics Policies and programs employed to prevent breeding by the "wrong" kinds of people. This included discouraging sexual activities through "education" and institutionalizing certain kinds of people to keep them from breeding.

Paternal grandparents The father or husband's parents.

Patriarchal family A hierarchical family structure in which the husband/father is dominant and the wife and/or children are subordinate to his authority.

Patriarchy An ideology and practice where male power and privilege equate with fathers' dominance and control over women and children in the home.

Patrilineage Descent traced through the paternal line to determine family and kin relations; the basic determinant of both heritage and inheritance in patriarchal societies that privilege the economic, social, and political power of men.

Polygyny The custom that one man may have more than one wife.

Pro-natal policies Policies aimed at maintaining or raising fertility. Conversely, anti-natalist policies are those aimed at bringing down high birth rates (i.e., "family planning policies").

Pronatalism An ideology promoting human reproduction and glorifying parenthood, especially motherhood as the principal "vocation" of all women. Pronatalists call upon the state to support policies and to create legislation that limits, or actually criminalizes, access to contraception and abortion, while also advocating state-mandated economic and social incentives to encourage marriage and childbearing. Closely entwined with the status of women, pronatalism was prominent in Canada in the immediate aftermath of the Great War. The roughly 66,000 casualties, many of whom were young men "in their prime," fathers and potential fathers, made reproduction the source of much social anxiety. Women's enfranchisement, the rise in female education and work opportunities, and the declining size of families also intensified pronatalist concerns and campaigns [see maternal feminist; eugenics, Family Allowances Act].

Public intimacy We usually think of intimacy as belonging to the private sphere of interpersonal relationships. Lauren Berlant (1997) uses the term to mean that intimate sexual relations are very much the concern of the state. An example of public intimacy is reflected in the 1967 statement by Pierre Trudeau that "there's no place for the state in the bedrooms of the nation."

Pure relationship Giddens's "pure relationship" describes an ideal relationship based in emotional and sexual intimacy, begun and continued for as long as it satisfies both partners. It relies on sexuality freed from reproduction, intimacy as central to love, and egalitarianism between partners.

Qualitative research/approach A non-numeric analysis of data intended to discover underlying meaning and explore relationships.

Quality time The term popularly used to describe the special time some working parents schedule to devote exclusively to their children.

Quasi-widowhood Feelings of grief, loss, and depression that women experience following their husband's placement in a long-term care facility.

Quiet Revolution The period of intensive political, economic, and sociocultural change characterizing the 1960s in the province of Quebec; known in French as the *Révolution tranquille*). It is associated with the election of Liberal Jean Lesage in June 1960, shortly after the death in office of arch-conservative Union Nationale premier Maurice Duplessis. It was characterized by the provincial government's campaign to "catch up" to the modern world by means of secularization, the creation of a welfare state, government control of natural resources, education and health care, and negotiations with the federal government for "opting out" of certain federal programs in favour of its own. Well over by the decade's end, the Quiet Revolution also saw the rise of the Parti Québécois as a viable separatist movement.

Racial profiling Stereotypical assumptions about race, ethnicity, colour, religion, or names that result in actions such arresting, searching, questioning, or beating particular groups of people.

Recession A term given to a sharp slow-down in the rate of economic growth, as distinct from a slump or depression, which is a more severe and prolonged downturn. Two successive declines in seasonally adjusted real gross domestic product (GDP) would constitute a recession.

Reconstruction Federal government plans for the transition to a peacetime economy after the Second World War. Planning took place during the war through the federal Committee on Post-War Reconstruction (1941–1944). The Department of Reconstruction was established in June 1944 to safeguard production and employment. Its transitional nature and the postwar economic boom meant that it was superseded by the Department of Resources and Development in 1950 [see Family Allowances Act].

Reproductive and genetic technologies The use of birth control pills, artificial insemination, in vitro fertilization, use of donor eggs, sex selection of fetuses, Viagra and its female equivalent, hormone replacement therapy, and other technologies.

Residential schools An extensive school system set up by the Canadian government in the 1880s and administered by the Roman Catholic, Anglican, Presbyterian, and United Churches. Intended to provide a nominal "white" education, the schools forcibly removed Aboriginal children from their families and communities, with the support of federal law, in order to disrupt the generational transmission of their languages and cultures. They were indoctrinated into Christianity, forbidden to use their own language and customs, their contact with parents and kin was severely restricted, and they were subjected to harsh rules, punishment, and physical labour. Their health was undermined by food deprivation, and inadequate clothing, heating, and sanitation. The mortality rate, and the extent of physical, sexual, and psychological repercussions at the hands of school staff, were horrendous. The individual, familial, and socio-economic repercussions persist to the present. On 11 June 2008, Prime Minister Stephen Harper issued a formal apology for the residential school system to First Nations communities on behalf of all Canadians [see Indian Act].

Respite care Short-term, temporary care, sometimes including overnight, designed to give families that include people with disabilities a break from caregiving.

Rite of passage A ritual the marks the movement of an individual from one status to another. A rite of passage usually has three segments. The first symbolizes the departure of the individual from the previous status. The second, liminality, includes the period when the individual is between statuses, and the third, incorporation, marks the entrance of the individual to the new status.

Rite of progression A ritual that recognizes the successful maintenance of a social status. For example, a birthday party marks the progression of an individual as she or he ages.

Royal Commission on the Status of Women An extremely important commission that with the release of its report in 1970 ushered in a new era in gender relations in Canada.

Sandwich generation Middle-generation cohorts sandwiched between older and younger cohorts in a population; more specifically, adults in mid-life (40–64 years) who have at least one child in the household and at least one living parent for whom they are the primary caregivers and who often resides in the household.

Scientific racism Resulted from mid-nineteenth century scientific developments, in particular Charles Darwin's evolutionary theory, that seemingly encouraged the racialization of the world's population. "Races" were defined as groups that shared certain biological characteristics, especially skin colour. From these physical traits, it was deduced that, in evolutionary terms, the white "race" represented the pinnacle of human achievement, while other "races" were progressively lower in the social hierarchy, the darkness of their skin a measure of their mental ability and "civilization." Scientific racism legitimized imperialism and the conquest and colonization of the "lesser races" by those deemed superior, especially the British [see eugenics].

Script theory Script theory states that there are sets of stereotypical actions expected in certain social situations. Scripts help people organize the world around them, providing predictability to social interactions.

Second-wave feminism A label applied to the women's movement of the 1960s and 1970s to distinguish it from the "first-wave feminism" of the late nineteenth–early twentieth century, which was focused on women's suffrage. Also known as the Women's Liberation movement, it was born of the turbulent

1960s New Left–inspired protest movements, especially those supporting civil rights, anti-racism, participatory democracy, and anti-war views, as well as the sexual revolution resulting from the introduction of the contraceptive pill in 1960. Among their key objectives, second-wave feminists fought for an end to employment discrimination, sexism, and violence against women, and called for affirmative action, pay equity, and reproductive choice, including the right to abortion [see maternal feminist].

Sensory impairments An impairment of any of the five senses. Unlike physical impairments, sensory impairments can be hard to detect; they can often be confused with learning or intellectual disabilities, so that the individual's educational provisions may not be appropriate until the individual is diagnosed.

Separation The end of a marriage or marriage-like relationship resulting from causes other than death.

Serial caregiving The adult child usually provides care to a parent after their own children have grown and left the home and prior to caring for a spouse, usually a wife caring for her husband.

Sexual citizen Someone who is not identified, by herself or by others, as heterosexual and who may have documents that prove a legal status, yet nonetheless remains outside the social privileges accrued from social belonging (e.g., the ability to freely discuss one's relationship or to express affection in public). A sexual citizen can also be someone who demands to be included in the citizenship body as not heterosexual.

Sexual minorities People who identify on the basis of non-heterosexuality, including those who identify as lesbian, gay, bisexual, trans-identified, two-spirited, intersexed, or queer.

Sexual scripts "Sexual scripting theory" was theorized by Simon and Gagnon (1986) to focus on ways that stereotypical scripts enable people to organize the social world and to predict meaningful social interactions.

Shiva The traditional Jewish mourning period, usually a week, during which the family refrains from its usual activities. During this period friends bring food and visit with the family.

Sifton, Clifford, (1861–1929) Represented Brandon, Manitoba, as a Liberal Member of Parliament during the reign of Sir Wilfrid Laurier (1896–1911). Sifton was the highly influential Minister of the Interior (1896–1905) in Laurier's Cabinet. He directed an aggressive and successful immigration campaign that resulted in the entry to Canada of roughly 1 million immigrants during the first decades of the twentieth century [see chain migration; Canada's Century; Chinese Immigration Act].

Skip-generation Those with grandparents and grandchildren but no middle (parental) generation.

Skip-generation households Grandchildren living with grandparents without the middle/parent generation being present.

Social capital The social networks and trust that allow for community members to co-ordinate their activities for mutual benefit.

Social convoy A model of support that involves a network of close family and friends who travel through life together, providing reciprocal social support.

Social democratic state One in which there is greater emphasis on government involvement in society and the economy—the raising of children is thought to be a collective responsibility, and consequently there tends to be more state government intervention and more generous benefits than in a liberal welfare state.

Social exchange theory Social exchange theory posits that people commodify a range of social characteristics, including physical attractiveness, youth, wealth, education, gender role, and social status and then offer their best traits in trade for traits they desire. This theory is used in studies of dating, cohabitation, and marriage partner choices.

Social Gospel An "umbrella" term used to signify activist, largely urban, middle-class, Protestant Christian reform campaigns focused on remedying the worst abuses of industrial capitalism. Commencing in the last quarter of the late nineteenth century, the Canadian movement peaked shortly after the Great War. It was inspired by similar progressive voluntarist movements in Great Britain and the United States. The Social Gospel included such diverse but related causes as child welfare, slum clearance, public health, municipal corruption, temperance, child and female labour, factory inspection, and the protection of animals [see maternal feminist].

Social learning theories Theories that predict links between modelling, rewards, punishments, and such behaviour as aggression.

Social legitimation Although a social group may gain political legitimation from the state, through laws and policies, which can result in benefits such as lower taxes or increased mobility in society, social approval or legitimation may still be withheld. For example, while the Canadian state legally legitimates same-sex marriage, polls indicate that it is not socially legitimated by the majority of Canadians.

Social minimum Refers to the financial resources needed by individuals and families to ensure a minimal standard of living in a given society at a given moment. The modern welfare state is premised on the provision of publicly funded institutions and policies to protect its citizens from falling below a reasonable "bottom" relative to others in that society [see reconstruction, Family Allowances Act].

Social model of disability From this view society is regarded as disabling for persons who have impairments. According to this model, disability refers to the social, environmental, and attitudinal oppression faced by persons with non-conformist bodies.

Social parenthood The practice and experience of parenthood by adults who have no biological connection to the children they are parenting.

Social reproduction "[T]he activities required to ensure day-to-day and generational survival" (Luxton, 1998).

Social responsibility family model Characterized by a concerted effort to minimize stratification on the basis of sex without distinguishing between types of relationships such as legal marriage or same-sex couples; they are all considered types of relationships where one is no more privileged than the other. The well-being of dependent children is the responsibility of parents and society; thus, all families are entitled to be supported by the state.

Social support The assistance (i.e., instrumental, emotional, and financial) that people give to one another. Sources can be either informal (i.e., family and friends) or formal (i.e., paid home-support service workers such as homemakers, companions).

Socialization The process by which individuals learn the norms and mores of a society.

Spock, Dr. Benjamin American paediatrician whose *Common Sense Book of Baby and Child Care*, first published in 1946, became the childrearing "Bible" of the Baby Boom generation. In seven editions, the last published in 1997 just before his death, the book sold almost 50 million copies internationally, in 42 languages. Unlike his predecessors, Spock advocated "instinctive" parenting; his critics contended that he advocated permissive childrearing, thereby fuelling the "youth revolt" of the 1960s [see generation gap].

Spousal caregiving The care provided by one's husband or wife.

Spousal violence Murder, attempted murder, sexual and physical assault, threats, criminal harassment, or other violent offence by a spouse or partner.

Spouse Legal definitions of spouse vary among provinces. Ontario defines spouses as married couples and couples who have cohabited for three years and/or are the parents of a child in a relationship of some permanence. Saskatchewan defines spouses as married spouses, or two people who have cohabited continuously for two years, or parents of a child.

Standard employment relationship A situation where the employee works full-time for one employer on the same premises and receives statutory benefits from that same employer; also called the male model of employment.

Status Indian The legal definition of who could be classified "Indian" under the Indian Act (1876). The Act specified that "Indian" referred to any man of Aboriginal heritage registered on the federal government's Indian Register as a member of a particular band; any offspring of a such a person; any woman, regardless of "race," currently or once married to such a person. Aboriginal women who married non-Aboriginal men, as well as any children of the union, lost Indian status. The Act denied Indian status to the Métis, persons of mixed Aboriginal and European descent, and the Inuit [see Indian Act].

Stem family An anthropological term that describes a household in which married adult children, typically the eldest male, reside with their spouse and their own children in the parental home.

Stepfamilies Families in which at least one of the children in the household is from a previous relationship of one of the parents; a cohabiting or legal union of two adults with at least one member bringing a child or children from previous relationships.

Survival tactics A term used by Berlant (1997), who contends that while we might question actions deployed by activists, we must understand the conditions under which people fight for their rights. For instance, it may be problematic for some sexual minorities to seek recognition through the institution of marriage since many sexual minorities do not gain from it and many do not want it. However, for some, recognition of same-sex marriage is emblematic of acceptance by the state, friends, and family—in short, it allows some to survive the penalties of non-recognition.

Suttee The Indian custom of a widow's burning herself on her husband's funeral pyre. This practice is against the law in India today.

Symbolic communitas Anthropologist Victor Turner developed this concept which refers to the sense of solidarity and belonging that emerges from the experience of public rites of passage in which the community expresses its support for the celebrants by its presence.

TABS (temporarily able-bodied) The notion that anyone may become disabled at any time. Unlike other identity categories, the line between "disabled" and "not disabled" is constantly in flux. This is particularly the case in an aging society.

Tar sands development One of the largest oil deposits in the world, located in Alberta. However, its extraction is extremely environmentally harmful.

Transnational, multi-local family/satellite family A family that finds itself (temporarily) separated and living across borders, in multiple locations.

Underemployment The inability to obtain a job commensurate with one's education or training qualifications.

Vertical extension Having more generations alive than was true in the past.

Violence Rough force in action, rough treatment causing harm or injury, and unlawful use of force.

Visible and invisible disabilities Visible disabilities are easily discerned by a second party or, in other words, their barriers are "visible," for example, using a wheelchair, walker, prosthesis, or oxygen. Invisible disabilities—which are not readily apparent—can include debilitating fatigue, pain, heart problems, depression, or neurological damage. A person may have both visible and invisible disabilities.

Visible minorities Persons, other than Aboriginal people, not white in race or colour.

Visible minority status Under the Employment Equity Act (1986), the concept of "visible minority status" was created in law and is defined as persons other than Aboriginal peoples who are non-Caucasian in race or non-white in colour. The following groups are included under this Act: Chinese, South Asians (e.g., East Indian, Pakistani, Punjabi, Sri Lankan), blacks (e.g., African, Haitian, Jamaican, Somali), Arab and West Asians (e.g., Egyptian, Iranian, Lebanese), Filipinos, Southeast Asians (e.g., Indonesians, Vietnamese, Cambodian), Latin Americans, Japanese, Koreans, and Pacific Islanders.

Wedsite Websites designed, primarily by brides, to communicate details about their forthcoming weddings. Wedsites emphasize the uniqueness of the couple and romantic aspects of the marriage proposal, and appear to be written by both members of the couple although the groom usually has little to do with them.

Welfare state A system of bodies of governance (e.g., federal, provincial) that offers social protection to citizens by redistributing, organizing, and ordering social policies and services according to the elected political party's agenda.

Whiteness A subordinate term is always defined in relation to its dominant counterpart. Identifying "whiteness," usually the dominant, unmarked term that serves to subordinate racial terms, destabilizes the non-visible minority (i.e., those of European ancestry are the dominant One that defines all Others).

Women's Christian Temperance Union The first women's social reform organization that attempted to apply Christian principles to the eradication of "the liquor evil." Founded in Ohio in 1873, the WCTU became an international organization the following year, when the first Canadian branch was established in Owen Sound, Ontario. In 1885, the WCTU became a national organization under the leadership of Letitia Youmans. It was the largest non-denominational women's organization of its time, though its membership consisted primarily of anglophone middle-class Protestant women, reflecting that of the larger Social Gospel movement [see maternal feminist; Social Gospel]. Many prominent Canadian suffragists of the time were WCTU members, and there was considerable overlap in its membership and that of other women's organizations of the time [see National Council of Women of Canada; Women's Institutes].

Women's Institutes Founded in Stoney Creek, Ontario, by maternal feminist and child welfare advocate Adelaide Hoodless in 1897. By 1913 the primarily rural-based institutes were established in all the provinces. In 1919, the Federated Women's Institutes of Canada was formed. The group's motto, "For Home and Country," indicates its focus on patriotism, rural life, and the concerns of women, children, and families [see maternal feminist; Social Gospel].

Women's lib The early name for second-wave feminism, which started in the 1960s.

Work–family balance The term used in organizational contexts to describe the family and workplace responsibilities of working parents.

Young elderly Those aged 65 to 74 years.

Zero population movement A social movement that started in the late 1960s advocating that the number of births should be restricted so that the human population would not outstrip the capacity of the earth to sustain humanity.

References

Aboriginal Affairs and Northern Development Canada. 2010. "Income Assistance Program." Available at http://www.aadnc-aandc.gc.ca/eng/1100100035256.

Adam, Barry D. 2004. "Care, intimacy and same-sex partnership in the 21st century," *Current Sociology* 52, 2: 265–279.

Adams, Mary Louise. 1997. *The Trouble with Normal: Postwar Youth and the Making of Heterosexuality*. Toronto: University of Toronto Press.

Adams, Michele, and Scott Coltrane. 2004. "Boys and men in families: The domestic production of gender, power and privilege," in Michael S. Kimmel, Jeff Hearn, and Robert W. Connell, eds, *The Handbook of Studies on Men and Masculinities*. Thousand Oaks, Calif.: Sage.

Agnell, Siri. 2008. "Pushing 50, solo—and living it up," *Globe and Mail*, 3 July, L1.

———. 2008a. "Tiny island nation seeks dry land," *Globe and Mail*, 13 Nov., A3.

Ahlgrim-Delzell, Lynn, and James R. Dudley. 2001. "Confirmed, unconfirmed, and false allegations of abuse made by adults with mental retardation who are members of a class action lawsuit," *Child Abuse & Neglect* 25: 1121–32.

Ahrons, Constance R., and Jennifer L. Tanner. 2003. "Adult children and their fathers: Relationship changes 20 years after parental divorce," *Family Relations* 52: 340–51.

Albanese, Patrizia. 2006. "Small town, big benefits: The ripple effect of $7/day child care," *Canadian Review of Sociology* 43, 2: 125–40.

———. 2007. "(Under)Valuing care work: The case of child care workers in small-town Quebec," *International Journal of Early Years Education* 15, 2: 125–39.

———. 2007a. "Quebec's $7 day Childcare: Some Preliminary Findings," in L. Tepperman and H. Dickinson, eds, *Reading Sociology: Canadian Perspectives*. Toronto: Oxford, pp. 102–4.

———. 2007b. "(Under)Valuing Care Work: The Case of Child Care Workers in Small-Town Quebec," *International Journal of Early Years Education* 15 (2): 125–39.

———. 2009. *Children in Canada Today*. Don Mills: Oxford University Press.

———. 2009a. "$7/Day, $7/Hour, 7 Days A Week: Juggling Commutes, Shift Work and Childcare in a Changing ('New') Economy," in J. Klaehn. ed., *Road Blocks To Equality*. Toronto: Black Rose Books, pp. 26–40.

———. 2011. "Addressing the Interlocking Complexity of Paid Work and Care: Lessons from Changing Family Policy in Quebec," in Krull and Sempruchs, eds, *Demystifying the Family/Paid Work Contradiction: Challenges and Possibilities*. Vancouver: University of British Columbia Press, pp. 130–43.

Alcohol and Seniors. 2005. Available at http://www.agingincanada.ca/enios%20Alcohol/1e6.htm; accessed 5 November 2008.

Allen, Katherine R., Rosemary Blieszner, and Karen A. Roberto. 2000. "Families in the middle and later years: A review and critique of research in the 1990s," *Journal of Marriage and the Family* 62: 911–26.

Allen, Richard. 1971. *The Social Passion: Religion and Social Reform in Canada, 1914–1928*. Toronto: University of Toronto Press.

Allen, Sarah M., and Kerry Daly. 2002. "The effects of father involvement: A summary of the research evidence," working paper. Carleton Place, Ont.: Father Involvement Initiative–Ontario Network.

———., and ———. 2007. *The Effects of Father Involvement: An Updated Research Summary of the Evidence*. Ottawa: Fatherhood Involvement Research Alliance.

Ambert, Anne-Marie. 1994. "An international perspective on parenting: Social change and social constructs," *Journal of Marriage and the Family* 56: 529–43.

———. 2002. *Divorce: Facts, Causes and Consequences*, rev. edn. Ottawa: Vanier Institute of the Family.

———. 2005. *Divorce: Facts, Causes, and Consequences*. Ottawa: Vanier Institute of the Family.

———. 2006. "One parent families: Characteristics, causes, consequences, and issues." Vanier Institute of the Family. Available at http://www.vifamily.ca/library/cft/oneparent.pdf.

———. 2006a. *Changing Families: Relationships in Context*, Canadian edn. Toronto: Pearson Education Canada.

———. 2009. *Divorce: Facts, Causes, and Consequences*. 3rd edition. Ottawa: Vanier Institute of the Family.

Andersen, Robert, and Tina Fetner. 2008. "Cohort differences in tolerance of homosexuality: Attitudinal change in Canada and the United States, 1981–2000," *Public Opinion Quarterly* 72: 311–30.

Anderson, Kim. 2001. *A Recognition of Being: Reconstructing Native Womanhood*. Toronto: Sumach Press.

Anderson, Tammy L., Caitlin Shannon, Igor Shyb, and Paul Goldstein. 2002. "Welfare reform and housing: Assessing the impact to substance abusers," *The Journal of Drug Issues* 2: 265–96.

Andren, S., and S. Elmstahl. 2005. "Family caregivers' subjective experiences of satisfaction in dementia care: Aspects of burden, subjective health and sense of coherence," *Scandinavian Journal of Caring Sciences* 19 (2): 157–68.

Andres, Lesley, and Maria Adamuti-Trache. 2008. "Life-course transitions, social class, and gender: A 15-year perspective on the lived lives of Canadian youth," *Journal of Youth Studies* 11: 115–45.

Angus Reid Poll. n.d. Available at http://www.angus-reid.com; accessed 12 March 2012.

Anisef, P., and K. Kilbride, eds. 2003. *Managing Two Worlds: The Experiences and Concerns of Immigrant Youth in Ontario*. Toronto: Canadian Scholar's Press.

Anisef, Paul, Robert S. Brown, Kelli Phythian, Robert Sweet, and David Walters. 2010. "Early school leaving among immigrants in Toronto secondary schools," *Canadian Review of Sociology* 47, 2: 103–28.

Anshen, Ruth Nanda. 1959. *The Family: Its Function and Destiny*. New York: Harper.

Antonucci, T.C., J.S. Jackson, and S. Biggs. 2007. "Intergenerational relations: Theory, research, and policy," *Journal of Social Issues* 63, 4: 679–93.

Antonucci, Toni, and Hiroko Akiyama. 1997. "Concern with others at mid-life: Care, comfort, or compromise?" in M.E. Lachman and J.B. James, eds, *Multiple Paths of Mid-life Development*. Chicago: University of Chicago Press, 147–69.

APA Online. 2008. "Elder abuse and neglect: In search of solutions." Available at http://www.apa.org/pi/aging/eldabuse.html; accessed 31 March 2008.

Aquilino, William S. 2005. "Impact of family structure on parental attitudes toward the economic support of adult children over the transition to adulthood," *Journal of Family Issues* 26: 143–67.

Arber, Sara, and Jay Ginn. 1995. "Gender differences in informal caring," *Health & Social Care in the Community* 3: 19–31.

———, and ———. 2004. "Aging and gender: Diversity and change," in C. Summerfield and P. Babb, eds, *Social Trends No. 34*. London: TSO.

Ariès, Philippe. 1962. *Centuries of Childhood*. New York: Alfred A. Knopf.

Ariza, Marina, and Orlandina de Oliveira. 2001. "Contrasting scenarios: Non-residential family formation patterns in the Caribbean and Europe," *International Review of Sociology* 11, 1: 47–61.

Armesto, Jorge C., and Ester R. Shapiro. 2011. "Adoptive gay fathers: Transformations of the masculine homosexual self," *Journal of GLBT Family Studies* 7, 1–2: 72–92.

Armitage, Andrew. 2003. *Social Welfare in Canada*, 4th edn. Toronto: Oxford University Press.

Armstrong, Elizabeth A., Laura Hamilton, and Paula England. 2010. "Is hooking up bad for young women?" *Contexts* 9: 22–7.

Arnup, Katherine. 1994. *Education for Motherhood: Advice for Mothers in Twentieth-Century Canada*. Toronto: University of Toronto Press.

Arthur, N., A. Chaves, D. Este, J. Frideres, and N. Hrycak. 2008. "Perceived discrimination by children of immigrant parents: Responses and resiliency," *Canadian Diversity* 6, 2: 79–83.

Asch, A., H. Rousso, and T. Jefferies. 2001. "Beyond pedestals: The lives of girls and women with disabilities," in H. Rousso and M. L. Wehmeyer, eds, *Double Jeopardy: Addressing Gender Equity in Special Education*. Albany, NY: SUNY Press, 13–48.

Ashbourne, L., K. Daly, and J.L. Brown. 2011. "Responsiveness in father–child relationships: The experience of fathers," *Fathering: A Journal of Theory, Research, and Practice About Men as Fathers* 9, 1: 69–86.

Auchmuty, Rosemary. 2004. "Same-sex marriage revived: Feminist critique and legal strategy," *Feminism & Psychology* 14, 1: 101–26.

Auliff, Lily. 2001. "Bringing up baby: Mothering with a disability," *WeMedia* 5, 1 (Jan.–Feb.): 66–9.

Baber, Ray E. 1953. *Marriage and the Family*. New York: McGraw-Hill.

Bagley, Christopher, and Kathleen King. 1991. *Child Sexual Abuse: The Search for Healing*. London: Tavistock.

Bailey, Martha. 2004. "Regulation of cohabitation and marriage in Canada," *Law & Policy* 26, 1: 153–75.

Baillargeon, Denyse. 1999. *Making Do: Women, Family and Home in Montreal during the Great Depression*. Waterloo: Wilfrid Laurier University Press.

Baird, B. 2007. "'Gay Marriage,' Lesbian Wedding," *Gay & Lesbian Issues and Psychology Review* 3 (3): 161–70.

Bajekal, M., D. Bland, I. Grewal, S. Karlsen, and J. Nazroo. 2004. "Ethnic differences in influences on quality of life at older ages: A quantitative analysis," *Ageing and Society* 24, 5: 709–28.

Bakan, Abigail B., and Daiva Stasiulis, eds. 1997. *Not One of the Family: Foreign Domestic Workers in Canada*. Toronto: University of Toronto Press.

Baker, Maureen. 1994. "Family and population policy in Québec: Implications for women," *Canadian Journal of Women and the Law/Revue Femmes et Droit* 7: 116–32.

———. 2001. *Families, Labour and Love*. Vancouver: University of British Columbia Press.

———. 2001a. "Definitions, cultural variations, and demographic trends," in Maureen Baker, ed., *Families: Changing Trends in Canada*. Toronto: McGraw-Hill Ryerson, pp. 3–27.

———. 2002. "Child poverty, maternal health and social benefits," *Current Sociology* 50, 6: 823–38.

———. 2008. "Improving child well-being? Restructuring child welfare programs in the liberal welfare states," *Canadian Journal of Family and Youth* 1, 1: 3–26

———. 2010. "Gendering 'child' poverty: Cross-national lessons for Canada in a deepening recession," *International Journal of Canadian Studies / Revue internationale d'études canadiennes* 42: 25–46.

Bala, Nicholas, and Rebecca Jaremko Bromwich. 2002. "Context and inclusivity in Canada's evolving definition of the family," *International Journal of Law, Policy and the Family* 16: 145–80.

Balbo, Laura. 1987. "Crazy quilts: Rethinking the welfare state debate from a woman's point of view," in Anne S. Sassoon, ed., *Women and the State*. London: Unwin Hyman.

Ball, J. 2009. "Fathering in the shadows: Indigenous fathers and Canada's colonial legacies," *The Annals of the American Academy of Political and Social Science* 634, 1: 29–48.

Bandura, Albert. 1973. *Aggression: A Social Learning Analysis*. Englewood Cliffs, NJ: Prentice-Hall.

Barbeau, Clayton C. 1971. *Future of the Family*. New York: Bruce Publishing.

Baril, Robert, Pierre Lefebvre, and Philip Merrigan. 2000. "Quebec family policy: Impact and options," *Choices: Family Policy* (IRRP) 6, 1: 4–52.

Barker, Richard W. 1994. *Lone Fathers and Masculinities*. Avebury, UK: Aldershot.

Barnes, Colin. 2003. "What a difference a decade makes: Reflection on doing "emancipatory" disability research," *Disability & Society* 18: 3–17.

Barnes, Sandra L. 2003. "Determinants of individual neighborhood ties and social resources in poor urban neighborhoods," *Sociological Spectrum* 23, 4: 463–97.

Barnett, O.W., Cindy L. Miller-Perrin, and Robin D. Perrin. 2005. *Family Violence Across the Lifespan: An Introduction*, 2nd edn. Thousand Oaks, CA: Sage.

Barnett, Rosalind C., Nancy L. Marshall, and Joseph H. Pleck. 1992. "Men's multiple roles and their relationship to men's psychological distress," *Journal of Marriage and the Family* 54, 3: 358–67.

Barraket, Jo, and Millsom Henry-Waring. 2008. "'Getting it on(line)': Sociological perspectives on e-dating" *Journal of Sociology*, 44: 149–65.

Barrett, A.E., and S.M. Lynch. 1999. "Caregiving networks of elderly persons: Variations by marital status," *Gerontologist* 39, 6: 695–704.

Bart, Pauline B., and Eileen G. Moran. 1993. *Violence against Women: The Bloody Footprints*. Newbury Park, Calif.: Sage.

Barth, R. 2001. "Policy implications of foster family characteristics," *Family Relations* 50, 1: 16–19.

Basen, Gwynne, Margrit Eichler, and Abby Lippman. 1993. *Misconceptions: The Social Construction of Choice and the New Reproductive and Genetic Technologies*, vol. 1. Hull, Que.: Voyageur.

Baumbusch, J.L. 2004. "Unclaimed treasures: Older women's reflections on lifelong singlehood," *Journal of Women and Aging* 16, 1/2: 105–21.

Baumrind, Diana. 1966. "Effects of authoritative parental control on child behaviour," *Child Development* 37, 4: 887–907.

Baxter, Leslie A., Dawn O. Braithwaite, and John H. Nicholson. 1999. "Turning points in the development of blended families," *Journal of Social and Personal Relationships* 16: 291–313.

BBC News. 2012. "California gay marriage ban nears US Supreme Court. *BBC News*, 31 July. Available at http://www .bbc.co.uk/news/world-us-canada-19072943; accessed 13 September 2012.

BC Institute against Family Violence. 1996. Overview of Family Violence. Available at http://www.bcifv.org/about/overview/3.shtml.

Bear, Shirley, with the Tobique Women's Group. 1991. "You can't change the Indian Act?" in Jeri Wine and Janice Ristock, eds, *Women and Social Change*. Toronto: James Lorimer.

Beaudin, Monique. 2012. "What Quebec's Parties are Offering in the 2012 Election," *Montreal Gazette*, 3 September.

Beaujot, Roderic. 1999. *Earning and Caring in Canadian Families*. Peterborough, Ont.: Broadview Press.

———. 2000. *Earning and Caring*. Peterborough, Ont.: Broadview Press.

———. 2004. "Delayed life transitions: Trends and implications." Ottawa: Vanier Institute of the Family.

———. 2005. "Families," in James J. Teevan and W.E. Hewitt, eds, *Introduction to Sociology: A Canadian Focus*, 8th ed. Toronto: Pearson, 221–49.

———. 2006. "Delayed life transitions: Trends and implications," in Kevin McQuillan and Zenaida Ravanera, eds, *Canada's Changing Families*. Toronto: University of Toronto Press, 105–32.

———, and Zenaida Ravanera. 2009. "Family Models for Earning and Caring: Implications for Child Care and for Family Policy," *Canadian Studies in Population* 36, 1–2: 145–66.

Beaupré, Pascale. 2008. *I Do. Take Two? Changes in Intentions to Remarry Among Divorced Canadians During the Past 20 Years*. Statistics Canada, Catalogue no. 86-630-X, July. Available at http://www.statcan.gc.ca/pub/89-630-x/2008001/article/10659-eng.pdf.

———, and Elisabeth Cloutier. 2007. "Navigating family transitions: Evidence from the General Social Survey, 2006" (Catalogue n. 89-625-XIE, No.002). Social and Aboriginal Statistics Division. Ottawa: Statistics Canada.

———, Heather Dryburgh, and Michael Wendt. 2010. "Making Fathers Count," *Canadian Social Trends* (8 June).

———, Pierre Turcotte, and Anne Milan. 2006. "When is junior moving out? Transitions from the parental home to independence," *Canadian Social Trends* 82: 9–15.

Beauvais, Caroline, and Pascale Dufour. 2003. "Articulation travail-famille: Le contre-exemple des pays dits 'libéraux'?" Canadian Policy Research Networks Family Network. Available at http://www.cprn.org.

Beauvoir, Simone de. 1989 [1949]. *The Second Sex*. New York: Vintage Books.

Béchard, Marcel. 2007. *Family Structure by Region* (revised). Ottawa: Statistics Canada.

Beck, Ulrich, and Elizabeth Beck-Gernsheim. 2002. *Individualization*. London: Sage.

Beck-Gernsheim, Elizabeth. 1998. "On the way to a post-familial family: From a community of needs to elective affinities," *Theory, Culture and Society* 15, 3–4: 53–70.

———. 2002. *Reinventing the Family: In Search of New Lifestyles*. Cambridge: Polity.

Behiels, Michael D. 1986. *Prelude to Quebec's Quiet Revolution*. Montreal and Kingston: McGill-Queen's University Press.

Behnia, Behnaz, and Édith Duclos. 2003. *Participation and Activity Limitation Survey, 2001: Children with Disabilities and Their Families*. Ottawa: Statistics Canada, Housing, Family and Social Statistics Division.

Belanger, A., and S. Gilbert. 2005. *The Fertility of Immigrant Women and Their Canadian-born Daughters*. Ottawa: Statistics Canada, Division of Demography, 127–51.

———, ———, and E. Malenfant. 2005. *Population Projections of Visible Minority Groups, Canada, Provinces and Regions, 2001–2017*. Ottawa: Statistics Canada.

Bell, D., and J. Binnie. 2000. *The Sexual Citizen: Queer Politics and Beyond*. Cambridge: Polity Press.

Bellis, Mark A., et al. 2012. "Prevalence and risk of violence against children with disabilities: A systematic review and meta-analysis of observational studies," *The Lancet* 30, 9845: 899–907.

Bennett, K.M. 2007. "'No sissy stuff': Towards a theory of masculinity and emotional expression in older widowed men," *Journal of Aging Studies* 21: 347–56.

Ben-Ze'ev, Aharon. 2004. *Love Online: Emotions on the Internet*. Cambridge: Cambridge University Press.

Benzeval, Michaela, and Ken Judge. 2001. "Income and health: The time dimension," *Social Science and Medicine* 52, 9: 1371–90.

Bergen, Raquel K. 1998b. "The reality of wife rape: Women's experiences of sexual violence in marriage," in Bergen (1998a: 237–50).

———, ed. 1998a. *Issues in Intimate Violence*. Thousand Oaks, Calif.: Sage.

Berkowitz, Dana, and William Marsiglio. 2007. "Gay men: negotiating procreative, father and family identities," *Journal of Marriage and Family* 69: 366–81.

Berlant, L., and M. Warner. 1998. "Sex in Public," *Critical Inquiry* 24: 547–66.

Berlant, Lauren. 1997. *The Queen of America Goes to Washington City: Essays on Sex and Citizenship*. Durham, NC: Duke University Press.

Bernard, Jessie. 1972. *The Future of Marriage*. New York: Bantam.

Bernhard, Judith K., Patricia Landolt, and Luin Goldring. 2008. "Transnationalizing families: Canadian immigration policy and the spatial fragmentation of care-giving among Latin American newcomers," *International Migration* 47, 2: 3–31.

——, ——, and ——. 2006. "Transnational, multi-local motherhood: Experiences of separation and reunification among Latin American families in Canada," *Policy Matters* 24: 1–7.

Bernstein, Elizabeth. 2007. *Temporarily Yours: Intimacy, Authenticity, and the Commerce of Sex*. Chicago: University of Chicago Press.

Berrardo, Felix M., and Hernan Vera. 1981. "The Groomal Shower: A Variation of the American Bridal Shower," *Family Relations* 30, 3: 395–401.

Bérubé, Alan. 2001. "How Gay Stays White and What Kind of White It Stays," in *The Making and Unmaking of Whiteness*, Birgit Rasmussen, Eric Klineberg, Irene Nexica, and Matt Wray, eds. North Carolina: Duke University Press.

Bezanson, Kate. 2006a. "Gender and the limits of social capital," *Canadian Review of Sociology and Anthropology* 43, 4: 427–43.

——. 2006b. *Gender, The State and Social Reproduction: Household Insecurity in Neo-liberal Times*. Toronto: University of Toronto Press.

——, and Meg Luxton. 2006. "Introduction: Social reproduction and feminist political economy," in K. Bezanson & M. Luxton, eds, *Social Reproduction: Feminist political Economy Challenges Neo-liberalism* (pp. 3–10). Montreal: McGill-Queen's University Press.

Bianchi, Suzanne M., et al. 2000. "Is anyone doing the housework? Trends in the gender division of household labor," *Social Forces* 79, 1: 191–228.

Bibby, Reginald. 2001. *Canada's Teens: Today, Yesterday and Tomorrow*. Toronto: Stoddart.

——. 2005. *Future Families Project: A Survey of Canadian Hopes and Dreams*. Ottawa: Vanier Institute of the Family.

Biblarz, Timothy, and Judith Stacey. 2010. "How does the gender of parents matter?" *Journal of Marriage and Family* 72: 3–22.

Bielski, Zosia. 2008 "Hard-up humanitarian seeks same," *Globe and Mail*, 13 November, L1, L4.

Bird, Joseph, and Lois Bird. 1971. "Marriage: A doubtful future," in Barbeau (1971: 1–10).

Bittman, Michael, and Jocelyn Pixley. 1997. *The Double Life of the Family: Myth, Hope and Experience*. St Leonard's, Australia: Allen and Unwin.

Blackford, Karen A. 1993. "Erasing mothers with disabilities through Canadian family-related policy," *Disability, Handicap & Society* 8: 281–94.

——. 1999. "Caring to overcome differences, inequities, and lifestyle pressures: When a parent has a disability," in K.A. Blackford, M. Garceau, and S. Kirby, eds, *Feminist Success Stories*. Ottawa: University of Ottawa Press, 279–87.

——. 1999a. "A child's growing up with a parent who has multiple sclerosis: Theories and experiences," *Disability & Society* 14: 673–85.

——, Heather Richardson, and Sarah Grieve. 2000. "Prenatal education for mothers with disabilities," *Journal of Advanced Nursing* 32, 4: 898–904.

Blain, Jenny. 1994. "Discourses of agency and domestic labor: Family discourse and gendered practice in dual-earner families," *Journal of Family Issues* 15, 4: 515–49.

Blake, Judith. 1972. "Here and beyond—the population crisis: The microfamily and zero population growth," in *College of Home Economics* (1972: 55–68).

Blakely, Kristin. 2008. "Busy brides and the business life: The wedding-planning industry and the commodity frontier," *Journal of Family Issues* 29, 5: 639–62.

Blau, P.M. 1964. *Exchange and Power in Social Life*. New York: John Wiley.

Block, Pamela, and Christopher Keys. 2002. "Race, poverty and disability: Three strikes and you're out! Or are you?" *Social Policy* 33, 1: 34–8.

Blossfeld, Hans-Peter, and Melinda Mills. 2001. "A causal approach to interrelated family events: A cross-national comparison of cohabitation, nonmarital conception and marriage," *Canadian Studies in Population* (special issue) 28, 2: 409–37.

Boden, S. 2003. *Consumerism, Romance, and the Wedding Experience*. Gordonsville, VA: Palgrave Macmillan.

Bogle, Kathleen A. 2008. *Hooking Up: Sex, Dating, and Relationships on Campus*. New York: New York University Press.

Bokma, Anne. 2008. "Being a foster-care family," *Canadian Living*. Available at http://www.canadianliving.com/ relationships/friends_and_family/being_a_foster_care_ family.php.

Bolin, K., B. Lindgren, and P. Lundborg. 2008. "Informal and formal care among single-living elderly in Europe," *Health Economics* 17, 3: 393–409.

Bonsang, E. 2009. "Does informal care from children to their elderly parents substitute for formal care in Europe?" *Journal of Health Economics* 28: 143–54.

Booth, T., and W. Booth. 1994. *Parenting under Pressure: Mothers and Fathers with Learning Difficulties*. Buckingham: Open University Press.

——, and ——. 1998. "The myth of the upside down family," in T. Booth and W. Booth, eds, *Growing Up With Parents Who Have Learning Difficulties*. London, Britain: Routledge, 146–68.

Bostock, Lisa. 2001. "Pathways of disadvantage? Walking as a mode of transport among low-income mothers," *Health and Social Care in the Community* 9, 1: 11–18.

Bott, Elizabeth. 1957. *Family and Social Networks*. London: Tavistock.

Bourassa, Carrie, Kim McKay-McNabb, and Mary Hampton. 2004. "Racism, sexism and colonialism: The impact on the health of Aboriginal women in Canada," *Canadian Woman Studies/les cahiers de la femme* 24, 1 (Fall): 23–9.

Bowker, Lee H., ed. 1998. *Masculinities and Violence*. Thousand Oaks, Calif.: Sage.

Boyd, M., and E. Grieco. 2003. "Women and migration: Incorporating gender into international migration theory," unpublished paper.

Boyd, Monica, and Doug Norris. 1995. "Leaving the nest? The impact of family structure," *Canadian Social Trends* (Autumn): 14–17.

Boyd, S.B., and C.F.L. Young. 2005. "From Same Sex to No Sex? Trends towards Recognition of (Same-Sex) Relationships in Canada," in *Open Boundaries*, B.A. Crow and L. Gotell, eds. Toronto: Pearson Prentice Hall.

Bradbury, Bettina. 1984. "Pigs, cows and boarders: Non-wage forms of survival among Montreal families, 1861–1881," *Labour/Le Travail* 14 (Autumn): 9–46.

———. 1993. *Working Families: Age, Gender, and Daily Survival in Industrializing Montreal*. Toronto: McClelland & Stewart.

———. 2000a. "Single parenthood in the past: Canadian Census categories, 1891–1951 and the "normal" family," *Historical Methods* 33, 4: 211–17.

———. 2000b. "Feminist historians and family history in Canada in the 1990s," *Journal of Family History* 25, 3: 362–82.

———. 2005. "Colonial comparisons: Rethinking marriage, civilization and nation in the nineteenth-century white settler societies," in Philip Buckner and R. Douglas Frances, eds, *Rediscovering the British World*. Calgary: University of Calgary Press, pp. 135–58.

Braithwaite, Dawn O. 1995. "Ritualized embarrassment at 'co-ed' wedding and baby showers," *Communication Reports* 8, 2: 145–57.

———, and Leslie A. Baxter. 1995. "'I do' again: The relational dialectics of renewing marriage vows," *Journal of Social and Personal Relationships* 12, 7: 177–98.

———, ———, and Anneliese M. Harper. 1998. "The role of rituals in the management of the dialectical tension of 'old' and 'new' in blended families," *Communication Studies* 49: 101–20.

———, Loreen N. Olson, Tamara D. Golish, Charles Soukup, and Paul Turman. 2001. "'Becoming a family': Developmental processes represented in blended family discourse," *Journal of Applied Communication Research* 29: 221–47.

Braithwaite, V. 1998. "Institutional respite care: Breaking chores or breaking social bonds?" *Gerontologist* 38, 5: 610–17.

Brandon, P.D., and D.P. Hogan. 2004. "Impediments to mothers leaving welfare: The role of maternal and child disability," *Population Research and Policy Review* 23: 419–36.

Brannen, Julia, and Ann Nilsen. 2006. "From fatherhood to fathering: Transmission and change among british fathers in four-generation families," *Sociology* 40, 2: 335–52.

———, and Peter Moss. 1991. *Managing Mothers: Dual Earner Households after Maternity Leave*. London: Unwin Hyman.

Brannigan, Augustine, William Gemmell, David J. Pevalin, and Terrance J. Wade. 2002. "Self-control and social control in childhood misconduct and aggression: The role of family structure, hyperactivity, and hostile parenting," *Canadian Journal of Criminology and Criminal Justice* 44, 2: 119–42.

Breitkreuz, R., D. Williamson, and K. Raine. 2010. "Dis-integrated policy: Welfare-to-work participants'

experiences of integrating paid work and unpaid family work," *Community, Work, & Family* 13, 1: 43–69.

Breitkreuz, Rhonda S. 2005. "Engendering citizenship? A critical feminist analysis of Canadian welfare-to-work policies and the employment experiences of lone mothers," *Journal of Sociology and Social Welfare* 32, 2: 147–65.

British Columbia Council for Families. 2011. "Quick facts on grandparenting." Available at http://www.bccf.ca/all/resources/quick-facts-grandparenting.

British Columbia Law Foundation and the Provincial Government. 2009. "Grandparents raising grandchildren, legal issues and resources, A brief B.C. introduction." (pamphlet).

British Columbia Law Institute and the Canadian Centre for Elder Law. 2010. "Care/Work: Law reform to support family caregivers to balance paid work and unpaid caregiving." BCLI Study Paper No. 4.

Brockmann, H., and T. Klein. 2004. "Love and death in Germany: The marital biography and its effect on mortality," *Journal of Marriage and Family* 66, 3: 567–81.

Bronfenbrenner, Urie. 1977. "Towards an experimental ecology of human development," *American Psychologist* 32: 513–31.

———, and Stephen Ceci. 1994. "Nature–nurture reconceptualized in developmental perspective: A bioecological model," *Psychological Review* 101: 568–86.

Brotherson, Sean, David Dollahite, and Alan Hawkins. 2005. "Generative fathering and the dynamics of connection between fathers and their children," *Fathering* 3: 1–28.

Brown, Lester R. 2003. *Plan B: Rescuing a Planet under Stress and a Civilization in Trouble*. New York: Norton.

Brown, Susan L. 2010. "Marriage and child well-being: Research and policy perspectives," *Journal of Marriage and Family* 72: 1059–77.

Brownridge, D., and S. Halli. 2003. "Double advantage? Violence against Canadian migrant women from developed nations," *International Migration* 41, 1: 29–46.

Brownworth, V. 1996. "Tying the knot or the hangman's noose: The case against marriage," *Journal of Lesbian, Gay and Bisexual Identity* 1: 91–8.

Buchignani, Norman, and Doreen M. Indra. 1985. *Continuous Journey: A Social History of South Asians in Canada*. Toronto: McClelland & Stewart.

Budgeon, Shelley. 2008. "Couple culture and the production of singleness," *Sexualities* 11, 3: 301–25.

Bulcroft, Kris, Richard Bulcroft, Linda Smeins, and Helen Cranage. 1997. "The social construction of the North American honeymoon, 1880–1995," *Journal of Family History* 22: 462–90.

Bumpass, Larry, and Hsien-Hen Lu. 2000. "Trends in cohabitation and implications for children's family contexts," *Population Studies* 54: 29–41.

Bumpus, Matthew F., Ann C. Crouter, and Susan M. McHale. 1999. "Work demands of dual-earner couples: Implications for parents' knowledge about children's daily lives in middle childhood," *Journal of Marriage and the Family* 61, 4: 465–76.

Burke, Stacie. 2001. "Marriage in 1901 Canada: An ecological perspective," *Journal of Family History* 26, 2: 189–219.

Burkhauser, Richard V., Philip Giles, Dean R. Lillard, and Johannes Schwarze. 2005. "Until death do us part:

An analysis of the economic well-being of widows in four countries," *Journals of Gerontology, Series B* 60, 5: S238–46.

Bushnik, Tracey. 2006. *Child Care in Canada* (Catalogue no. 89-599-MIE, No. 003). Children and Youth Research Paper Series. Ottawa: Statistics Canada.

Butler, J. 1997. *Excitable Speech: A Politics of the Performative*. New York: Routledge.

Butler, Judith. 1990. *Gender Trouble: Feminism and the Subversion of Identity*. New York: Routledge.

Calasanti, Toni M. 2006. "Gender and old age: Lessons from spousal care work," in T.M. Calasanti and K.F. Slevin, *Age Matters: Realigning Feminist Thinking*. New York: Routledge, 269–94.

———, and M.E. Bowen. 2006. "Spousal caregiving and crossing gender boundaries: Maintaining gendered identities," *Journal of Aging Studies* 20: 253–63.

———, and K.J. Kiecolt. 2007. "Diversity among late-life couples," *Generations* 31, 3: 10–17.

———, and Kathleen F. Slevin. 2006. "Introduction," in T.M. Calasanti and K.F. Slevin, eds, *Age Matters: Realigning Feminist Thinking*. New York: Routledge, 1–17.

Calder, Gillian. 2009. "Penguins and polyamory: Using law and film to explore the essence of marriage in Canadian family law," *Canadian Journal of Women & the Law*. 21, 1: 55–89.

Calhoun, C. 2003. Social Solidarity as a Problem for Cosmopolitan Democracy. Paper presented at the Identities, Affiliations, and Allegiances, Yale University, 3–4 October.

Calhoun, Cheshire. 2000. *Feminism, the Family and the Politics of the Closet*. New York: Oxford University Press.

Calliste, Agnes. 2003. "Black families in Canada: Exploring the interconnections of race, class and gender," in Marion Lynn, ed., *Voices: Essays on Canadian Families*, 2nd edn. Toronto: Thomson Nelson.

Campaign 2000. 2008. *Family Security in Insecure Times. The Case for a Poverty Reduction Strategy for Canada. 2008 Report Card on Child and Family Poverty in Canada*. Available at http://www.campaign2000.ca/rc/C2000%20Report%20 Card%20FINAL%20Nov%2010th08.pdf; accessed 29 November 2008.

———. 2011. *Revisiting Family Security in Insecure Times: 2011 Report Card on Child and Family Poverty in Canada*. Toronto: Family Service Toronto. Available at http://www.campaign2000.ca/reportCards/ national/2011EnglishReportCard.pdf.

———. 2012. "Canada's children told to fend for themselves." 29 March. Available at http://www.campaign2000.ca/ whatsnew/releases/Canada%27s%20children%20told%20 to%20fend%20for%20themselves.pdf.

———. 2012a. "Media Release: Canada Told to Stop Failing Its Children." Available at http://www.campaign2000.ca/ whatsnew/releases/MediaReleaseRCNov24En.pdf.

Campbell, Jacqueline C. 1992. "'If I can't have you, no one can': Power and control in homicide of female partners," in J. Radford and D.E.H. Russell, eds, *Femicide: The Politics of Woman Killing*. New York: Twayne, 99–113.

Campbell, Lara. 2009. *Respectable Citizens: Gender, Family, and Unemployment in Ontario's Great Depression*. Toronto: University of Toronto Press.

Campbell, Lori D., and Michael Carroll. 2007. "The incomplete revolution: Theorizing gender when studying men who provide care to aging parents," *Journal of Men and Masculinities* 9, 4: 491–508.

———, Ingrid Connidis, and Lorraine Davies. 1999. "Sibling ties in later life: A social network analysis," *Journal of Family Issues* 20, 1: 114–48.

———, and Anne Martin-Matthews. 2000. "Caring sons: Exploring men's involvement in filial care," *Canadian Journal on Aging* 19, 1: 57–79.

———, and ———. 2003. "The gendered nature of men's filial care," *Journals of Gerontology, Series B* 58, 6: S350–S358.

———, Jenny Ploeg, Candace L. Kemp, and Carolyn Rosenthal. 2007. "Who gets grandma's silver tea service?: The passing on of cherished family possessions." Paper presented at the *36th Annual Scientific and Educational Meeting of the Canadian Association on Gerontology*, Calgary, Alberta, 1–3 November 2007.

Campbell, Marie. 2003. "Dorothy Smith and knowing the world we live in," *Journal of Sociology and Social Welfare* 30, 1: 3–22.

Canada Revenue Agency. 2005. "About the Child Disability Benefit (CDB)." Ottawa: Government of Canada. Available at http://www.cra-arc.gc.ca/benefits/faq_cdb-e.html#q1; accessed 22 July 2005.

———. 2012. *Universal Child Care Benefit (UCCB)*. 20 September. Available at http://www.cra-arc.gc.ca/bnfts/ uccb-puge/menu-eng.html.

Canada's Aging Population. 2002. Minister of Public Works and Government Services. Available at http://dsp.psd.com-munication.gc.ca/Collection/H39-608-2002E.pdf; accessed 8 April 2008.

Canadian Association of Food Banks. 2007. *Hunger Count 2007*. Available at http://www.cafb-acba.ca.

———. 2008. *Hunger Facts 2008*. Toronto: Canadian Association of Food Banks.

Canadian Broadcasting Corporation. 2004. Indepth online news: "Day Care in Canada," 25 October.

Canadian Cancer Society. 2011. "Fight back to support caregivers. Handy facts about caregivers."

Canadian Centre on Disability Studies. 2008. *Visitability: Moving Towards Livable, Sustainable Housing*. Winnipeg, Manitoba.

Canadian Council on Social Development (CCSD). 2002. *The Canadian Fact Book on Poverty*. Ottawa: CCSD.

———. 2004. *One Million Too Many—Implementing Solutions to Child Poverty in Canada: 2004 Report Card on Child Poverty in Canada*. Ottawa: CCSD.

———. 2005. *Decision Time for Canada—Let's Make Poverty History: 2005 Report Card on Child Poverty in Canada*. Ottawa: CCSD.

———. 2006. "Economic Security: Poverty." CCSD's Stats and Facts. Available at http://www.ccsd.ca/factsheets/economic_ security/poverty/ccsd_es_poverty.pdf.

———. 2007. *It Takes a Nation to Raise a Generation: Time for a National Poverty Reduction Strategy: 2007 Report Card on Child and Family Poverty in Canada*. Ottawa: CCSD.

———. 2008. *Family Security in Insecure Times: The Case for a Poverty Reduction Strategy for Canada: 2008 Report Card on Child and Family Poverty in Canada*. Ottawa: CCSD.

———. 2009. *Poverty Reductions Policy and Programs: Poverty in Ontario—Failed Promise and Renewal of Hope*. Retrieved

12 April 2012. Available at http://www.ccsd.ca/Reports/ON_Report_FINAL.pdf.

———. n.d. "Families: A Canadian Profile." Retrieved 2 May 2012. Available at http://www.ccsd.ca/factsheets/family/.

Canadian Institute for Health Information. 2009. Experiences with primary health care in Canada. Analysis in Brief. http://www.cihi.ca/CIHI-ext-portal/pdf/internet/PDF_CSE_PHC_AIB_JUL09_EN.

———. 2010. Annual Report. The difference data makes. http://www.cihi.ca/CIHI-ext-portal/pdf/internet/ANNUAL_REPORT_2011_EN.

———. 2011. Health Care in Canada: A Focus on Seniors and Aging.

Canadian Policy Research Networks (CPRN/RCPP), Family Network. 2003. "Unique Quebec Family Policy Model at Risk," 26 November. Available at http://www.cprn.org.

Canadian Press. 2008. "Auditor: Foster care failing native children." *The Star.com*, 6 May. Available at http://www.thestar.com/News/Canada/article/422012.

Canadian Research Institute for the Advancement of Women. 2002. *Violence against Women and Girls Fact Sheet*. Ottawa: CRIAW/ICREF.

Canadian Study of Health and Aging Working Group. 1994. "Canadian Study of Health and Aging: Study Methods and Prevalence of Dementia," *Canadian Medical Association Journal* 150: 899–913.

Canadianwomen. n.d. The facts about violence against women. Available at http://www.canadianwomen.org/facts-about-violence.

Capponi, Pat. 1999. *The War at Home: An Intimate Portrait of Canada's Poor*. Toronto: Viking.

Caragata, Lea. 2003. "Neoconservative realities: The social and economic marginalization of Canadian women," *International Sociology* 18, 3: 559–80.

Card, C. 1996. "Against marriage and motherhood," *Hypathia* 11: 1–23.

Carr, D. 2004a. "Gender, preloss marital dependence, and older adults' adjustment to widowhood," *Journal of Marriage and Family* 66, 1: 220–35.

———. 2004b. "The desire to date and remarry among older widows and widowers," *Journal of Marriage and Family* 66, 4: 1051–68.

———. 2005. "The psychological consequences of mid-life men's social comparisons with their young adult sons," *Journal of Marriage and Family* 67: 240–50.

Carter, Sarah. 1999. *Aboriginal People and Colonizers of Western Canada to 1900*. Toronto: University of Toronto Press.

———. 2008. *The Importance of Being Monogamous: Marriage and Nation Building in Western Canada*. Edmonton: University of Alberta Press.

Carty, Linda. 1994. "African Canadian women and the state: 'Labour only, please,'" in Peggy Bristow, ed., *We're Rooted Here and They Can't Pull Us Up: Essays in African Canadian History*. Toronto: University of Toronto Press.

Castellano, Marlene Brant. 2002. *Aboriginal Family Trends: Extended Families, Nuclear Families, Families of the Heart*. Ottawa: The Vanier Institute of the Family.

Cavan, Ruth Shonle. 1963. *The American Family*. New York: Thomas Y. Crowell.

CBC News. 2004. "Canada's child care will improve, Dryden insists," 25 October. Available at http://www.cbc.ca/story/canada/national/2004/10/25/childcare_041025.html.

———. 2005. "Day care in Canada," 9 February. Available at http://www.cbc.ca/news/background/daycare/index.html.

———. 2007. "Victoria man in murder-suicide case had troubled past," 5 September. Available at http://www.cbc.ca/canada/british-columbia/story/2007/09/05/bc-oakbay.html.

———. 2011. "William, Kate, unite in fairy-tale wedding," 29 April. Available at http://www.cbc.ca/news/world/royalwedding/story/2011/04/29/royal-wedding-day.html

———. 2012a. "Canadian foster care in crisis, experts say," *CBC News*, 19 February. Available at http://www.cbc.ca/news/canada/story/2012/02/19/foster-care-cp.html.

———. 2012b. "Foster care report in Ontario urges cut-off age rise to 25," *CBC News*, 1 March. Available at http://www.cbc.ca/news/canada/toronto/story/2012/03/01/toronto-ontario-wards-state.html.

Centers for Disease Control and Prevention. 2002a. "Trends in sexual risk behaviors among high school students–United States, 1991–2001," *Morbidity and Mortality Weekly Report* 51: 856–859.

———. 2002b. "Youth risk behavior surveillance–United States, 2001," *Morbidity and Mortality Weekly Report* 51: 1–64.

Chang, Cyril F., and Shelley I. White-Means. 1991. "The men who care: An analysis of male primary caregivers who care for frail elderly at home," *Journal of Applied Gerontology* 10, 3: 343–58.

Chappell, M. 2007. "No relief in sight: Problematic substance use and women with disabilities in Canada," in N. Poole and L. Greaves, eds, *Highs & Lows: Canadian Perspectives on Women and Substance Use*. Toronto: Centre for Addiction and Mental Health, 79–89.

Chappell, N.L. 2008. "Comparing Caregivers to Older Adults in Shanghai," *The Asian Journal of Gerontology and Geriatrics* 3, 2: 57–65.

———, and H.A. Cooke. 2010. "Age related disabilities—Aging and quality of life," in J.H. Stone and M. Blouin, eds, *International Encyclopedia of Rehabilitation*. Available at http://cirrie.buffalo.edu/encyclopedia/en/article/189/.

———, Ellen Gee, Lynn McDonald, and Michael Stones. 2003. *Aging in Contemporary Canada*. Toronto: Prentice-Hall.

———, and M. Penning. 2012. *Health Inequalities in Later Life, Differences by Age/Stage. Final Report*. Ottawa: Public Health Agency of Canada.

———, and E. Pridham. 2010. *Age Friendly Communities (AFC)—Good for Caregivers*. Ottawa: Public Health Agency of Canada.

———, and R.C. Reid. 2002. "Burden and well-being among caregivers: Examining the distinction," *The Gerontologist* 42, 6: 772–80.

Chatters, Linda M., and Robert J. Taylor. 2005 "Religion and families," in Vern L. Bengston, Alan C. Acock, Katherine R. Allen, Peggy Dilworth-Anderson, and David M. Klein, eds, *Sourcebook of Family Theory and Research*. Thousand Oaks, Calif.: Sage.

Chatzky, Jean, and Amanda Gengler. 2005. "The blowout," *Money* 34, 5: 124–9.

Cheal, David. 1987. "'Showing them you love them': Gift giving and the dialectic of intimacy," *The Sociological Review* 35, 1: 150–69.

———. 1988a. *The Gift Economy.* New York: Routledge.

———. 1988b. "Relationships in time: Ritual, social structure, and the life course," *Studies in Symbolic Interaction* 9: 83–109.

———. 1991. *Family and the State of Theory.* Toronto: University of Toronto Press.

———. 1999. *New Poverty: Families in Postmodern Society.* Westport, Conn.: Greenwood.

———. 2002. *The Sociology of Family Life.* Houndmills, Basingstoke, Hampshire: Palgrave.

———. 2008. *Families in Today's World: A Comparative Approach.* London: Routledge.

Che-Alford, Janet, and Brian Hamm. 1999. "Under one roof: Three generations living together," *Canadian Social Trends* 53: 6–9. Available at http://dsp-psd.pwgsc.gc.ca/Collection-R/Statcan/11-008-XIE/0019911-008-XIE.pdf.

Chekki, Dan A. 1999. "Poverty amidst plenty: How do Canadian cities cope with rising poverty?" *Research in Community Sociology* 9: 141–52.

Chen, Wen-Hao, and Miles Corak. 2008. "Child poverty and changes in child poverty," *Demography* 45, 3: 537–53.

Cherlin, Andrew. 2004. "The deinstitutionalization of American marriage," *Journal of Marriage and the Family* 66: 848–61.

———, and Frank F. Furstenberg. 1994. "Stepfamilies in the United States: A reconsideration," *Annual Review of Sociology* 20: 359–81.

Chesley, N. 2011. "Stay-at-home fathers and breadwinning mothers gender, couple dynamics, and social change," *Gender and Society* 25, 5: 642–64.

Chesser, Barbara Jo. 1980. "Analysis of wedding rituals: An attempt to make weddings more meaningful," *Family Relations* 29: 204–9.

Chiang, N. "Astronaut families: Transnational lives of middle-class Taiwanese married women in Canada," *Social and Cultural Geography* 9, 5: 505–18.

Child Care Advocacy Association of Canada. 2007. "Women's employment patterns and the need for child care," Available at http://www.fafia-afai.org/files/fafia_ccaac_childcarefinal.doc.

———. 2011. With the Coalition of Child Care Advocates of British Columbia. "A Tale of Two Canadas: Implementing Rights in Early Childhood." February. Available at http://www.cccabc.bc.ca/res/rights/ccright_tale2can_brief.pdf?utm_source=+Advocacy+Update+February+6&utm_campaign=child+care+canada&utm_medium=archive.

———. 2012. "Child care—Solutions for children, families, communities and the economy: 2013 pre-budget consultation brief of the Child Care Advocacy Association of Canada." 9 August. Available at http://www.childcarecanada.org/documents/research-policy-practice/12/08/child-care-solutions-children-families-communities-and-econ; accessed 10 October 2012.

Child Space Statistics. 2007. Available at http://www.childcare-canada.org/sites/default/files/ccspacestatistics07_0.pdf.

Child Welfare Report of 2011, Canada. "Children's Well-Being: The Ontarian

Childcare Resource and Research Unit, Canada. 2007. "Child Care Space Statistics 2007." Available at http://www.childcarecanada.org/sites/default/files/ccspacestatistics07_0.pdf.

Chipperfield, J.G., and B. Havens. 2001. "Gender differences in the relationship between marital status transitions and life satisfaction in later life," *Journals of Gerontology* 56, 3: 176–86.

Choi, H., and N.F. Marks. 2008. "Marital conflict, depressive symptoms, and functional impairment," *Journal of Marriage and Family* 70, 2: 377–90.

Christiansen, Shawn, and Rob Palkovitz. 2001. "Why the 'good provider' role still matters: Providing as a form of paternal involvement," *Journal of Family Issues* 22: 84–106.

Chuang, S.S., and Y. Su. 2009. "Says who?: Decision-making and conflicts among Chinese-Canadian and mainland Chinese parents of young children," *Sex Roles* 60, 7–8: 527–36.

Chunn, Dorothy. 2003. "Boys will be men, girls will be mothers: The legal regulation of childhood in Toronto and Vancouver," in Nancy Janovicek and Joy Parr, eds, *Histories of Canadian Children and Youth.* Toronto: Oxford University Press.

Church, Elizabeth. 1999. "The poisoned apple: Stepmothers' experience of envy and jealousy," *Journal of Feminist and Family Therapy* 11: 1–18.

Cicirelli, Victor G. 2002. *Older Adults' Views on Death.* New York: Springer.

Citizenship and Immigration Canada. 2008. "Facts and figures 2007: Immigration overview: Permanent residents." Available at http://www.cic.gc.ca/english/resources/statistics/facts2007/01.asp.

Clark, W. 2006. "Interreligioius unions in Canada," *Canadian Social Trends*, 21 November: 17–24.

Cleveland, Gordon, Morley Gunderson, and Douglas Hyatt. 1996. "Child care costs and the employment decision of women: Canadian evidence," *Canadian Journal of Economics* 29, 1: 132–51.

———, ———, and ———. 2008. *New Evidence about Child Care in Canada: Use Patterns, Affordability and Quality.* 7 October. Montréal: Institute for Research on Public Policy.

Climateactionnetwork.ca. 2011. "Canada wins Fossil of the Year Award in Durban: Canadians in Durban hold moment of silence for the fifth Colossal Fossil in a row." Available at http://climateactionnetwork.ca/2011/12/09/canada-wins-fossil-of-the-year-award-in-durban; accessed 30 April 2012.

Cohen, G.D. 1999. "Marriage and divorce in later life: Editorial," *American Journal of Geriatric Psychiatry* 7, 3: 185–7.

Cohen, Marjorie Griffin. 2009. "Patriarchal relations of production in nineteenth-century Ontario," in Bonnie Fox, ed., *Family Patterns, Gender Relations.* Toronto: Oxford University Press, 85–96.

Cohen, Philip N. 2004. "The gender division of labor: 'Keeping house' and occupational segregation in the United States," *Gender & Society* 18, 2: 239–52.

———, and Lynne M. Caspar. 2002. "In whose home? Multigenerational families in the United States," *Sociological Perspectives* 45: 1–20.

Cohen, R. 2000. "'Mom is a Stranger': The Negative Impact of Immigration Policies on the Family Life of Filipina Domestic Workers," *Canadian Ethnic Studies* 32, 3: 76–89.

College of Home Economics, Iowa State University. 1972. *Families of the Future.* Ames: Iowa State University Press.

Collin, Chantal, and Hilary Jensen. 2009. *A Statistical Profile of Poverty in Canada.* Ottawa: Parliamentary Information and Research Service, Library of Parliament.

Collins, Patricia Hill. 1994. "Shifting the center: Race, class and feminist theorizing about motherhood," in Evelyn N. Glenn, Grace Chang, and Linda R. Forcey, eds, *Mothering: Ideology, Experience and Agency.* New York: Routledge.

———. 1999. "The meaning of motherhood in black culture and black mother–daughter relationships," in Maxine Baca Zinn, Pierrette Hondagneu-Sotelo, and Michael A. Messner, eds, *Through the Prism of Difference.* Boston: Allyn and Bacon.

———. 2000. *Black Feminist Thought: Knowledge, Consciousness, and the Politics of Empowerment,* 2nd edn. London and New York: Routledge.

———. 2004. *Black Sexual Politics: African Americans, Gender, and the New Racism.* New York: Routledge.

Collins, Stephanie Baker. 2005. "An understanding of poverty from those who are poor," *Action Research* 3, 1: 9–31.

Coltrane, Scott. 1996. *Family Man: Fatherhood, Housework, and Gender Equity.* New York: Oxford University Press.

———. 2000. "Research on household labor: Modeling and measuring the social embeddedness of routine family work," *Journal of Marriage and the Family* 62, 4: 1208–33.

———. 2003. "Fathering: Paradoxes, contradictions, and dilemmas," in Lawrence H. Ganong, ed., *Handbook of Contemporary Families: Considering the Past, Contemplating the Future.* Thousand Oaks, Calif.: Sage.

———, and Michele Adams. 2001. "Men's family work: Child-centered fathering and the sharing of domestic labor," in Nancy L. Marshall, ed., *Working Families: The Man of the American Home.* Berkeley: University of California Press.

Comacchio, Cynthia. 1993. *Nations are Built of Babies: Saving Ontario's Mothers and Children, 1900–1940.* Montreal: McGill-Queen's University Press.

———. 1999. *The Infinite Bonds of Family: Domesticity in Canada, 1850 to 1940.* Toronto: University of Toronto Press.

———. 2000. "'The History of Us:' Social Science, History, and the Relations of Family in Canada," *Labour/Le Travail* Special Millennium issue 46: 167–220.

Comeau, R. 1989. *Jean Lesage et l'éveil d'une nation: les débuts de la révolution tranquille.* Sillery, Que.: Presses de l'Université du Québec.

Community Action Toward Children's Health (CATCH). 2008. "Canada Still Needs Childcare." Available at http://www.catchcoalition.ca/UserFiles/File/Child_care_elections.

Conference Board of Canada. 2009. *Report Card on Child Poverty.* September. Available at http://www.conference-board.ca/hcp/details/society/child-poverty.aspx#_ftnref5.

Congleton, Roger D., and Feler Bose. 2010. "The rise of the modern welfare state, ideology, institutions and income security: Analysis and evidence," *Public Choice* 144: 535–55.

Connell, R.W. 1987. *Gender and Power: Society, the Person and Sexual Politics.* Stanford, CA: Stanford University Press.

Connidis, Ingrid A. 2001. *Family Ties and Aging.* Thousand Oaks, Calif.: Sage.

———. and Lori D. Campbell. 1995. "Closeness, confiding, and contact among siblings in middle and late adulthood," *Journal of Family Issues* 16: 722–45.

———. and Candace Kemp. 2008. "Negotiating actual and anticipated parental support: Multiple sibling voices in three-generation families," *Journal of Aging Studies* 22: 229–38.

———. and Julie A. McMullin. 1993. "To have or have not: Parent status and the subjective well-being of older men and women," *Gerontologist* 33: 630–6.

Connolly, Jennifer, Wyndal Furman, and Roman Konarski. 2000. "The role of peers in the emergence of heterosexual romantic relationships in adolescence," *Child Development* 71: 1395–408.

Conway, John. 2003. *The Canadian Family in Crisis,* 5th edn. Toronto: James Lorimer and Company.

Conway, Peg. 2006. "A modest wedding proposal," *U.S. Catholic* (November): 24–6.

Cook, Daniel Thomas. 2004. *The Commodification of Childhood.* Durham, NC: Duke University Press.

Cooke, Martin, and Amber Gazso. 2009. "Taking a life course perspective on social assistance use in Canada: A different approach," *Canadian Journal of Sociology* 34, 2: 349–72.

Cool, J. *Wage Gap Between Women and Men.* Publication no. 2010-30-E. Ottawa: Parliament of Canada, 2010. Available at http://www.parl.gc.ca/Content/LOP/ResearchPublications/2010-30-e.pdf; accessed 20 April 2012.

Coontz, Stephanie. 1993. *The Way We Never Were: American Families and the Nostalgia Trap.* New York: Basic Books.

———. 2005. *Marriage, a History: From Obedience to Intimacy or How Love Conquered Marriage.* New York, NY: Viking Penguin.

Cooper, Alvin, and Leda Sportolari. 1997. "Romance in cyberspace: Understanding online attraction," *Journal of Sex Education and Therapy* 22: 7–14.

Coote, Anne, Harriet Harman, and Patricia Hewitt. 1990. *The Family Way: A New Approach to Policy-Making.* London: Institute for Public Policy Research.

Copp, Terry. 1974. *The Anatomy of Poverty: The Condition of the Working Class in Montreal, 1897–1929.* Toronto: McClelland and Stewart.

Corak, Myles. 1999. *Death and Divorce: The Long-term Consequences of Parental Loss on Adolescents.* Research Paper Series, No. 135. Catalogue no. 11F0019MIE. Ottawa: Statistics Canada.

———, ed. 2004. *Generational Income Mobility in North America and Europe.* Cambridge: Cambridge University Press.

———. 2009. *Chasing the Same Dream, Climbing Different Ladders: Economic Mobility in the United States and Canada.* New York: The Pew Charitable Trusts.

———, Lori J. Curtis, and Shelley Phipps. 2010. *Economic Mobility, Family Background, and the Well-Being of Children in the United States and Canada* (Discussion Paper No. 4814). Bonn: Institute for the Study of Labor.

Correll, Shelley. 1995. "The ethnography of an electronic bar: The Lesbian Café," *Journal of Contemporary Ethnography* 24: 270–98.

Coser, Rose Laub. 1974. *The Family: Its Structure and Functions*, 2nd edn. New York: St Martin's Press.

Cossette, Lucie, and Édith Duclos. 2002. *Participation and Activity Limitation Survey: A Profile of Disability in Canada, 2001*. Ottawa: Minister of Industry, Statistics Canada.

Cossman, Brenda. 1996. "Same sex couples and the politics of family status," in Janine Brodie, ed., *Women and Canadian Public Policy*. Toronto: Harcourt Brace & Company, 223–53.

Cote, A., M. Kerisit, and M. Cote. 2001. *Sponsorship for Better or for Worse: The Impact of Sponsorship on the Equality Rights of Immigrant Women*. Ottawa: Status of Women Canada.

Cott, Nancy F. 2002. *Public Vows: A History of Marriage and the Nation*. Cambridge, MA: Harvard University Press.

Cotton, C., M. Webber, and Y. Saint-Pierre. 1998. *Should the Low Income Cutoffs Be Updated?* Ottawa: Statistics Canada, Catalogue no. 75F0002MIE-99009.

Cotton, S. 1999. "Marital status and mental health revisited: Examining the importance of risk factors and resources," *Family Relations* 48, 3: 225–33.

Coyle, Jim. 2006. "'A miserable existence' eked out behind the closed door of a bedroom," *Toronto Star*, 8 April, 1.

Cradock, Gerald. 2007. "The responsibility dance: Creating neoliberal children," *Childhood* 14, 2: 153–72.

Craig, Lyn. 2006. "Does father care mean fathers share? A comparison of how mothers and fathers in intact families spend time with children," *Gender and Society* 20, 2: 259–81.

Cranswick, C., and D. Thomas. 2005. "Elder care and the complexities of social networks," *Canadian Social Trends* (Summer): 10–15.

Cranswick, K. 2003. *Caring for an Aging Society*. Ottawa: Statistics Canada. Available at http://www.statcan. ca/english/freepub/89-582-XIE/index.htm; accessed 12 September 2008.

———. and D. Dosman. 2008. "Eldercare: What we know today," *Canadian Social Trends*. Ottawa: Statistics Canada, Catalogue no. 11-008-X, No. 86.

Crawford, Cameron. 2002. *Learning Disabilities in Canada: Economic Costs to Individuals, Families and Society*. North York: Roeher Institute.

Crawford, Maria, and Rosemary Gartner. 1992. *Woman Killing: Intimate Femicide in Ontario, 1974–1990*. Toronto: Women We Honour Action Committee.

Crawford, Mary, and Danielle Popp. 2003. "Sexual double standards: A review and methodological critique of two decades of research," *Journal of Sex Research* 40: 13–26.

Crittenden, Anne. 2010. *The Price of Motherhood: Why the Most Important Job in the World Is Still the Least Valued*. New York: Picador, 10th Anniversary Edition.

Crull, Marie C. 2008. *Following Sexual Abuse: A Sociological Interpretation of Identity Re-formation in Reflexive Therapy*. Toronto: University of Toronto.

CTV News. 2007. "Man sentenced in landmark elder abuse case." Available at http://www.ctv.ca/servlet/ArticleNews/story/CTVNews/20070320/elder_abuse_sentence_070320/20070320?hub=Canada; accessed 10 November 2008.

———. 2008a. "RESPs to be set up for children in foster care," 24 April. Available at http://www.ctv.ca/servlet/ ArticleNews/story/CTVNews/20080424/RESP_benefits_ 080424/20080424?hub=TopStories.

———. 2011. "Liberals pledge billion-dollar child care fund," *CTV News*, 31 March. Available at http://www. ctv.ca/servlet/ArticleNews/story/CTVNews/20110331/ ignatieff-election-110331/20110331?s_name=election2011.

———. 2012. "Data lacking on numbers, services for foster kids," *CTV News*, 19 February. Available at http://www.ctv.ca/CTVNews/Canada/20120219/ foster-care-data-canada-120219/.

CUPE Ontario. 2008. "Creator of Quebec child care system to be honoured on Child Care Worker Appreciation Day." 20 October. Available at http://www.cupe.on.ca/doc. php?document_id=572&lang=en.

Currie, Dawn H. 1998. "Violent men or violent women: Whose definition counts?" in Bergen (1998a: 97–111).

Curtis, Lori J., Martin D. Dooley, and Shelley A. Phipps. 2004. "Child well-being and neighbourhood quality: Evidence from the Canadian National Longitudinal Study of Children and Youth," *Social Science and Medicine* 58, 10: 1917–27.

Daatland, S.O., and A. Lowenstein. 2005. "Intergenerational solidarity and the family–welfare state balance," *European Journal of Aging* 2, 3: 208–12.

Daly, K., L. Ashbourne, and J.L. Brown. 2009. "Fathers' perceptions of children's influence: Implications for involvement," *The ANNALS of the American Academy of Political and Social Science* 624, 1: 61–77.

Daly, Kerry. 2004. *The Changing Culture of Parenting*. Ottawa: Vanier Institute of the Family.

———, and Rob Palkovitz. 2004. "Guest editorial: Reworking work and family issues for fathers," *Fathering* 2: 211–13.

Dandurand, Renée B., and Marianne Kempeneers. 2002. "Pour une analyse comparative et contextuelle de la politique familiale au Québec," *Recherches socio-graphiques* 43, 1: 9–78.

Daneback, Kristian, Al Cooper, and Sven-Axel Mansson. 2005. "An Internet study of cybersex participants," *Archives of Sexual Behavior* 34, 3: 321–28.

Darroch, Gordon. 2001. "Home and away: Patterns of residence, schooling, and work among children and never married young adults, Canada, 1871 and 1901," *Journal of Family History* 26, 2: 220–50.

Darvishpour, M. 2003. "Immigrant women challenge the role of men: How the changing power relationship within Iranian families in Sweden intensifies family conflicts after immigration," *Journal of Comparative Family Studies* 33, 2: 271–96.

Davids, Leo. 1971. "North American marriage: 1990," *The Futurist* 5, 2: 190–4.

Davidson, Kate S., Sara Arber, and Jay Ginn. 2000. "Gendered meanings of care work within late life marital relationships," *Canadian Journal on Aging* 19, 4: 536–53.

Davies, C., and D. Williams. 2002. "The Grandparent Study Report." AARP.

Davies, Megan. 2003. *Into the House of Old: A History of Residential Care in British Columbia*. Montreal: McGill-Queen's University Press.

Davies, Sharon, and Margaret Denton. 2002. "Economic well-being of older women who became divorced or separated in mid- or later life," *Canadian Journal on Aging* 21, 4: 477–93.

Daws, L. B. 2009. *Happily Ever After.com: The Construction of Identity on Wedding Websites*. Lexington, KY: University of Kentucky Press.

Dechêne, Louise. 1992. *Habitants and Merchants in Seventeenth Century Montreal*. Montreal: McGill-Queen's University Press.

DeJong Gierveld, J., T. Van Tilburg, and L. Lecchini. 1997. "Socio-economic resources, household composition and social network as determinants of well-being among Dutch and Tuscan older adults," *Genus* 53, 3–4: 75–100.

DeKeseredy, Walter S. 1996. "Patterns of family violence," in M. Baker, ed., *Families: Changing Trends in Canada*. Toronto: McGraw-Hill, 249–72.

———. 2011. *Violence Against Women: Myths, Facts, Controversies*. Toronto: University of Toronto Press

———, Shahid Alvi, and Martin D. Schwartz. 2006. "An economic exclusion/male peer support model looks as 'wedfare' and woman abuse," *Critical Criminology* 14: 23–41.

———, and Katharine Kelly. 1993. "The incidence and prevalence of women abuse in Canadian university and college dating relationships," *Canadian Journal of Sociology* 18: 137–59.

———, and Linda Macleod. 1997. *Woman Abuse: A Sociological Story*. Toronto: Harcourt Brace.

———, and Martin D. Schwartz. 1997. *Sexual Assault on the College Campus: The Role of Male Peer Support*. Thousand Oaks, Calif.: Sage.

———, and ———. 2008. "Separation/divorce sexual assault in rural Ohio: Survivor's perceptions," *Journal of Prevention and Intervention in the Community* 36: 105–20.

Delbès, C., and J. Gaymu. 2006. "Les femmes vieillissent seules, les homes vieillissent seules, les homes vieillissent à deux un bilan européen," *Population et Société* 419: 1–4.

Delphy, Christine. 1984. *Close to Home: A Materialist Analysis of Women's Oppression*. London: Hutchinson.

Dempsey, D. 2010. "Conceiving and negotiating reproductive relationships: Lesbian and gay men forming families with children," *Sociology* 44, 6: 1145–62.

Den Tandt, Michael. 2012. "PM must look beyond traditional nuclear family," *Calgary Herald*, 20 September.

Dentinger, Emma, and Marin Clarkberg. 2002. "Informal caregiving and retirement timing among men and women: Gender and caregiving relationships in later mid-life," *Journal of Family Issues* 23: 857–79.

Denton, F.T., and B.G. Spencer. 2010. "Changing prevalence in an aging population and some implications for the delivery of health care services," *Canadian Journal on Aging* 29, 1: 11–21.

Department of Justice Statistics. 2003. "Abuse of older adults: A fact sheet." Available at http://canada.justice.gc.ca/en/ps/fm/adultsfs.html; accessed 27 September 2004.

DePaulo, Bella M., and Wendy L. Morris. 2005. "Singles in society and science," *Psychological Inquiry* 16, 2–3: 57–83.

Derouin, J. 2004. "Asians and multiculturalism in Canada's three major cities," in C. Andrews, ed., *Our Diverse Cities* 1 (Spring): 58–62.

des Rivières-Pigeon, Catherine, Marie-Josèphe Saurel-Cubizolles, and Patrizia Romito. 2002. "Division of domestic work and psychological distress one year after childbirth:

A comparison between France, Quebec and Italy," *Journal of Community & Applied Social Psychology* 12: 397–409.

Desjardins, Bertrand, Alain Bideau, Guy Brunet, Hubert Charbonneau and Jacques Legare. 2000. "From France to New France: Quebec family names, past and present," *History of the Family* 5, 2: 215–27.

DesMeules, Marie, Donna Stewart, Arminée Kazanjian, Heather McLean, Jennifer Payne, and Bilkis Vissandjée, eds. 2003. *Women's Health Surveillance Report: A Multi-dimensional Look at the Health of Canadian Women*. Ottawa: Canadian Institute for Health Research. Available at http://www.phac-aspc.gc.ca/publicat/whsr-rssf/pdf/CPHI_WomensHealth_e.pdf; accessed 15 May 2005.

———, Linda Turner, and Robert Cho. 2004. "Morbidity Experiences and Disability Among Canadian Women," *BMC Women's Health* 4, Suppl. 1: S10. Available at http://www.biomedcentral.com/1472-6874/4/S1/S10.

Deutsch, Francine M. 1999. *Halving It All: How Equally Shared Parenting Works*. Cambridge, Mass.: Harvard University Press.

———, and S. Saxon. 1998. "Traditional ideologies, non-traditional lives," *Sex Roles* 38: 331–62.

Deven, Fred, and Peter Moss, eds. 2005. *Leave Policies and Research: Overviews and Country Notes*. Brussels: Centre for Population and Family Studies.

DeVerteuil, Geoffrey. 2005. "Welfare neighborhoods: Anatomy of a concept," *Journal of Poverty* 9, 2: 23–41.

Devine, Heather. 2004. *The People Who Own Themselves: Aboriginal Ethnogenesis in a Canadian Family, 1660–1900*. Calgary: University of Calgary Press.

Devine, M., and T. Earle. 2011. "Grandparenting: Roles and responsibilities and its implications for kinship care policies," *Vulnerable Children and Youth Studies* 6, 2: 124–33.

Di Leonardo, Micaela. 1987. "The female world of cards and holidays: Women, families and the world of kinship," *Signs* 12, 3: 440–53.

Dickason, Olive. 2010. *A Concise History of Canada's First Nations*, 2nd ed. Don Mills, ON: Oxford University Press.

Dienhart, Anna. 1998. *Reshaping Fatherhood: The Social Construction of Shared Parenting*. London: Sage.

DisAbled Women's Network (DAWN) Toronto. 1995. "The risk of physical and sexual assault," *Abilities: Canada's Lifestyle Magazine for People with Disabilities* 22 (Spring): 32–3.

———. 2003. "Factsheets on Women with DisAbilities."

Dobash, Emerson R., and Russell P. Dobash, eds. 1998. *Rethinking Violence against Women*. Thousand Oaks, Calif.: Sage.

———, and ———. 1979. *Violence against Wives: A Case against Patriarchy*. New York: Free Press.

———, ———, Kate Cavanagh, and Ruth Lewis. 1995. *Research Evaluation of Programmes for Violent Men*. Manchester, UK: Violence Research Unit.

Doe, Tanis. 1999. "Ecological view of prevention of violence," available at http://members.shaw.ca/dewresearch/others.html, accessed 17 March 2005.

Doherty, Gillian, Martha Friendly, and Jane Beach. 2003. *OECD Thematic Review of Early Childhood Education and Care: Canadian Background Report*. Paris: OECD.

Doherty, William, Edward Kouneski, and Martha Erickson. 1998. "Responsible fathering: An overview and conceptual framework," *Journal of Marriage and the Family* 60: 277–92.

Dosanjh, R., S. Deo, and S. Sidhu. 1994. *Spousal Abuse in the South Asian Community*. Vancouver: Mimeo.

Doucet, A. 2011. "'It's not good for a man to be interested in other people's children': Fathers and public displays of care," in Esther Dermott and Julie Seymour, eds, *Displaying Families: New Theoretical Directions in Family and Intimate Life*, pp. 81-101. London, UK: Palgrave MacMillan.

———, and L. Merla. 2007. "Stay-at-home fathering," *Community, Work, & Family* 10, 4: 455–73.

Doucet, Andrea. 1995. "Gender equality, gender differences and care: Toward understanding gendered labor in British dual earner households," PhD thesis, University of Cambridge.

———. 2000. "'There's a huge difference between me as a male carer and women': Gender, domestic responsibility, and the community as an institutional arena," *Community, Work and Family* 3, 2: 163–84.

———. 2001. "You see the need perhaps more clearly than I have: Exploring gendered processes of domestic responsibility," *Journal of Family Issues* 22, 3: 328–57.

———. 2004. "Fathers and the responsibility for children: A puzzle and a tension," *Atlantis: A Women's Studies Journal* 28, 2: 103–14.

———. 2006. *Do Men Mother?* Toronto: University of Toronto Press.

———. 2009. "Gender equality and gender differences: Parenting, habitus, and embodiment (The 2008 Porter Lecture)," *Canadian Review of Sociology* 46, 2: 103–21.

———. 2012. "The evolution of the stay-at-home dad" (op ed.), *Ottawa Citizen*, 18 June. Available at http://www.ottawacitizen.com/life/evolution+stay+home/6790417/story.html#ixzz1z5gDYTfT.

Dowd, Nancy E. 2000. *Redefining Fatherhood*. New York: New York University Press.

Downing, Joseph J. 1970. "The tribal family and the society of awakening," in Otto (1970a: 119–36).

Dozier, Raine, and Pepper Schwartz. 2001. "Intimate relationships," in Judith R. Blau, ed., *The Blackwell Companion to Sociology*. Malden, MA: Blackwell Publishing.

Dube, Rebecca. 2008. "The daddy shift," *Globe and Mail*, 24 June: L1–L2.

Dubinsky, Karen. 2010. *Babies Without Borders: Adoption and Migration Across the Americas*. Toronto: University of Toronto Press.

Duchesne, Louis. 2006. *La Situation Démographique au Québec—Bilan 2006 (Chapitre 5—La Fécondité)*. Québec: Institut de la Statistique du Québec.

Duck, Waverly O. 2012. "An ethnographic portrait of a precarious life: Getting by on even less," *The Annals of the American Academy of Political and Social Science* 642: 124–38.

Duffy, Ann, and J. Momirow. 1997. *Family Violence: A Canadian Perspective*. Toronto: Lorimer.

Dugan, Meg K., and Roger R. Hock. 2000. *It's My Life Now: Starting Over After an Abusive Relationship*. New York: Routledge.

Dumont, Micheline, Michèle Jean, Marie Lavigne, and Jennifer Stoddart. 1987. *Quebec Women—A History*. Toronto: Women's Press.

Dunbrack, Janet. 2003. *Respite for Family Caregivers—An Environmental Scan of Publicly-funded Programs in Canada*. Available at http://www.hc-sc.gc.ca/hcs-sss/pubs/home-domicile/2003-respite-releve/index-eng.php#a1.

Duncan, Greg J., and Jeanne Brooks-Gunn, eds. 1997. *Consequences of Growing Up Poor*. New York: Russell Sage Foundation.

Duncan, Simon, and Miranda Phillips. 2010. "People who live apart together (LATs)—how different are they?" *The Sociological Review* 58, 1: 112–34.

Dunlop, Rosemary, and Ailsa Burns. 1995. "The sleeper effect—Myth or reality?" *Journal of Marriage and Family*, 57: 375–86.

Dunn, P.A. 1991. "Accessible housing legislation and policies: A framework for future policy development," *Report of the CIB Expert Seminar on Building Non-Handicapping Environments*. Budapest: Independent Living Institute.

Dunne, Gillian. 2000. "Opting into motherhood: Lesbians blurring the boundaries and transforming the meaning of parenthood and kinship," *Gender & Society* 14, 1: 11–35.

———. 2000a. "Lesbians as authentic workers? Institutional heterosexuality and the reproduction of gender inequalities," *Sexualities* 3, 2: 133–48.

Duvall, Evelyn Millis, and Ruben Hill. 1948. *Reports of the Committee on the Dynamic of Family Interaction*. Washington: National Conference on Family Life.

———, and ———. 1988. "Family development's first forty years," *Family Relations* 37, 2: 127–34.

Duxbury, Linda, and Chris Higgins. 2002. *2001 National Work–Life Conflict Study: Report One*. Ottawa: Health Canada.

———, ———, and Karen L. Johnson. 2004. *The 2001 National Work–Life Conflict Study: Report Three—Exploring the Link between Work–Life Conflict and Demands on Canada's Health Care System*. Ottawa: Public Health Agency of Canada.

Eaton, Asia Anna, and Suzanna Rose. 2011. "Has dating become more egalitarian? A 35 year review using sex roles," *Sex Roles* 64: 843–862.

Ebaugh, H., and M. Curry. 2000. "Fictive kin associal capital in new immigrant communities," *Sociological Perspectives* 43, 2: 189–209.

Edin, Kathryn, and Laura Lein. 1997. *Making Ends Meet: How Single Mothers Survive Welfare and Low-Wage Work*. New York: Russell Sage Foundation.

Edwards, John N. 1967. "The future of the family revisited," *Journal of Marriage and the Family* 29, 3: 505–11.

eHarmony. Available at http://www.eharmony.com. Accessed 21 November 2008.

Ehrensaft, Diane. 2001. "The kinderdult: The new child born to conflict between work and family," in Rosanna Hertz and Nancy L. Marshall, eds, *Working Families: The Transformation of the American Home*. Berkeley: University of California Press, 304–22.

Eichler, Margrit. 1975. "The equalitarian family in Canada?" in P.S. Wakil, ed., *Marriage, Family and Society: Canadian Perspectives*. Toronto: Butterworths, 223–35.

———. 1983. *Families in Canada Today: Recent Changes and Their Policy Consequences*. Toronto: Gage.

———. 1997. *Family Shifts: Families, Policies and Gender Equality*. Toronto: Oxford University Press.

———, and Patrizia Albanese. 2007. "What is household work? A critique of assumptions underlying empirical studies of housework and an alternative approach," *Canadian Journal of Sociology* 32, 2: 227–58.

Elder, G.H., Jr. 1994. "Time, human agency, and social change: Perspectives on the life course," *Social Psychology Quarterly* 57, 1: 4–15.

Elections Canada. 2008. Estimation of Voter Turnout by Age Group at the 2008 Federal General Election. Available at http://www.elections.ca/res/rec/part/estim/estimation40_e.pdf.

Elkin, Frederick. 1964. *The Family in Canada: An Account of Present Knowledge and Gaps in Knowledge about Canadian Families*. Ottawa: Vanier Institute of the Family.

Elliot, Patricia, and Nancy Mandell. 1998. "Feminist theories," in Nancy Mandel, ed., *Feminist Issues: Race, Class and Sexuality*. Toronto: Prentice-Hall Allyn and Bacon Canada, 2–21.

Elliott, Katherine. 1970. *The Family and Its Future. A Ciba Foundation Symposium*. London: J.&A. Churchill.

Ellis, Desmond, and Walter S. DeKeseredy. 1997. "Re-thinking estrangement, interventions and intimate femicide," *Violence Against Women* 3, 6: 590–609.

Elze, Diane. 2003. "Gay, lesbian and bisexual youths' perceptions of their high school environments and comfort in school," *Children and Schools* 25: 225–39.

Emke, Ivan. 2002. "Why the sad face?: Secularization and the changing function of funerals in Newfoundland," *Mortality* 7, 3: 269–84.

Engels, Friedrich. 1972 [1884]. *The Origin of the Family, Private Property and the State*. New York: Pathfinder.

Engler-Stringer, Rachel, and Shawna Berenbaum. 2007. "Exploring food security with collective kitchens participants in three Canadian Cities," *Qualitative Health Research* 17, 1: 75–84.

English Federation of Disability Sport. 2004. "Count me in! Development framework 2004–2008." United Kingdom: Author.

English, Diana J., Richard Thompson, J. Christopher Graham, and Ernestine C. Briggs. 2005. "Toward a definition of neglect in young children," *Child Maltreatment* 10, 2: 190–206.

Enns, Ruth. 1999. *A Voice Unheard: The Latimer Case and People with Disabilities*. Halifax: Fernwood.

Environics Research Group. *Canadian Attitudes towards Disability Issues: 2004 Benchmark Survey*. Ottawa: Office for Disability Issues. Available at http://www.sdc.gc.ca/asp/gateway.asp?hr=/en/hip/odi/documents/attitudesPoll/benchmarkSurvey/toc.shtml&hs=pyp.

Epstein, Rachel. 2003. "Lesbian families," in Lynn, 2nd ed. (2003: 76–102).

———, ed. 2009. *"Who's Your Daddy?" And Other Writings on Queer Parenting*. Toronto: Sumach Press.

Errington, Elizabeth Jane. 1995. *Wives and Mothers, Schoolmistresses and Scullery Maids: Working Women in Upper Canada, 1790–1840*. Montreal: McGill-Queen's University Press.

Eshleman, J. Ross, and Susannah J. Wilson. 2001. *The Family*, 3rd Canadian edn. Toronto: Pearson Education.

Espiritu, Yen Le. 1997. *Asian American Women and Men: Labor, Laws and Love*. Thousand Oaks, CA: Sage Publications.

Este, D.C., and A. Tachable. 2009. "Fatherhood in the Canadian context: Perceptions and experiences of Sudanese refugee men," *Sex Roles* 60, 7–8: 451–5.

Evans, Patricia M., and Gerda R. Wekerle, eds. 1997. *Women and the Canadian Welfare State: Challenges and Change*. Toronto: University of Toronto Press.

Eyre, Stephen L., Emily Arnold, Eric Peterson, and Thomas Strong. 2007. "Romantic relationships and their social context among gay/bisexual male youth in the Castro District of San Francisco," *Journal of Homosexuality* 53, 4: 1–29.

Fahrni, Magda. 2005. *Household Politics: Montreal Families and Postwar Reconstruction*. Toronto: University of Toronto Press.

Faircloth, Charlotte. 2010. "What science says is best: Parenting practices, scientific authority and maternal identity," *Sociological Research Online Special Section on 'Changing Parenting Culture* 15 (4). Available at http://www.socresonline.org.uk/15/4/4.html.

Family Service Toronto. 2011. *Revisiting Family Security in Insecure Times: 2011 Report Card on Child and Family Poverty in Canada*. Toronto: Campaign 2000.

Fantino, Ana Marie, and Alice Colak. 2001. "Refugee children in Canada: Searching for identity," *Child Welfare* 80: 587–96.

Fantuzzo, John W., and Wanda K. Mohr. 1999. "Prevalence and effects of child exposure to domestic violence," *Future of Children* 9, 3: 21–32.

Farrell, Betty, Alicia VandeVusse, and Abigail Ocobock. 2012. "Family change and the state of family sociology," *Current Sociology* 60, 3: 283–301.

Farson, Richard E., Philip M. Hauser, Herbert Stroup, and Anthony J. Wiener. 1969. *The Future of the Family*. New York: Family Service Association of America.

Fast, Janet E., and Norah C. Keating. 2001. *Informal Caregivers in Canada: A Snapshot*. Ottawa: Health Canada.

———, ———, Leslie Oakes, and Deanna L. Williamson. 1997. *Conceptualizing and Operationalizing the Costs of Informal Elder Care*. NHRDP Project No. 6609-1963-55. Ottawa: National Health Research and Development Program, Health Canada.

Fawcett, G. 1996. *Living with Disability in Canada: An Economic Portrait*. Hull, Que.: Human Resources Development Canada.

———. 1998. "Canada's untapped workplace resource: People with disabilities," *Perception*. Ottawa, ON: Canadian Council on Social Development, 1–3.

Featherstone, B. 2003. "Taking fathers seriously," *British Journal of Social Work* 33, 1: 239–54.

Federal, Provincial, and Territorial Advisory Committee on Population Health. 1999. *Statistical Report on the Health of Canadians*. Ottawa: Health Canada and Statistics Canada.

Federal–Provincial Working Group on Social Development Research and Information. 1998. *Construction of a Preliminary Market Basket Measure of Poverty*. Ottawa: Federal Provincial Working Group.

Federation of Aboriginal Foster Parents. 2012. Available at http://www.fafp.ca/fosterparentinfo.shtml.

Feliciano, Cynthia, Belinda Robnett, Golnaz Komaie. 2009. "Gendered racial exclusion among white internet daters," *Social Science Research* 38: 39–54.

Felt, Lawrence, and Peter Sinclair. 1992. "'Everyone does it': Unpaid work in a rural peripheral region," *Work, Employment & Society* 6: 43–64.

Ferrao, Vincent. 2010. *Women in Canada: A Gender-based Statistical Report, Paid Work.* Ottawa: Statistics Canada. Available at http://www.statcan.gc.ca/pub/89-503-x/2010001/article/11387-eng.pdf; accessed 20 April 2012.

Feshbach, M. 2001. "Russia's Population Meltdown," *Wilson Quarterly* 2001, 25 (1): 15–21.

Fiese, Barbara H., Thomas J. Tomcho, Michael Douglas, Kimberly Josephs, Scott Poltrock, and Tim Baker. 2002. "A review of 50 years of research on naturally occurring family routines and rituals: Cause for celebration?" *Journal of Family Psychology* 16, 4: 381–90.

Finch, Janet, L. Hayes, J. Masson, J. Mason, and L. Wallis. 1996. *Wills, Inheritance, and Families.* Oxford: Oxford University Press.

Fineman, M. 2000. "Cracking the foundational myths: Independence, autonomy and self sufficiency," *Gender, Social Policy and the Law,* 13.

Finer, Lawrence B. 2007. "Trends in premarital sex in the United States, 1954–2003," *Public Health Reports* 122: 73–8.

Fingerman, Karen L. 2004a. "The role of offspring and in-laws in grandparents' ties to their grandchildren," *Journal of Family Issues* 25, 8: 1026–49.

———. Elizabeth L. Hay, and Kira S. Birdett. 2004. "The best of ties, the worst of ties: Close, problematic, and ambivalent social relationships," *Journal of Marriage and Family* 66: 792–808.

Finkelhor, David. 1986. *A Sourcebook on Childhood Sexual Abuse.* New York: Sage.

———. 1988. "The trauma of child sexual abuse: Two models," *Journal of Interpersonal Violence* 2, 4: 348–66.

Finnie, Ross. 1993. "Women, men, and the economic consequences of divorce: Evidence from Canadian longitudinal data," *Canadian Review of Sociology and Anthropology* 30: 205–41.

———. 2000. "The dynamics of poverty in Canada: What we know, what we can do," C.D. Howe Institute, Commentary No. 145 (Sept.).

Fisher, P. 2007. "A disabled San Jose mother fights again for right to raise child," *San Jose Mercury News.* San Jose, California: Disability Rights California: California's Protection and Advocacy System, 1–4.

Fleury, Dominique, and Myriam Fortin. 2006. *When Working is Not Enough to Escape Poverty: An Analysis of Canada's Working Poor.* Ottawa: Human Resources and Social Development Canada. Available at http://tamarackcommunity.ca/downloads/vc/When_Work_Not_Enough.pdf; accessed 23 March 2012.

Fleury, Ruth E., Criss M. Sullivan, and Deborah I. Bybee. 2000. "When ending the relationship does not end the violence," *Violence Against Women* 6, 12: 1363–83.

Folbre, Nancy. 1994. *Who Pays for the Kids? Gender and the Structures of Constraint.* London: Routledge, Chapman and Hall.

———. 2001. *The Invisible Heart: Economics and Family Values.* New York: New Press.

Food Banks Canada. 2011. "HungerCount: A comprehensive report on hunger and food bank use in Canada, and recommendations for change." Available at http://www.foodbankscanada.ca/getmedia/dc2aa860-4c33-4929-ac36-fb5d40f0b7e7/HungerCount-2011.pdf.aspx.

Forste, Renata. 2002. "Where are all the men? A conceptual analysis of the role of men in family formation," *Journal of Family Issues* 23: 579–600.

Foster, Deborah. 2005. "The formation and continuance of lesbian families in Canada," *Canadian Bulletin of Medical History* 22, 2: 281–97.

Foucault, Michel. 1990. *The History of Sexuality.* New York: Vintage Books.

Fournier-Savard, Patric. 2006. "Women with disabilities," *Women in Canada: A Gender-Based Statistical Report,* 5th ed. Ottawa: Minister of Industry.

Fox, Bonnie. 1993. "On violent men and female victims: A comment on DeKeseredy and Kelly," *Canadian Journal of Sociology* 18: 320–4.

———. 1998. "Motherhood, changing relationships and the reproduction of gender inequality," in Sharon Abbey and Andrea O'Reilly, eds, *Redefining Motherhood.* Toronto: Second Story Press.

———. 2001. "The formative years: How parenthood creates gender," *Canadian Review of Sociology and Anthropology* 38: 373–90.

———, and Meg Luxton. 2001. "Conceptualizing family," in Bonnie Fox, ed., *Family Patterns and Gender Relations.* Toronto: Oxford University Press.

Fraser Institute. 2001. *Measuring Poverty in Canada.* Vancouver: Fraser Institute.

Frean, Alexandra. 2005. "Unmarried families are more likely to fall apart," *The Times* (London, Ont.), 5 Feb.

Frenette, Marc, and R. Morissette. 2003. *Will They Ever Converge? Earnings of Immigrant and Canadian-born Workers over the Last Two Decades.* Ottawa: Statistics Canada Analytical Studies Research Paper Series.

Freud, Sigmund. 1974 [1920]. *Introductory Lectures on Psychoanalysis.* Middlesex, England: Penguin.

Friedan, Betty. 1963. *The Feminine Mystique.* New York: Norton.

Friendly, Martha, Jane Beach, Carolyn Ferns, and Michelle Turiano. 2007. *Early Childhood Education and Care in Canada 2006.* Toronto: Childcare Resource and Research Unit.

Fudge, Judy, and Leah Vosko. 2001. "Gender, segmentation and the standard employment relationship in Canadian labour law, legislation and policy," *Economic and Industrial Democracy* 22, 2: 218–310.

Fuller-Thomson, Esme. 2005. "Canada First Nations grandparents raising grandchildren: A portrait in resilience," *International Journal of Aging and Human Development* 60, 4: 331–42.

Fusick, Lisa. 2008. "Serving clients with hearing loss: Best practices in mental health counseling," *Journal of Counseling & Development* 86: 102–10.

Gadalla, Tahany M. 2008. "Gender differences in poverty rates after marital dissolution: A longitudinal study," *Journal of Divorce and Remarriage* 49, 3–4: 225–38.

Galarneau, Diane. 2005. "Earnings of temporary versus permanent employees," *Perspectives on Labour and Income*. Ottawa: Statistics Canada.

Galloway, Gloria. 2004. "Ottawa, provinces agree on child-care principles," *Globe and Mail*, 3 November, A11.

———. 2005a. "Dryden leaves the door open for separate childcare deals," *Globe and Mail*, 11 February, A4.

———. 2005b. "Money comes with no strings attached," *Globe and Mail*, 24 February, F3.

———. 2006. "Child-care proposal gives least to poorest," *Globe and Mail*, 26 April, A1, A7.

Gartner, Rosemary, Myrna Dawson, and Maria Crawford. 2001. "Confronting violence in women's lives," in B.J. Fox, ed., *Family Patterns, Gender Relations*, 2nd edn. Toronto: Oxford University Press, 473–90.

Gaunt, R. 2012. "Breadwinning moms, caregiving dads: Double standard in social judgments of gender norm violators," *Journal of Family Issues*, 4 April. Available at http://jfi.sagepub.com/content/early/2012/04/01/01925 13X12438686.

Gauthier, Anne Hélène. 1998. *The State and the Family: A Comparative Analysis of Family Policies in Industrialized Countries*. New York: Oxford University Press.

———. 2002. "The role of grandparents," *Current Sociology* 50: 295–307.

———. 2010. *The Impact of the Economic Crisis on Family Policies in the European Union*. Brussels: European Commission.

Gaymu, J., Ekamper, P., and G. Beets. 2007. "Qui prendra en charge les Européens âgés dependants en 2030?" *Population* 62: 789–820.

Gazso, A. 2007a. "Staying afloat on social assistance: Parents' strategies of balancing work and family," *Socialist Studies* 3, 2: 31–63.

Gazso, Amber. 2007b. "Balancing expectations for employability and family responsibilities while on social assistance: Low income mothers' experiences in three Canadian provinces," *Family Relations* 56: 454–66.

———. 2009a. "Mothers' maintenance of families through market and family care relations," in *Feminist Issues: Race, Class, and Sexuality*, edited by N. Mandell. Toronto: Pearson/Prentice Hall, pp. 219–46.

———. 2009b. "Reinvigorating the debate: Questioning the assumptions about and models of the 'family' in social assistance policy," *Women's Studies International Forum* 31, 2: 150–62.

Gee, Ellen, and Barbara A. Mitchell. 2003. "One roof: Exploring multi-generational households in Canada," in M. Lynn, ed., *Voices: Essays on Canadian Families*, 2nd edn. Scarborough, Ont.: Nelson Thomson Learning, 291–311.

Gelles, Richard J. 1987. *The Violent Home*, updated edn. Newbury Park, Calif.: Sage.

———. 1993. "Alcohol and other drugs are associated with violence—They are not its cause," in Gelles and Loseke (1993: 182–96).

———. 1994. "Introduction: Special issue on family violence," *Journal of Comparative Family Studies* 25, 1: 1–6.

———, and D.R. Loseke, eds. 1993. *Current Controversies on Family Violence*. Newbury Park, Calif.: Sage.

———, and Murray A. Straus. 1988. *Intimate Violence: The Causes and Consequences of Abuse in the American Family*. New York: Touchstone Books.

Gerodetti, Natalia. 2003. "'Disabling' femininities and eugenics: Sexuality, disability and citizenship in modern Switzerland," University of Lausanne.

Gerson, K. 2009. *The Unfinished Revolution: How a New Generation is Reshaping Family, Work, and Gender in America*. New York: Oxford University Press.

Gerson, Menachem. 1972. "Lesson from the kibbutz: A cautionary tale," in Howe (1972a: 326–40).

Gibbs, Jennifer, Nicole Ellison, and Rebecca Ditteiro. 2006. "Self-presentation in online personals: The role of anticipated future interaction, self-disclosure and perceived success in internet dating," *Communication Research* 33: 152–77.

Giddens, Anthony. 1992. *The Transformation of Intimacy: Sexuality, Love and Eroticism in Modern Societies*. Stanford, Calif.: Stanford University Press.

Gignac, Michel. 2002. *Guide to Family Support Needs*. Drummondville, Que.: Office des personnes handicapées du Québec, Direction des communications.

Gillespie, Kerry. 2006. "Ontario bans binding religious arbitration," *Toronto Star*, 15 February.

Gilligan, Carol. 1982. *In a Different Voice: Psychological Theory and Women's Development*. Cambridge, MA: Harvard University Press.

Gillis, John. 1996. *A World of Their Own Making: Myth, Ritual and the Quest for Family Values*. New York: Basic Books.

Gilmour, H., and J. Park. 2006. "Dependency, chronic conditions and pain in seniors," *Health Reports* 16: 21–31.

Ginn, Jay, and Sara Arber. 2002. "Degrees of freedom: Do graduate women escape the motherhood gap in pensions?" *Sociological Research Online* 7, 2.

Ginsburg, Gerlad P. 1988. "Rules, scripts and prototypes in personal relationships," in Steve Duck, Dale F. Hay, Stevan E. Hobfoll, William Ickes, Barbara M. Montgomery, eds, *Handbook of Personal Relationships: Theory, Research and Interventions*. Oxford, England: John Wiley & Sons, pp. 23–39.

Giordano, Peggy C., Monica A. Longmore, and Wendy D. Manning. 2006. "Gender and the meanings of adolescent romantic relationships: A focus on boys," *American Sociological Review* 71: 260–87.

Gladstone, James W., Ralph A. Brown, and Kerri-Ann J. Fitzgerald. 2009. "Grandparents raising their grandchildren: Tensions, service needs, and involvement with child welfare agencies," *International Journal of Aging and Human Development* 69, 1: 55–78.

Glaser, K., and E. Grundy. 2002. "Class, caring and disability: Evidence from the British Retirement Survey," *Ageing and Society* 22: 325–42.

———, Stuchbury, R., Tomassini, C., and J. Askham. 2008. "The long-term consequences of partnership dissolution for support in later life in the United Kingdom," *Ageing and Society* 28: 329–51.

Glass, Dee Dee. 1995. *All My Fault: Why Women Don't Leave Abusive Men*. London: Virago Press.

Gleason, Mona. 1999. *Normalizing the Ideal: Psychology, Schooling, and the Family in Postwar Canada.* Toronto: University of Toronto Press.

Glenn, Evelyn Nakano. 1994. "Social constructions of mothering: A thematic overview," in Evelyn Nakano Glenn, Grace Chang, and Linda Rennie Forcie, eds, *Mothering: Ideology, Experience and Agency.* New York: Routledge.

Glenn, Norval, and Elizabeth Marquardt. 2001. *Hooking Up, Hanging Out and Hoping for Mr. Right: College Women on Dating and Mating Today.* An Institute for American Values Report to the Independent Women's Forum.

Global Forum for Health Research. 2004. *Monitoring Financial Flows for Health Research.* Geneva: Global Forum for Health Research.

Globe and Mail. 2005. "Harper's prescription for choice in child care," 6 December, A22.

Goar, Carol. 2009. "Quebec shows the way on poverty," *Toronto Star,* 9 September. Available at http://www.thestar.com/comment/article/692619.

Godenzi, Alberto, Walter S. DeKeseredy, and Martin D. Schwartz. 2000. "Toward an integrated social bond/male peer support theory of woman abuse in North American college dating," unpublished paper.

Goetz, Anne Marie. 1995. "Institutionalizing women's interests and accountability to women in development," *IDS Bulletin* 26, 3: 1–10.

———. 1997. "Getting institutions right for women in development," in Goetz, ed., *Getting Institutions Right for Women in Development.* London: Zed Books.

Goffman, Erving. 1971. *Relations in Public.* New York: Harper Colophon Books.

Goldberg, Dan L. 2003. "Grandparent–grandchild access: A legal analysis," Department of Justice Canada Background paper 2003-FCY-15E. Available at http://canada.justice.gc.ca/en/ps/pad/reports/2003-FCY-15E.pdf; accessed 20 November 2005.

Goldscheider, Frances K. 1995. "Interpolating demography with families and households," *Demography* 32, 3: 471–80.

———, and Julie DaVanzo. 1989. "Pathways to independent living in early adulthood: Marriage, semiautonomy, and premarital residential independence," *Demography* 26: 597–614.

Golz, Annalee. 1993. "Family matters: The Canadian family and the state in the postwar period." *left history* 1, 2 (Fall): 9–49.

Goode, William J. 1972. "Social change and family renewal," in *College of Home Economics* (1972: 116–33).

———. 1995. "The theoretical importance of the family," in Mark Robert Rank and Edward L. Kain, eds, *Diversity and Change in Families: Patterns, Prospects and Policies.* Englewood Cliffs, NJ: Prentice-Hall, 1–14.

Goodhead, A., and J. McDonald. 2007. "Informal caregivers literature review: A report prepared for the National Health Committee." Health Services Research Centre, Victoria University of Wellington.

Gordon, Sean. 2005. "Kyoto enforcement may vary, Dion says," *Toronto Star,* 17 February, A3.

Gore, Carol. 2012. "Ontario elder abuse hotline in jeopardy," *Toronto Star,* 26 January, A1.

Gossage, Peter. 1999. *Families in transition: Industry and population in nineteenth-century Saint-Hyacinthe.* Montreal: McGill-Queen's University Press.

Government of Canada. 1984. *Sexual Offences against Children.* Ottawa: Minister of Supply and Services.

———. 2002. *Advancing the Inclusion of Persons with Disabilities: A Government of Canada Report.* Ottawa: Government of Canada, December.

———. 2003a. *Disability in Canada: A 2001 Profile.* Ottawa: Human Resources Development Canada, 1–65.

———. 2003b. "Education, employment and income of adults with and without disabilities—Tables," in Government of Canada (2003a).

———. 2005. *Employment Insurance (EI) and Maternity, Parental and Sickness Benefits.* Ottawa: Department of Human Resources and Skills Development. Available at http://www.hrsdc.gc.ca/asp/gateway.asp?hr=en/ei/types/special.shtml&hs=tyt#Maternity.

———. 2006. *The Human Face of Mental Health and Mental Illness in Canada.* Ottawa: Minister of Public Works and Government Services Canada, Cat. No. HP5-19/2006E.

———. 2007a. *Participation and Activity Limitation Survey.* Ottawa: Statistics Canada, 1–5.

———. 2007b. *Participation and Activity Limitation Survey 2006: Analytical Report.* Ottawa: Statistics Canada, Social and Aboriginal Statistics Division, 1–38.

———. 2007c. *Participation and Activity Limitation Survey 2006: Tables.* Ottawa: Statistics Canada, Social and Aboriginal Statistics Division, 1–93.

———. 2008. *Foster Care Report—September 2006: Children's Special Allowances.* Ottawa: Department of Human Resources and Social Development Canada. Available at http://www.hrsdc.gc.ca/en/publications_resources/social_policy/foster_care/page02.shtml.

———. 2008a. *Canada Pension Plan (CPP): Payment Rates.* Ottawa: Statistics Canada.

———. 2008b. *Participation and Activity Limitation Survey 2006: Labour Force Experience of People with Disabilities in Canada.* Ottawa: Statistics Canada, Social and Aboriginal Statistics Division, 1–22.

———. 2008c. *Participation and Activity Limitation Survey: Employment.* Ottawa: Statistics Canada.

———. 2008d. *Employment Insurance (EI) and Maternity, Parental and Sickness Benefits.* Ottawa: Department of Human Resources and Skills Development. Available at http://www.hrsdc.gc.ca/en/ei/types/special.shtml.

———. 2008e. *Foster Care Report—September 2006: Children's Special Allowances.* Ottawa: Department of Human Resources and Social Development Canada. Available at http://www.hrsdc.gc.ca/en/publications_resources/social_policy/foster_care/page02.shtml.

———. 2010. *Better Outcomes for First Nations Children: INAC's Role as a Funder in First Nations Child and Family Services Updated: July 2010.* Ottawa: Aboriginal Affairs and Northern Development Canada. Available at http://www.aadnc-aandc.gc.ca/DAM/DAM-INTER-HQ/STAGING/texte-text/cfsd1_1100100035211_eng.pdf.

———. 2011a. *Employment Insurance Coverage Survey—2010.* Ottawa: Statistics Canada. 27 June. Available at http://www.statcan.gc.ca/daily-quotidien/110627/dq110627a-eng.htm.

———. 2011b. *Federal–Provincial/Territorial National Child Benefit Program Initiative.* Ottawa: Treasury Board of Canada Secretariat. Available at http://www.tbs-sct.gc.ca/hidb-bdih/initiative-eng.aspx?Hi=42.

————. 2012a. *Employment Insurance Maternity and Parental Benefits*. Ottawa: Service Canada. Available at http://www.servicecanada.gc.ca/eng/ei/types/maternity_parental.shtml.

————. 2012b. *Children's special allowances (CSA) calculation sheet 2006–2013*. Ottawa: Canada Revenue Agency. Available at http://www.cra-arc.gc.ca/bnfts/cs/clc_2006_2012-eng.html.

Government of Canada. 2012c. *Canada Child Tax Benefit (CCTB) payment amounts—Tax years 2007 to 2011*. Ottawa: Canada Revenue Agency. Available at http://www.cra-arc.gc.ca/bnfts/cctb/cctb_pymnts-eng.html.

————. 2013. *Employment Insurance Maternity and Parental Benefits*. Ottawa: Service Canada. Available at http://www.servicecanada.gc.ca/eng/sc/ei/benefits/maternityparental.shtml.

————. Office for Disability Issues. 2004. *Advancing the Inclusion of Persons with Disabilities: A Government of Canada Report*. Ottawa: Social Development Canada.

Government of Ontario. 2011. "The Aboriginal Advisor's Report on the Status of Aboriginal child welfare in Ontario." Available at http://www.children.gov.on.ca/htdocs/English/topics/aboriginal/reports/child_welfare-2011.aspx.

Government of Quebec. 1999. *Report of the Auditor General to the National Assembly for 1998–1999, Summary*. Quebec City, ch. 4.

————. 2012. "1608 new subsidized childcare spaces—First projects accepted by the regional committees in six regions of Québec." Available at http://www.gouv.qc.ca/portail/quebec/pgs/commun/actualites/actualite/une/actualites_120709_services-de-garde/?lang=en.

Graff, E.J. 2004. *What Is Marriage For? The Strange Social History of Our Most Intimate Institution*. Boston: Beacon Press.

Graham, J.E., Rockwood, K., Beattie, B.L., Eastwood, R., Gauthier, S., Tuokko, H., and I. McDowell. 1997. "Prevalence and severity of cognitive impairment with and without dementia in an elderly population," *The Lancet* 349, 9068: 1793–6.

Graham-Berman, Sandra A., and Alytia A. Levendosky. 1998. "Traumatic stress symptoms in children of battered women," *Journal of Interpersonal Violence* 13, 1: 111–28.

Gratton, B.M., and E. Skop. 2007. "Immigrants, their children, and theories of assimilation: family structure in the United states, 1880–1970," *Historical Families* 12, 3: 203–22.

Green, Rebecca J., Patricia L. Williams, Shanthi C. Johnson, and Ilya Blum. 2008. "Can Canadian seniors on public pensions afford a nutritious diet?" *Canadian Journal on Aging* 27, 1: 69–79.

Greenwald, Harold. 1970. "Marriage as a non-legal voluntary association," in Otto (1970a: 51–66).

Grekul, J.M. 2002. *The Social Construction of the Feebleminded Threat: Implementation of the Sexual Sterilization Act in Alberta, 1929–1972*. Edmonton: University of Alberta Press.

Grello, Catherine M., Deborah P. Welsh, and Melinda S. Harper. 2006. "No strings attached: The nature of casual sex in college students," *Journal of Sex Research* 43: 255–67.

Griffin, Joan M., Rebecca Fuhrer, Stephen A. Stansfeld, and Michael Marmot. 2002. "The importance of low control at work and home on depression and anxiety: Do these effects vary by gender and social class," *Social Science and Medicine* 54, 5: 783–98.

Gross, Neil. 2005. "The detraditionalization of intimacy reconsidered," *Sociological Theory* 23: 3.

Grosz, Elizabeth. 1993. "Bodies and knowledges: Feminism and the crisis of reason," in Linda Alcoff and Elizabeth Potter, eds, *Feminist Epistemologies*. New York: Routledge, 187–215.

Grue, L., and K.T. Laerum. 2002. "'Doing motherhood': Some experiences of mothers with physical disabilities," *Disability & Society* 17: 671–83.

Grundy, E. 2006. "Ageing and vulnerable people: European perspectives," *Ageing and Society* 26: 105–34.

Guberman, N., J-P. Lavoie, L. Blein, and I. Olazabal. 2012. "Baby Boom caregivers: Care in the age of individualization," *The Gerontologist* 52, 2: 210–18.

Gudelunas, David. 2005. "Online personal ads: Community and sex, virtually," *Journal of Homosexuality* 49, 1: 1–33.

Guo, Guang, and Kathleen Mullan. 2000. "The mechanisms mediating the effects of poverty on children's intellectual development," *Demography* 37, 4: 431–47.

Guruge, S., P. Kanthasam, J. Jokarasa, T.Y.W. Wan, M. Chinichian, K.R. Shirpak, P. Paterson, and S. Sathananthan. 2010. "Older women speak about abuse and neglect in the post-migration context," *Women's Health and Urban Life* 9, 2: 15–41.

Guth, Tracy. 1999. "Why not renew your wedding vows?" *Good Housekeeping* 228, 3 (March): 162.

Haas, L., and M. O'Brien. "New observations on how fathers work and care: Introduction to the special issue—men, work and parenting—part I," *Fathering: A Journal of Theory, Research, and Practice About Men as Fathers* 8, 3 (2010): 271–5.

Haddad, Anton. 1996. "The sexual division of house-hold labour: Pragmatic strategies or patriarchal Dynamics. An analysis of two case studies," PhD thesis, York University.

Hall, David R. 2003. "The pure relationship and below replacement fertility," *Canadian Studies in Population* 30, 1: 51–69.

Halpern v. Canada (A.G.), [2002] O.J. No. 2714 (Ont. Sup. Ct. Blair, J.) [QL].

Hamilton, Graeme. 2004. "Quebec's sacred cow has quality issues," *National Post*, 9 December.

Hamilton, Kendall. 2007. "Renew your vows (without renewing your vows)," *Esquire* 148, 3: 92.

Hamilton, Laura, and Elizabeth A. Armstrong. 2009. "Gendered sexuality in young adulthood: Double binds and flawed options," *Gender & Society* 23: 589–616.

Hamilton, Roberta. 1995. "Pro-natalism, feminism, and nationalism," in Francois-Pierre Gingras, ed., *Gender and Politics in Contemporary Canada*. Toronto: Oxford University Press, 135–52.

Hamilton, Sylvia D. 1989. *Black Mother, Black Daughter*. Montreal: National Film Board of Canada.

Hanson Frieze, Irene. 2007. "Love and commitment," in George Ritzer, ed., *Blackwell Encyclopedia of Sociology*. New York: Blackwell Publishing.

Hanvey, Louise. 2002. *Children with Disabilities and Their Families in Canada: A Discussion Paper*. National Children's Alliance for the First National Roundtable on Children with Disabilities.

Harper's Bazaar. 2005 [1886]. "Mourning and funeral usage," *Harper's Bazaar*. Available at http://harpersbazaar.victorian-ebooks.com.

Harris, Olivia. 1981. "Households as natural units," in Kate Young, C. Walkowitz, and R. McCullagh, eds, *Of Damage and the Market: Women's Subordination in International Perspective*. London: CSE Books.

Harris, Richard. 2004. *Creeping Conformity: How Canada Became Suburban, 1900–1960*. Toronto: University of Toronto Press.

Harvey, Mark H. 2011. "Welfare reform and household survival: The interaction of structure and network strength in the Rio Grande Valley, Texas," *Journal of Poverty* 15, 43–64.

Hash, Kristina. 2001. "Caregiving and post-caregiving experiences of mid-life and older gay men and lesbians," PhD thesis, Virginia Commonwealth University.

Hassan, G., C. Rousseau, T. Measham, and M. Lashley. 2008. "Caribbean and Filipino adolescents' and parents' perceptions of parental authority, physical punishment, and cultural values and their relation to migratory characteristics," *Canadian Ethnic Studies* 40, 2: 171–86.

Hatala, Mark Nicholas, Daniel W. Baack, and Ryan Parmenter. 1997. "Dating with HIV: A content analysis of gay male HIV-positive and HIV-negative personal advertisements," *Journal of Social and Personal Relationships* 15, 2: 268–76.

Hatty, Suzanne E. 2000. *Masculinities, Violence and Culture*. Thousand Oaks, Calif.: Sage.

Hawkins, Alan J., and David C. Dollahite. 1996. *Generative Fathering: Beyond Deficit Perspectives*. Thousand Oaks, Calif.: Sage.

———, and ———, et al. 1993. "Rethinking fathers' involvement in child care: A developmental perspective," *Journal of Family Issues* 14, 4: 531–49.

Hayes, Sharon. 1996. *The Cultural Contradictions of Motherhood*. New Haven Yale University Press.

Health Canada. 1996. *Wife Abuse: The Impact on Children*. Ottawa: National Clearinghouse on Family Violence.

———. 1999. *Abuses and Neglect of Older Adults*. Available at http://www.hc-sg.gc.ca/hppb/familyviolence/html/agenegle.html; accessed 27 September 2004.

———. 2002. *The Family Violence Initiative: Five-Year Report*. Ottawa: National Clearinghouse on Family Violence.

———. 2008. *Changing Fertility Patterns: Trends and Implications*. Available at http://www.hc-sc.gc.ca/sr-sr/pubs/hpr-rpms/bull/2005-10-chang-fertilit/intro-eng.php, accessed 23 November 2008.

———. Division of Aging and Seniors. 2002. *Physical Activity and Older Adults*. Ottawa: Minister of Public Works and Government Services Canada.

Heath, Melanie. 2012. *One Marriage under God: The Campaign to Promote Marriage in America*. New York: New York University Press.

Heath, Sue. 2004. "Peer-shared households, quais-communes and neo-tribes," *Current Sociology* 52: 161–79.

Heaton, Tim B., Cardell K. Jacobson, and Kimberlee Holland. 1999. "Persistence and chance in decisions to remain childless," *Journal of Marriage and the Family* 61: 531–9.

Heisz, Andrew. 2007. *Income Inequality and Redistribution in Canada, 1976–2004*. Ottawa: Statistics Canada Analytical Studies Branch Research Paper Series.

Hell, Kyshah. 2001. "Victorian mourning garb," *Morbid Outlook*. Available at http://www.morbidoutlook.com/fashion/historical/2001_03_victorianmourn.html.

Henderson, Tammy L. 2005. "Grandparent visitation rights: Successful acquisition of court-ordered visitation," *Journal of Family Issues* 26, 1: 107–37.

Hendler, Darlene M. 1998. *Family Therapy with Families Who Have Special Needs Children*. Ottawa: National Library of Canada.

Henry, Frances, Carol Tator, Winston Mattis, and Tim Rees. 2000. "The ideology of racism," in Henry et al., *The Colour of Democracy: Racism in Canadian Society*. Toronto: Harcourt and Brace Canada, 15–34.

Henry, R.G., R.B. Miller, and R. Giarrusso. 2005. "Difficulties, disagreements, and disappointments in late-life marriages," *International Journal of Aging and Human Development* 61, 3: 243–64.

Hequembourg, A., and S. Brallier. 2005. "Gendered stories of parental caregiving among siblings," *Journal of Aging Studies* 19: 53–71.

Hetherington, Mavis, and Joan Kelly. 2002. *For Better or For Worse: Divorce Reconsidered*. New York: Norton.

Hewett, Heather. 2004. "My sister's family," *The Scholar and Feminist Online: Young Feminists Take on the Family*, Guest editors J. Baumgardner and A. Richards. Available at http://www.barnard.edu/sfonline/family/hewett_01.htm; accessed 7 May 2005.

Hiedemann, Bridget, Olga Suhomlinova, and Angela M. O'Rand. 1998. "Economic independence, economic status, and empty nest in mid-life marital disruption," *Journal of Marriage and the Family* 60: 219–31.

Hill, Reuben. 1964. "The American family of the future," *Journal of Marriage and the Family* 26, 1: 20–8.

Hill, Robert. 1958. "Generic features of families under stress," *Social Casework* 49: 139–50.

Hillier, Lynne, and Lyn Harrison. 2007. "Building realities less limited than their own: Young people practicing same-sex attraction on the internet," *Sexualities*, 10: 82–100.

Ho, S., A. Chan, J. Woo, P. Chong, and A. Sham. 2009. "Impact of caregiving on health and quality of life: a comparative population-based study of caregivers for elderly persons and noncaregivers," *The Journals of Gerontology* 64A: 873–9.

Hobbs, Edward C. 1970. "An alternate model from a theological perspective," in Otto (1970a: 25–42).

Hobson, Barbara. 2002. *Making Men into Fathers: Men, Masculinities and the Social Politics of Fatherhood*. Cambridge: Cambridge University Press.

Hochschild, Arlie Russell. 1972. "Communal living in old age," in Howe (1972a: 299–310).

———. 1989. *The Second Shift*. New York: Avon.

———. 1997. *The Time Bind*. New York: Metropolitan Books.

Hoffman, J. 2011. *Father Factors: What Social Science Tells us about Fathers and How to Work with Them*. Peterborough, Ontario: Father Involvement Research Alliance.

Hogan, D.B., MacKnight, C., and H. Bergman. 2003. "Models, definitions, and criteria of frailty," *Aging Clinical and Experimental Research* 15, Suppl. 3: 3–29.

Holland, Winifred. 2000. "Intimate relationships in the new millennium: The assimilation of marriage and cohabitation?" *Canadian Review of Family Law* 17: 114–50.

Holmes, Mary. 2004. "The precariousness of choice in the new sentimental order: A response to Bawin-Legros," *Current Sociology* 52: 251–7.

Holtzman, Mellisa. 2011. "Nonmarital unions, family definitions, and custody decision making," *Family Relations* 60, 5: 617–32.

Homans, G.C. 1974. *Social behavior: Its elementary forms.* New York: Harcourt Brace Jovanovich.

Hooyman, Nancy R., and H. Asuman Kiyak. 2005. *Social Gerontology: A Multidisciplinary Perspective.* Boston: Pearson.

Hossain, Ziarat. 2001. "Division of household labor and family functioning in off-reservation Navajo Indian families," *Family Relations* 50, 3: 255–61.

Hou, F. 2004. *Recent Immigration and the Formation of Visible Minority Neighbourhoods in Canada's Large Cities.* Ottawa: Statistics Canada.

Houle, R., and G. Schellenberg. 2008. *Remittance Behaviours among Recent Immigrants to Canada,* Statistics Canada, Ottawa.

Howard, Vicki. 2003. "A 'real man's ring': Gender and the invention of traditions," *Journal of Social History* 36, 4: 857–56.

———. 2006. *Brides, Inc.: American Weddings and the Business of Tradition.* Philadelphia: University of Pennsylvania Press.

Howe, Louise Kapp, ed. 1972a. *The Future of the Family.* New York: Simon & Schuster.

———. 1972b. "An introduction," in Howe (1972a: 11–24).

Howlett, Karen. 2004. "Families of disabled children to reunite Monday, judge says," *Globe and Mail,* 4 June, A13.

Hughes, Kate. 2005. "The adult children of divorce: Pure relationships and family values?" *Journal of Sociology* 41: 69–86.

Huisman, Kimberly A. 1996. "Wife battering in Asian American communities," *Violence Against Women* 2, 3: 260–83.

Hulchanski, David, and Joseph H. Michalski. 1994. *How Households Obtain Resources To Meet Their Needs: The Shifting Mix of Cash and Non-Cash Sources.* Toronto: Ontario Human Rights Commission.

Human Resources and Skills Development Canada (HRSCD). 2011a. *Disability in Canada: A 2006 Profile.* Available at http://www.hrsdc.gc.ca/eng/disability_issues/reports/disability_profile/2011/index.shtml.

———. 2011b. *Disability Facts about Education.* Ottawa: HRSDC.

———. 2012a. "Canadians in Context: Population Size and Growth." Available at http://www4.hrsdc.gc.ca/.3ndic.1t.4r@-eng.jsp?iid=35; accessed 25 April 2012.

———. 2012b. "Indicators of Well-Being: Family Life-Age of Mother at Childbirth." Available at http://www4.hrsdc.gc.ca/.3ndic.1t.4r@-eng.jsp?iid=75; accessed 25 March 2012.

Humble, Á,M. 2009. "The second time 'round: Gender construction in remarried couples' wedding planning," *Journal of Divorce and Remarriage* 50: 260–81.

———. 2013. "Moving from 'meh' to 'yay': Older same-sex couples get married in Canada," *Canadian Journal on Aging* 32, 2: Forthcoming.

———, A.M. Svonkovic, and A.J. Walker. 2008. "'The royal we': Gender ideology and assessment in wedding work," *Journal of Family Issues* 29, 1: 3–25.

Hunter, N. 1995. "Marriage, law and gender: A feminist inquiry," in *Sex Wars: Sexual Dissent and Political Culture,* L. Duggan and N. Hunter, eds (pp. 107–22). New York: Routledge.

Hurley, M.C. 2005. Bill C-38 The Civil Marriage Act, A Legislative Summary. Available at http://www.parl.gc.ca/About/Parliament/LegislativeSummaries/Bills_ls.asp?ls=c38&Parl=38&Ses=1; accessed 27 March 2012.

Hurst, Rachel. 2005. "'Disabled Peoples' International: Europe and the social model of disability," in Colin Barnes and Geof Mercer, eds, *The Social Model of Disability: Europe and the Majority World.* Leeds: Disability Press, 65–79.

Husaini, Z. 2001. *Cultural Dilemma and a Plea for Justice: Voices of Canadian Ethnic Women.* Edmonton: Intercultural Action Committee for the Advancement of Women.

Hutchinson, D.L. 1997. "'Out yet unseen': A racial critique of gay and lesbian legal theory and political discourse," *Connecticut Law Review* 29 (2): 590.

Iacovetta, Franca. 1992. *Such Hardworking People: Italian Immigrants in Postwar Toronto.* Montreal: McGill-Queen's University Press.

———. 2006. *Gatekeepers: Reshaping Immigrant Lives in Cold War Canada.* Toronto: Between the Lines.

Ibbitson, John. 2012. "New Canada: Land of immigrants with many families under the same roof," *Globe and Mail.* 20 September.

Ingoldsby, Bron, Suzanne Smith, and J. Elizabeth Miller. 2004. *Exploring Family Theories.* Los Angeles: Roxbury.

Institute of Marriage and Family Canada. 2009. "Cohabitation statistics," *Quick Stats: Social Policy Statistics at a Glance.* Ottawa.

Intergovernmental Panel on Climate Change. 2007. "Climate change 2007: Synthesis report. Summary for policymakers." Available at http://www.ipcc.ch/pdf/assessment-report/ar4/syr/ar4_syr_spm.pdf.

Irwin, Sharon Hope, and Donna S. Lero. 1997. *In Our Way: Child Care Barriers to Full Workforce Participation Experienced by Parents of Children with Special Needs—and Potential Remedies.* Wreck Cove, NS: Breton Books.

Iyenda, Guillaume. 2001. "Street food and income generation for poor households in Kinshasa," *Environment and Urbanization* 13, 2: 233–41.

Jacobson, Neil S., and John M. Gottman. 2001. "Anatomy of a violent relationship," in A.S. Skolnick and J.H. Skolnick, eds, *Family in Transition,* 11th edn. Boston: Allyn and Bacon, 475–87.

Jaffee, Peter G., David A. Wolfe, and Susan K. Wilson. 1990. *Children of Battered Women.* Newbury Park, Calif.: Sage.

James, Allison, and Adrian L. James. 2001. "Childhood: Toward a theory of continuity and change," *Annals of the American Association of Political and Social Sciences* 575: 25–37.

James, C. 2010. *Seeing Ourselves, Exploring Race, Ethnicity and Culture,* 4th edn. Toronto: Thompson Educational Publishing.

James, Estelle, Alejandra Edwards, and Rebecca Wong. 2003. *The Gender Impact of Pension Reform: A Cross Country Analysis.* Washington: World Bank.

Jamieson, Lynn. 1998. *Intimacy: Personal Relationships in Modern Societies.* Cambridge: Polity Press/Blackwell Publishers.

———. 1999. "Intimacy transformed? A critical look at the 'pure relationship'," *Sociology* 33, 3: 477–94.

———. 2007. "Intimacy," in George Ritzer, ed., *Blackwell Encyclopedia of Sociology*. New York: Blackwell Publishing.

Janke, Megan C., Galit Nimrod, and Douglas A. Kleiber. 2008. "Reduction in leisure activity and well-being during the transition to widowhood," *Journal of Women & Aging* 20: 83–98.

Janovicek, Nancy, and Joy Parr, eds. 2003. *Histories of Canadian Children and Youth*. Toronto: Oxford University Press.

Jarrett, Robin L., Stephanie R. Jefferson, and Jenell N. Kelly. 2010. "Finding community in family: Neighborhood effects and African American kin networks," *Journal of Comparative Family Studies* 41, 3: 299–328.

Jasinski, Jana L., and Linda M. Williams, eds. 1998. *Partner Violence: A Comprehensive Review of 20 Years of Research*. Thousand Oaks, Calif.: Sage.

Jedwab, J. 2004. "Diversity of marriage: Canadian opinion on cross-cultural marriage," unpublished paper.

Jensen, Jane. 2002. "Against the current: Child care and family policy in Quebec," in Sonya Michel and Riane Mahon, eds, *Child Care Policy at the Crossroads: Gender and Welfare State Restructuring*. New York: Routledge, 309–30.

———. 2003. *Redesigning the "Welfare Mix" for Families: Policy Challenges*. Ottawa: Canadian Policy Research Networks.

———. 2004. "Changing the paradigm: Family responsibility or investing in children," *Canadian Journal of Sociology* 29, 2: 169–92.

———, and Sherry Thompson. 1999. *Comparative Family Policy: Six Provincial Stories*. Ottawa: Canadian Policy Research Networks.

John, Daphne, and Beth Anne Shelton. 1997. "The production of gender among black and white women and men: The case of household labor," *Sex Roles* 36, 3 and 4: 171–93.

Johnson, H.M. 2003. "The disability gulag," *New York Times Magazine*, 1–15.

Johnson, Holly. 1995. "Risk factors associated with non-lethal violence against women by marital partners," in C.R. Block and R. Block, eds, *Trends, Risks and Interventions in Lethal Violence*, vol. 3. Washington: National Institute of Justice, 151–68.

———. 1996. *Dangerous Domains: Violence against Women in Canada*. Toronto: Nelson.

———, and Myrna Dawson. 2011. *Violence Against Women in Canada: Research and Policy Perspectives*. Toronto: Oxford.

———, and Vincent Sacco. 1995. "Researching violence against women: Statistics Canada's national survey," *Canadian Journal of Criminology* 37: 281–304.

Johnson, Jone. 2008. About.com. Available at http://womenshistory.about.com/od/diana/a/diana_wedding.htm; accessed 30 November 2008.

Johnson, Karen L., Donna S. Lero, and Jennifer A. Rooney. 2001. *Work–Life Compendium 2001: 150 Canadian Statistics on Work, Family and Well-Being*. Guelph, Ont.: Centre for Families, Work and Well-Being, University of Guelph.

Johnson, Michael P. 2008. *A Typology of Domestic Violence: Intimate Terrorism, Violent Resistance and Situational Couple Violence*. Boston: Northwestern University Press.

———, Janel M. Leone, and Yili Xu. 2008. "Violence in general survey data: The gender debate revisited—Again." Available

at http://www.personal.psu.edu/faculty/m/p/mpj/dvpage/html; accessed 13 March 2009.

Johnston, Lynda. 2006. "'I do down-under': Naturalizing landscapes and love through wedding tourism in New Zealand," *ACME: An International E-Journal for Critical Geographers* 5, 2: 191–208.

Jones, Anne C. 2003. "Reconstructing the stepfamily: Old myths, new stories," *Social Work* 48: 228–36.

Jones, Ross L. 1999. "The master potter and the rejected pots: Eugenic legislation in Victoria, 1918–1939," *Australian Historical Studies* 113: 319–43.

Juby, Heather, Céline Le Bourdais, and Nicole Marcil-Gratton. 2003. *Linking Family Change, Parents' Employment and Income and Children's Economic Well-Being: A Longitudinal Perspective*. Research Report 2003-FCY-2E. Ottawa: Department of Justice Canada.

———, N. Marcil-Gratton, and C. LeBourdais. 2003. "Yours, mine and ours: New boundaries for the modern stepfamily," *Transitions* 33, 4: 3–6.

———, ———, and ———. 2005. *Moving On: The Expansion of the Family Network after Parents Separate*. Ottawa: Department of Justice. Catalogue no. 2004-FCY-9E.

Kahn, R.I., and Toni C. Antonucci. 1980. "Convoys over the life course: Attachments, roles, and social support," *Life-Span Development and Behavior* 3: 253–86.

Kamo, Yoshinori. 2000. "Racial and ethnic differences in extended family households," *Sociological Perspectives* 43: 211–29.

Kane, R.L., J.G. Evans, and D. McFadyen. 1990. *Improving the Health of Older People: A World View*. New York: Oxford University Press.

Kanter, Rosabeth Moss. 1972. "'Getting it all together': Communes past, present, future," in Howe (1972a: 311–25).

Kapteyn, A. 2010. "What can we learn from (and about) global aging? Project Muse; Today's Research. Tomorrow's Inspiration," *Demography* 47, Suppl.: S191.

Kassel, Victor. 1970. "Polygyny after sixty," in Otto (1970a: 137–44).

Katz, Jonathan. 1995. *The Invention of Heterosexuality*. New York: Dutton.

———. 2006. *The Macho Paradox: Why Some Men Hurt Women and How All Men Can Help*. Naperville, Ill: Sourcebooks.

Katz, Michael. 1975. *The People of Hamilton, Canada West: Family and Class in a Mid-nineteenth Century City*. Cambridge: Harvard University Press.

Kaufman, Gayle. 2000. "Do gender role attitudes matter? Family formation and dissolution among traditional and egalitarian men and women," *Journal of Family Issues* 21: 128–44.

Kaufman, John, and Edward Zigler. 1993. "The intergenerational transmission of abuse is overstated," in Gelles and Loseke (1993: 209–21).

Kaufman-Kantor, Glenda, and Jana L. Jasinski. 1998. "Dynamics and risk factors in partner violence," in Jasinski and Williams (1998: 1–43).

———, and ———. *Out of the Darkness: Contemporary Perspectives on Family Violence* (1997). Calif.: Sage.

———, and Liza Little. 2003. "Defining the boundaries of child neglect: When does domestic violence equate with parental failure to protect?" *Journal of Interpersonal Violence* 18, 4: 338–55.

Kay, F. George. 1972. *The Family in Transition: Its Past, Present and Future Patterns.* Newton Abbot: David and Charles.

Kazemipur, A., and Shiva Halli. 2000. *The New Poverty in Canada: Ethnic Groups and Ghetto Neighbourhoods.* Toronto: Thompson Educational Publishing.

Keating, Norah C., Janet E. Fast, Judith Frederick, Kelly Cranswick, and Cathryn Perrier. 1999. *Eldercare in Canada: Context, Content, and Consequences.* Ottawa: Statistics Canada, Housing, Family and Social Statistics Division.

Keefe, J., and P. Fancey. 2000. "The Care Continues: Responsibility for elderly relatives before and after admission to a long term care facility," *Family Relations* 49, 3: 235–44.

———, J. Légaré, and Y. Carrière. 2007. "Older Canadians with disabilities: Projections of need and their policy implications," *Canadian Public Policy* 33 (special supplement on health human resources): S65–S80.

———, S. Vézina, J. Légaré, Y. Décarie, and G. Lefrançois. 2012. *Population Change and Lifecourse Strategic Knowledge Cluster.* London, ON: The University of Western Ontario.

Kelly, Katharine D. 1997. "The family violence and woman abuse debate: Reviewing the literature, posing alternatives," in A. Sev'er, ed., *Cross-Cultural Exploration of Wife Abuse.* Lewiston, NY: Edwin Mellen, 27–50.

Kelly, Liz, and Jill Radford. 1998. "Sexual violence against women and girls: An approach to an international overview," in Dobash and Dobash (1998: 53–73).

Kelly, Mary Bess. 2012. "Divorce cases in Civil Court, 2010–2011," *Juristat*, March 28.

Kemp, C.L., and C.J. Rosenthal. 2001. "The consequences of caregiving: Does employment make a difference?" *QSEP.* Research Institute for Quantitative Studies in Economics and Population.

Kemp, Candace. 2003. "The social and demographic contours of contemporary grandparenthood: Mapping the patterns in Canada and the United States," *Journal of Comparative Family Studies* 34, 2: 187–212.

———. 2004. "Grand expectations: The experiences of grandparents and adult grandchildren," *Canadian Journal of Sociology* 29, 4: 499–526.

———, Carolyn Rosenthal, Lori D. Campbell, and Jenny Ploeg. 2007. "'It totally tore the family apart': Exploring inheritance-related conflict in multigenerational families." Paper presented at the *36th Annual Scientific and Educational Meeting of the Canadian Association on Gerontology*, Calgary, Alberta, 1–3 November 2007.

Kempf, Herve. 2007. "Tar sands development is a global environmental disaster," *CCPA Monitor* 14, 7: 45–7.

Kendall-Tackett, Kathleen, and Roberta Marshall. 1998. "Sexual victimization of children: Incest and child sexual abuse," in Bergen (1998a).

Kennedy, Gerard. 1995. *The Circumstances and Coping Strategies of People Needing Food Banks.* Toronto: Daily Bread Food Bank.

Kenney, Catherine. 2004. "Cohabiting couple, filing jointly? Resource pooling and U.S. poverty policies," *Family Relations* 53, 2: 237–47.

Kenworthy, Lane, and Jonas Pontusson. 2005. "Rising inequality and the politics of redistribution in affluent countries," *Perspectives on Politics* 3, 3: 449–71.

Kerr, Don, Melissa Moyser, and Roderic Beaujot. 2006. "Marriage and cohabitation: Demographic and socioeconomic differences in Quebec and Canada," *Canadian Studies in Population* 33: 83–117.

Kerstetter, Steve. 2012. "Scrapping welfare council is a cheap shot by a government that doesn't care about the poor," *The Star*, 8 April. Available at http://www.thestar.com/opinion/editorialopinion/article/1157655-scrapping-welfare-council-is-a-cheap-shot-by-a-government-that-doesn-t-care-about-the-poor.

Kevles, Daniel J. 1995. *In the Name of Eugenics: Genetics and the Uses of Human Heredity.* Cambridge, Mass.: Harvard University Press.

Kiernan, Kathleen. 2002. "Cohabitation in western Europe: Trends, issues, and implications," in Alan Booth and Ann C. Crouter, eds, *Just Living Together: Implications of Cohabitation on Families, Children, and Social Policy.* Mahwah: Lawrence Erlbaum Associates, pp. 3–31.

Killoran, Carrie. 1994. "Women with disabilities having children: It's our right too," *Sexuality and Disability* 12: 121–6.

King, Tamara. 2008. "Photographers snap pictures of brides in unexpected places," *Daily Gleaner*, 20 October.

King, V., and M.E. Scott. 2005. "A comparison of cohabiting relationships among older and younger adults," *Journal of Marriage and Family* 67, 2: 271–85.

Kirshbaum, M., and R. Olkin. 2002. "Parents with physical, systemic, or visual disabilities," *Sexuality and Disability* 20: 65–80.

Kirton, D. 2001. "Love and money: Payment, motivation and the fostering task," *Child and Family Social Work* 6: 199–208.

Kitterod, Ragni Hege. 2002. "Mothers' housework and childcare: Growing similarities or stable inequalities?" *Acta Sociologica* 45, 2: 127–49.

Klebanov, Pamela Kato, Jeanne Brooks-Gunn, and Greg J. Duncan. 1994. "Does neighborhood and family poverty affect mothers' parenting, mental health and social support?" *Journal of Marriage and the Family* 56, 2: 441–55.

Klinkenberg, Dean, and Suzanna Rose. 1994. "Dating scripts of gay men and lesbians," *Journal of Homosexuality* 26, 4: 23–35.

Kneen, Brewster. 1999. *Farmageddon: Food and the Culture of Biotechnology.* Gabriola Island, BC: New Society Publishers.

Knowles, Valerie. 2007. *Strangers at Our Gates: Canadian Immigration and Immigration Policy, 1540–2006.* Rev. edn Toronto: Dundurn.

Kobayashi, K., D. Cloutier-Fisher, and M. Roth. 2009. "Making meaningful connections: A profile of social isolation and health among older adults in small town and small city British Columbia," *Journal of Aging and Health* 21, 2: 374–97.

Kobayashi, Karen M. 1999. "*Bunka no tanjyo* (emergent culture): Continuity and change in older *nisei* (second generation) parent–adult *sansei* (third generation) child relationships in Japanese Canadian Families," PhD thesis, Simon Fraser University.

Korinek, Valerie. 2000. *Roughing It in the Suburbs: Reading Chatelaine Magazine in the Fifties and Sixties.* Toronto: University of Toronto Press.

Kornberger, Rhonda, Janet E. Fast, and Deanna L. Williamson. 2001. "Welfare or work: Which is better for Canadian children?" *Canadian Public Policy* 24, 4: 407–21.

Koropeckyj-Cox, Tanya. 2002. "Beyond parental status: Psychological well-being in middle and old age," *Journal of Marriage and Family* 64: 957–71.

Koss, Mary P., and Sarah L. Cook. 1993. "Facing the facts: Date and acquaintance rape are significant problems," in Gelles and Loseke (1993: 104–19).

————, Christine A. Gidycz, and Nadine Wisniewski. 1987. "The scope of rape: Incidence and prevalence of sexual aggression and victimization in a national sample of higher education students," *Journal of Consulting and Clinical Psychology* 55, 2: 162–70.

Kosteniuk, Julie G., and Harley D. Dickinson. 2003. "Tracing the social gradient in the health of Canadians: Primary and secondary determinants," *Social Science and Medicine* 57, 2: 263–76.

Kozuch, Patricia, and Teresa M. Cooney. 1995. "Young adults' marital and family attitudes: The role of recent parental divorce, and family and parental conflict," *Journal of Divorce and Remarriage* 23: 45–62.

Krahn, Harvey. 1991. "Non-standard work arrangements," *Perspectives on Labour and Income* (Statistics Canada) 4, 4: 35–45.

————. 1995. "Non-standard work on the rise," *Perspectives on Labour and Income* (Statistics Canada) 7, 4: 35–42.

————, Graham S. Lowe, and Karen D. Hughes. 2007. *Work, Industry, and Canadian Society*, 5th edn. Toronto, Ont.: Thomson/Nelson.

Kramer, B.J. 2000. "Husbands caring for wives with dementia: A longitudinal study of continuity and change," *Health & Social Work* 25: 97–107.

Krashinsky, Michael. 2001. "Are we there yet? The evolving face of child care policy in Canada," *Transition* 31, 4: 2–5.

Kremarik, Frances. 2000. "Urban Development." Special Issue: 100 Years of Education. *Canadian Social Trends*, 59 (Winter): 18–22.

Krogh, Kari, and Mary Ennis. 2005. *A National Snapshot of Home Support from the Consumer Perspective: Enabling People with Disabilities to Participate in Policy Analysis and Community Development*. Winnipeg: Council of Canadians with Disabilities.

Krüger, Helga, and René Levy. 2001. "Linking life courses, work, and the family: Theorizing a not so visible nexus between men and women," *Canadian Journal of Sociology* 26, 2: 145–66.

Krull, Catherine. 2003. "Pronatalism, feminism and family policy in Quebec," in M. Lynn, ed., *Voices: Essays on Canadian Families*, 2nd edn. Toronto: Nelson Thomson, ch. 11.

————. 2007. "Placing families first: The state of family policies in *la belle province*," *Canadian Review of Social Policy* 50: 93–102.

————. 2012 "Does 'the family' exist?" in M.J. Hird and G. Pavlich, eds, *Questioning Sociology: Canadian Perspectives*, 2nd edn. Toronto: Oxford University Press, pp. 90–102.

————, and Justyna Sempruch, eds. 2011. *Demystifying the Family/Work Contradiction: Challenges and Possibilities*. Vancouver: UBC Press.

————, and ————. 2011a. "Diversifying the Model, Demystifying the Approach: The Work-Family Debate Reopened," in C. Krull and J. Sempruch, eds, *Demystifying the Family/Paid Work Contradiction: Challenges and Possibilities*. Vancouver: University of British Columbia Press, pp. 1–11.

————, and ————. 2011b. *A Life in Balance? Reopening the Family-Work Debate*. Vancouver: University of British Columbia Press.

Kurz, Demie. 1995. *For Richer, For Poorer: Mothers Confront Divorce*. New York: Routledge.

————. 1996. "Separation, divorce and woman abuse," *Violence Against Women* 2, 1: 63–81.

Kuttai, Heather. 2010. *Maternity Rolls: Pregnancy, Childbirth and Disability*. Halifax and Winnipeg: Fernwood Publishing.

Kvande, E. 2009. "Work–life balance for fathers in globalized knowledge work. Some insights from the norwegian context," *Gender, Work and Organization* 16, 1: 58–72.

Laaroussi, M. 2006. "Le nous familial vecteur d'insertion pour les familles immigrantes," *Canadian Themes* (Spring): 72–5.

Laberge A-M, J. Michaud, A. Richter, E. Lemyre, M. Lambert, B. Brais, and G.A. Mitchell. 2005. "Population history and its impact on medical genetics in Quebec," *Clinical Genetic* 68, 4: 287–301.

Lafrenière, S.A., C. Yves, L. Martel, and A. Bèlanger. 2003. "Dependent seniors at home: Formal and informal help," *Health Reports*. Statistics Canada Catalogue No. 82-003-XIE. 14(4): 31–9.

Laghi, Brian. 2005. "Poll finds gender gap on daycare," *Globe and Mail*, 8 December, A4.

Lamb, M. E. *The Role of the Father in Child Development*. New York: John Wiley and Sons, 2004.

————, and Randal D. Day, eds. 2004. *Reconceptualizing and Measuring Father Involvement*. Mahwah, NJ: Lawrence Erlbaum Associates.

Lamphere, Louise. 1987. *From Working Daughters to Working Mothers: Immigrant Women in a New England Community*. Ithaca, NY: Cornell University Press.

Landis-Kleine, C., Linda Foley, Loretta Nall, P. Padgett, and L. Walters-Palmer. 1995. "Attitudes toward marriage and family held by young adults," *Journal of Divorce and Remarriage* 23: 63–73.

Laner, Mary, and Nicole Ventrone. 2000. "Dating scripts revisited," *Journal of Family Issues*, 21: 488–500.

Langford, Wendy. *Revolutions of the Heart: Gender, Power and the Delusions of Love*. London: Routledge.

Langlois, S., J. Baillargeon, G. Caldwell, G. Fréchet, M. Gauthier, and J. Simard. 1992. *Recent Social Trends in Québec, 1960–1990*. Montreal and Kingston: McGill-Queen's University Press.

Lareau, Annette. 2002. "Invisible inequality: Social class and childrearing in black families and white families," *American Sociological Review* 67: 747–76.

Laroche, D. 2005. *Aspects of the context and consequences of domestic violence: Situational couple violence and intimate terrorism in Canada in 1999*. Available at http://www.stat.gouv.qc.ca/bul/conditions_vie/AspectViolen_an.pdf; accessed 22 July 2009.

LaRossa, Ralph. 1988. "Fatherhood and social change," *Family Relations* 37: 451–8.

———. 1997. *The Modernization of Fatherhood*. Chicago: University of Chicago Press.

Lashewicz, B., G. Manning, M. Hall, and N. Keating. 2007. "Equity matters: Doing fairness in the context of family caregiving," *Canadian Journal on Aging* 26, Suppl. 1: 91–102.

Laslett, Peter. 1984. *The World We Have Lost*, 3rd ed. New York: Scribner's Sons.

Laughlin, L. "Who's Minding the Kids? Child Care Arrangements: Spring 2005/Summer 2006," *Current Population Reports*. Washington: US Census Bureau. Available at http://www.census.gov/prod/2010pubs/p70-121.pdf; accessed 20 April 2012.

Laumann, Edward O., John H. Gagnon, Robert T. Michael, and Stuart Michaels. 1994. *The Social Organization of Sexuality: Sexual Practices in the United States*. Chicago: University of Chicago Press.

Lavalife. 2008. www.lavalife.com Accessed 21 November 2008.

Lavigne, Marie. 1986. "Feminist reflections on the fertility of women in Québec," in Roberta Hamilton and Michèle Barrett, eds, *The Politics of Diversity: Feminism, Marxism and Nationalism*. London: Verso, 303–21.

Le Bourdais, Céline, and Évelyne Lapierre-Adamcyk. 2004. "Changes in conjugal life in Canada: Is cohabitation progressively replacing marriage?" *Journal of Marriage and Family* 66, 4: 929–42.

———, and Annie Sauriol. 1998. "La Part des Peres dans la Division du Travail Domestique au Sein des Familles Canadiennes [Father's Share in the Division of Domestic Labor among Canadian Families]," *Etudes et Documents* No. 69. Montreal, Quebec: INRS-Urbanisation.

Leacock, Eleanor. 2009. "Women in an egalitarian society: The Montagnais-Naskapi of Canada," in Bonnie Fox, ed., *Family Patterns, Gender Relations*. Toronto: Oxford University Press, 43–54.

Lee, Kevin. 2000. *Urban Poverty in Canada*. Ottawa: Canadian Council on Social Development.

Leeson, G.W. 2004. "National background report for Denmark," *Eurofamcare*. Oxford. (European Union funded project).

Lefebvre, Pierre, and Philip Merrigan. 2003. "Assessing family policy in Canada: A new deal for families and children," *Choices: Family Policy* 9: 5.

Lehmann, Peter. 1997. "The development of post-traumatic stress disorder (PTSD) in a sample of child witnesses to mother assault," *Journal of Family Violence* 12, 3: 241–57.

Leichliter, Jami S., Anjani Chandra, Nicole Liddon, Kevin A. Fenton, and Sevgi O. Aral. 2007. "Prevalence and correlates of heterosexual anal and oral sex in adolescents and adults in the United States," *Journal of Infectious Diseases* 196: 1852–59.

Lenon, S. 2008. *A White Wedding? The Racial Politics of Same-Sex Marriage in Canada*. Toronto: University of Toronto Press.

Letkemann, Paul G. 2004. "First nations urban migration and the importance of 'urban nomads' in Canadian plains cities: A perspective from the streets," *Canadian Journal of Urban Research* 13, 2: 241–56.

Levendosky, Alytia A., and Sandra A. Graham-Bermann. 2001. "Parenting in battered women: The effects of domestic violence on women and their children," *Journal of Family Violence* 16, 2: 171–92.

Levesque, L., S. Cossette, and L. Lachance. 1998. "Predictors of the psychological well-being of primary caregivers living with a demented relative: A one-year follow-up study," *Journal of Applied Gerontology* 17, 2: 240–58.

Levett, Carl. 1970. "A parental presence in future family models," in Otto (1970a: 161–82).

Levin, Irene. 2004. "Living apart together: A new family form," *Current Sociology* 52: 223–40.

Levinson, David. 1989. *Family Violence in Cross-Cultural Perspective*. Newbury Park, Calif.: Sage.

Lewis, Charlie. 1986. *Becoming a Father*. Milton Keynes, UK: Open University Press.

Lewis, Jane. 2003. *Should We Worry about Family Change?* Toronto: University of Toronto Press.

———, Marilyn Porter, and Mark Shrimpton, eds. 1988. *Women, Work and the Family in the British, Canadian and Norwegian Offshore Oil Fields*. London: Macmillan.

Li, L., and J.A. Ford. 1998. "Illicit drug use by women with disabilities," *American Journal of Drug and Alcohol Abuse* 24: 405–18.

Li, P. 2001. "The market worth of immigrants' educational credentials," *Canadian Public Policy* 27, 1: 23–38.

———. 1998. *The Chinese in Canada*, 2nd edn. Toronto: Oxford University Press.

Lightman, Ernie S., Andrew Mitchell, and Dean Herd. 2008. "Globalization, precarious work, and the food bank," *Journal of Sociology and Social Welfare* 35, 2: 9–28.

———, ———, and ———. 2010. "Cycling on and off of welfare in Canada," *Journal of Social Policy* 39, 4: 523–42.

Lin, I-Fen. 2008. "Consequences of parental divorce for adult children's support of their frail parents," *Journal of Marriage and Family* 70, 1: 113–28.

Lindsay, Colin. 1999. *A Portrait of Seniors in Canada*, 3rd edn. Ottawa: Statistics Canada, Catalogue no. 89-519-XPE.

———. 2008. "Canadians attend weekly religious services less than 20 years ago," *Matter of Fact* (June). Ottawa: Statistics Canada.

Linton, Ralph. 1959. "The natural history of the family," in Anshen (1959: 30–52).

Lipman, Ellen L., and David R. Offord. 1997. "Psycho-social morbidity among poor children in Ontario," in Duncan and Brooks-Gunn (1997: 239–87).

Lippman, Abby. 1993. "Worrying—and worrying about—the geneticization of reproduction and health," in G. Basen, M. Eichler, and A. Lippman, eds, *Misconceptions*, vol. 1. Quebec City: Voyageur Publishing, 39–65.

Little, Margaret Hillyard. 2011. "The increasing invisibility of mothering," in C. Krull and J. Sempruch, *A Life in Balance? Reopening the Family-Work Debate*. Vancouver: University of British Columbia Press, pp. 194–205.

———. 2001. "A litmus test for democracy: The impact of Ontario welfare changes on single mothers," *Studies in Political Economy* 66: 9–36.

Liu, L. W. 2012. "Transnational Eldercare and Kin Maintenance: Chinese Immigrants and Informal Learning on Emotion Work," in E. Judd and J. Zhang, eds, *Mobility and Migration in China and the Asia Pacific Region*. Beijing: Intellectual Property Publishing House, pp. 106–26.

———. and Don Kerr. 2003. "Family change and the economic well-being of recent immigrants to Canada," *International Migration* 41, 4: 113–40.

———, ———, and Roderic Beaujot. 2006. *Children and Youth in Canada: Recent Demographic Changes* (Discussion Paper No. 06-07). London, Ontario, Canada: University of Western Ontario, Population Studies Centre.

Llewellyn, Gwynnyth, David McConnell, and Luisa Ferronato. 2003. "Prevalence and outcomes for parents with disabilities and their children in an Australian court sample," *Child Abuse & Neglect* 27: 235–51.

Lofaro, Tony. 2008. "Son killed mother in 'fit of anger, insanity'," *Ottawa Citizen*, 27 March 2008.

London, Andrew S., Ellen K. Scott, Kathryn Edin, and Vicki Hunter. 2004. "Welfare reform, work-family trade-offs, and child well-being," *Family Relations* 53, 2: 148–58.

Lookingglass.com. 2002. "Parents with Disabilities," retrieved 29 April 2003.

Lopata, Helen. 1981. *Occupation: Housewife*. New York: Oxford University Press.

Lovell, Vicky, and Gi-Taik Oh. 2005. "Women's job loss and material hardship," *Journal of Women, Politics, and Policy* 27, 3–4: 169–83.

Lupton, Deborah, and Lesley Barclay. 1997. *Constructing Fatherhood: Discourses and Experiences*. London: Sage.

Lustbader, W. 1996. "Conflict, emotion, and power surrounding legacy," *Generations* 20, 3: 54–7.

Luxton, Meg. 1980. *More than a Labour of Love: Three Generations of Women's Work in the Home*. Toronto: Women's Press.

———. 1998. *Families and the Labour Market: Coping Strategies from a Sociological Perspective*. Ottawa: Canadian Policy Research Networks.

———. 2001. "Family coping strategies: Balancing paid employment and domestic labour," in B. Fox, ed., *Family Patterns, Gender Relations*, 2nd edn. New York: Oxford University Press, pp. 318–37.

———. 2011. *Changing Families, New Understandings*. Ottawa: Vanier Institute of the Family (June).

———, and June Corman. 2001. *Getting By in Hard Times: Gendered Labour at Home and On the Job*. Toronto: University of Toronto Press.

———, and Leah F. Vosko. 1998. "The census and women's work," *Studies in Political Economy* 56 (Summer): 49–82.

Lynn, Marion, ed. 2003. *Voices: Essays on Canadian Families*, second edition. Toronto: Thomson Nelson.

Lyonette, C., and L. Yardley. 2003. "The influence on carer wellbeing of motivations to care for older people and the relationship with the care recipient," *Ageing and Society* 23, 4: 487–506.

M. v. H., [1999] 2 S.C.R. 3 (S.C.C.).

McCalla, Douglas. 2005. "A world without chocolate: Grocery purchases at some Upper Canada country stores, 1808–1861," *Agricultural History* 79, 2: 147–72.

McCann, Larry. 1999. "Seasons of labor: Family, work and land in a nineteenth century Nova Scotia shipping community," *History of the Family* 4, 4: 485–527.

McCarthy, Michelle. 2000. "Consent, abuse and choices: Women with intellectual disabilities and sexuality," in R. Traustadottir and K. Johnson, eds, *Women with Intellectual Disabilities: Finding a Place in the World*. London: Jessica Kingsley Publishers.

———, and David Thompson. 1996. "Sexual abuse by design: An examination of the issues in learning disability services," *Disability & Society* 11: 205–17.

McCloskey, Donna. 2001. "Caring for Canada's kids," *Transition Magazine* 31, 4: 1–2.

McConnell, D., and G. Llewellyn. 2000. "Disability and discrimination in statutory child protection proceedings," *Disability & Society* 15: 883–95.

McCracken, Molly. 2004. "Women need safe, stable, affordable housing: A study of social housing, private rental housing and co-op housing in Winnipeg." Prairie Women's Health Centre of Excellence, Winnipeg.

McCubbin, H.I., and J.M Patterson. 1983. "Family transition: Adaptation to stress," in H.I. McCubbin and C.R. Figley, eds, *Stress and the Family*, vol. 1: *Coping with Normative Stress*. New York: Brunner/Mazel, 5–25.

McDaniel, Susan. 2002. "Women's changing relations to the state and citizenship," *Canadian Review of Sociology and Anthropology* 39, 2: 125–49.

———. 2005. "The family lives of the middle-aged and elderly in Canada," in Maureen Baker, ed., *Families: Changing Trends in Canada*. Toronto: McGraw-Hill Ryerson, 181–99.

———, and Paul Bernard. 2011. "Life course as a policy lens: Challenges and opportunities," *Canadian Public Policy* 37 (1): S1–S13.

———, and Lorne Tepperman. 2007. *Close Relations: An Introduction to the Sociology of Families*, 3rd edn. Toronto: Pearson Prentice Hall.

McDill, T., S.K. Hall, and S.C. Turell. 2006. "Aging and creating families: Never married heterosexual women over forty," *The Journal of Women & Aging* 18, 3: 37–50.

Macdonald, C.L. 2011. *Shadow Mothers: Nannies, Au Pairs, and the Micropolitics of Mothering*. Berkeley, CA: University of California Press.

McDonald, L., A. Collins, and J. Dergal. 2006. "The abuse and neglect of adults in Canada," in R. Alaggia and C. Vine, eds, *Cruel but not Unusual*. Waterloo, ON: Wilfrid Laurier, 425–66.

McDonald, Lynn, and A.L. Robb. 2004. "The economic legacy of divorce and separation for women in old age," *Canadian Journal on Aging* 23 (supplement): S83–97.

Macdougall, Brenda. 2010. *One of the Family: Métis Culture in Nineteenth-Century Northwestern Saskatchewan*. Vancouver: UBC Press.

MacDougall, Brian. 2000. *Queer Judgments: Homosexuality, Expression, and the Courts in Canada*. Toronto: University of Toronto Press.

McFate, Katherine. 1995. "Western states in the new world order," in McFate, *Poverty, Inequality, and the Future of Social Policy*. New York: Russell Sage Foundation.

McGarry, K. 1999. "Intervivos transfers and intended bequests," *Journal of Public Economics* 73: 321–51.

———, and R.F. Schoeni. 1997. "Transfer behavior within the family: Results from the Asset and Health Dynamics

Survey," *Journals of Gerontology*, Series B 52 (Special Issue): 82–92.

MacGregor, Tracy E., Susan Rodger, Anne L. Cummings, Alan W. Leschied. 2006. "The needs of foster parents: A qualitative study of motivation, support, and retention," *Qualitative Social Work* 5, 3: 351–68.

MacIntosh, H., E.D. Reissing, and H. Andruff. 2010. "Same-sex marriage in Canada: The impact of legal marriage on the first cohort of gay and lesbian Canadians to wed," *The Canadian Journal of Human Sexuality* 19, 3: 79–90.

McKeen, Wendy. 2001. "Shifting policy and politics of federal child benefits in Canada," *Social Politics* 8, 2: 186–90.

MacKenzie, P., L. Brown, M. Callahan, and B. Whittington. 2005. "Grandparents raising their grandchildren." Paper presented at the Canadian Association on Gerontology, Halifax, NS.

Mackinnon, Catharine A. 1982. "Feminism, Marxism, method and the state: An agenda for theory," *Signs* 7 (Spring): 515–44.

McLaren, Angus. 1986. "The creation of a haven for 'human thoroughbreds': The sterilization of the feeble-minded and the mentally ill in British Columbia," *Canadian Historical Review* LXVII: 127–50.

———. 1990. *Our Own Master Race: Eugenics in Canada, 1885–1945*. Toronto: McClelland and Stewart Inc.

———, and Arlene Tigar McLaren. 1997. *The Bedroom and the State: The Changing Practices and Politics of Contraception and Abortion in Canada, 1880–1997*, 2nd edn. Toronto: Oxford University Press.

McLeod, Jane D., and Michael J. Shanahan. 1996. "Trajectories of poverty and children's mental health," *Journal of Health and Social Behavior* 37, 3: 207–20.

McMullin, Julie Ann. 2005. "Patterns of paid and unpaid work: The influence of power, social context, and family background," *Canadian Journal on Aging* 24, 3: 225–36.

McRoberts, Kenneth. 1988. *Quebec: Social Change & Political Crisis*. Toronto: McClelland.

Mader, Jill. 2007. "More young adults living with parents". Available at http://novanewsnet.ukings .ca/nova_ news_3588_12891.html; accessed 29 November 2008.

Madibbo, A. 2010. "The African francophone identities within the francophone diaspora," in T. McCauley and J. Hill, eds, *Canadian Society: Global Perspectives*. Oshawa: de Sitter Publications, pp. 87–94.

Magnus, G. 2009. *The Age of Aging: How Demographics are Changing the Global Economy and Our World*. New York: John Wiley and Sons.

Mahoney, Janis, and Linda M. Williams. 1998. "Sexual assault in marriage: Prevalence, consequences and treatment of wife rape," in Jasinski and Williams (1998: 113–62).

Maki, Krystle. 2011. "Neoliberal deviants and surveillance: Welfare recipients under the watchful eye of Ontario Works," *Journal of Surveillance and Society* 9, 1: 47–63.

———. Forthcoming, 2013. "Welfare surveillance, neoliberal policy and the never-deserving single mother," in Joanne Minaker and Bryan Hogeveen, eds, *Criminalized Mothers, Criminalizing Motherhood*. Demeter Press: Toronto.

Malacrida, C. 2005. "Discipline and dehumanization in a total institution: Institutional survivors' descriptions of a time-out room," *Disability & Society* 20: 523–38.

———. 2007. "Negotiating the dependency/nurturance tightrope: Dilemmas of disabled motherhood," *Canadian Review of Sociology* 144: 469–93.

———. 2009. "Performing motherhood in a disablist world: Dilemmas of motherhood, femininity and disability," *International Journal of Qualitative Studies in Education* 23: 99–117.

———. 2009a. "Discipline and Dehumanization in a Total Institution: Institutional Survivors' Description of Time-out Rooms," in *Rethinking Normalcy: A Disability Studies Reader*, Tanya Titchkosky and Rod Michalko, eds. Toronto: Canadian Scholars' Press Inc.

Malec, Christine. 1993. "The double objectification of disability and gender," *Canadian Woman Studies* 13, 4: 22–3.

Malenfant, E., A. Lebel, and L. Martel. 2010. *Projections of the Diversity of the Canadian Population*. Minister of Industry. No. 91-551-X, Ottawa.

Man, G. 2007. "Racialization of gender, work, and transnational migration: The experience of Chinese immigrant women in Canada," in S. Hier and S. Bolaria, eds, *Race and Racism in 21st Century Canada*. Peterborough: Broadview Press, pp. 235–52.

Mandell, Denna. 2002. *Deadbeat Dads: Subjectivity and Social Construction*. Toronto: University of Toronto Press.

Mandell, Nancy, and Ann Duffy. 2000. *Canadian Families: Diversity, Conflicts and Change*, 2nd edn. Toronto: Nelson Thomson.

Mann, M. 2009. "Disproportionate and unjustifiable: Teen First Nation mothers and unstated paternity," *Canadian Issues* (Winter): 31–6.

Mann, R. 2009. *Evolving Family Structures, Roles and Relationships in Light of Ethnic and Social Change*. Oxford University: Oxford Institute of Ageing.

Manning, Wendy, Peggy Giordano, and Monica Longmere. 2006. "Hooking up: The relationship contexts of 'non-relationship' sex," *Journal of Adolescent Research* 21: 459–84.

Marcil-Gratton, Nicole. 1999. "Lone parents and their children," *Transition Magazine* 29: 1.

———, and Celine Le Bourdais. 1999. *Custody, Access and Child Support: Findings from the National Longitudinal Survey of Children and Youth*. Ottawa: Department of Justice Canada, Child Support Team.

———, ———, and Evelyn Lapierre-Adamcyk. 2000. "The implications of parents' conjugal histories for children," *Canadian Journal of Policy Research* 1: 32–40.

Marcus, Ivan G. 2004. *The Jewish Life Cycle: Rites of Passage from Biblical to Modern Times*. Seattle: University of Washington Press.

Margolis, Maxine. 2009. "Putting mothers on a pedestal," in Bonnie Fox, ed., *Family Patterns, Gender Relations*. Toronto: Oxford University Press, 119–35.

Marks, Loren, and Rob Palkovitz. 2004. "American fatherhood types: The good, the bad and the un-interested," *Fathering* 2: 113–29.

Marks, Nadine F. 1995. "Mid-life marital status differences in social support relationships with adult children and psychological well-being," *Journal of Family Issues* 16: 5–28.

———, and James David Lambert. 1998. "Marital status continuity and change among young and mid-life adults:

Longitudinal effects on psychological well-being," *Journal of Family Issues* 19: 652–86.

Marmot, Michael G., and George Davey Smith. 1997. "Socio-economic differentials in health: The contribution of the Whitehall studies," *Journal of Health Psychology* 2, 3: 283–96.

Maroney, Heather J. 1992. "Who has the baby? Nationalism, pronatalism and the construction of a 'demographic crisis' in Quebec, 1960–1988," *Studies in Political Economy* 39: 7–36.

Marshall, Dominique. 2006. *The Social Origins of the Welfare State: Québec Families, Compulsory Education, and Family Allowances, 1940–1955*. Translated by Nicola Doone Danby. Waterloo: Wilfrid Laurier University Press.

Marshall, Katherine. 1993. "Dual earners: Who's responsible for the housework?" *Canadian Social Trends* 31 (Winter): 11–14.

———. 1998. "Stay-at-home dads," *Perspectives on Labour and Income* 10 (1): 9–15. Available at http://prod.library. utoronto.ca/datalib/codebooks/cstdsp/71f0004xcb/2003/ pe_archive_sa/english/1998/pear19980100015ia01.pdf; accessed 20 March 2012.

———. 2003. "Benefiting from extended parental leave," *Perspectives on Labour and Income* (Statistics Canada) 4, 3: 5–11.

———. 2006. "Converging gender roles," *Perspectives* 7, 7: 5–17. Available at http://www.statcan.ca/english/freepub/75-001-XIE/10706/art-1.htm.

———. 2008. "Fathers' use of paid parental leave," *Perspectives on Labour and Income* 9 (6): 5–14.

———. 2011. "Generational change in paid and unpaid work," *Canadian Social Trends* 92: 13–24.

Marsiglio, W., and K. Roy. 2012. *Nurturing Dads: Social Initiatives for Contemporary Fatherhood*. New York: Russell Sage Foundation.

———, et al. 2000. "Scholarship on fatherhood in the 1990s and beyond," *Journal of Marriage and the Family* 62, 4: 1173–91.

Martel, Edith, Benoit Laplante, and Paul Bernard. 2005. "Unemployment and family strategies: The mitigating effects of the transition from unemployment insurance to employment insurance," *Recherches Sociodemographiques* 46, 2: 245–80.

Martel, L., and J. Légaré. 2001. "Avec ou sans famille proche a la vieillesse: Une description du réseau de soutien informel des personnes âgées selon la présence du conjoint et des enfants," *Cahiers quebecois de demographie* 30: 89–114.

Martin, B. 1994. "Extraordinary homosexuals and the fear of being ordinary," *Differences* 6 (2–3): 100–25.

Martin, Karin A. 1996. *Puberty, Sexuality, and the Self: Boys and Girls at Adolescence*. New York: Routledge.

Martin-Matthews, Anne. 1999. "Widowhood: Dominant renditions, changing demography, and variable meaning," in S.M. Neysmith, ed., *Critical Issues for Future Social Work Practice with Aging Persons*. New York: Columbia University Press, pp. 27–46.

Mason, M., S. Harrison-Jay, G.M. Svare, and N.H. Wolfinger. 2002. "Stepparents: De facto parents or legal strangers?" *Journal of Family Issues* 23, 4: 507–22.

Matas, Robert. 2005. "Questions of funding dog talks on national child-care program," *Globe and Mail*, 12 February, A6.

Matthews, Sarah H. 2002. *Sisters and Brothers/Daughters and Sons: Meeting the Needs of Older Parents*. Bloomington, IN: Unlimited Publishing.

Maximova, Katerina. 2004. *Memorandum for the Minister—Family-Friendly Policies in Quebec*. Ottawa: Government of Canada, Social Policy Research.

Maytree Conversations. 2012. "Increase the Canada Child Tax Benefit to $5,000," 13 April. Available at http://maytree. com/blog/tag/canada-child-tax-benefit.

Mead, George Herbert. 1967 [1934]. *Mind, Self and Society*. Chicago: University of Chicago Press.

Mead, Margaret. 1949. *Male and Female: A Study of the Sexes in a Changing World*. New York: Dell Publishing, Laurel Editions.

Meert, Henk, Pascale Mistiaen, and Christian Kesteloot. 1997. "The geography of survival: Household strategies in urban settings," *Journal of Economic and Social Geography* 88, 2: 169–81.

Meissner, Martin, et al. 1975. "No exit for wives: Sexual division of labour and the culmination of house-hold demands," *Canadian Review of Sociology and Anthropology* 12, 4: 424–39.

Mendelson, Michael, Ken Battle, and Shari Torjman. 2009. *Canada's Shrunken Safety Net: Employment Insurance in the Great Recession*. Ottawa: Caledon Institute of Social Policy.

Menec, Verena H. 2003. "The relation between everyday activities and successful aging: A six-year longitudinal study," *Journals of Gerontology*, Series B 58: S74–82.

Menon, Vinay. 2012. "Rihanna, Brown send 'dreadful' message," *Toronto Star*, 24 February, L1, L7.

Merali, Noorfarah. 2009. "Experiences of South Asian brides entering Canada after recent changes to family sponsorship policies," *Violence Against Women* 15, 3: 321–39.

Mercier, Michael, and Christopher Boone. 2002. "Infant mortality in Ottawa, Canada, 1901: Assessing cultural, economic and environmental factors," *Journal of Historical Geography* 28, 4: 486–507.

Merkle, Erich R., and Rhonda A. Richardson. 2000. "Digital dating and virtual relating: Conceptualizing computer mediated romantic relationships," *Family Relations* 49: 187–92.

Messias, DeAnne K. Hilfinger, Margaret K. DeJong, and Kerry McLoughlin. 2005. "Expanding the concept of women's work: Volunteer work in the context of poverty," *Journal of Poverty* 9, 3: 25–47.

Miall, Charlene, and Karen March. 2003. "A comparison of biological and adoptive mothers and fathers: The relevance of biological kinship and gendered constructs of parenthood," *Adoption Quarterly* 6: 7–39.

Michalski, Joseph H. 2003a. "The economic status and coping strategies of food bank users in the Greater Toronto area," *Canadian Journal of Urban Research* 12, 2: 275–98.

———. 2003b. "Housing affordability, social policy and economic conditions: Food bank users in the Greater Toronto area, 1990–2000," *Canadian Review of Sociology and Anthropology* 40, 1: 65–92.

Michelson, William, and Lorne Tepperman. 2003. "Focus on home: What time-use data can tell about caregiving to adults," *Journal of Social Issues* 59: 591–610.

Milan, Anne. 2000. "100 Years of Families." *Canadian Social Trends*, 56 (Spring).

———, and Brian Hamm. 2003. "Across the generations: Grandparents and grandchildren," *Canadian Social Trends* (Winter): 2–9. Ottawa: Statistics Canada.

———, and ———. 2004. "Mixed unions," *Canadian Social Trends* 73: 2–6.

———, H. Maheux, and T. Chui. 2010. *A Portrait of Couples in Mixed Unions*, No. 89. Ottawa: Statistics Canada.

———, and M. Vézina. 2011. *Senior Women. Women in Canada: A gender-based statistical report*. Ottawa: Statistics Canada, Catalogue no. 89-503-X.

———, ———, and C. Wells. 2007. *Family Portrait: Continuity and Change in Canadian Families and Households in 2006*. Ottawa: Statistics Canada. at http://www12.statcan.ca/english/census06/analysis/famhouse/index.cfm.

Milkie, Melissa A., and Pia Peltola. 1999. "Playing all the roles: Gender and the work balancing act," *Journal of Marriage and the Family* 61, 4: 476–90.

Millar, Paul. 2010. "Punishing our way out of poverty: The prosecution of child-support debt in Alberta, Canada," *Canadian Journal of Law and Society* 25, 2: 149–65.

Miller, J.R. 1996. *Shingwauk's Vision: A History of Native Residential Schools*. Toronto: University of Toronto Press.

Miller, James. 2003. "Out family values," in Lynn, second edition (2003: 103–30).

Miller, T. 2011. "Falling back into gender? Men's narratives and practices around first-time fatherhood," *Sociology* 45, 6: 1094–109.

Miller, Vincent. 2008. "New media, networking and phatic culture," *Convergence: The International Journal of Research into New Media Technologies* 14: 387–400.

Milligan, Kevin. 2002. "Quebec's baby bonus: Can public policy raise fertility?" *Backgrounder* 57. Toronto: C.D. Howe Institute. Available at http://www.cdhowe.org/pdf/milligan_backgounder.pdf.

Milne, A., and E. Hatzidimitriadou. 2003. "'Isn't he wonderful?': Exploring the contributions and conceptualization of elder husbands as carers," *Ageing International* 28: 389–407.

Mincy, Ronald B., and Allen T. Dupree. 2001. "Welfare, child support and family formation," *Child and Youth Services Review* 23, 6 and 7: 577–601.

Minister of Finance, Canada, Hon. James M. Flaherty, P.C., M.P. 2012. "Economic Action Plan 2012." Tabled in the House of Commons, Canada. Available at http://www.budget.gc.ca/2012/plan/pdf/Plan2012-eng.pdf.

Ministère de l'Emploi, de la Solidarité sociale et de la Famille. 2005. "Financial support for childcare." Available at http://www.messf.gouv.qc.ca/Index_en.asp.

Ministère de la Famille et de l'Enfance du Québec. 1999. *Family Policy: Another Step towards Developing the Full Potential of Families and Their Children*. Quebec City: Les Publications du Québec.

Ministère de la Famille et des Aînés. 2011. *Analyse comparative des politiques en matière familiale dans les provinces canadiennes*. June. Available at http://www.mfa.gouv.qc.ca/fr/publication/Documents/analyse_politiques_fam.pdf.

———. 2012. "La politique familiale au Québec." Available at http://www.mfa.gouv.qc.ca/fr/Famille/politique-familiale/pages/index.aspx.

Ministère des Finances. 2009. *Budget 2009–2010: Status Report on Québec's Family Policy*. Available at http://www.budget.finances.gouv.qc.ca/Budget/2009-2010/en/documents/pdf/FamilyPolicy.pdf.

Ministry of Social Affairs and Health. 2006. Social Welfare in Finland. Brochures of the Ministry of Social Affairs and Health. Available at http://pre20090115.stm.fi/aa1161155903333/passthru.pdf.

Miranda, V. "Cooking, Caring and Volunteering: Unpaid Work Around the World," *OECD Social, Employment and Migration Working Papers, No. 116*. Paris: OECD Publishing. doi: 10.1787/5kghrjm8s142-en.

Mitchell, Barbara A. 1998a. "The refilled nest: Debunking the myth of family in crisis," paper presented at the ninth annual John K. Friesen Conference, "The Overselling of Population Aging," Simon Fraser University, 14–15 May.

———. 1998b. "Too close for comfort? Parental assessments of 'boomerang kid' living arrangements," *Canadian Journal of Sociology* 23: 21–46.

———. 2006. *The Boomerang Age: Transitions to Adulthood in Families*. Edison, NJ: Aldine

———. 2009. *Family Matters: An Introduction to Family Sociology in Canada*. Toronto: Canadian Scholar's Press Inc.

———, and Ellen M. Gee. 1996. "'Boomerang kids' and mid-life parental marital satisfaction," *Family Relations* 45: 442–8.

———, Andrew V. Wister, and Ellen M. Gee. 2002. "There's no place like home: An analysis of young adults' mature co-residency in Canada," *International Journal of Aging and Human Development* 54: 57–84.

Mitchell, David, and Sharon Snyder. 2003. "The eugenic Atlantic: Race, disability, and the making of an international eugenic science, 1800–1945," *Disability & Society* 18: 843–64.

Mitchell, P.J. 2012. "A wedding isn't a marriage, it just starts one," *eReview: Latest Developments in Family Friendly Research* 12, 3. Ottawa: Institute of Marriage and Family Canada.

Moen, Phyllis. 1991. "Transitions in mid-life: Women's work and family roles in the 1970s," *Journal of Marriage and the Family* 53: 135–50.

Moffat, Alistair, and James F. Wilson. 2011. *The Scots, A Genetic Journey*. Edinburgh: Birlinn.

Mongeau, Paul, Janet Jacobsen and Carolyn Donnerstein. 2007. "Defining dates and first date goals: Generalizing from undergraduates to single adults," *Communication Research* 34: 526–47.

Monsebraaten, Laurie. 2008. "Copy Quebec daycare, PQ leader says," *Toronto Star*, 24 October.

Montemurro, Beth. 2002. "'You go 'cause you have to': The bridal shower as a ritual of obligation," *Symbolic Interaction* 25, 1: 670–92.

———. 2003. 'Sex symbols: The bachelorette party as a window to change in women's sexual expression," *Sexuality and Culture* 7, 2: 3–29.

————. 2005. "Add men, don't stir: Reproducing traditional gender roles in modern wedding showers," *Journal of Contemporary Ethnography* 34: 6–35.

————. 2006. *Something Old, Something Bold: Bridal Showers and Bachelorette Parties*. Piscataway, NJ: Rutgers University Press.

Montenegro, Xenia P. 2004. "The divorce experience: A study of divorce at mid-life and beyond," Report published by the AARP, May.

Montgomery, Sue. 2008. "Foster parents charged: Accused of sexually abusing children," *The Montreal Gazette*, 15 April. Available at http://ww.canada.com/montrealgazette/news/story.html?k=15566&id=3f601e2f-9c6f-4734-a02a-1e738f5cb113.

Montigny, Edgar-A. 1993. *Foisted Upon the Government? State Responsibilities, Family Obligations, and the Care of the Dependent Aged in Late Nineteenth-Century Ontario*. Montreal: McGill-Queen's University Press.

Montreal Diet Dispensary. 1998. *Budgeting for Basic Needs and Budgeting for Minimum Adequate Standard of Living*. Montreal.

Moore, D., and L. Li. 1998. "Prevalence and risk factors of illicit drug use by people with disabilities," *Journal on Addictions* 7: 93–102.

Moore, Eric, and Andrejs Skaburskis. 2004. "Canada's increasing housing affordability burdens," *Housing Studies* 19, 3: 395–413.

Moore, Maureen. 1989. "Female lone parenting over the life course," *Canadian Journal of Sociology* 14, 3: 335–52.

Morgan, David H.J. 1996. *Family Connections: An Introduction to Family Studies*. Cambridge: Polity Press.

Moriarty, J., and J. Butt. 2004. "Social support and ethnicity in old age," in A. Waker and C. Hagan Hennessy, eds, *Quality of Life in Old Age*. Maidenhead, UK, Open University Press.

Morissette, R., X. Zhang, and M. Drolet. 2002. "Wealth Inequality," *Perspectives* 2, 3: 1–18.

Morissette, René, and Garnett Picot. 2005. "Low-paid work and economically vulnerable families over the last two decades" (Catalogue no. 11F0019MIE-No. 248). Analytical Studies Branch Research Paper Series. Ottawa: Statistics Canada. Available at http://www.statcan.ca/english/research/11F0019MIE/11F0019MIE2005248.pdf.

————, and Xuelin Zhang. 2006. "Revisiting wealth inequality," *Perspectives on Labour and Income* 7, 12: 5–16.

————, ————, and Marie Drolet. 2002. *The Evolution of Wealth Inequality in Canada, 1984–1999*. Ottawa: Statistics Canada, Business and Labour Market Analysis Division.

Morris, Jenny. 2001. "Impairment and disability: Constructing an ethics of care that promotes human rights," *Hypatia* 16, 5: 1–16.

Morris, Lydia. 1985. "Local social networks and domestic organisations: A study of redundant steelworkers and their wives," *Sociological Review* 33, 2: 327–42.

Morris, Marika. 2001. *Gender-Sensitive Home and Community Care and Caregiving Research: A Synthesis Paper*. Ottawa: Women's Health Bureau, Health Canada.

Moser, Caroline. 1993. *Gender Planning and Development: Theory, Practice and Training*. London: Routledge.

Mosoff, J. 1995. "Motherhood, madness and law," *University of Toronto Law Journal* 45: 107–42.

Mulcahy, Meghan, and Nico Trocme. 2010. "Children and Youth in Out-of-Home Care in Canada." Centres of Excellence in Research for Children's Well-being. Available at http://www.cecw-cepb.ca/sites/default/files/publications/en/ChildrenInCare78E.pdf.

Mullin, A. 2003. "Disability theory, children, and care," in *The Canadian Philosophical Association at the Congress of Humanities of Social Sciences*. Halifax: CPA, 1–18.

Murdie, R.A. 2008. "Diversity and concentration in Canadian immigration: Trends in Toronto, Montreal and Vancouver, 1971–2006," *Research Bulletin* 42: 1–12, Centre for Urban and Community Studies. Toronto: University of Toronto.

Murdock, George P. 1949. *Social Structure*. New York: Macmillan.

Myers, David G. 1993. *Social Psychology*. New York: McGraw-Hill.

Myles, John. 2000. "The maturation of Canada's retirement income system: Income levels, income inequality and low income among older persons," *Canadian Journal on Aging* 19, 3: 287–316.

Nakonezny, Paul A., Wayne H. Denton. 2008. "Marital relationships: A social exchange theory perspective," *American Journal of Family Therapy* 36 (5): 402–12.

National Advisory Council on Aging (NACA). 2004. *The NACA position on Alzheimer disease and related dementias*. Ottawa: Minister of Public Works and Government Services Canada.

National Center on Elder Abuse. 2005. Available at http://www.ncea.aoa.gov/ncearoot/MainSite/pdf/publication/FinalStatistics050331.pdf; accessed 10 March 2008.

National Clearinghouse on Family Violence (NCFV), Family Violence Prevention Division. 1993a. *Family Violence against Women with Disabilities*. Ottawa: Health and Welfare Canada. Available at http://www.phac-aspc.gc.ca/ncfv-cnivf/familyviolence/pdfs/fvawd.pdf.

————. 1993b. *Family Violence and People with a Mental Handicap*. Ottawa: Health and Welfare Canada. Available at http://dsp-psd.pwgsc.gc.ca/Collection/H72-22-13-1993E.pdf.

————. 2000. *Abuse of Children with Disabilities*. Ottawa: Health and Welfare Canada. Available at http://www.phac-aspc.gc.ca/ncfv-cnivf/familyviolence/html/nfntsdisabl_e.html.

————. 2004. *Violence against Women with Disabilities*. Ottawa: Health and Welfare Canada. Available at http://www.phac-aspc.gc.ca/ncfvcnivf/familviolence/html/femdisabus_e.html.

National Council of Welfare. 2004. *Welfare Incomes 2003*. Ottawa: Minister of Public Works and Government Services Canada. Available at http://www.ncwcnbes.net/htmdocument/reportWelfareIncomes.

————. 2004a. *Poverty Profile 2001*, vol. 122. Ottawa: Minister of Public Works and Government Services Canada.

————. 2006. *Number of People on Welfare: Fact Sheet*. Ottawa: Minister of Public Works and Government Services Canada.

————. 2006a. *Welfare Incomes 2005*. Ottawa: Minister of Public Works and Government Services Canada. Available at http://www.ncwcnbes.net/documents/researchpublica-tions/ResearchProjects/WelfareIncomes/2005Report_Summer2006/ReportENG.pdf.

———. 2006b. *Brief to the Standing Committee on Human Resources, Social Development and the Status of Persons with Disabilities concerning Factors Aggravating Poverty*.

———. 2007a. *Poverty Statistics 2004*. Ottawa: Minister of Public Works and Government Services Canada. Available at http://www.ncwcnbes.net/documents/researchpublica-tions/ResearchProjects/PovertyProfile/2004/PovertyRates-FamiliesENG.pdf.

———. 2007b. *We Still Need a National Anti-Poverty Strategy: National Council of Welfare (NCW) Response to the 2007 Federal Budget*. Ottawa: Minister of Public Works and Government Services Canada. Available at http://www.ncwcnbes.net/documents/publicstatements/FederalBudgets/2007_Response ToBudgetENG.pdf.

———. 2007c. *Solving Poverty: Four Cornerstones of a Workable National Strategy for Canada*, Volume 126. Available at http://www.ncwcnbes.net/documents/researchpublications/ResearchProjects/NationalAntiPovertyStrategy/2007Report-Solving Poverty/ReportENG.pdf.

———. 2008. *Welfare Incomes 2006 and 2007*. Ottawa: Minister of Public Works and Government Services Canada. Available at http://www.ncwcnbes.net/documentsresearchpublications/OtherPublications/2008Report-WelfareIncomes2006-2007/Report-WelfareIncomes2006-2007E.pdf.

———. 2010. *Welfare Incomes 2009*. Ottawa: National Council of Welfare. Available at http://www.ncw.gc.ca/l.3bd.2t.1ils@-eng.jsp?lid=331.

———. 2011. *The Dollars and Sense of Solving Poverty*. Ottawa: National Council of Welfare.

———. 2012. *A Snapshot of Racialized Poverty in Canada*. Ottawa: National Council of Welfare.

Nativevillage.org. 2012. "21st Century Poverty Facts and Stats." Available at http://www.nativevillage.org/Messages%20from%20the%20People/21st%20poverty_facts_and_stats.htm; accessed 25 April 2012.

Navaie-Waliser, M., P.H. Feldman, D.A. Gould, C. Levine, A.N. Kuerbis, and K. Donelan. 2002. "When the caregiver needs care: The plight of vulnerable caregivers," *American Journal of Public Health* 92, 3: 409–13.

Nazroo, J., M. Bajekal, D. Blane, and I. Grewal. 2004. "Ethnic Inequalities," in A. Walker and C. Hagan Hennessy, eds, *Growing Older: Quality of Life in Old Age*. Maidenhead, UK, Open University Press, pp. 35–59.

Neimeyer, Robert A., Holly G. Prigerson, and Betty Davies. 2002. "Mourning and meaning," *American Behavioral Scientist* 46, 2: 235–51.

Nelson, Adie. 2006. *Gender in Canada*. Toronto: Pearson Prentice Hall.

Nelson, Fiona. 1996. *Lesbian Motherhood: An Exploration of Canadian Lesbian Families*. Toronto: University of Toronto Press.

Nelson, J. 2010. "Your wedding, by Martha Stewart," *Canadian Business* 83, 3: 18.

Nett, Emily M. 1988. *Canadian Families, Past and Present*. Toronto: Butterworths.

Netting, Nancy. 2006. "Two lives, one partner: Indo-Canadian youth between love and arranged marriages," *Journal of Comparative Family Studies*, 37: 129–46.

Newman, T. 2002. "Young carers and disabled parents: Time for a change of direction?" *Disability & Society* 17: 613–25.

News Release. 2011. "Caregiver Recognition Act would recognize caregivers' contribution to families, communities: Rondeau." News Release—Manitoba. Available at http://news.gov.mb.ca/news/index.html?item=11580.

Ney, Philip G. 1992. "Transgenerational triangles of abuse: A model of family violence," in E.C. Viano, ed., *Intimate Violence: Interdisciplinary Perspectives*. Bristol, UK: Taylor and Francis, 15–26.

Neysmith, Sheila. 1995. "Power in relationships of trust: A feminist analysis of elder abuse," in M. MacLean, ed., *Abuse and Neglect of Older Canadians: Strategies for Change*. Toronto: Thompson.

Ngo, H. V. 2009. "Patchwork, sidelining and marginalization: Services for immigrant youth," *Journal of Immigrant and Refugee Studies* 7, 1: 82–100.

———, and B. Shleifer. 2005. "Immigrant children and youth in focus," *Canadian Issues* (Spring): 29–33.

Nimkoff, Meyer F. 1947. *Marriage and the Family*. Boston: Houghton Mifflin.

Novak, Mark, and Lori Campbell. 2009. *Aging and Society: A Canadian Perspective*, 6th ed. Scarborough, Ont.: Nelson.

O'Brien, Margaret. 1987. "Patterns of kinship and friendship among lone fathers," in Charlie Lewis and Margaret O'Brien, eds, *Reassessing Fatherhood: New Observations on Fathers and the Modern Family*. London: Sage.

———. 2005. *Shared Caring: Bringing Fathers in the Frame*. Manchester, UK: Equal Opportunities Commission.

O'Brien, Mary. 1981. *The Politics of Reproduction*. Boston: Routledge.

O'Connor, D. 1999. "Living with a memory-impaired spouse: (Re)cognizing the experience," *Canadian Journal on Aging* 18, 2: 211–35.

———, A. Phinney, A. Smith, J. Small, B. Purves, E. Drance, M. Donnelly, H. Chaudhury, and L. Beattie. 2007. "Personhood in dementia care," *Dementia* 6, 1: 122–42.

O'Donnell, J.M., W.E. Johnson, Jr., L.E. D'Aunno, and H.L. Thorton. 2005. "Fathers in child welfare: Caseworkers' perspectives," *Child Welfare* 84, 3: 387–414.

O'Hara, Kathy. 1998. *Comparative Family Policy: Eight Countries' Stories*. Canadian Policy Research Networks, no. 15734. Ottawa: Renouf Publishing.

O'Sullivan, Lucia F., Mariah Mantsun Cheng, Kathleen Mullan Harris, and Jeanne Brooks-Gunn. 2007. "I wanna hold your hand: The progression of social, romantic and sexual events in adolescent relationships," *Perspectives on Sexual and Reproductive Health* 39: 100–7.

O'Toole, Corbett Joan, and Tanis Doe. 2002. "Sexuality and disabled parents with disabled children," *Sexuality and Disability* 20: 89–102.

OACAS. 2011. *Children's Well-Being: The Ontarian Perspective, Child Welfare Report 2011*. Toronto: Ontario Association of Children's Aid Societies. Available at http://www.oacas-groups.org/uploads/cwr/11childwelfarereporteng.pdf.

Oakley, Ann. 1974. *Housewife*. London: Allen Lane.

Ochocka, J., and R. Janzen. 2008. "Immigrant parenting: A new framework of understanding," *Journal of International Migration and Integration* 6, 1: 85–112.

Oderkirk, Jill. 1992. "Food banks," *Canadian Social Trends* 24, 6: 6–14.

OECD, Directorate for Education. 2004. *Early Childhood Education and Care Policy. Canada: Country Note.* Paris: OECD.

———. 2011. Better Life Index 2011—Canada. Paris: OECD. Available at http://oecdbetterlifeindex.org/countries/canada/.

Office for Disability Issues. 2001. *Disability in Canada: A 2001 Profile.* Gatineau, Que.: Human Resources Development Canada.

———. 2003. *Defining Disability: A Complex Issue.* Gatineau, Que.: Human Resources Development Canada.

Office of the Prime Minister. 2004. "Speech from the Throne" and "Reply to the Speech from the Throne," 5 October. Available at http://pm.gc.ca/eng.ftddt.asp.

Ogburn, W.F., and M.F. Nimkoff. 1955. *Technology and the Changing Family.* Boston: Houghton Mifflin.

Ogrodnik, L. 2007. *Family Violence in Canada: A Statistical Profile.* Ottawa: Statistics Canada.

Oliver, M. 1996. "Defining impairment and disability: Issues at stake," in C. Barnes and G. Mercer, eds, *Exploring the Divide.* Leeds: The Disability Press, 29–54.

Oliver, Michael. 1996a. "The Social Model in Context," in *Understanding Disability: From Theory to Practice.* Hampshire and New York: Palgrave, pp. 30–42.

Olsen, R. 1996. "Young carers: Challenging the facts and politics of research into children and caring," *Disability & Society*, 11.

Ontario Advisory Council on Senior Citizens. 1993. *Denied Too Long: The Needs and Concerns of Seniors Living in First Nation Communities in Ontario.* Toronto.

Openparliament.ca. 2012. "Nycole Turmel on Helping Families In Need Act," 27 September. Available at http://openparliament.ca/debates/2012/9/27/nycole-turmel-1/only.

———. 2012a. Bill C-44. Available at http://openparliament.ca/bills/41-1/C-44/?page=2.

Orava, Tammy A., Peter J. Mcleod, and Donald Sharpe. 1996. "Perceptions of control, depressive symptomatology and self-esteem of women in transition from abusive relationships," *Journal of Family Violence* 11: 167–86.

Organisation for Economic Co-operation and Development (OECD). 2004. *Early Childhood Education and Care Policy: Canada Country Note.* Paris: OECD.

———. 2008. *OECD Health Data: How Does Canada Compare?* Available at http://www.oecd.org/dataoecd/46/33/38979719.pdf.

Orleans, Myron, and Florence Wolfson. 1970. "The future of the family," *The Futurist*: 48–9.

Oswald, Ramona Faith. 2000. "A member of the wedding?: Heterosexism and family ritual," *Journal of Social and Personal Relationships* 17: 349–68.

———. 2001. "Religion, family, and ritual: The production of gay, lesbian, bisexual, and transgender outsiders-within," *Review of Religious Research* 43, 1: 39–50.

———, and Elizabeth A. Suter. 2004. "Heterosexist inclusion and exclusion during ritual: A 'straight versus gay' comparison," *Journal of Family Issues* 25, 7: 881–99.

Otto, Herbert A., ed. 1970a. *The Family in Search of a Future: Alternate Models for Moderns.* New York: Appleton-Century-Crofts.

———. 1970b. "Introduction," in Otto (1970a: 1–9).

———. 1972. "New light on human potential," in College of Home Economics (1972: 14–25).

Owram, Doug. 1996. *Born at the Right Time: A History of the Baby Boom Generation.* Toronto: University of Toronto Press.

Pacaut, Philippe, Celine Le Bourdais, and Benoit Laplante. 2011. "The Changing Impact of Conjugal Status and Motherhood on Employment across Generations of Canadian Women," *Canadian Studies in Population* 38, 3–4: 105–32.

Pacey, Michael. 2002. "Living alone and living with children: The living arrangements of Canadian and Chinese-Canadian seniors," SEDAP Research Paper 74. Hamilton, Ont.: McMaster University.

Pagelow, Mildred D. 1985. "The battered husband syndrome: Social problem or much ado about little?" in N. Johnson, ed., *Marital Violence.* London: Routledge & Kegan.

Pahl, Ray E. 1984. *Divisions of Labour.* Oxford: Blackwell.

———, and David J. Pevalin. 2005. "Between family and friends: A longitudinal study of friendship choice," *The British Journal of Sociology* 56, 3: 433–50.

———, and Liz Spencer. 2004. "Personal communities: Not simply families of 'fate' or 'choice'," *Current Sociology* 52, 2: 199–221.

Paish, S., and J. Kwok. 2005. "Undue hardship: How much accommodation is enough?" in The Canadian Institute, ed., *Duty to Accommodate.* Vancouver: Fasken Martineau, 1–27.

Palameta, B. 2003. "Who pays for domestic help?" *Perspectives on Labour and Income*: 39–42.

———. 2004. "Low income among immigrants and visible minorities," *Perspectives on Labour and Income* 5: 4.

Palmer, Bryan. 2008. *Canada's 1960s: The Ironies of Identity in a Rebellious Era.* Toronto: University of Toronto Press.

Palmer, Kimberly. 2008. "For richer or poorer?" *U.S. News and World Report*, 15 September, 145, 6: 86.

Pappone, Jeff. 2005. "Tech workers in 'sandwich generation' often most squeezed," *Ottawa Business Journal.* Available at http://www.ottawa businessjournal.com/305596806034971.php; accessed 4 May 2004.

Paraskevas, Joe. 2004. "Survivor pension denial upheld," *Vancouver Sun*, 29 October.

Park, Deborah C., and John P. Radford. 1998. "From the case files: Reconstructing a history of involuntary sterilization," *Disability & Society* 13: 317–42.

Parkatti, T. 2004. "Services for supporting family carers of elderly people in Europe: characteristics, coverage and usage: National background report for Finland," *Eurofamcare.* (European Union funded project).

Parkin, A., and M. Mendelsohn. 2003. *A New Canada: An Identity Shaped By Diversity.* Montreal: Centre for Research on Information on Canada.

Parks, Malcolm R., and Lynne D. Roberts. 1998. "'Making MOOsic': The development of personal relationships online and a comparison to their off-line counterparts," *Journal of Social and Personal Relationships* 15, 4: 517–37.

Parsons, Talcott. 1955. "The American family: Its relations to personality and to the social structure," in Talcott Parsons and Robert F. Bales, eds, *Family Socialization and Interaction Process.* Glencoe, Ill.: Free Press.

———. 1967. *Sociological Theory and Modern Society.* New York: Free Press.

———, and Robert Bales. 1955. *Family, Socialization and Interaction Process.* New York: Free Press of Glencoe.

Patterson, Annette, and Martha Satz. 2002. "Genetic counseling and the disabled: Feminism examines the stance of those who stand at the gate," *Hypatia* 17: 118–42.

Patterson, Christopher, and Elizabeth Podnieks. 1995. "A guide to the diagnosis and treatment of elder abuse," in M. Novak, ed., *Aging and Society: A Canadian Reader.* Toronto: Nelson.

Paul, Eden. 1930. *Chronos or the Future of the Family.* London: Kegan Paul, Trench, Trubner and Co.

Paul, Elizabeth L., Brian McManus, and Allison Hayes. 2000. "Hookups: Characteristics and correlates of college students' spontaneous and anonymous sexual experiences," *Journal of Sex Research* 37: 76–88.

Peacock, Lindsey. 2012. "Cost of daycare across Canada," 21 August. Available at http://www.shawconnect.ca/money/features/Cost_of_daycare_across_Canada.aspx.

Pegg, Shawn. 2007. *HungerCount 2007.* Toronto: Canadian Association of Food Banks.

———, and Diana Stappleton. 2012. *HungerCount 2012.* Toronto: Food Banks Canada.

Pence, Ellen, and Michael Paymar. 1993. *Education Groups for Men Who Batter: The Duluth Model.* New York: Springer.

Pendakur, R. 2000. *Immigrants and the Labour Force.* Montreal and Kingston: McGill-Queen's University Press.

Penning, M., and N.L. Chappell. 2010. *Health Inequalities among Adults in Later Life: Review of Issues, Promising Practices and Upstream Health Interventions in Responding to Aging and Older People in Canada.* For the Public Health Agency of Canada, June.

Penning, M.J. 1998. "In the middle: Parental caregiving in the context of other roles," *Journal of Gerontology* 53B: S188–97.

Pennington Phil, and Barbara Pennington. 2001. *A Healing Divorce: Transforming the End of Your Relationship with Ritual and Ceremony.* Online publication: Author.

Pérusse, Dominique. 2003. "New maternity and parental benefits," *Perspectives on Labour and Income* 4, 3: 12–15.

Peters, Yvonne, and Karen Lawson. 2002. *The Ethical and Human Rights Implications of Prenatal Technologies: The Need for Federal Leadership and Regulation.* Winnipeg: Prairie Women's Centre of Excellence.

Phipps, Shelley. 2003. *The Impact of Poverty on Health: A Scan of Research Literature.* Ottawa: Canadian Institute for Health Information.

———, and Peter Burton. 1995. "Sharing within families: Implications for the measurement of poverty among individuals in Canada," *Canadian Journal of Economics* 28: 177–204.

Phua, Voon Chin, and Gayle Kaufman. 2003a. "The crossroads of race and sexuality: Date selection among men in Internet 'personal' ads," *Journal of Family Issues* 24, 8: 981–94.

Picard, Andre. 2005a. "Flame retardants building up within us," *Globe and Mail,* A19.

———. 2005b. "Obese moms risk having babies with birth defects," *Globe and Mail,* A15.

Picot, Garnett, and F. Hou. 2003. *The Rise in Low-Income Rates among Immigrants in Canada.* Analytic Studies Research Paper Series 11F0019MIE2003198. Ottawa: Statistics Canada, Analytic Studies Branch.

———, and John Myles. 2005. *Income Inequality and Low Income in Canada: An International Perspective.* Analytical Studies Research Paper Series 11F0019MIE2005240. Ottawa: Statistics Canada, Analytic Studies Branch.

———, ———, and Wendy Pyper. 1998. "Markets, families and social transfers: Trends in low income among the young and old, 1973–1995," in Miles Corak, ed., *Labour Markets, Social Institutions and the Future of Canada's Children.* Ottawa: Statistics Canada, Catalogue no. 890553–XPB, 11–30.

———, M. Zyblock, and Wendy Pyper. 1999. *Why Do Children Move into and out of Low Income: Changing Labour Market Conditions or Marriage and Divorce?* Analytic Studies Research Paper Series 11F0019MIE1999132. Ottawa: Statistics Canada, Analytic Studies Branch.

Pike, Martha. 1980. "In Memory of: Artifacts Relating to Mourning in Nineteenth Century America," *Journal of American Culture* 3, 4: 642–59.

Pillemer, Karl. 1993. "The abused offspring are dependent: Abuse is caused by the deviance and dependence of abusive caregivers," in Gelles and Loseke (1993).

———, and Jill J. Suitor. 2002. "Explaining mothers' ambivalence toward their adult children," *Journal of Marriage and Family* 64: 602–13.

Pinquart, M., and S. Sorensen. 2003. "Differences between caregivers and noncaregivers in psychological health and physical health: A meta-analysis," *Psychology of Aging* 18: 250–67.

Piva, Michael. 1976. *The Condition of the Working Class in Toronto, 1900–1921.* Montreal: Concordia University.

Platt, John. 1972. "A fearful and wonderful world for living," in *College of Home Economics* (1972: 3–13).

Platt, L. 2010. *Ethnicity and Family: Relationships Within and Between Ethnic Groups.* University of Essex: Institute for Social and Economic Research.

Pleck, Joseph H. 1985. *Working Wives, Working Husbands.* London: Sage.

———. 1987. "American fathering in historical perspective," in Michael Kimmel, ed., *Changing Men: New Directions in Research on Men and Masculinity.* Newbury Park, Calif.: Sage.

Ploeg, Jenny, Lori Campbell, Candace Kemp, Carolyn Rosenthal, and Lorna DeWitt. 2007. "The unwritten 'rules' guiding inheritance decisions." Paper presented at the 36th Annual Scientific and Educational Meeting of the Canadian Association on Gerontology, Calgary, Alberta, 1–3 November 2007.

———, ———, Margaret Denton, Anju Joshi, and Sharon Davies. 2004. "Helping to build and rebuild secure lives and futures: Financial transfers from parents to adult children and grandchildren," *Canadian Journal on Aging* 23 (Supplement): S113–25.

Podoluk, Jenny. 1968. *Incomes of Canadians*. Ottawa: Dominion Bureau of Statistics.

Polikoff, N. 2008. *Beyond (Straight and Gay) Marriage*. Boston: Beacon Press.

Polivka, Anne E., and Thomas Nardone. 1989. "On the definition of 'contingent work'," *Monthly Labor Review* 112, 12: 9–16.

Pollak, Otto. 1972. "Family functions in transition," in College of Home Economics (1972: 69–78).

Pollock, Linda. 1983. *Forgotten Children*. Cambridge: Cambridge University Press.

Ponti, Michael. 2008. "Special considerations for the health supervision of children and youth in foster care," *Paediatrics & Child Health* 13, 2: 129–32.

Pottie-Bunge, V. 2002. "National trends in intimate partner homicides, 1974–2000," *Juristat* 22.

———, and A. Levett. 1998. *Family Violence in Canada: A Statistical Profile*. Ottawa: Canadian Centre for Justice Statistics.

Prentice, Alison, Paula Bourne, Gail Cuthbert Brandt, Beth Light, Wendy Mitchinson and Naomi Black. 1988. *Canadian Women: A History*. Toronto: Harcourt Brace.

Press Release. 2012. "Harper government welcomes vote on Helping Families in Need Act." 2 October. Available at http://www.msnbc.msn.com/id/49265526/ns/business-press_releases/t/harper-government-welcomes-vote-helping-families-need-act/#.UHWd-VHcwyw.

Preston, Samuel. 1984. "Children and the elderly: Divergent paths for America's dependents," *Demography* 21: 435–58.

Prilleltensky, O. 2004. "'My child is not my carer': Mothers with physical disabilities and the well-being of children," *Disability & Society* 19: 209–23.

Pruchno, R. 2012. "Not your mother's old age: Baby boomers at age 65," *The Gerontologist* 52, 2: 149–52.

Pruett, Kyle. 2000. *Fatherneed: Why Father Care Is As Essential As Mother Care for Your Child*. New York: Broadview Press.

Public Health Agency of Canada. 2003. Canadian incidence study of reported child abuse and neglect. Available at http://www.phac-aspc.gc.ca/cm-vee/csca-ecve/pdf/childabuse_final_e.pdf; accessed 8 November 2008.

———. 2010. "Chapter 3: The Health and Well-being of Canadian Seniors." Available at http://www.phac-aspc.gc.ca/cphorsphc-respcacsp/2010/fr-rc/cphorsphc-respcacsp-06-eng.php; accessed 22 August 2012.

Raddon, Mary Beth. 2003. *Community and Money: Men and Women Making Change*. Montreal: Black Rose Books.

Rainwater, Lee, Tim Smeeding, and John Coder. 2001. "Child poverty across states, nations and continents," in K. Vleminckx and Tim Smeeding, eds, *Child Well-Being, Child Poverty and Child Poverty in Modern Nations: What Do We Know?* Bristol, UK: Policy Press, 33–74.

Raj, A., and J. Silverman. 2002. "Violence against immigrant women," *Violence Against Women* 8, 3: 367–98.

Ranson, Gillian. 1998. "Education, work, and family decision making: Finding the right time to have a baby," *Canadian Review of Sociology and Anthropology* 35, 4: 517–33.

———. 2004. "Paid work, family work and the discourse of the full-time mother," in Andrea O'Reilly, ed., *Mother Matters: Motherhood as Discourse and Practice*. Toronto: Association for Research on Mothering.

Rapoport, R., and L. Bailyn. 1996. *Relinking Life and Work: Toward a Better Future*. New York: Ford Foundation.

Rappoport, Anat, and Ariela Lowenstein. 2007. "A possible innovative association between the concept of intergenerational ambivalence and the emotions of guilt and shame in care-giving," *European Journal of Ageing* 4: 13–21.

Rees, Elizabeth. 1995. "Christian widowhood," *New Blackfriars* 76, 896: 393–40.

Régie des rentes du Québec. 2005. "Family Benefits." Available at http://www.rrq.gouv.qc.ca/an/famille/10.htm.

———. 2012a. "Child assistance measure." Available at http://www.rrq.gouv.qc.ca/en/programmes/soutien_enfants/paiement/Pages/montant.aspx.

———. 2012b. "A handicapped child." Available at http://www.rrq.gouv.qc.ca/en/enfants/enfant_handicape/Pages/enfant_handicape.aspx.

Reid, Carrie. 2007. "The transition from state care to adulthood: International examples of best practices." *New Directions for Youth Development* 113: 33–49.

Reid, Julie, Sinikka Elliott, and Gretchen Webber. 2011. "Casual hookups to formal dates: Refining the boundaries of the sexual double standard," *Gender & Society* 25, 5: 545–68

Reid, R.C., K.I. Stajduhar, and N.L. Chappell. 2010. "The impact of work interferences on family caregiver outcomes," *Journal of Applied Gerontology* 29, 3: 267–89.

Reimann, R. 1997. "Does biology matter? Lesbian couples' transition to parenthood and their division of labor," *Qualitative Sociology* 20, 2: 153–85.

Reimer, Bill. 2006. "The informal economy in non-metropolitan Canada," *Canadian Review of Sociology and Anthropology* 43, 1: 23–49.

Reinders, H.S. 2008. "Persons with disabilities as parents: What is the problem?" *Journal of Applied Research in Intellectual Disabilities* 21: 308–14.

Reinelt, C., and M. Fried. 1993. "'I am this child's mother': A feminist perspective on mothering with a disability," in M. Nagler, ed., *Perspectives on Disability: Text and Readings*. Palo Alto, Calif.: Health Markets Research, 195–202.

Reitsma-Street, M., Josie Schofield, Brishkai Lund, and Colleen Kasting. 2001. *Housing Policy Options for Women Living in Urban Poverty: An Action Research Project in Three Canadian Cities*. Ottawa: Status of Women Canada.

Renzetti, Claire M. 1998. "Violence and abuse in lesbian relationships: Theoretical and empirical issues," in Bergen (1998a: 117–28).

Reppucci, N. Dickon, and J. Jeffrey Haugaard. 1993. "Problems with child sexual abuse: Prevention programs," in Gelles and Loseke (1993: 306–22).

Rer-Stier, D. 1996. "Coping strategies of immigrant parents: Directions for family therapy," *Family Process* 35: 363–76.

Research on Aging, Policies and Practice (RAPP). 2010. "Gender differences in family/friend caregiving in Canada." November.

Rhode, Deborah L. 1989. *Justice and Gender: Sex Discrimination and the Law*. Cambridge, Mass.: Harvard University Press.

Ribeiro, O., C. Paúl, and C. Nogueira. 2007. "Real men, real husbands: Caregiving and masculinities in later life," *Journal of Aging Studies* 21: 302–13.

Ricciuto, Laurie E., and Valerie S. Tarasuk. 2007. "An examination of income-related disparities in the nutritional quality of food selections among Canadian households from 1986–2001," *Social Science and Medicine* 64, 1: 186–98.

Rich, Adrienne. 1993. "Compulsory heterosexuality and the lesbian experience," in Henry Abelove et al., eds, *The Lesbian and Gay Studies Reader*. New York: Routledge, 227–54.

———. 1995. *Of Woman Born: Motherhood as Experience and Institution*. New York: Norton.

Richards, Gwendolyn, and Sherri Zickefoose. 2008. "Alberta RCMP deny threats made before murder–suicide." Canada.com. Available at http://www.canada.com/topics/news/national/story.html?id_20a2d384-b235-40ed-b85b-fe0d6cd09b3b; accessed 10 November 2008.

Richardson, Diane. 1998. "Sexuality and citizenship," *Sociology* 32, 1: 83–100.

———. 2005. "Desiring sameness? The rise of a neoliberal politics of normalisation," *Antipode* 37 (3): 515–35.

Richardson, Jack. 1996. "Canada and free trade: Why did it happen?" in Robert Brym, ed., *Society in Question*. Toronto: Nelson.

Richie, Beth E., and Valli Kanuha. 2000. "Battered women of colour in health care system: Racism, sexism and violence," in A. Minas, ed., *Gender Basics: Feminist Perspectives on Women and Men*, 2nd edn. Belmont, Calif.: Wadsworth.

Ridington, Jillian. 1989. "Beating the odds: Violence and women with disabilities," Vancouver: DAWN Canada. Available at http://www.dawncanada.net/odds.htm, accessed 28 September 2004.

Rietschlin, John. 2005. Personal communication, Office for Disability Issues, 24 Aug.

Risman, Barbara. 1998. *Gender Vertigo: American Families in Transition*. New Haven, CT: Yale University Press.

Ristock, J.I. 2002. *No More Secrets: Violence in Lesbian Relationships*. New York: Routledge.

Robb, R., M. Denton, A. Gafni, A. Joshi, J. Lian, C. Rosenthal, and D. Willison. 1999. "Valuation of unpaid help by seniors in Canada: An empirical analysis," *Canadian Journal on Aging* 18, 4: 430–46.

Roberts, R.E.L., and V.L. Bengston. 1996. "Affective ties to parents in early adulthood and self-esteem across 20 years," *Social Psychology Quarterly* 59: 96–106.

Robinson, Bryan E., and Robert L. Barret. 1986. *The Developing Father: Emerging Roles in Contemporary Society*. New York: Guilford.

Robinson, Clyde C., Barbara Mandleco, Susanne Frost Olsen, and Craig H. Hart. 1995. "Authoritative, authoritarian, and permissive parenting practices: Development of a new measure," *Psychological Reports* 77: 819–30.

Robinson, Lynne M., Lynn McIntyre, and Suzanne Officer. 2005. "Welfare babies: Poor children's experiences in forming healthy peer relationships in Canada," *Health Promotion International* 20, 4: 342–50.

Robison, J., R. Fortinsky, A. Kelppinger, N. Shugrue, and M. Porter. 2009. "A broader view of family caregiving: Effects of caregiving and caregiver conditions on depressive symptoms, health, work, and social isolation," *Journals of Gerontology* 64B, 6: 788–98.

Rocher, Guy. 1962. "Patterns and status of French Canadian women," *International Social Science Journal* 14, 1: 131–7.

Rockwood, K., and A. Mitnitski. 2007. "Frailty in relation to the accumulation of deficits," *Journal of Gerontology* 62A, 7: 722–7.

Rodgers, Karen. 1994. "Wife Assault in Canada: The Findings of a National Survey," *Juristat* 14, 9.

———. 2000. "Wife assault in Canada," *Canadian Social Trends* 3: 237–42.

Rodriguez-Garcia, D. 2007. *Intermarriage Patterns and Socio-Ethnic Stratification among Ethnic Groups in Toronto*. Toronto, CERIS Working paper No. 60.

Roeher Institute. 1994. *Violence and People with Disabilities: A Review of the Literature*. North York, Ont.: Roeher Institute, for the National Clearing House on Family Violence.

———. 1995. *Harm's Way: The Many Faces of Violence and Abuse against Persons with Disabilities in Canada*. North York, Ont.: Roeher Institute.

———. 2000a. *Beyond the Limits: Mothers Caring for Children with Disabilities*. North York, Ont.: Roeher Institute.

———. 2000b. *Count Us In: A Demographic Overview of Childhood and Disability*. North York, Ont.: Roeher Institute.

Rollings-Magnusson, Sandra. 2008. "Flax seed, goose grease, and gun powder: Medical practices by women homesteaders in Saskatchewan (1882–1914)," *Journal of Family History* 33, 4: 388–410.

Rose Floral and Greenhouse. 2008. *Wedding Anniversary Symbols*. Available at http://www.rosefloral.com/wedding.htm.

Rose, Susan J., and William Meezan. 1995. "Child neglect: A study of the perceptions of mothers and child welfare workers," *Children and Youth Services Review* 17, 4: 471–86.

Rosenberg, George. 1970. "Implications of new models of the family for the aging population," in Otto (1970a: 171–86).

Roseneil, Sasha. 2006. "On not living with a partner: Unpicking coupledom and cohabitation," *Sociological Research Online* 11: 3.

Rosenfeld, Michael J. 2007. *The Age of Independence: Interracial Unions, Same-Sex Unions, and the Changing American Family*. Cambridge: Harvard University Press.

Rosenthal, Carolyn, and P. Dawson. 1991. "Wives of institutionalized husbands," *Journal of Aging and Health* 3, 3: 315–34.

Ross, Jonathan. 2006. "Get real about child care: Why Harper feels he can go to the polls on the issue." *The Tyee*, 20 Apr. Available at http://thetyee.ca/Views/2006/04/20/RealChildCare.

Ross, M.M., C. Rosenthal, and P.G. Dawson. 1994. "The continuation of caregiving following the institutionalization of elderly husbands," in *National Advisory Council on Aging, Marital Disruption in Later Life*. Catalogue no. H71-3/17-1994E. Ottawa: Minister of Supply and Services, 23–32.

———, ———, and ———. 1997a. "Spousal caregiving in the institutional setting: Task performance," *Canadian Journal on Aging* 16, 1: 51–69.

———, ———, and ———. 1997b. "Spousal caregiving in the institutional setting: Visiting," *Journal of Clinical Nursing* 6, 6: 473–83.

Rossi, A.S., and P.H. Rossi. 1990. *Of Human Bonding: Parent–Child Relations across the Life Course*. Hawthorne, NY: Aldine de Gruyter.

Rotermann, Michelle. 2007. "Marital breakdown and subsequent depression," *Health Reports* 18, 2: 35. Ottawa: Statistics Canada, Catalogue 82-003

Rothman, Barbara Katz. 1989. "Women as fathers: Motherhood and childcare under a modified patriarchy," *Gender & Society* 3, 1: 89–104.

Roussel, Jean-Francois. 2003. "Roman Catholic religious discourse about manhood in Quebec: From 1900 to the Quiet Revolution," *Journal of Men's Studies* 11, 2: 145–56.

Roy, C. 2004. "Relatives get off easier for abuse, survey finds," *Toronto Star*, 7 July, B2.

Roy, F. 2006. "From she to she: Changing patterns of women in the Canadian labour force," *Canadian Economic Observer*: 3.1–3.10.

Roy, Kevin M. 2004. "You can't eat love: Constructing provider role expectations for low-income and working-class fathers," *Fathering* 2: 253–76.

Roy, Laurent, and Jean Bernier. 2007. *Family Policy, Social Trends and Fertility in Quebec: Experimenting with the Nordic Model?* Government of Quebec: Ministère de la Famille, des Aînés et de la Condition Féminine.

RSVP. Available at http://www.rsvp.com.au; accessed 21 November 2008.

Rubin, Lillian B. 1983. *Intimate Strangers: Men and Women Together*. New York: Harper and Row.

Ruddick, Sara. 1995. *Maternal Thinking: Towards a Politics of Peace*. Boston: Beacon Press.

Rush, George, and Nancy Dillon. 2009. "Not the first time Chris Brown abused me, Rihanna tells police," *New York Daily News*. Available at http://articles.nydailynews.com/2009-02-12/gossip/17916817_1rihanna-chris-brown-cops.

Russell, Diana E.H. 1989. "Sexism, violence and the nuclear mentality," in Russell, ed., *Exposing Nuclear Fallacies*. New York: Pergamon, 63–74.

———, and Rebecca M. Bolen. 2000. *The Epidemic of Rape and Child Sexual Abuse in the United States*. Thousand Oaks, Calif.: Sage.

Russell, R. 2007. "The work of elderly men caregivers: From public careers to an unseen world," *Men & Masculinities* 9, 3: 298–314.

Sabells, Jerald. 1983. "Child abuse in residential institutions and community programs for intervention and prevention," *Child Abuse & Neglect* 7: 473–5.

Sager, Eric. 2000. "The Canadian Families Project and the 1901 census," *Historical Methods* 33, 4: 179–84.

———. 2001. "Introduction: The Canadian Families Project," *Journal of Family History* 26, 2: 157–61.

———, and Peter Baskerville, eds. 2007. *Household Counts: Canadian Households and Families in 1901*. Buffalo: University of Toronto Press.

Sanchez, Laura, and Elizabeth Thomson. 1997. "Becoming mothers and fathers: Parenthood, gender, and the division of labor," *Gender and Society* 11, 6: 747–72.

Sanders, G. 2010. "The dismal trade as culture industry," *Poetics* 38: 47–68.

Sangster, Joan. 1995. *Earning Respect: The Lives of Working Women in Small-Town Ontario, 1920–1960*. Toronto: University of Toronto Press.

———. 2001. "Women's activism and the state," in Sharon Ann Cook, Lorna McLean, and Kate O'Rourke, eds, *Framing Our Past: Canadian Women's History in the Twentieth Century*. Montreal: McGill-Queen's University Press.

Saris, A., and J. Potvin. 2008. "Shar'ia in Canada: Family dispute resolution among Muslim minorities in the west." Unpublished paper, Montreal.

Sarlo, Christopher. 2008. *What is Poverty? Providing Clarity for Canada*. Vancouver: Fraser Institute.

Satzewich, Vic. 1993. "Migrant and immigrant families in Canada: State coercion and legal control in the formation of ethnic families," *Journal of Comparative Family Studies* 24, 3: 315–38.

Saul, Jennifer Mather. 2003. *Feminism: Issues and Arguments*. New York: Oxford University Press.

Sauvé, R. 2002. *The Current State of Canadian Family Finances*. Ottawa: Vanier Institute of the Family.

———. 2008. *The Current State of Canadian Family Finances 2007 Report*. Ottawa, Ontario: The Vanier Institute of the Family, 1–30.

Saxton, Marsha, Mary Ann Curry, Laurie E. Powers, Susan Maley, Karyl Eckels, and Jacqueline Gross. 2001. "'Bring my scooter so I can leave you': A study of disabled women handling abuse by personal assistance providers," *Violence Against Women* 7: 393–417.

Schacher, Stephanie Jill, Carl F. Auerbach, and Louise Bordeaux Silverstein. 2005. "Gay fathers expanding the possibilities for us all," *Journal of GLBT Family Studies* 1, 3: 31–51.

Schafer, Gabriele. 2008. "Romantic love in heterosexual relationships: Women's experiences," *Journal of Social Science*, 16: 187–97.

Schellenberg, G. 2004. *The retirement plans and expectations of non-retired Canadians 45 to 59*. (Catalogue No. 11F0019MIE). Ottawa: Statistics Canada.

Scheper-Hughes, Nancy. 1992. *Death without Weeping: The Violence of Everyday Life in Brazil*. Berkeley: University of California Press.

———. 1999. "(M)Other love: Culture, scarcity and maternal thinking," in Maxine Baca Zinn, Pierrette Hondagneu-Sotelo, and Michael A. Messner, eds, *Through the Prism of Difference*. Boston: Allyn and Bacon.

Schimmele, Christoph M., and Zheng Wu. 2011. "Cohabitation and social engagement," *Canadian Studies in Population* 38: 23–36.

Schmitz, Cristin. 2004. "B.C. ruling puts fault into no-fault divorce," *National Post*, 27 September.

Schulz, David A. 1972. *The Changing Family: Its Function and Future*. Englewood Cliffs, NJ: Prentice-Hall.

Schwartz, Martin D., and Walter S. DeKeseredy. 1997. *Sexual Assault on the College Campus: The Role of Male Peer Support*. Thousand Oaks, Calif.: Sage.

———, ———, W.C. Tait, and S. Alvi. 2001. "Male peer support and routine activities theory: Understanding sexual assault on the college campus," *Justice Quarterly* 18: 701–27.

Scott, Ellen K., Kathryn Edin, Andrew S. London, and Rebecca Joyce Kissane. 2004. "Unstable work, unstable income: Implications for family well-being in the era of time-limited welfare," *Journal of Poverty* 8, 1: 61–88.

Scully, Diana. 1990. *Understanding Sexual Violence*. Boston: Unwin.

Sears, W., and M. Sears. 2001. *The Attachment Parenting Book, A Commonsense Guide to Understanding and Nurturing Your Baby*. London: Little, Brown and Company.

Seeley, John, R., Alexander Sim, and Elizabeth W. Loosely. 1956. *Crestwood Heights: A Study of the Culture of Suburban Life*. Toronto: University of Toronto Press.

Séguin, Rhéal. 2008. "Make babies, ADQ urges Quebec women," *Globe and Mail*, 13 March. Available at http://www.amren.com/mtnews/archives/2008/03/make_babies_adq.php.

———, and Gloria Galloway. 2004. "Some provinces skeptical about federal daycare plan," *Globe and Mail*, 2 November, A6.

Seniors Resource. 2005. Available at http://www.seniorsresource.ca/docs/conference_Report.pdf; accessed 10 April 2008.

Settersten Jr., Richard A. 1999. *Lives in Time and Place: The Problems and Promises of Developmental Science*. Amityville, NY: Baywood.

———. 2007. "Passages to adulthood: Linking demographic change and human development," *European Journal of Population* 23: 251–72.

Sev'er, Aysan. 1996. "Current feminist debates on wife abuse: Some policy implications," *Sonderbulletin* (Berlin: Humboldt University Press): 121–37.

———. 1997. "Recent or imminent separation and intimate violence against women: A conceptual overview and some Canadian examples," *Violence Against Women* 3, 6: 566–89.

———, ed. 1998. *Frontiers in Women's Studies: Canadian and German Perspectives*. Toronto: Canadian Scholars' Press.

———. 1999. "Exploring the continuum: Sexualized violence by men and male youth against women and girls," *Atlantis* 24, 1: 92–104.

———. 2002a. *Fleeing the House of Horrors: Women Who Have Left Their Abusive Partners*. Toronto: University of Toronto Press.

———. 2002b. "A feminist analysis of flight of abused women, plight of Canadian shelters: Another path to homelessness," *Journal of Social Distress and the Homeless* 11: 307–24.

———. 2009. "More than wife abuse that has gone old: A conceptual model for violence against the aged in Canada and the US," *Journal of Comparative Family Studies* 40, 2: 279–92.

Seymour, Anne. 1998. "Aetiology of the sexual abuse of children: An extended feminist perspective," *Women's Studies International Forum* 21, 4: 415–27.

Sharlin, S., and V. Moin. 2001. "New immigrants' perception of family life in origin and host cultures," *Journal of Comparative Family Studies* 32, 3: 405–18.

Sharma, Ursala. 1986. *Women's Work, Class and the Urban Household: A Study of Shimla, North India*. London: Tavistock.

Shehan, Constance L., and Jeffrey W. Dwyer. 1989. "Parent–child exchanges in the middle years: Attachment and autonomy in the transition to adulthood," in J.A. Mancini, ed., *Aging Parents and Adult Children*. Lexington, Mass.: Lexington Books, 99–116.

Sheldon, Alison. 2005. "One world, one people, one struggle? Towards the global implementation of the social model of disability," in Colin Barnes and Geof Mercer, eds, *The Social Model of Disability: Europe and the Majority World*. Leeds: Disability Press, 115–40.

Shelton, Beth Anne, and Daphne John. 1993. "Does marital status make a difference?" *Journal of Family Issues* 14, 3: 401–20.

———, and ———. 1996. "The division of household labor," *Annual Review of Sociology* 22: 299–322.

Shiota, M.N., and R.W. Levenson. 2007. "Birds of a feather don't always fly farthest: Similarity in big five personality predicts more negative marital satisfaction trajectories in long-term marriages," *Psychology and Aging* 22, 4: 666–75.

Shissler, A. Holly. 2006. "Marriages made on Madison Avenue?" *Journal of Women's History* 18, 4: 118–22.

Shiva, Vandana. 2000. *Stolen Harvest: The Hijacking of the Global Food Supply*. Cambridge, Mass.: South End Press.

Shorter, Edward. 1977. *The Making of the Modern Family*. New York: Basic Books.

Shows, Carla, and Naomi Gerstel. 2009. "Fathering, class, and gender: A comparison of physicians and emergency medical technicians," *Gender and Society* 23, 2: 161–87.

Silver, Cynthia. 2000. "Being there: The time dual-earner couples spend with their children," *Canadian Social Trends* 57: 26–9.

Silverstein, M., S.J. Conroy, H. Wang, R. Giarrusso, and V.L. Bengtson. 2002. "Reciprocity in parent–child relations over the adult life course," *Journal of Gerontology*, Series B 57, 1: S3–13.

Simon, William, and John H. Gagnon. 2003. "Sexual scripts: Origins, influences and changes," *Qualitative Sociology* 26, 4: 491–7.

Simons, Paula. 2008. "Praiseworthy step will help families: Generous package of benefits means successful adoptions for children in care," *The Edmonton Journal*, 25 November.

Sims, Andrew. 2005. *Ecological Debt: The Health of the Planet and the Wealth of Nations*. London: Pluto Press.

Single in the City. 2008. Available at http://www.singleinthecity.ca; accessed 21 November 2008.

Skinner, B.F. 1948. *Walden II*. New York: Macmillan.

Slade, Daryl. 2011. "Father's gay partner gets custody of girl, 8," *National Post*, 26 October, A7.

Small, Mario Luis. 2006. "Neighborhood institutions as resource brokers: Childcare centers, inter-organizational ties, and resource access among the poor," *Social Problems* 53, 2: 274–92.

Smart, C. 1984. "Ties that bind," *Canadian Journal of Law and Society* 9 (1): 15–38.

———, and Bren Neale. 1999. *Family Fragments?* Malden, Mass.: Polity Press.

Smeeding, Tim, Lee Rainwater, and John Coder. 2002. "United States poverty in a cross-national context," in Sheldon H. Danziger and Robert H. Haveman, eds, *Understanding Poverty*. New York and Cambridge, Mass.: Russell Sage Foundation and Harvard University Press, 162–89.

Smiler, Andrew. 2008. "'I wanted to get to know her better': Adolescent boys' dating motives, masculinity ideology and sexual behaviour," *Journal of Adolescence* 31: 17–32.

Smith, B. 1997. "Where has gay liberation gone? An interview with Barbara Smith," in *Homo Economics: Capitalism, community, and lesbian and gay life*, A. Gluckman and B. Reed, eds. London: Routledge.

Smith, Dorothy. 1993. "The 'Standard North American Family': SNAF as an ideological code," *Journal of Family Issues* 14: 50–65.

Smith, E. 2004. *Nowhere to Turn? Responding to Partner Violence against Immigrant and Visible Minority Women.* Ottawa: Canadian Council on Social Development.

Smith, Ekuwa, and Andrew Jackson. 2002. *Does a Rising Tide Lift All Boats?* Ottawa: Canadian Council on Social Development.

Smith, J.A. 2009. *The Daddy Shift: How Stay-at-Home Dads, Breadwinning Moms, and Shared Parenting Are Transforming the American Family.* Boston: Beacon Press.

Smith, Miriam. 2007. "Framing same-sex marriage in Canada and the United States: Goodridge, Halpern and the national boundaries of political discourse," *Social and Legal Studies* 16, 1: 5–26.

Smith, Theresa. 2012. "Census: Data glitch affects numbers on gay marriage," *Canada.com*, 19 September. Available at http://www.canada.com/Census+Data+glitch+affects+numbers+marriage/7266536/story.html; accessed 27 September 2012.

Smock, Pamela J., and Wendy D. Manning. 2004. "Living together unmarried in the United States: Demographic perspectives and implications for family policy," *Law and Policy* 26: 87–117.

Snarey, John. 1993. *How Fathers Care for the Next Generation: A Four Decade Study.* Cambridge, Mass.: Harvard University Press.

Snell, A. 2008. "Grand(re)parents," *Family Connections* 12, 1.

Snell, James G. 1991. *In the Shadow of the Law: Divorce in Canada, 1900–1939.* Toronto: University of Toronto Press.

———. 1996. *The Citizen's Wage: The State and the Elderly in Canada, 1900–1951.* Toronto: University of Toronto Press.

Snow, Rebekah and Katherine Covell. 2006. "Adoption and the best interests of the child: The dilemma of cultural interpretations," *The International Journal of Children's Rights* 14: 109–17.

Sokoloff, Natalie J., and Dupont Ida. 2005. "Domestic violence at the intersections of race, class, and gender," *Violence Against Women* 11: 38–64.

Song, X., A. Mitniski, and K. Rockwood. 2010. "Prevalence and 10-year outcomes of frailty in older adults in relation to deficit accumulation," *Journal of the American Geriatrics Society* 58, 4: 681–7.

South, S.J., and G. Spitze. 1994. "Housework in marital and nonmarital households," *American Sociological Review* 59, 3: 327–47.

Special Senate Committee on Aging Final Report. 2009. *Canada's Aging Population: Seizing the Opportunity.* The Honourable Sharon Carstairs, P.C., Chair. The Honourable Wilbert Joseph Keon, Deputy Chair. April.

Spitzer, Denise, Anne Neufeld, Margaret Harrison, Karen D. Hughes, and Miriam Stewart. 2003. "Caregiving in transnational context: 'My wings have been cut; where can I fly?'" *Gender & Society* 17: 267–86.

Sprecher, Susan. 2001. "Equity and social exchange in dating couples: Associations with satisfaction, commitment, and stability," *Journal of Marriage and the Family* 63: 599–613.

———. 2009. "Relationship initiation and formation on the Internet," *Marriage & Family Review* 45: 761–82.

Stacey, Judith. 1990. *Brave New Families: Stories of Domestic Upheaval in Late Twentieth-Century America.* Boston: Basic Books.

———. 2006. "Gay parenthood and the decline of fatherhood as we knew it," *Sexualities*, 9: 27–55.

———, and Timothy Biblarz. 2001. "(How) does the sexual orientation of parents matter?" *American Sociological Review* 66: 159–83.

Stack, Carol. 1974. *All Our Kin: Strategies for Survival in a Black Community.* New York: Harper and Row.

Stanley, Timothy J. 2011. *Contesting White Supremacy: School Segregation, Anti-Racism, and the Making of Chinese Canadians.* Vancouver: University of British Columbia Press.

Stark, Evan. 2007. *Coercive Control: How Men Entrap Women in Personal Life.* New York: Oxford.

———, and Anne Flitcraft. 1996. *Women at Risk: Domestic Violence and Women's Health.* London: Sage.

Stasiulis, Daiva. 2005. "The Active Child Citizen: Lessons from Canadian Policy and the Children's Movement," in *Polis, Revue Camerounaise de Science Politique* 12.

———, and Abigail Bakan. 2005. *Negotiating Citizenship: Migrant Women in Canada and the Global System.* Toronto: University of Toronto Press.

Statistics Canada. 1984. *Canada's Lone Parent Families.* Ottawa: Statistics Canada.

———. 1996. *1996 Census Dictionary.* Available at http://www.statcan.ca/english/freepub/92-351-UIE/04fam.pdf.

———. 1997. "Who cares? Caregiving in the 1990s," *The Daily*, 19 Aug. Available at http://epe.lac-bac.gc.ca/100/201/301/daily/daily-h/1997/97-08/97-08-19/d970819.htm.

———. 2000. *Women in Canada: A Gender-Based Statistical Report.* Ottawa: Statistics Canada.

———. 2001. *2001 Census Dictionary.* Available at http://www12.statcan.ca/english/census01/Products/Reference/dict/index.htm.

———. 2002. *Changing Conjugal Life in Canada.* Ottawa: Statistics Canada, Housing, Family and Social Statistics Division.

———. 2002a. *Profile of Canadian Families and Households: Diversification Continues.* Catalogue no. 96F0030XIE2001003. Ottawa: Ministry of Industry.

———. 2002b. "Changing conjugal life in Canada," *The Daily*, 11 July.

———. 2002c. "Divorces," *The Daily*, 2 December.

———. 2002d. *Labour Force Survey, Annual Average 2002/Family Characteristics of Single Husband–Wife Families.* Ottawa: Statistics Canada.

———. 2002e. "The evolution of wealth inequality in Canada: 1984–1999," *The Daily*, 22 February.

———. 2002f. *2001 Participation and Activity Limitation Survey: Education, Employment and Income of Adults with and without Disabilities—Tables.* Ottawa: Statistics Canada.

———. 2002g. *2001 Participation and Activity Limitation Survey: Education, Employment and Income of Adults with and without Disabilities.* Ottawa: Statistics Canada.

———. 2002h. "Homicides," *The Daily*, 25 September.

Statistics Canada. 2003. *Women in Canada: Work Chapter Updates.* Ottawa: Ministry of Industry.

———. 2003a. "Report on the demographic situation in Canada—2003." Available at http://www.statcan.ca/english/ads/91-209-XPE/highlights.htm.

————. 2003b. "Marital status of Canadians, 2001 census: Common-law status, age group and sex" Available at http://www.statcan.ca/bsolc/english/beolc?catno=95F0405X.

————. 2003c. "Marriages, 2001," *The Daily*, 20 November.

————. 2003d. "The people: Common-law," *Canada e-Book*. Ottawa: Statistics Canada.

————. 2003e. *The Canadian Labour Market at a Glance*. Ottawa: Statistics Canada.

————. 2003f. *Women in Canada: Work Chapter Updates*. Ottawa: Statistics Canada.

————. 2004. "Divorces, 2001 and 2002," *The Daily*, 4 May.

————. 2004a. "The sandwich generation," *The Daily*, 28 September.

————. 2004b. "Mixed unions," *The Daily*, 8 June.

————. 2004c. "Births," *The Daily*, 19 April.

————. 2005. "Births," *The Daily*, 12 July.

————. 2005a. "Divorces," *The Daily*, 8 March.

————. 2005b. *The Canadian Labour Market at a Glance*. Ottawa: Statistics Canada.

————. 2005c. *Income Trends in Canada*. Ottawa: Statistics Canada.

————. 2005d. *Family Violence in Canada: A Statistical Profile*. Ottawa: Canadian Centre for Justice Statistics.

————. 2006. *Women in Canada: Work Chapter Updates*. Ottawa: Statistics Canada.

————. 2006a. "The wealth of Canadians: An overview of the results of the survey of financial security 2005." Statistics Canada Pension and Wealth Research Paper Series Catalogue 13F0026MIE.

————. 2006b. *2006 Census: Family portrait: Continuity and change in Canadian families and households in 2006: National portrait: individuals*. Available at http://www12.statcan.ca/census-recensement/2006/as-sa/97-553/index-eng.cfm

————. 2007. "Marriages, 2003," *The Daily*, 17 January.

————. 2007a. *Family Portrait: Continuity and Change in Canadian Families and Households in 2006, 2006 Census*. Ottawa: Statistics Canada, Demography Division.

————. 2007b. "Quarterly demographic estimates: January to March 2007, Preliminary." Available at http://www.statcan.ca/english/freepub/91-002-XIE/91-002-XIE2007001.pdf.

————. 2007c. "2006 Census: Families, marital status, households and dwelling characteristics," *The Daily*, 12 September. Available at http://www.statcan.ca/Daily/English/070912/d070912a.htm; accessed 12 September 2008.

————. 2007d. "Distribution of total income, by economic family type, 2006 constant dollars, annual." CANSIM Table 202-0401.

————. 2007e. "Participation and activity limitation survey," *The Daily*, 3 December.

————. 2007f. *2006 Participation and Activity Limitation Survey: A Profile of Disability in Canada, 2006—Technical and Methodological Report*. Ottawa: Statistics Canada.

————. 2007g. *2006 Participation and Activity Limitation Survey: A Profile of Disability in Canada, 2006—Analytical Report*. Ottawa: Statistics Canada.

————. 2007h. *2006 Participation and Activity Limitation Survey: A Profile of Disability in Canada, 2006—Tables*. Ottawa: Statistics Canada.

————. 2007i. "Census families by number of children at home." Available at http://www.statcan.gc.ca/

tables-tableaux/sum-som/l01/cst01/famil50a-eng.htm; accessed 20 April 2012.

————. 2007j. *Women in Canada: A Gender-Based Statistical Report*, 5th ed. Ottawa: Statistics Canada. Statistics Canada. Available at http://www5.statcan.gc.ca/access_acces/archive.action?loc=/pub/89-503-x/89-503-x2005001-eng.pdf; accessed 6 January 2012.

————. 2007k. "Census snapshot of Canada: Families," *Canadian Social Trends*.

————. 2007l. *Immigrants in Canada: A Portrait of the Foreign-born Population, 2006 Census*, Catalogue no. 97-557-XCB2006006. Available at http://www12.statcan.ca/census-recensement/2006/as-sa/97-557/pdf/97-557-XIE2006001.pdf.

————. 2008. *Report on the Demographic Situation in Canada 2005 and 2006*. Ottawa: Statistics Canada.

————. 2008a. "Table 1 families by family structure, Canada and regions, 2001 and 2006. Ottawa: Statistics Canada. Available at http://www.statcan.ca/english/research/89-625-XIE/2007001/tables/tab1-en.htm.

————. 2008b. "Induced abortions," *The Daily*, 21 May.

————. 2008c. "Births 2006," *The Daily*.

————. 2008d. *The Children of Older First-time Mothers in Canada: Their Health and Development*. Ottawa: Statistics Canada. Available at http://www.statcan.ca/english/research/89-599-MIE/89-599-MIE2008005.pdf.

————. 2008e. *Report on the Demographic Situation in Canada, 2005 and 2006*. Ottawa: Statistics Canada. Available at http://www.statcan.ca/english/freepub/91-209-XIE/91-209-XIE2004000.pdf.

————. 2008f. "Births, 2006," *The Daily*, 26 September.

————. 2008g. "2006 Census: Ethnic origin, visible minorities, place of work and mode of transportation," *The Daily*, 2 April.

————. 2008h. 2006 Census website. Available at http://www12.statcan.ca/english/census06/analysis/famhouse/ind4a.cfm; accessed 17 September 2008.

————. 2008i. *Labour Force Information*. Ottawa: Ministry of Industry.

————. 2008j. *2006 Participation and Activity Limitation Survey: A Profile of Disability in Canada, 2006—Labour Force Experience of People with Disabilities in Canada*. Ottawa: Statistics Canada.

————. 2008k. *2006 Participation and Activity Limitation Survey: A Profile of Disability in Canada, 2006—Families of Children with Disabilities*. Ottawa: Statistics Canada.

————. 2008l. *2006 Participation and Activity Limitation Survey: A Profile of Disability in Canada, 2006—Tables (Part V)*. Ottawa: Statistics Canada.

————. 2008m. *Family Violence in Canada: A Statistical Profile*. Ottawa: Canadian Centre for Justice Statistics.

————. 2008n. *Aboriginal Peoples in Canada in 2006: Inuit, Métis and First Nations, 2006 Census*, Catalogue no. 97-558-XIE. Available at http://www12.statcan.ca/english/census06/analysis/aboriginal/pdf/97-558-XIE 2006001.pdf.

————. 2008o. "Divorces in Canada, 2005." *The Daily*. 18 November.

————. 2008p. Table 106-9013 - Induced abortions in hospitals and clinics, by area of residence of patient, Canada, provinces and territories, annual, CANSIM (database). Available at http://www5.statcan.gc.ca/cansim/a01;jsessio

nid=EA00A29DADB23FCF0BED38F1FC9BAE0A?lang=
eng&p2=33.

———. 2009. "Earnings and Incomes of Canadians Over the
Past Quarter Century," *2006 Census: Earnings*. Available
at http://www12.statcan.ca/census-recensement/2006/
as-sa/97-563/p10-eng.cfm; accessed 22 March 2012.

———. 2009a. *Canada at a Glance. International Comparisons*.
Available at http://www45.statcan.gc.ca/2009/
cgc0_2009_009-eng.htm.

———. 2010. *Census Dictionary 2006*. (Catalogue no. 92-566-
X). Ottawa: Minister of Industry.

———. 2010a. "Visual census, Income and earnings, Canada."
Available at http://www12.statcan.ca/census-recense-
ment/2006/dp-pd/fs-fi/index.cfm?Lang=ENG&TOPIC_
ID=7&PRCODE=01; accessed 22 March 2012.

———. 2010b. *Population Estimates 1971–2010*. Ottawa,
Statistics Canada.

———. 2010c. *Perceived Mental Health*. Available at http://www.
statcan.gc.ca/pub/82-229-x/2009001/status/pmh-eng.htm.

———. 2010d. "Paid work," in *Women in Canada: A Gender-
Based Statistical Report*. Catalogue no. 89-503-X. Ottawa:
Statistics Canada.

———. 2011. "Individual Internet Use and E-Commerce."
Available at http://www.statcan.gc.ca/daily-quotidien/
111012/dq111012a-eng.htm.

———. 2011a. *Portrait of Families and Living Arrangements
in Canada, 2011 Census*, Catalogue no. 98-312-X2011001.
Available at http://www12.statcan.ca/census-
recensement/2011/as-sa/98-312-x/98-312-x2011001-
eng.cfm.

———. 2011b. *Fifty Years of Families in Canada: 1961 to 2011*.
Catalogue no. 98-312-X2011003. Available at http://www12
.statcan.gc.ca/census-recensement/2011/as-sa/98-312-x/
98-312-x2011003_1-eng.cfm.

———. 2011c. *Canadian Households in 2011: Type and Growth*.
Catalogue no. 98-312-X2011003. Available at http://www12
.statcan.gc.ca/census-recensement/2011/as-sa/98-312-x/
98-312-x2011003_2-eng.cfm.

———. 2011d. "Fathers Day by the Numbers." Ottawa:
Statistics Canada. Available at http://www42.statcan.
gc.ca/smr08/2011/smr08_157_2011-eng.htm; accessed
20 April 2012.

———. 2011e. "Homicide in Canada," *The Daily*, 26 October.

———. 2011f. "Family violence in Canada: A statistical profile,"
The Daily, 27 January.

———. 2011g. "Shelters for abused women," *The Daily*,
27 January.

———. 2012. *Family Violence in Canada: A Statistical Profile*.
CTA: 85-224-X.

———. 2012a. "Portrait of families and living arrangements in
canada," *Analytical Document*. (Cat no. 98-312-X2011001).
Ottawa: Statistics Canada.

———. 2012b. "Fifty years of families in Canada: 1961 to 2011,"
Census in Brief. (Cat no. 98-312-X2011003). Ottawa: Statistics
Canada. Available at http://www12.statcan.gc.ca/census-
recensement/2011/as-sa/98-312-x/98-312-x2011003_
1-eng.pdf.

———. 2012c. *2011 Census of Population Families and Living
Arrangements in Canada: Concept Brief* (July 12, 2012).
Available at http://www42.statcan.gc.ca/smr10/pdf/
smr10_2011_002-eng.pdf; accessed 27 July 2012.

———. 2012d. "Age groups and sex of foster children, for both
sexes, for Canada, provinces and territories." Available at
http://www12.statcan.gc.ca/census-recensement/2011/
dp-pd/hltfst/fam/Pages/highlight.cfm?TabID=1&Lang=E&
Asc=1&PRCode=01&OrderBy=999&Sex=1&tableID=304.

———. 2012e. "Living arrangements of young adults aged 20
to 29," *Families, households and marital status, 2011 Census
of Population*. Cat no. 98-312-X2011003. Ottawa: Statistics
Canada. Available at http://www12.statcan.gc.ca/census-
recensement/2011/as-sa/98-312-x/98-312-x2011003_
3-eng.pdf.

Statistics Canada and Status of Women Canada. 2012. *Women
in Canada: A Gender-based Statistical Report*, 6th edn.
Ottawa, Minister of Industry.

Steckley, J., and B. Cummins. 2001. *Full Circle: Canada's First
Nations*. Toronto: Prentice-Hall.

Steed, Judy. 1994. *Our Little Secret: Confronting Child Sexual
Abuse in Canada*. Toronto: Random House.

Steinberg, Laurence, and Susan B. Silverberg. 1987. "Influences
on marital satisfaction during the middle stages of the family life cycle," *Journal of Marriage and the Family* 49: 751–60.

Stephens, William. 1963. *The Family in Cross-Cultural
Perspective*. New York: Holt, Rinehart and Winston.

Stevens, Noreen. 2006. "The brides of Stephen Harper,"
Winnipeg Free Press, 30 April. Available at http://www.equal-
marriage.ca/resource.php?id=488.

Stewart, Susan D. 2010. "Children with nonresident parents:
Living arrangements, visitation, and child support," *Journal
of Marriage and Family* 72, 5: 1078–91.

Stoller, Eleanor Palo. 1994. "Teaching about gender: The experience of family care of frail elderly relatives," *Educational
Gerontology* 20, 7: 679–97.

Stoller, Frederick H. 1970. "The intimate network of families as
a new structure," in Otto (1970a: 145–60).

Stone, L.O., C.J. Rosenthal, and I.A. Connidis. 1998. *Parent–
Child Exchanges of Supports and Intergenerational Equity*.
Ottawa: Ministry of Industry.

Stratton, Dorothy C., and Alinde J. Moore. 2007. "Fractured
relationships and the potential for abuse of older men,"
Journal of Elder Abuse and Neglect 19: 75–97.

Straus, Murray, and Richard J. Gelles. 1990. *Physical Violence in
American Families: Risk Factors and Adaptations to Violence in
8145 Families*. New Brunswick, NJ: Transaction.

———, ———, and Suzanne K. Steinmetz. 1986. "The mar-
riage license as a hitting license," in A.S. Skolnick and
J.H. Skolnick, eds, *Family in Transition*, 5th edn. Boston:
Little, Brown, 290–303.

———, S. Hamby, S. Boney-McCoy, and D. Sugarman. 1996.
"The revised Conflict Tactics Scale (CTS2): Development
and preliminary psychometric data," *Journal of Family Issues*
17: 283–316.

Strong, Bryan, Christine DeVault, and Theodore F. Cohen.
2005. *The Marriage and Family Experience: Intimate
Relationships in a Changing Society*, 9th edn. Belmont, Calif.:
Thomson Wadsworth.

Strong-Boag, Veronica. 1991. "Home dreams: Women and
the suburban experiment in Canada, 1945–60," *Canadian
Historical Review* 72.

———. 2006. *Finding Families, Finding Ourselves: English
Canada Encounters Adoption, from the Nineteenth Century to
the 1990s*. Don Mills: Oxford University Press.

———. 2011. *Fostering Nation? Canada Confronts its History of Childhood Disadvantage*. Waterloo: Wilfrid Laurier University Press.

Struthers, James. 1983. *No Fault of Their Own: Unemployment and the Canadian Welfare State, 1914–1941*. Toronto: University of Toronto Press.

Stum, M.S. 2000. "Families and inheritance decisions: Examining non-titled property transfers," *Journal of Family and Economic Issues* 21, 2: 177–202.

Sullivan, Maureen. 2004. *The Family of Woman: Lesbian Mothers, Their Children, and the Undoing of Gender*. Berkeley: University of California Press.

Sun Sentinel. 2008. *Sun Sentinel*, 2 December, 17a.

Sun, Shirley Hsiao-Li. 2008. "Housework and gender in nuclear versus extended family households: Experiences of Taiwanese immigrants in Canada," *Journal of Comparative Family Studies* 39, 1: 1–17.

Sutherland, Neil. 1997. *Growing Up: Childhood in English Canada from the Great War to the Age of Television*. Toronto: University of Toronto Press.

———. 2000. *Children in English-Canadian Society: Framing the Twentieth-Century Consensus*, 2nd edn. Waterloo: Wilfrid Laurier University Press.

Swain, Phillip A., and Nadine Cameron. 2003. "'Good enough parenting': Parental disability and child protection," *Disability & Society* 18: 165–77.

Swan, Suzanne C., and David I. Snow. 2006. "The development of a theory of women's use of violence in intimate relationships," *Violence Against Women* 12: 1026–45.

Swenson, Don. 2008. *The Religion and Family Link: Neo-Functionalist Reflections*. New York: Springer.

———, Jerry G. Pankhurst, and Sharon K. Houseknecht. 2005. "Links between families and religion," in Vern L. Bengston, Alan C. Acock, Katherine R. Allen, Peggy Dilworth-Anderson, and David M. Klein, eds, *Sourcebook of Family Theory and Research*. Thousand Oaks, CA: Sage.

Swidler, Ann. 2001. *Talk of Love: How Culture Matters*. Chicago: University of Chicago.

Sykorova, D. 2008. "Childlessness in old age: The social integration of childless seniors," *Sociologicky Casopis-Czech Sociological Review* 44, 1: 113–38.

Szinovacz, Maximiliane E., and Adam Davey. 2004. "Honeymoons and joint lunches: Effects of retirement and spouse's employment on depressive symptoms," *Journals of Gerontology*, Series B 59, 5: P233–45.

Talaga, Tanya, and Laurie Monsebraaten. 2008. "Benefit bypasses foster kids," *Toronto Star*, 18 February. Available at http://action.web.ca/home/crru/rsrcs_crru_full.shtml?x=113991.

Talbani, Aziz, and Parveen Hasanali. 2000. "Adolescent females between tradition and modernity: Gender role socialization in South Asian immigrant culture," *Journal of Adolescence* 23: 615–27.

Tarasuk, Valerie S. 2001. "Household food insecurity with hunger is associated with women's food intakes, health and household circumstances," *Journal of Nutrition* 131, 10: 2670–6.

———, and Naomi Dachner. 2009. "The proliferation of charitable meal programs in Toronto," *Canadian Public Policy* 35, 4: 433–50.

———, and Joan M. Eakin. 2003. "Charitable food assistance as symbolic gesture: An ethnographic study of food banks in Ontario," *Social Science and Medicine* 56, 7: 1505–15.

Tarleton, B., and L. Ward. 2007. "'Parenting with support': The views and experiences of parents with intellectual disabilities," *Journal of Policy and Practice in Intellectual Disabilities* 4: 194–200.

Tarlow, B.J., S.R. Wisniewski, S.H. Belle, M. Rubert, M.G. Ory, and D. Gallagher-Thompson. 2004. "Positive aspects of caregiving: Contributions of the REACH project to the development of new measures for Alzheimer's caregiving," *Research on Aging* 26, 4: 429–53.

Taylor, Janelle S., Linda L. Layne, and Danielle F. Wozniak. 2004. *Consuming Motherhood*. New Brunswick, NJ: Rutgers University Press.

Teelucksingh, C., and G. Galabuzi. 2005. *Working Precariously: The Impact of Race and Immigrant Status on Employment Opportunities and Outcomes in Canada*. Ottawa: Canadian Race Relations Foundation.

Tessema, S. 1992. *Substance Abuse among People with Disabilities*. Edmonton: Alberta Alcohol and Drug Abuse Commission, 1–61.

Tézli, Annette, and Gauthier, Anne. 2009. "Balancing Work and Family in Canada: An Empirical Examination of Conceptualizations and Measurements," in *Canadian Journal of Sociology/Cahiers Canadiens de Sociologie* 34, 2: 433–61.

Thamm, Robert. 1975. *Beyond Marriage and the Nuclear Family*. San Francisco: Canfield Press.

The Canadian Caregiver Coalition. 2008. *A Framework for a Canadian Caregiver Strategy*. Available at www.ccc-ccan.ca.

The Canadian Encyclopedia. 2009. *Historica Dominion*. Available at http://www.thecanadianencyclopedia.com/index.cfm?PgNm=TCESSubjects&Params=A1.

Thekaekara, Mari Marcel. 2005. "Weakened coast was prime target," *Manchester Guardian Weekly*, 8.

Thomas, Carol. 1997. "The baby and the bathwater: Disabled women and motherhood in social context," *Sociology of Health and Illness* 19: 622–43.

———. 1999. *Female Forms: Experiencing and Understanding Disability*. Philadelphia: Open University Press.

Thompson, Clive. 2008. "I'm so totally, digitally close to you," *New York Times Magazine*, 7 September, 42–7.

Thompson, Elizabeth. 1999. "Daycare woes ignored: Auditor report blasts lack of supervision," *Montreal Gazette*, 10 December, F7.

Thomson, Dale C. 1984. *Jean Lesage and the Quiet Revolution*. Toronto: Macmillan.

Thorne, Barrie. 2001. "Pick-up time at Oakdale Elementary School: Work and family from the vantage points of children," in Rosanna Hertz and Nancy L. Marshall, eds, *Working Families: The Transformation of the American Home*. Berkeley: University of California Press.

Thun, B. 2007. "Disability rights frameworks in Canada," *Journal of Individual Employment Rights* 12, 351–73.

Tibbetts, Janice. 2008. "Divorced pair must share future debt," *National Post*, 13 June.

Tilly, Louise A., and Joan W. Scott. 1987. *Women, Work and Family*. New York: Holt, Rinehart and Winston.

————, and ————. 2009. "The Family Economy in Modern England and France," in Bonnie Fox, ed., *Family Patterns, Gender Relations*. Toronto: Oxford University Press, 56–84.

Torjman, Sherri. 1999. "Crests and crashes: The changing tides of family income security," in Maureen Baker, ed., *Canada's Changing Families: Challenges to Public Policy*. Ottawa: Vanier Institute of the Family, 69–88.

Toronto Star. 2012. "Federal budget 2012: Ottawa axes National Council on Welfare." Available at http://www.thestar.com/news/canada/politics/article/1154445–federal-budget-2012-ottawa-axes-national-council-on-welfare.

Townsend, Nicholas. 2002. *The Package Deal: Marriage, Work and Fatherhood in Men's Lives*. Philadelphia: Temple University Press.

Transken, Si. 2011. "Noises and unwanted odours in old closets," in A. Sev'er, and J. Trost, eds, *Skeletons in the Closet: A Sociological Analysis of Family Conflicts*. Toronto: Wilfrid Laurier University Press, pp. 139–55.

Treas, Judith, and Leora Lawton. 1999. "Family relations in adulthood," in M. Sussman, S.K. Steinmetz, and G. Peterson, eds, *Handbook of Marriage and the Family*. New York: Plenum Press, 425–38.

Tremain, Shelley, ed. 1996. *Pushing the Limits: Disabled Dykes Produce Culture*. Toronto: Women's Press.

Tringo, J.L. 1970. "The hierarchy of preference toward disability groups," *The Journal of Special Education* 4: 295–306.

Trocmé, Nico, Della Knoke, and Cindy Blackstock. 2004. "Pathways to overrepresentation of Aboriginal children in Canada's child welfare system," *Social Science Review* 78, 4: 577–600.

Trussell, Dawn, and Susan Shaw. 2007. "'Daddy's gone and he'll be back in October': Farm women's experiences of family leisure," *Journal of Leisure Research* 39, 2: 366–87.

Tsang, A. Ka Tat, Howard Irving, Ramona Alaggia, Shirley B.Y. Chau, and Michael Benjamin. 2003. "Negotiating ethnic identity in Canada: The case of 'satellite children'," *Youth & Society* 34, 3: 359–84.

Turcotte, Martin, and Grant Schellenberg. 2007. *A Portrait of Seniors in Canada*. Statistics Canada: Social and Aboriginal Statistics Division.

Turcotte, Pierre, and Frances Goldscheider. 1998. "Evolution of factors influencing first union formation," *Canadian Studies in Population* 25, 2: 145–73.

Turner, R.J., D. Lloyd, and J. Taylor. 2006. "Physical disability and mental health: An epidemiology of psychiatric and substance disorders," *Rehabilitation Psychology* 51: 214–23.

Turton, Jackie. 2008. *Child Abuse, Gender and Society*. New York: Routledge.

Twenge, Jean M., W. Keith Campbell, and Craig A. Foster. 2003. "Parenthood and marital satisfaction: A meta-analytic review," *Journal of Marriage and the Family* 65: 574–83.

Tye, Diane, and Ann Marie Powers. 1998. "Gender, resistance and play: Bachelorette parties in Atlantic Canada," *Women's Studies International Forum* 21, 5: 551–61.

Tyyskä, Vappu. 2001. *The Long and Winding Road: Adolescents and Youth in Canada Today*. Toronto: Canadian Scholars' Press.

Unger, D. 2010. *Men Can: The Changing Image and Reality of Fatherhood in America*. Philadelphia: Temple University Press.

UN Ratifications (n.d.). Available at http://www.bayefsky.com/pdf/canada_t1_ratifications.pdf; accessed 20 October 2008.

UNICEF Canada. 2012. "Canada can do more to protect its children from poverty, new UNICEF report." Available at http://www.unicef.ca/en/press-release/canada-can-do-more-to-protect-its-children-from-poverty-new-unicef-report.

————. 2000. *A World Fit for Children: Millennium Development Goals Special Session on Children Documents the Convention of the Rights of the Child*. New Delhi, India: UNICEF.

————. 2008. Available at http://www.unicef-irc.org/databases/transmonee/2008/Tables_TransMONEE.xls; accessed 29 November 2008.

————. 2012. "Relative Income Poverty among Children in Rich Countries." Innocenti Working Papers 2012-01. Available at http://www.unicef-irc.org/publications/655.

United Nations (UN). 1993. Declaration on the Elimination of Violence Against Women (DEVAW). Available at http://www.un.org/womanwatch/daw/devaw; accessed 24 May 2001.

United Nations Development Program (UNDP). 1995. *The Human Development Report*. New York: Oxford University Press.

————. 1998. *Human Development Report 1998*. New York: Oxford University Press.

Ursel, Jane. 1992. *Private Lives, Public Policy: 100 Years of State Intervention in the Family*. Toronto: Women's Press.

US Census Bureau. 2008. *World Population Trends*. Available at http://www.census.gov/ipc/www/idb/worldpopinfo.html; accessed 23 November 2008.

Valkyrie, Zek Cypress. 2011. "Cybersexuality in MMORPGs: Virtual sexual revolution untapped," *Men and Masculinities* 14, 1: 76–96.

Valpy, Michael, Caroline Alphonso, and Rheal Seguin. 2006. "Same-sex vote likely to be tight," *Globe and Mail*, A1, A4.

Valverde, Mariana. 1991. *The Age of Light, Soap and Water: Moral Reform in English Canada, 1885–1925*. Toronto: McClelland and Stewart.

————. 1993. "Heterosexuality: Contested ground," in Bonnie Fox, ed., *Family Patterns, Gender Relations*. Toronto: Oxford University Press, 189–94.

————. 2006. "A New entity in the history of sexuality: The respectable same-sex couple," *Feminist Studies* 32 (1): 155–62.

————. 2009. "Heterosexuality: Contested ground," in *Family Patterns, Gender Relations*, B. Fox, ed. Toronto: Oxford University Press, pp. 212–18.

van den Hoonaard, D. 1997. "Identity foreclosure: Women's experiences of widowhood as expressed in autobiographical accounts," *Ageing and Society* 17, 5: 533–51.

————. 2001. *The Widowed Self: Older Women's Journey through Widowhood*. Waterloo, Ont.: Wilfrid Laurier University Press.

————. 2010. *By Himself: The Older Man's Experience of Widowhood*. Toronto: University of Toronto Press.

Van Die, Marguerite. 2005. *Religion, Family and Community in Victorian Canada*. Montreal: McGill-Queen's University Press.

————, and ————. 2008. "Informal care and health care use of older adults," *Journal of Health Economics* 23: 1159–80.

Van Houtven, C.H., and E.C. Norton. 2008. "Informal care and Medicare expenditures: testing for heterogeneous treatment effects," *Journal of Health Economics* 27: 134–56.

van Solinge, H., and K. Henkens. 2005. "Couples' adjustment to retirement: A multi-actor panel study," *Journals of Gerontology*, Series B 60B, 1: S11–20.

Vanier Institute of the Family. 2004. *Profiling Canada's Families III*. Ottawa: Vanier Institute.

———. 2006. "Family facts." Available at http://www.vifamily.ca/library/facts/facts.html.

———. 2008. "Definition of family." Ottawa: Vanier Institute of the Family. Available at http://www.vifamily.ca/about/definition.html.

———. 2008a. *Family Facts*. Available at http://www.vifamily.ca/library/facts/facts.html#couple, accessed 18 November 2008.

———. 2010. *Families Count: Profiling Canada's Families*. Ottawa: Vanier Institute of the Family. Available at http://www.vanierinstitute.ca/families_count_-_profiling_canadas_families_iv.

———. 2011. "Marriage Rates Continue to Drop." Ottawa: Vanier Institute of the Family. Available at http://www.vanierinstitute.ca/modules/news/newsitem.php?ItemId=82

———. 2012. "Our Approach to Family—Definition of Family." Available at http://www.vanierinstitute.ca/definition_of_family#.UBfg8bRfF9k; accessed 31 July 2012.

Veblen, Thorstein. 1994. *The Theory of the Leisure Class*. New York: Penguin Classics.

Vincent, Carole. 2000. "Editor's note," *Choices: Family Policy* (IRRP) 6, 1: 2–3.

Violence Against Women Survey (VAWS). 1993. *The Daily*, 18 Nov. Ottawa: Statistics Canada, Catalogue no. 11–001.

Vitaliano, P.P., J. Zhang, and J.M. Scanlan. 2003. "Is caregiving hazardous to one's physical health? A meta-analysis," *Psychological Bulletin* 129, 6: 946–72.

Vosko, Leah F. 2000. *Temporary Work: The Gendered Rise of a Precarious Employment Relationship*. Toronto: University of Toronto Press.

———. 2010. *Managing the Margins: Gender, Citizenship, and the International Regulation of Precarious Employment*. Toronto: Oxford University Press.

———, and L. Clark. 2009. "Canada: gendered precariousness and social reproduction," *Comparative Perspectives Database Working Paper Series, 2009*. Available at http://libgwd.cns.yorku.ca/cpdworkingpapers/; accessed 20 April 2012.

———, Nancy Zukewich, and Cynthia Cranford. 2003. "Precarious jobs: A new typology of employment," *Perspectives on Labour and Income* 4, 10: 16–26.

Vozoris, Nicholas, Barbara Davis, and Valerie Tarasuk. 2002. "The affordability of a nutritious diet for households on welfare in Toronto," *Canadian Journal of Public Health* 93, 1: 36–40.

Wakeford, Nina. 2000. "Cyberqueer," in David Bell and Barbara M. Kennedy, eds, *The Cybercultures Reader*. New York: Routledge, pp. 403–15.

Walby, Sylvia. 1994. "Is citizenship gendered?" *Sociology* 28, 2: 379–95.

Waldron, Florencemae. 2005. "Battle over female (in)dependence: Women in New England Quebecois migrant communities," *Frontiers: A Journal of Women Studies* 26, 2: 158–205.

Walker, Alexis, and Lori McGraw. 2000. "Who is responsible for responsible fathering?" *Journal of Marriage and the Family* 62: 563–9.

Wall, G., and S. Arnold. 2007. "How involved is involved parenting? An exploration of the contemporary culture of fatherhood," *Gender and Society* 21, 4: 508–27.

Wall, Glenda. 2004. "Is your child's brain potential maximized? Mothering in an age of new brain research," *Atlantis* 8: 41–50.

Wall Street Journal. 2012. "Gay marriage makes Washington State ballot," *Wall Street Journal*, 14 June. Available at http://online.wsj.com/article/SB10001424052702303410404577464793812361230.html; accessed 13 September 2012.

Walmsley, J. 2005. "Institutionalization: A historical perspective," in K.J.A.R. Traustadottir, ed., *Deinstitutionalization and People with Intellectual Disabilities*. Philadelphia: Jessica Kingsley Publishers, 50–65.

Walters, L., W. Warzywoda-Krusznska, and T. Gurko. 2002. "Cross-cultural studies of families: Hidden differences," *Journal of Comparative Family Studies* 33, 3: 433–50.

Walton-Roberts, M., and G. Pratt. 2005. "Mobile modernities: A South Asian family negotiates immigration, gender, and class in Canada," *Gender, Place, & Culture: A Journal of Feminist Geography* 12, 2: 173–95.

Walton-Roberts, Margaret. 2004. "Rescaling citizenship: Gendering Canadian immigration policy," *Political Geography* 23: 265–81.

Walzer, Susan. 1996. "Thinking about the baby: Gender and divisions of infant care," *Social Problems* 43: 219–34.

Ward, Russell, and Glenna Spitze. 1996. "Will the children ever leave? Parent–child coresidence history and plans," *Journal of Family Issues* 17: 514–39.

———, and ———. 1998. "Sandwiched marriages: The implications of child and parent relations for marital quality in midlife," *Social Forces* 77: 647–66.

Ward-Griffin, C., and V. Marshall. 2003. "Reconceptualizing the relationship between 'public' and 'private' eldercare," *Journal of Aging Studies* 17: 189–208.

Wargon, Sylvia. 1997. *Children in Canadian Families*. Ottawa: Statistics Canada.

Warrick, Gary. 2008. *A Population History of the Huron-Petun, A.D. 500–1650*. New York: Cambridge University Press.

Waters, Johanna L. 2001. "Migration strategies and transnational families: Vancouver's satellite kids." Working Paper Series, No. 01–10. Vancouver: Vancouver Centre of Excellence, Research on Immigration and Integration in the Metropolis. Available at http://ceris.metropolis.net/frameset_e.html.

Wates, M. 1997. *Disabled Parents: Dispelling the Myths—A National Childbirth Trust Guide*. Cambridge: Trust Publishing.

Wattie, Chris. 2008. "Lesbian's children to be returned to Britain," National Post, 25 July, A3.

Wearing, Betsy. 1984. *The Ideology of Motherhood*. Sydney: George Allen and Unwin.

Webb, Adrienne, Sharon Doyle Dreidger, and Mark Cardwell. 1994. "A new diversity," *Maclean's* 107, 25: 34.

Weeks, Jeffrey, Catherine Donovan, and Brian Heaphy. 1999. "Everyday experiments: Narratives of non-heterosexual relationships," in Elizabeth B. Silva and Carol Smart, eds, *The New Family?* London: Sage.

———, ———, and ———. 1999. "Partners by choice: Equality, power and commitment in non-heterosexual relationships," in Graham Allen, ed., *The Sociology of the Family: A Reader.* Oxford: Blackwell.

———, ———, and ———. 2001. *Same Sex Intimacies: Families of Choice and Other Life Experiments.* London: Routledge.

Weikart, Richard. 2004. *From Darwin to Hitler: Evolutionary Ethics, Eugenics, and Racism in Germany.* New York: Palgrave Macmillan.

Wendell, Susan. 1996. *The Rejected Body: Feminist Philosophical Reflections on Disability.* New York and London: Routledge.

West, Candace, and Don Zimmerman. 1987. "Doing gender," *Gender and Society* 1: 125–51.

Weston, Kath. 1991. *Families We Choose: Lesbians, Gays, Kinship.* New York: Columbia University Press.

Whelan, Christopher T., and Bertrand Maitre. 2007. "Income, deprivation and economic stress in the enlarged European Union," *Social Indicators Research* 83, 2: 309–29.

White, James, and David Klein. 2008. *Family Theories*, 3rd ed. Los Angeles: Sage.

White, Lynn. 1994. "Coresidence and leaving home: Young adults and their parents," *Annual Review of Sociology* 20: 81–102.

Whitehurst, R.N. 1975. "Alternate life styles and Canadian pluralism," in P. S. Wakil, ed., *Marriage, Family and Society: Canadian Perspectives.* Toronto: Butterworths, 433–45.

Whyte, Martin King. 1990. *Dating, Mating and Marriage.* New York: Aldine de Gruyter.

Widmer, Eric. 2010. *Family Configurations: A Structural Approach to Family Diversity.* Burlington, VT: Ashgate.

Wilkie, Jane. 1993. "Changes in U.S. men's attitudes toward the family provider role, 1972–1989," *Gender & Society* 7: 261–79.

Wilkins, Russell, and Gregory J. Sherman. 1998. "Low income and child health in Canada," in David Coburn, Carl D'Arcy, and George M. Torrance, eds, *Health and Canadian Society: Sociological Perspectives.* Toronto: University of Toronto Press, 102–9.

Williams, Cara. 2000. "Income and expenditures." Special Issue: 100 Years of Education. *Canadian Social Trends*, 59 (Winter).

———. 2005. "The sandwich generation," *Canadian Social Trends* 77: 16-24.

Williams, J.C. 2010. *Reshaping the Work-Family Debate: Why Men and Class Matter.* Cambridge, MA: Harvard University Press.

Williams, Kristi, and Debra Umberson. 2004. "Marital status, marital transitions, and health: A gendered life course perspective," *Journal of Health and Social Behavior* 45: 81–98.

Williamson, Deanna L., and Fiona Salkie. 2005. "Welfare reforms in Canada: Implications for the well-being of preschool children in poverty," *Journal of Children and Poverty* 11, 1: 55–76.

Willms, J. Douglas. 2002. *Vulnerable Children: Findings from Canada's National Longitudinal Survey of Children and Youth.* Edmonton: University of Alberta Press.

Willson, Andrea E., Kim M. Shuey, and Glen H. Elder, Jr. 2003. "Ambivalence in the relationship of adult children to aging parents and in-laws," *Journal of Marriage and Family* 65: 1055–72.

Wilmott, Helen. 2007. "Young women, routes through education and employment and discursive constructions of love and intimacy," *Current Sociology* 55: 446–66.

Wilson, Beth, with Emily Tsoa. 2001. *HungerCount 2001: Food Bank Lines in Insecure Times.* Toronto: Canadian Association of Food Banks.

Wilson, Brian, and Shannon Jette. 2005. "Making sense of the cultural activities of Canadian youth," in Nancy Mandell and Ann Duffy, eds, *Canadian Families: Diversity, Conflict and Change*, 3rd edn. Toronto: Thomson Nelson.

Wilson, Daniel, and David Macdonald. 2010. *The Income Gap between Aboriginal Peoples and the Rest of Canada.* Ottawa: Canadian Centre for Policy Alternatives.

Wilson, Margo, and Martin Daly. 1993. "Spousal homicide risk and estrangement," *Violence and Victims* 8: 3–15.

———, and ———. 1994. "Spousal homicide," *Juristat* 14: 1–15.

Winch, Robert F. 1970. "Permanence and change in the history of the American family and some speculation as to its future," *Journal of Marriage and the Family* 32, 1: 6–15.

Wister, A.V. 2005. *Baby Boomer Health Dynamics, How Are We Aging?* Toronto: University of Toronto Press.

Wittig, Monique. 1993. "One is not born a woman," in Henry Abelove et al., eds, *The Lesbian and Gay Studies Reader.* New York: Routledge, 103–9.

Wolak, Janis, and David Finkelhor. 1998. "Children exposed to partner violence," in Jasinski and Williams (1998: 73–111).

Wolbring, Gregor. 2001. *Folgen Der Anwendung Genetischer Diagnostik Fuer Behinderte Menschen.* Enquete-Kommission des deutschen Bundestages: Recht und Ethik der modernen Medizin. Calgary: University of Calgary.

Wolfe, D., L. Zak, and S. Wilson. 1986. "Child witness to violence between parents: Critical issues in behaviour and social adjustment," *Journal of Abnormal Child Psychology* 14, 1: 95–102.

Wolfson, E. 1996. "Why we should fight for the freedom to marry: The challenges and opportunities that will follow a win in Hawaii," *Journal of Gay, Lesbian and Bisexual Identity* 1: 70–89.

Wollstonecraft, Mary. 1988 [1792]. *A Vindication of the Rights of Women.* New York: Norton.

Woolley, Frances. 1998. "Work and household transactions: An economist's view," in David Cheal, Frances Woolley, and Meg Luxton, eds, *How Families Cope and Why Policymakers Need to Know.* Ottawa: Canadian Policy Research Networks Study No. F12, 27–55.

———. 2004. "Why pay child benefits to mothers?" *Canadian Public Policy* 30, 1: 47–69.

World Health Organization. 2003b. "What are the main risk factors for disability in old age and how can disability be prevented?" Available at http://www.euro.who.int/document/E82970.pdf.

Worth, Heather, Alison Reid, and Karen McMillan. 2002. "Somewhere over the rainbow: Love, trust and monogamy in gay relationships," *Journal of Sociology*, 38: 237–53.

Worts, Diana. 2005. "'It just doesn't feel like you're obviously in': Housing policy, family privacy, and the reproduction of social inequality," *Canadian Review of Sociology and Anthropology* 42: 445–65.

Wouters, Cas. 2002. "The quest for new rituals in dying and mourning: Changes in the we–I balance," *Body & Society* 8, 1: 1–27.

Wu, Zheng. 2000. *Cohabitation: An Alternative Form of Family Living.* Toronto: Oxford University Press.

———, and C.M. Schimmele. 2007. "Uncoupling in later life," *Generations* 31, 3: 41–6.

———, and Margaret Penning. 1997. "Marital instability after midlife," *Journal of Family Issues* 18: 459–78.

———, and Randy Hart. 2002. "The effects of marital and non-marital union transition on health," *Journal of Marriage and the Family* 64: 420–32.

———, Feng Hou, and Christoph M. Schimmele. 2008. "Family structure and children's psychosocial outcomes," *Journal of Family Issues* 29, 12: 1600–24.

Wyatt, Nelson. 2005. "Quebec to operate parental leave plan," *Globe and Mail*, 2 March, A5.

Yee, J.L., and R. Schulz. 2000. "Gender differences in psychiatric morbidity among family caregivers: A review and analysis," *The Gerontologist* 40: 147–64.

Yeung, W. Jean, and Sandra L. Hofferth. 1998. "Family adaptations to income and job loss in the US," *Journal of Family and Economic Issues* 19, 3: 255–83.

Yllö, Kersti A., and Michel Bograd, eds. 1988. *Feminist Perspectives on Wife Abuse.* Newbury Park, Calif.: Sage.

Young, C.L. 2006. "What's sex got to do with it? Tax and the 'family' in Canada," *Journal of the Australasian Tax Teachers Association* 2 (1).

———, and S. Boyd. 2006. "Losing the feminist voice? Debates on the legal recognition of same sex partnerships in Canada," *Feminist Legal Studies* 14 (2): 213–40.

Zaidi, Arshia U., and Muhammad Shuraydi. 2002. "Perceptions of arranged marriages by young Pakistani Muslim women living in a Western society," *Journal of Comparative Family Studies* 33, 4: 495–514.

Zavella, Patricia. 1987. *Women's Work and Chicano Families: Cannery Workers of the Santa Clara Valley.* Ithaca, NY: Cornell University Press.

Zhang, Xuelin. 2003. *The Wealth Position of Immigrant Families in Canada.* Ottawa: Statistics Canada, Business and Labour Market Analysis Division.

Zima, Bonnie T., Regina Bussing, and Maria Bystritsky. 1999. "Psychological stressors among sheltered homeless children: Relationship to behavioural problems and depressive symptoms," *American Journal of Orthopsychiatry* 69, 1: 127–33.

Zimmerman, Carle C. 1947. *Family and Civilization.* New York: Harper & Brothers.

Zuzanek, Juri. 2001. "Parenting time: Enough or too little?" *Canadian Journal of Policy Research* 2, 2: 125–33.

Index

paternal leave benefits: in Quebec, 311
patriarchal family, 231, 345
patriarchy, 72, 279, 345
patrilineage, 28, 345
Paul, Eden, 319–20
Pence, Ellen and Michael Paymar, 279
Pennington, Phil and Barbara, 162–63
"people first" language, 252
persons with disabilities/disabled
    persons, 248–49, 252; aging and,
    133, 249; children and youth, 252–59;
    labour force participation and,
    266–67; lack of support for, 266;
    parents, 259–63; violence and abuse
    and, 263–66
Persons with Disabilities Online, 269
Piaget, Jean, 17
Picot, Garnett and John Myles, 195
Picot, Garnett et al., 186, 196–97
pill, the, 37
Pillemer, Karl, 278
plural marriage. See polygamy
policy, parenting and social/workplace,
    71; see also family policy; social
    policy
Polikoff, Nancy, 220
Pollak, Otto, 322
polygamy, 12, 55, 86
polygyny, 322, 345
population, growth in global, 325–26,
    326, 329
population, of Canada: by age, 127; aging,
    126; diversity of, 229; fertility rate
    and, 230; foreign-born, 227; visible
    minorities, 231, 232
poverty, 146, 185, 234; Aboriginal peoples
    and, 234; alleviating adult, 301; among
    families in later life, 194–95; child,
    196–97, 204, 205, 296; consequences
    of, 203–4, 205; coping with and
    surviving, 199–203; definitions of,
    186–87; disability and, 266; employ-
    ment and, 302; explanations for, 186;
    families with disabled children and,
    254–55; family types and, 301; food
    banks and, 302; foster children and,
    299; health and, 203–4; infant and
    child mortality and, 26;
    leading to disability, 255; lone-parent
    families and, 103; shortcomings of
    income-based measures of, 197–99;
    varying status over life course,
    196–97; visible minorities or racial-
    ized peoples, 197; welfare programs
    and, 191–94; whether worsened in
    Canada, 186–90
poverty rate, 301, 302
power: exchange theory and, 16; Marxism
    and, 14, 15
predictions, about the family: current,
    336–37; extrapolation from trends

into the future, 327; family specialists'
    future family, 327, 329; identifying
    societal changes and reflecting on
    their importance for the family, 327,
    329; impact of inventions, 327, 328;
    past, 318–19, 319–27, 336; projection
    from generational changes, 327–28;
    tentative, 329–32; various bases
    for, 327–29; worldwide changes,
    329–32
pregnancy, vulnerability to abuse, 285
premarital sex, 56
pre-wedding rituals, 148–51; bridal
    showers, 148–49
Price of Motherhood, The (Crittenden), 180
probate, 89
production, modes of, 14
progression, rites of, 148, 347
pronatalism, 31, 345–46; in Quebec, 308
Proposition 8, 210
Protestant Church, 49
provincial governments: benefits for
    children in state care, 298, 299;
    child and family policies and, 293,
    301–2, 314; child benefits and, 297;
    child care and, 80–81; divorce and,
    88–89; early learning and child-care
    program, 312; family law and, 222;
    formal care to assist families, 140;
    maternity benefits and, 294; National
    Child Benefit Supplement clawback,
    297; regulated child-care and, 305;
    same-sex marriage and, 212, 213;
    social assistance programs, 67–68
Prince Edward Island, 281
Public Health Agency of Canada, Living
    with Disabilities, 269
public intimacy, 346
public policy, family change and, 196–97;
    see also family policy
pure relationship, 50, 51, 346

qualitative research methods, 13, 346
quality time, 346
Quebec: amounts of family-policy
    disbursements, 310–11; birth rate in,
    308; child allowance in, 308–9; child
    care in, 80, 179, 306, 309, 310, 315;
    common-law unions in, 39, 49; critics
    of family policies in, 310; employabil-
    ity of parents, 311; family allowance
    in, 309; family policy in, 271, 301–2,
    305, 307–12; law, 94; parental leave in,
    311; policies for supporting families
    and reducing poverty, 301–2; pro-natal
    policies, 308; Quiet Revolution,
    37, 49, 308, 346; success of family
    policies in, 311–12; tax benefits for
    families, 310
Quebec Pension Plan, 195
Queen Victoria, 162

queer theory, 19
Quiet Revolution, 37, 49, 308, 346

racialized peoples, poverty and, 197,
    301, 303
racial profiling, 243, 346
racism: in immigration policy, 28;
    scientific, 28, 347
Radio-Canada, 36
Raj, A. and J. Silverman, 240
Ranson, Gillian, 70, 71
recessions, economic, 185–86, 187, 190,
    200, 302, 346
reconstruction, 33, 346
Reid, Carrie, 299
Reid, Julie, Sinikka Elliott, and Gretchen
    Webber, 57
Reid, R.C. et al., 136
religion: marriage rituals and, 147–48;
    separation and divorce and, 87;
    service attendance, 148
Religious Coalition for Equal Marriage
    Rights, 215
remarriage, 6, 30, 48, 86, 119
remittances, 81
Report Card on Child Poverty in
    Canada, 303
Report on Social Security for Canada
    (Marsh), 32
Report on the Health of Canadians, 203
reproduction, past predictions
    about, 325
reproductive and genetic technologies,
    120, 328, 346; new, 50, 345; past
    predictions about, 326; predictions
    about, 333–34
residence, 235–36
residential mobility, 99
residential schools, 28–29, 234, 237,
    346–47
respite care, 140, 347; children with
    disabilities and, 257–58
retirement, 116, 128; end of mandatory,
    126, 128; leisure time and, 128
"la revanche des berceaux" ("revenge of
    the cradle""), 307
Rhode, Deborah, 180
Rick v. Brandsema, 102
Rihanna, 277, 282, 289
Risman, Barbara, 51
rituals, 145, 163; marriage, 145, 147–48,
    148–51; mourning, 162; rites of pas-
    sage, 148, 347; rites of progression,
    148, 347; rites of separation, 145,
    161–63
Roberts, Robin, 218
Rodriguez-Garcia, 2007, 245
Roeher Institute, 255, 256, 257, 264
Roman Catholic Church: on divorce, 30;
    in Quebec, 49; on widowhood, 161
Rooney, Rebekah, 216, 217